Sports and the Law

Sports and the Law

A Modern Anthology

Edited by

Timothy Davis
Alfred D. Mathewson
Kenneth L. Shropshire

Carolina Academic Press
Durham, North Carolina

42384816

ISBN 0-89089-734-4
LCCN 99-65466

CAROLINA ACADEMIC PRESS
700 Kent Street
Durham, North Carolina 27701
Telephone (919) 489-7486
Fax (919) 493-5668
E-mail: cap@cap-press.com
www.cap-press.com

Printed in the United States of America

Contents

Part V — Drug Testing

Prologue

Sports law literature has evolved over the last twenty years as writers have successfully grappled with the myriad of legal and quasi-legal issues that arise in the context of sports. As a result of their efforts, scholars addressing these topics have heightened our understanding of the complex factual, legal and social issues that sports matters generate. This anthology seeks to continue this development. It includes excerpts, primarily of law review articles, that address the broad dimensions of sports and the law.

This anthology may supplement principal texts used in sports, sports management and sports law courses at the law school, undergraduate and graduate levels. It is sufficiently comprehensive, however, for use as a primary text. The materials contained in the anthology provide a depth of coverage that is difficult, if not impossible, to achieve in class due to time constraints. It makes accessible to students articles, book excerpts and other materials, such as government documents, that can enhance their understanding of topics traditionally covered in sports law and management classes, as well as topics that typically escape class coverage.

Given our multiple objectives, it is not surprising that we have selected excerpts that perform multiple functions. A principal focus of certain of the excerpts is to explain the current status of the law. Rather than simply focus on doctrinal matters, however, many of the articles and book excerpts examine the variables (e.g., economic and social) that have influenced the development of the law of sports. Relatedly, this anthology attempts to acquaint readers with contrasting views on controversial issues confronting sports. In this regard, the anthology appropriately begins with differing perspectives on whether "sports law" represents a discrete substantive area of law. In subsequent chapters, differing views are presented on issues ranging from the use of Title IX to increase athletic participation opportunities for women to the debate regarding the antitrust status of professional sports leagues. In addition, the anthology includes articles that introduce the larger context within which to view the world of sport as it relates to the law.

A more discrete, but nevertheless important, goal of this anthology is to serve as an accessible reference source for frequently cited or discussed materials. For example, included within the chapter on intercollegiate athletics are excerpts from major studies (e.g., the 1929 Carnegie Report on Intercollegiate Athletics) of intercollegiate athletics. Also included are government documents such as the NCAA-Justice Department Consent Decree regarding learning disabled student-athletes and the OCR Letter of Clarification concerning the three-pronged test for assessing compliance with Title IX gender equity requirements.

What became apparent in our review of articles, books and other materials for inclusion in this anthology is the breadth and quality of contemporary scholarship in the sports context. We attribute this in part to the growing number of quality sports and entertainment law journals that provide increased opportunities for publication. We also noted, however, the proliferation of sports related scholarship published in highly respected mainstream journals. These phenomena suggest the multi-dimensional nature of sports related scholarship and the significance of legal issues that arise in the sports context.

The proliferation of sports related scholarship made our task of determining which works to include all the more difficult. We attempted to include most of what we characterized as groundbreaking articles, those which offer novel and interesting perspectives. Nevertheless this anthology does not represent a collection of the "best" sports law articles given that many such articles have been omitted. Many of these excellent articles were omitted because of length limitations. In other instances, groundbreaking articles were not included because a subsequently published article expanded or updated the information presented therein. Page limitations also caused us to omit substantive topics as well; we attempt to note these in the chapters in which they would have been included.

In order to include as much of the substance of articles as possible, most footnotes have been omitted. Where footnotes are included, original footnote numbering is retained. An * represents an original note included by the editors.

The editors thank the many authors and copyright holders who granted permission to reprint edited versions of their work. We also acknowledge the research assistance provided by the following students: at Southern Methodist— Louis Hakim; at Pennsylvania—Scott Rosner, Sharese Bullock and Michelle McMeans; and at New Mexico—Carolyn Ramos and Mark Saltman. We also express our gratitude for the secretarial assistance provided by Sharon Magill, Sarina Arnold, Lisa Kmetz, Andrea King and Theresa Montoya. Finally, we acknowledge the support of our respective families.

Part I

Sports in Law and Society

Chapter 1

Sports Law or
Sports and the Law?

Introduction

What is sports law? This question is frequently posed to academics and practitioners with more than a tangential interest in addressing legal issues that arise in the context of sport. Attempts to respond to this question often take on an apologetic and defensive air suggesting the non-existence of a separately identifiable body of substantive law that can be called sports law.

The articles in this chapter present varying perspectives on the question of whether common law and legislative developments in the sports environment amount to a substantive body of law that warrants the sports law designation. Although Professor Shropshire acknowledges developments that support the notion of sports law, he concludes that the body of law in the sports context has not reached a point of maturation such that a "unique substantive corpus" exists that can be categorized as sports law. Showing that the "sports law" or "sports and the law" debate has not been confined to the United States, Professor Simon Gardiner favors the former designation. He points to the increasing body of judicial and legislative law specific to sport as support for his position. Noting that this is an ongoing debate, Gardiner also considers the theoretical and practical implications of the sports law designation.

Kenneth L. Shropshire, Introduction: Sports Law?
35/2 American Business Law Journal 181 (1998)*

What is sports law?

....

The bulk of sports law scholarship, particularly in recent years, focuses on sports issues impacted by the antitrust and labor laws. The contemporary focus on the labor exemption to the antitrust laws has raised issues not seen before in any other substantive context. This present focus evolved from basic issues of tort and contract.

One scholar provides the following broad definition of the field:

Sports law is an amalgamation of many legal disciplines, ranging from antitrust to tax law. These disciplines are applied to facts arising from sports context and are supplemented by case law nuances and a growing body of state and federal statutes specifically applicable to sports. Sports law, with its wide variety of legal aspects, probably encompasses more areas of the law than any other discipline. Sports law is also a dynamic field of the law with new issues arising on an almost daily basis due to court decisions, new legislation and regulations.[4]

Before discussing the contents of this volume, there is one small debate—not raging but present—that those unfamiliar with the field may not be aware of . Should this area of study be referred to as "sports law" or "sports and the law"? I believe the latter is more appropriately descriptive of this body of law. Sports law implies that there exists a unique substantive corpus that can be neatly categorized such as is the case with contracts, torts, or property, for example. There is a little law that is unique to sports alone. Even the exemption to the antitrust laws with regard to its application to baseball might equally be characterized as antitrust law. The growing sports-only corpus is that of federal and state statutes impacting sports. Laws at the state level regulating boxing, for example, have long been with us. The number of sports agent regulatory statutes has grown to a fairly large number as well. And although federal statutes impacting sports are rare, they do exist and new, unlikely-to-be-passed legislation is introduced annually. Thus, what we normally mean when we say "sports law" is sports and the law that impacts that industry.

When I first began teaching a sports law course in 1981, people would ask "What's that, contracts?" Most today understand the focus is much broader. Some even immediately recognize the potential capstone value of a course that, in varying incarnations, can bring in a broad array of substantive areas. Contract issues as well as remedies are immediately recognizable. We read about athletes and contract disputes on a daily basis. The antitrust and labor issues, particulary with the labor strife in sports these days, is readily identifiable as well. Torts is a rich sector of sports jurisprudence, too, as are some closely related criminal cases. The not-so-obvious possibilities include issues related to stadium and arena construction, enterprise governance, and even estate and taxation issues.

Simon Gardiner, Birth of a Legal Area: Sport and the Law or Sports Law?
5 Sport & Law Journal 10 (1997)*

INTRODUCTION

In Britain, a recurring issue that has been discussed in the Sport and the Law Journal since its inception, has been whether the subject should be identified as

---

4. Dean Robert P. Garberinio, *So You Want to Be a Sports Lawyer, or Is It a Player Agent, Player Representative, Sports Agent, Contract Advisor or Contract Representative*, 1 VILL. SPORTS & ENT. L.F. 11 (1994).

* Copyright 1997 by Simon Gardiner. Used by permission. All rights reserved. This article is a modified extract from *Sports Law: Text and Materials* by Simon Gardiner, Alexandra Felix, Mark James, John O'Leary, and Roger Welch.

'sport and the law' or whether it is more accurate to talk of an identifiable area of 'sports law'. In the context of the increasing body of case law concerning sporting issues and legislation that has been specifically developed for sport generally and sports such as football in particular, the time is right to start to rigorously analyse this issue.

Initially it is useful to consider the support found amongst British writers for the former position favouring the designation 'sport and the law'.

EDWARD GRAYSON
Sport and the Law

> No subject exists which jurisprudentially can be called sports law. As a sound-bite headline, shorthand description, it has no juridical foundation; for common law and equity creates no concept of law exclusively relating to sport. Each area of law applicable to sport does not differ from how it is found in any other social or jurisprudential category...When sport hits the legal and political buffers, conventional and ordinary principles affecting the nature of the appropriate sporting issue concerned including parliamentary legislation are triggered into action.[1]

CHARLES WOODHOUSE
The Lawyer in Sport: Some Reflections

> I have often said there is no such thing as sports law. Instead it is the application to sport situations of disciplines such as contract law, administrative law (disciplinary procedures), competition law, intellectual property law, defamation and employment law.[2]
> ....
> ....

JOHN BARNES
Sports and the Law in Canada

> Sports law deals with the state interests and the resolution of conflicts according to general legal norms. Sports maintain internal rules and structures to regulate play and organize competition. In sports law, the wider legal system impinges on this traditionally private sphere and subjects the politics of the sports game to the politics of the law game. The result is a double drama as the deep human concern for play combines with the concern for social justice. Sports law addresses basic ethical issues of freedom, fairness, equality, safety and economic security. The subject matter of sports law includes state control and subsidy of sport, rights of access, disciplinary powers and procedures, commercial and property rights, employment relations and compensation for injuries. Sports law is grounded in the material dimensions of sport and includes a study of the life and times of its heroic practitioners.[3]
> .... A country where the recognition of the development of sports law occurred at a similar time to Britain at the end of the 1960s and early 1970s is Australia:

---

1. Edward Grayson, *Sport and the Law*, 2nd ed. (London: Butterworths, 1994), xxxvii.
2. Charles Woodhouse, "The Lawyer in Sport: Some Reflections," *Sport and the Law Journal* Vol.4, No.3 (1996).
3. John Barnes, *Sports and the Law in Canada*, Toronto: Butterworths (1996), p 2-3.

HAYDEN OPIE

Sports Associations and their Legal Environment

"Sports law" is one of those fields of law which is applied law as opposed to pure or theoretical law. Rather than being a discipline with a common legal theme such as criminal law, equity or contract law, sports law is concerned with how law in general interacts with the activity known as sport. Hence, the label applied law. Yet there is an increasing body of law which is specific to sport. This produces debate among scholars over whether one should use the term sports law, which indicates a legal discipline in its own right, or "sport and law" which reflects the multifarious and applied nature of the field. No doubt the general public would regard this as one of those sterile debates which are so attractive to inhabitants of ivory towers-if the public bothered to think about it![4]

. . . .

SPORT AND THE LAW OR SPORTS LAW?

These four accounts present alternative views on this issue: sport and the law or sports law? Grayson believes there is no such identifiable area of sports law. Woodhouse agrees. In a qualified way Barnes agrees, stating that "there is really no distinct 'sports law', but the proliferation of sports legislation, litigation and arbitral decisions has led to some special doctrine."[5] Opie believes that it is possible to see a recognisable sports law, an applied area of law, and notes the debate concerning whether an 'identifiable legal subject' exists has occurred in other developing and burgeoning areas.

I think this last position is the correct one. This subject area of law is part of a process that has happened to all legal areas in the past. Labor or employment law is a subject area that has only achieved relatively recent recognition. It has its origins in contract law in the employment context, but no one would doubt that with the plethora of legislation during the post-war era regulating the workplace, it has become a subject area in its own right. Passing through various incarnations such as industrial law, it is now a mature legal subject.

Of course the process by which legal areas are identified, constituted and named is a complex one and often to some extent arbitrary. There is no official recognition procedure. It is a process of legal practitioners and academics recognising the growing application of law to a new area of social life. Computer law is a good example to analogise with sports law. It is a relatively new legal subject, where specific laws dealing with this new technology are recent developments. In Britain two pieces of legislation, The Data Protection Act 1984 concerning access to information on computers, and the Computer Misuse Act 1991, concerning criminalisation of unauthorised access to computer systems, have developed due to the inadequacies of the existing law to effectively regulate. As far as unauthorised access to computers, or hacking, as it is commonly known, unsuccessful attempts had been made to apply the law of criminal damage to penalise such activities. The need for new legislation was overwhelmingly supported.

A significant body of computer law has developed. It falls into the 'applied law' classification that Opie describes. The development of legal areas which involves

---

4. Hayden Opie, *Sports Associations and their Legal Environment*, 1996.
5. Barnes, 2 n. 4 (1996).

essentially the application of pure legal areas in the context of a human activity, in this case sport, move from a loose association such as sport and the law to a more recognisable body of law such as sports law. It is *true* to say that it is largely an amalgam of interrelated legal disciplines involving such areas as contract, taxation, employment, competition and criminal law, but dedicated legislation and case law has developed and will continue to do so. As an area of academic study and extensive practitioner involvement, the time is right to accept that a new legal area has been born- sports law.

A LEGAL THEORY FOR SPORTS LAW

What is now needed is increased examination of why law is involved increasingly in sport - a legal theory of sports law. Here are a few suggestions:

1. It is not difficult to identify that large areas of sports law are concerned with the regulation of commercial activities in sport. Both Barnes and Opie provide clear commercial reasons, amongst others, for law's greater involvement in North America and Australia. There does seem to be a strong complementary relationship between greater regulation of sport by the law and its increased commercialisation and commodification. This has happened in the sense of increased marketability of sport in terms of advertising and sponsorship together with greater professionalisation of sport....It is too easy just to consider the commercial causes of legal intervention in sport. In Britain and elsewhere, there are other reasons too that need to be evaluated.

2. The legal regulation of sport reflects the general increase in regulating new areas of social life. In sport this leads to inter-action between different levels of normative rules. Sports law is an area on the periphery of the legal domain, and as such, the law's role in regulating sport is opening ethical concerns and continual analysis, debate and evaluation.

3. Lawyers, as adept as ever, have seen sport as a social field ripe for colonisation and exploitation. An important part of this process is the ability of lawyers to develop new areas of work. The involvement of lawyers in sport can be compared with their involvement in other environments where their participation is contested. As Bankowski and Mungham argue concerning tribunals of both a legal and a wider quasi-legal nature:

> *The creation and maintenance of legal problems by lawyers follows a...pattern...when 'proper' becomes synonymous with 'legal' and 'paid' then there is created a pressure to abandon extra-legal means of dispute settlement in favour of legal ones.*[6]
>
> ....

4. Many 'problems' in sport such as drug use and violence are presented as 'moral panics' in need of legal regulation. This fits in with the view espoused by such writers as Alan Hunt and Steve Redhead that increasingly law is best understood as a regulatory process that interacts with other quasi-legal and nonlegal normative mechanisms. Sport is the latest social area or field to come increasingly under the gaze of the law. Moral panics are where problems are socially constructed and amplified, largely by the media, as in urgent need of legal regulation.

---

6. Zenon Bankowski & Geoff Mungham *Images of Law,* (1976), 62.

A major issue with the intervention of the law into new 'sporting arenas' is the dangers of juridification, where what are intrinsically social relationships between humans within a 'social field' become imbued with legal values and become understood as constituting a legal relationship - social norms become legal norms.[8] If a dispute then befalls the parties, a legal remedy is seen as a primary remedy. This will invariably change the nature and perception of the dispute and the relational connection between the parties.

CONCLUSION

So these are some suggested reasons and causes of greater legal intervention in sport. But there is still a need for a clear theoretical perspective to place these competing causes within. I will leave you with two theoretical models of law's intervention. They may not necessarily be oppositional and can be potentially complementary.

The first model is that the law's involvement is an extension along the road of the civilising process in sport in addition to the internal constitutive sports rules. The law is providing a functional role in the context of the modern commercial complexity of sport. This fits in with a functionalist perspective on sport and society. This complements the view that has been expressed that law will save sport from its modern ills.

The second model is that the law is a form of regulatory power, a form of control. This fits in with a critical perspective on sport and society, with law reflecting power relations in society and sport.

Which is the most persuasive? Is law a neutral mechanism intervening for the betterment of sport or is its use a form of power and control? Further work is needed in developing a systematic theoretical model of sports law.

One last point can be made: the phenomenon of the greater activity of lawyers in sport is one of course that can fit into both models. A cynical view is that lawyers will always follow where there is work and where money can be made.

---

8. *See* Pierre Bourdieu *The Force of Law: Towards a Sociology of the Juridical Field,* 38 HASTINGS LAW REVIEW 814 (1987).

Chapter 2

Sports as a Microcosm of Law and Society

Introduction

Sport is often characterized as representing a microcosm of society. According to sociologist Harry Edwards, sport reflects and recapitulates America's evolving social realities. Sociologists Stanley Eitzen and George Sage make similar observations in proposing that sport provides a useful institution for examining the complexities of the larger society because it represents a microcosm of the society in which it is embedded. In a 1998 issue of *The Nation*, the first in the magazine's history to focus on sport, the editor notes that "if sport is a powerful expression, it is also an expression of power." Assigning a figure of $350 billion as the gross national sports product, the editor adds that in terms of popular culture, nothing enters the public consciousness on such a scale as sport. Writing in the same issue of *The Nation*, Professor Gerald Early notes the pervasive influence of sport in shaping national ideology.

In the first contribution to this chapter, which also served as a foreword to a symposium that focused on sports law as a reflection of society's laws and values, Professor Matthew Mitten expresses sentiments consistent with the perspectives noted above. He proposes that a reciprocal relationship exists between sport and societal values. In this regard, he argues that sport both reflects and contributes to shaping societal values. In the legal "arena," the use of sports metaphors illustrates the value-shaping influence of sport. Indeed, two scholars recently observed that "[sp]orts metaphors are commonly used in everyday language, as well as in the jargon of business, law and other disciplines which involve conflict and challenge."[1] The use of sports metaphors in legal discourse is explored in Professor Elizabeth Thornburg's detailed and thought provoking examination of this theme. She critically explores the considerable degree to which sports metaphors, similar to those of war and sex, "lie behind substantive, procedural, and ethical rules that reward competition and discourage greater cooperation," in litigation. In so doing, she provides further support for the proposition that sport contributes to and reflects the values that shape societal and legal norms.

---

1. Maureen Archer & Ronnie Cohen, *Sidelined on the (Judicial) Bench: Sports Metaphors in Judicial Opinions*, 35/2 AM. BUS. L.J. 225, 231 (1998).

Matthew J. Mitten, Foreword to Symposium:
Sports Law as a Reflection of Society's Laws and Values
38 South Texas Law Review 999 (1997)*

Sports constitute an important cultural phenomena and play a pervasive role in our society. Virtually every American has viewed or participated in some form of competitive sport during the course of their lives. Millions of people annually attend sporting events and millions more avidly keep abreast of the day's sports events, which are the subject of extensive coverage by print, television, and radio media. Our favorite players, teams, and events provide an important source of identification for us.

Former United States Supreme Court Justice Earl Warren stated, "I always turn to the sports page first. The sports page records people's accomplishments; the front page, nothing but man's failure."[1] The sports field provides the setting for many triumphs and some of the proudest accomplishments of both men and women. Sports simultaneously embodies and encourages the development of many positive societal values. Sports participation demonstrates that success requires discipline, commitment, motivation, and hard work. Moreover, it requires and encourages teamwork and cooperation, and provides an opportunity to perform to the best of one's ability, develop a sense of fair play, and enhance physical fitness.

On the other hand, sports, like the rest of society, has a negative side—reflecting values that adversely impact American culture. There is often an over-emphasis on winning in sports and the single-minded pursuit of its accompanying economic rewards. In some instances, powerful groups within sports have acted to further their own objectives and have exploited others by neither engaging in teamwork nor playing fairly. Inconsistent with sport's inherent positive values, some people have been the victims of blatant or subtle discrimination, limiting their opportunities to participate in athletics or its governing structure.

Although sports has a special place in our culture, it mirrors society's values. There is a reciprocal relationship between sports and societal values. Sports incorporates society's existing values and reinforces these values on the playing field, in its rules, and through its established institutions. Sports also exports its principles and the lessons learned from participating in athletics and its governance to society in general.

Our laws, which are significantly influenced by value and policy considerations, play an important role in the regulation of society and its sport constituent. General private and public law principles are often applied to regulate amateur and professional sports. Sometimes these laws have been applied appropriately to further society's positive values while, at other times, they have been construed to reflect or further society's negative values. In some instances, certain aspects of sports or those involved in the sports industry have received preferential legal treatment, or conversely, have been denied adequate legal protection.

Despite its significant cultural role in society, sports has historically not been the subject of serious academic study. Thus, an important opportunity presents it-

---

1. *See* ALEC LEWIS, THE QUOTABLE QUOTATIONS BOOK 262 (1980).

self. The objective of this symposium is to provide a forum for discussion of various legal, philosophical, and sociological issues concerning the regulation of sports and to suggest reforms that are necessary to advance positive values within sports and society....

.... [Professor Mitten's summary of the articles that comprise the symposium issue is omitted. — ed.].

Elizabeth G. Thornburg, Metaphors Matter: How Images of Battle, Sports, and Sex Shape the Adversary System
10 Wisconsin Women's Law Journal 225 (1995)*

Even its name begins to tell the story: the *adversary* system. American court procedure is labeled in a way that implies a fight or a contest, highlighting the conflict rather than the resolution. Technically, "adversary system" merely means that "neutral and passive factfinders...resolve lawsuits on the basis of evidence presented by contending litigants during formal adjudicatory proceedings."[1] The phrase connotes more than its technical definition, however. A complex web of metaphor pervades the idea of the adversary system in a way that captures the hearts and minds of the lawyers who function within that system. In case law, academic literature, professional literature, and in popular culture, a trial is a battle and the lawyer the client's champion; a trial is a sports contest and the lawyer the client-team's winning coach or star player. Metaphors transform the trial lawyer from a mere person who presents information favorable to his client to a triumphant hero and change the other party to the dispute into the enemy. This metaphorical fixation on the combative, non-cooperative aspect of dispute resolution and the suppression of any duty to other litigants, the court system, or the community, contributes to a professional role that is severely out of balance.

....

This article collects and analyzes, for the first time, a kind of lawyer talk that is uniquely revealing about legal culture. It will begin by discussing the nature and effect of metaphors in society, using insights from recent psychological literature concerning the power of metaphor. The article will then survey and analyze the dominant metaphors for the adversary system and for the role of trial lawyers within that system. Further, the article will suggest some of the reasons for the powerful hold these metaphors have on American legal culture.

Next, the article will assess the impact of the metaphors on the behavior and identity of the people who work within the adversary system. It will argue that although the competitive metaphors sometimes promote good behavior, they more often foster unacceptable actions and attitudes. They disguise situations in which the parties should be able to achieve a cooperative or different vision of their dispute. Metaphors lie behind substantive, procedural, and ethical rules that reward competition and discourage greater cooperation; they keep us from seeing the ex-

---

1. Stephan Landsman, Readings on Adversarial Justice: The American Approach to Ajudication 1 (1988).

tent of problems within the adversary system and possible solutions to those problems. Therefore, the article will conclude by suggesting that we adopt and nurture new metaphors that will emphasize those parts of the adversary system that are obscured by the currently dominant metaphors of war, sports, and sex.

I. THE NATURE AND EFFECT OF METAPHORS

....

A metaphor is "a figure of speech containing an implied comparison, in which a word or phrase ordinarily and primarily used for one thing is applied to another."[14] In making such a comparison, the speaker says that one thing has certain traits of the other. If a metaphor says, then, that "all the world's a stage," it says that there are some things about the world that are like a dramatic production. Metaphor thereby provides new ways of understanding experience.

Most people first learned to think about metaphor as a mere poetic or rhetorical device, something to make the use of words more colorful or persuasive. Modern psychological and linguistic researchers, however, have demonstrated that metaphor is much more fundamental, not a matter of words but a matter of thought. Indeed, most of anyone's ordinary conceptual system is metaphorical in nature. Each culture has unique foundational metaphors which play a part in shaping the way members of that culture conceptualize their experience. Identifying those metaphors provides valuable clues about how a society thinks about things and defines its reality.

The pervasiveness of metaphor and the way in which it organizes thought processes can be illustrated by examining a simple metaphorical system—for example, up-down spatialization metaphors. In American culture, things that are desirable tend to be associated with "up" while things that are undesirable are associated with "down." Thus happy is up and sad is down. (I'm feeling *up*. That *boosted* my spirits. I'm *depressed*. My spirits *sank*.)...These spatial metaphors are rooted in physical and cultural experience, and they are not universal. In some cultures, balance or centrality play a much more important role than in our up-down culture. But within any one culture, it is very difficult to conceptualize experience outside of these metaphorical constructs. It would seem incoherent, as in "I'm appealing this case to a lower court" or "I'm feeling narrow." The metaphors come to limit the way people think and the way they perceive their physical and social realities.

Metaphors not only structure experience, they do so selectively. Since they compare things that are not in fact identical, metaphors emphasize some traits of their subject and exclude others. In forcing us to focus on one aspect of a concept, a metaphor can keep us from focusing on other aspects of the concept that are inconsistent with that metaphor. For example, a fundamental conceptual metaphor in American society is "Argument is War." (Your claims are *indefensible*. I *attacked* his argument. I *shot* his argument down. I will *win* the argument.) This metaphor structures the actions we perform in arguing; we attack and defend, we have strategies, we see the person we are arguing with as an opponent. The metaphor emphasizes the battling aspect of arguing. At the same time, the war metaphor obscures the cooperative aspects of arguing. For example, people who

---

14. WEBSTER'S NEW WORLD DICTIONARY 852 (3rd College ed. 1988).

argue are giving each other their time, a valuable commodity, in an effort at mutual understanding.

Metaphors are thus powerful cultural tools. They structure the way we perceive reality, and they structure it in a way that chooses to emphasize certain parts of our experience at the expense of others. They do both of these things in a way that we hardly notice:

> Anything that we rely on constantly, unconsciously, and automatically is so much part of us that it cannot be easily resisted, in large measure because it is barely even noticed. To the extent that we use a...conceptual metaphor, we accept its validity. Consequently, when someone else uses it, we are predisposed to accept its validity. For this reason, conventionalized...metaphors have persuasive power over us.[26]

Without a careful awareness of our dominant metaphors, then, and without competing alternate metaphors, people act and think on the basis of "limited comprehension masquerading as the whole truth."[27]

Because metaphors are so powerful and so potentially deceptive, we must examine carefully the metaphors that structure our experience of litigation. By studying the metaphors we can learn something about our concept of dispute resolution; we can see what the metaphors emphasize and what they hide.

II. METAPHORS FOR THE ADVERSARY SYSTEM

....

Metaphors so pervade our language about litigation that it is almost impossible to talk about a trial without using metaphors. There are a variety of metaphors available, but the ones that by far dominate our formal, public discussion of litigation are the ones comparing litigation to war, sports and, to a lesser degree, sex. Metaphors are used knowingly and unknowingly, as descriptions and as criticisms, but they are always used.

A. *Wars and Fighting*

Litigation is commonly referred to as a war, or more often as a battle. The other battle metaphors flow from this premise. For example, some refer to the roles that trial lawyers play in this war. They can be heroes, hired guns, gladiators, warriors, champions, generals, lone gunfighters, or the man on the firing line. Like soldiers, lawyers can be seasoned or battle-tested....

Other metaphors describe litigation activities in warlike terms. Parties arm themselves, draw battle lines, offer or refuse quarter, plan preemptive strikes, joust, cross swords, undertake frontal assaults, win by attrition, seek total annihilation of their enemies, marshal forces, attack, and sandbag their opponents....

....

...War provides a rich source domain for trial metaphors, providing words for process and participants and communicating the message that a hostile and competitive attitude is an important characteristic of the adversary system. The same is true of the sports metaphors.

---

26. LATKOFF & TURNER, *supra* note 15, at 63.
27. MILNER S. BALL, LYING DOWN TOGETHER: LAW, METAPHOR, AND THEOLOGY 22 (1985).

B. *Sports and Games*

Game metaphors describing litigation are not quite as straightforward as the war metaphors. Probably because games have a less serious connotation, courts that recognize parallels between trials and games sometimes affirm and sometimes deny the accuracy of the metaphor. In other words, when making an outright comparison, courts will sometimes say that litigation is a "game," "sport," or "contest," and sometimes will say that it is not. Even when courts negate the metaphor (e.g. "a lawsuit is not a game of chess"), they do so because they have recognized something in the parties' behavior that *does* evoke qualities of the game in question. And in describing litigation activities, courts and commentators often use sports and game metaphors.

Some sports metaphors, like war metaphors, have to do with roles. They portray trial lawyers as game players, boxers, team members, or forensic athletes. Judges, not surprisingly, are referees or umpires.

Other metaphors compare lawsuits to particular sports or games: blind man's bluff, hide and seek, chess, a game of chance, a game of wits and strategy, a cat and mouse game, a poker game, a football game, a boxing match, tennis, fishing, a tug of war, dice, a race, hunting, Monopoly, and even a confidence game. Metaphors using sports as a reference for litigation activities are also common. For example, litigants sometimes play with one hand tied behind their backs, skate close to the edge, strike a blow, lay their cards on the table, go close to the line, bluff, coach witnesses, ask for an extra inning, or get an elbow in the eye.

Sports metaphors also illustrate litigation strategy. As in war, the goal is to win. The players must know the rules of the game. Lawyers employ stratagems and devices; they need gamesmanship and game plans. As in chess, successful litigators make moves and need defensive gambits; as in cards, they need a poker face; as in wrestling, they "go to the mat." Litigators can be hard hitting, play rough, or play tough but fair. It is currently extremely popular, despite frequent criticism, to play hardball.

Games also provide metaphors for the location of litigation. It can be in an arena, an obstacle course, or the omnipresent level playing field. Finally, there are metaphors, primarily from card games, for the things lawyers use to play the litigation game: wild cards, bargaining chips, high stakes, and high cards.

C. *Sex and Sexuality*

The sexual metaphors for litigation are much more underground than the other metaphors and therefore harder to document. One hears them mostly in lawyers' offices and in continuing legal education speeches. These metaphors, however, definitely exist. In part, they are tied to the system of war metaphors, since sexual imagery has long been a part of the world of warfare. They are also part of a conceptual system that links male sexuality with conquest, sex with power. For these sexual metaphors are not images of mutually pleasurable adult relationships; they are images of domination and aggression.

....

...[S]exual metaphors for the adversary system further glamorize and reinforce the adversarial nature of the war and sports metaphors, and the cultural overlap of the metaphors add a suggestion of sexual victory to their images.

III. MESSAGES FROM THE METAPHORS

The war, sports, and sex metaphors portray the judicial system as highly competitive, bi-polar (win/lose), and client-centered. The litigants have no relationship to each other except as adversaries and their ends are completely antithetical. The purpose of litigation is to win, to be better than the opposing party. In achieving this goal, the only duty is to the client; anyone else who wanders into the war zone or playing field can protect herself only by hiring her own champion. And by winning the litigation battles and games, the litigator powerfully demonstrates his manhood.

A. *Competition and Victory*

The war metaphors are, by their very nature, competitive. Battles have *sides* who *compete* against each other. In addition, the combative setting can excuse misbehavior because it occurs "in the heat of battle." There is also a feeling of righteousness involved in the competition. The warrior/competitor is "constantly fighting [but] never at fault."[166]

The complex use of game metaphors also reinforces competitive values and behavior. The sin here is not playing too hard, but failing to take the game seriously. Many judges state that litigation is *not* a game because the game image fails to recognize the seriousness of the competition or suggest that the outcome might be somewhat random. Nevertheless, metaphors describing game activities are frequently used to describe what goes on in litigation, and are used approvingly to describe the strategic and competitive aspects of lawsuits. The most popular metaphor is boxing, a sport in which hurting the opponent is part of the game. In fact, litigation metaphors primarily refer to two-sided sports in which the player either wins or loses (boxing, football, baseball, chess) rather than cooperative games or games having multiple winners.

Analogies to team sports could be used to highlight the value of working together, the reality that everyone loses sometimes, and the idea that there are better and worse ways of losing and winning. These implications of the sports metaphors, however, do not tend to appear in discussions of litigation. Most of the messages about interactions with one's own team drop out and the metaphors focus only on the opponent. In doing so, the metaphors stress winning at all costs rather than fair play and rules.

As noted above, the sex metaphors merely reinforce the aggressive and competitive overtones of the war and sports metaphors. They smack more of conquest than of romance, and have to do with dominance rather than relationship. Further, the metaphors equate achieving sexual intercourse with victory, so much so that anything that threatens the ability of the lawyer-participants to compete threatens their masculinity.

Occasionally, the metaphoric systems are used to indicate that competition has been carried too far. For example, when adversariness exceeds normally-accepted parameters it is called "Rambo" litigation. This is only a half-hearted pejorative term, since John Rambo is the hero of action-adventure movies, and the violence toward enemies and bystanders in those movies is presented as admirable rather than morally ambiguous. The image of the lawyer as Sylvester Stallone swinging through the jungle may not, in fact, deter much adversary behavior. The sports

---

166. MARK GERZON, A CHOICE OF HEROES: THE CHANGING FACE OF AMERICAN MANHOOD 14 (1982).

counterpart of Rambo litigation is "hardball" litigation. Again, this is only partly successful as a reproach. Hardball, after all, is what the big kids get to play when they graduate from the juvenile (and female?) game of softball. Probably for this reason, the "hardball" metaphor is sometimes used admiringly. Some critical uses of the metaphors are less ambivalent, as when a court condemns "Pearl Harbor tactics" or "kamikaze tactics."

The game metaphors occasionally refer to the rules of the game, but the use of metaphors to describe cheating is uncommon. Cases do contain references to "hitting below the belt" or "dealing from the bottom of the deck," but they do not occur with any frequency. One case filled with football metaphors referred to a "flag on the play."[177] A foul, however, is an expected part of a football game for which one merely takes his penalty and goes on (rather like a routine discovery sanction). Only a large number of penalties or a penalty at a crucial moment seems to be considered outcome determinative in football. In basketball, fouling an opponent is often part of a team's strategy. The "foul" metaphor thus operates to make low-level rule violations a part of the system rather than to encourage scrupulous allegiance to the rules.

B. *Client Supremacy*

Because of the emphasis on competing and winning, the only role for the lawyer reflected in the metaphors is to further the desires of the client — the lawyer's "side" or "team." A general commanding troops would never help his opponent, nor would a football coach send plays to the other team. To do so would be unthinkable, not only unnecessary but also treasonous.

Similarly, there is no lively metaphor within these systems depicting concern for non-litigants. In a war, injuries to non-combatants may be inevitable, and in the game metaphors, non-players are invisible except for the judge-referee. War and sports metaphors stressing a duty to the judicial system itself, to the extent they exist at all, tend to be weak ones. There are war metaphors depicting extreme behavior, such as "Rambo litigation" or "scorched earth tactics," but these carry with them at least grudging admiration. There is no metaphor representing the warrior's responsibility to use the "minimum necessary force."[180]

C. *Lawyer Role*

. . . .

The combination of war, sports, and sex metaphors also indicates strongly that the world of litigation is populated solely by men. In this culture, the participants in war and sports are generally pictured as male (despite the real life participation of women in both worlds). Similarly, the metaphors' use of male sexuality suggests that litigators are male. These metaphors refer exclusively to heterosexual male sexuality, thus excluding all others from the metaphorical lawyer world, or forcing them into a stereotypical male role.

In real life, of course, women are lawyers and judges and clients. But they are invisible in this metaphorical paradigm. To fit into existing war/sports/sex talk, they must speak in male metaphors and tell male stories. It may be that the in-

---

177. Laxey v. Louisiana Bd. of Trustees, 22 F.3d at 622.
180. JOHN KEEGAN, THE FACE OF BATTLE 51 (1976).

creasing presence of women in the profession will ultimately motivate changes in the dominant metaphors and the adoption of newer, more inclusive ones. Presently, however, the metaphors do not reflect the presence of women in litigation.

D. *Suppression of Harm and Objectification of Participants*

Real battles involve more than a general concocting strategy. Real battles also involve pain and suffering, death and destruction. These traits of war, however, are largely ignored in the litigation metaphors. The metaphors describing litigation spring from popular culture rather than from complex reality.

....

Similarly, the sports metaphors function to emphasize strategy and hide moral ambiguity. Since sports are a socially acceptable way of releasing aggressive impulses, if litigators use the sports metaphor then they suggest that the aggressiveness of litigation is likewise acceptable. The metaphors highlight the glamour of sports, the risk, the strategy, the victories. They do not mention greed, pain, mud, sweat, broken bodies, illegal drug use, or student athletes deprived of a meaningful education.

Further, both war and sports metaphors create dehumanizing roles for everyone except the lawyer-hero. The closest to human a party comes is to be a "combatant." More often they are things: ammunition; weapons; bombs; high cards. Still more often they are just invisible. The only important role is that of the lawyer, who creates the strategy and bravely directs the battle or quarterbacks the team.

IV. CULTURAL SUPPORT FOR THE METAPHORS

....

The pervasiveness of metaphors in legal discourse is powerful. The metaphors themselves make it difficult to even think about litigation in non-competitive terms, and they provide an aura of glamour to those competitive activities. They are also powerful because the metaphors' vision of dispute resolution is consistent with other conceptual underpinnings of American society. First, the adversary metaphors are compatible with liberal political theory and the competitive, free market economic system. Second, the metaphors parallel cultural and psychological archetypes. Third, the metaphors reinforce cultural concepts of male identity. Fourth, the behavior portrayed metaphorically is consistent with the instrumental vision of the law conveyed in legal education, lawyer training, and legal realist philosophy. Finally, there is a personal financial appeal to the competitive metaphors. The economics of law practice, created by client pressure for undivided lawyer loyalty, encourage the kind of behavior depicted by the metaphors.

....

V. THE EFFECT OF ADVERSARY METAPHORS

....

Not many things are all bad, and the battle and sports metaphors do have some redeeming social value. When they encourage lawyers to rise above self interest, they operate for the good. When they make it possible for a fact finder to render a decision based a greater amount of clearly-presented information, they operate for the good. Unfortunately, the metaphors also cause problems. Taken together, they make lawyers overly adversarial in carrying out the tasks of formal litigation, and they obscure the possibility of mutually beneficial solutions. They subvert attempts to modify rules of procedure and ethics in ways that could decrease the benefit of adversarial gamesmanship. They submerge any concept of cooperative behavior or community values. And, at least for some, they take a personal toll on the lawyer's private self.

....

VI. THE NEED FOR NEW METAPHORS

....

Metaphors highlight, but they also hide. Our metaphors for the adversary system limit us to a system based on hierarchy, competition, and binary results. They depend on concepts of social contract and market forces rather than trust and mutual respect. The war, sports, and sex metaphors control our very idea of litigation, so much so that anyone proposing a less adversarial approach has had to create the idea of a different system. Scholars talking about cooperative strategies, mutually acceptable solutions, or win/win results are almost forced to talk about "alternative dispute resolution" rather than litigation. A more varied set of metaphors might allow litigators to see litigation, mediation, settlement, and trial as potential parts of a single process for reconciling the interests of their clients. In this process it would be sometimes appropriate to compete, sometimes appropriate to cooperate, but always necessary to be fair and honest.

This vision of a single, less adversarial process will require some changes in procedure and ethics rules in order to become a reality. Changes in the rules alone, however, will not be enough; attitudes need to change as well. As long as lawyers believe that when they are doing "litigation" their job is to be almost-Rambo, any changes in the rules will re-locate but not eliminate strategic behavior. Changes in the law and changes in the metaphors must go hand in hand.

Sometimes, it is possible to nurture new metaphors. New metaphors can alter the perceptions and actions of people within a culture. A different set of metaphors for the adversary system might transform trial lawyers' conception of their work, and thus the way they go about it. These metaphors need to change the existing conceptual system in a way that highlights what the adversary comparisons hide. They should emphasize cooperation and responsibility to others. They should provide active and important roles for parties and witnesses rather than transforming them from people into things (e.g. ammunition and high cards). They should also be more gender neutral metaphors that do not conjure images of people and activities that are predominantly male.

....

VII. CONCLUSION

The metaphors trial lawyers use influence their identities as professionals. They shape the way those lawyers perceive reality and the way they behave when carrying out their professional duties. The metaphors for the adversary system consistently stress the competitive, partisan features of dispute resolution at the expense of any other qualities or potential qualities of litigation. These metaphors are used so pervasively and so consistently that many people have ceased to notice that they are only metaphors and not definitions.

The metaphors need to change so that a more complete picture of dispute resolution can emerge. They need to change so that rulemakers are better able to see problems and solutions in the litigation process. They need to change so that trial lawyers must face their conflicting roles within the judicial system rather than suppressing the less appealing prospect of divided loyalties. New metaphors can demonstrate that the competitive parts of litigation are not the only parts, that unmitigated competition does not always benefit even the client, and that the client is not the only person whose interests are important. New metaphors will not erase the social and economic pressures to maximize client desires, but they can still serve a purpose.

....

Part II

Professional Sports

Chapter 3

The Structure and Governance of Sports Leagues

Introduction

Perhaps more than any other area of sports, the legal issues that arise at the professional level are closely aligned with the economics of the industry. If one understands the economics, the legal points of contention are more readily predictable. The dominant economic structure of team sports is the "league." Thus, the selections below begin with a discussion of the law's impact on running a sports league and its franchises.

Many of the basic economic issues residing within professional sports are discussed in the materials that follow. For example, revenues from national television contracts represent a major economic engine for professional sports leagues. The manner in which these revenues are divided is also of great importance. The National Football League is the most "socialistic" of all; teams share their television revenues equally. The other sports leagues place a greater reliance on local television revenues. Thus, in football, the additional revenues from a new facility, particularly from luxury boxes, may be the lone route to greater individual team financial success rather than television revenue. In other sports, an improved local television contract, for example, can improve the bottom line. No such option exists in the NFL. The readings that follow demonstrate the extent to which the nature of these relationships influence legal disputes among NFL owners.

Similarly, live gate receipts are of varying degrees of importance for all professional sports leagues. In recent years it has become clear that the larger markets in baseball, for example, not only have an "advantage" over smaller markets due to the greater revenue potential for local television deals, but due to the potential for greater attendance, which also translates into higher revenues. Once again, football, with fewer games, and greater revenue sharing, is less dependent on the live gate for individual franchise success. Articles in this chapter, as does the Vogel excerpt, examine the role of these economic and other arrangements in shaping the contours of the law.

Section (2) below discusses one of the keys to sports league governance, the league commissioner. The power of this individual to make decisions and act is constrained by both the courts and the guidelines prescribed by the owners of league franchises. Matthew B. Pachman's article, *Limits on the Discretionary Powers of the Professional Sports Commissioners*, focuses on the power this individual has in the various sports leagues.

Section (3) employs one article to explore the extent of the actual monopoly power possessed by professional sports leagues. Professor Stephen Ross's, *Monopoly Sports Leagues* excerpt looks broadly at how the law relevant to sports leagues drives their success. He also explores how various stakeholders, including fans and cities, are impacted by the monopoly status of sports leagues.

Perhaps the key structural issue discussed in the literature and the courts since the early 1980s has been the single entity status of professional sports leagues. Quite simply, there must be at least two parties in order to violate the U.S. antitrust laws. Thus, an ideal defense is that a sports league, albeit a group of about thirty separate enterprises, is for antitrust purposes, a single entity, a league. Much has been written on this subject. The essence of this debate is captured in articles by Professors Gary Roberts and Lee Goldman. The Goldman article is particularly valuable for its summary of the view of other key scholars in the debate. Section (4) describes the litigation in the most recent iteration of this single entity debate. For a thorough discussion of the most recent issues, *see*, PAUL C. WEILER & GARY R. ROBERTS, SPORTS AND THE LAW: CASES, MATERIALS AND PROBLEMS 495-498 (2d ed. 1998).

With the foregoing considerations in mind, this Chapter begins with Harold Vogel's overview of the finances and economics of professional sports leagues. We wish to note that while the focus of this chapter is on teams sports, many of the issues that impact team sports are also relevant to athletes involved in individual sports such as golf and tennis. Issues relevant to those athletes are covered in chapters, *infra*, on torts, crimes, drugs and Olympic sports.

The economics of sports is examined in many articles and other works, in addition to those cited above. A classic economic examination of sports leagues is provided by James Quirk and Mohammed El Hodiri, *The Economic Theory of a Professional Sports League*, chapter one in GOVERNMENT AND THE SPORTS BUSINESS (Roger Noll ed. 1977).

Other noteworthy readings in this area include: Andrew L. Lee, *The Bosman Case: Protecting Freedom of Movement in European Football*, 19 FORDHAM INT'L L.J. 1255 (1996); Jeffrey A. Rosenthal, *The Football Answer to the Baseball Problem: Can Revenue Sharing Work?*, 5 SETON HALL L.J. 419 (1995); Jonathan C. Latimer, *The NBA Salary Cap: Controlling Labor Costs Through Collective Bargaining*, 44 CATH. U.L. REV. 205 (1994); Andrew Zimbalist, BASEBALL AND BILLIONS: A PROBING LOOK INSIDE THE BIG BUSINESS OF OUR NATIONAL PASTIME (Basic, 1992); James Quirk and Rodney D. Fort, PAY DIRT: THE BUSINESS OF PROFESSIONAL TEAM SPORTS (Princeton U. Press, 1992); Michael S. Jacobs, *Professional Sports Leagues, Antitrust, and the Single-Entity Theory: And Defense of the Status Quo*, 67 IND. L.J. 25 (1991); Thane N. Rosenbaum, *The Antitrust Implications of Professional Sports Leagues Revisited: Emerging Trends in the Modern Era*, 41 U. MIAMI L. REV. 729 (1987); David Harris, THE LEAGUE: THE RISE AND DECLINE OF THE NFL (Bantam Books, 1986); Glenn M. Wong, *Of Franchise Relocation, Expansion and Competition in Professional Sports: The Ultimate Political Football*, 9 SETON HALL LEGIS. J. 7 (1985).

1. The Economics of Professional Team Sports

Harold L. Vogel, Entertainment Industry Economics: A Guide for Financial Analysis
263-274 (Cambridge University Press, 4th Edition 1998)*

Sports
It ain't over 'til it's over. — Yogi Berra

In sports today, chances are the game's not over 'til there's another television commercial.

... The exposition underscores the importance of links to broadcasting, cable, and wagering segments, and illustrates how tax-law considerations are at the core of many sports business decisions. But it also indicates why professional sports may be the only business "where the owners want regulation, and labor — the players — want the free market."

....

The most striking feature of the modern sports business is how dependent it has become on broadcasting and cable industry revenue growth. Indeed, in the absence of this electronic-media coverage and the fees so generated, many fewer professional teams and probably many fewer fans would have been created: There were 42 professional sports franchises, mostly in the Northeastern United States, in 1960, and well over 100 franchises spread all over the country by 1995. Moreover, in the 1980s alone, the annual number of hours of sports programming aired by the three major networks and cable systems rose from 4,600 to over 7,300.

All of this growth began with, and has been largely governed by, the Sports Broadcasting Act, which Congress passed in 1961. This legislation gave sports leagues the right to act as a cartel (free of any antitrust sanction) in bargaining with television networks, and has had a beneficial effect on development of interest in all professional sports.

But although sales of transmission rights for sporting events are still heavily weighted toward over-the-air broadcasters, as the cable subscriber base has grown to two-thirds of television homes, cable has become much more important as a source of team revenues. In fact, by the mid-1980s, major boxing events had already become the province of pay-per-view cable, and other sports offerings had become the mainstay for primarily advertiser-supported cable networks. It thus seems that cable could eventually become a foremost licensee of rights to major sporting events such as the World Series and the Super Bowl.

To a large degree, then, it is the expectation of steadily increasing aggregate broadcast and cable rights prices in local, national, and international markets that has made investments in professional sports so attractive for major media and entertainment companies or for those wealthy private investors able to take advantage of favorable tax treatments. In contrast, the appreciation potential of broadcast rights for collegiate and other amateur sports events appears to be more limited.

....

The wagering connection

Wagering has always been an integral part of sports because a contest is always more exciting when spectators are personally involved in the outcome. Indeed, betting on virtually any type of match, from baseball through boxing, is legal and well developed in Nevada (and also in England). Everywhere else in the United States, however, legal sports betting is largely limited to racetracks (horses and dogs) or to jai alai (in Connecticut and Florida). Still, the absence of legal sanction has not stopped people from risking tens of billions of dollars each year on the results of football, baseball, basketball, hockey, boxing, and automobile racing.

The spice that wagering adds to spectator sports is, moreover, also immediately reflected in increased demand for coverage by electronic and print media. The potential for high ratings leads sponsors to pay high prices for commercial time, and leads stations, networks, and cable systems to then bid aggressively for rights to distribute the programs. Because revenues generated from sales of these rights are essential to the operation of spectator-sports enterprises, wagering indirectly provides important financial underpinnings by creating demand for information that would otherwise be of narrow interest.

11.2 Operating characteristics

Revenue sources and divisions

As Scully...notes, "all professional sports leagues restrict entry, assign exclusive franchise territory, and collude on a revenue-sharing formula." And although each professional sport or team may have its own special problems and circumstances, each shares concerns over: (a) the potential for tax-shelter, stadium-lease, and transfer pricing benefits for franchise owners, (b) the prices received for broadcast and cable rights, and (c) the cost of player salaries. Nevertheless, each of the three major sports (football, baseball, and basketball) has evolved differently with regard to these fundamentally common concerns. Football, for example, has always been highly dependent on network-television money—a fact that became especially evident in the early 1980s when the National Football League (NFL) signed a $2 billion, five-year contract with the networks that was for the first time sufficiently large to provide each club with a profit before counting gate receipts. A financial cushion on this order of magnitude clearly permits revenues to be shared among all teams— each gets an equal share of media and licensing revenues and 40% of gate receipts at away games—and furthermore insulates owners from the normal adverse financial consequences of prolonged mismanagement, incompetence, or competition. As a result—despite considerable disparity in on-field performances—the richest NFL team has usually generated only about 20% more gross revenue than the poorest.

Moreover, until recently, football's allocation arrangements—which contained elements of immunity, or exemption from antitrust laws also seen in baseball— tended to reduce aggressive bidding for star athletes and to diminish the general usefulness of free-agency status for players. This is in contrast to the traditional situation in baseball and basketball, where free-agency status has long been effective and has led to the signing of many multimillion-dollar-per-year contracts.

The operating structures of baseball and basketball have also differed markedly from that of football because a lesser percentage of total revenues in baseball and basketball has been shared by the teams, and because market size and gate receipts have historically been much more important determinants of profitability. In both sports,... ticket sales have typically accounted for approximately 40% of total revenues, with concession income from parking fees, advertising, and beer, peanut, and hot-dog sales accounting for only a small part of total income.

Nevertheless, as of the late-1990s, salary-cost pressures and slower growth of media-rights prices appear to be gradually pushing revenue-sharing and salary-cap agreements of all the major sports into closer conformity.

Labor issues

Player salary costs in professional sports have, in recent years, often accounted for as much as 60% of total team operating expenses. And it is thus not surprising to find that many conflicts between players and owners have involved player compensation issues.

But, in fact, the stormy and well-publicized labor relationships that characterize modern professional sports can probably be best understood in the context of several landmark legal decisions, the most significant of which was *Federal Baseball Club of Baltimore v. National League,* argued in the U.S. Supreme Court in 1922. At the time, big league baseball was essentially operated as a cartel in which teams agreed not to hire away each others' players. Nevertheless, this case provided baseball clubs with continued immunity from antitrust laws and thus with the ability to hold on to young players as team property for the duration of their playing careers. Under these conditions, players had no choice but to accept whatever salaries the team owners decided was fair.

Toolson v. New York Yankees in 1953 presented the court with yet another opportunity to correct the obvious economic imbalances, but again the justices decided that baseball was entitled to a special status, and they passed the responsibility for any changes on to a reluctant Congress that, until recently, was satisfied with the status quo.

However, legal challenges by players against the owners finally began to succeed in the 1970s. Although the Major League Baseball (MLB) reserve clause (that originated in 1887) held up under appeal in 1972 in the case of Curt Flood *(Curt Flood v. Bowie Kuhn* (1971)), free agency was approved in late 1975 in what came to be known as the Messersmith Decision.

Prior to this decision, a team would sign a contract with a player for a brief period, usually one season and, under the so-called reserve system, could then hold on to the player for much longer by exercising options to extend contract terms. The system effectively eliminated competition and suppressed player salaries. It also created a valuable property right for the club owners. But after Messersmith, baseball players could, under much less restrictive conditions, become free agents and bargain with other clubs once their contracts expired.

Football and basketball, of course, were never granted the special antitrust immunity of baseball. Yet as Michener... has noted, both sports often acted as if they were immune. Indeed, in both sports, although an athlete could in theory become a free agent after "playing out his option" on a reduced salary, an indemnity system (wherein the player's new team had to compensate his previous team) effectively reduced the player's value to a prospective new owner of his contract.

The court decisions of the 1970s gave athletes the right to negotiate for higher compensation with teams other than their own, and contract terms are no longer necessarily extended beyond an initial period. As a result, in all major sports, but especially in baseball, the implementation of free-agency has significantly raised the level of player compensation...while also bolstering player representation unions.

Soccer, of course, has yet to attain the status of a major sport in the U.S., but is *the* major sport for the rest of the world. As might be expected, rapid growth of global private broadcast interests has led to a media, marketing, and player-compensation structure for professional soccer that is beginning to resemble that of the other major sports.

11.3 Tax-accounting and valuation

Tax issues

From an economic point of view, the tax loopholes that provide benefits to professional team owners make little sense. As Zimbalist...has noted:

(a) The overwhelming share of the value of a franchise is derived not from players' contracts, but from the monopoly rent that is generated from belonging to a league that confers exclusive territorial rights. The value of these territorial rights does not diminish over time.

(b) The value of players does not depreciate over time. Most players reach peak performance beyond the midpoint of their careers.

Despite such economic advantages, however, in many cases it would be difficult for high-income owners to justify investments in professionals sports franchises if it were not for the tax benefits that may also accrue. It is thus worthwhile to at least outline the major tax concepts.

Historical development Prior to 1954 there was a uniform practice of signing players to one-year contracts and of then expensing the acquisition costs of such player contracts during the year of play. In 1954, however, the IRS made a distinction between purchase of a single player's contract and purchase of substantially the entire roster of a baseball club's contracts acquired at one time. In the former case, expensing the cost over one year would remain appropriate; but in the latter, the aggregate amount assignable to players' contracts was to be capitalized and then expensed over the useful life of the assets.

These rulings remained in effect until 1967, when the IRS reconsidered treatment of individual player contracts in light of baseball's reserve clause, which effectively tied a player to a team for his entire career despite the one-year term of his contract. A team's effective long-term control over its athletes implied, according to the IRS, that the cost of individual players' contracts ought also to be capitalized and then expensed over the useful life of the asset.

Then, in the early 1970s, guidelines pertaining to professional-football expansion agreements provided favorable tax treatment to franchise owners. Of greatest importance was the IRS allowance that payments from new teams to established teams could be allocated between the franchise cost and the cost of player contracts for the veterans picked in the expansion draft. Because proceeds allocated to franchise cost were to be treated as capital gains, while proceeds allocable to player contracts were subject to recapture (of tax benefits by the IRS), owners were naturally provided with incentive to allocate as much as possible to franchise costs.

Because most clubs were (and still are) owned by private individuals or by a small number of partners, owners' income from other sources could then be sheltered as long as the franchise was held as a sole proprietorship, partnership, or so-called subchapter-S corporation (or subsidiary of a profitable privately held corporation). All that needed to be done was to buy a franchise and to then allocate a large percentage (say 80%-90%) of the purchase price to player contracts. The resulting large write-downs and reported losses would provide substantial tax savings, and after a few years, the franchise could be sold at a gain....

In effect, prior to the mid-1970s, player-contract depreciation deductions would be converted into capital gains because sellers would allocate most of the purchase price to the franchise asset and very little to player contracts, and buyers would allocate a large portion of the purchase price to depreciable player contracts.

Current treatments   By 1976, concern about potential abuses of professional franchise ownership had risen to the point that Congress felt it necessary to take corrective action against overstating the basis for depreciation, claiming large tax losses despite positive cash flows, and avoidance of depreciation recapture on players who had retired or were otherwise eliminated from the roster. The new law specified that franchise buyers and sellers would have to agree on an allocation formula, that no more than 50% of the purchase price of a franchise would be allocable to player contracts, and that there would be special recapture provisions designed to prevent the stocking of a team with new players possessing substantially undepreciated contracts just before sale of a franchise.

Since 1976, several important court decisions have further defined the tax and accounting ramifications in this area, but issues involving the tax deductiblity of television and cable rights amortizations have not until recently been settled.

....

11.4 Sports economics

Franchise owners have argued that their cartel agreements to block competition are needed to uphold franchise values. Such arguments stand on weak legal ground, but make economic sense in that restriction on the number of clubs and maintenance of territorial exclusivity tends to support the relative and absolute quality of play. That is, professional sports contests would attract fewer fans if the quality of play were low and the uncertainty of the game results were to be reduced.

An interesting early mathematical model of a professional league was presented in Quirk and Hodiri.... This model employed concepts such as a team's inventory of playing skills and cost per unit of playing skills acquired. Assuming that a league is in steady-state equilibrium (the stock of playing skills of each team remains fixed over time), and that franchise owners are motivated solely by profits from operations, the following conclusions were reached:

(a) Franchises located in areas with high drawing potential have stronger teams than franchises in low-drawing-potential areas.
(b) On balance, franchises in low-drawing-potential areas sell players to franchises in high-drawing-potential areas.
(c) If local television revenues are ignored, the distribution of playing strengths among teams is independent of the gate-sharing arrangements.

(d) The higher the share of television and radio revenues accruing to the home team, the higher the costs of players, and the smaller the chance of survival for low-drawing-potential franchises.

In addition, many other studies of sports economics broadly suggest that:

A strong positive correlation between economic and athletic performance exists;

Restrictive labor market practices such as reserve clauses have been used by clubs to extract monopsony rents from player services;

Under free-agency, player compensation rates generally reflect marginal revenue production expectations;

The earnings distribution in individual sports is more skewed than in team sports.

Athletes and teams respond to incentives as predicted by general economic theory.

11.5 Concluding remarks

Sports will continue to be a highly visible and important entertainment segment tightly linked to the broadcasting, cable, and wagering industries. As such, the tools and methods of economic analysis used in those sectors can be readily applied in the study of sports economics. The major trends currently include the following:

More sharing of network-broadcast and cable revenues by professional baseball, basketball, and hockey teams

Emergence of large local and regional cable networks that support collegiate and individual athletic events

Greater emphasis on player mobility and player rights as reserve-clause control by owners is weakened

Significantly increased bargaining power of pay-cable networks and pay-per-view promoters relative to broadcast networks in obtaining distribution rights to major sporting events.

---

2. The Commissioner

Matthew B. Pachman, Limits on the Discretionary Powers of Professional Sports Commissioners: A Historical and Legal Analysis of Issues Raised by the Pete Rose Controversy
76 Virginia Law Review 1409 (1990)*

. . . .

I. THE OFFICE OF THE COMMISSIONER

The most appropriate place to begin an analysis of the breadth of sports commissioner power is with a description of the office itself. This description involves

---

an examination of the provisions of the league charter that outline the commissioner's powers and responsibilities as well as a consideration of the motives behind the creation of the commissioners office. It is helpful to look at the history of the commissioner's office before examining the relevant provisions of the league charter, primarily because historical debate shaped the current charter constructions. The intent of league charter drafters is important to judicial review of commissioner actions in much the same way that legislative intent is important to judicial review of ambiguous statutes. Judges will look to the intent of charter drafters to help determine the meaning of the often ambiguous phrases in league agreements enumerating commissioner powers and limitations.

Because baseball had the first commissioner, and because the office was created in part as a response to a public scandal, the principles, opinions, and debates surrounding the genesis of the commissioner's post are fairly well documented. For this reason, baseball, of all the sports, is the best vehicle to examine the genesis of the commissioner's office. The other major league sports, perhaps without the same degree of urgency, later created their commissioner posts in order to solve similar league governance problems.

In 1903, the National League and the American League were established as the "major leagues" for professional baseball.[22] The "National Agreement" entered into by the two leagues led to the creation of a "National Commission" composed of three baseball personalities. In addition to general supervisory control of professional baseball, the National Agreement granted the Commission "the power to interpret and carry out the terms and provision [sic] of the National Agreement, as well as the ability to enact and enforce fines and suspensions."[24] The fact that Commission members generally had vested interests in particular ball clubs, however, raised questions of fairness and integrity which hampered the Commission's effectiveness. This, in addition to a series of related squabbles and controversies, created a receptive environment for the appointment of a single, impartial commissioner of baseball.

The infamous Chicago Black Sox scandal of 1920 provided the final impetus for the creation of a commissioner's office. The scandal involved eight members of the Chicago White Sox who were accused of accepting gamblers' money to "throw" the 1919 World Series. The Black Sox scandal decreased public confidence in a sport already beleaguered due to the absence of a neutral decision-maker. Significantly, a conflict of interest related to the Black Sox scandal highlighted the dubious nature of the fledgling Commission. August Herrmann, the Commission chairman and acting president of the Cincinnati Reds, the club that had beaten the tainted White Sox in the 1919 World Series, received serious criticism for not investigating the scandal with as much intensity as the situation warranted. In a document entitled the "Lasker Plan," a number of club owners called for replacing the Commission with a single leader of unquestionable reputation who was in no way connected with baseball and whose "mere presence would as-

---

22. Major League Baseball News Release, The Commissionership—An Historical Perspective 4 [hereinafter News Release, The Commissionership] (available through the public relations office of Major League Baseball as part of its press kit entitled "The Commissioners"). For a more accessible history of the baseball commissioner's office, see Charles O. Finley & Co. v. Kuhn, 569 F.2d 527, 532-35 (7th Cir.), *cert. denied*, 439 U.S. 876 (1978).

24. *Id.*

sure that public interests would first be served, and that...as a natural sequence, all existing evils would disappear."[30]

The club owners achieved many of their goals when they successfully convinced Judge Kenesaw Mountain Landis to become the first commissioner of professional baseball. The Judge had gained recognition in the baseball world due to his involvement in a 1914 antitrust challenge brought by the upstart "Federal League" against a number of other established leagues. Landis had a reputation as a "hanging judge," and his demonstrated willingness to challenge such powerful figures as John D. Rockefeller, labor leader Big Bill Haywood, and even Kaiser Wilhelm I made him an ideal candidate to whip baseball into shape. He began his term as commissioner by suspending for life the players involved in the Black Sox scandal, even though they had been exonerated of criminal charges in court.

The new Major League Agreement formalized the reconstituted governance system and granted the commissioner the authority: to be the final arbiter of disputes between leagues and clubs and disputes involving players; to impose punishment and pursue legal remedies for any conduct of league personnel that he determined to be detrimental to the best interests of the game; to resolve disagreements over proposed amendments to the rules; and "to take such other steps as he might deem necessary and proper in the interest and morale of the players and the honor of the game."[35] In an especially significant provision, the club owners expressly waived any rights to challenge the commissioner's rulings in court, "no matter what would be the severity of the new Commissioner's discipline...."[36]

The Major League Agreement clearly provided Landis with much latitude within which to work, and any doubt about whether Landis would use his power to its limits was quickly dispelled. He forcefully implemented his mandate to clean up baseball and thereby improve its image, and the team owners ultimately allowed him to define the broad powers of his office....

It is clear from the strict reliance on the system set up by the Major League Agreement of 1921, and from the broad interpretation Commissioner Landis was allowed to give to the Agreement, that Major League Baseball intended for its Commissioner to have absolute power, and that questions of scope and due process were apparently of little concern. In *Milwaukee American Association v. Landis*,[46] the court confirmed this conclusion when it observed that "[t]he various agreements and rules...disclose a clear intent upon the part of the parties to endow the commissioner with all the attributes of a benevolent but absolute despot and all the disciplinary powers of the proverbial *pater familias*."

Former Baseball Commissioner Bowie Kuhn has pointed out that, at the time Landis served as commissioner, people tended to accept quietly the acts of those in leadership positions, but that after World War II ended, baseball owners became increasingly willing to challenge commissioner authority. In 1944, the year of Landis's death, the Major League Charter was changed in two significant respects: first, clubs would be free to challenge commissioner actions in the courts;[47]

---

30. *Id.*

35. Major League Agreement art. I, §§ 2-4 (1988) (on file with the Virginia Law Review Association).

36. *Id.*

46. 49 F.2d 298, 299 (N.D. Ill. 1931).

47. News Release, The Commissionership, *supra* note 22, at 6.

and second, conduct which did not violate a specific league rule could not be found by the commissioner to be "detrimental to the best interests of baseball."[48]

These limitations on the power of the baseball commissioner did not last long, however. When he retired in 1964, Commissioner Ford Frick convinced the club owners to resurrect the policy of prohibiting court challenges to the commissioner's actions. In addition, the proviso allowing the commissioner to take action *against any act* that he believed to be "not in the best interests of baseball" was restored.[49] The repeal of the restrictions on commissioner activity, together with the reaffirmation of the older provisions by the League's owners increased and strengthened the control the commissioner exerted over baseball. It also demonstrated that these rather strict provisions enjoyed modern day validity, and were not reserved solely for Landis, or for the negative circumstances under which he took office.[50]

. . . .

Not every sports league has a charter as simple as the baseball charter. In football, for example, article VIII of the constitution and bylaws of the National Football League (NFL) describes the powers of the commissioner in a very detailed manner.[56] The NFL charter specifically states the punishments its commissioner may impose. If none of those punishments adequately address a certain case, the NFL commissioner, in what is a significant departure from the approach in baseball, must seek the approval of an executive committee to deviate from the punishments allowed by the charter.

While the punishment of being barred for life is specifically mentioned only in relation to gambling offenses, section 8.13(D) of the NFL Constitution allows the commissioner to bar anyone from professional football if that person is "guilty of conduct detrimental to the best interest of the League or professional football." In this regard, the NFL commissioner's power seems quite similar to that of his baseball counterpart.

In any case where players are involved, sports league rules are tempered by collective bargaining agreements which generally take the form of the "standard player contract."[60] Because a collective bargaining agreement takes precedence over the league constitution in the case of a dispute, one must look to the standard player contracts in order to determine the extent of commissioner power in any individual case. In general, these contracts tend to restate the commissioner's blanket authority to take action based on conduct which he determines to be "detrimental" to the game.[61] An exception is found in the National Basketball As-

---

48. News Release, The Commissionership, *supra* note 22, at 6. This change, according to Commissioner Frick, was intended to be a written codification of a restriction that even Landis believed applied to the "best interests" clause. F. Frick, *supra* note 49, at 211.

49. *See* News Release, The Commissionership, *supra* note 22, at 7.

50. The commissioner's powers increased further during the tenure of Peter Ueberroth to the point that "the two league presidents were required to answer to the commissioner with respect to administrative matters." News Release, The Commissionership, *supra* note 22, at 8.

56. *See* National Football League Constitution and Bylaws art. VIII [hereinafter NFL Const.], *reprinted in* 1 R. BERRY & G. WONG, LAW AND BUSINESS OF THE SPORTS INDUSTRIES 511-14 (1986).

60. *See* 1 R. BERRY & G. WONG, *supra* note 56, at 139, 510-11.

61. *See* Hochberg & Blackman, *supra* note 59, at 11-70. Some of these clauses are more specific than others. The baseball standard player contract merely states that "Player and Club agree to be bound by...the Constitution and By-Laws of the League...pertaining to

sociation (NBA) standard player contract. The provisions of that document indicate that NBA players acknowledge the commissioner's right to suspend them for activities related to gambling, but that other "detrimental" activities are restricted to punishment by fine. Since this caveat has not been tested in court, its effect on suspensions for nongambling activities is unknown.

A commissioner may not violate the agreements that determine the scope of his office. Similarly, regardless of intent, league rules may not violate the law. As in legislative interpretation, however, the intentions of the league's founders may aid courts in their efforts to determine the meaning of ambiguous phrases in league charters....

II. LEGAL CONSTRAINTS ON A COMMISSIONER'S POWER

A. The "Best Interests" Clause

Although a sports commissioner has almost absolute power to enforce the rules governing his sport, courts will not hesitate to interfere with commissioner activities in areas where the commissioner has acted outside the bounds of his authority. [The author's discussion of the "best interests" clause and restrictions on acting beyond authority is omitted. — ed.]

....

B. Due Process Constraints on Commissioner Actions

While courts have shown almost complete deference when defining the scope of professional sports commissioners' powers, most judicial decisions recognize that commissioners are restrained by the requirement of due process.[132] Because of their hesitancy to become involved in the internal affairs of private organiza-

---

Player conduct...and [by] the decisions of the Commissioner of Baseball." *Id.* at 26.

The NFL contract is far more specific:

Player recognizes the detriment to the League and professional football that would result from impairment of public confidence in the honest and orderly conduct of NFL games or the integrity and good character of NFL players. Player therefore acknowledges his awareness that if he accepts a bribe or agrees to throw or fix an NFL game; fails to promptly report a bribe offer or an attempt to throw or fix an NFL game; bets on an NFL game; knowingly associates with gamblers or gambling activity; uses or provides other players with stimulants or other drugs for the purpose of attempting to enhance on-field performance; or is guilty of any other form of conduct reasonably judged by the League Commissioner to be detrimental to the League or professional football, the Commissioner will have the right, but only after giving Player the opportunity for a hearing at which he may be represented by counsel of his choice, to fine Player in a reasonable amount; to suspend Player for a period certain or indefinitely; and/or to terminate this contract.

Id. at 14.

The standard Major Indoor Soccer League player contract follows this form as well: Player acknowledges that if he...is guilty of any...form of conduct reasonably judged by the Commissioner to be detrimental to the League or professional soccer, the Commissioner has the right, after giving Player the opportunity for a hearing, to fine Player in a reasonable amount; to suspend Player for a period certain or indefinitely; and/or to terminate this contract.

Id. at 68.

132. *See, e.g.,* Crouch v. National Ass'n for Stock Car Racing, 845 F.2d 397, 401 (2d Cir. 1988).

tions, courts have shied away from setting out specific due process standards. The definition of the due process requirements placed on commissioners is of tremendous importance, however, as was evidenced by its central role in the *Rose v. Giamatti* controversy.

As a general rule, courts avoid intervention in questions involving voluntary associations and the enforcement of their bylaws or disciplinary rules. This hands-off approach squares well with the underlying justifications for the existence of private systems of arbitration, i.e., streamlining the dispute resolution process and ensuring that conflicts are resolved by experts.... [The remainder of this section discusses specific due process cases.—ed.].

....

CONCLUSION

The confusion experienced during the Pete Rose saga over the scope of professional sports league commissioner power was justified. The law in this area is unclear although certain generalizations may be drawn. As was discussed above, it is unlikely that a court will restrict any actions a commissioner takes under a "best interests" clause. Only if a commissioner fails to observe minimal procedural requirements in the exercise of his duties, and their exercise affects the rights of league personnel, will his broad powers be restricted. Among the most important restraints is the requirement that the commissioner not be biased to the point that he has prejudged the facts of a particular case. The case of *Rose v. Giamatti* illustrated what happens when a commissioner is not conscientious about observing these limits.

Courts should be careful to respect the intent of the founders of sports league governance systems and to allow commissioners broad discretion to take actions necessary to preserve the integrity of their sport. On the other hand, while courts might once have accorded Commissioner Kenesaw Mountain Landis boundless authority, the modern judicial system, out of respect for the rights of those subject to a commissioner's discipline, does not and should not allow today's commissioners to be the "czars" they once were.

---

3. Monopoly Power

Stephen F. Ross, Monopoly Sports Leagues
73 Minnesota Law Reiew 643 (1989)*

Politicians and the public often view sports as a luxury or pure recreation. Major professional sports are businesses, however, and their impact on the economy warrants national attention. The cost to taxpayers of subsidizing sports teams' facilities runs into the hundreds of millions of dollars annually. League decisions concerning the location of franchises have significant impacts on local

---

economies. The allocation of players among teams interests every fan who desires that the hometown team acquire the talent necessary to make the team a championship contender rather than an also-ran. Decisions on the broadcasting of games have a profound effect on consumers/fans. Imagine, for example, the public reaction if next year's Super Bowl were available only on a paycable station!

The economic policy of the United States, as expressed in our antitrust laws, provides that firms should compete in an open and free marketplace to supply consumers with the best possible product at the lowest possible price and to allocate society's resources efficiently. Professional baseball and, to a lesser degree, football are shielded from the antitrust laws. The Supreme Court expressly exempted Major League Baseball from the antitrust laws.[5] The National Football League (NFL) achieved its monopoly status in 1966 when Congress enacted a specific statute permitting the league to merge with its one major rival, the American Football League (AFL).[6]

Economic theories underlying the federal antitrust statutes suggest that monopolies result in higher prices, lower output, and a transfer of wealth from consumers to the producer/monopolist. Therefore, when economic or political considerations lead Congress to suspend application of the antitrust laws for particular industries, some form of government regulation designed to protect consumers from the harms that monopolists inflict almost always accompanies such exemptions. Major League Baseball and the NFL are glaring exceptions to this practice. They operate as monopolists with no significant governmental check upon their ability to exercise monopoly power.

The results of these policy decisions exempting professional baseball from antitrust scrutiny and allowing professional football to achieve monopoly status through merger have been predictable. As lessees of stadiums built and paid for by taxpayers' dollars, sports monopolists obtain favorable contract terms that require the public treasury to subsidize stadium operations. Monopoly sports leagues grant fewer franchises than would exist in a competitive market. To hold salary levels below the competitive level, leagues adopt restrictions on the mobility of players that limit the efficient allocation of players among teams. On the horizon, the distinct possibility exists that sportscasts will shift from free television to cable, forcing fans to pay for what they now receive for free. Finally, monopoly sports leagues tolerate inefficient and wasteful management practices by franchise owners that leagues facing the pressure of competition could not endure.

. . . .

I. MONOPOLY SPORTS LEAGUES HARM TAXPAYERS, FANS, AND PLAYERS

Monopoly sports leagues and their member teams operate in a variety of markets. Local owners of stadiums, usually public stadium authorities, lease their facilities to individual teams. Leagues organize, with limited membership, to sponsor exhibitions of major league talent. Teams contract for the services of players. Leagues and individual teams sell the broadcast rights for these exhibitions to radio, television, or cable stations or networks.

---

5. Federal Baseball Club v. National League, 259 U.S. 200 (1922).
6. Act of Nov. 8, 1966, Pub. L. No. 89-800, 80 Stat. 1515 (1966) (codified as amended at 15 U.S.C. §§ 1291-1293 (1982)).

In each of these markets, the monopoly sports leagues or their member teams exercise monopoly power. No league other than Major League Baseball features franchises that regularly can fill between one and three million seats over eighty-one dates. No league other than the NFL can fill stadiums to near or total capacity for eight Sundays. Localities regard neither a minor league professional baseball team, nor a major college football program, nor a professional football team in a new league as a sufficient substitute for their fans. As a result, local officials and civic groups organize to beseech the monopoly sports leagues for expansion franchises. A special exemption from the antitrust laws permits league members to agree among themselves to limit the games they each televise and to offer a single package of broadcast rights to television networks. For many fans, no acceptable substitutes for Major League Baseball and NFL televised contests exist. Monopoly sports league members agree among themselves to limit competition for the services of players; for most professional athletes, no other employment offers a realistic alternative to professional sports. This portion of the Article details the injury that local treasuries, fans, and players suffer because of the exercise of monopoly power Major League Baseball and the NFL possess.

A. TAXPAYER SUBSIDIES

United States cities eagerly seek professional sports franchises. The teams confer "major league" prestige upon the city, its citizens, and its public officials. Many believe that a franchise brings the city significant economic benefits as well. To attract and retain sports teams in their communities, local governments find it necessary to provide the franchises with substantial subsidies, paid for out of the public treasury. Franchises may insist on large subsidies because cities lack bargaining power when dealing with members of monopoly sports leagues.

Tax subsidies may take a number of forms. These typically include rents priced below the economic value of a facility or forgone taxes on stadium property. Other types of subsidies include the development and construction of new stadiums and improved highway and parking facilities

. . . .

Team owners use their significant advantage in bargaining power to extract subsidies from local treasuries. The number of cities desiring teams greatly exceeds the number of major league franchises. Incumbent owners thus use the threat of relocation to a city currently without a major league franchise to extort concessions from local taxpayers. . . .

In addition, leagues use the scarcity of franchises to wring concessions out of potential expansion cities. For example, in 1975, the NFL, after considering proposals from a host of cities, tentatively decided to expand to Tampa and Seattle. When the initial terms Seattle offered for the lease of its publicly-owned stadium were not to the League's liking, the NFL did not mention Seattle in its expansion franchise announcements. Seattle officials soon succumbed to League pressure and shortly thereafter the NFL announced that Seattle would be the latest expansion franchise. Similarly, Baseball Commissioner Bowie Kuhn explained to a Louisiana member of Congress that although the league was considering New Orleans as a possible expansion city, the city's inability to afford parking facilities and other concessions created a roadblock to expansion.

Some may claim that cities bemoaning the need either to pay tax subsidies or to lose a team have only themselves to blame for poor bargaining. The cities, the argument goes, could protect themselves adequately by entering into long-term leases with the professional sports franchise. The possibility of long-term contracts, however, does not solve the problems that the scarcity of teams creates. Precisely because of the bargaining power that monopoly sports league franchises have over cities, franchise owners usually refuse to enter into long-term leases. For example, when Oakland agreed to provide the Raiders with the stadium improvements owner Al Davis demanded, the city requested a long-term lease to secure bond financing for those improvements, but Davis absolutely refused.

Even if a city were able to negotiate a long-term lease, the team's owner simply could break the lease, pay damages for breach of contract, and receive an indemnity from a new city. Although some courts have found damages an inadequate remedy and have granted injunctive relief to prevent a team from breaching its lease,[36] many other courts, even in the home city of the franchise, have refused to do so.[37] This area of the law is so uncertain that most city officials will grant the concessions demanded rather than risk litigation.

Other observers claim that the league as a whole will protect a city's interests adequately by preventing a team's owner from moving solely to secure more favorable concessions from another city. Indeed, leagues have acted periodically to prohibit a franchise from relocating in search of increased subsidies. The NFL attempted to bar the Oakland Raiders from moving to Los Angeles,[39] and Baseball Commissioner Peter Ueberroth acted to prevent the Minnesota Twins from moving to the Tampa Bay area. Monopoly leagues occasionally, or even frequently, may find it in their self-interest to prohibit franchises from moving, although critics of the leagues can point to other factors that might explain such actions. Such moves may be unpopular among voters in the other cities that currently have franchises, thus exposing the leagues to the risk of legislative retribution. When a team threatens to leave a major media market for a smaller market, television ratings on the league's network package may suffer and the league therefore may act to protect its ratings. Moreover, franchise moves may decrease fan loyalty to the detriment of the league as a whole.

Nevertheless, taxpayers cannot rely on monopoly sports leagues for adequate protection. There is no reason to expect that franchise owners routinely will interfere with their joint-venturers' efforts to make more money at the taxpayers' expense. In fact, leagues often have permitted franchises to move when cities without teams offer more lucrative opportunities. The most famous example is the Dodgers' move from Brooklyn to almost 300 acres of free land in Los Angeles. Perhaps a more typical exercise of league authority involved construction of the Hubert H. Humphrey Metrodome in Minneapolis. The Minnesota Vikings desired a domed stadium, but the owners' efforts to get legislative approval of that costly project stalled. When the NFL discovered that opponents of the domed stadium believed that acquiescing to the Vikings' demand was unnecessary because the League would not permit the team to move, Commissioner Pete Rozelle held a

---

36. *See, e.g.*, City of New York v. New York Jets Football Club, Inc., 90 Misc. 2d 311, 316, 394 N.Y.S.2d 799, 803 (Sup. Ct. 1977).

37. *See, e.g.* HMC Management Corp. v. New Orleans Basketball Club 375 So.2d 700, 707-12 (La. Ct. App. 1979), *cert. denied*, 379 So. 2d 11 (La. 1980).

39. *Raiders*, 726 F.2d at 1385.

special press conference emphasizing the League's willingness to permit the Vikings to move if efforts to obtain a new stadium failed.

Economic theory suggests that if sports leagues did not hold monopoly power in the stadium market, taxpayers would fare better. The existence of competing sports leagues would significantly reduce subsidies. An incumbent team, with its reservoir of good will and fan loyalty, still would obtain some subsidies to prevent it from moving. A city's knowledge that a rival league probably would replace the franchise eagerly, however, would limit the amount of the subsidy. Moreover, competing sports leagues can be expected to expand. As the number of desirable cities without a major league team dwindles, a city's current team will be less able to set off a bidding war by threatening to relocate.

Rival leagues battled for sole rights to an expansion city on only one occasion in recent history: in 1960 both the NFL and the fledgling AFL sought to establish a franchise in Houston. In contrast to the demands upon taxpayers described above, Houston Oilers owner Bud Adams secured a five-year lease on an existing stadium by promising to spend $150,000 of his own money to expand the seating capacity. Twenty-seven years later, with a secure membership in a monopoly sports league, the same Bud Adams threatened to relocate the Oilers to Jacksonville, relenting only after the Houston Astrodome's operator agreed to add, at *its* expense, an additional 10,000 seats and seventy-two sky boxes, as well as granting Adams a more favorable lease.

Experience demonstrates that Major League Baseball and the NFL have monopoly power in negotiating with stadium authorities for the lease of public sporting arenas and that the monopoly sports leagues exercise that power to the detriment of taxpayers. Economic theory, buttressed by the one example in which two rival leagues both sought to enter a new market, confirms that divestiture of monopoly sports leagues into competing economic entities will significantly reduce taxpayer subsidies. Compensation would decrease the ability of team owners to demand that stadiums be built or renovated at public expense and similarly would increase the ability of stadium authorities to secure rent that would cover the cost of operating arenas.

B. INSUFFICIENT EXPANSION

One benefit of a free enterprise system is that the market usually responds to increased consumer demand for a product by spurring increased output of the product. Monopoly sports leagues, in contrast, exercise their power deliberately to hold down the number of available franchises. As a result, fans in cities without Major League Baseball or NFL franchises lose the opportunity to have a team that they may call their own. Leagues exploit fans in cities with franchises by threats of relocation to the many "have-not" areas. Of course, fans in markets capable of supporting expansion franchises but unable to obtain them suffer the major harm of not having a team to follow. Monopoly sports leagues have significant economic incentives to keep the number of franchises below the number that would exist in a free market. The fewer the franchises, the more incentive for have-not cities to provide generous tax subsidies to induce an existing team to relocate....

Even owners with no intention of relocation their own teams have powerful incentives to resist expansion. Limiting the number of teams enhances the value of each franchise.... With more owners, each owner gets a smaller piece of the "pie." Although expansion franchises pay huge sums of money to the existing owners as the price of entry, the smaller share of television revenue offsets the benefit of the one-time entry fee in just a few years.

When a market can support multiple teams, monopoly sports league owners are unlikely to agree to an expansion that jeopardizes a fellow owner's local territorial monopoly.... It is no surprise, then, that the location of two franchises within large metropolitan areas is more likely to occur when there are separate competing leagues....

Some expansion may be sound strategy even for a monopolist. Limited expansion can be a potent political tool. As a monopolist, the NFL faces difficulties when important initiatives cannot go forward without congressional exemptions from the antitrust laws. The NFL has had considerable success in persuading Congress to grant such exemptions and invariably has used expansion teams as a political reward to key legislators....

The NFL also has nonpolitical incentives for permitting limited expansion. If the NFL leaves too many obvious markets without a franchise, the NFL opens itself to challenge from a rival league. In 1960, for example, the NFL occupied only thirteen of the thirty-one available markets for major professional football franchises.[78] As a result, the AFL was able to enter the market in 1960 and to compete successfully with the NFL.

Because the NFL and Major League Baseball are now so large, however, the threat of entry by a new league featuring franchises in locations currently without teams no longer deters either league from creating an artificial scarcity of franchises.... Even if a new league could find room...the new league would face greater difficulties in competing with today's [NFL] than the AFL faced in 1960 with the thirteen-franchise league. Moreover...a dominant sports league can more easily engage in predatory practices to rebuff new entrants than can a similarly dominant monopolist in a more typical industry. Fear of entry by a rival league therefore no longer deters a monopoly sports league from deliberately restricting the number of its members in order to maintain and exploit its monopoly power.

. . . .

It is difficult, if not impossible, to ascertain precisely the optimal number of franchises in major league sports. Economic models can predict, for example, the population characteristics necessary to produce a given amount of revenue for a team that wins half its games. Models cannot predict, however, whether that revenue is sufficient to enable the owners to make a normal return on their investment. Profitability depends on player salary levels, revenue from national broadcast rights, and other factors unascertainable in advance and not necessarily constant as the number of franchises increases.

. . . .

Some empirical evidence nevertheless shows, at least with regard to baseball, that monopoly sports leagues can comfortably expand. Baseball should expand to any market in which an average team can draw one and one-half million fans per season. This proposition is supported by the 1986 season, in which only nine of the current twenty-six teams drew fewer fans, and by recent evidence indicating that well-managed franchises achieve profitability even when their home atten-

---

78. *See* AFL v. NFL, 205 F. Supp. 60, 62, 76 (D.Md. 1962), *aff'd*, 323 F.2d 124 (4th Cir. 1963).

dance is lower.... Finally, several commentators have noted that very large metropolitan areas probably can accommodate additional expansion teams.

The major policy argument against expansion is a lack of "sufficient player talent to produce a proper caliber of play in expanded leagues." Any expansion reduces the average caliber of major league players somewhat. Even if this reduction in quality noticeably affects the fans' enjoyment of the game, however, the dramatic increase in satisfaction in the new expansion cities will usually counterbalance any decreased satisfaction among fans in cities with teams. If live gate attendance measures enjoyment, expansion and the alleged dilution of player quality does not appear to have a negative impact on the fans' enjoyment of the game. For example, overall attendance increased in 1962, 1969, and 1977 after each Major League Baseball expansion. Similarly, overall attendance at NFL games increased after each expansion. Indeed, when the National Hockey League (NHL) expanded overnight from six to twelve teams in 1967, overall attendance at NHL games continued to increase, despite the significant decrease in player quality one would expect with such a rapid expansion.

. . . .

Fans in areas without franchises suffer without a local team. Monopoly sports league owners, however, face strong economic incentives not to expand, but rather deliberately to restrict the number of available franchises. Economic models nonetheless predict that Major League Baseball, for example, easily could expand. With competing leagues, fans in expansion cities would have something to cheer about.

C. INEFFICIENT ALLOCATION OF PLAYERS

Sports fans should prefer a system of allocating players among teams that gives their own favorite team the opportunity to win the championship, but at the same time provides for close, competitive games. To maximize both fan attendance at games and ratings for broadcasts, thereby maximizing revenue, leagues have an incentive to establish player allocation systems that create the greatest fan interest. A monopoly league, however, has an anti-consumer incentive for establishing a player allocation system. In sports in which all teams are members of a single league, teams can agree among themselves on rules that create a monopsony [107] in the acquisition of players. Monopoly leagues therefore can create systems of allocating players that do not enhance the fans' enjoyment of the game, but instead allow league owners artificially to hold down player salaries. These restrictions, of course, have the most direct impact on players. In addition, however, these systems do not allocate players to maximize fan interest. This negative impact on the fans may be of greater importance, but often is overlooked.[108]

The following section will discuss systems of allocating players....

The player allocation systems that Major League Baseball and the NFL adopted have provided fodder for extensive debate in court,[119] before congressional committees, and among academics. This Article's thesis suggests that mo-

---

107. *Monopsony* is the flip side of monopoly—a single firm buying goods or services from sellers.

108. *See, e.g.*, Mackey v. NFL, 407 F. Supp. 1000, 1006-07 (D.Minn. 1975)...*aff'd in part, rev'd in part*, 543 F.2d 606 (8th Cir. 1976).

119. *See, e.g.*, Flood v. Kuhn, 407 U.S. 258, 269-282 (1972).

nopoly sports leagues, under the present scheme, employ inefficient player allocation systems that harm fans. Competing leagues have much less incentive to adopt
such allocation systems, although they might desire to impose some restraints on
the free market to promote exciting, competitive seasons. Unfortunately, both industry defenders and critics in the debate do not currently share this view that existing players allocation systems harm fans. Rather, the consensus viewpoint is
that player restraints do not result in an inefficient allocation of players. Industry
defenders of the current restraints argue that the rules promote competitive balance and thus increase fan interest in the sport. Critics charge that the restraints
have no effect, positive or negative, on player allocation, and serve only to exploit
the players. Those on both sides of this chasm are incorrect.

1. The Desirability of Competitive Balance

Virtually all commentators on this subject agree that "competitive balance" is
a desirable goal for a sports league. Competitive balance occurs when "there is
relative parity among the member teams and...each team has the opportunity of
becoming a contender over a reasonable cycle of years and a reasonable chance of
beating any other team on any given night."[125]

Competitive balance in a league and the close competition it creates chance
fans' enjoyment of sporting events. Economists Roger Noll and Henry Demmert
have demonstrated empirically that attendance increases when championship
races are closely contested. Similarly, courts have recognized that sports leagues
have a unique interest in maintaining competitive balance.[128] The key issue in assessing player mobility restrictions therefore is their effect on competitive balance.

2. Restraints Historically Imposed on Player Mobility Harm Competitive Balance

The reserve clause and the Rozelle Rule are inefficient because cash is superior
to barter as a means of allocating goods in a market.[130] Under these rules, any
change in the current allocation of players effectively is limited to a direct transaction among two or three teams at most. In many circumstances, the rules therefore result in an inefficient allocation of players.

Suppose, for example, that Baseball Team A has a surplus of outfielders, but
needs relief pitching. If Team B happens to have extra relievers but is weak in the
outfield, a trade may result. Suppose that Team B can part with a reliever, however,
but needs a power-hitting pinch hitter, and that Team C has a power-hitting pinch
hitter but needs a utility infielder. In theory, some complex deal involving a number
of teams might be arranged, but the transaction costs would be significant. Cash is
simply more efficient than trading as a means of allocating players. Team A would
pay a premium for relief pitchers, but not for outfielders. Team B could acquire a
free agent pinch hitter. Team C could acquire the utility infielder it needs. In this
way, all three teams would improve their player talent and satisfy their fans.

Relying on trades or other forms of noncash direct transactions also is inefficient and anti-consumer in situations in which a team, perhaps because of bad
luck or poor management decisions, has a current shortage of talented players. In

---

125. Philadelphia World Hockey, Inc. v. Philadelphia Hockey Club, Inc., 351 F. Supp 462,
486 (E.D. Pa. 1972).
128. Mackey v. NFL, 543 F.2d 606, 621 (8th Cir. 1976).
130. R. Ekelund & R. Tollison, Microeconomics 14-15 (2d ed. 1988).

such cases, trades are unlikely to be helpful because a team usually must give up quality players to obtain quality players. Intelligent drafting and development of young talent takes a long time. In a free market, however, an owner recognizing that improved player quality will result in increased attendance could get immediate results by acquiring top players in the open market. Thus, fans of teams with inferior talent clearly suffer from restrictions on player mobility. At the same time, dominant teams with excess talent have no incentive—if cash sales are difficult—to transfer a surplus player to a team that may value the player more. It is ironic that a rule supposedly designed to promote competitive balance actually appears to impede poorer teams' efforts to improve themselves and to become more competitive.

. . . .

Owners in a monopoly league willingly adopt inefficient player allocation schemes because their own profits from eliminating competitive player salaries far exceed any losses due to diminished fan interest in their sport. For example, attendance at Major League Baseball games rose fifty-seven percent, from 29,789,913 in 1975, the last year of the reserve clause, to 46,824,379 in 1985, showing a strong increase in fan attendance after *Messersmith* substantially eliminated the reserve clause. Salaries rose to a competitive level at the same time, however, with the average player's salary increasing from $44,676 to $371,157. In constant dollars, this amounts to a 316 percent increase in costs. Thus, although players and, most important, fans, profit from free agency for baseball veterans, owners do not.

Accordingly, monopoly sports leagues have adopted many rules that increase the league's power in the player market significantly, but which have little effect on league competitiveness.[154] For example, a reserve clause that eliminates almost all free player mobility is unnecessary to achieve competitive balance. If certain teams become dominant—because of location, winning tradition, or size of the market—a league can foster competitive balance by temporarily prohibiting the dominant teams from signing free agents. A system that allows poorer teams to draft players from the rosters of the more successful teams, with minimal compensation paid to the dominant franchise, also could correct any competitive imbalance free agency caused. Also, some form of revenue sharing among franchises could address the fear that teams in cities with larger markets would dominate teams from smaller markets.

Substantial restraints on free agency . . . hurt fans and competition. This is true as a theoretical matter: a cash economy is simply a more efficient way to allocate goods and services than a barter economy. It is also true as an empirical matter: under Major League Baseball's recent regime of free agency, competitive balance and exciting pennant races have flourished; under baseball's ill-fated reserve clause and football's continuous restraints on mobility, there are fewer new champions and greater dominance by a few teams.

3. The Leagues' Thesis: Player Allocation Will Be Distorted Absent Significant Restraints on Player Mobility

League officials argue that restrictions on player mobility serve to promote competitive balance and to enhance fan interest. They observe that the size of the

---

154. *See* Mackey v. NFL, 543 F.2d at 622.

various markets in which major league franchises play differs widely, resulting in a disparity in the revenue each team obtains from live gates and broadcasts. The leagues fear that without restrictions on player mobility, the richer teams in major media markets will outbid their poorer rivals for the best players and dominate the league, ruining competitive balance and reducing fan interest.[163] Significantly, monopoly leagues often have avoided adopting other rules—such as restrictions on investments in player development, coaches, or executive talent—that may significantly increase competitive balance, but do not provide the dividend of monopsonization of the player market.

League officials vigorously reject the contention that an open market will allocate players efficiently.[165] They claim that free agents will flock to cities with the richest teams or owners—to 'glamor' cities like New York, Los Angeles, and Miami—and to teams with winning records. The league's critics have denied this claim with equal vigor....

Veteran Major League Baseball players were not subject to any significant restraints on mobility during a period from 1976 through 1985. An examination of the actual movement of free agents during this ten-year period tests the league officials' claims that unrestricted player mobility results in an exodus of talent to contenders in warm-weather cities with large populations. First, a multiple regression analysis assessed the impact of the net movement of free agents each year, characterizing each franchise by the population of its home city, previous year's place in the standings, and median temperature in April. This analysis revealed no systematic relationship between a franchise's place in the standings and its ability to sign free agents. Multiple regression analysis also revealed only a very weak positive relationship that was not statistically significant, over the entire ten-year period, between both temperature and population and a franchise's net success in signing— versus losing—players in the free agent market. Even if valid, the analysis shows that a city that is eight degrees warmer than another city will sign only one more free agent *over a ten-year period*, hardly cause for concern. Moreover, franchises in the larger cities have a limited edge in attracting free agents in an open market; for every additional million residents, a team will sign fewer than one free agent a decade. Indeed, over the decade of active free agency, the Los Angeles Dodgers and the New York Mets *lost* more free agents than they signed.

....

4. The Critics' Thesis: Restraints Have No Effect on Competitive Balance

The reserve clause, the Rozelle Rule, and other significant restraints on a free market for players have come under extensive attack from academics who claim that the restraints have no effect on the allocation of players, but merely allow owners in monopoly sports leagues to act collusively so as to reduce the salaries paid to players. These critics argue that a free market does exist because a team can sell a player's contract to another team. The only difference between a system using a reserve clause and a free market system, they maintain, is that under the former, the premium needed to acquire a player is paid to the player's prior team,

---

163. *See Smith v. Pro Football*, 420 F. Supp. at 746.
165. *See Smith v. Pro Football*, 420 F. Supp. at 745-46; *see also Mackey v. NFL*, 543 F.2d at 621.

not to the player himself. These critics conclude that the owners' desire for monopsony power alone motivates any restrictions on player mobility.

This argument has two flaws. First, these critics falsely assume that teams freely sell player contracts among themselves. Second, the critics fail to recognize that some restraints on player mobility may be necessary to achieve competitive balance.

. . . .

In a free market, a player will go to the team that places the highest value on his services. For example, if Rickey Henderson were playing for the Seattle Mariners, but the New York Yankees valued him most highly, he would sign with the Yankees when his contract expires. Acquiring Henderson will, of course, please Yankee fans and further enrich the New York franchise. The acquistion might also, however, make the Yankees too dominant in the American League East, thereby decreasing the enjoyment, and possibly the attendance, of the fans in other American League East cities. In theory, if the adverse marginal effect of the trade upon the Yankees' American League East rivals were greater than the marginal benefits to New York, then the Red Sox, Orioles, Blue Jays, Indians, Tigers, and Brewers could all get together and pay Seattle not to sell Henderson to the Yankees. In reality, however, the high transaction costs would prohibit this arrangement. An inefficient allocation of resources results: fans on the whole would be worse off if Henderson moved to the Yankees than if he stayed in Seattle. Maximizing fan interest may necessitate some generalized restraint to prevent players from moving freely to the team that values them most highly.

. . . . [A discussion of rival league and minor league restraints is omitted. — ed.].

D. PRESERVING OPPORTUNITIES TO WATCH GAMES ON
FREE TELEVISION

Competition forces firms operating in a free market to lower the price of their goods and services to cost, although many consumers willingly would pay far in excess of that price. Economists refer to the difference between the maximum amount consumers would pay and the actual price as *consumer surplus*. As one of its principal functions, antitrust laws prevent firms from engaging in tactics that shift wealth from consumers to producers by robbing consumers of this surplus.

Few markets permit consumers to enjoy a greater amount of surplus than the telecasting of major professional sports. The NFL broadcasts virtually all of its games on free television. Each Major League Baseball team broadcasts a large number of its games on free television. Any fan with a television set can watch all post-season playoff contests, the World Series, and the Super Bowl.

As technology makes it more feasible for monopoly sports leagues to capture this surplus, many observers predict that these leagues will do so. . . .

This anticipated shift to cable probably will have several effects. First, some fans no longer will be willing and able to view games they now can see for free. Second, because many fans will be willing to pay to watch their favorite team on television, there will be a significant transfer of wealth from fans to league owners. Fees cable networks generate from charging a few dollars per household for top games will translate into offers to the NFL for broadcast rights that will more than offset the resulting decrease in revenues from contracts with free television networks. . . .

. . . .

Not every league decision to shift some games to cable is necessarily inefficient and contrary to the fans' best interest. A cable contract may allow a league to televise nationally some contests— Sunday night football, for example—that do not attract the attention of the major networks. In such a case, fans benefit by gaining the option of watching a cablecast of a contest that otherwise would not be broadcast at all.

Competing leagues would be unlikely, however, to shift to cable if free television has a strong interest in obtaining broadcast rights. Each team's football games would continue to be telecast on free television back to home markets; networks would continue to feature nationally the top weekly games; large numbers of baseball games and a featured game-of-the-week also would remain on free television, as would all post-season contests. This is because if one league shifted to cable, a rival league could remain on free television and pick up many new viewers. A monopoly league, in contrast, would face no retribution in the market for a decision to shift to cable in order to capture the large consumer surplus.

E. INEFFICIENT MANAGEMENT

Another of the myriad benefits of competitive markets is their tendency to force firms to operate efficiently, providing the highest quality of goods and services to consumers at the lowest possible cost. Indeed, firms that introduce innovations and quality control are rewarded with greater sales, sometimes at premium prices, and higher profits. Firms that operate less efficiently lose business to rivals.

Owners of teams in monopoly sports leagues, however, have substantial room to engage in inefficient behavior. Mounting a challenge to an entrenched monopoly sports league through the creation of a new league is costly and difficult. As a result, monopoly sports leagues do not face the retribution of the marketplace for inefficient decisions about expansion, franchise relocation, player allocation systems, and many other matters.

In fact, monopoly sports leagues are more harmful to consumers and more inefficient than other monopolies. A single corporation that monopolizes an industry may enjoy 'the quiet life,'[237] but its managers otherwise will strive to maximize profits for the corporation as a whole. By contrast, franchises are not organized to maximize overall league profits; rather, franchisers join a league to maximize their own individual profits.... Thus, owners might reject innovations that would be in the best interest of Major League Baseball or the National Football League as a whole. Each league's adoption of roles that require a three-fourths majority to approve any major innovation exacerbates this problem....

Legislative hearings and academic writings recount numerous examples of innovations that a minority of owners blocked because of their individual self-interest at the expense of the league and, indirectly, fans. For example, a minority of baseball owners from the larger markets repeatedly has rejected proposals to increase revenue sharing despite the sports leagues' contention that revenue sharing promotes competitive balance and is thus good for the sport....

Defenders of the leagues—especially those affiliated with the NFL—staunchly insist that sports leagues are "single entities." Commissioner Pete Rozelle has testified that the league "is as much of a common enterprise and a business partnership as any law firm partnership." Similarly, Professor Gary Roberts has written

---

237. *See*, Hicks, *Annual Survey of Economic Theory: The Theory of Monopoly*, 3 Econometrica 1, 8 (1935).

that "[o]nly with the total cooperation of every league member on every aspect of league operations can there be a league product...." Whatever significance this argument may have in other contexts, the league remains nonetheless a collective of owners who have interests that do not always serve the league as a whole.

League officials—most notably NFL Commissioner Pete Rozelle—have worked tirelessly and with some success to persuade owners to act in the interests of the league as a whole, to engage in "Leaguethink," as author David Harris has described it.[249] Nevertheless, in many cases, a monopoly league accepts intolerable inefficiencies because the owners do not wish to act against one of their own. If a competitive league entered the market with an efficient front-office management team, no incumbent league would permit Baltimore (now Indianapolis) Colts owners Robert Irsay to call plays from his owners' box even though he had no experience in football, or allow a former owner's wife, who had no experience and had developed a reputation for incompetence, to manage the franchise in the nation's second largest market. Nor would the league tolerate continued misman-agement of the Philadelphia Eagles by owner Leonard Tose as he sought to stay one step ahead of creditors seeking repayment of gambling debts....

As with other abuses of monopoly power, fans are the primary victims of inefficient management. Loyal fans of local teams, having no marketplace alternative to which they can turn, have little choice but to endure whatever management chooses to do. The dilemma facing proud fans who must suffer or cease patronizing teams they love is precisely the dilemma that competition, as enforced through antitrust policy, is designed to avoid.

4. Single Entity Status

Lee Goldman, Sports, Antitrust, and the Single Entity Theory
63 Tulane Law Review 751 (1989)*

I. INTRODUCTION

This Article addresses whether section 1 of the Sherman Act[1] should be applied to joint actions by members of professional sports leagues....

....

Each section 1 challenge to league restraints poses the same threshold issue: whether the league member teams are capable of unlawful agreement. Although teams are separate legal entities, they are all part of a greater entity, the league, and must cooperate on many issues to produce the league product. Accordingly, leagues and commentators have posited that it is the league, not the individual

---

249. D. HARRIS, THE LEAGUE: THE RISE AND DECLINE OF THE NFL 14 (1986).

* Originally published in 63 Tul. L. Rev. 751-797 (1989). Reprinted with the permission of the Tulane Law Review Association, which holds the copyright. All rights reserved.

1. 5 U.S.C. § 1 (1982 & Supp. IV 1986). Section 1 of the Sherman Act provides, in relevant part: "Every contract, combination..., or conspiracy, in restraint of trade or commerce...is declared to be illegal."

member clubs, that is the relevant "firm" for antitrust purposes. They conclude that no section 1 violation can occur when the league member teams make decisions regulating internal league affairs because there is no plurality of firms sufficient to support a finding of contract, combination, or conspiracy under section 1.

Most courts that have reviewed challenges to intraleague agreements have not directly confronted the so-called single entity defense, but have assumed, without actually deciding, that sports leagues were plural entities. Two relatively recent court of appeals decisions have specifically rejected the defense.

Despite the virtually uniform unwillingness of the courts to adopt the single entity defense, the validity of the defense apparently remains an open issue. The courts of appeals in *Los Angeles Memorial, Coliseum Commission v. National Football League*[19] and *North American Soccer League v. National Football League*[20] relied, in part, on the intra-enterprise conspiracy doctrine to support a finding of agreement. The intra-enterprise conspiracy doctrine, however, was overruled by the Supreme Court in *Copperweld Corp. v. Independence Tube Corp.*[22] Several commentators have since argued that the validity of the single entity defense must be reconsidered in light of Copperweld. The three major commentators to focus exclusively on the single entity issue have each urged that the defense be recognized in virtually all cases.

. . . .

This Article finds that *Copperweld* does not support a complete single entity defense for sports leagues, but does provide some general guidelines to determine single entity status. In particular, this Article advocates that co-venturers should not be treated as a single entity unless either (1) a single entity has the right to exercise day-to-day control over all participants in the venture or (2) the jointly created entity produces a new product and the co-venturers are acting on behalf of the joint entity without implicating any independent economic interest of a co-venturer. Applying these standards to sports leagues compels the conclusion that most intraleague decisions are properly subject to section 1 review.

II. BACKGROUND

. . . . [The author's discussion of the National Football League's history and structure is omitted. — ed.].

B. *Judicial Treatment of the Single Entity Theory*

Despite the critical importance of determining whether leagues should be treated as single entities, surprisingly few cases have directly addressed this issue. The Supreme Court has yet to rule on the question. To some, two early district court cases[40] appeared to accept the leagues' argument that league members should be treated as a single entity. Those cases, however, can be read alternatively as merely finding that the challenged conduct had no anticompetitive effects. The vast majority of sports cases have simply assumed that league members were capable of agreement.

---

19. 726 F.2d 1381 (9th Cir.), *cert. denied*, 469 U.S. 990 (1984).
20. 670 F.2d 1249 (2d Cir.), *cert. denied*, 459 U.S. 1074 (1982).
22. 467 U.S. 752 (1984).
40. Levin v. National Basketball Ass'n, 385 F. Supp. 149 (S.D.N.Y. 1974); San Francisco Seals, Ltd. v. National Hockey League, 379 F. Supp. 966 (C.D. Cal. 1974).

The only two court of appeals decisions that have specifically discussed the single entity issue found league members capable of agreement. In *North American Soccer League v. National Football League*,[44] a professional soccer league challenged the NFL's cross-ownership ban that precluded members from owning teams in other professional sports leagues. The Second Circuit tersely rejected the NFL's single entity argument. Citing a long list of primarily intra-enterprise conspiracy and sports restraints cases, the court stated: "The theory that a combination of actors can gain exemption from [section] 1 of the Sherman Act by acting as a 'joint venture' has repeatedly been rejected by the Supreme Court and the Sherman Act has been held applicable to professional sports teams by numerous lesser federal courts." The court also feared that characterizing the league as a single entity would create a loophole which would allow a league to escape antitrust liability for agreements when the benefits to the league were outweighed by the agreements' anticompetitive effects. The court found such a result particularly inappropriate because the cross-ownership ban did not merely protect the NFL as a league, but shielded discrete economic entities—individual teams— from competition in their home territories.

The league's single entity theory received more extended discussion, as well as notoriety, in *Los Angeles Memorial Coliseum Commission v. National Football League*.[48] That case involved the hotly contested move by the Oakland Raiders to Los Angeles. The Coliseum and the Raiders challenged League Rule 4.3, which prohibited any league member from moving its franchise without the prior approval of three-fourths of the existing member clubs. The court of appeals, in a two to one opinion, affirmed the lower court's decision directing a verdict against the league on the single entity issue and approved the jury's finding that Rule 4.3 was an unreasonable restraint of trade under section 1 of the Sherman Act.

The appellate court's single entity analysis focused on and approved of the three grounds relied upon by the district court. First, the court indicated that the league's argument would be inconsistent with the numerous cases finding that other league restraints, such as the cross-ownership ban, the draft, and the "Rozelle rule," violated section 1. Second, the court found the league's argument inconsistent with the Supreme Court's intraenterprise conspiracy cases. Although the court acknowledged that those cases were the subject of much criticism, it felt bound by them because "they remain the law." The court also found that the league could not satisfy the Ninth Circuit's exception to the intra-enterprise conspiracy doctrine for multiple corporations in which one individual or corporation sets corporate policies. The court reasoned that NFL policies were not set by one parent, but by the separate teams acting jointly. Finally, the court found that the teams' separate profits and losses supported the conclusion that the teams were independent entities. The court recognized the necessity for cooperation between teams, but found that the necessity for otherwise independent business entities to cooperate had never sufficed to preclude scrutiny under section 1. Judge Williams vociferously dissented. He found that NFL clubs did not compete in any meaningful sense, but were profoundly interdependent, and argued that the majority's failure to reconcile properly the organizational and operational aspects of the league enterprise with economic realities severely threatened consumer welfare. No ap-

---

44. 670 F.2d 1249 (2d Cir.), *cert. denied*, 459 U.S. 1074 (1982).
48. 726 F.2d 1381 (9th Cir.), *cert. denied*, 469 U.S. 990 (1984).

pellate court has decided the single entity issue since *Los Angeles Memorial Coliseum Commission*.

Despite the consistent unwillingness of the judiciary to adopt the single entity theory and the extensive analysis provided by the Ninth Circuit for its rejection, commentators have reasonably argued that there are legitimate bases for questioning existing law: the absence of a Supreme Court ruling on the subject; the partial reliance on the now repudiated intra-enterprise conspiracy doctrine by the only two appellate courts to address the issue directly; and Judge Williams' vigorous dissent in *Los Angeles Memorial Coliseum Commission*.

III. THE COMMENTATORS' VIEWS

All of the major articles exclusively addressing the single entity issue have recommended that leagues be treated as single entities for most, if not all, league decisions. The views of these commentators are analytically interesting, but ultimately unpersuasive and potentially dangerous. There are flaws common to all of their works, but the thoroughness of their efforts and their independent insights justify individual treatment of each commentator's views.

A. *Professor Roberts*

Professor Roberts has been the most ardent supporter of the single entity defense for sports leagues.[63] He is sharply critical of reliance on separate team ownership as a basis for treating league decisions as agreement under section 1. According to Professor Roberts, teams are not "true" economic competitors. No revenue is generated by a single team operating independently, but it derives solely from the team's membership in the wholly integrated operation of the league. "Separate" ownership, the revenue sharing scheme, and the internal "competition" that both engender are mere manifestations of the league decision to structure its operations so that each member performs optimally. That a league could form and choose to operate without separate ownership or with complete revenue sharing highlights to Professor Roberts that club ownership is not separate ownership in any meaningful antitrust sense, but is merely the right of a "partner" to share in the revenue of the integrated league operations.

The fundamental error of those focusing on separate ownership to determine whether leagues should be treated as separate entities, according to Professor Roberts, is their failure to consider antitrust policy. Because the Sherman Act is primarily, if not exclusively, a statute designed to maximize consumer welfare, whether sports leagues should be treated as single entities is properly determined by an analysis of which approach is most consistent with consumer welfare. Of course, Professor Roberts concludes that treating all league decisions as those of a single entity best satisfies the goal of consumer wealth maximization.

Professor Roberts' detailed and well-written articles persuasively underscore the need for cooperation among league members. The coproductive nature of leagues should permit team decisions on behalf of the league when the teams are acting as an executive committee or board of directors without implicating their independent marketplace identities. When teams have personal stakes as a result

---

63. *See* Roberts, *supra* note 23; Roberts, *supra* note 24; *see also* Roberts, *supra* note 18, at 968-70.

of their separate ownership and separate profits and losses, however, joint decisions should be considered agreements for the purposes of section 1.

Professor Roberts' contrary conclusion rests, in part, on an unwillingness to accord current league structure sufficient weight. The twenty-eight member clubs are separate legal entities— some are corporations, some are partnerships, and some are sole proprietorships. No two clubs have a common owner. Indeed, the Constitution and Bylaws of the NFL prohibit a member club from having any financial interest, directly or indirectly, in a competing club. The clubs share a large part, but not all, of their revenues. They do not share their profits and losses. Each club is managed independently, having control over its own day-to-day decisionmaking concerning ticket prices, the acquisition and salaries of players, coaches, and administrators, the terms of its stadium lease and equipment purchases, and the sale of local radio and preseason television rights. The teams' profits and losses are widely disparate as a result of these independent decisions.

Nevertheless, Professor Roberts argues that while separate ownership is not a misleading description for most purposes, the reality of league economics and the inability of clubs to generate revenue outside the league makes this independence meaningless for antitrust purposes.

Although member clubs do not generate revenue outside the integrated enterprise, the same can be said about many joint enterprises whose members are treated as separate entities for antitrust purposes. For example, most independent franchisees, such as McDonald's franchisees, do not generate revenue outside the parent franchisor's enterprise. Moreover, the success of franchisees, like that of league member clubs, depends on the success of the integrated enterprise as well as the performance of its members. Customers have learned to expect a level of quality and value at any McDonald's. This is one reason for eating at a McDonald's franchise. If some franchisees fail to maintain that level of quality and value, the enterprise's reputation is diminished and the success of all franchisees is undermined. Indeed, almost every vertically integrated enterprise can be said to rely on the integrated enterprise's existence to produce revenue. Yet where the co-venturers are separately owned, independently controlled, and have separate profits and losses, they are treated as independent, and competition can lead to more efficient market allocation of resources. Of course, the corproductive nature of the integrated enterprise may result in a more sympathetic analysis of covenants between co-venturers, but such covenants are nonetheless agreements for the purpose of section 1.

It is also legally irrelevant that the league could have chosen to structure itself to discourage competition by completely sharing revenues or by eliminating separate ownership. A manufacturer could choose to vertically integrate and eliminate the independence of its distributors. If it does not do so, however, an agreement with its distributors on price is per se illegal resale price maintenance. General Motors, Ford, and Chrysler could have entered the market as a single automobile company (assuming they were ready to enter at the same time). They did not. They cannot now act as a single enterprise. More generally, the analysis of whether there is an agreement for antitrust purposes must take the marketplace as it currently exists, not as it hypothetically might have been.

In short, Professor Roberts' attempts to dismiss the significance of the member clubs' independent ownership and profits and losses are unconvincing. His consumer welfare standard is equally problematic.

Professor Roberts' consumer welfare model for determining single entity status does not depend on an analysis of whether the particular practice being challenged enhances efficiency or furthers consumer welfare. Rather, Professor Roberts' standard rests on whether consumer welfare is generally enhanced over the long run by assuming that the organization's internal management decisions are adopted in furtherance of organizational efficiency.

This consumer welfare test is unpredictable and sweeps too broadly. Any organization may simultaneously make decisions that enhance and detract from consumer welfare. Under the Roberts standard, a determination of whether an organization is a single entity seems to require a court to decide which type of decision is likely to predominate. Professor Roberts eschews the rule of reason due to the difficulty of determining the effect of a single restraint. Yet his standard apparently requires an analysis of the likely effects of all possible restraints. Even if those restraints and likely effects could be isolated, it is unclear how one could balance such unquantifiable data. Furthermore, Professor Roberts' all-or-nothing approach accepts purely harmful restraints merely because there are net beneficial effects from cooperation. There is no requirement that the anticompetitive agreements be reasonably necessary to produce the benefits, and no consideration is given to less restrictive alternatives available to achieve the same beneficial effects.

Classification of an organization that may have mixed goals illustrates the difficulties. Trade associations are designed to enhance industry efficiency. Typical association activities include cooperative industrial research, market surveys, development of new uses for products, mutual insurance, joint representation before legislative and administrative agencies, publication of trade journals, and joint advertising and publicity. Yet the same associations can also be mechanisms for price fixing or boycotting of industry competitors. Which activity predominates? If the trade association's overriding organizational goal is defined as improving industry performance and competitiveness, Professor Roberts' standard would apparently immunize from section 1 attack explicit price fixing and boycotts by such associations.

A fundamental problem with Professor Roberts' standard is its inability to distinguish between the formation of the enterprise or joint venture and the enterprise's terms. For example, if General Motors has a plant that is about to close due to inefficient operation, and Toyota is unable to sell large numbers of cars due to quotas, a General Motors/Toyota joint venture may enhance consumer welfare. When General Motors and Toyota agree on the price of their joint product, it would not be illegal because the joint venture would be considered a single enterprise and the price agreement an essential ancillary term. Yet there is little doubt that an agreement giving the automakers' joint venture an exclusive sales territory, although enterprise enhancing, would simultaneously reduce competition between General Motors and Toyota and constitute illegal market division. Professor Roberts' failure to distinguish the validity of an enterprise or joint venture from its terms is inconsistent with a long line of Supreme Court precedent.

Consideration of franchisor/franchisee or manufacturer/distributor relationships highlights the problems with and potential impact of Professor Roberts' standard. Presumably, a manufacturer or franchisor structures the internal management decisions of the enterprise to enhance the organization's efficiency. Indeed, the belief that the enterprise's profit motive furthers consumer welfare has justified the sympathetic treatment accorded vertical restraints. Yet no one has suggested that manufacturer/distributor or franchisor/franchisee agreements are not agreements for the purpose of section 1. To do so, as application of Professor Roberts' standard seems to, would make resale price maintenance, as well as vertical nonprice restraints, per se legal.

The problems with Professor Roberts' standard derive from his critical assumption that where there is a valid single enterprise, any decision enhancing the enterprise will benefit consumer welfare. This assumption ignores the possibility that the enterprise's members have independent economic interests. Decisions that enhance the enterprise may simultaneously distort market forces at the public's expense by reducing the horizontal competition that co-venturers would otherwise face. For this reason, a personal stake outside the enterprise by one of its members has long been recognized as a basis for finding an agreement for the purpose of section 1. Teams' independent interests aside, Professor Roberts' assumption still fails. League interests and the public interest are not coextensive. It is hard to see how an agreement to fix ticket prices, which certainly enhances the enterprise, benefits consumer welfare. Similarly, agreements restricting the sale of pay television rights may enhance league revenues, but reduce the output of televised football to the public's detriment. Even agreements lowering league members' costs may not benefit consumer welfare if the result is an artificial allocation of market resources.

In sum, Professor Roberts' standard is unpredictable and inconsistent with Supreme Court authority. It takes a narrow view of consumer welfare and threatens to legalize vertical restraints, including resale price maintenance, and overrule the personal stake exception to the intra-enterprise conspiracy rule.

Whatever the shortcomings of the general standard for determining single entity status, Professor Roberts would argue that such disadvantages pose no difficulty for determining the status of sports leagues because the leagues' existence is essential to the production of the entertainment product, and no single team is capable of producing anything of economic value on its own; thus there is no independent competition to restrain.

Professor Roberts' basic premise, however, is false. Teams are capable of producing a sports entertainment product outside a league venture. Indeed, before the NFL was formed, teams traveled the country playing individual football games. Individual sports clubs such as the Harlem Globetrotters basketball team or the King and his Court softball team have profitably traveled the world presenting exhibitions. Many college teams, such as Notre Dame's football teams, are major attractions without league membership. Further, the name recognition developed in college makes professional barnstorming even more feasible now than it was historically. The success of exhibitions involving the United States Olympic basketball team is illustrative.

It may be that league membership enhances the product presented by sports teams. The league product may even be considered a separate or new product. That, however, merely serves to justify the venture; it does not immunize all of the venture's terms from section 1 attack nor distinguish a long line of Supreme Court precedent.

Professor Roberts' concern with consumer welfare is laudable. Leagues do present an entertaining product, and many of their restraints are essential for, or beneficial to, the efficient conduct of their business. It is not necessary, however, to find the league and its members a single entity for all purposes in order to preserve such restraints. A section 1 violation requires a showing that an agreement exists and that the agreement unreasonably restrains trade. If league restraints promote competition more than they hinder it, such restraints can be upheld under the rule of reason.[98] The rule of reason allows for individualized determinations of harms and benefits. Equally important, the rule of reason would not result in the reversal of well-established law and the creation of precedent that other industries could use to avoid application of section 1 to their collective actions.

Professor Roberts acknowledges that beneficial internal management policies should survive a rule of reason test. He objects, however, that a full-blown rule of reason proceeding is costly and unpredictable. Although a rule of reason inquiry can in some cases be costly and unpredictable, there is no reason why it should be any more so for sports leagues than it is in other areas where the rule of reason must be applied. Additionally, many sports cases are easily disposed of, without distorting single entity theory, through a standing analysis, application of the labor exemption, or a "quick look" rule of reason inquiry.

Nevertheless, Professor Roberts is concerned that judicial review of internal league governance through a rule of reason analysis will result in frivolous lawsuits. The courts, however, have already shown an ability to deal with such claims through summary judgment. Although sports leagues should not have to be in court on frivolous claims at all, that problem is more properly dealt with by awarding Rule 11 sanctions than by distorting the single entity analysis.

In summary, Professor Roberts' analysis fails to give sufficient weight to the current league structure of separate ownership with separate profits and losses, or to acknowledge teams' independent economic interests; takes a naive view of sports teams' ability to produce a product on their own; fails to distinguish between an enterprise's existence and its terms; erroneously assumes joint enterprises will protect consumer welfare; and does not adequately acknowledge the dual requirement of agreement and restraint of trade for a section 1 violation. As a result, the standard that he suggests threatens to undermine existing case law in a wide variety of areas.

.... [Professor Goldman's critique of the views of Professor Grauer is omitted. Goldman describes Professor Roberts views as a refinement of Grauer's earlier work. Consequently Professor Goldman posits that Grauer's model is subject to many of the shortcomings ascribed to Roberts' model. —ed.].

C. Professor Weistart

Professor Weistart recognizes that teams within a league both compete and cooperate. He does not support a complete single entity defense, but argues that teams should be treated as a single entity when they operate "with such economic interdependence that [they] should be allowed to enjoy the economic freedom af-

---

98. There are two basic approaches to determining the legality of an agreement alleged to restrain trade. A per se rule allows a court to find certain agreements illegal without elaborate inquiry into the precise harm they have caused or the business justification for their use. The truncated analysis is justified by the belief that agreements subject to per se treatment have such a pernicious effect on competition and lack any redeeming value that their unreasonableness may be presumed. Northern Pac. R.R. v. United States, 356 U.S. 1, 5 (1958). By contrast, the rule of reason requires a consideration of the nature, purpose, and effect of any challenged agreement before a decision is made about its legality. Chicago Board of Trade v. United States, 246 U.S. 231, 238 (1918).

forded other more traditional collections of capital, such as partnerships and corporations."[145]

Focusing on the court of appeals' single entity analysis in *Los Angeles Memorial Coliseum Commission*, Professor Weistart finds that the court overvalued the independence of sports franchises and the significance of separate profits and losses, and underweighed the extent to which teams require joint cooperation. Professor Weistart also finds the cases relied upon by the court of appeals distinguishable and views the Supreme Court's decision in *Copperweld* as support for finding that it is not necessarily desirable to increase competition between components irrevocably bound in a common economic venture.

Nevertheless, Professor Weistart, unlike Professors Roberts and Grauer, recognizes that teams do compete economically, at least to some extent, and acknowledges that adopting a single entity defense has several dangers. Still, he ultimately rejects analysis under the rule of reason as too unpredictable. Fearing complete exemption from section 1, however, Professor Weistart suggests as a potential limit on the single entity defense the distinction drawn by Judge Williams in his dissenting opinion in *Los Angeles Memorial Coliseum Commission*. The league should be treated as a single entity when marketing its product ("downstream output"), but should be subject to section 1 in its relationships with players and suppliers ("upstream flow").

Professor Weistart's arguments downplaying the significance of the separate legal status of member clubs, with separate profits and losses, contains many of the same arguments and flaws as Professors Roberts' and Grauer's analyses. Professor Weistart, like Professor Roberts, questions the ability of member clubs to produce independently anything of value. He challenges the abiality of a disgruntled league member to join a new league, as suggested by the *Los Angeles Memorial Coliseum Commission* court, observing that such a move would interfere with the expectations of the club's players and violate their contracts. Similarly to Professor Grauer, Professor Weistart argues that the separate profits and losses are little different from the unequal division of profits that can exist among partners in an accounting or law partnership. He adds that the differences between the two are even further diminished if the economic effect of league cooperative behavior is fully recognized. Professor Weistart views the sharing of revenues and the player draft as subsidies from successful teams to unproductive ones nearly equivalent to the sharing of profits and losses.

The notion that teams are not able to produce anything of independent value has previously been dispelled. The assertion that players can not be switched between leagues is factually questionable and ultimately meaningless. Players may be under personal services contracts that must be honored, or may choose to continue playing, fearing unemployment if faced with limited free agency and team player limits. More fundamentally, whether players would choose to remain with the club is irrelevant. The issue is whether a team, not exactly the same team, has independent value. An independent Toyota distributor can not sell Toyotas if its distributorship is terminated. It does not follow that it is incapable of producing anything of independent value. The distributor can still obtain other cars to sell. Similarly, a team can always hire other players.

---

145. Weistart, *supra* note 23, at 1044.

The analogy to a law partnership has previously been rejected. Emphasizing league revenue sharing and player drafts does not strengthen the analogy. The extent of revenue sharing, although substantial, has often been overstated. Relying on the player draft to support single entity status is little more than bootstrapping. The draft is itself a form of restraint that has been subject to challenge as an illegal agreement between separate entities. Most importantly, the argument misperceives the significance of separate profits and losses. Where there are separate profits and losses, as opposed to sharing of common revenue, there is a greater personal stake or independent interest that justifies treating the entity members as separate decisionmakers.

Professor Weistart's attempt to distinguish the line of cases that his, as well as Professors Roberts' and Grauer's, single entity analysis would overrule is equally unavailing. Professor Weistart argues that sports leagues can not produce a product without cooperation and that the member entities are "inherently interdependent in a financial sense." By contrast, the collective efforts of the defendants in *Associated Press v. United States*,[167] *United States v. Sealy*,[168] and *NCAA v. Board of Regents*[169] were ones of mere convenience. The co-venturers in those cases were relatively indifferent to the success or failure of their partners.

Once again, Professor Weistart's distinction is factually questionable and legally irrelevant. The defendants in *Associated Press*, *Sealy*, and *NCAA* were not indifferent to the financial success of their joint venturers. Nationwide news coverage for many members could have been compromised if a member of AP had been forced to withdraw. The joint venturers undoubtedly were also more than indifferent to whether their coventurer was *The New York Times* or *The New York Post*. The co-venturers in *Sealy* also had a significant degree of financial interdependence. Not only was the capital of its members necessary to support Sealy, but each member's success and reputation depended on the quality of production of its co-venturers. To a lesser extent, co-venturers may have been concerned that the failure of their partners might result in a loss of market penetration that would harm the remaining venturers. Similarly, NCAA members had an interest in the success of their co-venturers, much like sports leagues do. A more successful opponent promises greater exposure and gate revenues. Although, as Professor Weistart notes, there are a greater number of potential competitors in college than in professional sports, games are scheduled years in advance so each member club's ability selectively to choose worthy opponents is nevertheless limited.

It might be argued that sports teams' greater financial interdependence is illustrated by the possibility of direct financial assistance or support between teams. Such support, however, is extremely rare, and in the NFL, may be nonexistent. Certainly teams, unlike traditional partnerships, have no legal liability for the contractual obligations or debts of other teams.

In any event, financial interdependence is not a sound basis for finding that a group of co-venturers is a single entity. Many manufacturers or franchisors provide analogous financial support, through loans or the renegotiation of contracts, to their distributors or franchisees. To call the vertically integrated enterprise a single entity would make all vertical restraints per se legal, contrary to existing law.

---

167. 326 U.S. 1 (1945).
168. 388 U.S. 350 (1967).
169. 468 U.S. 85 (1984).

Finally, Professor Weistart argues that the greater unitary nature of sports leagues is suggested by the *Copperweld* Court's repeated emphasis of the "sudden joining together" of otherwise independent economic forces' as the basis for a finding of agreement. Clubs within a league, he reasons, were never wholly independent actors, at least in modern times. There is no "sudden joining." Typically, then, the option available to the marketplace, according to Professor Weistart, is not league activity versus independent teams, but rather league activity versus having these same resources devoted to a nonfootball venture. He concludes that when viewed in this light, "the league is not a venture that has the net effect of depriving consumers of the benefit of independent centers of competition."

Some sports leagues, such as the NFL, of course, have resulted from the sudden joining of independent economic forces. The weakness in Professor Weistart's argument, however, is more than factual. The choice Professor Weistart posits, between league activity or no football, begs the question. The true choice depends on what the law says is a violation of the Sherman Act. The more accurate dichotomy might be a league with some independence and cooperation, or no football. More important, Professor Weistart misreads *Copperweld*. The emphasis on the sudden joining of economic forces must have been concerned with the elimination of otherwise independent decisionmakers, whether or not they were literally pre-existing. If a manufacturer and a distributor, or a franchisor and its franchisees, entered the market at the same time, resale price maintenance would still not be legal.

The fundamental problem with Professor Weistart's thesis, however, is not his attempt to accentuate the extent to which sports leagues are unitary and to minimize their degree of independence. Rather, the problem is framing the single entity issue as requiring determination of the relative degree of cooperation and competitiveness. The central issue should be simply whether independent interests are implicated. Many cooperative ventures are fully integrated, yet the joint venturers are not treated as a single entity because the law recognizes the potential influence of their independent economic interests. Once again, a manufacturer and distributor, or franchisor and franchisee, can not agree on resale prices. Similarly, the GM/Toyota joint venture can not prohibit its co-venturers from selling their own cars at a price below the jointly established entity price, even if such a restriction is entity enhancing.

To the extent Professor Weistart intends to weigh the degree of cooperation required versus the amount of independence that exists, he is creating a balancing test with no guidelines. How are such unquantifiable variables to be weighed? By what standard? Professor Weistart is seemingly aware of this problem because he suggests Judge Williams' arbitrary input/output market distinction as a guideline. This distinction, however, has little correlation to the amount of cooperation required between entities. More importantly, it is totally unworkable. For example, Professor Weistart suggests that the location restrictions challenged in *Los Angeles Memorial Coliseum Commission* are marketing (output market) restraints. Yet the restraints have an obvious effect on the negotiation of stadium leases. If teams can not transfer locations without league approval, every team becomes a monopsonist in the local stadium market. Conversely, Weistart suggests that labor or supplier restraints are input market restraints where the single entity defense might not be recognized. Such restraints, however, are typically justified as necessary for marketing the league's product. For example, the league claims that player restraints are necessary for league balance, and that without restraints, its product is less desirable. In short, virtually all sports restraints impact both up-stream and downstream markets.

Professor Weistart acknowledges that the single entity defense has its dangers and that league interests, at least theoretically, can be protected by a rule of reason analysis. Ultimately, however, he chooses a single entity rule which in practice could approach a complete single entity defense. The result is once again a standard that effectively ignores the independent interests of co-venturers and threatens to overrule established precedent in both sports and nonsports cases.

IV. A SYNTHESIS AND PROPOSED ANALYSIS

The National Football League, like all professional sports leagues, exhibits a dual financial and decisionmaking structure. On the one hand, clubs are separate legal entities with a large degree of autonomy for day-to-day decisionmaking. They are responsible for most personnel, stadium, concessions, and local radio broadcasting decisions. They bear the economic consequences of these decisions in the form of individual operating costs and revenues. On the other hand, many league decisions must be made collectively. League members must agree on the rules of play as well as the scheduling of games. Many other league decisions are made collectively to enhance the joint product. Rules prohibiting gambling are but a simple example. The financial consequences of these collective decisions are incurred jointly and distributed among the clubs through extensive revenue sharing. Clubs are, to a large extent, financially interdependent as a result.

Although the commentators pay lip service to the dual structure of sports leagues, the common thread is an attempt to denigrate the independent aspects and focus solely on the cooperative and interdependent aspects of sports leagues. Teams are only superficially independent, it is said, because they do not produce anything of independent value outside the league. Of course they do not. League rules prohibit teams from attempting to stage exhibitions. The league does not want to have to compete with its own members for attendance and media coverage. The ability of teams to stage exhibitions, however, can not be reasonably doubted. Teams historically have barnstormed. The success of exhibitions staged in England, where fans have little knowledge of the NFL product, suggests that teams could currently succeed without an NFL. Indeed, if exhibitions were not feasible, there would be no need for a rule prohibiting them. The success of college sports events, which are little more than isolated exhibitions with rankings provided by outside services, further supports the feasibility of exhibitions without league restraints. Moreover, many distributors operate exclusively for one manufacturer and therefore also do not produce anything of value outside the joint enterprise. They are still recognized as more than superficially independent when separately incorporated and responsible for their own profits and losses.

Nevertheless, by demeaning the independent aspect of league operations, it becomes easier to make what is the critical assumption of the single entity proponents—that league decisions are designed to benefit the joint enterprise and therefore benefit consumer welfare. This assumption, however, is flawed at both ends. Once it is recognized that teams have independent economic interests, it can no longer be assumed that league decisions are made solely to benefit the joint enterprise. This is especially true, as Professor Roberts himself has previously recognized, where league decisions can be effectively made by a minority of teams, as is commonly the case. More critically, it is also false that decisions benefitting the joint enterprise benefit consumer welfare. Collective team decisionmaking is a poor surrogate for the free operation of the marketplace because teams' views of consumer welfare or allocative efficiency are distorted by their interest in redistribution of wealth. As suggested previously, restrictions on pay television broadcasting may enhance the league product or diminish output. The league, however, is not in a good position to decide which predominates because it will be motivated by the monopoly profits that the restriction can provide. Ticket price determinations, particularly in two-team cities, perhaps more sharply reveal that team and consumer interests do not coincide.

Although the commentators' analyses are fundamentally flawed, their concern with consumer welfare is valid and is an important contribution of their work. Some collective decisions may be necessary to maintain the benefits of the joint enterprise. For example, a boycott of players found to have gambled on league games may preserve a league's integrity. Similarly, leagues have argued that player restraints are necessary to prevent wealthy teams in large cities (where revenues from attendance will be greatest) from dominating the player market and creating a competitive imbalance that undermines the entire league.

Consumer welfare, however, is not sacrificed by recognizing teams' independent interests and rejecting a complete single entity defense. Once it is decided that teams are multiple decisionmakers, it is still necessary to demonstrate that their decision was an unreasonable restraint of trade to establish a section 1 violation. The cooperative and interdependent aspects of the league will entitle it to review under the rule of reason. Many restraints will easily pass scrutiny under that standard. Truly efficient decisions should not be sacrificed.

The objection to a complete single entity defense, however, is more than one of form. Although the result under the rule of reason will often be the same as if the league were treated as a single entity, this may not always be the case. Some restraints may not survive a rule of reason review. More importantly, the analysis suggested by the single entity theorists threatens to have an impact on sports and antitrust law well beyond the determination of the legality of individual restraints.

The most immediate impact may be on sports players' associations. Currently, if the players' union and management agree on certain player restrictions such as the draft or reserve system, management is immune from antitrust challenge under the nonstatutory labor exemption. The league has a strong incentive to bargain with the union to protect itself from antitrust suits. If the league is considered a single entity, labor restraints will be immune from challenge whether or not the union has agreed to them. Teams will have little incentive to bargain with the union. The outcome of the 1987 NFL strike suggests that the teams' power vis-a-vis the players' association will result in teams dictating terms to the players, and quite possibly, the dissolution of the players' association.

The potential impact of the single entity defense is not limited to the sports arena. As has been suggested throughout this Article, most of the arguments for treating leagues as single entities apply equally well to firms that are in a vertical relationship such as manufacturers and distributors or franchisors and franchisees. There, too, firms are interdependent and joint decisions are generally designed to benefit the enterprise and, ultimately, consumer welfare. Treating such firms as single entities would make vertical restraints, whether price or nonprice, per se legal. The impact does not stop there. Hospital staff privilege decisions may be affected. A medical staff that predatorily denied admitting privileges to a competing doctor may be found incapable of agreement and therefore exempt from section 1 liability. Additionally, joint venture precedents would seemingly be overruled. As a result, competitors may be able legally to impose anticompetitive restraints, merely by including such restrictions in otherwise beneficial joint venture agreements. In short, in addition to threatening existing sports relationships, the single entity defense posited by Professors Roberts, Grauer, and Weistart poses a dangerous precedent for a diverse range of substantive areas.

Nevertheless, it does not necessarily follow that leagues should never be treated as single entities. As Professors Roberts, Grauer, and Weistart persuasively demonstrate, teams' cooperation helps produce a new product. A league is more than a series of isolated games. The interrelationship among the 224 regular season and 9 playoff games, culminating in the Super Bowl, makes the NFL a far more exciting and attractive product than any individual game. No individual team can produce the same league product. The whole is truly greater than the sum of its parts. Some decisions must be jointly made if this new product can exist. It would make no more sense to find an illegal agreement when the executive committee, composed of member teams, decides on the commissioner's salary, than it would to find a per se illegal price fix when GM and Toyota agree on the price at which they sell their jointly produced Nova.

Although such decisions could be quickly upheld under the rule of reason even if single entity status were completely rejected, this Article prefers recognizing a very limited single entity defense. Such a defense might marginally simplify litigation and increase predictability without sacrificing the public's interest in a competitive marketplace. Additionally, recognizing single entity status in a limited set of situations may be most consistent with existing law.

The scope of such a single entity theory is suggested by the Supreme Court's decision in *Copperweld*. A corporation and its wholly owned subsidiary were charged with conspiring to exclude a competing tube manufacturer from the market. Flatly rejecting the intra-enterprise conspiracy doctrine, the Court held that a parent and its wholly owned subsidiary were incapable of agreement under section 1 of the Sherman Act. The Court reasoned that such "agreements" did not deprive "the marketplace of the independent centers of decisionmaking that competition assumes and demands," but were really "unilateral behavior flowing from decisions of a single enterprise." An ideal single entity test, therefore, should seek to preserve independent centers of decisionmaking when they exist, but should classify strictly unilateral decisions as those of a single entity.

Copperweld also established that where a single entity has the legal authority to control the day-to-day actions of all other entities, there is but one center of decisionmaking. The Court indicated that a parent and its wholly owned subsidiary have a complete unity of interest because

> their general corporation actions are guided or determined not by two separate corporate consciousnesses, but one....With or without a formal 'agreement,' the subsidiary acts for the benefit of the parent, its sole shareholder....
>
> ....They share a common purpose whether or not the parent keeps a tight rein over the subsidiary; the parent may assert full control at any moment if the subsidiary fails to act in the parent's best interests.

In short, *Copperweld* found single entity status based on the parent's legal control over its subsidiary.

Accordingly, this Article proposes to treat multiple enterprises as single entities if either (1) a single entity has the right to exercise day-to-day control over all participants, or (2) the jointly created entity produces a new product and the co-venturers are acting on behalf of the joint entity without implicating any of their independent economic interests. Part one of this test derives exclusively from *Copperweld's* focus on legal control. Where a single entity has day-to-day control, an agreement between the companies does not add anything to the market power of the first company or deprive the marketplace of an independent center of decisionmaking. The second part of the proposed standard recognizes that an entity must act through its agents, but adheres to the well-established rule that conspiracy is possible where the agent has an independent personal stake. Part two is also consistent with *Copperweld*. If independent entities make decisions that do not implicate their independent economic interests, there is effectively only one decisionmaker. Conversely, when one of the venturers' personal stake or independent interest is implicated by the enterprise decision (in a more than derivative manner), there is no longer a unity of interest. There are independent centers of decisionmaking and consequently, single entity treatment should be rejected.

The suggested standard acknowledges that cooperation can be beneficial, yet recognizes that dual interests can influence joint decisions to the public's detriment. The standard, however, does not attempt to balance the extent to which agreements involve independent and cooperative interests. Such balancing is reserved for the rule of reason. Once it is clear that independent interests are present, there are multiple decisionmakers, and the presumption is that the marketplace should be allowed to control. Single entity status is denied. If the agreement is truly necessary or beneficial, it should still be found legal under the rule of reason. This standard does not jeopardize sports unions or create revolutionary changes in existing law. It is consistent with *Copperweld* and sports, the personal stake exception, vertical restraints, hospital staff privileges, and joint venture cases.

Applying this Article's test to sports leagues reveals that some, but not many, league decisions should be treated as those of a single entity. The currently existing major sports leagues do not have day-to-day control over their member clubs. Although the leagues have extensive powers to prevent actions detrimental to themselves, their affirmative powers are far less sweeping. For example, the commissioner cannot enter into a stadium lease for the club, require specific salaries for particular players, or force the hiring of any particular coach. Therefore, single entity status must rest on joint decisions not implicating teams' independent interests. Decisions on league office operating costs such as the Commissioner's salary should satisfy this standard. Teams merely act as agents for the leagues and do not have interests implicated by such costs that do not derive solely from each team's pro rata share of league revenues and expenses. Accordingly, such decisions should be treated as those of a single entity. Similarly, most playing rules decisions should not implicate teams' independent interests. Leagues should be treated as single entities for those decisions, unless a plaintiff can reasonably allege that the league's decision was influenced, at least in part, by the teams' independent interests. On the other hand, player mobility restraints, team location restrictions, and franchise expansion decisions will likely be alleged to implicate individual team interests—in particular, the teams' interest in reduced input costs. In those cases, it would be necessary to ask whether there was a good faith basis for believing that the independent interest may have influenced the league's decision. Again, the parameters for the inquiry could be provided by precedent in the personal stake exception area. A plaintiff should not have to show that the individual team and league interests conflicted. If the league's decisions might have been influenced by teams' independent economic interests, which should usually be the case, single entity status should be denied. The league's restraint should be subject to rule of reason review.

V. CONCLUSION

The single entity determination is critical to the analysis of virtually every sports restraint. Commentators have almost uniformly urged that leagues should be treated as single entities for the purposes of section 1 of the Sherman Act. This Article has examined and rejected the arguments advanced by those commentators and has proposed an alternative analysis. The limited single entity test proposed should ideally balance the league's and the public's interests. In any event, this Article makes clear that a complete single entity defense is untenable and its potential effects profound.

Sports leagues are big businesses. They are run for profit and have a great impact on the American culture. They should not be allowed to operate without the judicial supervision required in virtually every other business. When individual owners with independent economic interests form agreements, the reasonableness of those agreements should be subject to antitrust review. Judge Williams' dissent in *Los Angeles Memorial Coliseum Commission* predicted that "[h]olding that the N.F.L. is not a single entity...will spell the end of sporting leagues...and countless other associations."[217] Four years have passed and the world continues rotating on its axis, sports teams compete, and joint venturers produce new products. There is simply no reason to undermine players' associations and upset existing law with arguments built on attractive buzzphrases and faulty premises, merely to protect or enhance the profits of a select group of wealthy sports entrepreneurs.

Gary R. Roberts, The Antitrust Status
of Sports Leagues Revisited
64 Tulane Law Review 117 (1989)*

In the early 1980s, four major law review articles were written challenging the holding in *Los Angeles Memorial Coliseum Commission v. National Football League (Raiders II)*[2] that every internal governance rule or decision of a sports league automatically constituted a "contract, combination..., or con-

---

217. Los Angeles Memorial Coliseum Comm'n v. National Football League, 726 F.2d 1381, 1408 (9th Cir.) (Williams, J., dissenting), *cert. denied*, 469 U.S. 990 (1984).

* Originally published in 64 Tul. L. Rev. 117-145 (1989). Reprinted with the permission of the Tulane Law Review Association, which holds the copyright. All rights reserved.

2. 726 F.2d 1381 (9th Cir.), *cert. denied*, 469 U.S. 990 (1984).

spiracy" of the individual member teams of the league within the meaning of section 1 of the Sherman Act.[3] I wrote two of these four articles, one in the *UCLA Law Review*[4] and the other in the *Tulane Law Review*.[5] A third article, in the *Michigan Law Review*, was written by Professor Myron Grauer.[6] Professor John Weistart authored the fourth article in the *Duke Law Journal*.[7] Although these four articles differed in some respects, the fundamental position advanced in each was that in most or all league governance cases, the league, not the individual club, is the relevant firm for purposes of antitrust analysis, and, therefore, league rules are not appropriately reviewed on a case-by-case rule of reason basis because the section 1 "plurality of actors" element is not satisfied.

For several years, these four articles, which took the position that leagues were generally single firms, were the only major scholarly efforts dealing with this issue. However, a recent article by Professor Lee Goldman in the *Tulane Law Review* has undertaken to defend the *Raiders II* view that each league member team is an independent firm for section 1 purposes.[8] In so doing, Professor Goldman attempts to characterize and then to refute in order my, Professor Grauer's, and Professor Weistart's arguments. While Professor Goldman's effort is thorough and commendable—indeed, it is probably the best that can be done to support that particular view—it is nonetheless incorrect. This Article briefly attempts to explain why.

Professor Goldman's article represents the first effort by any commentator or court opposing single entity status for leagues to deal seriously with this complicated issue on any but the most superficial rhetorical level. Thus, although the rebuttal to his arguments might be gleaned by a very careful reading of the earlier articles noted above, a response directed specifically to his arguments will focus the debate. This is particularly true since Professor Goldman's article properly demonstrates that the debate essentially boils down to a single issue—whether league member clubs have any economic interests independent of the league. Thus, this issue needs to be explored thoroughly.

I. FRAMING THE ISSUE

The ultimate issue here is not whether leagues are single entities or a collection of independent firms; rather, it is whether or not the internal rules and decisions of leagues ought to be immune from case-by-case rule of reason review under section 1. I argue that league governance rules and decisions should be beyond the

---

3. Section 1 of the Sherman Act provides in relevant part: "Every contract, combination in the form of trust or otherwise, or conspiracy, in restraint of trade or commerce among the several States, or with foreign nations, is declared to be illegal." 15 U.S.C. § 1 (1982).

4. Roberts, *Sports Leagues and the Sherman Act: The Use and Abuse of Section 1 to Regulate Restraints on Intraleague Rivalry*, 32 UCLA L. REV. 219 (1984).

5. Roberts, *The Single Entity Status of Sports Leagues Under Section 1 of the Sherman Act: An Alternative View*, 60 TUL. L. REV. 562 (1986).

6. Grauer, *Recognition of the National Football League as a Single Entity Under Section 1 of the Sherman Act: Implications of the Consumer Welfare Model*, 82 MICH. L. REV. 1 (1983).

7. Weistart, *League Control of Market Opportunities: A Perspective on Competition and Cooperation in the Sports Industry*, 1984 DUKE L.J. 1013.

8. Goldman, *Sports, Antitrust, and the Single Entity Theory*, 63 TUL. L. REV. 751 (1989).

scope of section 1. I do not claim that they are necessarily lawful. Such rules and decisions might still constitute monopolization, attempts to monopolize, or conspiracies to monopolize, which are all condemned under section 2. Also, when leagues or members of leagues enter into agreements with third parties outside of the league, those agreements would of course be subject to section 1 review under the rule of reason. However, purely internal league rules or decisions that merely define the product that the league joint venture will produce, designate who will produce it, and outline when, where, and how it will be produced are merely the normal business decisions of the only economic entity capable of making those production decisions and as such ought to be beyond the reach of section 1.

Having said this, I am indifferent about whether the single entity theory is the device used to arrive at this proper application of section 1 to sports leagues. As I have more recently explained in a third article,[10] the same doctrinal result can be achieved conceptually and politically more easily by a proper application of the doctrine of ancillary restraints or by holding that intraleague agreements, which relate only to the production or marketing of the league product, inherently implicate no competition that is protectable by antitrust law. Which of these three legalistic characterizations the courts employ matters not. What is important is that the courts adopt some doctrinal vehicle to allow leagues to win on dispositive pretrial motion when only purely intraleague governance rules or decisions are being challenged.

All three possible doctrinal vehicles that I have suggested (single entity, ancillary restraints, or inherent noncompetition) achieve the proper result because each recognizes and is premised on the fundamental facts distinguishing a sports league from any other type of business organization in our economy: (1) that the product of a league cannot be produced by any one member team, but rather is only produced by the complete integration and cooperation of each and every member of the league; and (2) that a league member team does not and cannot lawfully have any relevant independent productive function outside its existence as a wholly integrated member of the league.

As discussed below, Professor Goldman's failure to recognize or understand the second of these two crucial facts is the major source of our disagreement and flaws his analysis. Presumably, this difference between us would also cause him to reject the ancillary restraints and inherent noncompetition theories. Thus, rather than debate the single entity theory, we should focus on the more fundamental question of whether the inherent structure of a sports league is such that antitrust policy is better served by having league governance matters reviewed on a case-by-case basis under the rule of reason or by having them automatically treated as lawful under section 1. With this question as the focus, we can concentrate on the one fundamental disagreement—whether, in fact, member teams of a sports league legitimately have or can have interests separate from those of the league.

II. ESTABLISHING THE GOVERNING STANDARDS

A. Consumer Welfare Must Govern the Analysis

---

10. Roberts, *The Evolving Confusion of Professional Sports Antitrust, the Rule of Reason, and the Doctrine of Ancillary Restraints*, 61 S. CAL. L. REV. 943 (1988).

Supreme Court decisions over the past decade and a half have established that the Sherman Act is designed almost exclusively to maximize consumer welfare. Even most populist dissenters from this approach, who believe that social and political goals should also play some role in antitrust enforcement, acknowledge that consumer welfare is and should be the primary goal. Therefore, consumer welfare analysis should determine whether or not internal league rules will be treated as per se legal. To allow the analysis to turn on some other standard that has no relationship to the overriding consumer welfare policy of antitrust law would be arbitrary, irrational, and illegitimate.

B. Professor Goldman's Alternative Policy Objective—Enhancing Player Union Bargaining Leverage

Professor Goldman expressly acknowledges that the "concern with consumer welfare is valid." Furthermore, he frames his arguments around that assumption. For example, he attacks my position on the ground that it does not further consumer welfare. He also argues that league rules that promote efficiency more than they injure competition should be found lawful under the rule of reason. And he employs a methodology to justify his conclusion that is based on the consumer welfare analysis outlined in *Copperweld Corp. v. Independence Tube Corp.*[17] However, while Professor Goldman is willing to frame much of his argument in consumer welfare terms, he is strongly motivated by other policy objectives. More specifically, Professor Goldman's primary policy objection to treating league rules as per se legal has nothing to do with consumer or antitrust policy. The only adverse impact he identifies for the sports industry from adopting the single entity approach is as follows:

> The most immediate impact may be on sports players' associations. Currently, if the players' union and management agree on certain player restrictions such as the draft or reserve system, management is immune from antitrust challenge under the nonstatutory labor exemption. The league has a strong incentive to bargain with the union to protect itself from antitrust suits. If the league is considered a single entity, labor restraints will be immune from challenge.... Teams will have little incentive to bargain with the union. The outcome of the 1987 NFL strike suggests that the teams' power vis-a-vis the players' association will result in teams dictating terms to the players, and quite possibly, the dissolution of the players' association.[18]

Then, in his concluding sentence, Professor Goldman states, "There is simply no reason to undermine players' associations and upset existing law with arguments built on attractive buzz-phrases and faulty premises, merely to protect or enhance the profits of a select group of wealthy sports entrepreneurs." In short, Professor Goldman opposes the single entity theory because it would deprive player unions of a valuable collective bargaining weapon—that is, it undermines antitrust suits as a device for redistributing wealth from "wealthy sports entrepreneurs" to wealthy athletes.

If Professor Goldman is seriously advancing this concern as a basis for requiring every league rule of decision to be subjected to rule of reason review, then our

---

17. 467 U.S. 752 (1984).
18. Goldman, *supra* note 8, at 792 (footnotes omitted).

difference is fundamental. Allowing suits against leagues to survive pretrial dismissal to strengthen a player union's collective bargaining position in no way furthers, and arguably injures, consumer welfare. Notwithstanding those who claim all law is indeterminate, it is illegitimate to structure antitrust doctrine without regard for, and perhaps in derogation of, antitrust policy solely to rearrange labor-management relationships to suit Professor Goldman's or a court's personal political preferences. If the NFL Players Association cannot obtain the bargaining concessions it (and apparently Professor Goldman) wants from the League, it is not a matter of antitrust concern. This is particularly so since Congress has expressed in three separate statutes, the Clayton Act,[22] the Norris-LaGuardia Act,[23] and the National Labor Relations Act,[24] that federal labor policy requires labor and management to bargain in good faith over all terms and conditions of employment, free from interference by antitrust courts and other government agencies that might try to alter the bargaining leverage of parties or to impose a particular substantive term.[25]

If single entity status for antitrust purposes were to turn on whether or not unionized employees would gain leverage to extract more concessions in collective bargaining from wealthy (i.e., evil) employers, then employment terms offered by every corporation, partnership, and sole proprietorship having wealthy equity owners, not to mention every multi-employer bargaining group, would be a "conspiracy" of the individual shareholders, directors, partners, or employees and subject to case-by-case rule of reason review. Such a rule is not the law and has never seriously been claimed to be the law. Professor Goldman's position is simply a surreptitious effort to advance a political objective under the guise of antitrust enforcement.

The extent that player associations should be allowed to use antitrust suits to enhance their collective bargaining leverage is more properly debated within the context of when the labor exemption(s) should apply to protect leagues in such cases. Courts and commentators have always framed that issue as when and to what extent labor policy is inconsistent with and takes priority over antitrust policy.[26] That issue, however, assumes that antitrust policy is implicated in the first place. To suggest, as Professor Goldman does, that antitrust doctrine itself should be shaped without regard for antitrust policy, to circumvent the express labor policies of private bargaining and freedom of contract by realigning the relative bargaining positions of labor and management in the sports industry, is simply untenable.

C. Professor Goldman's Concern for Stare Decisis

---

22. Ch. 328, 38 Stat. 730 (1914) (codified as amended at 15 U.S.C. §§ 12-27. (1982) and 29 U.S.C. § 52 (1982)). The specific sections of the Act relevant for sports labor exemption purposes are § 6, 15 U.S.C. § 17.

23. Ch. 90, 47 Stat. 70 (1932) (codified as amended at 29 U.S.C. §§ 101-115).

24. The National Labor Relations Act (NLRA) was first passed as the Wagner Act, ch. 372, 49 Stat. 449 (1935) (codified as amended at 29 U.S.C. §§ 141-187). The Taft-Hartley Act amendments to the NLRA were passed as ch. 120, 61 Stat. 136 (1947). The Labor-Management Reporting and Disclosure Act was passed as Pub. L. No. 86-257, 73 Stat. 519 (1959).

25. I have developed this argument thoroughly in an article focussing on the application of both the statutory and non-statutory labor exemptions to the antitrust laws as they apply to sports league player restraints. *See* Roberts, *supra* note 20.

26. *See, e.g.*, Mackey v. National Football League, 543 F.2d 606, 614 (8th Cir. 1976), *cert. dismissed*, 434 U.S. 801 (1977).

Professor Goldman offers one additional reason for rejecting the single entity position—that it would be "a dangerous precedent" that might revolutionize antitrust law by making all vertical restraints, professional peer review decisions, and joint venture agreements per se legal. This fear is probably overstated.... [T]hat I could accomplish so easily what the likes of Robert Bork, Frank Easterbrook, Richard Posner, William Baxter, and others have tried (with limited success) to do for decades is doubtful. In any event, to the extent the theory for immunizing internal sports league rules from case-by-case rule of reason review might serve to avoid judicial anticonsumer excesses... it is further justified. Serving as a vehicle for exposing bad precedent is hardly an indictment.

But one need not favor legitimizing all vertical restraints, professional peer review decisions, and joint venture agreements under all circumstances (as I do not) to support the treatment of league rules as per se legal under section 1. The error of Professor Goldman's assertion in this respect is the same one that undercuts his entire analysis; he fails to see the fundamental difference between a sports league and a variety of other business entities—namely, that unlike distributors of a particular product brand, sister franchisees, traditional joint venture partners, and members of a trade association or peer review board, the member teams in a sports league are inherently incapable (so long as they remain members of any league) of having legitimate economic interests independent of and in conflict with those of the league. Thus, Professor Goldman's claim that the single entity theory will revolutionize antitrust law (presumably for the worse) is premised on his erroneous view that sports leagues are materially identical to all these other types of business organizations. This premise is the same one upon which he bases his entire consumer welfare argument. It is to that issue that we must therefore turn.

III. RESOLVING THE ISSUE

To his credit, Professor Goldman is the first commentator opposing single entity status for sports leagues who does not base his argument on the separate organization and "ownership" of the league member teams. As I advocated in my earlier article in the *Tulane Law Review*, the Supreme Court's 1984 decision in *Copperweld Corp. v. Independence Tube Corp.*[32] renders invalid any doctrinal position on the issue of what constitutes multiple entities for section 1 purposes based on purely formalistic factors like separate organization and/or ownership, which have no necessary relationship to the antitrust policy of advancing consumer welfare.[33] "[W]hether an enterprise is a single firm or a collection of separate firms should depend on its inherent structural characteristics and the economic realities of its operations, not on the manner in which it voluntarily chooses to structure and operate itself."[34]

Professor Goldman does not disagree with this position. Instead, he argues that it is inappropriate to treat leagues as single firms because in voting on league rules or decisions, the individual member clubs may be motivated by their independent economic interests. In other words, he believes that every league rule or decision should be subject to rule of reason review because every league vote may reflect

---

32. 467 U.S. 752 (1984).
33. *See* Roberts, *supra* note 4, at 586-89.
34. *Id.* at 586.

the effort of the individual member clubs to suppress competition among themselves rather than enhance the efficiency of the league as a whole....

Professor Goldman deserves credit for raising the level of the debate over whether internal league rules and decisions should be per se legal under section 1. He makes a consumer welfare-based argument, and his basic legal premise is correct. When two or more "persons" enter into a productive relationship of some kind (be it a trade association, a joint venture, a partnership, or a corporation) but retain wholly independent productive functions, agreements governing the joint enterprise should be reviewed under a rule of reason analysis to determine if and to what extent they have anticompetitive implications for the market(s) in which the joint ventures act independently and should be competing. Thus, our disagreement over whether internal league rules and decisions should be per se legal or subject to case-by-case rule of reason review is not over the legal standard, but rather over a single, albeit complex, fact—whether member clubs of a sports league have legitimate economic interests of their own, independent of the league and each other. I say they do not; Professor Goldman says they do. On this factual disagreement, the ultimate issue turns.

At various points, Professor Goldman focuses on three different generic types of independent economic interests that a league might arguably have: (1) interests in some product wholly unrelated to the league's product that a team might produce independently, (2) interests in random exhibition games that league members potentially could produce by playing other teams that might or might not be league members, and (3) interests in the league's joint venture product itself. While Professor Goldman at one point or another relies on each of these different types of alleged independent team interests, he never clearly identifies or differentiates them and at times jumps from one to another as if all three were analytically identical. Whether this "moving target" approach reflects a deliberate debating strategy or simply his failure to appreciate the distinction is unclear. Nevertheless, when each purported type of independent team interest is separately defined and examined, none provides a legitimate basis for subjecting internal league governance rules to case-by-case rule of reason review.

A. Independent Team Interests in Economic Activity Other Than Producing he League Product

1. True Independent Economic Interests

Of course, cooperating participants in a business enterprise (whether it be a trade association, a traditional joint venture, a partnership, or a corporation) might have economic interests other than those in the cooperative or joint enterprise. To use one of Professor Goldman's examples, General Motors and Toyota can form a joint venture to produce Novas, but they each can (and do) operate wholly independent businesses that produce cars, trucks, automotive parts, and other products. Two or more lawyers can form a partnership or professional corporation for practicing law, but they can each independently own and operate other businesses like a bar review course or a restaurant.

All of the joint venture/trade association cases that Professor Goldman cites to support his view that "independent interests" require rule of reason review, and that he claims require rejection of the single entity approach, involve these kinds of truly independent economic interests—as do the professional peer review board cases. In *Associated Press v. United States*,[39] the newspaper members of the joint venture news gathering service independently produced and sold newspapers in their respective communities. In *Silver v. New York Stock Exchange*,[40] the stockbroker members of the joint venture stock exchange independently produced brokerage and investment advice services. In *United States v. Topco Associates*,[41] the grocery store members of the bulk buying and trademarking joint venture independently operated grocery stores and sold a wide range of grocery products. In *Broadcast Music, Inc. v. Columbia Broadcasting System*,[42] the individual composer and author members of the blanket licensing joint venture independently were able to sell copyright licenses for their own separate works. And in *NCAA v. Board of Regents*,[43] the individual college members of the NCAA trade association independently produced and sold both educational products and a range of athletic entertainment products in several different sports. In each case, the members of the cooperative enterprise conducted independent business activity in a market other than that of the productive activity of the joint enterprise, and the questioned agreement implicated competition in the market in which that independent activity was carried on. Thus, the challenged agreement in each of these cases required some evaluation of how it affected competition in the market(s) that some or all of the members conducted their independent activities.

The same reasoning does not apply to sports leagues. No member team in a league produces a product wholly independent of the league. Conceivably, a corporation or partnership that owns a franchise in a league (*e.g.*, the Minnesota Vikings Football Club, Inc.) might also own and operate an oil refinery, a trucking company, or a grocery store, but to my knowledge, none ever has. Therefore, league member teams themselves engage in no truly independent competition that a league rule might reduce.

It is true that often the people or entities ("persons") owning teams in a league also wholly or partially own or operate other entities that do engage in independent business activity. Because wholly owned (and arguably predominantly commonly owned) related corporate entities must be regarded as one firm for antitrust purposes, valid antitrust concerns could exist if a league rule or decision had anticompetitive spillover effects into a market in which a "person" related to a league member team independently competed. Thus, to use an extreme example, if the NFL adopted a rule fixing the territories that any "person" related to an NFL team could sell crude oil, undoubtedly this rule would be an agreement among the separate oil companies controlled by various NFL owners like Lamar Hunt, Bud Adams, and Leon Hess. However, this rule would not be an internal league governance rule, and no one would contend that it was per se legal under section 1.

One could imagine a case in which truly independent interests were implicated by a league rule, particularly because some "persons" related to league member teams can and do own independent businesses also involved in the sports industry— for example, stadiums or arenas, sports magazines or newspapers, radio or

---

39. 326 U.S. 1 (1945).
40. 373 U.S. 341 (1963).
41. 405 U.S. 596 (1972).
42. 441 U.S. 1 (1979).
43. 468 U.S. 85 (1984).

television stations, tennis or golf tournaments, racetracks, and/or franchises in other sports leagues. Although I have never heard of a league rule or decision that even arguably had the effect of reducing competition in a market in which a "person" related to a league member team independently competed, it is not inconceivable that one could.

What is undisputed is that no section 1 case brought against a sports league to date has involved a league rule or decision that implicated competition involving the wholly independent economic activity of one or more member teams (including related "persons"). League rules like those governing eligibility standards for players, the team for which each player will play, the location of the various league members' home games, the number of league members, who will own the member teams, the size of each team's roster, how league revenues will be shared, and who will hold the league's broadcasting rights and under what terms and conditions, clearly do not (or at least have never been alleged to) diminish competition faced by one or more of the member teams in any market unrelated to the league. If some—as yet nonexistent—case implicating truly independent economic activity were to arise, it would be appropriate not to find the league rule per se legal. Until then, the "personal stake" or "independent interest" argument based on truly independent team interests has no application to sports leagues.

2. Pseudo-Independent Activity

There is another type of economic activity that Professor Goldman claims individual teams could engage in outside of the league structure—the production of exhibition or barnstorming games in the same sport in which the league operates, carried on, in each case, in conjunction with other teams that may or may not be members of the same league. Professor Goldman notes: "[individual] [t]eams are capable of producing a sports entertainment product outside a league venture. Indeed, before the NFL was formed, teams traveled the country playing individual football games."[47] Today, however, no team in any major sports league actually engages in the business of staging those kinds of exhibitions. Thus, no team has an actual independent interest of this type that might be affected by a league rule or decision.

Professor Goldman's argument, however, is apparently not that the teams in fact have this kind of independent interest today. Professor Goldman acknowledges that today no clubs produce anything of value outside the structure of the league, but he claims this is so only because "[l]eague rules prohibit teams from attempting to stage exhibitions," and that "[t]he ability of teams to stage exhibitions...can not be reasonably doubted." He then claims, in the next paragraph, that leagues should not be treated like single entities because they have independent economic interests, which, coming immediately after his discussion about a team's potential for staging exhibition games, strongly implies that it is this potential for playing exhibitions that he believes gives rise to the requisite independent economic interest upon which his argument is based.

This argument is simply wrong. Individual member teams in a league do not have any legitimate economic interest in the potential for playing nonleague exhibition games. While metaphysically someone could assemble a team of athletes and arrange exhibition contests with other teams, a league member team cannot

---

47. *See* Goldman, *supra* note 8, at 771 (footnotes omitted).

lawfully decide unilaterally to play such games. Professor Goldman himself notes that league rules prevent member teams from playing games outside the league structure, as do the collective bargaining agreements between the league and players unions and the individual contracts each club has signed with its players. But even beyond these prohibitive contractual and labor law obligations, if a league member team is engaged in the business of producing and selling exhibition games in competition with the league's joint venture product, that activity would constitute a breach of the team's fiduciary duty of loyalty to the joint venture and/or an unlawful expropriation of league assets (like the league's trademark and goodwill and rights created in player contracts). As Professor Goldman notes, "The league does not want to have to compete with its own members for attendance and media coverage,"[54] and partnership/joint venture law requires that it not have to. Therefore, not only do member teams in a league have no independent economic interest in the business of playing exhibitions, they cannot lawfully have such an interest. And even if they could, no suit brought to date against a league rule or practice has involved or alleged diminished competition in a market in which league members might sell barnstorming games. Whether such interests do or can exist is simply a strawman.

Professor Goldman, however, argues that the obligation of league member teams to play within the structure of the league is beside the point....Professor Goldman states: "[W]hether players would choose to remain with the club is irrelevant. The issue is whether a team, not exactly the same team, has independent value."[57] However, it is Professor Goldman who misses the point. Of course some hypothetical team of athletes might have independent interests and be a relevant firm for section 1 purposes, but this debate is not about the status of a hypothetical barnstorming team; it is about whether league member teams should be treated as independent firms. To say that the Minnesota Vikings should be regarded as a separate firm for section 1 purposes because some hypothetical team of athletes, not bound by the Vikings' contractual obligations and fiduciary duties, might have independent economic interests in exhibition games is nonsense.

Every business firm's individual employees, partners, or directors could hypothetically engage in economic activity in competition with the firm were it not for their contractual obligations and traditional duties of loyalty. But when those individuals do not in fact and legally cannot have this type of independent economic interest, there is no justification for treating them as centers of independent economic power separate and apart from the enterprise of which they are an integral part. Professor Goldman's argument, if valid, would render every business organization employing more than a single individual to be a conspiracy of independent economic actors, all of whom, in theory (but not in fact or law), could independently compete with the primary enterprise.

Because league member teams do not and cannot play games outside of the league structure, rules governing the production and marketing of the league's joint venture product, including defining player eligibility, allocating players among the member teams, establishing where each team will play its league home games, determining how many teams there will be and who will own them, set-

---

54. Goldman, *supra* note 8, at 789.

57. *See* Goldman, *supra* note 8, at 784.

ting roster size, and allocating league revenues cannot possibly cause anticompetitive effects in markets in which member teams have independent interests in producing exhibition games. Indeed, no plaintiff has ever alleged diminished competition in such a market. Thus, to the extent Professor Goldman's argument relies on this hypothetical or pseudo-independent economic interest, it is invalid.

B. *Interests Relating to the Production and Marketing of the Joint Venture Product*

Professor Goldman's above-noted arguments about independent team interests notwithstanding, no plaintiff has ever challenged a league rule or decision under section 1 on the ground that it diminished competition in a market in which one or more of the league's teams competed independently of the league venture. With two bizarre and, for present purposes, irrelevant exceptions,[58] plaintiffs' antitrust claims have always alleged that the challenged rule diminished competition between the league's member clubs in some aspect of the production or marketing of the league's joint venture product. His analysis and the types of league rules he believes ought to be subjected to case-by-case rule of review show that Professor Goldman relies primarily on a team's interest in producing and selling the league entertainment product as the basis for finding independent club interests.

I take sharpest exception with Professor Goldman on this point. Indeed, my primary emphasis in the two prior single entity articles was precisely that member clubs of a league do not have any legitimate independent economic interests in the league product. Apparently, I was unsuccessful because Professor Goldman repeats the *Raiders II*[59] court's mistake by arguing that matters like stadium leases, player mobility restraints, and franchise location and expansion decisions implicate independent economic interests. Without fully repeating every line and nuance of my earlier arguments, let me briefly try to set forth the crucial facts that undercut Professor Goldman's position.

First, the league product is not simply a group of isolated games. It is, to use the NFL as the example, an annual matrix of 224 wholly interrelated regular season games, each of which counts in the league standings and leads to nine playoff games, culminating in the Super Bowl championship. Every one of the these 233 games is an integral and necessary component of the league's entertainment product that affects every league member team. None of these individual games could be produced as part of the league product, or would have any significant economic value, but for the willingness of every team in the league to play when, where, and against whom they are scheduled; to pay a proportionate share for the officials and equipment used in every NFL game; to recognize the results of every NFL game; and to allow each game to be played under the imprimatur and trademark of the NFL in which each team has an equal ownership interest. Thus, while every team does not equally share the responsibilities for putting on a particular game, each game is the joint product and the joint property of every team, just as the product of every joint venture is inherently the joint product of every joint venture partner.

Second, since each team has an ownership interest in every game, every dimension of the production and marketing of every game must be expressly or tacitly

---

58. *See supra* note 46.
59. 726 F.2d 1381 at 187-90.

agreed upon by every team in the league. As a result, who the other joint venture partners will be; where, when, and under what rules each games will be played; what players will participate for each team and how much they will be paid; what price will be charged for admission and for broadcast rights; how the revenues derived will be divided; and every other aspect of every game are all matters in which every league member has an inherent interest and right to control.

Of course, the league could not administratively and politically involve directly, and obtain unanimous consent from, every team in every decision affecting every game. Therefore, the joint venture partners (*i.e.*, the teams) have established a set of operating rules in the league's governing constitution whereby each team agrees in advance to accept the decisions of others on a wide variety of matters. It is not that each team does not have an inherent right to be involved in these decisions; it is simply that efficiency and good business require the delegation of many decisions. Accordingly, NFL decisions concerning the pricing of broadcast rights to games, the hiring and salary of game officials, the scheduling of game times and opponents, the making of arrangements for the Super Bowl, and the disciplining of employees who violate established rules of conduct are all delegated to a staff person—the Commissioner. Decisions about ticket prices for individual games and stadium lease arrangements for each game are delegated to the home team of every game. Decisions about whom to hire as team executives, coaches, and players..., how much to pay these employees, and when and where each team will practice are delegated to each individual team. Decisions concerning where each team will play its home games, what the playing field rules will be, how both gate and broadcast revenues will be shared among the league members, and a panoply of terms and conditions of player employment... are not delegated at all, but are retained by the full league partnership—although every club agrees to accept a decision on these matters, regardless of its own position, if three-fourths of the partners vote to change the status quo or more than one-fourth votes to retain it. In each case, decision-making authority rests with the party whom the league members collectively believe is generally in the best position to make the decision most efficiently.

Simply because each member team has, to maximize the efficiency of the joint business, agreed to delegate decision-making on many matters to the Commissioner or to individual clubs does not mean that it has no inherent property right in every league game. Professor Goldman argues that *Copperweld* suggests that an entity is single if it "has the right to exercise day-to-day control over all participants,"[61] and that is correct. But the key point that *Copperweld* makes is that single entity status hinges on the right to exercise such control, not whether, in fact, the entity elects to exercise that control. Undoubtedly, a league joint venture, by virtue of its inherent property right in every league game, has the legal right to assume control over any and every decision affecting the jointly owned league product. Generally, under the various league constitutions, the league could instantly assume complete control over every aspect of every team's day-to-day operations with a three-fourths vote of the members.

Third, because every club has an economic interest and property right in every league game, each could be required to share equally in the costs of and receive an equal share of the revenues from every league game (by having all costs paid and

---

61. *Id*. at 795.

all revenues collected by the league office). This requirement, however, would be foolish. Obviously the responsibility for putting on each game falls most heavily on the two participating teams, particularly the home team, to whom many decisions about teams and games have been delegated. To encourage each club to field the best team athletically, to maintain costs at reasonable levels, and to promote and market its home games, the league partners have permitted each club to bear most of the costs and reap most of the revenue rewards of its decisions. This decentralized form of cost and revenue sharing...is important also because the league's product necessitates maintaining the appearance of honest and vigorous athletic competition between the league partners.

The unique nature of the competitive athletic product...has caused sports leagues to adopt a more decentralized form of management structure and profit/risk sharing than any other type of business. This extreme decentralization and athletic competition apparently creates the illusion that the joint venture partners have independent economic interests. This illusion, in turn, has led courts and Professor Goldman mistakenly to believe that the teams are separate firms for antitrust purposes. It also has led courts and sports leagues themselves to claim unjustifiably that league members have no liability for the contract and tort liabilities of other league members. However, the appearance of independent team interests is still an economic illusion. In recognition of this situation, the *Copperweld* Court stated that "whether or not the [league] keeps a tight rein over the [clubs]; the [league] may assert full control at any moment if [an individual club] fails to act in the [league's] best interests."[65]

While decentralization in leagues is greater than in other types of businesses, it is only different in degree, not in kind. Virtually every business firm decentralizes decision-making and creates positive incentives for efficient performance (*e.g.*, profit sharing, promotions, raises, bonuses, perquisites, trips to Hawaii) and/or negative penalties for inefficient performance (*e.g.*, firing, demotions, public reprimand)....Simply because leagues are more decentralized than other types of joint ventures and partnerships does not permit the conclusion that each individual joint venturer has acquired an independent legal interest in some part of the inherently joint league product. Perhaps the clearest lesson of the Supreme Court's *Copperweld* decision is that whether a group of related "persons" has a common interest or independent interests (*i.e.*, is a single entity or multiple entities for section 1 purposes) turns solely on the inherent nature of the economic relationship, not on differences in organizational form adopted in the pursuit of optimal efficiency.

. . . .

In any other industry, it is unimaginable that every agreement between joint venturers that affects only the production and marketing of the joint venture product can be reviewed on a case-by-case rule of reason basis. Of course, to the extent individual venturers engage in economic activity that is truly independent of the venture and their agreements have competitive spillover effects into those other markets, the agreements must be reviewed under the rule of reason to see if the procompetitive productive efficiencies generated for the joint venture product are offset by the anticompetitive allocative inefficiencies in the other independent

---

65. *Copperweld*, 467 U.S. at 771-72 (simply substituting "league" for "parent" and "clubs" for "subsidiary").

markets. This statement is Professor Goldman's basic premise, and he is correct. But, as noted in the previous section, internal league governance rules of the type with which we are concerned do not implicate any market or economic interests that are truly independent of the league. These league governance rules, which are merely limitations on the intra-enterprise rivalry that decentralized league operations allow, simply do not involve any legitimate independent economic interests.

Professor Goldman inadvertently condemns his own position in his frequent use of the General Motors-Toyota joint venture example. On one occasion, he notes the "[a]n agreement between General Motors and Toyota that neither will sell its own cars below the price of their joint product, the Nova, enhances their joint enterprise, yet has unacceptable potential for price restraints benefitting their independent market identities."[71] He later states that "the GM/Toyota joint venture can not prohibit its co-ventures from selling their own cars at a price below the jointly established entity price." All of this is correct—GM and Toyota could not lawfully agree on the price at which they sell their independently produced cars. So too sports leagues could not, as single firms, agree on the price at which their club owners sell oil products or otherwise injure competition in a market in which their owners operate newspapers or television stations; but the league rules with which we are concerned do not do that.

Professor Goldman, however, on another occasion states: "When General Motors and Toyota agree on the price of their joint product, it would not be illegal because the joint venture would be considered a single enterprise and the price agreement an essential ancillary term." And later he says that "[i]t would make no more sense . . . to find a per se illegal price fix when GM and Toyota agree on the price at which they sell their jointly produced Nova." Again, he is exactly correct. But in admitting that GM and Toyota are a single entity when they reach agreements on the price and other matters related to their joint product, he is rebutting himself. Agreements among league member teams that relate to the locations at which their jointly owned league product will be produced (*i.e.*, franchise location), the terms and conditions of employment of the personnel that will actually produce the product (*i.e.*, player mobility rules), or any other league governance rule that has ever been challenged, are exactly the same thing as the agreement between GM and Toyota relating to the price (or plant location or employee working conditions) of their jointly produced car.

. . . .

IV. CONCLUSIONS

Professor Goldman claims that the courts "have already shown an ability to deal with [frivolous] claims through summary judgment."[77] He also states: "If league restraints promote competition more than they hinder it, such restraints can be upheld under the rule of reason,"[78] and that "[t]ruly efficient decisions should not be sacrificed." Thus, Professor Goldman has strong faith in the ability of the judiciary to deal with rule of reason cases correctly and efficiently. (He apparently has been in different courtrooms than I). But the competence of the judiciary is not the issue, and Professor Goldman's above-quoted statements miss the point.

---

71. Goldman, *supra* note 8, at 776 (*emphasis added*).
77. *Id.* at 774.
78. Goldman, *supra* note 8, at 772.

Regardless of the ability of courts to engage in rule of reason review, no one seriously argues that every internal business decision made by the agents, employees, or equity owners of corporations and traditional partnerships involving only the production and marketing of the firm's product should be subject to such case-by-case review. Those decisions have no potential for diminishing consumer welfare except to the extent they hinder the firm's efficiency because of bad judgment, but no one has ever suggested that section 1 outlaws stupidity or allows a court to substitute its business judgment for that of a firm's managers. Thus, Professor Goldman's assertions about the ability of courts to reach correct and efficient decisions, even if true, beg the question by assuming the very fact that he is trying to prove—that leagues are not single firms, or more correctly, that internal league governance decisions should not be considered per se legal under section 1 for whatever doctrinal reason.

But Professor Goldman has commendably furthered the debate on this crucial issue by recognizing that it turns entirely on whether or not the member clubs of a sports league have any independent economic or competitive interests that might be promoted by league governance rules or decisions. If they do have such independent interests, their mutual agreements potentially implicate independent competition required by section 1 and should be reviewed under the rule of reason. If they do not, then their agreements are merely the decisions of inherently integrated subunits of a single productive enterprise that are immune from section 1 review. Professor Goldman's primary error is his frequently asserted but factually and analytically unsupported claim that the teams do have such independent interests.

Although Professor Goldman never precisely identifies the nature of the interests he believes member clubs independently have, he implicitly posits three different types. In fact, however, none justifies his assertion. First, there are no truly independent actual interests that justify rule of reason review of governance rules or decisions. No team itself engages in any economic activity unrelated to the business of the league, and while member teams of various leagues are related to other firms that carry on businesses other than producing the league's sports entertainment product, no one has ever alleged that the teams have voted on league governance rules to further these interests.

Second, no league member team has any actual interest in producing isolated exhibition games or games in another league, and any hypothetical interests a league member might have in producing those games are illegitimate. Such activity outside of the league structure would violate both the team's contract with the league and the traditional duty of loyalty owed by a joint venture partner not to compete against the venture and not to take venture assets for individual gain.

Third, and most significantly, because every game played within the league structure is an integral part of the league product that is jointly produced and owned by every member team, no team has any legitimate right unilaterally to make any decision relating to any aspect of the production and marketing of the joint venture product. To enhance the quality of the league product and the profitability of the league, the league members have mutually agreed to operate in a highly decentralized structure, in which many inherently joint decisions are delegated to individual clubs, and in which costs and revenues are divided accordingly. But any incentives this decentralization creates for the individual member teams provide no basis for finding that the league is dispossessed of its inherent authority to govern every aspect of its business by joint decision of its joint venturers (all of whom inherently have an equal and indivisible interest in the entire league product). In short, the only legitimate economic interests member clubs have in decisions affecting only the production and marketing of the jointly owned league product are inherently joint interests held by every league member. Professor Goldman's own analogies to other joint ventures, like that of General Motors and Toyota, underscore this fact.

Because the teams have no independent economic interests that they can further by their participation in governing their jointly owned league, league governance rules present no rule of reason issue. Putting leagues to the expense of defending every governance rule adversely affecting some plaintiff, making them run the risk of having misguided or ill-motivated courts overturn generally efficient league rules, and distorting their management judgments because of this risk, all when there is no basis for finding any meaningful anticompetitive effects, can only injure consumer welfare to the detriment of antitrust policy. Those league rules should be per se legal under section 1, and concerns about the wealth of club owners, the bargaining power of player unions, or the market power of the league venture should be addressed through other more appropriate legal and political vehicles.

Chapter 4

Owner Control Over Athletes, Ownership and Franchise Location

Introduction

This chapter explores another level of league governance—the role of the sports franchise owner. The governance of a sports franchise owner, even over his or her own franchise, is riddled with constraints. In this regard, there is no question that being an owner in sports is quite different from owning, for example, a dry cleaning business, and not just because of the differences in the public profiles of the owners. The dry cleaning business owner has little or no control over a similar business opening up on the same street, let alone in the same city or country. Moreover, a dry cleaner can relocate, for any business reason, provided his or her economic circumstances allow him or her to do so. Such is not the case with a professional sports franchise.

The selections in this chapter examine varying aspects of professional sports franchise ownership. In section (1), James Brennan discusses one of the key issues in early sports law literature, the inability of owners to enforce personal service contracts through the equitable remedy of specific performance. The distinction between athlete employees in sports compared with employees in other businesses is related to the uniqueness of the talent of even the least talented professional athlete. Brennan identifies the issues that courts have addressed in determining the appropriate rules for the enforcement of player contracts. Another means of exerting control over players is the use of salary caps. An informative article that addresses this issue is Christopher D. Cameron and J. Michael Echevarria, *The Plays of Summer: Antitrust, Industrial Distrust, and the Case Against a Salary Cap for Major League Baseball*, 22 FLA. ST. U.L. 827 (1985). Additional issues regarding the control of players, such as free agency, are discussed in Chapter 5, *infra*.

In section (2) the focus shifts to the ability of the owners to intervene in the operations of a fellow owner's club. The framework for the limitations imposed on this ability is reflected in the section on the commissioner above. The article by L. Patrick Auld serves further to illustrate the extent of this power as exercised through sports leagues, with regard to controlling specific owner activities.

Finally, section (3) examines what is often the leading issue on sports business pages—sports franchise relocations. The initial article, *The Super Bowl and the Sherman Act: Professional Team Sports and the Antitrust Laws*, provides a brief historic overview of the issue. The law governing sports franchise relocations has spawned considerable legal scholarship since that 1967 entry. This is due, in part, to the diverse areas of substantive law, e.g. contracts, antitrust, and eminent domain, that the topic implicates. Illustrative of the genre of scholarship is the article by Professors Matthew J. Mitten and Bruce W. Burton. The single entity debate, set forth in section (4) of Chapter 3 in articles by Professors Goldman and Roberts are also valuable in understanding the franchise relocation issue.

Don Kowet, The Rich Who Own Sports
3-8 (Random House 1977)*

Once upon a time, in the ancient republic of Rome, people were caught up in a fad called *hippomania*—*a* madness for horses. The leading chariot drivers enjoyed the adulation showered today on Joe Namath and Reggie Jackson and Rick Barry and Bobby Orr. The drivers belonged to four teams—Whites, Blues, Reds and Greens. They dressed in "uniforms"—tunics dyed in their team colors. Nearly every Roman citizen rooted for one team or another; White fans, for example, wore white tunics and white scarves to broadcast their allegiance. Fans at the Circus Maximus sat in groups, shouting encouragement, waving placards and team insignias, just the way fans do today in stadiums and arenas across the country. Each team was owned by a large corporation, similar to those that own, say, the Dallas Cowboys and the Kansas City Chiefs. And all four teams were organized into a league run by the four corporations, just the way modern baseball owners run the major leagues.

As the popularity of the races soared, the drivers started making demands. Almost two thousand years before Catfish Hunter got $3.75 million for switching teams, an ex-slave named Diocles got 35 million sesterces ($1.8 million) for switching stables. "Decent men groan to see this former slave earn an income that is one hundred times that of the entire Roman Senate," moaned one contemporary sportswriter.

Eventually, as the empire replaced the republic, the league expanded. Races were increased to twenty-four a day, and eight franchises were added, then another four, for a total of sixteen. The owners of Roman franchises had discovered that by charging millions of sesterces in entry fees, they could turn selling franchises into a profitable business. To make the sport more exciting, as expansion had made it more profitable, the owners began to tolerate, and finally to encourage, violence for its own sake. Just as in modern hockey, the chariot races became marred by collisions and fistfights and deliberate fouls and injuries. The day of the gladiators wasn't far off. In A.D. 79, to attract fans to the newly built Roman Colosseum, promoters staged a bizarre spectacle: a team of Amazon women fought a team of Pygmy men, to the death. Fortunately, the stakes were lower in 1973, when—to attract fans to the newly built Houston Astrodome—an Amazon named Billie Jean King beat a pygmy named Bobby Riggs at tennis.

The Roman franchise owners, of course, didn't have TV to promote their product. Ten years ago the three networks were broadcasting between 540 and 550 hours of sports a year. Now the three commercial networks bombard us with 1,000 hours of baseball and table-top tennis and football and demolition derby

---

and basketball and barrel jumping and ice hockey and dart throwing. TV created a new set of Diocleses, whose cost-accounted grins gleam at us above cans of shaving cream, under a lathery shampoo. It created new leagues. In promoting the modern version of *hippomania,* TV turned our Sundays from days of rest into days of anxiety. It caused Kiwanis clubs and Boy Scout troops and Parent-Teacher Associations to reshuffle their Monday night meetings, so entranced had their members become by the hypnotic monotone of Howard Cosell. As they had in Rome, multimillionaire tycoons infiltrated American sports, joining the old guard who had started their franchises as a hobby, on a shoestring.

....

Perhaps a kind of dementia has always been a quality of sports ownership. Showman Harry Frazee was labeled downright crazy when, in 1920, he sold Babe Ruth to the New York Yankees to pay for the Broadway fiascos he had financed. Jake Ruppert, who bought Ruth from Frazee's Boston Red Sox, was in turn considered odd because he thought there was a relationship between beer (the beer manufactured by his brewery) and baseball.

....

It took Walter O'Malley to bring a modern method to the madness of sports ownership. O'Malley expanded baseball's horizon to the West Coast, and provided an early object lesson to modern owners when he brought the Los Angeles City Council to its knees over the issue of a stadium in Chavez Ravine. Then came two millionaires from Texas: Lamar Hunt, frustrated in his effort to start a new team, invented a whole new *league,* while he was still in his twenties; Clint Murchison, only a few years older, started a new team, then invented a new way to operate it—with computers, and an alert eye for collateral profits. At the same time, Roy Hofheinz, a man with more political clout than cash, was brokering an alliance between Texas and professional baseball; he built the first domed stadium, then saw his empire crumble, all the while indulging his bizarre taste for period furniture.

Perhaps the most striking figure among...owners is a man who made an unexpected fortune selling health insurance to doctors. Charlie Finley never gained much fame in insurance, but once he bought a baseball team his wildly contradictory behavior made him more famous than most players. He was by turns the advocate of new promotional stunts and fan comfort, deserter of a city, enemy of the Players Association, firer of managers, critic of the press, enemy of the Commissioner and defender of owner rights. And his baseball team happened to be just about the best in the game.

Two other owners who came to wealth late in their lives showed themselves almost as irrepressible as Finley himself. Ewing Kauffman became owner of a baseball team on a fortune made from ground-up oyster shells. And Ray Kroc, whose hamburgers are sold at every crossroads in America, once grabbed the public-address microphone at his team's first home game and denounced his players for their inept performance.

....

The whole boom in sports and the wild increase in the number of teams available to own was the work of the one-eyed monster called television. Noticing this fact, corporate businessmen in the 1960's declared sports a part of the entertainment industry. The Madison Square Garden Corporation, once merely the owner of a malodorous arena and the teams that played there, built a new complex suitable for ice shows, circuses, live musical events, movies and political conventions. Their hockey and basketball players played alternate nights with acrobats and trained seals. CBS, the original patron of televised pro football, even got into the ownership business, paying the bills for the fast-declining baseball Yankees for a few years before selling the team at a loss. The marriage of broadcasting and sports seems more stable on a local level. Cowboy Gene Autry combines interests in radio, television and his sports team, as do several other owners.

    ....

History may not spin in cycles. The twentieth-century franchise owner may not, after all, be leading pro sports down the perilous path cleared by his Roman counterpart. But there are some eerie resemblances. The Super Bowl and the World Series seem to have at least as much pomp and pageantry as a Roman circus. The increasing strife between players and owners is mirrored by Diocles' statement two millennia earlier: "I do not care that I am exploited," he said. "I exploit those that exploit me." And an unusual number of the new "emperors" of sport were at one time professional musicians: Ray Kroc and Jack Kent Cooke were dance-band pianists; Gene Autry, a Western singer. We can only be thankful that none of them was a fiddle player.

---

1. Over Athletes

James T. Brennan, Injunction Against Professional Athletes Breaching Their Contracts

34 Brooklyn Law Review 61 (1967)*

Professional sports are big business, and the industry appears to be growing by leaps and bounds. The entire industry is founded upon contract. While from the overall organizational standpoint the leagues are of prime importance, the contract between the ball club and the athlete goes to the heart of the everyday operation of professional sports.

Specific performance has traditionally been considered an extraordinary remedy for the breach of a contract. However, the trend is to make specific performance more readily available as an alternative remedy for breach of contract.[1] As to personal service contracts, the rule has been that such contracts will not be specifically enforced. Likewise the general rule has been that a contract to render personal service exclusively to one employer will not be indirectly enforced by injunction against serving for any other employer. Yet since the famous case of *Lumley v. Wagner*,[4] injunctions have been issued against individuals enjoining their accepting employment to render services for another in breach of their contract....

    ....

---

1. See UCC § 2-716. Comments 1 and 2.
4. 1 DeG., M & G 604 (1852 ch. App.).

The leading case for the availability of specific performance against an athlete is *Philadelphia Ball Club v. Lajoie.*[6] Lajoie's contract, in clause 5, provided several alternative remedies to the ball club in case of his breach. They were expulsion from the club, damages, specific performance, or injunction against breach. While clause 17 gave the club the right to terminate on 10-days written notice, Lajoie could be bound to his contract under clause 19 for a minimum of three years if the club exercised its options.[7] And it might be argued that under the option contained in the contract, the club on each renewal was entitled to a contract with a further two-year option in it. This would mean that Lajoie had sold his services to the club for life or such lesser time as the club at its option might desire. However, the club apparently only exercised its option for a year and sought to restrain Lajoie from playing ball with any other club during the period covered by the contract. The club alleged that "the defendant's services were unique, extraordinary, and of such a character as to render it *impossible* to replace him; so that his breach of contract would result in irreparable loss to the plaintiff...." The injury to the plaintiff would be irreparable because no certain pecuniary standard existed for the measurement of damages. In this instance Lajoie was rather clearly a person of unique or exceptional skill, and he would be in direct competition with his former employer in the same city. Specific performance was not decreed, but the injunction was rather clearly intended to force Lajoie to play for the plaintiff if he desired to continue to play baseball. There is hardly any practical difference between an injunction and a decree of specific performance against an athlete.

In *Central New York Basketball, Inc. v. Barnett*[8] the court was presented with the case of a better-than-average or near star player. In the season prior to his breach, Barnett had ranked 19th in his league of approximately 100 players in scoring, but he was not among the players in the East-West All Star Game on January 17, 1961, nor was he named in the U.S. Basketball Writers' All-NBA Team for 1961. Barnett's contract likewise had an option clause[9] which the club exercised and which gave rise to the dispute. The most natural construction of this op-

---

6. *Ibid.*
7. Clause 19 of the contract provided:

> It is hereby expressly understood and agreed for the consideration above mentioned, that the party of the first part, or its assigns shall have the option or right to renew this contract with all its terms, provisions and conditions for another period of six months, beginning April 15, 1901, and for a similar period in two successive years thereafter, and the said party of the second part hereby agrees to perform similar services and be subject to all the obligations, duties and liabilities prescribed in this contract for the period or periods of such renewal or renewals, provided only that written notice of the exercise of such option of renewal be served upon the said party of the second part prior to the 15th day of October of the current year of this contract and of the current year of and renewal thereof.

8. 190 Ohio Op. 2d 130, 181 N.E.2d 506 (C.P. 1961).
9. The clause provided:

> 22. (a) On or before September 1st (or if a Sunday, then the next preceding business day) next following the last playing season covered by this contract, the Club may tender to the Player a contract for the term of that season by mailing the same to the Player at his address following his signature hereto, or if none be given, then at his last address of record with the Club. If prior to the November 1 next succeeding said September 1, the Player and the Club have not agreed upon the terms of such contract, then on or before 10 days after said November 1, the club shall have the right by written notice to the Player at said address to renew this con-

tion clause would seem to be that the club had the right to a renewal contract with an option clause in it. Barnett and the Cleveland Club argued that the contract provided for perpetual service and was in consequence void. The plaintiff argued that it was entitled to only one renewal contract under the clause. The court applied the rule of construction that if the language of a contract is susceptible to two constructions, one of which will render the contract void and the other which will render it valid, the language is to be construed in favor of the validity of the parties' agreement. Hence, the injunction could run for no more than one year, which is what the Syracuse Nationals had asked for.

Whether or not the injunction would issue thus depended upon whether Barnett was a "player of great skill and whose talents and abilities as a basketball player are of special, unique, unusual and extraordinary character."[10] This, both Barnett and the Cleveland Club denied. The court found as a matter of fact that, "whether Barnett ranks with the top basketball players or not, the evidence shows that he is an outstanding professional basketball player of unusual attainments and exceptional skill and ability, and that he is of peculiar and particular value to plaintiff."[11] While it did not rely upon Barnett's contractual representations that he had exceptional and unique skill and ability as a basketball player, the court did see fit to quote these representation clauses from both contracts in its opinion. Concerning these clauses, the court said, "The aforesaid provisions are contained in uniform players' contracts and it would seem that mere engagement as a basketball player in the N.B.A., or A.B.L., carries with it recognition of his excellence and extra-ordinary abilities."

. . . .

The question then remains whether average or marginal professional athletes may be restrained from breaching their contracts. Are even their skills sufficiently exceptional and unique to authorize the granting of an injunction against their breach of contract? This question has been answered in the affirmative. In *Winnipeg Rugby Football Club v. Freeman*[14] no option clause was directly involved. The player defendants had signed their contracts with Winnipeg on January 8, 1955, and their contracts with the Cleveland Browns on February 6, 1955. The player defendants could be regarded as good prospects for a professional football team, but they had not even demonstrated their ability to make a professional football team. Neither player ever became a star or better than average professional football player. At the time of the suit for the injunction, the court stated:

> In view of the acknowledged difference between college and professional football, and even between the Canadian League and the current National League, it seems reasonable to observe that appraisal of skill and unique ability of a player, as they relate to contracts of this type, must depend somewhat upon his

---

tract for the period of one year on the same terms, except that the amount payable to the Player shall be such as the Club shall fix in said notice; provided, however, that said amount shall be an amount payable at a rate not less than 75% of the rate stipulated for the preceding year.

10. Central New York Basketball, Inc. v. Barnett, 190 Ohio Op. 2d 130, 181 N.E.2d 506, 507 (C.P. 1961).

11. *Id*. at 514.

14. 140 F. Supp. 365 (N.D. Ohio 1955).

prospects and potential. Otherwise such a contract with a college football player seldom would stand up for the professional club that first signed him.[15]

As Coach Sherman did not think Winnipeg was in a class with the NFL teams, the court found that as to the Winnipeg club, the defendant players had special skills and exceptional ability and that they were of peculiar value to the Winnipeg Club.

The result of the case may have been partially a result of the player defendants not notifying Winnipeg of their contract with the Browns until it was too late for Winnipeg to replace them with players of equal ability.

. . . .

Conclusion

It would appear that every individual who signs a contract as a professional athlete whether merely a prospect, . . . , a better than average player or a star will be subject to an injunction against breach of contract. While the language of the cases speaks of exceptional knowledge, skill or ability, the cases in fact ignore the limitations inherent in this language. The reason appears to be an undemonstrated and unlitigated assumption on the part of the courts that professional athletics would collapse as an industry economically or competitively if injunctions against breach were not issued. Personally, I see little justification and no proof for this assumption. Obviously, other similar occupations have functioned satisfactorily without the remedy of injunction against breach of contract. And, indeed, provision is made for a player to play out his option under the standard professional football contract. Professional football does not appear to have suffered irreparable harm from not tying up its players indefinitely. Even when an injunction is issued, it is normally only for one year. This merely means that the complaining club may obtain indirect specific performance by means of an injunction for one season. For these reasons the author concludes that sufficient reason for granting an injunction does not exist in view of the very considerable reasons of social policy against specific enforcement of personal service contracts whether this specific enforcement is accomplished directly or indirectly.

An alternative reason for granting the injunctions . . . was the difficulty of measuring the damages caused by players' breaches of their contracts. Firstly, it must be conceded that only in very rare instances will any considerable financial harm be done to a professional athletic team by a single player breaching his contract. Certainly no one could convincingly argue that the teams involved would have suffered financial harm by the players' breaches. . . . Even in the case of a star such as Ted Williams, it is doubtful whether a ball club would suffer financial harm should the star jump to another team. The dubiousness of the harm must be considered in the light of the limitations on consequential damages for the breach of a contract in accordance with the rule in *Hadley v. Baxendale*.[20] Certainly these difficulties in determining damages have not been interpreted as authorizing injunctions against the breach of other types of contracts. If they had been, specific performance would be the general rule in contract cases rather than the exception.

---

15. *Id.* at 366.
20. 9 Exch. 341 (1854).

A reasonable amount as stipulated damages in athletes' contracts should adequately indemnify clubs in cases of breach of contract by players; and liquidated damages would remove the substantial public policy objections to enforced performance of personal service contracts. A liquidated damage clause would also probably be at least as effective a deterrent to contract breach by professional athletes as the present remedy of injunction.

However, it must be noted that there is a definite trend in the modern case law toward providing specific performance as an alternative remedy available to the aggrieved party for breach of all types of contracts. Thus the availability of injunction as a remedy against a player's breach of contract is in step with the times. At present the only instance when an injunction may not be available against a player is when the contract is interpreted as providing that the renewal option entitles the club to a further renewal option in the renewed contract. In such an instance the contract is in fact one for perpetual service and should be unenforceable by injunction. However, it is doubtful that a court would ever interpret an option clause in a player's contract in this manner, particularly in view of the court's decision in the *Barnett* case.

---

2. Over Individual Owners

L. Patrick Auld, Ownership Control over Professional Sports Teams' Payrolls: Could Anyone Have Stopped Tom Werner from Dismantling the San Diego Padres?
12 University of Miami Entertainment & Sports Law Review 129 (1995)*

....

II. THE PERCEIVED PROBLEM

Most observers would concede that an owner of a major league sports team should have a great deal of autonomy to determine how the business of the franchise ought to be conducted. However, certain forms of ownership action draw intense negative public reaction. This phenomena is perhaps most pronounced when the owner's actions appear directed toward improving the owner's financial "bottom line" at the fans' expense....

During the 1992 season, the ownership group of the San Diego Padres, led by Tom Werner, determined that it should engage in cost-cutting measures. The absence of a full public disclosure of the team's budget figures and accounting practices makes it unclear whether the team was losing money, whether it was projected to lose money or whether the team was simply not as profitable as the owners desired....

In order to achieve the desired savings, the club's front office engineered a massive payroll cut. By mid-summer 1993, the Padres had eliminated $25-30 million

---

in salaries from their annual budget. In the process, the Padres either traded or released at least six starting position players and four top pitchers. At times, the Padres' revamped starting lineup featured nine players with less than five years combined major league experience and a combined salary less than the single lowest paid player on the field for the opposing team. As a result of the moves, the team went from contending for the National League's West Division crown in 1992 to losing over one hundred games in 1993. The apparent dismantling of the team angered many of the Padres' season ticketholders, fans, and players. Additionally, damage to the game's competitive balance disturbed others, including major league players' union officials and fans at large. The following section examines whether the various interested parties have legitimate reasons for feeling aggrieved by such drastic unilateral ownership action. The final section considers the types of recourse available to critics of ownership action.

III. IS THE PERCEIVED PROBLEM REALLY A PROBLEM AT ALL?

....

The argument that regulation of ownership action is too difficult is only one justification for a laissez-faire approach in this area. Another similar, but conceptually distinct, argument might be that sports franchise owners have the right to do whatever they wish as a function of their property right in their team.[19] Under this rationale, Werner would be privileged to field a losing team in the interest of making money, if he so desired. However, this argument fails to recognize the monopolistic characteristics of major league sport organization and the distinctive connection fans have to sports teams. Both of these factors should arguably temper an owner's autonomy. In addition, owners have enmeshed themselves in a complex web of contractual relationships involving players, municipalities, other owners, and even fans. These entanglements limit the owner's right to act unilaterally in many contexts and could even compromise an owner's right to exclusive oversight of personnel and payroll. The section which follows catalogs the specific legal challenges owners might face given the cartel-like organization of their business, the unique relationship between fans and sports, and existing contractual arrangements.

IV. POTENTIAL RESPONSES OF PARTIES AGGRIEVED BY OWNERSHIP ACTION

The exercise of decision-making authority by an individual owner affects a wide range of parties, including players, fans, and other owners. Not surprisingly, conflict has often arisen between these various parties. Historically, each of the different constituencies has sought to vindicate its claims in different ways. The subsections which follow discuss the various responses available to the different parties affected by an owner's management of payroll and personnel.

A. Fan Boycotts and Direct Pressure: The Market Solution

Market discipline is perhaps the most basic constraint upon ownership action. Under the market rationale, those persons who do not approve of ownership action can "vote with their feet" by not attending games or more likely in today's

---

19. This position is seldom explicitly articulated, but it has historically informed baseball owners' responses to challenges to their autonomy. *See generally* MARVIN MILLER, A WHOLE DIFFERENT BALL GAME: THE SPORT AND BUSINESS OF BASEBALL (1991).

world, vote with their remote controls by not watching games. The free market theory posits that lower fan attendance and viewership will lead to lower revenues for the owner. Ultimately, this trend would force ownership to change its approach to structuring the club. From this perspective, fans could indirectly regulate the amount of money an owner would invest in the club's payroll.

In order to effectuate the market sanction more rapidly, fans must organize. The financial pressure must be complemented by protests, media campaigns and other forms of direct pressure. In San Diego, such efforts included a letter-writing campaign to the *San Diego Union-Tribune*, calls to local radio talk shows, and protests both inside and outside of the Padres' stadium. Protesters displaying banners, such as "TRADE WERNER" and "BLUE LIGHT SPECIAL! 75% OFF!," were ejected from the stadium. These actions drew protests from the American Civil Liberties Union. Faced with the threat of a First Amendment lawsuit, the Padres agreed not to remove banners criticizing the team. Similar threats had produced mixed results in previous conflicts. The effectiveness of such suits will generally turn upon whether the stadium is controlled at least in part by a governmental or quasi-governmental body.

Because the market sanctions, even when supplemented by direct pressure, seem insufficient to constrain ownership action, interest in other forms of action remains. Indeed, in San Diego, despite the organized efforts cited above and the concurrent precipitous drop in attendance to a league-low 20,000 per game, the Werner payroll reductions continued. The chief problem with applying the market rationale to major league baseball is that the presupposed elements of the free market are simply not present. Because of the major league sports owner's guarantee of revenue through the existing systems of league-wide revenue sharing and his insulation from competition through the cartel arrangement, the fans' ability to create financial pressure is severely curtailed.

Contrary to the market hypothesis, the Padres do not earn revenue in direct proportion to the number of fans who come to watch the Padres or who choose to watch the Padres on local television. Because certain revenues, such as network television contracts, expansion fees and product licensing revenue are shared in some league-wide fashion, the Werner Group can take home a large block of revenue, and perhaps, more importantly, enjoy rising franchise value, without substantial support in San Diego. Werner thus becomes a classic free rider. He contributes little to the value of the team or the league as a whole, but he profits from the investments and efforts of others. This free rider problem could, in fact, serve as the basis for fiduciary duty actions.

Finally, the Padres virtually guaranteed position as the only major league baseball team in San Diego also undermines the effectiveness of the market solution. Since there are no close substitutes for major league baseball, fans in San Diego must pay a severe price for boycotting the team. This problem is magnified by the unique connection between fans and their local sports teams:

> If you reside in or near a city with a professional sports franchise, it is likely that you are one of the faithful who follow your team, swell with pride when they win the big game, or take it a little personally when they lose. Your team is the "home" team.... When standings are published in your newspaper's sports section, teams are not listed as "Eagles," "Redskins," "Cardinals," etc., but rather "Philadelphia," "Washington," "Phoenix," etc. It is your city's integrity

at stake every time your team takes the field. This is the way it has been since ancient Greek cities vied for Olympic championships.[31]

The Werner Group can never mismanage the Padres out of the majors (and thus lose its share of league-wide revenues), nor can another club enter the league to compete against Werner in San Diego. As a result, the Padres are quite literally the only game in town when it comes to major league baseball and thus, the existing market may not afford fans a legitimate mechanism for responding to ownership actions.

B. The Commissioner's Office: Internal Regulation

The commissioner's office has traditionally served as the key complement to the market check on ownership action. The position of commissioner emerged in major league baseball following the alleged World Series fix of 1919. The major league owners agreed that they needed a strong system of internal regulation headed by a respected leader to restore and to preserve the integrity of the sport. The notion of the noble commissioner empowered to protect the "best interests of the game" arose out of this controversy. Because of the commissioner's broad mandate, it is not surprising that many parties seeking to restrain individual owners appealed to the office.

....

Today the commissioner's office no longer offers an avenue for fans or others concerned about major league baseball's competitive balance to contest ownership action. The baseball commissioner's office experienced a continual ebbing of authority throughout the last decade. The last person to hold the position, Fay Vincent, was driven from office by disgruntled owners in 1992. Vincent, and the office itself, collapsed under the weight of the central paradox embedded in the system of internal regulation: what happens when the commissioner's duty to regulate the sport conflicts with his or her responsibility to serve the owners? Even prior to Vincent's ouster, observers questioned whether a commissioner could ever adequately protect interested third parties because of the office's ties to ownership:

Accordingly, even though commissioners are intended to be the guardians of their sports and often do have very broad powers to act (and often do act) 'in the best interests' of those sports, it can be argued that the public's interests are really secondary to those of ownership in the appointment and regulation of commissioners. The recent developments in major league baseball appear to confirm these concerns.

Bud Selig, owner of the Milwaukee Brewers, has assumed the administrative duties of the commissioner's office and the owners have pushed him to remain in the post. Not surprisingly, Selig has refused to intervene in any manner in San Diego. The hands-off approach to the controversy in San Diego will likely continue if and when a new commissioner is selected. The owners appear committed to formally limiting the office's powers. As a result, the commissioner will have very little leverage to constrain ownership excesses; indeed, that is the very point of the changes.

Despite its current demise in baseball and its inherent ownership-bent, the commissioner's office may ultimately return as one of the key mechanisms for

---

31. Harris, *supra* note 1, at 255.

policing the actions of individual owners. The commissioner can take informal action, negotiate settlements and mediate disputes. These approaches allow more refined responses to conflicts arising among owners and between owners and third parties than do the blunt instruments of litigation or legislation. The owners would clearly prefer self-regulation to ad hoc supervision by courts or legislatures. If faced with a credible threat from one of the sources discussed below, the owners might opt to re-invigorate the commissioner's office in the hopes of diffusing the movement for external regulation.

C. Antitrust Suits: Leveling the Playing Field Between Owners and Fans

If fans cannot securely protect their interests through the current market for major league baseball or through existing forms of internal regulation, such as the commissioner's office, what alternatives might be available? This subsection and the next consider how fans might challenge owners through the legal system, as other interested parties, such as players, have in other contexts. Given the cartel-like characteristics of major league baseball organization, an antitrust action represents perhaps the most obvious resolution for fans aggrieved by the actions of the Werner Group. Such a suit would likely involve a challenge to the league's restrictions on market entry and forms of revenue sharing. As previously noted, these horizontal restraints limit the San Diego fans' ability to secure their preferences in the market. Fans could seek to employ the antitrust laws to create a marketplace in which fans' voices could be heard.

The first difficulty fans would face in litigating an antitrust claim against the Padres and the major leagues is, of course, baseball's so-called antitrust exemption. The exemption emerged in *Federal Baseball Club of Baltimore v. National League of Professional Baseball Clubs, Inc.*,[44] and was based on the Supreme Court's narrow view of interstate commerce. The Court refused to extend this immunity to other professional sports. However, the Court has declined to withdraw baseball's protection from antitrust scrutiny. The exemption was most recently reaffirmed in an opinion by Justice Blackmun in the case of *Flood v. Kuhn*.[45]

The case law, from *Federal Baseball* through *Flood*, may not present an absolute bar to an antitrust suit in the Padres scenario. *Flood* and many of the previous antitrust challenges against baseball (and other professional team sports for that matter) involved a challenge to the reserve system which indefinitely bound players to one team. A federal judge recently ruled, in *Piazza v. Major League Baseball* that the *Federal Baseball* exemption may only apply to issues involving the reserve system. In *Piazza*, members of the Tampa Bay-St. Petersburg investment group, which sought to purchase the San Fransisco Giants in 1992, had alleged that Major League Baseball, Inc.'s monopolization of the market for major league professional baseball teams and its restraints upon the transfer and movement of franchises violated antitrust laws.

Piazza may represent the first sign of a new judicial attitude toward baseball's antitrust status. This development results from a lack of satisfaction with the *Flood* rationale and a recognition that baseball's organization has flaws in need of regulation. This potentially new judicial attitude toward antitrust claims over

---

44. 259 U.S. 200 (1922).
45. 407 U.S. 258 (1972).

major league baseball should also be viewed against a backdrop of threatened congressional revocation of the *Federal Baseball* exemption. Grumbling in Congress over baseball's specialized protection from antitrust liability may well signal the federal courts to rein in the owners' autonomy. Thus, even without the passage of new legislation, antitrust challenges to major league baseball's structure, such as those that might arise from the conflict in San Diego, might be viable.

Padres' fans would likely face other difficulties should they pursue an antitrust suit. First, Congress specifically waived antitrust liability in connection with professional sports league's negotiation of league-wide television contracts.[52] This exemption may undermine any claims based upon the sharing of revenue from network contracts. Second, fans would likely face a challenge to their standing to sue. It may be difficult for Padres' fans to demonstrate, in tangible terms, how the horizontal restrictions damage them. One possibility is to bring the suit through a prospective alternative ownership group who could claim that the league's cartel arrangement unjustly excluded it. Finally, parties challenging the organization of professional sports leagues face difficult issues of proof, particularly given the courts' typical application of rule of reason, rather than per se analysis, in such cases. Despite its limitations, an antitrust suit by fans in San Diego would likely spark a more careful examination of the situation by the league.

D. *Suits by Fans and Season Ticketholders: Private Enforcement of Public Trust Fiduciary Duties and Money Damage Actions*

Antitrust represents only one avenue through which aggrieved fans in San Diego might attack the actions of the Werner Group. One author, John Harris, has suggested that professional sports franchises should be conceived of as public trusts, where fans are beneficiaries and owners are trustees.[55] Harris derives this relationship from two sources: fans' perceptions of ownership and public investment in franchises. Harris argues that this relationship imposes responsibilities analogous to trustee-beneficiary fiduciary duties upon franchise owners. These duties include the duty to reinvest in the team, the duty to furnish information to the public and the duty to manage the team's resources carefully. Harris perceived that these duties would be implicated in a scenario such as the one which has developed in San Diego. In Harris' view " [i]t might be a violation of a trust, if, for example, team ownership, following a title-winning season, traded its valuable players only to reduce salaries in order to make more profit for management."

Harris fails to outline how these duties might be enforced in practice. One possibility is that any fan who could demonstrate the requisite attachment to the team could claim standing to sue based on Harris' concept of beneficial ownership. Such a scheme of private enforcement raises a host of questions about potential overburdening of the court system. Such concerns could be mitigated by restricting enforcement actions to public representatives, such as governmental bodies. Even under this system, questions could properly be raised about the capability of courts to evaluate strategic sports personnel decisions.

Harris' scheme also requires significant modifications and/or expansions of traditional trust doctrines. The Restatement (Second) of the Law of Trusts imposes

---

52. *See* Sports Broadcasting Act, 15 U.S.C. §§ 1291-95. Some of the bills introduced into Congress would also eliminate this exemption. *See, e.g.*, 1993 U.S. House Bill 1549.

55. Harris, *supra* note 1.

upon trustees a duty "to administer the trust *solely* in the interest of the beneficiary."[60] Arguably, any owner who earns a profit, either through the operation of
the team or through resale, breaches this duty. The returns earned by the
owner/trustee's management of the franchise should either be reinvested in the
team or disbursed to fans in forms such as lower ticket prices. Courts deciding a
fiduciary duty suit against a professional sport franchise owner would be hard-
pressed to invalidate some, but not all, forms of profit-taking by owners without
mutilating existing trust doctrine.

Further, in order for a public trust to arise, the holder of the property must
make a "manifestation of an intention to create the [public trust]."[61] A court
could conceivably create an implied or constructive trust, but such action would
require some finding of fraud or an inequitable result. At an analytical level, the
theory behind the judicial creation of a constructive public trust intersects with
the argument for an eminent domain action by a municipality. Given the doctrinal
inconsistencies likely to arise through the modification and expansion of trust law
into the sports franchise context, eminent domain actions may represent a preferable course. Indeed, such actions appear more likely to vindicate the public investment interest Harris' discussed in drawing the trust analogy.

Even if the public trust theory proves unworkable, individual fans should not
be left without legal recourse. Season ticketholders should be able to protect their
personal financial investment in the team (as distinguished from public investment
in the team through stadium deals) by maintaining money damage actions based
on modified theories of misrepresentation (false advertising) or breach of warranty, if an owner makes drastic changes to the franchise. In essence fans were
promised a certain product (in the Padres' case- "major league" baseball) and attracted by promises of performances by Fred McGriff, Gary Sheffield and Benito
Santiago. Instead, they received an arguably inadequate substitute.

The Werner Group responded to the threat of such suits by offering season ticketholders a sell-back option during the 1993 season. The management acknowledged that its offseason promotional material which promised that the "nucleus of
the club" would remain in San Diego may have misled fans. Hundreds of fans accepted the refund offer within the first few weeks after the club made it. With the
rise of more complex ticket arrangements, such as the lifetime seat licensing agreements used by the National Football League's expansion Carolina Panthers, the
grounds for these suits should be even further strengthened. The economic impact
of such suits upon the team's management would also rise significantly.

E. Labor Negotiation: Bargaining for Minimum Team Payrolls

Fans are not the only parties who feel aggrieved by the developments in San
Diego. Players also have raised complaints of harm, ranging from the psychological damage associated with playing on a poor team and losing long-time teammates, to more subtle forms of financial damage. Tony Gwynn and Andy Benes,
the Padres' only remaining superstars, have both voiced their anger over the
Werner Group's payroll cuts. Players who have been dealt away or who simply
play in the league might also have a grievance with the Padres. By effectively with-

---

60. Restatement (Second) of the Law of Trusts § 170(1) (1959).
61. Restatement (Second) of the Law of Trusts § 348 (1959).

drawing from the market for high-caliber (or arguably, even moderately talented) players, the Padres have cut the overall demand for such players by 3-4%. This constriction of demand for playing talent will likely have a negative overall effect on players' salaries. The recent comments of Major League Baseball Players' Union representative, Don Fehr, suggest that this development has not gone unnoticed.[70]

Previously, players who were disgruntled about management's decisions had only one option: to stage an individual holdout. Now, with the emergence of collective bargaining, new avenues of action are available. Gone are the days of ownership domination over players. The cost of strikes and the owners' desire to secure antitrust exemption through the collective bargaining agreement (for sports other than major league baseball), have combined to level the playing field between owners and players.

In major league baseball, players concerned about developments in San Diego can make the creation of floors on team expenditures part of the collective bargaining agreement. Fehr's comments, noted above, and the union's growing interest in a broad range of issues beyond the staple concerns of free agency and pension protection, suggest that the player's union may be prepared to make these types of demands. Not only might these demands be made, but also, they might succeed as part of a larger player-owner revenue sharing/salary cap arrangement. The owners' chief negotiator, Richard Ravitch, has expressed an interest in combatting the perceived "small-market" team problem and increasing revenue sharing between the owners. In addition, a floor on team's player payrolls would protect the owners from the free-riding owner problem. Players have successfully bargained to limit ownership autonomy in many areas, there is little reason to believe that they would be less able to secure protection from owners seeking to profit by fielding underfinanced teams.

F. Fiduciary Duties and Free Riders: Enforcement by Owners, Players and Municipalities

As the introduction noted, professional sports franchise owners have entered into complex contractual relationships with their fellow owners, players, and governmental entities. These arrangements are often difficult to label, but may in fact create fiduciary duties between the parties. The law surrounding fiduciary obligations is complex and often ambiguous. As two experts on the subject noted, "[l]egal theorists and practitioners have failed to define precisely when a [fiduciary] relationship exists, exactly what constitutes a violation of this relationship, and the legal consequences generated by such a violation."[78] This uncertainty may complicate the issues of fiduciary liability in the professional sports context, but it need not undermine the availability of this potential cause of action.

These experts also note that partnership and joint venture arrangements are among business relationship paradigms which trigger mutual fiduciary obligations. Commentators have suggested that while professional sports leagues do not identically match any business organizational form, they most closely parallel

---

70. Fehr cited the rise of owners who are "not interested in fielding competitive teams" as one of the union's top concerns. Maske, *supra* note 17.

78. Robert Cooter and Bradley Friedman, *The Fiduciary Relationship: Its Economic Character and Legal Consequences*, 66 N.Y.U. L. Rev. 1045, 1045-46 (1991).

partnerships. Courts have generally taken a functional, rather than a formalistic, approach in determining if the parties to an agreement have created a fiduciary relationship:

> It is the subject, and not the name of the arrangement between (the parties) which determines their legal relationship toward each other, and if, from a consideration of all the facts and circumstances, it appears that the parties intended, between themselves, that there should be a *community of interest of both the property and profits of a common business or venture*, the law treats it as their intention to become partners, in the absence of other controlling facts.[81]

Owners would appear to meet this definition, at least as to most elements of the venture of putting on professional sports events.

In addition, courts have recognized that because of the interdependence between franchises, individual owners owe each other fiduciary duties.[82] Such liability makes sense in the Padres scenario. The Werner Group's actions affect road attendance, television ratings, and sales of merchandise, all of which affect the other owners' pocketbooks. Further, the Padres' decisions clearly affect the competitive balance of the league and thus jeopardize the success of the entire enterprise.

Establishing a business relationship possessing the fiduciary duties of loyalty and care between the parties does not end the investigation. As noted above, the boundaries of these duties are unclear and difficult issues of proof would remain for an owner claiming breach (particularly regarding the effect of uncompetitive teams on overall league revenues). It is clear, however, that pursuit of individual profit by one partner or joint venturer at the expense of another will often run afoul of fiduciary principles. In a classic statement on the subject of fiduciary duties, Judge (later Justice) Cardozo stated:

> Joint venturers, like copartners, owe to one another, while the enterprise continues, the duty of the finest loyalty. Many forms of conduct permissible in a workaday world for those acting at arm's length, are forbidden to those bound by fiduciary ties. A trustee is held to something stricter than the morals of the marketplace. Not honesty alone, but the punctilio of an honor the most sensitive, is then the standard of behavior.[83]

Thus, an owner who slashed his or her payroll in the interest of higher individual profits, but at the expense of lower league-wide revenues, might well violate his or her duties to the other league owners. Whether these interests would spark action or cause owners to avoid acting against each other for fear of undermining their own autonomy is questionable.

Individual owners may also hold fiduciary ties to the league's players. [I HAVE NOT SEEN THE ASSERTION ARGUED ANYWHERE ELSE.] The sharing of revenue between players and owners creates a type of joint venture arrangement in which players have a direct contractual stake in seeing the league's overall revenues rise. Given the legal emphasis upon "the community of interests" regarding profits and property, and the well-established principle that such fiduciary business rela-

---

81. Vohland v. Sweet, 433 N.E.2d 860, 864 (Ind. App. 1982) (emphasis added).

82. *See* Professional Hockey Corp. v. World Hockey Ass'n, 143 Cal. App. 3d 410, 415-16, 191 Cal. Rptr. 773, 776-77 (1983).

83. Meinhard v. Salmon, 249 N.Y. 458, 459, 164 N.E. 545, 546 (1928).

tionships may be formed by parties who supply skill, labor, and capital, the players would have a strong claim of partner or co-venturer status. Again, such liability makes sense; when an individual owner fails to contribute to, or damages, the value of league by fielding an uncompetitive team, the owner directly damages the players who receive a set percentage of league-wide revenues. Players in leagues which are already involved in player/owner revenue sharing arrangements, perhaps without a sufficient floor on individual team payrolls, might bring fiduciary duty suits against owners, such as Werner, who are building low-budget teams.

Players would face the same difficult issues of proof as owners. In addition, because the players' union is a party to the collective bargaining agreement with the owners, the union would likely have to bring an action to enforce the fiduciary duties. Should the union be unamenable to the requests of players from under-financed clubs, these players might lodge duty of fair representation claims against the union. Given the union's concern for the impact of uncompetitive teams on league-wide salaries, such player-union conflicts seem unlikely.

Governmental bodies might also file fiduciary duty suits against individual owners who slash payrolls. Municipalities, in particular, frequently provide substantial subsidies, often in the form of friendly stadium deals, to professional sports franchises. Governmental officials might argue that such arrangements create joint ventures which carry some mutual fiduciary duties. Because the interdependence and revenue sharing elements of the owner-owner and owner-player contexts are less apparent in the owner-government context, courts may be unreceptive to fiduciary suits brought by governmental bodies.

G. Eminent Domain Actions by Municipalities: From Joint Ventures to Hostile Takeovers

While governmental entities would likely have a difficult time winning a fiduciary duty suit against a sports franchise owner, they may have a much more powerful form of legal recourse, an eminent domain action. If fans, angry over ownership decisions, created pressure on their representatives, a municipality might opt to seize the local team. Such action would in effect accomplish the goals of Harris' public trust theory.

Two municipalities, Oakland and Baltimore, have attempted to utilize eminent domain authority to block relocations of their local professional football franchises. The California Supreme Court upheld Oakland's authority to take intangible property such as a sports franchise under the eminent domain statute,[90] but subsequently, a lower court ruled that the taking violated the dormant commerce clause.[91] The court in the Baltimore case did not reach either of the above issues, but instead rejected the city's claim on somewhat narrow jurisdictional grounds.

While the decision in *Raiders II* would appear to bar action by the city of San Diego in this case, other jurisdictions might not follow the California state court's interpretation of the Commerce Clause.[93] A recent Supreme Court decision, which arguably narrowed the dormant commerce clause, might increase this pos-

---

90. City of Oakland v. Oakland Raiders, 32 Cal.3d 60, 183 Cal. Rptr. 673 (1982) (Raiders I).

91. City of Oakland v. Oakland Raiders, 174 Cal. App. 3d 414, 220 Cal. Rptr. 673 (1982) (Raiders II).

93. See Raiders II, *supra* note 91.

sibility.[94] Regardless of its ultimate success, the mere threat of an eminent domain action may cause an owner to reconsider his or her tactics.

V. CONCLUSION

A familiar sports cliche states that "the game belongs to the fans." While this claim may be true on some metaphysical level, it seldom resolves the specific controversies which arise in the world of professional sports. Franchise owners' pretensions of absolute autonomy are equally inapposite. Another somewhat metaphysical concept, the notion that property should be construed as a bundle of rights, provides a more helpful framework for analyzing these conflicts. The Padres are a complex entity created by the capital of the Werner Group and the other league owners, the labor of the league's players, the facilities and services of the city of San Diego, and the support of fans. Thus, one should not be surprised that all of the above parties can assert a variety of colorable legal rights regarding how the "property" in question should be handled. The legal system serves the world of sports, not because it will resolve each of these claims, but rather because it may. The shadow cast by the law encourages the various constituencies to cooperate with each other and thereby preserve the enterprise they combined to create.

---

3. Over Franchise Locations

(a) Background

Comment, The Super Bowl and the Sherman Act: Professional Team Sports and the Antitrust Laws
81 Harvard Law Review 418 (1967)*

. . . .

The emergence of professional sports as a major industry highlights the question of whether the peculiar practices of the trade meet the demands of the antitrust laws. The antitrust laws express a national faith that competition is the most appropriate and most efficient regulator of economic activity, that the demands of the market should determine the price and quantity of goods and services and the division of the consumer's dollar among the factors of production. Application of this policy to professional sports, however, presents special difficulties because, while the teams are in some respects normal individual economic units seeking to sell a service to the public, economic competition between teams is clearly not acceptable as the sole determinant of their behavior. Professional sports leagues present a unique form of economic organization, whose members must compete fiercely in some respects and cooperate in others. The end product

---

94. CTS Corp. v. Dynamics Corp. of America, 481 U.S. 69 (1987).
   * Copyright by Harvard Law Review Association. Used with permission. All rights reserved.

of the teams is competition on the playing field. But the demands of producing the best sports competition often require cooperative action rather than competition in the economic sphere. Where it is alleged that the structure of an industry makes such combinations economically desirable, the courts have generally decided the lawfulness of its arrangements under the antitrust laws by balancing the alleged economic benefits against the potential evils and have allowed reasonable restraints, even when they fall into a category usually regarded as per se illegal. This Note will suggest a pattern for such an antitrust analysis....

....

III. RESTRAINTS ON OWNERS AND POTENTIAL OWNERS

A. Entry

The clubs are the profit-making, and, in many respects, the decision-making units in professional sports; the league, a nonprofit association made up of the member clubs, however, provides the framework within which the individual clubs provide their "product," league sports. Entry into sports leagues and hence into the industry is by no means free. Generally, new entrants are admitted only if a high percentage of the member clubs vote to admit the applicant.[42] As an organization which makes possible a product no single unit could produce, a league is comparable to a joint venture; as a group which sets standards for the industry and regulates competition among the clubs, it is comparable to a trade association. Usually when the structure of an industry mystifies anticompetitive cooperation through a trade association, the courts require at least that the organization be open equally to all reasonably qualified persons or firms who seek membership[43] so that the market rather than the self interest of those already in the business will determine the number of firms in the industry.

Despite this general rule, absolutely free entry is not, and scarcely could be, required of sports leagues.[44] A new sports team deals with the existing teams as well as with the public. At the very least, they must include it on their schedules and, under existing league structures, they must also share certain revenues with it. These relationships would justify controls on entry which would be unacceptable where a new entrant would be a completely independent unit. A further justification for entry controls arises from the pervasive problem of maintaining a balance of team strengths, which must be done during expansion of the league as well as in normal operation. The existing teams control the current players through the option restraints described above. If the new teams were forced to build from new talent alone it would take years for them to give the established teams a real contest, and in the meantime the entire league would suffer from lack of interest in one-sided contests. To avoid this situation — which would probably mean virtu-

---

42. *E.g.,* American League Const. art. 3.1(b) (1966) (three-fourths); NFL Const. art. 3.I(b) (1966) (vote of 13 of 16 members); NHL Const. art. 3.3 (1947) (three-fourths).

43. *See* Associated Press v. United States, 326 U.S. I (1945); United States v. Terminal R.R. Ass'n, 224 U.S. 383 (1912).

44. *See* Deesen v. Professional Golfers' Ass'n of America, 358 F.2d 165 (9th Cir.), *cert. denied*, 385 U.S. 846 (1966) (upholding reasonable limits on PGA membership); Note, *Concerted Refusals To Deal Under the Federal Antitrust Laws*, 71 HARV. L. REV. 1531, 1540 (1958).

ally no expansion of existing leagues the leagues — stock new teams from existing teams.[45] Obviously, the existing teams cannot be required to transfer players to a prospective entrant at his mere request, so existing clubs can legitimately defend some control over the frequency of expansion and the beneficiaries of the transfers.

The exercise of this legitimate control over entry should, however, be carefully examined, for there would seem to be a built-in bias against expansion, which would bring dilution of the existing teams' position as one of a very few suppliers of a highly demanded service. More specifically, an increase in the number of teams would mean a smaller percentage of shared television and other revenues for each,[46] and a division of publicity and interest among more units. In addition, if more than one city or syndicate is bidding for a new franchise, the power of the league to choose the successful applicant is subject to abuse.

Many of the problems associated with more rapid expansion seem surmountable. If balance is maintained, the dilution in ability of players seems not to affect the fans' interest in a sport; professional football is booming although it has gone from 12 to 25 teams in the last seven years, with an inevitable dispersion of talent. Similarly, more teams need not mean a fatal decline in the excitement of the championship race; the league can be divided into smaller conferences, as the NFL has been this year, giving teams a chance to compete for lower level "championships" as well as for the ultimate prize as the best professional team in the sport.

It is a customary objective of antitrust law to promote free entry and expansion of supply as demand rises. Accordingly, in principle, a league should be required by the courts to base its decisions about expansion on how fast the league can expand without serious injury to the sport as a whole and to allocate new franchises on the basis of a rational comparison among applicants. These standards would, however, be extremely difficult for a court to apply, except in extreme cases. To avoid the uncertainties of judicial supervision of the details of expansion, it might be appropriate to leave expansion decisions to the existing league, but use antitrust policy to foster new leagues. Historically, existing leagues have reacted to competition by expansion, so even if the new league did not survive, there would be a greater number of teams than before.

B. Sale of Franchises

Restrictions on the sale of franchises are of two types: an absolute prohibition of certain classes of owners, and a requirement that all sales be approved by the league. These controls by competitors over sale of teams could be defended as protecting the integrity of the sport by preventing gambling interests from acquiring teams, by barring a single individual from owning two supposedly competing teams, and by guarding against other forms of conflict of interest. In addition, supervision of sales by the other teams might insure that the new owner had finances strong enough to support a competitive team and to enable him to look to the long run interest of the sport.

---

45. The usual procedure is for the new club to pay a fee for the privilege of picking some of the less talented players from the rosters of the established clubs.

46. Of course, if expansion produced higher total revenues the actual income of each team from shared sources would not decline. Like other oligopolists, however, club owners may prefer stability at low total income to the uncertainties of expanding the market.

One may, however, be skeptical whether the other league owners are efficient at detecting potential illegal ownership or conflicting interests, and they may not themselves be very convincing in the role of disinterested advocates of their sports' long run good. Some of the restrictions, such as the NFL's policy of no corporate ownership, seem unrelated to any identifiable purpose, except perhaps to preserve the romantic "sport, not a business" atmosphere. Many of the legitimate controls on transfer of ownership — no gamblers, owners of other teams, or under-financed buyers — could be secured by league rule, enforceable by injunction, without subjecting every sale to general review by the other owners. Restraints on leaving any business tend to discourage entry, and experience in sports suggests that the sale restrictions are easily subject to abuse, for the power has been used to punish mavericks in a league and to interfere with the business decisions of potential buyers.[53] The tenuousness of the alleged legitimate purposes, the availability of alternatives, the serious restrictive effects on entry, and the possibility of abuse all suggest that these restraints on sale are not sufficiently justified by the peculiarities of the industry to survive antitrust challenge.

C. Movement of Franchises

Another set of restraints limits an owner's ability to move his franchise. One league prohibits moving teams altogether;[54] the others require that moves be approved by an extraordinary majority of the owners.[55] If the proposed move is to an area near an existing team, there is usually provision for a veto by that team.[56] Territorial restraints are traditionally considered per se illegal, for the division of markets necessarily has the effect of eliminating competition. There seems to be no reason why these restraints are particularly justified in the sports context, at least when a team is moving into virgin territory. Control of movement is somewhat more justified in the case of a team wishing to move into a city already occupied by another team, since the incumbent team might be sufficiently weakened by the competition to weaken the entire league. In most cases, however, the economic self interest of the moving team would seem sufficient to avoid burdening an area with more teams than it can support, and it is highly unlikely that a team

---

53. The sale of the Philadelphia Athletics baseball team is an example of the use of the veto power to force the sale of the team to a man who would move the team rather than to a group that would have kept the team in Philadelphia. See N.Y. Times, Oct. 16, 1954, at 20, col. I; Oct. 18, 1954, at I, col. 7; Oct. 29, 1954, at 30, col. I; Nov. 5, 1954, at 25, col. I; Nov. 9, 1954, at 33, col. I.

54. NHL Const. art. 4.2 (1947).

55. National League Const. & Rules art. 3.I (1962) (three-fourths); American League Const. art. 3.2 (1966) (three-fourths); Major League Rules I(c)(I), 1966 BLUE BOOK 507 (when one major league club wishes to enter a city with a population less than 2,400,000 in which the other league has a club, it must obtain the consent of three-fourths of the clubs in the other league) ; NFL Const. art. 4.2(A) (1966) (13 of 16 members); AFL By-Laws art. 4, § 6 (1964) (three-fourths vote for sale of franchise; would probably be construed to cover franchise shifts as well).

56. National League Const. & Rules art. 3.2 (1962) (ten miles); American League Const. art. 3.2 (1966) (one hundred miles); Major League Rules I (c) (I) (iii), 1966 BLUE BOOK 507 (club of one league cannot move within five miles of the stadium of a club in other league unless that club agrees); NFL Const. arts. 4.1, 4.3 (1966) (generally an exclusive right to play football within 75 miles) AFL By-Laws art. 4, § 2 (1964) (city in which the club plays); NHL Const. art. 4.1(c) (1947) (fifty miles).

would move into a city capable of supporting only one team with the intent of pushing out an established team, for the old team would have the benefit of established loyalties and, probably, the best stadium or arena.

With jet travel, scheduling would seem to be feasible no matter where the team located within the United States or Canada. Further, the vagueness of the rule makes it prone to use as a weapon of reprisal against unpopular owners.[59] The only defensible argument for the rule is that fan loyalty and trust will be lost if teams move from city to city despite adequate support. But when that very case has arisen — the shift of an adequately supported franchise in the hope of making a fast buck — both baseball leagues have allowed the move.[60] Indeed, owners are unlikely to take a stand to protect the fans' interests since they may wish to move their franchises in the future. Thus, devices which restrict an owner's ability to shift his franchise at least to a new territory — should be held illegal.[61]

....

(b) Private and Public Law

Matthew J. Mitten and Bruce W. Burton, Professional Sports Franchise Relocations from Private Law and Public Law Perspectives: Balancing Marketplace Competition, League Autonomy, and the Need for a Level Playing Field
56 Maryland Law Review 57*

INTRODUCTION

....

The Article's thesis is that free market principles generally should govern the relationship between a host city and its professional sports franchises and should determine the most efficient locations of franchises. However, limited federal statutory remedies should be available to protect a host city's benefit of the bar-

---

59. Bill Veeck, who had antagonized his fellow club owners by his irreverent approach to baseball and his demand for a sharing of television revenue, was blocked in repeated efforts to move his team to a more profitable location. N.Y. Times, Mar. 4, 1953, at 32, col. 5; Mar. 17, 1953, at 32, col. I; Sept. 28, 1953, at 28, col. I. Only after he sold the club was approval granted for it to move. N.Y. Times, Sept. 30, 1953, at I, col. 4....

60. The most recent example was the shift of the Braves from Milwaukee to Atlanta despite extraordinary although somewhat declining support in Milwaukee. Brief for Respondent at 2, State v. Milwaukee Braves, Inc., 31 Wis. 2d 699, 144 N.W. 2d I, *cert. denied,* 385 U.S. 990 (1966).

61. An owner would of course have standing to challenge a league decision preventing him from moving. Perhaps the city to which the aborted move would have been made could also sue, alleging lost commerce. Municipal criticism of franchise shifts is, however, more likely to come from "abandoned" cities, where league approval of a team's departure only ratifies an individual team's decision. In that case it is hard to see how any restraint of trade is involved.

gain and to prevent taxpayer and fan exploitation. Congressional regulation is necessary to protect taxpayers and fans by leveling the playing field between a team owner and its current or prospective host city.

I. COMMON LAW PRINCIPLES

A. Symbiotic Relationships

If a local team plays in a publicly owned facility, the legal relationship between a host community and a professional sports franchise is that of a landlord and tenant. The team covenants to play its home games in an arena or stadium for a designated number of years and to pay rent to the facility owner or operator out of revenues derived from that activity. Ancillary revenues generated from the sale of concessions, parking, souvenirs, and other items are allocated between the franchise and its lessor in agreed percentages. The specifics of the parties' respective rights and obligations under the lease arrangement are subject to negotiation and agreement like most other commercial transactions.

In fact, the nature of the relationship between a host community and a professional team extends beyond the parameters of the ordinary, commercial, landlord-tenant lease because a sports franchise often receives a multi-million dollar subsidy from state and local taxpayers. In recent years, local governments have spent, or have offered to spend, millions of dollars to retain, or attract, sports franchises. In effect, taxpayers are investors in the local sports franchises, but they do not share directly in team profits.

Most sports facilities are publicly owned, there customarily being no incentive for wholly privately financed construction. This is particularly true because the costs of facility development and maintenance usually exceed the revenues generated, and it is usually not possible for team owners, or other private parties, to capture all of the positive economic externalities that arise from maintaining a team in the community. The vast public cost and its accelerating pace is staggering. From 1975 to 1990, cities and states spent an aggregate $1.2 billion in tax revenues to construct or improve arenas and stadiums housing professional sports teams. Since 1992, cities have spent an additional $1 billion on professional sports facilities, with another $5 billion to be spent within five years if all planned construction occurs. Huge additional public subsidies in the form of government financing of roads and other necessary infrastructure around a playing facility are also expended. In 1988, two economists estimated that a city's total financial contribution to a new stadium project can easily exceed $100 million. That figure is undoubtedly higher today.

What accounts for such extraordinary public investment? Although other private businesses and public facilities, such as performing arts theaters and museums, receive public subsidies, tax abatements, or both, professional sports franchises are unique in energizing some core of tribalism in local residents through the teams' ability to develop a bond with a community and to symbolize its identity and spirit.

These intangibles create enormous bargaining leverage in favor of owners. Teams are able to gain favorable lease terms and other concessions because local governing officials want to avoid the loss of community pride and esteem that occurs when a franchise relocates. Customarily, teams pay rents below competitive market rates. Moreover, heavy public subsidization of a franchise's playing facility significantly contributes to the team's revenue-generating capacity, thereby increasing its profitability.

Thus, a professional sports franchise that plays its games in a publicly owned facility has a symbiotic relationship with its host city; the franchise benefits from public funds spent in connection with the facility, and the team constitutes a unique form of community entertainment that is irreplaceable if lost. It is appropriate to characterize a city as a consumer and renter of a sports franchise, rather than viewing the team as merely a lessee of a publicly owned facility. This is a particularly apt description because the primary community benefits of hosting a franchise are intangible psychological values and the corresponding entertainment option the team provides. A city's loss of a franchise is perceived as devastating to its image, and unlike love, it may not be better to have had and lost a team than never to have had one in the first place.

.... [A discussion in which the authors conclude that a city-franchise relationship is not a joint venture is omitted. —ed.].

C. Franchisor-Franchisee Relationship of Team and City

In determining the respective rights and obligations of a professional sports team and its host city, the nature of the parties' relationship justifies treating it like other well-recognized business relationships, whereby one party's financial investment in a commercial endeavor inures to the benefit of the other. A city essentially "rents" a league franchise by providing public subsidization, thereby enabling its citizens to consume professional sports entertainment. The relationship between a professional team and its host city is compellingly similar to a franchising arrangement; both extend beyond the typical landlord-tenant relationship and involve a type of symbiotic commercial venture. Therefore, common law principles governing the franchisor-franchisee relationship appear sufficiently analogous to apply here. The team owner functions as a "franchisor" in locating its team (subject to league approval) and the host city as a "franchisee" in housing a team. However, such common law principles may be of limited value in governing the parties' relationship.

Absent applicable statutory provisions, the express terms of the franchise agreement govern the franchisor-franchisee relationship. Courts are reluctant to impose obligations on a franchisor inconsistent with the express terms of the franchise agreement. Most courts hold that a franchisor does not owe a general fiduciary duty to its franchisee, because the relationship is viewed as the product of arm's length commercial dealing, despite any disparity of bargaining power in the franchisor's favor. Thus, a professional sports franchise is legally able to place its own economic interests above the public welfare of its host community if it does so in a manner consistent with the written agreements governing the parties' relationship.

Some courts have implied a contractual duty of good faith and fair dealing in franchise agreements to prevent a franchisor from reducing or destroying the franchisee's ability to receive the economic benefits of the parties' business relationship. Whereas imposition of a fiduciary duty "requires a party to place the interest of the other party before his own," a duty of good faith and fair dealing "merely requires the parties to 'deal fairly' with one another." It is appropriate to impose a duty of good faith and fair dealing on the owner of a professional sports franchise in its business relationship with the team's host city. As in the more typical franchise relationship, the team owner's or franchisor's superior bargaining power enables it to take unfair advantage of its host city or franchisee.

Imposing this implied duty may prevent a team owner from depriving a host city of its return on millions of dollars in playing facility-related public subsidies. However, the post hoc judicial application of an implied duty of good faith and fair dealing in this context will create uncertainty, interfere with freedom of contract, and may result in inconsistent obligations established by different state courts. Federal legislation offers a uniform and predictable measure of protection to host cities and would be a better and more effective alternative to a common law duty, developed on a case-by-case basis.

D. The Right to Breach a Contract

.... Even when courts have imposed an obligation of implied good faith to perform a commercial contract, breach of this duty has given rise to contractual, rather than tort, liability. Tort liability usually arises only if a franchisor makes fraudulent material representations to induce a franchisee to enter into an agreement, or if the franchisor enters into a contract with no intention of fully performing its contractual duties.

Judicial application of the foregoing principles would allow a team owner to breach a stadium lease agreement by relocating its club to another city prior to the lease's expiration in exchange for the payment of contract damages caused by the breach. Tort damages may be recovered only if the team owner knowingly provided false assurances that the team would not be relocated prematurely and did so to obtain certain promises or actions from city officials. A team owner's refusal to perform its obligations under the lease would not, in itself, establish his intent not to perform fully at the time the lease was executed—a showing that is necessary to recover tort damages. Under these circumstances, the city's recovery for loss of a sports franchise will usually be limited to contract damages.

Merely allowing a city to recover contract damages for the premature loss of a team does not provide adequate compensation for the city's lost "benefit of the bargain" in providing the public, financial inducements necessary to attract or retain a sports franchise. Aside from specified amounts of rent and income from ancillary revenues, such as parking and concessions, the city's economic benefits from hosting a sports franchise are difficult to determine and are probably too speculative to recover as contract damages. The city's real benefits of the bargain are the highly valued, intangible benefits noted above. A professional sports team is a unique community asset that cannot be readily replaced....

E. Injunctive Relief and Specific Performance

Courts have suggested that a stadium lease is the most effective means of protecting a community's investment in the playing facility that houses a professional franchise. Because contract damages do not provide an adequate remedy at law for breach of a lease with a publicly owned playing facility and the premature relocation of a team causes irreparable harm to a city and its fans, some courts have enjoined teams from scheduling and playing home games outside their host cities. In *City of New York v. New York Jets Football Club, Inc.*,[74] a New York State

---

74. 394 N.Y.S.2d 799 (Sup. Ct. 1977).

trial court preliminarily enjoined an NFL team from violating a municipal stadium lease that expressly prohibited the team from playing home games in any other city or location while the lease was in effect. The court noted that the lease granted the city a right to injunctive relief against a threatened breach. After weighing the equities, the court held that injunctive relief was necessary to prevent irreparable harm to the "welfare, recreation, prestige, prosperity and trade and commerce" of the city's residents.

.... [The authors' discussion of the limitations imposed on specific performance and injunctive relief as available remedies is omitted. — ed.].

F. Non-Renewal of Contract with Host City

....

If a lease between a sports franchise and the operator of a publicly owned playing facility has a definite duration without any obligation for renewal, there is no common law precedent or applicable statute requiring a team owner to keep the team in its host city after its playing-facility lease expires. Notwithstanding a government entity's substantial investment of public money in constructing or improving a playing facility for the purpose of retaining or attracting a professional team, a court may not require the team to remain in its host city beyond the termination date of the lease, even if necessary to enable the government to recoup its investment, nor may the court award damages if the team departs.

....

The foregoing discussion illustrates judicial reluctance to make aggressive use of the common law to rewrite the express terms of a commercial transaction to prevent unfairness or financial hardship, even when a significant disparity of bargaining power exists between the parties. Courts have demonstrated a tendency not to reallocate the risks of loss by interfering with the parties' contract. Moreover, it is uncertain whether specific performance and injunctive relief will be judicially recognized as remedies for a professional team's breach of a lease with a publicly owned playing facility.

II. PRIVATE MARKETPLACE COVENANTS FOR PROTECTION OF THE CITY

A. Preventive Law—Private Ordering

....

In the sophisticated business and legal arrangements made between private owners and commercial tenants, there have been solutions developed that can be applied to most of the seemingly knotty questions which plague a team-city relationship. In the private marketplace, a variety of agreements have evolved with commercially creative provisions crafted to maximize the protection of the parties and to minimize their exposure to unexpected loss. These private arrangements allow for carefully nuanced adaptations suitable to a wide variety of individual circumstances involving professional sports franchises—a preferable alternative to judicial policing of the parties' contract by implying terms upon which the parties never agreed.

A city's true interest lies in sharply defining its goals and performing a cost-benefit analysis that assesses the need to attract or retain a particular franchise. This is the same discipline that any private developer of office buildings, shopping malls, or medical campuses must undertake before committing private resources to a new project. The fiduciary relationship between city officials and the tax-paying electorate should push these officials fully into the private marketplace model as far as analyzing and structuring the city's relationship with a professional sports franchise. Only after a cost-benefit analysis has been performed can the net burden of the relationship be identified to the city, and only then can the ultimate financial risk of the city and its resources be considered clearly. With this in mind, a set of adaptive principles, taken from the law of the private marketplace, may be useful in addressing some of the more persistent problems that arise between the city and team owners.

B. Approaching the End of the Term: Notification and Negotiation Structures

For the protection of both city and team during the critical final years of any lease arrangement under which the team uses a city-owned facility, it is vital to have crafted a "no surprises" set of notifications that provides a structure for the timing of negotiations. The same type of approach is frequently used when a major occupant of office or commercial space is nearing the end of its lease term and the parties have previously negotiated for covenants of mutual protection.

For example, provisions can easily be devised requiring that the team, as tenant, give notice to the city, as landlord, of the team's desire to renegotiate, terminate, move, or otherwise make a material change in status at the end of the current lease term. These notifications are common when a commercial tenant has committed for a fixed term of years, but wishes to enjoy a series of special renewal or other options that would allow the tenant to continue to enjoy the leasehold site if it is successful.... Failure of a team to notify the city of the team's desire to change its status before one year prior to the end of the lease could cause an automatic five-year renewal. The renewal would be governed by the previous terms and conditions and would take place at the city's election when the original term expires. These provisions would tend to "smoke out" problems that a tenant, such as a sports franchise owner, may have with the arrangement; focus both parties' attention on the matter; and provide ample time for seeking a variety of mutually acceptable solutions.

Notification covenants should also include a grant to the city of an exclusive right to negotiate with the team for a fixed period of months.... Upon expiration of the six-month period, and without some agreement having been reached, the team would be free to negotiate simultaneously with other cities.

This type of structured approach avoids the risk of the team's making a "midnight evacuation" if the parties have not held genuine negotiations, or if the city has been passive or nonforthcoming during the period leading up to the expiration of the lease term. Forcing the issues to be addressed in a timely fashion is obviously a benefit to the host city. Similarly, a team owner benefits from having a level of certainty as to when and how it may negotiate with other cities....

C. Early Departures

A structure for advance notification and negotiations can be included for any proposed departure from the host city, regardless of when this might become an issue in the mind of the team ownership. If team ownership is contemplating the breach of its lease agreement in the fifteenth year of a thirty-year term, it would still be obligated to give notice and to negotiate for a fixed period before any rival negotiations were legally permitted. To enforce this obligation, the parties could craft the notice and negotiation covenants as preconditions to the team's departure and include a covenant offering the host city explicit remedies, such as specific performance for the term of the lease, injunctive relief, or heightened damages, if the team departs at any time without adhering to this structured notification and negotiation provision. The virtues of crafting a structure that provides a high degree of certainty regarding notices, negotiation time, and remedies are apparent.

....

D. Rights of First Refusal: Tenant Protections

Rights of first refusal, which could be crafted to protect either party, can be modeled on traditional commercial tenant protections....

During the life of the lease, a city may decide to privatize the sports facility. In an era of devolving functions from government to private parties, the privatization of a city or county sports facility is certainly conceivable. The city may decide to sell the facility or convey it by long-term ground lease, or otherwise, to a third party. If this should occur, the team could be faced with a potentially undesirable new landlord or be unable to realize the increased projected values from what may have proven to be a very successful facilities site. The team may feel that capturing these values, which its own sports success has helped to create, is a wise business choice.

Accordingly, it would be seen by most owners as highly desirable for the team to hold a right of first refusal from the city as part of its agreement. This desire may provide the government with a wedge-issue incentive to get teams to amend existing agreements in order to provide the protective procedures desired by cities as a quid pro quo for granting teams a first refusal call on any transfers of interest in the sports facilities they occupy.

The call would operate in the traditional fashion. In the event that the city sought to sell or otherwise transfer all or any part of the sports facility, the team would have a right of first refusal for a specified period. The covenant would require the city to offer to make all transfers to the team on identical terms and conditions as transfers contemplated to a third party. This would allow a team to avoid a potentially hostile lessor in the future. More enticing, the team could capture for itself the economic benefits of any increased values which have accrued to the facility site—values which presumably provided the marketplace incentive for the third party to negotiate with the city.

....[Discussion of the mechanics of such a scenario is omitted.—ed.].

E. Rights of First Refusal: Protections for the City

Risk for the city comes about in one of two ways. Typically, a city finds itself at risk when a team accepts a proposal from a rival city to relocate the franchise at some future time. However, a second possibility exists that may place a significant public interest at risk: ownership transfers involving the team. This usually arises when the team is not a publicly traded entity, but rather, is closely held. In the event of a sale of all or some of the control group of the team to a third party, the city may have an interest in acquiring that which is being offered for sale.

As in so many other business arrangements, special covenants can be crafted to prevent a proposed change in team ownership or management that the city would view as hostile to its long-range best interests without the city's having had an opportunity to protect its interests in the marketplace.

1. Protections When the Team Wishes to Move to a Rival City.—....The city could hold a right for a specified period, during which the city may match the terms of the rival's offer. Sometimes, in the realities of the marketplace, the rival's offer simply cannot be matched....If so, the team may move, and the result would simply reflect the economic reality of the marketplace.

....

2. If the Team Wishes to Sell Control of Management.—A host city may feel uncomfortable if the team occupying the city's facility is to be sold and replaced by new team ownership. The city may be faced with seeking to preserve the team at its current facility while new team management is hostile to that goal. Perhaps the new control group favors moving the franchise to a different city. Accordingly, a city might decide that exercising a right of first refusal would be appropriate to forestall this result. For the city to become the owner of a sports franchise—perhaps only temporarily, because the city may well inspire a group of local investors to become the ultimate new owners—the city will need a right of first refusal. This covenant simply achieves through private means the result sought by eminent domain actions against teams....

F. Liquidated Damages

The "passive landlord," whose only economic interest is collecting rentals, has no claim for breach of lease damages beyond the present value of the future rents. City-team relationships are not this simplistic. If a team moves to a rival city, the most significant risk of incurring major damages would stem from the host city's unpaid indebtedness on the land and buildings that constitute the facility....

Under these circumstances, the most direct measure of liquidated damages would be the unpaid portion of the public indebtedness. This calculation would be rather simple, and liquidated damages could easily be tied to the team's payment of the present value of the unamortized public bonds. Fine tuning this arrangement with a cap to protect the team, or the absence thereof, would force negotiators for the city and the team to focus ex ante upon the direct costs to be borne by each if the team departs before the debt incurred to develop the sports facility is paid.

....

G. Variables: Revenue Participations

In a matter closely related to liquidated damages, teams frequently negotiate for a monopoly, or at least a participation, in all facility revenues. Sometimes this takes the form of revenues generated from the sale of refreshments, liquor, or merchandise; parking; catering; or funds accruing from the rental of skyboxes and similar facilities. These participations in favor of the tenant need to be included in calculations or departure covenants, as they may represent a major stream of income from which both the city and tenant have received or plan to receive profits.

These items can be formulized based on revenues from recent operating years or fixed by agreement at the original term of the lease, as is often customary in commercial retail leases. The formula also can be adjusted continually for operating experiences, inflation, and other factors. This formalization, though more difficult than simply looking to the amortization pattern of public bonds, is fre-

quently done in the private marketplace and is certainly well within the knowledge and ability of most commercial lawyers. Finally, ADR devices can be used to
resolve any unforeseen variables in application of the damages formula.

H. Periodic Estoppel Certificates

In a commercial leasing relationship, a tenant will frequently supply, periodically or upon request, estoppel certificates for the use and protection of the commercial landlord. Conversely, some tenants can require certificates from landlords
regarding certain matters, particularly those involving computations of shared
operating costs. Because of the need for assurances regarding exclusive negotiating rights and the possibility of a dynamic formula for liquidated damages, the
parties might include a covenant requiring an exchange of annual or periodic
estoppel certificates....
....

I. Confidentiality, Arbitration, and Mediation

Although local or state "open meeting" statutes and "open records" laws may
make confidentiality of negotiations and other items impossible, a municipal government should consider seeking covenants of confidentiality regarding certain
matters involving the local team and the sports facility. The parties should, at
least, identify those items sensitive enough to remain confidential and not subject
to widespread media dissemination. For example, teams will be likely to have a
strong desire not to reveal publicly the identities of offerors that have sought to
purchase ownership or control of the franchise. The problem of protecting such
legitimate requests for confidentiality needs to be addressed.

A city may find it advantageous to remove discussions of rights of first refusal,
resolution of disputes about liquidated damages, and resolution of disputes about
the structure of notification and negotiation from the public limelight, and possibly from the sensationalism of the courtroom. This can be accomplished by including appropriate mediation and arbitration clauses in the agreements with the
team owner. It would be relatively simple to identify the most sensitive issues and
to allow them to be addressed, at least in the first instance, by confidential mediation. It might also be possible to structure clauses requiring binding arbitration of
specific issues in the event that mediation fails. Rules of confidentiality may stand
a better chance of being enforced and respected during the arbitration or mediation process than when such questions are resolved before the local or federal
courtroom, the chambers of the city council, the legislature, or the media.

J. Game Plan for City

In summary, the practices used in the private economy pertaining to negotiations for long-term arrangements between developers and commercial tenants
offer a number of devices that can be creatively adapted to address the issues between a city and a major league franchise occupying its sports facility. Even if the
final resolution of some covenants reaches an impasse, and some elements are
thus not addressed in the final agreements between the city and the team, forcing
the public agenda to focus on these issues should have a significant, healthy effect.
Rather than rushing into an agreement for the sake of landing or retaining a
major league team, relying on little more than bullish high hopes and civic ap-
petites, a city would be well served to take a hard-headed look at the potential

consequences to the community of the departure, perhaps many decades later, of a local sports franchise. The analog to the courtship between the city and its team is not a "prenuptial agreement," but rather, the commercially creative arrangements of the business marketplace. Preventive law through private ordering, like preventive medicine, can frequently ensure maximum health.

III. MAJOR LEAGUE MONOPOLY POWER CREATES DISPARITY OF BARGAINING POWER.

.... [The authors' discussion of the monopoly nature of sports leagues is omitted.—ed.].

B. League Monopoly Power and Its Effects

....

While the granting of geographically exclusive franchises benefits a league and its member teams, it places cities that desire to host a team at a significant disadvantage in contract negotiations. There are few regular, long-term uses for a large playing facility, particularly an outdoor stadium that only generates substantial revenues as the venue for a major league sports franchise. Because the aggregate demand for teams exceeds the available supply, and because a city can only negotiate with one team per major league sport at a time, clubs are able to extract public funds from government entities for the team's own private benefit.

The disparity between the number of major league professional sports franchises and the number of cities desiring to host them has spawned some classic monopoly characteristics—opportunistic behavior by teams, bidding wars among communities for a limited supply of teams, and an inability of cities to protect the interests of their taxpayers and fans solely by contract. The threat of relocation gives the owners of professional teams substantial leverage in negotiations with cities seeking to retain or attract a sports franchise. Franchise owners often shop their teams to competing cities in an effort to increase their profits, largely at taxpayer expense. A sports franchise can extract a monopoly price from a community by insisting on millions of dollars of publicly financed subsidies, such as reduced rental fees, playing facility or infrastructure improvements, or new arenas or stadiums.

Economists believe that teams which play home games in publicly owned facilities pay below free market rents. Through the effective use of bargaining leverage, a franchise owner is able to appropriate to itself many of a city's economic benefits of hosting a team....

....

Losing or attracting a sports franchise may have an impact on an elected official's political future. To satisfy prevailing public opinion and to further their political ambitions, elected officials may not fully consider the costs and benefits to the community of providing millions of dollars in public subsidies to a sports franchise. The adverse effects of committing taxpayer funds over a long period, without ensuring that the community's interests are safely protected, may not manifest themselves until after the politician has left office.

....

D. League Response to Franchise Relocations

....

Leagues and individual team owners have a series of economic contradictions at work within their relationships. Because of the importance of maintaining stable franchises and preventing unwarranted team movements, leagues require super-majority *de jure* approval before a franchise is permitted to relocate; however, this is often a meaningless requirement *de facto*. Individual franchise owners often lack a significant economic incentive to protect a host city's interests. Because owners share gate receipts and national television revenues, it is in their collective interest to keep franchises in, or allow franchises to move to, communities offering the highest potential sources of shared revenues. Moreover, freely permitting franchise movement enables all member teams to use the threat of future relocation to enhance their bargaining power in stadium negotiations with their host cities. An owner must also consider the possibility that voting against a fellow owner's relocation may cause the fellow owner to disapprove of future efforts to move another team.

Professional leagues historically have not made vigorous efforts to prevent franchise movements. One commentator has observed: "There is no reason to expect that franchise owners routinely will interfere with their joint-venturers' efforts to make more money at the taxpayers' expense." From 1950 through 1982, seventy-eight franchise movements occurred in the four major league professional sports. Most league attempts to block franchise relocations were directed at owners, such as Charlie Finley, Bill Veeck, and Al Davis, who were perceived as mavericks. Apparently, "personal animosity" and other factors motivated these actions, rather than an honest desire to protect a host city's interests.

Since 1982, when the NFL and its members were found to have violated the antitrust laws by voting against the proposed move of the Oakland Raiders to Los Angeles, leagues have been forced to consider potential legal liability for attempting to prevent franchise relocation. In 1983, the NHL was sued for rejecting the sale of the St. Louis Blues to a group that planned to move it to Saskatoon, Saskatchewan. The Ralston Purina Company, which owned the Blues at the time, sought $60 million in antitrust damages from the league. The NHL subsequently approved the sale of the Blues to a local consortium that kept the team in St. Louis, and the antitrust suit was ultimately settled. The operator of the stadium that houses the St. Louis Rams recently filed an antitrust suit against the NFL, alleging that conditioning league approval of the team's move from Los Angeles on the payment of a $29 million relocation fee harmed the stadium operator's economic interests. The now Oakland Raiders sued the NFL on antitrust grounds for alleged unlawful interference with the team's 1995 move from Los Angeles back to Oakland.

IV. ANTITRUST CLAIMS BY CITIES

The relocation of a major league professional sports team causes psychological distress and a sense of loss to the fans of the former host city. The government entity that owns the playing facility may be left with a significant amount of debt incurred to attract or retain the franchise. Taxpayer dollars are used to pay outstanding facility-related debt, while the franchise, which derived the benefits of taxpayer subsidization, has no legal obligation to remain or pay damages, absent an agreement to do so.

A city's inability to protect its taxpayers' financial investment and prevent fan exploitation by a team owner's opportunistic behavior is the product of a major professional sports league's monopoly power. As previously discussed, both the undersupply of major league franchises and the excess demand by cities give each team owner strong leverage in playing facility lease negotiations. The threat of relocation is an incentive to obtain favorable terms and concessions at taxpayer expense.

Cities, as owners of stadiums, and states, in their sovereign capacity, have sought relief under the antitrust laws for harm caused by franchise relocation. This section of the Article discusses the inappropriateness of using the antitrust laws to regulate a professional league's determination of the total number and geographical location of franchises.

A. Loss of Team by Franchise Relocation

1. Standing and Antitrust Injury Requirements.—The objective of the antitrust laws is to prevent, or to allow recovery for, economic losses caused by anticompetitive commercial activity. An antitrust plaintiff must prove actual or threatened harm to its economic interests as a result of the defendant's antitrust violation. A city must show that the anticompetitive conduct of a professional sports league and its member franchises has harmed the city's proprietary interests. For example, lease revenues and revenues associated with the operation of a publicly owned stadium that are lost as a result of the relocation of a professional sports franchise satisfy the economic damages requirement. A government body cannot recover damages for injury to its general economy that has been caused by the movement of a sports franchise out of its jurisdiction.

The antitrust laws do not permit recovery of damages for personal injury. Disappointed local fans cannot recover for any emotional distress resulting from the home team's movement to another city. . . .

Although the Clayton Act expressly permits "any person" who has suffered economic loss from an antitrust violation to bring suit, the Supreme Court has held that the plaintiff must be either a consumer or a competitor in the restrained market. This standing requirement has the practical effect of precluding parties only "tangentially affected by an antitrust violation" from bringing a claim for harm caused by anticompetitive activity. In the context of antitrust litigation surrounding the relocation of sports franchises, federal courts have held that a stadium owner or operator has standing to claim that a professional league's rules or conduct restrain its ability to compete with rival stadiums to house a league team.

In *Los Angeles Memorial Coliseum Commission v. National Football League (Raiders II)*,[289] the Ninth Circuit upheld a trebled $14.5 million antitrust damages award in favor of a football stadium. The stadium suffered economic loss from the NFL's efforts to prevent the Oakland Raiders from honoring its contract to relocate to Los Angeles and play its home games in the plaintiff's stadium. Rejecting the league's contention that the plaintiff had no standing because its injury was too remote from the antitrust violation, the court observed: "Football stadia constitute a special market distinguished from those comprised by, say, hotels, laundering establishments, or limousine services, by their indispensable and intimate connection with professional football and football teams."

Raiders II limited the class of potential plaintiffs that may recover antitrust damages for economic loss caused by the relocation of a professional sports franchise. A city must have a direct economic stake in hosting a sports franchise, such

---

289. 791 F.2d 1356 (9th Cir. 1986).

as the ability to earn rent from the lease of a publicly owned playing facility.[294] The court's distinction between a stadium and local businesses that only indirectly derive a financial benefit from the presence of a professional team suggests that any other economic loss that a city and its inhabitants suffer from the relocation of a professional sports franchise, such as a reduced tax base, is not compensable under the antitrust laws.

More important, even if a city satisfies the economic injury and standing requirements, it can obtain an injunction or recover damages under the antitrust laws only if its harm is caused by an anticompetitive effect in a properly defined market as a result of a professional team's relocation. This is known as the "antitrust injury" requirement. *Raiders II* implicitly recognizes that cities compete to host professional sports franchises and to house them in publicly owned stadiums and that the antitrust laws encourage such free market competition. Thus, it appears virtually impossible for a city to prove that it has suffered an antitrust injury after it has lost a professional team because the franchise owner accepted a better stadium deal from another city. That type of harm flows from increased competition, rather than decreased competition, for which the federal antitrust laws do not provide a remedy.

. . . .

In an eminent domain proceeding, one court has held that permitting the city to take a professional sports franchise through condemnation proceedings unduly interfered with a professional sports league's national geographical dispersal of its teams. In *City of Oakland v. Oakland Raiders (Oakland III)*,[302] the California Court of Appeals ruled that the City of Oakland's use of state eminent domain laws to prevent the Raiders from moving to Los Angeles violated the Commerce Clause. Because the NFL's member teams provide nationwide entertainment and are financially interdependent, the court recognized the league's legitimate need to determine the location of its teams. Observing that "[a]n involuntarily acquired franchise could, at the local government's pleasure, be permanently indentured to the local entity," the court concluded that "[t]his is the precise brand of parochial meddling with the national economy that the commerce clause was designed to prohibit." Although not an antitrust case, *Oakland III* implicitly recognized that market competition among cities should be left free of local interference that would determine the geographical location of professional sports franchises. Moreover, the case buttressed the principle of using private ordering, not eminent domain, to achieve this result through a "call mechanism."

2. *Merits of Claim.*—Holding that matters of internal league governance are outside the scope of section 1 of the Sherman Act, courts initially provided professional sports leagues with broad authority to regulate franchise relocation. In *San Francisco Seals, Ltd. v. National Hockey League*,[309] a 1974 case, a federal district court dismissed a team's antitrust claim against other league members for prohibiting the team's relocation to Vancouver. The court found that league teams "are not competitors in the economic sense," but rather are "all members of a single unit competing as such with other similar professional leagues." Because a sports league cannot exist without cooperation on matters such as the geographi-

---

294. *Id.*
302. *Id.*
309. 379 F. Supp. 966 (C.D. Cal. 1974).

cal location of franchises, the court found that the requisite conspiracy among independent economic competitors did not exist as a matter of law.

Although the Supreme Court has not resolved this issue, the prevailing judicial view among circuit courts is that the member teams of a professional sports league are separate and independent economic entities whose collective action is subject to section 1 scrutiny. It is reasoned that each team acts to further its individual economic interests rather than the league's common interests; therefore, teams are capable of conspiring among themselves. As the First Circuit recently observed: "NFL member clubs compete in several ways off the field, which itself tends to show that the teams pursue diverse interests and thus are not a single enterprise under s 1."[315] This line of authority allows a team owner to challenge, on antitrust grounds, a collective decision by other league teams not to allow the owner's franchise to relocate.

In *Los Angeles Memorial Coliseum v. National Football League (Raiders I)*,[316] the Ninth Circuit upheld a jury finding that the collective refusal of league member teams to approve the 1980 proposed move of the Oakland Raiders to Los Angeles violated the antitrust laws. The court initially concluded that the defendants were "an association of teams sufficiently independent and competitive with one another" to be covered by section 1 of the Sherman Act. An NFL rule required the approval of three-quarters of the league's teams before a franchise was permitted to relocate into another team's designated home territory. With five abstentions, NFL owners voted 22-0 against the proposed relocation of the Raiders into the territory of the Los Angeles Rams.

The challenged NFL rule was found to be a means of establishing exclusive geographical territories among economic competitors, thus interfering with a team owner's right to do business where it pleased. Although team owners have a legitimate collective interest in protecting the league's integrity and attractiveness as an entertainment product by controlling the geographical placement of franchises, the court held that a standardless relocation approval requirement would not necessarily accomplish these objectives. The owners' refusal to allow the Raiders to relocate restrained economic competition unreasonably between league teams. The Ninth Circuit suggested that in order to withstand an antitrust challenge by a franchise owner or stadium authority, a league must have objective franchise relocation standards that are no more restrictive than necessary to protect its legitimate interests.

Allowing a former host city to bring an antitrust claim against a league and its members for merely permitting a franchise to relocate to another city creates conflicting legal obligations. *Raiders I* limits a league's authority to govern franchise relocation and creates potential exposure to antitrust treble damages for disapproving a team's move to another city. Therefore, it is inconsistent with *Raiders I* to permit a jilted city to use antitrust law as a sword against a league for failing to prevent a franchise from relocating.

Raiders I not only appears to preclude a city that has lost a professional sports team from prevailing in an antitrust action; it also gives the "green light" to franchise free agency and encourages opportunistic behavior by team owners. *Raiders I* creates uncertainty regarding a league's legal ability to prevent franchise reloca-

---

315. *Sullivan*, 34 F.3d at 1099.
316. 726 F.2d 1381 (9th Cir. 1984).

tion and increases the likelihood that a franchise owner will move the team to another city if the host city does not satisfy the owner's demands. Thus, *Raiders I* reinforces, rather than ameliorates, the disparity of bargaining power between franchise owner and host city.

In the context of franchise relocation, a professional league should be viewed as an economically interdependent entity whose decisions are outside of the scope of section 1 of the Sherman Act. The success of a league depends upon exciting on-field competition between evenly matched teams that are financially viable. An exclusive geographical territory for each league team appears necessary to ensure the league's economic stability. Moreover, it is unlikely that league teams in the same metropolitan area engage in any significant economic competition for fan support. A team owner's decision to relocate its franchise in pursuit of individual economic gain may harm the league's collective interests. League franchise relocation restrictions are necessary internal regulations to protect host cities' interests, to preserve the good will of the fans, and to secure the league's geographic stability. These underlying purposes require that the league not be subject to antitrust challenges, as asserted in *Raiders I*, by teams seeking to engage in opportunistic behavior.

B. No Right to Obtain Replacement Team

Cities that formerly lost an NFL sports franchise have, ironically, filed antitrust suits claiming that NFL efforts to interfere with an existing team's agreement to relocate to one of these communities unreasonably restrains trade. The operator of a new stadium housing the St. Louis Rams has sued the NFL and its member teams for conditioning the move of the Rams from Los Angeles on the payment of a $29 million relocation fee, which the plaintiff claims deprived it of substantial economic benefits under its lease with the Rams. The City of Baltimore also filed an antitrust suit against the NFL in an effort to force the league to approve an agreement with the owner of the Cleveland Browns to move his team to Baltimore. Thus, the paradox: cities like St. Louis and Baltimore are suing to preserve the very system that allowed them to be jilted by opportunistic owner behavior in the first place, and that may jilt them again in the future.

These lawsuits are patterned after the successful Raiders antitrust litigation, and they contend that league efforts to prevent or hinder franchise relocation represent a concerted, illegal refusal to deal with a city that has reached an agreement to host a league team. Judicial recognition of these types of claims will preserve unbridled, free market competition among cities for professional sports franchises, but will also have the adverse effect of encouraging franchise free agency, to the detriment of host cities. In addition, such recognition would preclude a league from preventing franchise moves that are contrary to the collective best interests of its member teams.

1. Antitrust Injury Requirement—Although an antitrust claim arising out of a league's refusal to permit an existing team to relocate is viable under current law, a city probably could not successfully assert that a league's failure to provide a replacement team for a lost franchise violates antitrust laws. In two cases, federal courts have held that a league's denial of an application for an expansion franchise is not an antitrust violation. Although these cases involve efforts by an existing sports franchise to gain admission to a major professional league, they seem to apply equally to a city seeking to host a team.

In *Mid-South Grizzlies v. National Football League*,[341] the Third Circuit rejected a former World Football League team's claim that the NFL's denial of the Grizzlies' application for an expansion franchise in Memphis violated section 1 of the Sherman Act. While conceding that NFL member teams could legitimately refuse to deal with a team seeking admission to the league by "applying objective, rational and fair decisional criteria," the plaintiff asserted that there was no valid basis for rejecting its application, as it had satisfied the league's criteria. The court initially ruled that the 1966 congressional approval of the merger between the NFL and the AFL did not require the league to share its dominant market power with all applicants. The court also held that denial of the plaintiff's application for an NFL franchise would not cause any actual or potential injury to economic competition among league teams, as none of them was in the same market area as the proposed Memphis franchise. Observing that the plaintiff's exclusion from the NFL left Memphis available as the site of a franchise for a rival league, the court stated that the NFL's conduct was "patently pro-competitive."

In *Mid-South Grizzlies*, the Third Circuit properly concluded that a league's refusal to admit new member teams does not reduce economic competition among NFL teams or in the broader professional football market. This ruling is consistent with the correct position that collective league member decisions on franchise location issues should not be subject to section 1 of the Sherman Act. Because it would hamper a league's ability to protect its interests in a manner that enhances the image and attractiveness of its product to consumers, allowing a section 1 claim by a disappointed applicant or city would not further the antitrust law's paramount objective of preserving interbrand competition among competing forms of entertainment.

2. Legal vs. Illegal Use of Monopoly Power.—Although it is appropriate to view a league as a single entity in making franchise location and expansion decisions, the mere fact that a league has monopoly power does not violate section 2 of the Sherman Act. Monopoly power has been judicially defined as the ability to affect the product price charged to consumers or to exclude competitors from the market. A violation of section 2 occurs only if a monopolist abuses its power by illegally acquiring or maintaining its market dominance.

Despite disagreement over whether a sports league is a natural monopolist, lawfully acquired or maintained aspects of the league's monopoly position are not subject to antitrust challenge. For example, Congress approved the 1966 merger between the NFL and AFL. MLB has a judicially created antitrust exemption that effectively immunizes its monopoly status.

The federal antitrust laws do not affirmatively require a monopolist professional sports league or its member teams to deal fairly with a current or prospective host city. A sports franchise's demand that a city pay a monopoly price in the form of multi-million dollar public subsidization of a playing facility does not violate the antitrust laws. A city's loss of, or inability to attract, a sports franchise is often the direct result of the city's failure to make the best offer to the team's owner. Notwithstanding the league's limitation on the supply of franchises in the supply-demand equation, any economic harm to a city caused by competition among communities to attract a team is not compensable under the antitrust laws.

---

341. 720 F.2d 772 (3d Cir. 1983).

Even a monopolist has the right to unilaterally select its customers. A refusal to deal with an existing or potential customer is lawful unless a monopolist is seeking to establish or maintain its market dominance by excluding a rival from the market. It is unlikely that a professional sports league's mere unwillingness to locate a franchise in a city is an abuse of the league's monopoly power, actionable under the antitrust laws. In fact, a dominant league's refusal to award a franchise to a city or group of cities with the necessary population base and playing facilities to support a team arguably creates an opportunity for a rival league to form, although the history of successful rival leagues is not encouraging.

In *Seattle Totems Hockey Club, Inc. v. National Hockey League*,[364] the Ninth Circuit held that a league's denial of an application for an expansion franchise did not violate section 2 of the Sherman Act's prohibition against monopolization. The court found no antitrust injury because there was no showing that the plaintiff's exclusion from the league reduced competition among existing league teams. The court ruled that the league's challenged conduct was not an effort to monopolize professional hockey in North America, because the plaintiff was "not competing with the NHL; [it was] seeking to join it."[367]

This is consistent with the classic judicial interpretations of section 2 of the Sherman Act as prohibiting the abuse of monopoly power by unfair exclusionary practices that harm a monopolist's competitors. Aggressive competition on the merits resulting from the production of an attractive product for which there is strong public demand is legal even if it creates reduced market opportunities for a monopolist's rivals. Most antitrust suits asserting section 2 claims against a dominant professional sports league have been brought by a competing league complaining about exclusion from the market, rather than by a city that has been unable to retain or attract a major league team in a particular sport.

There has been one federal antitrust action brought by a city threatened with the loss of a professional sports team. In *Buffalo v. Atlanta Hawks Basketball, Inc.*,[371] the City of Buffalo, which owned the arena leased by the NBA Buffalo Braves, asserted a section 2 claim against the NBA and its member teams after the Braves announced its intention to relocate to North Hollywood, Florida. The complaint alleged that the NBA was monopolizing major league professional basketball by (1) restraining the market for player services through its draft procedure, uniform player contracts, and player boycotts; (2) impeding the development of a rival league by negotiating a merger with the American Basketball Association (ABA); and (3) placing NBA franchises in each major advertising market, even if some locations were unprofitable. The case was settled before resolution of its merits, after the Braves chose to remain in Buffalo.

The Atlanta Hawks Basketball suit appeared to challenge indirectly the proposed dissolution of the ABA and the entry of some of its member teams into the NBA. The City of Buffalo's primary contention was that the elimination of competition between the NBA and ABA harmed the city's ability to retain or attract a major league professional basketball franchise. It thus appears that the City of Buffalo was not claiming a legal right to host an NBA franchise, nor was it claim-

---

364. 783 F.2d 1347 (9th Cir. 1986).

367. *Totems*, 783 F.2d at 1350.

371. Civil No. 76-0261 (W.D.N.Y., filed June 15, 1976) discussed in Weistart & Lowell, *supra* note 167, at s 5.11, 716-19.

ing that the NBA's refusal to provide a replacement team, if the Braves relocated, violated the antitrust laws. Buffalo's complaint clearly identifies the underlying cause of franchise free agency and opportunistic behavior by team owners as being an undersupply of major league professional teams in comparison to the demand by cities to host such teams, and it asserts that antitrust law is the solution to this market imbalance. This central issue was not resolved when the case was settled.

3. *Preserving Competition vs. Requiring Fairness.*—part from seeking damages for its economic harm, a city that has lost a popular and well- supported sports franchise as a result of its relocation generally desires to obtain another league team as a replacement. In *State v. Milwaukee Braves, Inc.*, [378] the State of Wisconsin alleged that the National League and its member baseball clubs violated state antitrust law by allowing the Milwaukee Braves to move to Atlanta and by refusing to provide a replacement team in Milwaukee. The trial court issued an injunction barring the Braves from relocating unless the league granted a franchise to a group that sought to operate a major league baseball team in Milwaukee.

The trial court made several material findings of fact, including (1) the National League and the American League and their respective member teams collectively have monopoly power over major league professional baseball, thereby giving them "unlimited power and discretion to determine the location of" franchises; (2) expansion by the National League was feasible; (3) the Braves franchise had been profitable in Milwaukee; (4) Milwaukee had the economic and population bases needed to support a major league baseball team; (5) the National League had no objective standards for evaluating the propriety of franchise relocations or any procedure to enable cities faced with the loss of a team an opportunity to be heard; and (6) the move of the Braves to Atlanta would cause a substantial economic loss to Milwaukee's metropolitan area.

The trial court heard testimony that MLB "is an operation in a sense quasi public in nature," and the court cited the league's "persistent refusal to expand." The court also heard testimony that, from the perspective of a host community, the loss of a baseball franchise "would be a detriment where there was a benefit before."[387] The court held that the defendants unreasonably exercised monopolistic control over major league baseball and engaged in a concerted refusal to deal with a consumer in violation of state antitrust law.

In deciding not to restore competitive conditions in the baseball industry, the court noted that the common law declared certain businesses, "because they were monopolies, to be 'effected with the public interest' and therefore subject to judicially imposed rules of reasonable behavior." As an alternative to facilitating competition by dissolving the league, the trial court permitted the league to continue its monopoly status, but required the league "to respond in a responsible and reasonable manner in matters pertaining to the transfer and allocation of franchises."[390] The court awarded the plaintiff $5000 in damages and ordered the National League to place a baseball franchise in Milwaukee.

On appeal, the Wisconsin Supreme Court reversed the trial court's judgment. Assuming that the defendants' conduct violated the Wisconsin antitrust laws, the

---

378. 1966 Trade Cas. (CCH) ¶ 71,738 (Wis. Cir. Ct.), *rev'd on other grounds*, 144 N.W.2d 1 (Wis. 1966).

387. Id. at 82,376.

390. *Id*. at 82,406.

appellate court properly held that the use of state law to require the National League to expand the number of its franchises conflicts with the Supremacy and Commerce Clauses of the United States Constitution. Because MLB has a common law exemption from the federal antitrust laws, the court ruled that application of state antitrust law to league decisions regarding franchise location and league membership would conflict with national policy and violate the Supremacy Clause. Observing that government regulation of a professional sports league requires uniformity, the court also concluded that applying Wisconsin law to prevent the National League from allowing the Braves to relocate and refusing an application for a Milwaukee franchise would violate the Commerce Clause.

The *Milwaukee Braves* trial court improperly used state antitrust law to accomplish a laudable, but nonantitrust law objective, namely, imposing a fairness requirement on a professional sports league in making franchise relocation and expansion decisions as a means of protecting a host city's interests. Assuming the appropriateness of characterizing a league as a single entity regarding matters of internal governance, the move of the Braves to Atlanta and the National League's refusal to grant Milwaukee an expansion franchise were not the products of anticompetitive conduct. There was no allegation or finding that the defendants impeded the formation of a rival league or prevented the American League from placing a team in Milwaukee. Rather, the State of Wisconsin merely contended that the National League chose to no longer have a team in Milwaukee.

The primary focus of antitrust law is to enhance consumer welfare by prohibiting anticompetitive conduct. It is important to consider the welfare of all consumers who are affected by the relocation of a sports franchise. Although the fans of a city losing a sports franchise are harmed, the fans of a city gaining a franchise are benefitted. Accordingly, it is extremely difficult, if not impossible, for a court to measure accurately the net consumer welfare effects of a sports franchise relocation. Milwaukee Braves illustrates an unwarranted intrusion, in the form of an antitrust claim, by local politics and emotion into a dispute involving conflicting claims to the same team by different communities.

Antitrust law is concerned with prohibiting anticompetitive acts that impair the operation of a free market. It is not designed to enable activist judicial regulation of private business and the second-guessing of business judgment, particularly parochial second-guessing in a charged atmosphere of disappointed fans and cities. Neither is antitrust law grounded in appeals to "fairness," which are not at the core of antitrust policy. The limited focus of antitrust law in a judicial proceeding does not consider harm caused by "unfairness," unless it flows from anticompetitive conduct. Whether it is fair for a sports franchise to move out of a city or how a city should be compensated for noneconomic harm caused by a team's relocation are important issues, but they should not be resolved by courts in antitrust suits.

The *Milwaukee Braves* trial court's finding that MLB is "quasi public in nature" demonstrated an erroneous mix of common law doctrine—subjecting a public utility to judicial control—with antitrust principles. The court attempted to engage in affirmative regulation of a private monopolist's conduct, regulation that is normally undertaken, pursuant to legislative authority, by a specialized administrative body. Private businesses subject to this form of regulation are typically monopolists whose activities are vital to basic public welfare. Although the presence of a major league team may provide significant economic and psychological benefits to its host community, a professional sports franchise is not vital to the public welfare as is the provision of energy, transportation, telephone service, food, shelter, or sanitation. Neither Congress nor state legislatures have established a regulatory framework governing professional sports leagues. It is, therefore, inappropriate for a court to affirmatively regulate a private business enterprise such as a professional sports league, which does not provide a public utility service. Those constraints are most appropriately the province of private ordering between the city and the team.

4. *Remedies for Anti-Competitive League Conduct.*—The *Milwaukee Braves* trial court's affirmative remedy of forced league expansion was improper because expansion did not establish or restore a competitive market for major league professional baseball franchises harmed by an antitrust violation. At best, this relief is a step toward equalizing the available supply of major league franchises in a given sports league with the collective demand of cities for teams.

Artificially interfering with the output decisions of private business by judicial fiat is not appropriate under antitrust principles. This interference runs contrary to antitrust law's objective of preserving a free market that determines supply and demand for products. Requiring a league to expand may have the anticompetitive effect of inhibiting the formation of a rival league by foreclosing potential franchise locations.

The normal equitable remedy to correct conduct that restrains trade is an injunction prohibiting the continuation of the activity. Courts generally grant affirmative injunctive relief requiring an antitrust violator to do business with another party only if necessary to correct harm to the competitive market system caused by the violation.

A single-league monopoly at the major league level for baseball, basketball, football, and hockey has been the historical norm. Although new rival leagues periodically have been established, they have not provided viable competition to a dominant league or remained in existence for any sustained period. This exacerbates the problem of franchise free agency and opportunistic behavior.

.... [A discussion of Professor Stephen Ross' proposal to break-up major sports leagues is omitted.—ed.].

V. PROPOSALS TO LEVEL THE PLAYING FIELD

The principal goals of any proposal to remedy the harm to taxpayers and fans caused by franchise free agency and opportunistic behavior by team owners should include (1) preserving marketplace competition as the optimal method of allocating a limited number of professional sports franchises; (2) strengthening league authority to protect its members' collective interests and host cities' investments in their local teams; and (3) requiring fairness to prevent exploitation of taxpayers and fans. These proposals appropriately balance the interests of all concerned parties and provide a solution that furthers national policy objectives.

Congressional legislation is necessary to correct the problem of externalities imposed on a host city's taxpayers and fans when a professional sports league exercises its monopoly power to limit the supply of franchises in a destructive combination with a franchise owner that engages in opportunistic behavior. During its tenure in a host city, a privately owned sports franchise often reaps the benefits of public subsidization, while not having to bear the costs imposed on the community after the team relocates. A team owner generally chooses to move to another city to enhance profitability. A city may be faced with continuing to pay off playing facility or infrastructure bond indebtedness, while bearing the cost of other externalities, such as a reduced tax base and disruption of ancillary business activity and employment after a professional sports franchise departs for greener pastures.

The unfortunate reality is that the marketplace, if left entirely alone, will not equalize the supply of, and demand for, professional sports franchises in order to eliminate the significant disparity of bargaining power between a city and team owner, nor will the current marketplace effectively require a sports franchise to bear the public costs that its relocation creates.

Current legal regimes fail to deal effectively with the problem. Private law may be inadequate to safeguard a city's interests because city officials may not have the political strength, will power, or foresight to insist on appropriate contract terms to ensure that the city receives the full benefit of its bargain from providing multi-million dollar public subsidization to host a sports team. An incumbent government official may agree to provide millions in public subsidization to reap an immediate gratification—the political benefits of retaining or attracting a team—but will escape downstream accountability for allowing a sports franchise to drain the local treasury. Even if appropriate contractual provisions are considered and requested, a city may lack the bargaining power necessary to obtain a franchise owner's agreement.

In the private law context of commercial transactions, courts generally hold parties to the express terms of their agreement and are reluctant to impose implied obligations, even if necessary to remedy an imbalance of bargaining power. Although, if proved with reasonable certainty, damages may be recovered for breach of a playing facility lease, it is uncertain whether judicially compelled specific performance is an available remedy to prevent a team from prematurely departing and depriving its host city of the agreed upon term of the team's stay.

The current public law regime also does not provide an appropriate measure of protection for a host city's taxpayers and fans. Applying antitrust law to interfere with a league's business judgment concerning franchise location and expansion decisions does not further the antitrust policy objectives of preserving the competitive process as a means of allocating scarce resources, while maximizing consumer welfare.

Rather than alleviating the negative effects of externalities on cities created by a major professional league's monopoly power, current federal law contributes to the problem. Congress approved the 1966 merger between the AFL and NFL, thereby reducing competition among those leagues to establish football teams in all cities with the population and economic bases to support a franchise. The same federal statute authorizes the NBA, NFL, NHL, and MLB to pool their television rights and divide television revenues. This legislation makes it easier for teams to move from large market cities to medium and small market cities because a relocating franchise shares, on a pro rata basis, any reduction in national television revenues from these moves. The Raiders litigation impedes a league's ability to restrict a member team from abandoning a host city despite a demonstrated history of community support for the team.

The federal tax laws provide special benefits to owners of professional sports franchises. Professional sports is the only industry in which player salaries may be claimed as depreciable capital assets. Player contracts are considered to be capital assets that can be depreciated over the average length of the player's career. In general, up to fifty-percent of the purchase price of a sports franchise may be allocated to player contracts. This facilitates characterizing appreciation in franchise value as a capital gain and enables the team owner to take advantage of favorable tax treatment. Because many sports franchises are part of conglomerates of unrelated businesses, creative accounting can be used to selectively include different parts of the team's operation in various enterprises to minimize overall tax liability. In addition, tax-exempt municipal bonds are frequently used to finance playing facilities for professional teams, thereby providing another form of taxpayer subsidization that benefits sports franchise owners.

There are several potential bases for federal legislation to protect host cities and their taxpayers and fans from exploitation by owners of professional teams. Pursuant to its authority to regulate interstate commerce, Congress may govern the conduct of the members of national professional sports leagues. Congress may also modify the antitrust laws, the tax laws, or both to strengthen league authority to restrict franchise relocations, to provide a disincentive for profitable teams to move, and to enable cities to protect themselves from harm caused by franchise free agency and opportunistic behavior.

Consistent with the belief that a solution to this problem be based on free market and private law principles to the greatest extent possible, Congress should enact legislation effective enough to correct existing problems, yet least intrusive upon a sports league's autonomy to govern itself and a franchise owner's property rights. Before discussing these recommendations, it is important to identify some legislative proposals that appear to be unwarranted.

. . . . [The authors' critique of Congressional and other proposed legislation to regulate sports franchise relocations is omitted. — ed.].

B. Level the Bargaining Table

"[F]reedom of contract begins where equality of bargaining power begins."[509]

1. *Limited League Antitrust Immunity.*—The objective of any congressional legislation should be to "create a level playing field for all participants," and "government must involve itself only so far as to make the position of the owners and the cities at the bargaining table equal." The first step in accomplishing this objective is to strengthen a league's authority to prevent franchise free agency and opportunistic behavior by individual team owners. Congress should modify the antitrust laws to immunize professional sports league rules governing franchise relocations and actions taken thereunder from antitrust challenge. A league's internal franchise location decisions should not be subject to review under the antitrust laws.

Several House and Senate bills introduced in 1995 and 1996 propose that professional sports league decisions on franchise movement be immunized from antitrust scrutiny. The Fans Rights Act of 1995,[512] introduced in the Senate by Ohio Senators John Glenn and Michael DeWine and Washington Senator Slade Gorton and in the House of Representatives by Ohio Congressman Louis Stokes, would provide this exemption. In addition, the Fan Freedom and Community Protection Act of 1996;[514] the Professional Sports Franchise Relocation Act of 1996,[515] spon-

---

509. Oliver Wendell Holmes, Jr., *quoted in* GEORGE SELDES, THE GREAT QUOTATIONS 229 (1967).

512. S. 1439, 104th Cong. (1995); H.R. 2699, 104th Cong. (1995).

514. H.R. 2740, 104th Cong. (1995).

sored by Pennsylvania Senator Arlen Specter; and the Professional Sports Antitrust Clarification Act of 1996,[516] sponsored by South Carolina Senator Strom Thurmond, also would provide antitrust immunity.

.... [The authors' discussion of the details of these bills is omitted. — ed.].

Permitting a league to exercise its autonomy in determining the location of its franchises, without the potential for antitrust challenge or judicial oversight of its decisions, will not, alone, create the necessary incentive to discourage franchise free agency and opportunistic behavior. Merely "allowing the fox to guard the hen house" will not ensure that the interests of a host city's taxpayers and fans are protected adequately. Congress should enact the following proposals to satisfy this objective.

2. *Publicly Traded Ownership.*—League antitrust immunity for franchise relocation decisions should be conditioned upon a league's allowing publicly traded ownership of a minority interest in each franchise. In addition to providing a franchise with an infusion of local capital, this would enable fans and investors to have an ownership interest in a local team and some voice in its management. It would also be more difficult for a profitable franchise to abandon its host city and engage in opportunistic behavior. To prevent the short-term profit motives of a franchise's shareholders from adversely affecting the team's competitiveness and the league's collective long-term interests, restrictions could be placed on the size of any individual's stock holdings, and the total extent of public ownership could be limited to a minority percentage.

....

3. *Collective League Decisions on Revenue Sharing.*—Collective league decisions requiring the sharing of each franchise's locally generated revenues and all nationally generated revenues among all league teams should be immunized from antitrust challenge by a team owner. The primary impetus behind franchise free agency in the NFL is the availability of certain locally generated revenues, such as the rental of luxury suites and the sale of personal seat licenses, which are kept by a team owner and not shared with other owners. This creates a strong economic incentive for a franchise owner to relocate, or threaten to relocate, to obtain a new stadium, or improvements to an existing stadium, thus enhancing revenues generated from these local sources.

4. *Model Lease Terms by Cities.*—Congress should also provide antitrust immunity to enable cities to collectively establish model terms for playing facility leases necessary to protect a host city's taxpayers and fans. Under existing federal law, cities are subject to antitrust liability for collectively agreeing on uniform lease terms. Cities should be permitted to band together to protect their mutual interests in order to counteract a league's monopoly power. If a league should have antitrust immunity for franchise location decisions, cities should have a corresponding antitrust exemption for their joint efforts to develop model lease terms to protect cities' interests.

.... [A discussion of tax-exempt debt service is omitted. — ed.].

....

---

515. S. 1625, 104th Cong. (1996).
516. S. 1696, 104th Cong. (1996).

CONCLUSION

Public law does not solve the problem of opportunistic behavior by sports franchise owners who generate bidding wars and abandon their host cities for other venues, often contrary to both league and host-city interests. Present ordering of city-team arrangements by private law mechanisms may be inadequate because of existing league monopoly power that creates a disparity of bargaining power in favor of team owners. The solution is to make narrow, tactical changes in public law by congressional legislation so that the private ordering of these relationships may be given fuller effect. Individual team owners should not be allowed to harm a host city's fans and taxpayers or defy a league's collective interests by opportunistic or exploitative conduct designed primarily to enhance the economic value of the owner's franchises.

———

Chapter 5

Labor Law and Player Associations

Introduction

The problems involving labor relations in sports have long been discussed in the law reviews. This scholarship initially examined the applicability of federal labor laws to organizing activities in sports. Such scholarly attention seemed warranted given a long standing ruling that baseball was not a part of interstate commerce. Management used the Supreme Court's decision in *Federal Baseball*, as well as subsequent holdings, to argue against the application of the National Labor Relations Act to professional baseball. Eventually federal labor law was deemed applicable to labor and management in the business of sports.

The labor law discourse in sports, beyond the issue of applicability, serves as the ideal primer for understanding the competing goals of antitrust and labor law policy in the United States. In recent years, the dominant theme addressed in the literature has been the non-statutory labor exemption to the federal antitrust laws. The scholarship in this regard has emphasized issues such as the point at which an agreement that is reached through the collective bargaining process expires. The possibilities raised in a long line of cases range from the date of expiration of the collective bargaining agreement, the date impasse is reached, the date impasse is reached with regard to individual issues, to the decertification of the relevant players association. These cases, and the analyses of them, are integral to understanding the negotiating strategies and tactics of both labor and management in today's collective bargaining process, both within and outside of the sports industry.

The opening excerpt from an article by Professors Robert Berry and William Gould discusses the theories that provide the foundation for application of federal labor law to sports. The article also explains the source of the non-statutory labor exemption to the antitrust laws. In order to understand the non-statutory labor exemption in sports, one must first understand the development of the exemption outside of the sports context. Berry and Gould provide this background. An early scholarly treatment of the intersection of labor and antitrust law is Michael Jacobs and Ralph Winter, *Antitrust Principles and Collective Bargaining: Of Superstars in Peonage*, 81 YALE L.J. 1 (1971).

The second article, by Dylan Carson, examines sports specific court rulings regarding the non-statutory labor exemption to the antitrust laws. The article concludes with an overview of the Supreme Court's current view regarding the timing of the expiration of the terms of a collective bargaining agreement. For an extended discussion of this issue *see*, Gary Roberts, *Symposium: Antitrust in the Professional Sports Industry: the Supreme Court Gets it Right for the Wrong Reasons*, 42 ANTITRUST BULL. 595 (1997).

Robert C. Berry and William B. Gould, A Long Deep Drive to Collective Bargaining: Of Players, Owners, Brawls, and Strikes
31 Case Western Reserve Law Review 685 (1981)*

. . . .

THE ELYSIAN FIELDS, Canton's mud patch, the peach basket in Springfield, and ice ponds across Canada produced the beginnings of organized team sports in baseball, football, basketball, and hockey. These early teams evolved into professional sports.

. . . . [Discussion of the structure of the sports industry and the relevant participants is omitted. —ed.].

C. The Pick-and-Roll: Labor

. . . .

Until 1969..., it was unclear that the National Labor Relations Board (the Board) would take jurisdiction over professional sports. The Board had characterized horse racing as a local activity beyond its purview. Baseball umpires then began pressing for Board recognition. Baseball was not the best sport to advance the cause of sports unions, since the umpires faced the *Federal Baseball*[181] precedent and Justice Holmes' declaration that baseball was not interstate activity. As expected, the baseball leagues relied on Holmes' declaration, urging that the Board's jurisdiction under the federal labor law be limited to businesses engaged in interstate commerce and controlled by the employers. The leagues argued further that, without Board regulation, the industry would be subject to many different labor laws depending on the locality in which the dispute arose. The Board, however, accepted the union's argument:

> The system appears to have been designed almost entirely by employers and owners, and the final arbiter of internal disputes does not appear to be a neutral third party freely chosen by both sides, but rather an individual appointed solely by the member club owners themselves. Moreover, it is patently contrary to the letter and spirit of the Act for the Board to defer its undoubted jurisdiction to decide unfair labor practices to a dispute settlement system established unilaterally by an employer or group of employers.

The Board also observed that many employees—other than those involved in the petition for representation filed in the case—were not involved in any kind of self-regulation system.[185] If the Board declined jurisdiction over the industry, such employees would be deprived of any representation or dispute settlement machinery. The Board, examining the legislative history, found no intent to exclude sports when Congress refused to include baseball under the antitrust laws.

. . . .

---

    181. 259 U.S. 200 (1922).
    185. 180 N.L.R.B. at 191.

This decision coincided roughly with the first collective bargaining agreements forged between the nascent players union and the various major league teams. According to Larry Fleischer, director of the NBPA in 1962, it was not until 1966 that the owners were willing to talk with him. In 1967, however, the players and NBA owners entered into the first collective bargaining agreement in professional sports history. Agreements in baseball and football followed shortly thereafter. The MLBPA reached an agreement with the owners in 1968, shortly after the arrival of the influential Marvin Miller as director of the MLBPA. The agreement was modest compared to those made subsequently, but it provided some significant gains for the players. The agreement raised the minimum salary to $10,000, provided for arbitration of grievances, and demanded a study committee to examine the reserve clause. Both the NFL and the about-to-be merged, AFL, completed similarly significant, yet rudimentary, agreements a few months later. With collective bargaining agreements in these three sports and agreements in hockey soon to follow, the union movement in professional team sports was a pervasive reality, although the strength of these associations had not been tested fully. All leagues showed a similar pattern; their early agreements skirted many tough issues and each succeeding agreement weakened traditional management prerogatives. Powers and rights slowly shifted away from the owners to include the players as well.

The ascendancy of players associations and the advent of collective agreements were based, in part, on a growing sentiment among the players that their grievances were being ignored and the unanimity was needed. Fortunately for the players, there were people available from whom they could seek advice on resolving these grievances.

In addition to a growing awareness of the possible strengths of collective efforts, three types of concerted action helped develop the potency of collective bargaining in sports. The first type of concerted action was the strike weapon. The second...was antitrust litigation. Finally, the third, an outgrowth of collective bargaining, was the arbitration of grievances and salary disputes arising under the collective agreement (rights disputes). While the second and third approaches, particularly baseball salary arbitration, have achieved the most obvious gains, strikes and threats to strike should not be underestimated.

The first indication players would strike for their rights surfaced in the NBA in early 1964. Upset over the owners' position regarding contributions to be made to the newly established player pension fund, the players threatened a boycott at the league's All-Star game. The players delayed the start of the contest for several minutes until, in a locker room confrontation, they received guarantees that the owner would take positive action.

The first full-scale, league-wide strike occurred in the NFL in the fall of 1968. As with the NBA dispute four years earlier, the bone of contention was the owners' contribution to the pension fund. This contribution was the sole issue preventing the first collective agreement in football, and negotiations became difficult and heated. After reaching an impasse in negotiations, the players boycotted the preseason training camps. The owners then retaliated with a lockout. Only then, with the battle lines firmly drawn, did the sides agree to talk. Within a few days, the parties reached an agreement. It was not a long or bitter strike, but the boycott and resulting lockout influenced the parties' willingness to resume talks and reach an agreement.

Baseball has seen numerous threats of strikes and, particularly in light of the 1981 strike, more than its share of actual ones. The first threat was in 1969 when the parties disagreed on the percentage of receipts the players' pension fund should receive from the leagues' national television contract. A short-lived training camp boycott resulted. Again in 1972, pension issues led to a walkout that delayed the start of the baseball season for several days. Games were canceled and, under the agreement that was eventually reached, were never rescheduled. This episode was followed by a lockout during spring training in 1967 and by a walkout in the waning stages of the baseball preseason in 1980, with the threat of a full-scale strike in May of that year. The proposed 1980 strike was narrowly averted by a new collective bargaining agreement that granted several additional benefits to players but postponed a decision on the thorny free-agent question. When the members of the joint player-owner committee appointed to study the question could not agree, the owners announced that they would implement their proposal for a free agent system which had been included provisionally in the 1980 accord. The players responded by declaring a strike. Although delayed by legal maneuvering, the strike was called in June, 1981 and continued to August, setting record for sports strikes. The success of the strike and the declaration of winners and losers will continue to be debated. It is evident, however, that the strike succeeded in stimulation awareness that a labor dispute could threaten a league's existence or, at a minimum, the conclusion of a playing season. Thus, while neither the player boycotts nor lockouts by owners have been unqualified successes, they have prodded the two sides toward reaching new agreements, as evidenced by the 1981 baseball agreement and the agreements in years past.

In 1974, however, a football strike was definitely a failure—and nearly a disaster. The collective bargaining agreement at issue that year had expired, and the owners and players were far from agreement, particularly over any changes in player mobility rules. The players voted to strike, and most of them did strike. Rookies were urged not to report to training camps, but many reported. Other aspiring professional players arrived on the scene and were labeled "scabs" by the striking players. Public sentiment was assuredly against the players. The players' position weakened daily as more of them relinquished the fight and reported to preseason camp. After forty-four days, the strike ended in a whimper, with all players returning to camp under a fourteen day moratorium that became moot when the players decided not to resume the strike at the end of the period.

If the players had not initiated a second line of attack, the union movement in football might have died. Although dissention racked the players association there was still the antitrust weapon. The decision in *Kapp v. NFL*[201] held early promise, but it was so diffuse that its ultimate effects were uncertain. This diffusion did not exist in *Mackey v. NFL*[202] and its companion case, *Alexander v. NFL*.[203] After an extended trial, the players scored an important triumph in *Mackey* and scored

---

201. 390 F. Supp. 73 (N.D. Cal. 1974), *aff'd*, 586 F.2d 644 (9th Cir. 1978), *cert. denied*, 441 U.S. 907 (1979).

202. Mackey v. NFL, 407 F. Supp. 1000 (D. Minn. 1975), *modified*, 543 F.2d 606 (9th Cir. 1976), *cert. dismissed*, 434 U.S. 801 (1977). For a discussion of *Mackey*, see notes 276-95 *infra* and accompanying text.

203. [1977-2 TRADE CASES ¶ 72,983], D. Ct. Minn. (1977).

again in *Alexander*. The direct result of these cases was a multimillion dollar cash settlement and owners' promise to negotiate a new collective pact. It has been suggested that the players had the owners' backs to the wall and yet did not exact a sufficient settlement in their 1977 collective bargaining agreement. At this point, it is important only to note that antitrust was a direct, powerful, and most influential force in moving sports management and labor toward collective bargaining. In addition to football, this force has affected basketball and hockey.

Baseball, of course, was different, particularly with *Federal* Baseball[207] and *Flood*[208] casting lengthy shadows over its business methods. Since antitrust was not available in this sport, the viable alternative was arbitration. In 1973, the players association and the owners negotiated several arbitration provisions in the new collective bargaining agreement. These provisions were the portent of change for the national pastime.

In 1974, Oakland pitcher Jim "Catfish" Hunter and Oakland's owner, Charles O. Finley, had a confrontation. Hunter had finished the previous season with an impressive 25-13 win-loss record. The twenty-eight-year-old pitcher had been a twenty game winner for four consecutive seasons and had compiled a total of eighty-eight wins during his four years with the Oakland A's. The A's and Hunter had agreed on a two year contract whereby $50,000 of Hunter's salary would be paid to him directly and the remaining $50,000 would be paid to a deferment plan of Hunter's choice. Hunter had requested a specific deferred payment provision which would enable him to avoid immediate tax liability. Finley agreed to the provision but later discovered that he, personally, would incur resultant tax liability. Finley insisted that the contract clause did not require him to assume this burden. During the 1974 season, consequently, Hunter routinely received the portion of his salary that was to be paid directly to him, but the deferred payments were not made to the designated investment company. The season ended with the deferred payments still not made, despite Hunter's repeated requests. Hunter claimed that Finley's failure to make payments constituted a breach of contract, thus enabling the pitcher to exercise his right to terminate the contract. Hunter then announced that since he had no contract, he was a free agent. Finley insisted that no free agent question was involved, that the only dispute concerned the method of payment, and that the dispute was merely a matter of contract interpretation. Finley offered the other $50,000 to Hunter as direct payment, but Hunter rejected this offer as contrary to his contractual rights.

The case was submitted under the applicable collective bargaining procedures to Arbitrator Peter Seitz. Seitz ruled in Hunter's favor, finding no ambiguity in the contract language outlining the club's obligations. According to Seitz, the club failed to perform, thus enabling Hunter rightfully to terminate. The arbitrator rejected Finley's contention that no breach could occur until the arbitration established whether the club was obligated to meet Hunter's demands. Seitz further ruled that Hunter no longer had a valid contract with the A's. Hunter was, therefore, a free agent and could entertain offers from any other major league club.

On December 31, 1974, the "Catfish" accepted an offer from the New York Yankees for an unprecedented salary package. Hunter received a $1 million signing bonus, $150,000 salary per year for five years, life insurance benefits worth

---

207. 259 U.S. 200 (1922).
208. 407 U.S. 258 (1972).

$1 million, and a substantial amount of deferred compensation. Only later was it learned that the bidding for Hunter had exceeded the Yankee's offer. At trial in the Joe Kapp case, evidence disclosed that Hunter rejected a $3.8 million offer from the Kansas City Royals. This testimony, by Hunter's lawyers, was admitted for the limited purpose of showing how open competition for players might affect salaries. This evidence apparently did not impress the *Kapp* jury, since it awarded no damages to Kapp even though he had been forced to deal in something less than a free market. Later events, however, have demonstrated the value of free agency to players. Perhaps the Hunter situation was a harbinger, but it involved special circumstances. An obstinate owner materially breached a contract, thus freeing his star player. These circumstances are rare.

The players needed to mount a frontal attack on baseball's reserve system. This attack came, at length, through the grievances of pitchers Andy Messersmith of the Los Angeles Dodgers and Dave McNally of the Montreal Expos. These players claimed to be free agents, contending that the sacred reserve clause was only a one-year option. When their request to be declared free agents was denied, a grievance was filed.

The league and clubs asserted that the contract had not expired because, under the option clause, the contract created a new option. As long as the clubs duly "reserved" their players each year, new options would be created perpetually. The owners not only contested the grievance on the merits but also contended that the matter was not properly the subject of arbitration. To support this contention, the owners referred to the 1973 Basic Agreement, article XV, which stipulated that the agreement "does not deal with the reserve system." The agreement further stated that contractual language should not prejudice the position of either side. The owners' position was that article XV deprived the arbitrator of power to arbitrate on the core of the reserve system. As the arbitrator noted: "This system of reservation of exclusive control is historic in baseball and is traceable to the early days of the organized sport in the 19th century." If the arbitrator accepted management's interpretation of article XV, he would be confronted with a paradox. On the one hand, the standard players contract was incorporated in the basic agreement and part of the core of the reserve system, as characterized by the league, was in that contract. On the other hand, the owners relied on the language of article XV to mean that the agreement did not "deal" with the reserve system. Arbitrator Seitz noted that the legality of the reserve clause was at issue in *Flood*, that the parties had "agreed to disagree" about its continuation from the 1968 agreement onward, and that the reserve system remained, therefore, "untouched" and in existence. The arbitrator accordingly found that the contract provisions represented a type of "cease fire" over the issue while the matter was litigated. Since the basic agreement incorporated the players contract, and since the players contended they were free agents once their individual contracts expired, the arbitrator found that he did, in fact, have authority to resolve the dispute.

The arbitrator interpreted the Uniform Players Contract language, which provided for renewal "for the period of one year," as a renewal clause which "does not warrant interpreting the section as providing for contract renewal beyond the contract year." "When that year comes to an end, the Player no longer has contractual duties that bind him to the Club." In light of the considerable impact the award would have on the parties, the arbitrator repeatedly urged them to negotiate a new system. Realistically, the owners were faced with two alternatives. The first alternative was to allow McNally and Messersmith to become free agents. This decision would have allowed the owners to argue that the principle of stare decisis, not being as embedded in the arbitration system as in the judiciary, would not bind another arbitrator to Arbitrator Seitz' interpretation of the collective bargaining agreement. This option would have created uncertainty, especially given the expiration of the collective agreement and the imminent expiration of numerous individual contracts. The owners' second option was to negotiate more vigorously with the association about changes in the reserve system—a process initiated in the summer of 1976.

The owners, however, chose to litigate. This choice was made despite the arbitrator's indication that he would resolve the issue adversely to the owners and despite the Supreme Court's declaration in the *Steelworkers Trilogy*[229] that the courts will not reverse a labor arbitration award in the absence of "clear infidelity" to the agreement. Not surprisingly, the courts, pursuant to the *Steelworkers* standards, affirmed the award. The Court of Appeals for the Eighth Circuit in *Kansas City Royals Baseball Corp. v. Major League Baseball Players Association*[230] concluded that the arbitrator had jurisdiction to resolve the issue. *Steelworkers Trilogy* instructed that courts only should conclude that an issue cannot be arbitrated when there is explicit language or bargaining history excluding the issue from the arbitration clause. Accordingly, arbitrability—one of the more difficult issues presented—was resolved against the owners. The court noted that article XV and its predecessor, article 14, were adopted as both sides maneuvered in anticipation of the *Flood* case. The association was willing to negotiate language which indicated it had not addressed the free agent issue. The association was concerned that the players, unhappy with the handling of the reserve clause issue, might initiate litigation on the duty of fair representation. The association wanted to avoid this issue while *Flood* was pending. The owners wanted to utilize the labor exemption defense in the *Flood* litigation[234] to establish that the agreement addressed the issue.[235] The court concluded that "manifest infidelity," a prerequisite for finding that the arbitrator erroneously interpreted the agreement, was not present.

These rulings prompted new collective bargaining. Excluding those players bound by long term contracts, the owners faced the prospect that all players would become free agents at the end of the 1976 season, or soon thereafter, because of the Seitz award and its affirmance in *Kansas City Royals*. The Eighth Circuit, following *Mackey*, urged the parties to resolve their problems through collective bargaining:

> [W]e intimate no views on the merits of the reserve system. We note, however, that club Owners and the Players Association's representatives agree that some form of a reserve system is needed if the integrity of the game is to be preserved

---

229. *United Steelworkers v. American Mfg. Co.*, 363 U.S. 564 (1960), United Steelworkers v. Warrior & Gulf Navigation Co., 363 U.S. 574 (1960); United Steelworkers v. Enterprise Wheel & Car Corp., 363 U.S. 593 (1960).

230. 532 F.2d 615 (8th Cir. 1976).

234. *Id.* at 624.

235. *Id.* at 625.

and if public confidence in baseball is to be maintained. The disagreement lies over the degree of control necessary if these goals are to be achieved. Certainly, the parties are in a better position to negotiate their differences than to have them decided in a series of arbitrations and court decisions. We commend them to that process and suggest that the time for obfuscation has passed and the time for plain talk and clear language has arrived. Baseball fans everywhere expect nothing less.[237]

The call for collective bargaining was sounded over issues most critical to the lifeblood of professional sports. Free agency and resultant compensation, full arbitration of grievances, the draft of nonleague players, and even the rules of the games were all potential roadblocks to successful negotiation. Aided by concerted union activities, antitrust litigation, and an arbitrator who severed the reserve lock in baseball, labor law and labor relations moved to the forefront. Sports was no longer merely the business of giving exhibitions; it was a complex of industries, each with challenges to meet in the 1980's.

III. The Labor Law of Sports

The long drive to collective bargaining in professional sports has culminated in agreements of pervasive impact on the industries. These industries now address most issues of vital importance to both labor and management. The approaches taken by different leagues in their respective agreements reflect, to a degree, fundamental variations among the sports leagues themselves. As to some provisions, however, it is unclear whether they are responses to the exigencies of a particular sport or whether labor and management simply have recast old themes, without regard to future realities and needs. Nonetheless, labor law and labor relations are at the forefront in influencing league operations. A labor law of sports is developing and is preeminent today as legal catalyst for the industries.

This section concentrates on the most significant developments. First, there is a growing body of case law encouraging both labor and management to opt for collective bargaining. These cases underscore the benefits attainable through the labor exemption of the antitrust laws, both as insulation for management and a bargaining leverage for the players. Second, there are major trends toward collective bargaining covering such issues as player mobility, the possible range of mandatory subjects of bargaining, and arbitration as a labor-management dispute resolution process. Finally, there are the unresolved issues, the most notable of which are continuing problems over definition and control of the bargaining unit and questions about exclusivity in sports labor dealings. These analyses describe the heart of the present situation and foreshadow the discussion in the Article's final section concerning the future of labor law in the sports industries.

A. Collective Bargaining and the Antitrust Labor Exemption

As in American labor management relations law generally, labor litigation in the sports industry must refer to the antitrust litigation which preceded it. The historical context for antitrust litigation is considerably different for sports than for other industries. In industrial relations, the courts utilized the antitrust laws as a repressive weapon and attempted to thwart trade union organizations and their

---

237. 532 F.2d at 632.

collective bargaining goals. In contrast, trade unions or players associations in professional sports have benefitted from the modern labor-antitrust cases. Despite the legal restraints otherwise imposed on the union, the courts have provided athletes an advantage in their battle to gain credibility at the bargaining table and to negotiate effectively over player mobility issues.

1. Background Cases

The antitrust cases begin with *United States v. Hutcheson*[242] in which the Court held that if a union acts in its own "self-interest" and does not combine with non-labor groups, its conduct is immunized from antitrust liability. Under this exemption, the Court invoked the policies of other modern labor legislation, such as the Clayton Antitrust Act[244] and the Norris-LaGuardia Act[245] to interpret antitrust legislation in a manner compatible with some aspects of contemporary trade union behavior. The Court concentrated on the antitrust laws, which prohibit practices designed to suppress or eliminate competition between firms, and the labor laws, which promote freedom of association among workers to foster the collective bargaining process and to remove labor cost competition between firms.

In *Allen Bradley Co. V. Local 3, IBEW*,[248] the Court held that union-employer agreements aimed at boycotting unorganized local contractors and manufacturers and barring the importation of equipment manufactured outside of the local area, were a combination which constituted a conspiracy to monopolize the trade. The Court noted that the labor and antitrust statutes sometimes promoted separate and competing policies. The policy of preserving a competitive business economy, for example, may conflict with the policy of preserving "the rights of labor to organize to better its conditions through the agency of collective bargaining."[250] In *Allen Bradley*, the unlawful conspiracy was between labor and nonlabor groups and was aimed at controlling the marketing of goods and services.

. . . .

The next two major decisions were made in 1965. These cases represent the so-called nonstatutory exemption of antitrust liability where the union, through an agreement with an employer group, attempts to promote its interests and, in so doing, induces restraints in a product market. The first case was *UMW v. Pennington*[253] in which a coal company cross-claimed in a suit by the trustees of the Welfare and Retirement Fund to recover royalty payments owed under the agreement. The cross-claim alleged an unlawful conspiracy between the UMW Welfare and Retirement Fund trustees and the large coal operators to violate the antitrust laws. The argument, essentially, was that the union agreed with the large coal operators to abandon its established stand against mechanized equipment and technological innovation in the mines in exchange for higher wages and royalty payments. The union allegedly imposed a wage and benefit package that smaller operators could not meet. It was further alleged that the union engaged in a collusive bidding agreement designed to drive such operators from the market.

---

242. 312 U.S. 219 (1941).
244. Clayton Act of 1914, §§1-26, 15 U.S.C. §§12-27 (1976).
245. Norris-LaGuardia Act §§1-15, 29 U.S.C. §§101-115 (1976).
248. 325 U.S. 797 (1945).
250. *Id.* at 811.
253. 381 U.S. 657 (1965).

Justice White, writing for two other Justices, noted that national labor law sanctioned multiemployer bargaining. Such bargaining was held not to violate the antitrust laws in that a union might "as a matter of its own policy and not by agreement with all or part of the employers of that unit, seek the same wages from other employers."[257] Justice White, in contrast to Justice Goldberg's position in his separate opinion, rejected the view that an agreement was immunized because its subject matter constituted a mandatory subject of bargaining for labor and management under the National Labor Relations Act (NLRA).[259] Despite the mandatory nature of issues, the nonstatutory exemption would not prevail where the resulting agreement imposed terms on small employers that revealed the "predatory" intent of unions and large employers to injure the small employers. Additionally, if the agreement interfered with the union's ability to act in its self-interest, it was unlawful. The *Allen Bradley* and *Pennington* cases dramatize a single, recurrent theme in sports cases. There is great judicial concern about possible injury to a third party not immediately involved in the union-employer relationship. This concern was for nonunion and nonlocal manufacturers and contractors in *Allen Bradley*; in *Pennington*, it was for the small coal operators.

The second 1965 Supreme Court decision, *Local 189, Amalgamated Meat Cutters v. Jewel Tea Co.*,[263] indicated that public injury due to product restraints could give rise to antitrust liability when trade unions negotiated such restraints. In *Jewel Tea*, an employer refused to sign a multiemployer collective bargaining agreement which litigated the hours for the sale of meat. The Court's plurality opinion initially rejected the argument that the subject matter involved in the union's demand was a mandatory bargaining subject within the meaning of the NLRA. Second, the Supreme Court declared that courts should not defer to the primary jurisdiction of the Board because courts are not "without experience in classifying bargaining subjects as terms of conditions of employment." The Court also found deference to the Board particularly inappropriate where the "controlling legal issue" was "wholly unrelated" to determinations in which the Board normally engages, such as unfair labor practice orders. Finally, the Court noted that if the parties were remitted to the Board's primary jurisdiction, there was a "substantial probability" that the plaintiff might be left without jurisdiction, either because the statute of limitations expired or because no unfair labor practice existed.

The Court, in finding no antitrust liability, weighed the legitimacy of the union's claim that the impact of the subject matter on employment opportunities significantly affected its members against the argument that the union's demands restrained product consumption and thus injured a third party. Because the union's interest in protecting its members' employment opportunities was "immediate" and "legitimate," the labor exemption was deemed applicable and immunized the union from antitrust liability. The third party in *Jewel Tea* was the consuming public, which could not purchase goods at convenient hours. In the sports case, the injured party is either the player, a competing league which is injured in its ability to attract players, or the consuming public. The peculiar relevance of *Jewel Tea* to the sports case is best seen by reference to leading cases involving

---

257. 381 U.S. at 664.
259. *Id.* at 664-65. *But see id.* at 710 (Goldberg, J., dissenting).
263. 381 U.S. 676 (1965).

league- imposed restraints on player mobility. Another important theme in *Pennington*, *Jewel Tea*, and their antecedents is the statutory exemption which concerns a union's self interest as a prerequisite to antitrust immunity. In *Jewel Tea*, the Court attempted to define self-interest. When the agreement is "intimately related to wages, hours, and working conditions"[273] and the union members' concern is "immediate and direct,"[274] an agreement "pursuant to what the labor unions deemed to be in their own labor union interests"[275] is appropriate.

....

Dylan M. Carson, The *Browning* of Sports Law: Defining the Survival of the Labor Exemption After Expiration of Bargaining Agreements
30 Suffolk University Law Review 1141 (1997)*

....

I. INTRODUCTION

....

Over the past several decades, players and owners in professional sports have fiercely contested the issues of how and when the exemption applies to protect collectively bargained league rules and practices.[10] Recent litigation has focused on the limits to the nonstatutory exemption application after a collective bargaining agreement has expired and further negotiations fail to produce a new agreement. Until recently, the Court had never clearly delineated the exact nature and boundaries of the exemption or considered it in the context of labor disputes in professional sports.[12] Finally, in 1996 the Supreme Court, in *Brown v. Pro Football, Inc.*,[13] settled the much-litigated issue of the exemption's survival after parties reach an impasse in collective bargaining.

.... [A discussion of the background of non-statutory labor exemption is omitted. - ed.].

C. *Development of the Nonstatutory Labor Exemption in Professional Sports*

1. *The Contempt for Player Restraints*

.... [Background discussion of player restraints is omitted. - ed.].

2. *Playing Defense with the Nonstatutory Exemption: The Mackey Test*

---

273. 381 U.S. at 689.

274. *Id.* at 691.

275. *Id.* at 688.

10. *See, e.g.,* Wood v. NBA, 809 F.2d 954, 956-57 (2nd Cir. 1987).

12. *See* Brown v. Pro Football, Inc., 50 F.3d 1041, 1048 (D.C. Cir. 1995) (noting Court's cases only mark labor exemption's general boundaries), *aff'd*, 116 S. Ct. 2116 (1996).

13. 116 S. Ct. 2116 (1996).

In the first major antitrust suit to bring the nonstatutory labor exemption to a federal court of appeals, *Mackey v. National Football League*,[83] the National Football League (NFL) raised the exemption as a defense in a player challenge to the league's reserve rule as a per se antitrust violation.[84] Named after the NFL's commissioner, the "Rozelle Rule" empowered the commissioner to require a team signing a "free agent" to compensate the player's former club with players, draft picks or cash. The rule created uncertainty for teams about the compensation the commissioner would require and effectively deterred clubs from signing free agents.[86] As a result, the rule forced players to either re-sign with their original team or leave football.[87] Initially, the United States District Court for the District of Minnesota sided with the NFL players, finding that the Rozelle Rule violated the Sherman Act, under both the per se and rule of reason tests, as an unreasonable restraint of trade in the form of a group boycott and concerted refusal to deal with players. The court rejected the the NFL's argument that the nonstatutory exemption immunized the Rozelle Rule from antitrust liability because the Rule was part of collective bargaining agreement between team owners and the players' union.

On appeal, the United States Court of Appeals for the Eighth Circuit articulated a three-prong test for determining whether the nonstatutory exemption applies to a collectively bargained restraint of trade.[90] The exemption would apply if, and only if: the restraint primarily affects only parties to the collective bargaining relationship; the restraint concerns a mandatory subject of bargaining; and the restraint results from bona fide arm's-length bargaining.[91] Applying its test, the *Mackey* court held that the exemption did not immunize the Rozelle Rule because it failed the third prong. Specifically, the NFL unilaterally promulgated the restraint on competition in the market for players' services instead of gaining the union's consent to the restraint through collective bargaining.

Declining to grant antitrust immunity, the court then held that the Rozelle Rule constituted an unreasonable restraint of trade in violation of the Sherman Act. The court reasoned that the restraint failed the rule of reason test because it was more restrictive than necessary and unjustified by the business purposes of reimbursing teams for player development costs and maintaining competitive balance in the league. Although the *Mackey* court held the exemption inapplicable to the league's restraint, the court established that teams may invoke the exemption in appropriate circumstances, reasoning that the Supreme Court intended the exemption's benefits to extend to both parties of a collective bargaining agreement.[96]

. . . .

---

83. 407 F. Supp. 1000 (D. Minn. 1975), *aff'd in part and remanded*, 543 F.2d 606 (8th Cir. 1976).

84. *Id.* at 1002-03.

86. *See id.* at 1006-07.

87. *See id.*

90. *See* Mackey v. NFL, 543 F.2d 606, 614 (8th Cir 1976).

91. *Id.* The *Mackey* court supported its three prong test by citing to *Jewel Tea, Pennington,* and *Connell,* but provided no reasoning for why it articulated the three prongs as it did. *Id.; see Antitrust Issues, supra* note 6, § 19.06[4][b], at 19-50 to 19-51 (labeling *Mackey* controversial decision because assertion counterintuitive that agreement not product of bona fide bargaining).

96. *Mackey v. NFL,* 543 F.2d 606, 612-13 (8th Cir. 1976).

4. Coming of Age: The Nonstatutory Exemption in the 1980s

During the 1980s, the teams in the National Basketball Association (NBA) recovered from near financial ruin and prospered with the help of a salary cap that limited team payrolls. Before the ink dried on the 1983 collective bargaining agreement between the NBA and the National Basketball Players Association, a college player selected in the annual draft filed an antitrust action alleging the salary cap and draft violated Section 1 of the Sherman Act.[104] In *Wood v. National Basketball Ass'n*,[105] the federal district court applied the *Mackey* test and held that the nonstatutory labor exemption immunized the draft and salary cap from antitrust liability. On appeal, the Second Circuit affirmed, holding the collectively bargained restraints exempt from antitrust scrutiny, but not as a result of applying the *Mackey* test. The court declined to differentiate between the statutory and nonstatutory exemptions or consider the parameters of the nonstatutory exemption.[108] Instead, without relying on *Mackey*, the court applied a general exemption that would deny any player's antitrust claim against a collective bargaining agreement, reasoning that "no one seriously contends that the antitrust laws may be used to subvert fundamental principles of our federal labor policy."[109] The *Wood* court also reasoned that applying "a wholly unprincipled, judge-made exception [to antitrust immunity]...created for professional athletes" would cause the collapse of federal labor policy by exposing all collective bargaining agreements to antitrust challenge.[110]

. . . .

5. The Effect of the Expiration of the Collective Bargaining Agreement

The circuit courts in *Wood*, *McCourt* and *Mackey* each considered the antitrust immunity of player restraints included in collective bargaining agreements then in effect. But it was not until 1987, in *Bridgeman v. National Basketball Association*,[116] that a federal district court considered whether the nonstatutory labor exemption applied to restraints contained in an expired collective bargaining agreement. In *Bridgeman*, a group of NBA players filed an antitrust action challenging the league's draft, salary cap, and right of first refusal after the 1983 collective bargaining agreement expired and the league and union failed to reach a new agreement.... [T]he United States District Court for the District of New Jersey determined that the novel issue of the application of the nonstatutory labor exemption after expiration of the collective bargaining agreement required a standard modified from the reasoning in *Mackey*.[119]

Balancing the competing labor and antitrust policies, the *Bridgeman* court ruled that the nonstatutory exemption survives as long as the employer does not change the restraint and reasonably believes the next collective bargaining agreement will include the restraint "or a close variant of it."[120] The court then denied both motions for summary judgment because issues of material fact existed over

---

104. *See* Wood v. NBA, 602 F. Supp. 525, 526-27 (S.D.N.Y. 1984).

105. 602 F. Supp. 525 (S.D.N.Y. 1984), *aff'd*, 809 F.2d 954 (2d. Cir 1987).

108. *See Wood*, 809 F.2d at 959.

109. *Id.*

110. *Wood*, 809 F.2d at 961.

116. 675 F. Supp. 960 (D.N.J. 1987).

119. *See id.* at 963-65.

120. *See id.* at 967 & n.6.

whether the NBA reasonably believed the next collective bargaining agreement would include the salary cap and draft. Initially, both the owners and players declared victory after the court's decision. Ultimately, the parties settled the Bridgeman case with a new collective bargaining agreement that continued the salary cap, draft, and right of first refusal.

a. Powell v. National Football League: The Eighth Circuit's Approach

A scenario similar to *Bridgeman* unfolded in professional football when the NFL Players Association (NFLPA) challenged the NFL's right of first refusal system as a Sherman Act violation after the 1982 collective bargaining agreement containing the provision expired in 1987 and the parties reached impasse. In *Powell v. National Football League*,[125] as in *Mackey*, the United States District Court for the District of Minnesota considered whether the labor exemption applied to the players union's challenge to restraints on the labor market. The court rejected the *Bridgeman* standard, concluding that accommodation of the conflicting antitrust and labor policies requires that the exemption survive to immunize a term relating to a mandatory bargaining subject until the parties bargain to impasse over that term. Accordingly, the court denied the league's motion for partial summary judgment and stayed the remaining motions for summary judgment because an issue existed as to whether the parties had bargained to impasse over the player restraint system.[128]

In an interlocutory appeal of the district court's denial of summary judgment to the Eighth Circuit, the NFL prevailed on the labor exemption issue.[129] The *Powell* court, responding to the question left open by *Mackey*, held that the nonstatutory exemption protects restraints "conceived in an ongoing collective bargaining relationship" from antitrust scrutiny.[130] The *Powell* court rejected the district court's standard that would subject an employer's unilateral conduct after impasse to antitrust liability when, under the NLRA, an employer may lawfully implement pre-impasse proposals once the parties reach a deadlock in negotiations.[131] Instead, the court reasoned that the "level playing field" of the "labor arena," where Congress intended parties to exert their respective economic forces in good faith bargaining free from the intervention of courts, provides the league and its players the proper framework to settle their dispute without the threat of the Sherman Act.[132] On appeal, the Supreme Court declined to review the decision.[133]

In response to the *Powell* court's immunization of the NFL's right of first refusal system from antitrust attack and suggestion that the exemption would not apply in the absence of a collective bargaining relationship, the NFLPA decertified as a union. With the bargaining relationship dissolved, several NFL players, led by New York Jets running back Freeman McNeil, challenged the league's modi-

---

125. 678 F. Supp. 777 (D. Minn. 1988), *rev'd*, 930 F.2d 1293 (8th Cir. 1989).

128. *Id.* at 789.

129. *See* Powell v. NFL, 930 F.2d 1293, 1295 (8th Cir. 1989).

130. *Compare id.* at 1303 (finding national labor policy overrides antitrust policy when agreement expired) *with* Mackey v. NFL, 543 F.2d 606, 618 n.18 (8th Cir. 1976) (stating unnecessary for court to decide whether exemption extends beyond agreement).

131. *See Powell*, 930 F.2d at 1302.

132. *See Powell*, 930 F.2d at 1302-03 & n.11 (citing Wood v. NBA, 809 F.2d 954, 959 (2d. Cir. 1987).

133. *See* Powell v. NFL, 498 U.S. 1040, 1040 (1991) (denying certiorari)....

fied "Plan B" free agency system as an antitrust violation. In *McNeil v. National Football League*,[136] the players gained a significant victory, and proceeded to trial, when the United States District Court for the District of Minnesota ruled that the nonstatutory exemption does not apply in the absence of a collective bargaining relationship. A jury found that the Plan B free agency system violated the rule of reason as substantially anticompetitive in the market for football player services, and more restrictive than reasonably necessary to achieve competitive balance in the NFL.[138] Shortly thereafter, the NFL settled the case and formed a seven-year collective bargaining agreement in 1993, bringing extended labor peace to professional football.

.... [Discussion of *National Basketball Association v. Williams*, 145 F.3d 684 (2d Cir. 1995), *cert. denied*, 116 S. Ct. 2546 (1996) is omitted - ed.].

c. Brown v. Pro Football, Inc.: The D.C. Circuit's Call

In *Brown v. Pro Football, Inc.*,[154] the dispute over the scope of the nonstatutory labor exemption began in 1989 when the NFL owners decided to impose a $1,000 per week salary cap for players on "developmental squads," over the NFLPA's objection that each NFL player, including developmental ones, had the right to negotiate his own salary. In response to the NFLPA's antitrust suit, the NFL asserted that the nonstatutory labor exemption protected its unilateral change in the terms of employment after bargaining to impasse on the topic. The United States District Court for the District of Columbia disagreed, however, and held that the nonstatutory labor exemption did not survive past the expiration of the collective bargaining agreement.[157] Further, without the exemption, the court granted summary judgement to the players on the issue of antitrust liability, holding that the club's agreement to fix salaries failed under rule of reason analysis. A jury then awarded damages of $10 million, which the court trebled to $30 million.[159]

On appeal, a divided panel of the United States Court of Appeals for the District of Columbia Circuit reversed the award, holding that the non-statutory labor exemption protects restraints imposed through collective bargaining as long as a collective bargaining relationship exists. Chief Judge Edwards stated that "restraints on competition lawfully imposed through the collective bargaining process are exempted from antitrust liability so long as the restraints primarily affect only the labor market organized around the collective bargaining relationship."[161] The court noted that if the exemption did not extend as long as a collective bargaining relationship existed, then unions could "invoke the antitrust laws and their threat of treble damages to gain an advantage in bargaining over a salary provision about which union members do not care deeply enough to strike."[162] According to the court, this result would impermissibly shift the balance of power under federal labor law from a position of neutrality toward favor-

---

136. 777 F. Supp. 1475 (D. Minn. 1991).

138. *See* McNeil v. NFL, 1992 WL 315292 (No. 4-90-476), at *1-*2 (D. Minn. Sept. 10, 1992).

154. 782 F. Supp. 125 (D.D.C. 1991), *rev'd*, 50 F.3d 1041 (D.C. Cir. 1995), *aff'd*, 116 S. Ct. 2116 (1996).

157. *Id*. at 139.

159. *See* Brown v. Pro Football, Inc., 50 F.3d 1041, 1045 (D.C. Cir. 1995)

161. *Id*.

162. *Id*. at 1052.

ing unions. Instead, the court's definition of the exemption's scope gives employees in a labor dispute the choice of either invoking the protection of the labor laws or—by forgoing unionization or decertifying their union—seeking antitrust law relief.

In a dissenting opinion, Circuit Judge Wald argued that the majority decision tilts the balance of collective bargaining power in the employers' favor by compelling unions to choose between unionization and antitrust relief. Judge Wald opined that the potential for employer imposition of restraints if bargaining fails gives employees "powerful incentives not to engage in collective bargaining at all," thereby undermining the labor laws' central purpose of promoting collective bargaining as the primary means for achieving industrial peace.[166] Accordingly, Judge Wald distinguished between bargaining "tactics" and "terms."[167] She stated that post-impasse tactics, such as strikes and lockouts, deserve antitrust protection because of their value in creating pressure to reach an agreement, while unilaterally implemented terms that could last indefinitely do not merit the same protection as a substitute for agreement.[168]

.... [T]he Clinton Administration urged the Supreme Court to hear the players' appeal from the *Brown* decision, arguing that a broad interpretation of the nonstatutory labor exemption "may do serious harm to the nation's antitrust and labor policies."[170] On December 8, 1995, the Supreme Court granted the players' petition for certiorari.

6. *Playing on the Highest Court in the Land*: Brown *Defines Exemption's Limits*

In *Brown v. Pro Football, Inc.*,[172] the Court finally resolved the issue of whether leagues may invoke the exemption to defend against a players' union suit during negotiations to reach a new collective bargaining agreement. In an 8-1 decision penned by Justice Breyer, the *Brown* Court essentially agreed with the D.C. Circuit's majority opinion. The Court held that as long as the parties to a multi-employer collective bargaining relationship engage in lawful conduct under the federal labor laws, the labor exemption protects that conduct. Specifically, the Court found that employers in a multi-employer bargaining group, like the NFL, have the right to implement new terms and conditions of employment after impasse without incurring antitrust liability because labor law permits this collective bargaining manuever.

The *Brown* Court began by noting that the nonstatutory labor exemption reflects the history of federal labor law jurisprudence and the congressional objective of substituting "legislative and administrative labor-related determinations for judicial antitrust-related determinations as to the appropriate legal limits of industrial conflict."[177] Further, considering the conflict between labor and antitrust law policy, the Court commented that logically "it would be difficult, if not impossible, to require groups of employers and employees to bargain together,

---

166. *Id.* at 1059.

167. *See id.* at 1066-69 (discussing importance of protecting bargaining tactics but not terms).

168. *See id.* at 1067-68.

170. Linda Greenhouse, *Justices to Hear Players' Case Against N.F.L.*, N.Y. TIMES, Dec. 9, 1995, at A2.

172. 116 S. Ct. 2116 (1996).

177. *See* Brown v. Pro Football, Inc., 116 S. Ct. 2116, 2120 (1996).

but at the same time to forbid them to make among themselves or with each other any of the competition-restricting agreements potentially necessary to make the process work."[178] Moving from the exemption's roots to its scope, the Court found that multi-employer bargaining, "a well-established, important, pervasive method of collective bargaining," enjoyed the same treatment as a single employer regarding the nonstatutory exemption. Accordingly, the Court concluded that the antitrust laws do not apply to collective bargaining where employers in a bargaining group may agree on bargaining proposals and terms to impose in the event of an impasse. The Court admonished that to permit antitrust scrutiny of post-impasse bargaining tactics would "introduce instability and uncertainty into the collective bargaining process, for antitrust law often forbids or discourages the kind of joint discussions and behavior that the collective-bargaining process invites or requires."[181] Despite the Court's directive that the labor exemption includes within its scope union-employer agreements and lawful bargaining activity, the Court did not intend its holding "to insulate from antitrust review every joint imposition of terms by employers, for an agreement among employers could be sufficiently distant in time and in circumstances from the collective-bargaining process that a rule permitting antitrust intervention would not significantly interfere with that process."[182]

Justice Breyer considered the argument that antitrust courts might attempt to evaluate specific types of employer agreements and find them "reasonable" under antitrust law when justified by by bargaining necessity. The Court reasoned, however, that allowing nonexpert antitrust judges and juries to determine rules for the collective bargaining process would undermine the NLRB's role as administrative interpreter of federal labor law. In addition, the Court noted that this scenario would contravene the labor laws' objective of preventing courts from employing antitrust laws to define what constitutes "socially or economically desirable collective-bargaining policy."[185]

The Court then specifically rejected several alternative limitations on the labor exemption's scope.[186] Initially, the Court refused to endorse the player's theory that the nonstatutory labor exemption should apply only to union-employer agreements, and not to employer agreements in the absence of an union consent. The Court reasoned that labor unions often will not, and should not, consent to multi-employer bargaining practices, such as lockouts and the use of temporary replacements, that are lawful under labor law. Further, the Court dismissed the Solicitor General's argument that impasse in bargaining marks the proper expiration for termination, because "[l]abor law permits employers, after impasse, to engage in considerable joint behavior, including joint lockouts and replacement hiring."[189] The Court also rejected the theory advanced in Judge Wald's dissent that the exemption should encompass post-impasse agreement about bargaining "tactics," but not employer agreement about imposing "terms."[190] Finally, the

178. *Brown*, 116 S. Ct. at 2120.
181. *Id*. at 2123.
182. *See* Brown v. Pro Football, 116 S. Ct. 2116, 2127 (1996).
185. *Id*.
186. *See* Brown v. Pro Football, Inc., 116 S. Ct. 2116, 2123-25 (1996).
189. *Brown*, 116 S. Ct. at 2124.
190. *Id*. at 2125 (citing Brown v. Pro Football, Inc., 50 F.3d 1041, 1066-69 (D.C. Cir.

Court dismantled the players' argument that the "special" nature of professional sports and its bargaining relationships justify different treatment under the non-statutory labor exemption.

In dissent, Justice Stevens stated that the nonstatutory exemption served the purpose of ensuring that "unions which engage in collective bargaining to en-hance employees' wages may enjoy the benefits of the resulting agreements."[192] Justice Stevens argued that, contrary to the majority's holding, the exemption's purpose did not provide "justification for exempting from antitrust scrutiny col-lective action initiated by employers to depress wages below the level that would be produced in a free market."[193] Further, Justice Stevens claimed the majority ig-nored several special features of the case in rendering its decision, including the unique bargaining position of the NFL developmental squad players, the NFL's concession that it imposed the salary cap to help police its owners on roster size rules, and the lack of bargaining engaged in before the league declared an im-passe. Reminding that Congress remained "free to act to exempt the anticompeti-tive employer conduct" involved in the case, Justice Stevens stressed that the Court should not "stretch the limited exemption that we have fashioned to facili-tate the express statutory exemption created for labor's benefit so that unions must strike in order to restore a prior practice of individually negotiating salaries."[195]

III. ANALYSIS

A. *The Scope of the Nonstatutory Labor Exemption Before* Brown

The nonstatutory labor exemption provides a necessary resolution to the fun-damental conflict between antitrust policy and labor policy by sanctioning the an-ticompetitive activity that federal labor statutes allow. Unfortunately for courts dealing with the nonstatutory labor exemption in the professional sports context, the Supreme Court did not delineate how and when the nonstatutory labor ex-emption applies to labor market restraints until *Brown*. Instead, the Court had fo-cused on the narrow factual issue of whether a negotiating union may invoke the exemption when defending its collective bargaining agreement from antitrust challenge of third parties.

The contexts in which the Supreme Court considered the nonstatutory labor exemption differ factually from the setting in which unions and employers in pro-fessional sports have battled over the application of the exemption. Unlike *Pen-nington* and *Jewel Tea*, which involved unions as defendants and employers' com-petitors as plaintiffs, professional sports cases have primarily involved multi-employer bargaining units and leagues as defendants and the collectively bargaining employees as plaintiffs. In the absence of clear guidance and factual similarity, courts resolving disputes in the sports labor arena failed to reach a con-sensus on how properly to accommodate federal antitrust and labor policy. With *Powell*, *Williams* and the D.C. Circuit's decision in *Brown*, however, three circuit courts had concluded that labor policy trumps antitrust law while parties main-

---

1995) (Wald, J., dissenting)).
    192. *Id.* at 2129 (Stevens, J., dissenting).
    193. *Id.*
    195. *Id.* at 2134.

tain a bargaining relationship. These cases differed only in that in *Williams* and *Powell*, the teams maintained the status quo of the collectively bargained restraints after expiration of the agreement, while in *Brown*, the NFL imposed new terms and conditions of employment after reaching impasse in further negotiations.

B. Brown's *Accommodation of Labor and Antitrust Policy*

With *Brown*, the Supreme Court has now resolved the contentious issue of whether multi-employer bargaining units, like sports leagues, may invoke the nonstatutory labor exemption when labor unions file antitrust suits during negotiations to reach a new collective bargaining agreement. The National Football League's victory in Brown effectively enhances the bargaining leverage of leagues because unions will no longer have the antitrust weapon they have wielded in the past with success....

C. *The Aftermath of* Brown *on the Sports Labor Landscape*

....

When the current collective bargaining agreements in football, basketball and hockey expire, the issue of how and when the bargaining relationship between a union and league terminates may prove central to any labor dispute or antitrust suit. Already, in a moment of labor peace in all four major professional sports, a group of professional soccer players, represented by the same attorneys that counsel the NFLPA and NBPA, have foregone unionization and filed an antitrust suit against Major League Soccer and its system for controlling player salaries.

IV. CONCLUSION

The conflict between the federal labor and antitrust laws has played a fascinating role in the development of American jurisprudence in the twentieth century. While Congress designed the Sherman Act to thwart the ambitious designs of big business, labor unions found themselves the frequent target of antitrust scrutiny. Congressional efforts to enact legislation to exempt labor unions from the scope of the antitrust laws initially failed to protect them. The Supreme Court articulated the nonstatutory labor exemption to ensure unions maintained the benefits of their collective bargaining, but employers have enjoyed the primary fruits of this exemption.

In the labor relations of professional sports leagues, the exact scope of nonstatutory labor exemption perplexed judges and scholars for years. For the benefit of all sports fans, the Supreme Court's decision in *Brown* has cleared up the conflict over the exemption's application after expiration of a collective bargaining agreement. Labor peace now pervades in professional sports, but tumult will surely return. By brightly drawing the battle lines for teams and players that bargain collectively, the *Brown* decision may keep the words strike and lockout out of the sports page headlines for the foreseeable future.

Chapter 6

The Regulation of Sports Agents

Representing players as a sports agent is viewed by many as participating in the glamorous side of the business of sports. The Academy Award winning movie, *Jerry Maguire,* in portraying player agents as stars in their own right, contributed to such perceptions. Unfortunately, the glamorization of the sports agent may understate the importance of this participant in the sports industry. The significance of sports agents is underscored by the diverse roles that they assume — roles that require expertise in a wide array of subject areas. As noted in a recent publication: "[t]here are many functions that an agent can provide for the athlete. These functions might include: contract negotiations, tax planning, financial planning, money management, investments, estate planning, income taxation, preparation, incorporating the client, endorsements, sports medicine consultations, physical health consultations, post-career development, career and personal development counseling, legal consultations and insurance matters." Walter T. Champion, Jr., *Attorneys Qua Sports Agents: An Ethical Conundrum*, 7 MARQ. SPORTS L.J. 349, 351-52 (1997). As noted in the aforementioned article, the multiple dimensions of an agent's representation of his or her client also creates potential ethical issues for lawyers who serve as sports agents.

The multiple functions provided by sports agents has contributed to the call for the regulation of sports agents. The debate concerning public regulation of player agents is also, however, an outgrowth of problems identified with them. Unfortunately, sports pages are riddled with stories of agents making improper cash payments, and offering other inducements such as clothing, automobiles and prostitutes, to student athletes as a part of the agent's client development efforts. Notorious incidents such as those involving businessman Raul Bey's attempt to secure representation of Florida State University football players by giving them cash and allowing several players to participate in a private shopping spree at a Foot Locker athletic store are detailed in Ricardo J. Bascuas, *Cheaters, Not Criminals: Antitrust Invalidation of Statutes Outlawing Sports Agent Recruitment of Student Athletes*, 105 YALE L.J. 1603 (1996). These forms of conduct not only conflict with NCAA principles of amateurism and rules prohibiting compensation for athletic participation, but increasingly run afoul of state law. Consequently, it is not surprising that much of the scholarship regarding sports agents has focused on governmental efforts to regulate the manner in which sports agents conduct their business. A valuable work that examines early governmental regulatory efforts, their rationale and content is Lionel Sobel's, *The Regulation of Sports Agents: An Analytical Primer*, 39 BAYLOR L. REV. 701 (1987).

The articles in this chapter are intended to provide an overview of certain of the issues identified above involving this key participant in the sports industry. In the first selection, Landis Cox's discussion of *United States v. Norby Walters*, 997 F.2d 1219 (1993), provides the vehicle for exploring the major government prosecution stemming from sports agents' improper interaction with student-athletes. Although the future use of mail fraud statutes in this context is questionable given that the government's success at the district court level in *Norby* was reversed at the appellate level, the article describes an important moment in the evolution of legal attempts to regulate the sports agent business. The chapter concludes with a selection by Professor Jan Stiglitz, who proposes an alternative to regulation — agent deregulation. Informative articles not included herein, but which provide helpful insight into the issue of agent regulation include: James Malone and Daren Lipinsky, *The Game Behind the Games: Unscrupulous Agents in College Athletics and California's Miller-Ayala Act*, 17 Loy. L.A. Ent. L.J. 413 (1997); and, Miriam Benitez, *Of Sports Agents and Regulations—the Need for a Different Approach*, 3 Ent. & Sports L.J. 199 (1986).

Landis Cox, Note, Targeting Sports Agents with the Mail Fraud Statute: *United States v. Norby Walters & Lloyd Bloom*
41 Duke Law Journal 1157 (1992)*

. . . .

In *United States v. Walters*,[6] sports agents Walters and Bloom faced charges of mail fraud[7] for their involvement in a scheme of signing college football players to professional representation contracts before the players' college eligibility expired. The two agents offered top college players money, cars, gifts, and trips in exchange for the players agreeing to be represented by the agents in their professional football careers. The players signed post-dated contracts, which were placed in a safe until their college eligibility expired.

The Walters and Bloom plan caused the players to violate the rules of the National Collegiate Athletic Association (NCAA), the private governing body of college sports... The NCAA can sanction players and universities for rule infractions, yet the NCAA has no authority to sanction agents who interfere with the rules.

In seeking the convictions of Walters and Bloom, the U. S. government advanced a novel interpretation of the mail fraud statute. The government argued that the agent's plan of signing college athletes in violation of the NCAA rules constituted a scheme to defraud universities of their property interests in athletic scholarships. The mails were used in furtherance of this scheme when the players lied on eligibility forms that were later mailed by their schools to regional athletic conferences in accordance with NCAA rules. Never before had a university's interest in athletic scholarships been held to constitute property under the mail fraud statute.... At the conclusion of the trial, the jury found the agents guilty of defrauding two universities.[14]

---

6. No. 88 CR 709 (N.D. Ill. Apr. 13, 1989).
7. 8 U.S.C. § 1341 (1988).
14. Steve Fiffer, *Two Sports Agents Convicted of Fraud and Racketeering*, N.Y. Times,

The Walters and Bloom trial represents a watershed period in the area of college sports and the law. It marks the first time that federal criminal law has been used to target the activities of aggressive sports agents who violate NCAA rules. On appeal, the Court of Appeals for the Seventh Circuit reversed the convictions and remanded the case for new trials, but did not address the challenge to the government's interpretation of the mail fraud statute.[16] The mail fraud statute thus appears to exist as a new tool to target aggressive agents who violate NCAA rules such as Walters and Bloom. Indeed, in the wake of the Walters and Bloom trial, other sports agents have been prosecuted for mail fraud.

. . . .

I. THE TRIAL

The trial of sports agents Norby Walters and Lloyd Bloom on charges of mail fraud, conspiracy, racketeering, and extortion lasted over six weeks, and followed a two-year investigation by both the FBI and a federal grand jury.[18] Although the indictment mentioned some thirty schools as "victims" of the Walters and Bloom scheme, the trial focused on only eight of the schools—Michigan, Michigan State, Iowa, Purdue, Illinois, Notre Dame, Texas, and Temple.

The media treated the trial as "high drama" and a "window into the abuses of big-time sports in higher education." From the opening statements, the prosecution and defense told very different stories of what the case concerned. The prosecution's opening statement focused on the two agents and their alleged connections with organized crime, and on the supposed victims of the scheme, the universities, and their "strict requirements" for awarding scholarships. The defendants' opening statements framed the case in the broader setting of the college sports system. They questioned the integrity of the system—where NCAA rule violations run rampant and are frequently committed by the universities themselves in pursuit of millions of dollars in potential revenues. The tension between the prosecution's and defendants' view of the case was evident throughout the trial, as illustrated by the following warning given to counsel from Judge Marovich: "When I indicated to you that this is going to be a criminal trial and not a morality play, that's what I'm talking about. I am not going to visit ever [sic] sin, real and imaginary, that has occurred in intercollegiate sports." Despite Judge Marovich's admonitions, the trial of Walters and Bloom did indeed become a morality play.

. . . . [A detailed discussion of the role of the various parties in the dispute is omitted. - ed.].

II. THE TREND TOWARD ADOPTING THE MAIL FRAUD STATUTE.

A. The Government's Theory of Mail Fraud in the Walters and Bloom Case: Stretching the Statute Beyond Its Limit

1. Background of the Mail Fraud Statute. The mail fraud statute provides that it is illegal to use the mails "for the purpose of executing" a "scheme to defraud."[175] Thus, there are two basic elements to the crime of mail fraud: (1) a

---

Apr. 14, 1989, at A1, A31.

16. *See* United States v. Walters, 913 F.2d 388 (7th Cir. 1990).

18. Judge Marovich presided at trial, which took place in a federal district court in Chicago. Transcript, United States v. Walters, No. 88 CR 709 (N.D. Ill. Apr. 13, 1989)...

"scheme to defraud"; and (2) use of the mails to "execute" the scheme. The broad language of the statute, along with the sparse legislative history of the original statute, has left the scope of the mail fraud statute to judicial interpretation. Through the years, courts have expansively interpreted the mail fraud statute.

The broad scope of the mail fraud statute has been the subject of much debate. On the one hand, the statute has been heralded as a catch-all provision to fight against crime-the prosecutor's "first line of defense."[178] Chief Justice Warren Burger cited the mail fraud statute as a valuable stop-gap measure that allowed crime to be punished before Congress had time to pass specific legislation. On the other hand, critics have faulted the expansive reading of the mail fraud statute because (1) it violates due process by subjecting defendants to criminal liability without fair warning that their actions are criminal, (2) it creates tension within the separation of powers doctrine, and (3) it raises the problems associated with "overcriminalization."

One hotly contested subject in the debate over the proper scope of the mail fraud statute was the development of the "intangible rights" doctrine. Under the "intangible rights" doctrine, the public was deemed to have a right in honest government. The doctrine was used to prosecute corrupt public government officials with mail fraud on the theory that they had "defrauded the public of its right to 'honest government.'"[182] In 1987, the Supreme Court seemed to have resolved the debate over the "intangible rights" doctrine in favor of the critics with two decisions, *McNally v. United States*[183] and *Carpenter v. United States*.[184] In *McNally*, the Court held that the mail fraud statute extended only to schemes to defraud *money or property*.[185] Thus, the Court reversed to convictions of government officials in Kentucky who allegedly diverted commissions from Kentucky's workers' compensation insurance business to forward their own financial interests. The Court stated that "[i]f Congress desires to go further, it must speak more clearly than it has." In 1988, Congress did just that by amending the mail fraud statute to define "scheme to defraud" to include "a scheme or artifice to defraud another of the intangible rights of honest services."[188]

In *Carpenter*, the Court fine-tuned the definition of property by holding that "*McNally* did not limit the scope of [section] 1341 to tangible as distinguished from intangible property rights." The Court upheld the mail fraud conviction of

---

175. The mail fraud statute, 18 U.S.C. § 1341 (1988), provides, in relevant part:
   Whoever, having devised or intending to devise any scheme or artifice to defraud, or for obtaining money or property by means of false or fraudulent pretenses, representations, or promises...for the purpose of executing such scheme or artifice or attempting so to do, places in any post office...any matter or thing whatever to be sent or delivered by the Postal Service...or knowingly causes to be delivered by mail according to the direction thereon...any such matter or thing, shall be fined not more than $1,000 or imprisoned not more than five years, or both.
   Id.
178. United States v. Maze, 414 U.S. 395, 405 (1974) (Burger, C.J., dissenting).
182. Rod J. Rosenstein, Recent Developments, *Mail Fraud: Termination of the "Intangible Rights" Doctrine*, 11 Harv. J.L. & Pub. Pol'y 286, 286.
183. 483 U.S. 350 (1987).
184. 484 U.S. 19 (1987).
185. *See McNally*, 483 U.S. at 356-60.
188. Anti-Drug Abuse Act of 1988, Pub. L. No. 100-690, § 7603, 102 Stat. 4148, 4508 (codified at 18 U.S.C. § 1346 (1988)).

defendant R. Foster Winans, who had disclosed financial information from his "Heard on the Street" column in the *Wall Street Journal* to investors who traded on the information. The Court held that the *Wall Street Journal* had a property interest in the intangible property of confidential business information. It further ruled that a scheme to defraud under the mail fraud statute does not require "monetary loss," but can consist of the deprivation of "exclusive use" of such property.[190] In light of the Court's apparent restriction and refinement of the mail fraud statute in *McNally* and *Carpenter*, the government advanced its new theory of mail fraud against Walters and Bloom. This Note will now analyze judicial acceptance of the government's novel theory of the mail fraud statute in the Walters and Bloom case.

2. *Judicial Acceptance of the Government's New Theory of Mail Fraud.* The government's new theory of mail fraud was accepted by two courts as well as by the jury in the Walters and Bloom trial. In *United States v. Walters (Walters I)*,[192] the court rejected the defendants' motion to dismiss the mail fraud indictment on several grounds. The case proceeded to trial, where a jury found Walters and Bloom guilty of the mail fraud charges for two of the four schools named as victims. The agents' convictions were reversed on appeal and the case was remanded on account of trial error. The appellate court's decision did not comment on the government's mail fraud theory. As a result of the appellate ruling, Walters and Bloom were granted separate trials. In *United States v. Walters (Walters II)*,[194] a new court in the same district denied Walters's motion to dismiss the mail fraud indictment for many of the same reasons expressed in *Walters I*.

In *Walters I*, the defendants argued that their scheme did not satisfy the mailing element of the mail fraud statute. As stated earlier, one of the two elements of mail fraud is use of the mails "for the purpose of executing the scheme."[196] The mailing requirement has been construed by the courts to mean that defendant must have "caused" the mailing, and the mailing must be "in furtherance" of the scheme. Defendants argued that they did not cause the mailings because neither they nor the student-athletes personally mailed the eligibility forms.[198] The defendants further protested that the mailings were too far removed from the scheme to satisfy the "in furtherance" requirement.[199]

The court held that Walters and Bloom met both of these requirements. First, the court recognized the well-established rule that a defendant "causes" the use of the mails as long as such use was "reasonably foreseeable" to one in the defendant's position. The court held that the use of the mails was reasonably foreseeable because the student-athletes had to sign eligibility forms that would be sent to the athletic conferences. However, the court did not discuss whether it was reasonably foreseeable for Walters and Bloom to know about these eligibility forms in the first place. This omission is a weakness in the *Walters I* opinion. Second, the court ruled that the "in furtherance" requirement was satisfied because "the mailings of the documents...are an expected part of the scheme and the mailings

---

190. *See id.* at 26-27.

192. 711 F. Supp. 1435 (N.D. Ill. 1989), *rev'd*, 913 F.2d 388 (7th Cir. 1990).

194. 775 F. Supp. 1173 (N.D. Ill. 1991).

196. *See supra* notes 175-76 and accompanying text.

198. *See Walters I*, 711 F. Supp. at 1439.

199. *See id.*

clearly further the scheme."[203] The court noted that a jury could reasonably conclude that concealment was essential to the agents' scheme. If the schools had truthful information, they could have declared the athletes ineligible to compete. The court explained that such a situation "could seriously affect a particular athlete's value to defendants."

Although the court seems to reason correctly that mailing the false eligibility forms to the athletic conferences helped the agents conceal their plan, this focus on the mailing element begs the question: Was the agents' plan a "scheme to defraud" as prohibited by the mail fraud statute? Even though there are weaknesses in the *Walters I* analysis of the mailing element, it is equally important to focus on judicial treatment of the "scheme to defraud" element.

Under *McNally*, the "scheme to defraud" must involve the deprivation of a protectible property interest. In *Walters I*, defendants argued that the mail fraud indictments should be dismissed because the agents' plan did not deprive the universities of property within the meaning of *McNally*. The court rejected defendants' *McNally* arguments. The court noted that the indictment alleged two types of property deprivation due to the agents' scheme: (1) money and property in the form of the scholarships; and (2) the universities' "right to control" the allocation of a limited number of scholarships to athletes.

The court in *Walters I* reasoned that the first alleged property deprivation, the scholarship money and property, clearly satisfied the *McNally* requirement. The court rejected Walters's protest that the schools were not defrauded of the scholarship money or property because the schools suffered no economic loss.[209] Walters argued that the schools would have paid out the same amount of money in scholarships regardless of the agents' plan—the scholarships would just be awarded to other athletes. He further explained that the schools received what they paid for—football players. Moreover, because the agents' plan was not discovered until after the football season, the schools did not lose any revenues from the sport.

Walters's position was supported by dicta in *United States v. Holzer*.[211] In *Holzer*, the United States Court of Appeals for the Seventh Circuit reversed the mail fraud conviction of a state judge who accepted bribes because the conviction was based on the "intangible rights" doctrine invalidated by *McNally*.... The *Walters I* court acknowledged the logical appeal of the *Holzer* dicta, but declined to follow it. Instead, the court cited *Carpenter* for the rule that a victim need not suffer monetary loss under the mail fraud statute—it is enough if the victim lost the "right to control" or the "right to exclusive use" of the property.

In *Walters II*, Walters advanced a new argument regarding the *McNally* requirement. Citing post-*McNally* decisions, Walters argued that the mail fraud statute only applies where the "goal" of the scheme is to obtain money or property through fraud. After a careful review of the cases, the court rejected Walters's interpretation. The court commented: "A more sensible interpretation of the statute would indicate that a scheme is devised 'for obtaining' money or property when the defendant knows that its success requires a specific fraudulent deprivation of money or property."[219]

---

203. *Walters I*, 711 F. Supp. at 1440.
209. *Id.*
211. 840 F.2d 1343 (7th Cir. 1988).
219. *Walters II*, 775 F. Supp. at 1179.

Both *Walters I* and *Walters II* recognized a second, separate type of property deprivation in addition to the scholarships—the "right to control" the distribution of a limited number of athletic scholarships. Initially, it appeared that *Walters I* was not going to acknowledge this intangible right as a separate property right. Yet the opinion stated that the "intangible property right to control disposition of property is protected by the mail fraud statute" under the *Carpenter* rationale. The court concluded that the universities' loss of the "right to control" distribution of the scholarships was the "gist" of the alleged fraudulent scheme. The *Walters II* opinion also concluded that the universities' loss of the right to control the allocation of athletic scholarships due to the agents' scheme constituted a "brand new [property] deprivation."[223]

Both *Walters I* and *Walters II* erroneously stretched *Carpenter*'s holding that intangible property can be protected by the mail fraud statute. The intangible property interest recognized in *Carpenter*—the right to exclusive use of confidential business information—is much different than the intangible right to control the allocation of athletic scholarships. The opinion in *Carpenter* noted that confidential business information, itself intangible property, has long been recognized as property. Furthermore, the opinion stressed that the confidential business information constituted "news matter" and "stock in trade" that could be bought and sold like any other commodity. These attributes of property emphasized in *Carpenter* are notably lacking in the right to control the allocation of athletic scholarships.

The cases cited in *Walters I* in support of applying *Carpenter* to the right to control the allocation of athletic scholarships can be distinguished. In *United States v. Lytle*,[226] the government alleged a scheme by a bank employee to defraud the bank of money by making loans in violation of the bank's lending rules. *Lytle* is consistent with *Carpenter* in that the bank was in the business of making loans, just as the *Wall Street Journal* was in the business of providing financial information to its readers. Unlike the situation in *Carpenter*, the universities are not in the business of awarding athletic scholarships; rather, they are in the business of providing education. *United States v. Cooper*[227] and *United States v. Thomas*[228] involved the fraudulent deprivation of wages secured through an employer-employee relationship. Like confidential business information, an employer's interest in wages has been recognized by the law as protectible property. The athletic scholarships do not fit into the category of wages. The scholarships represent an award to the athlete of tuition, room, board, books, and fees. In return, the athlete agrees to participate on the football team. Although the scholarships are contracts and have economic value, their value, unlike wages, is not based on the free-market system. The NCAA rules support the position that athletic scholarships are not wages. Furthermore, in other situations, courts have rejected treating the university and student-athlete as an employer-employee relationship. These distinctions undermine the argument that the universities have an economic interest in scholarships equal to an employer's economic interest in wages. Whereas an employer's loss of the "right to control" affects his interests as a property holder, a university's loss of the "right to control" affects its interest only as a regulator.

---

223. *Walters II*, 775 F. Supp. at 1179.
226. 677 F. Supp. 1370 (N.D. Ill. 1988).
227. 677 F. Supp. 778 (D. Del. 1988).
228. 686 F. Supp. 1078 (M.D. Pa. 1988).

Although no court has considered precisely the property issue presented in the sports agents' case, the situation is similar in many respects to mail fraud cases that involve the fraudulent issuance of licenses or permits in the regulatory context. The typical fact pattern in these cases involves an applicant who falsifies information on his or her application for a license or permit, just as the athletes in the Walters and Bloom case lied on the NCAA eligibility forms. Courts have generally refused to extend the reach of the mail fraud statute to protect the property interest in the permit itself. These courts have reasoned that, although a governmental permit may be property in the hands of the person who receives it, licensing authorities have no property interest in licenses or permits. One court that arrived at the contrary result based its opinion on the fact that the issuer was "in the 'business'" of conveying such permits.[235] . . .

   . . . .

The *Walters I* and *Walters II* analyses of the *McNally* objections indicate that the courts had to strain to fit the alleged property deprivation caused by the sports agents into the mail fraud statute. The opinions erroneously extended *Carpenter* to reach intangible property not before recognized at common law. Furthermore, the courts distinguished or ignored case law that suggested a contrary and better-reasoned approach. Judicial acquiescence in the latest expansion of the mail fraud statute is misguided.

3. *Errors in Mail Fraud Theory Revealed at Trial.* The trial of Walters and Bloom exposed further errors with the government's theory of mail fraud. Under the "scheme to defraud" requirement, the government had to prove that Walters and Bloom had the specific intent to defraud the universities of a protectible property interest. The trial revealed that the agents lacked the specific intent to engage in a scheme to defraud the universities. Thus, the mail fraud charges should have been dismissed.

A meaningful definition of the term "scheme to defraud" is lacking in mail fraud jurisprudence. One oft-cited opinion defines "to defraud" broadly as "wronging one in his property rights by dishonest methods or schemes" and "usually signif[ying] the deprivation of something of value by trick, deceit, chicane or overreaching."[243] As the trial disclosed, Walters and Bloom did not specifically intend to "wrong" the universities by obtaining the scholarships. Nor did Walters or Bloom have the specific intent to deprive the universities of the economic value of the scholarships or the "right to control" the allocation of the scholarships. Walters and Bloom did intentionally act to sign college athletes to representation contacts in violation of the NCAA rules. They knew that their plan would have to be concealed from the universities in order for the players to continue to play collegiate athletics. But knowledge of concealment is different than possessing the criminal intent to defraud someone of his property.

   . . . .

[Discussion of related case of *Abernathy v. State* omitted. - ed.].

The government's theory of mail fraud may be tenable under a very broad reading of the statute. Yet, as *Walters I* and *Walters II* illustrate, the statute must be stretched to absurd limits. Such a broad reading is unsound for legal reasons.

---

235. United States v. Novod, 923 F.2d 970 (5th Cir. 1991).
243. Hammerschmidt v. United States, 265 U.S. 182, 188 (1924).

Furthermore, the expansion of the mail fraud statute should be rejected based on policy reasons...
[Discussion of the author's thesis on why expansion of the mail fraud statute should be rejected is omitted. - ed.].

Jan Stiglitz, A Modest Proposal: Agent Deregulation
7 Marquette Sports Law Journal 361 (Spring 1997)*

I. INTRODUCTION

Over the last decade, sports journalists, college coaches, athletic directors, and NCAA officials have expressed the notion that the sports industry is plagued by "unethical" agents. This "problem" has spawned a steady stream of legislation and regulation specifically designed to clean up the industry. The author continues to question, however, whether this regulatory approach makes any sense. In fact, it is time to consider a whole new approach: deregulation. Just as some have suggested decriminalization as a legitimate approach to the drug problem, the purpose of this essay is to suggest that deregulation is the best solution to some of the problems commonly associated with sports agents.

II. THE NATURE OF THE PROBLEM

Before proceeding with the argument and analysis, it is essential to carefully define the nature of the problem being discussed. With the exception of attorney solicitation, the author does not suggest deregulation or decriminalization of the kind of conduct that is generally prohibited outside the world of sports agentry. Defrauding clients or stealing their money should be illegal and offenders should be punished. But this kind of conduct is not what gets most of the attention. Rather, the problem that is invariably being discussed when one reads or hears about unethical agents relates to actions by agents which lead to the loss of collegiate eligibility for the athlete or NCAA sanctions for the athlete's institution. This essay suggests that the solution is not to generate additional rules and statutes to further punish athletes, institutions or agents, but to look at the existing rules and statutes to see whether any real wrong has been done.

III. THE ATHLETE-AGENT RELATIONSHIP

The starting point for analysis is the player-agent relationship because that relationship is the focal point for most complaints. These complaints are usually the result of a violation of the NCAA's prohibition against an athlete entering into a contract with an agent. The NCAA's rules on this point are quite clear:

> 12.3.1. GENERAL RULE. An individual shall be ineligible for participation in an intercollegiate sport if he or she has ever agreed (orally or in writing) to be represented by an agent for the purpose of marketing his or her athletics ability or reputation in that sport.

... 12.3.1.1. REPRESENTATION FOR FUTURE NEGOTIATIONS. An individual shall be ineligible per 12.3.1 if he or she enters into a verbal or written agreement with an agent for representation in future professional sports negotiations that are to take place after the individual has completed his or her eligibility in that sport.[4]

Thus, the NCAA's rules prevent the athlete from entering into a contractual relationship with an agent. An agent who induces a player into violating that rule is considered to be unethical. Does that make sense? Or should that ethical rule be changed?

In answering that question, we should consider the answer to another question: at what point should we expect and, therefore, allow a player to consult with an agent and enter into a formal relationship? To answer this we should put ourselves in the position of the athlete.

Assume that you are a college football player at Notre Dame and that you have just finished your junior year. The National Football League (NFL) is about to conduct its draft and you are trying to decide whether to enter the draft and forgo your senior year. You know that you can not test the waters and see how you do in the draft because the NCAA will declare you to be ineligible if you make yourself eligible for the draft. Who do you want to talk to about this decision? Who is in the best position to give you advice on what is best for you?

Several possibilities come to mind. First, you can turn to your parents. But are your parents likely to have concrete information about your chances of getting selected in the draft, the round in which you are likely to go, the team or teams which might draft you, the salary you might expect, the chance of injury if you stay in school, or the quality of people playing your positions who are in this year's draft as compared to next year's?

Another person you might consult is your coach. But again, one might ask what concrete information your coach would have. His or her job is to study his or her own team and to scout high school players. Your coach doesn't study the NFL. In addition, since we are assuming that you are a good player, your coach has a vested interest in having you stay at Notre Dame for as long as possible.

The NCAA does allow a school to create a "professional sports counseling panel" to advise students about professional careers. This panel may review a proposed professional contract, assist the student in the selection of an agent, and even visit with agents and teams to help determine an athlete's market value. But the NCAA rules expressly provide that panel members must be full time employees of the institution. Although the rules limit the panel membership to only one member, who is employed in the athletic department, this does not completely eliminate bias. As long as the institution has a vested, financial interest in encouraging the student to stay, full time employees of the institution may not be wholly neutral.

What other persons, thus, have the expertise to analyze the draft and determine whether it makes sense to stay at Notre Dame or go into the draft? Agents. In reality, there are only two groups of people who study the players' market: agents and people who work for NFL teams. Because NFL teams also have interests that

---

4. NCAA BYLAWS, art. 12.3.1, 12.3.1.1, *reprinted in* 1996-1997 NCAA MANUAL 100-101 (1996).

might be in direct opposition to the best interests of the players, agents are proba-bly the best sources of information.

At this point, one could legitimately question whether there are inherent con-flicts between the interests of players and agents. However, if one looks at the big picture, then the answer is no. A player wants to maximize his or her financial op-portunities and freedom of choice. In other words, a player wants to be rich and happy. Agents are also interested in maximizing a player's financial interests be-cause agent compensation is generally a percentage of an athlete's salary. To that extent, players and agents inherently possess the same interests.

Furthermore, good agents are also united in interest with players when it comes to freedom of choice. The happier a client is, the less likely he or she will change agents and the more likely he or she will recommend that friends sign with that agent.

Does that mean that there is never a conflict between the interests of a player and an agent? Of course not. However, the issue is not whether the agent is the only voice that should be heard. The real question is whether it is in the athlete's best interest to have that voice available. Moreover, the reality is that an athlete will not hear only one agent's opinion. The top athletes will be getting solicited (and thus getting advice) from a number of agents.

Skeptics of this analysis should consider an alternate hypothetical. Suppose the NCAA had a rule which stated:

> An individual shall be ineligible for participation in an intercollegiate sport if he or she has ever agreed (orally or in writing) to be treated by a non-university physician for the purpose of determining his or her physical condition and whether he or she should continue to play or instead should seek additional treatment.

People would agree that such a rule would be outrageous. But why is such a rule different from the "no agent" rule?

As in the draft situation, an athlete with a medical problem may need critical advice from an outside expert—neither the athlete nor his or her parents would necessarily know what medical treatment is best. Similarly, as in the draft situa-tion, there is good reason for the athlete to be wary of taking advice from any per-son affiliated with the team or institution. This is because a team doctor may be judged on how quickly he or she gets players back out on the field.

Would our sense of outrage be eliminated if the NCAA also allowed the athlete to get assistance from a school sponsored medical panel, like the professional sports counseling panel? Not if the rules still prohibited the student from engag-ing the professional services of an independent physician.

One might question whether the author has presented a fair analogy. Medical services may be more critical than the services provided by an agent. But, just as a college athlete might prefer to consult with the Jobe/Kerlan clinic in Los Angeles for a question about whether surgery is required on a knee, that same athlete might think that retaining an agent with Leigh Steinberg's experience and exper-tise is equally important.

Thus, when an agent signs a player who is still eligible and that player loses his or her eligibility, who is the real villain? The agent who is filling a legitimate need, or the NCAA that has imposed a rule which has no inherent justification? If it's the latter, isn't deregulation more appropriate than expanding a system of state regulation which takes private NCAA rules and turns them into public law?

IV. ACCEPTANCE OF MONEY IN EXCHANGE FOR ENTERING A CONTRACT

Another frequently cited ethical problem is the agent who pays the athlete for the privilege of representing that athlete. Again, this practice is specifically proscribed by the NCAA's rules:

> 12.3.1.2 BENEFITS FROM PROSPECTIVE AGENTS. An individual shall be ineligible per 12.3.1 if he or she (or his or her relatives or friends) accepts transportation or other benefits from any person who wishes to represent the individual in the marketing of his or her athletics ability.[16]

Similar restrictions exist in professional sports representation. For example, the National Basketball Players Association (NBPA) prohibits agents from:

> (b) Providing or offering a monetary inducement (other than a fee less than the maximum fee contained in the standard fee agreement...) to any player (including rookies) or college athlete to induce or encourage that person to utilize his services;[17]

These are the rules which make it "unethical" for an agent to give a player a suitcase full of money. But why do these rules exist? Why should it be unethical?

At this point, the analysis needs to be divided into two separate questions. First, is there anything inherently wrong with paying a player for the right to represent that player? This question cuts across sports and deals with both the amateur and professional athlete. The second question relates to the specific problem of payment to a supposedly non-professional athlete. The answer to both questions are the same.

V. PAYING FOR THE RIGHT TO REPRESENT AN ATHLETE

As argued previously, if we have a student/inventor who wants to market a product but doesn't have the capital to get that product to market, it would not be unethical for an investor to give that inventor money in order to develop and market the product. This is basic capitalism.

Even in the sports world, we seem to generally allow capitalism. When NIKE decided that it could make money by marketing its products through Tiger Woods, it was not unethical for NIKE to offer Tiger Woods millions of dollars for the right to use his name and likeness.

To the extent that an agent wants to "invest" in the future income of a player, it can be to the mutual benefit of both the player and the agent to allow such a relationship. Why should it be unethical?

One can't deny that such an arrangement could be quite helpful to an athlete. Suppose, for example, a college football player is not happy with the NFL team that has drafted him or with the amount of money that he is being offered. The

---

16. NCAA Bylaws, art. 12.3.1.2, *reprinted in* 1996-1997 NCAA Manual 101 (1996).

17. NBPA Regulations Governing Player Agents, sec. 3 [Standard of Conduct for Player Agents in Providing Services Governed by These Regulations], subdivision B: Prohibited Conduct Subject to Discipline (as amended June, 1991).

average recent graduate faced with this problem would not have the financial resources to enable him to "hold out" in an attempt to get a better offer or force a
team to trade his draft rights. If that athlete was allowed to obtain financial support from an agent, the balance of power might shift.

Certainly, the teams would not like that possibility. To the extent that the players associations have obtained benefits in collective bargaining for giving these
draft systems a labor antitrust shield, the associations might have legitimate reasons to assist the teams in the preservation of those systems. But that does not
mean that an agent who wants to violate this rule and helps his client challenge
the restraints of the draft system is inherently unethical.

One person familiar with the genesis of this rule indicated that the NBPA, in
drafting this rule, was concerned that the practice of paying for representation
was "unseemly." But, there is a big difference between unseemly and unethical.

That same person indicated that the NBPA was also concerned that a player
entering the draft was "vulnerable" and that only the less established agents
would pay for the right to represent a player. However, just because this is not
something that a David Falk or a Leonard Armato would do, does not mean that
a person who was willing to do it would provide inadequate representation.

Moreover, a market with a rule that allowed initial payments would either give
the more successful agents like Falk and O'Neal another competitive edge or enable others to break into the business. If one believes in the free enterprise system,
increased competition among service providers (agents) should benefit the customers (athletes). Thus, once again, deregulation is as appropriate a response as
increased regulation.

VI. PAYMENTS TO COLLEGE ATHLETES

When it comes to amateur athletics, there is an entirely different set of considerations. To the extent that there is a legitimacy to maintaining amateurism in college athletics, one could argue that payments to athletes should be prohibited. But
for many reasons, the notion of amateurism in college athletics is a joke.

First, college athletics is a billion-dollar industry. At best, it is only amateur for
the players. Second, college athletes are already being compensated for their athletic ability. They get free tuition and room and board. So, why do we draw the
line at additional funds? Or, to paraphrase an old punch line, we know what they
are—we are just discussing the price.

In recent years, the question of additional compensation for college athletes
has been explored and a number of practical arguments have been raised against
it. For example, payment of money to a college athlete might have tax consequences for the athlete and the institution, might have expensive Title IX consequences, and might require workers' compensation coverage. However, allowing
the athletes to get payment from sources outside the university would not raise
any of those problems. In fact, the NCAA has recently authorized student athletes
to work outside the school in order to earn extra money.

Why restrict an athlete's ability to make extra money? If anything, the NCAA's
position makes it even more difficult for the student-athlete to benefit from his or
her educational experience. A student-athlete's extensive practice, game and travel
schedule puts him or her at an educational disadvantage. Allowing the athlete the
"right to work" while denying that athlete the right to accept an advance on his or
her future professional earning potential only adds to an educational disadvantage.

Allowing athletes to accept money from an agent who wants to buy representational rights also has some benefits. We know that many college athletes do not succeed in professional sports. Most never even get drafted. If we allow all athletes to sell their representational rights, some of those athletes who don't make it to the professional level will at least get some financial reward for their time and effort. Since many of these same athletes don't complete their degree program, perhaps this money could be used to help them graduate after they have finished playing their sport.

In addition, payments might be critical for those players who are in their junior year and who want to complete school but fear that an injury during their senior year will prevent them from pursuing a professional career. Currently, the NCAA allows a student to borrow money in order to buy disability insurance. Why not allow the athlete to have that insurance funded for him by an agent?

VII. SOLICITATION

The third area where the agent player relationship is the subject of criticism for unethical behavior by an agent is solicitation. The problem here is that licensed attorneys are generally prohibited from soliciting clients. Agents who are not attorneys are not bound by such ethical rules. However, because it is in the best interests of athletes to have the most competent representation possible, it does not make sense that the ethical rules give a competitive advantage to non-attorney agents, who generally are not as well trained as lawyers to deliver the kinds of services that are beneficial to athletes. Thus, it is better to eliminate the state bar anti-solicitation rules.

An analysis of these no-solicitation rules must consider why they were initially advocated. The United States Supreme Court has focused its attention on the question of attorney advertising and solicitation, and concluded that certain forms of advertising are protected commercial speech, but that state bars can ban in-person solicitation. In *Ohralik v. Ohio State Bar Association*, the Supreme Court noted that the ban on solicitation "originated as a rule of professional etiquette rather than as a strictly ethical rule."[29] In *Ohralik*, the American Bar Association defended the no solicitation rule on three grounds: 1) to prevent overreaching and undue influence, 2) to protect an individual's privacy rights, and 3) to avoid situations where a lawyer's judgment would be "clouded" by financial self-interest.[30] In sustaining the constitutionality of an outright ban on in-person solicitation, the Supreme Court relied, primarily, on the problem of overreaching, noting that the "potential for overreaching is significantly greater when a lawyer, a professional trained in the art of persuasion, personally solicits and unsophisticated, injured or distressed lay person."[31]

In the context of solicitation to secure an athlete's representational rights, none of the reasons for a no solicitation rule are persuasive. Unlike an accident victim, who is facing sudden and unexpected physical and financial problems, an athlete's need for professional representation is to maximize a financial potential that is the culmination of years of planning and effort.

---

29. *Id*. at 460.
30. *Id*. at 461.
31. *Id*. at 465.

In this context, rather than focusing on the potential problems engendered by the "unique features of in-person solicitation," we should consider the unique benefits of in-person solicitation. . . . .

It is also important to distinguish the athlete's situation from that of the more typical potential client because the athlete is going to be solicited by non-attorney agents. Thus, the rule merely protects the athlete from one group of solicitors.

Similarly, in *Bates v. State Bar of Arizona*,[34] the Supreme Court noted that a "consumer's concern for the free flow of commercial speech often may be far keener that his concern for urgent political dialogue." The court further stated that "commercial speech serves to inform the public of the availability, nature, and prices of products and services, that thus performs an indispensable role in the allocation of resources in a free society."[36] Those comments certainly resonate in the context of NCAA Division I football and basketball. Arguably, a Heisman Trophy candidate is much more likely to care about the NFL draft than President Clinton's position on Bosnia. That candidate is also more likely to want to compare the benefits of representation by Leigh Steinberg, a licensed attorney, with representation by an agent who is not trained and licensed to practice law.

In truth, Steinberg, as an established agent, is not going to be at a competitive disadvantage. Prospective clients will seek him out. But, young attorneys who want to break into the business are at a disadvantage. If they do not already know an athlete, there is virtually no legitimate way to break into the business as an attorney. Many work around the rule by setting up a separate sports agency business. However, if the use of an alter ego is legitimate, than the no solicitation rule is essentially useless. If the use of an alter ego is not legitimate, than we are forcing a segment of the bar to break the rules and be labeled as "unethical" without justification.

VIII. CONCLUSION

A charge that an individual is acting in an unethical manner is and should be serious. If we want that charge to have meaning, it should not be leveled against those who violate rules that have no justification. Thus, it is appropriate to look at the rules as well as the violators. Do the rules serve a useful function? Are they protecting a class of people or institutions who need or who are worthy of protection? Do they restrict activity that is, in the absence of the rules, perfectly appropriate? The problem of the unethical agent is a problem created by the rules—not by those who break the rules.

---

34. 433 U.S. 350 (1977).
36. *Id.*

Chapter 7

Societal Issues

Introduction

The professional sports industry is not immune to the problems impacting society at large. Issues that confront sport and society such as drug abuse and equitable treatment of impaired athletes are the subject of other chapters of this anthology. The articles in this chapter address societal issues in sports, that at times, receive a higher degree of attention because they involve this high profile industry. At other times, these issues seem to be ignored either because of the discomfort in addressing them or because the wrongdoer is a high profile athlete.

Despite the appearance of equity (and in some cases dominance) by minority athletes on the playing field, they remain under-represented in the front offices and ownership ranks of sports franchises. Articles by Professors Edward Rimer and Kenneth Shropshire offer empirical evidence of the absence of African Americans and other racial minorities from leadership and ownership positions in professional sports. Professor Shropshire joins other scholars in proposing that the denial of such opportunities is an adverse consequence of the persistence of racism in sports. In this regard, he challenges popular beliefs that the elimination of the overt racism that excluded blacks from majority professional sports teams leveled the playing field in front offices. Borrowing from themes of critical race analysis, Professor Shropshire concludes that unconscious racism, which manifests in conduct such as the refusal of sports franchise owners to afford African Americans access to positions of power in organizations, limits high-level opportunities for African Americans in sports.

The Rimer and Shropshire articles discuss racism in professional sports on the management levels; legal scholarship has paid scant attention to the extent to which race impacts individual athletes at the professional level. An article of note that has such an emphasis is a recent publication by Jack F. Williams and Jack A. Chambless, *Title VII and The Reserve Clause: A Statistical Analysis of Salary Discrimination in Major League Baseball*, 52 U. MIAMI L. REV. 461 (1998).

Given reports that appear in the popular press, acts of domestic violence by professional athletes are receiving increased notoriety. Notable recent episodes of such violence include misdemeanor assault charges filed against a well-known football quarterback for allegedly choking his wife, the arrest of a football defensive lineman for punching his four-month pregnant girlfriend, and the arrest of the manager of a professional baseball team for allegedly hitting his wife in the face. An article in the September 6, 1998 issue of the NEW YORK TIMES examined factors that may contribute to off-the-field acts of aggression by athletes. Another recent article that appeared in an October 20, 1998 issue of USA TODAY suggested that notwithstanding the increased attention given to criminal conduct, including domestic violence engaged in by professional athletes, the problem remains understated. Indeed, questions regarding whether and the reasons why athletes, in contrast to non-athletes, may or may not possess a propensity to engage in criminal and assaultive conduct is generating considerable debate as scholars and other commentators turn their attention to this topic.

The article by Lawrence Schoen attempts to shed light on certain of these questions in his examination of the advantages and disadvantages of professional sports league enactment of domestic violence policies. The article by Professor Timothy Davis and Tonya Parker, which appears in Chapter 13 *infra*, offers additional insights into this issue. The same is true of an article by Anna L. Jefferson, *The NFL Domestic Violence: The Commissioners Power to Punish Domestic Abusers*, 7 SETON HALL J. SPORT L. (1997).

Unlike its collegiate counterpart, at the professional level, scholarship regarding gender discrimination is virtually non-existent. With the emergence of the American Basketball League and Women's National Basketball Association this area is ripe for future scholarship. Similarly, the difficulties of women in obtaining traditional male positions as umpires and referees and other sporting officials should be explored in greater depth than they have been in the past.

The problem of gambling is important enough to note separately here as well. The excerpt in the introduction to the Professional Team Sports section by Harold Vogel establishes elements of the monetary role of wagering on sporting events. The dominant issues in gambling at the professional level are addressed by understanding the power of the Commissioner as set forth in Chapter 3. Thus we refrain from including a gambling specific article. It was gambling, after all, in the Black Sox scandal that occurred in 1920, which caused the office of the commissioner to be created in the first place. It is the commissioner who has the power to act in cases of gambling by athletes or even where athletes associate with gamblers as was alleged against New York Jets football great Joe Namath. An article that deals with the commissioner's power with an emphasis on gambling is Thomas J. Ostertag, *From Shoeless Joe To Charley Hustle: Major League Baseball's Continuing Crusade Against Sports Gambling*, 2 SETON HALL J. SPORT L. (1992)

New technologies, particularly internet gambling are becoming more important in this area, as well. Articles on this topic include: Mark G. Tratos, *Gaming on the Internet*, 3 STAN. J. L BUS. & FIN. 101 (1997); Harley J. Goldstein, *On-Line Gambling: Down to the Wire?* 8 MARQ. SPORTS L.J. 1 (1997).

---

1. Race and Gender

Jay J. Coakley, Sport in Society: Issues & Controversies
211-214 (Irwin McGraw-Hill 6th ed. 1998)*

Chapter 8. Gender: Is equity the only issue?

. . . .

Participation patterns among women

Writing in *Newsweek* magazine, Frank Deford noted in 1996 that what "has happened in the last generation to women in sports has been nothing short of revolutionary—and those who would seek to understand the 21st century woman dismiss [sports] at their peril." I would add that since the early 1970s, the single most dramatic change in the world of sport has been the increased participation of girls and women. This has occurred in many countries around the world, especially those with reasonably strong postindustrial economies. But even in traditional, labor-intensive, poor countries, women have begun to push for new opportunities to play sports on their own terms (Cohen, 1993). Despite resistance in some countries, girls and women around the world now participate in a variety of school, community and club programs that didn't even exist twenty-five years ago.

WHY PARTICIPATION HAS INCREASED

Five major factors account for recent increases in sport participation among girls and women in North America and other parts of the world:

1. new opportunities
2. government legislation demanding, equal treatment for women in public programs
3. the women's movement
4. the health and fitness movement
5. increased media coverage of women in sports

New opportunities. The primary reason more girls and women participate in sports today is that there are more opportunities than ever before. Prior to the mid-1970s, many girls and women did not play sports for one simple reason: teams and programs didn't exist. Young women today may not realize it, but few of their mothers had the opportunities they now enjoy in their schools and communities. Teams and programs developed over the past two decades have uncovered and cultivated interests ignored in the past. Girls and women still do not receive an equal share Of sport resources in most organizations and communities, but their increased participation clearly has gone hand in hand with the development of new opportunities. The majority of these new opportunities owe their existence to some form of political pressure or government legislation.

Government legislation. People tend to complain about government regulations, but literally millions of girls and women would not be playing sports today if it were not for liberal local and national legislation mandating new opportunities. Various policies and rules have come into existence as a result of concerted efforts to raise legal issues and apply pressure on political representatives. These efforts have been made by individuals and groups committed to the struggle to achieve fairness in sports. For example, in the United States, it took years of lobbying before Congress passed Title IX of the Educational Amendments in 1972. Title IX declared, "No person in the United States shall, on the basis of sex, be excluded from participation in, be denied the benefits of, or be subjected *to* discrimination under any educational program or activity receiving federal financial assistance." The men who controlled athletic programs in high schools and colleges objected to this "radical" idea and delayed the enforcement of Title IX for five years after it was passed into law. Many claimed that equity was impractical and burdensome. They apparently thought they were entitled to be "more equal" than women when it came to sports. And they passionately resisted equality by claiming they were now going to be victims of equality!

In 1984, after six years of enforcement and progress, the U.S. Supreme Court strengthened the resistance to Title IX. It ruled that the law did not apply to school athletic programs because the schools and the students were the true recipients of federal funds, not the athletic programs (even though the programs were sponsored by the schools). Consequently, eight hundred cases of alleged discrimination under investigation at the U.S. Department of Education's Office for Civil Rights were dropped or narrowed (Sabo, 1988). It then took Congress another four years to pass (over President Reagan's veto in March 1988) the Civil Rights Restoration Act, which again mandated equal opportunity in *all* programs in any organization receiving federal money. This was helpful, but this act did not contain enough incentives for schools and other sport organizations to make positive changes; nor did it encourage people to challenge inequities in the courts.

Then, in 1992, the U.S. Supreme Court ruled that if schools intentionally violated Title IX, the injured parties could sue for financial damages. This ruling enabled many young women in schools and even women coaches to make schools and other public organizations accountable in establishing gender equity in sports. The result has been that people have become much more sensitive to the need to take girls and women into account when it comes to sports. People still resist the law, but they leave themselves open to lawsuits when they do. And this state of affairs has led a few men in Congress to suggest in 1996 that new rules are needed to protect current funding for the most traditional of all men's sports: football. Progress has been made, but the struggle continues (Bruce, 1993; Carpenter, 1993; Shaw, 1995; Staurowsky, 1996).

The Canadian experience has been similar (see Hall, 1996; Lenskyj, 1988). After a Royal Commission on the Status of Women was established in 1970, studies were done to document the existence of inequality, and conferences were held to identify issues and set priorities. In 1980, the Fitness and Amateur Sport Women's Program was established. It provided a combination of government-funded programs, training, and policy development opportunities for women. This program, along with other federal and provincial programs and pressures from feminist advocacy groups, led to the 1986 publication of *Women in Sport: A Sport Canada Policy*, which outlined national policy on women in sport. This document not only set the official goal of equality of opportunity for women at all levels of sport, but also called for a specific action-oriented program to achieve this goal. Thus Canada became the first noncommunist country to have an official policy on women in sport.

Other countries have followed (Hargreaves, 1994). But in many of them, especially those with traditional and/or religion-based cultures, change has been very slow. Official power in these countries rests in the hands of men, and they often see women's sport participation as disruptive of the social or moral order. Women in these countries have had to be persistent and politically creative to produce even minor changes.

The women's movement. The worldwide women's movement over the past thirty years has emphasized that females are enhanced as human beings when they have opportunities to develop their intellectual *and* physical abilities. This idea has encouraged women of all ages to pursue their interests in sports, and it has led to the creation of new interests among those who, in the past, never would have thought of participating in sports (Fasting, 1996). The women's movement also has helped redefine occupational and family roles for women, and this has provided more women with the time and resources needed for sport participation. As the ideals of the women's movement have become more widely accepted, and as male control over the lives and bodies of women has weakened, more women have been choosing to play sports. More change is needed, especially in poor countries and among low-income women, but the choices now available to women are less restricted than they once were.

A number of politically influential women's sport organizations have emerged in connection with the women's movement. In the U.S., for example, the Women's Sport Foundation has become an important lobbying group for change. Women-Sport International is a new organization designed to assist people around the globe in their efforts "to bring about positive change for girls and women in sport and physical education." A group of women delegates from eighty countries met in Brighton, England, in 1994 to discuss "women, Sport and the Challenge of Change," and unanimously passed a declaration of global gender equity principles. What has come to be known as the "Brighton Declaration" is now used by women in a number of countries to apply pressure on their governments and sport organizations to make new spaces for girls and women in sports. Lobbying efforts by representatives from these and other groups led to the inclusion of statements related to sports and physical education in the official Platform for Action of the U.N.'s Fourth World Conference on Women held in Beijing, China, in 1996. These statements called for new efforts to provide sport and physical education opportunities to promote the education, health, and human rights of girls and women in countries around the world. What started out as the radical thinking of a few now has become a widely accepted global effort to promote and guarantee sport participation opportunities for girls and women (Hargreaves, 1994).

The health and fitness movement. Since the mid-1970s, increased awareness of health and fitness has encouraged women to become involved in many physical activities, including, sports. Although much of the emphasis in this movement has been tied to the traditional feminine ideal of being thin and sexually attractive to men, there also has been an emphasis on the *development of physical strength and competence.* Muscles have become more widely accepted as desirable attributes among women of all ages. Traditional standards still exist, as illustrated by many clothing fashions and marketing strategies associated with women's fitness. But many women have moved beyond those standards and given priority to physical competence and the good feelings that go with it rather than trying to look like anorexic models in fashion magazines.

Furthermore, many transnational corporations, such as Nike and Reebok, recently have jumped from the women's fitness and appearance bandwagon to the fitness and sport bandwagon. Even though their ads are designed to sell clothes, shoes, and even sweat-proof makeup, they present strong messages intended to "appeal to women's enthusiasm for sports as a symbol of female liberation and power" (Conniff, 1996). And they have encouraged sport participation in the process.

Increased media coverage of women's sports. Even though women's sports are not covered as often or in the same detail as men's sports (see chap. 12), girls and women now can see and read about the achievements of women athletes in a wider range of sports than ever before. Seeing women athletes on television and reading about them in newspapers and magazines encourages girls and women to be active as athletes themselves. As girls grow up, they often want to see what is possible before they experiment with and develop their own athletic skills. This is the case because many of them still receive mixed messages about becoming serious athletes; their vision of the athletic woman gets clouded by swimsuit models in *Sports Illustrated* and other powerful images emphasizing the "need" to be thin and sexually appealing to men. Under these cultural conditions, the media coverage of everything from professional women's basketball to synchronized swimming helps girls and young women conclude that sports are human activities, not male activities.

Media companies, like their corporate counterparts that sell sporting goods, have begun to realize that women really do make up half the world's population, and, therefore, half the world's consumers. NBC, the U.S. television network that covered the 1996 Summer Olympic Games in Atlanta, experienced great ratings success when it targeted women during its 175 hours of coverage. Many men complained about this new approach, since they liked it better when their interests were the only ones that mattered in sports media coverage. But we can expect to see the real existence of women athletes and spectators acknowledged in the media coverage of the future, and that coverage clearly will change the images that all of us associate with sports and athletic achievement. (Gunther, 1996)

In summary, it is clear that increased opportunities, government legislation, the women's movement, the health and fitness movement, and increased media coverage given to women's sports and women athletes have combined to encourage sport participation among girls and women. These changes are part of the growing awareness that girls and women cannot be denied equal sport participation opportunities.

Edward Rimer, Discrimination in Major League Baseball: Hiring Standards for Major League Managers, 1975-1994
20(2) Journal of Sport & Social Issues 118 (May 1996)*

In 1975, the Cleveland Indians hired Frank Robinson to be their manager, the first Black to hold such a position in major league baseball. This occurred 28 years after Jackie Robinson had successfully integrated professional baseball. As befalls most managers, Frank Robinson was fired and, subsequently, was rehired by two other teams. Although other Blacks have become managers and there have been several Hispanic managers, there remains a belief that minorities are not given an equal opportunity to assume administrative and managerial positions in the major leagues.

This belief is fueled in part by the behavior of baseball officials. In 1987, Al Campanis, an executive for the Los Angeles Dodgers, stated on national television that Blacks lacked the "necessities" to manage or perform well in administrative po-

---

sitions. The former commissioner, Peter Ueberroth, hired Harry Edwards to develop and implement a plan to get more minorities into higher level positions. In 1992, it was reported that there were only 21 Blacks in the more than 500 front office department positions in major league baseball. Marge Schott, the owner of the Cincinnati Reds who was accused of uttering racial and ethnic slurs, was suspended from baseball for 1 year. According to data collected by the Center for the Study of Sport in Society, in 1994, 36% of the players were either Black or Latino, yet Asians, Blacks, and Hispanics comprised only 17% of the front-office employees and 22% of the club on-field staff. After the conclusion of the 1994 season, six teams changed managers. One minority manager was fired (Hal McRae), no minorities were hired, and, of the six nonminorities hired, three had recently been fired. This has led sportswriters to consider the behavior of baseball owners to be unperturbed stubborn racism and their efforts to rectify past practices as a pathetic charade.

The purpose of this article is twofold. First, I analyze the backgrounds of those individuals who were managers during the past 20 years (1975-1994) to ascertain what were the implicit standards, if any, that the owners used in making their hiring decisions. Second, having identified such standards, I compare the backgrounds of Black, White, and Hispanic managers to determine whether the standards were applied equally to all managers.

DISCRIMINATION IN BASEBALL

Previous research on discrimination in baseball has focused on three areas: positional segregation (known as stacking), entry barriers for players, and salary differentials. These are inextricably linked, as salary is tied to performance, and the performance expectations for certain positions are distinct. Nevertheless, a body of research has been developed that indicates that Blacks are stacked into certain positions and must outperform Whites to enter and remain at the major league level.... [The author's discussion of earlier studies of discrimination is omitted. —ed.].

This study differs from previous work in that it seeks to determine what were the standards used to hire managers and whether such standards were applied equally to Blacks, Hispanics, and Whites. The focus is on the hiring actions of the teams, and on whether the qualifications were applied uniformly to all who became managers, rather than on the behaviors of individuals seeking managerial positions.

Historically, employers have used two methods to screen out and discriminate against applicants for certain positions. Applicants may be asked to possess some non-job-related attributes. Courts have continually ruled that employers must demonstrate that the requirements for a job must be essential for its successful completion.

Second, these job-related requirements must be applied equally to all applicants. Personnel management law is replete with edicts that standards must be applied equally in diverse areas such as hiring, firing, compensation, and benefits. In fact, current human resource management theory posits that other functions, such as performance appraisal, also suffer when dissimilar standards are used to evaluate employees. Employers have been able to defend their personnel actions when they have been able to demonstrate that the qualifications are job related and applied equally to all applicants.

Rather than explore indirect relationships between several aspects of baseball management to uncover the incidence and cause of discrimination (e.g., stacking in playing positions may lead to opportunities and/or stacking in coaching positions, which may affect opportunities for minorities to be managers), this study attempts to determine whether the job-related requirements were applied equally to all who became managers between 1975 and 1994. In this manner, we would have some indication as to how the courts might rule should an individual seek legal remedies against a team alleging discriminatory hiring/promotion practices.

This is accomplished by comparing the prior job-related work experiences of Whites, Blacks, and Hispanics who were managers during the past 20 years, 1975-1994. The purpose of this study is to ascertain whether White, Black, and Hispanic professional baseball players had to possess different attributes to be hired as major league managers. Further, I discuss the extent to which these different hiring standards may preclude or facilitate future success as a manager.

MANAGERIAL SKILLS, KNOWLEDGE, AND ABILITIES

Managers need to possess a knowledge of baseball so that they can make strategic decisions as the game progresses. This normally involves setting the starting lineup, determining the starting pitching rotation, and determining when to pinch hit, remove the pitcher, and numerous other options (steal, hit-and-run, etc.) that may occur during a game. Whereas the average fan may have some rudimentary understanding of these aspects of the game, the manager is expected to make these decisions while being cognizant of his team's abilities as well as what the opposition will do to counter his actions. This knowledge of the game can be gained by anybody playing the game. It is not limited to those who play for specific teams or at certain positions.

Managers also serve as teachers, assisting their players in some of the finer points of the game. Aspects of hitting, fielding, and pitching are all within the purview of the manager. It is common to hear players give credit to their managers and to see photographs in the newspapers (particularly during spring training) of a manager holding a bat and demonstrating a swing or gripping a bat while a circle of players is gathered around him. Managers must also possess leadership abilities. Although their specific styles may differ, managers must be able to instill in their players the confidence and loyalty to perform at their peak performance levels. The ability to teach and be an effective leader is not limited to certain types of players. The literature on both teaching and leadership indicates that there is more than one effective style, and a cursory review of baseball history indicates that infielders, outfielders, pitchers, and catchers have been effective managers.

Whereas knowledge of the job, knowledge of the jobs of those they supervise (the players), and the ability to lead are quite similar to the case of generic management, baseball is unique in that the prior job-related experiences of managers (as players and/or coaches) are readily available and easily quantifiable. The ability to quantify performance has been an essential part of the studies on salary discrimination. Here, however, prior records are evaluated in terms of qualifications for the job as manager. Three distinct prior job-related experiences are analyzed. Specifically, I compare the records of the managers as players, focusing on longevity and several career performance statistics to measure their knowledge of major league baseball and potential ability to be major league managers.

Longevity provides the individual with a greater opportunity to learn about the game, leadership techniques, and the like. Managerial experience at the minor league level is used to assess previous opportunities to exercise leadership, and major league coaching background is used as a measure of their teaching and instructional expertise.

THE MANAGERIAL POOL, 1975-1994

Between 1975 and 1994, 140 different individuals held the position of manager of a major league baseball team. Of these 140, 39 had managed prior to 1975; Frank Robinson was the only new manager to begin the 1975 season. In 1975, there were 24 teams. Two teams were added to the American League in 1977, and two teams were added to the National League in 1993. During this 20-year time period, major league teams changed managers 210 times, creating an average of more than 10 opportunities per year for major league teams to hire new managers. Of the 24 managers who started the 1975 season, none was managing the same team at the conclusion of the 1994 season. Of the original 24 managers in 1975, 20 were subsequently rehired by other teams after being terminated. There was a constant turnover of managers, thus providing ample opportunity for the hiring of Black and Hispanic managers.

Of the 140 managers, there were 7 Black managers (Don Baylor, Dusty Baker, Larry Doby, Cito Gaston, Hal McRae, Frank Robinson, and Maury Wills) and 5 foreign-born Hispanic managers (Felipe Alou, Preston Gomez, Marty Martinez, Tony Perez, and Cookie Rojas). In addition, 12 individuals managed fewer than 42 games or 25% of a full season. Marty Martinez, who managed 1 game with Seattle in 1986, is the only Black or Hispanic who managed fewer than 42 games. Many of these individuals who managed a limited number of games were hired on an interim basis. This is taken into account when I compare their managerial experiences.

RESULTS

MANAGERS AS MAJOR LEAGUE PLAYERS

The most notable prerequisite to being a major league manager is to have played in the major leagues. By performing at the major league level, players demonstrate their abilities under the most repetitive conditions and gain firsthand knowledge of how the game is played and the performance required to succeed at the highest level.

Of the 140 managers, 25 never played at the major league level. Of the remaining 115, 6 were pitchers. Consistent with earlier findings, most played second base or short stop (47), followed by catcher (25)....[A]ll 25 who did not have major league experience as players were White. All 6 managers who were pitchers in the major leagues were White.

A comparison of the experience of White, Black, and Hispanic managers as major league players reveals that the Black and Hispanic managers have had more extensive and productive careers than have their White counterparts. This is true even after eliminating from the comparison all of the White managers who never played at the major league level....

Even after excluding White managers who never played at the major league level and therefore raising the mean experience for Whites, Black managers have approximately twice as much major league experience as do White managers (i.e., 84% longer, 136% more games, and 159% more at bats). The major league careers of Hispanic managers are 42% longer, having played in 72% more games and with 82% more plate appearances.

Because there is a limited number of Black and Hispanic managers compared to White managers, and because the analysis includes the entire population, no test for statistical significance was performed. I did calculate the standard deviation of each mean to reveal the extent to which there is variation within the White, Black, and Hispanic managers. The greatest variance is among the Hispanic managers, whereas the least is among the Black managers.

.... As with career longevity, Black and Hispanic managers outperformed the White managers in all offensive categories [as major league players]. Blacks, on average, scored more than twice as many runs and had 176% more hits, 406% more home runs, 249% more runs batted in, and a batting average 7% higher than did White managers. Hispanics also outperformed White managers, but not to the same extent as did the Black managers: 88% more runs, 91% more hits, 163% more homeruns, 120% more runs batted in, and a batting average 5% higher than those of White managers. Interestingly, there is less variance among White managers regarding the performance criteria, with Hispanics showing the greatest variance.

MINOR LEAGUE MANAGERIAL EXPERIENCE

In addition to being a player, managing at the minor league level is often considered a prerequisite for obtaining a major league managerial job. It is as a manager that the individual gains experience in game strategy, leadership, and interactions with team administration. Of the 140 managers, almost 70% had managed at the minor league level....

Felipe Alou, Frank Robinson, and Preston Gomez are the only minority major league managers with prior experience as minor league managers....

Whereas the length of experience and performance appears similar, the percentage of Blacks and Hispanics with minor league managerial experience is less than the percentage of Whites with minor league managerial experience. The variance between those who have managed at the minor league level is also similar.

    ....

DISCUSSION

Standard employment practices compel employers to demonstrate that requirements for a position are job related and that such job requirements are applied equally to all candidates for the position. Baseball managers need to have a knowledge of the game, the ability to teach, and the ability to lead. I identified three prior job-related experiences that are likely to provide the individual with these necessary skills, knowledge, and abilities: major league playing experience, minor league managerial experience, and major league coaching experience.

All but one of the men who managed between 1975 and 1994 had some experience as either a major league player, a minor league manager, or a coach of a major league team. The lone exception, Atlanta Braves owner Ted Turner, managed for one game in 1977. It thus appears that these three conditions are used by teams as part of the hiring process and are considered to be job-related prerequisites for employment as a manager. It is also evident from the analysis that these three qualifications are not considered to be an absolute requirement. Only 55 of the 140 managers (39%) had experience in all three areas studied. Some combination of playing experience, minor league managerial experience, and major league coaching experience is deemed appropriate to be hired as a manager.

The requirement that a manager have major league playing experience was not applied equally to all who were managers between 1975 and 1994. All Black and Hispanic managers had to have played at the major league level and had to have had longer and more productive careers as players than was the case with White managers. This is true even after eliminating from consideration the 25 White managers who never played major league baseball. Only 80% of the White managers had major league playing experience, whereas 100% of the minority managers had performed at the major league level. The data reveal that heightened expectations regarding length of time in the major leagues were applied consistently to all Black managers.

Previous studies would lead one to conclude that this difference in the performance standards is attributable to position segregation. Seven of the minority managers were primarily outfielders (58% of all minority managers as compared to only 9% of White managers were outfielders), and outfielders have consistently had to be more productive in terms of offensive performance. The data reveal, however, that minority outfielders who became managers had longer and more productive careers than did White outfielders who became managers.

The seven minority outfielder/managers played an average of 17 years compared to 12 for the White outfielder/managers; the average number of games played was 1,981 compared to 1,302 for Whites; the average number of runs scored was 1,033 compared to 610 for Whites; the average number of hits was 1,938 compared to 1,284 for Whites; the average number of home runs was 272 compared to 96 for Whites; and the average number of runs batted in was 1,058 compared to 506 for Whites. The batting average of the White outfielder/managers was higher, however, .286 compared to .281.

Between 1975 and 1994, only 18 outfielders became managers. This is consistent with previous research regarding position centrality. However, the total playing, coaching, and minor league managerial experience of minority and White outfielders is different. The minority outfielder/managers spent an average of 23 years as player, coach, and minor league manager; whereas the average was 17 years for the White outfielders with major league playing experience who became managers. There were several White managers who were outfielders but had not played at the major league level.

Minority outfielders who became managers were coaches for an average of 4 years, whereas the White outfielder/managers were coaches for an average of 2 years. Only 28% of the minority outfielder/managers had minor league managerial experience, whereas 55% of the White outfielder/managers managed at the minor league level. The average number of years of managing in the minor leagues was almost equal: 1.8 for the minority outfielders and 2.7 for the White outfielders. The limited number of Black or Hispanic managers who played positions other than outfielder precludes any meaningful comparison to the White managers.

The data show that no marginal Black players, either those who did not make it to the major leagues or those who had limited major league careers, were ever selected to be major league managers during the past 20 years. Although it is not known with any certainty who may have applied for these positions, there are several Blacks with limited playing careers who became coaches but never became managers (e.g., Tommie Aaron, Gene Baker, Curt Motton, and, most recently, Tom Reynolds).

A cursory look at the White managers who did not play at the major league level indicates that a lengthy playing career cannot be considered an essential prerequisite for superior performance as a manager. Two of the more successful managers in the past and present, Earl Weaver and Jim Leyland, are among the 25 who never played major league baseball. This leads one to consider the impact on the effectiveness of minority managers who, it appears, are required to possess certain characteristics that are not necessarily correlated with success as a manager. Further analysis of the relationship between a manager's playing career and managerial record is necessary.

The situation is somewhat reversed when we examine managerial experience in the minor leagues. Although it is the weakest of the three elements (only 69% of all managers had minor league managerial experience), the majority of Black and Hispanic managers did not have an opportunity to manage in the minor leagues. The length and performance of those who did are similar for Blacks, Whites, and Hispanics.

Star players may be hesitant to spend time in the minor leagues, even if it is as the manager of the team. Data on player performance at the major league level indicate that most of the minority managers could be considered star players. Offers to coach at the major league level may appeal to both the player and team, as the player is more visible to the fans. It should be noted that there are numerous star White players who became managers without first obtaining managerial experience in the minor leagues. Yogi Berra, Alvin Dark, Toby Harrah, and Pete Rose are some of the more prominent to follow this career path. Further study is needed to determine the extent to which being a minor league manager provides invaluable experience that is not obtained by either playing or coaching.

. . . .

The large variance in the means for player longevity, performance categories, and years and games managed in the minor leagues indicates the absence of precise prerequisite criteria. A total of 65 managers (46%) had experience in two of the three categories. In addition, 20 were players and minor league managers, 30 were players and had prior coaching experience, and 15 had managed minor league teams and coached. Previous studies of managerial performance have taken into account the abilities of the players managed and the teams' won-lost records (Horowitz, 1994; Jacobs & Singell, 1993; Kahn, 1993; Porter & Scully, 1982), and neglected to include the backgrounds of the individual managers. Porter and Scully's evaluation of managers with 5 or more years of experience between 1961 and 1980 determined that Earl Weaver, Sparky Anderson, and Walter Alston were the most efficient. Horowitz's methodology also concluded that Weaver and Alston were among the best major league managers. Given that these three had limited, if any, major league experience as players (Alston, 1 at bat; Anderson, 1 year with 477 at bats; Weaver, no major league playing experience), we should be cautious before assuming that playing can substitute for minor league or coaching experience. To the extent that Blacks and Hispanics have longer playing careers and limited coaching and previous managerial experience, they may be at a disadvantage in terms of the training and background necessary to succeed as a manager. Further study is needed to determine what combination of the three job-related activities is most closely related to superior performance as a manager. Additionally, further study is needed to determine whether and to what extent the position played at the major league or minor league level affects the number of years considered appropriate experience and, therefore, the need to be a minor league manager or major league coach before becoming a major league manager.

This study examined the background of all major league managers from 1975 through 1994. Specifically, it compared the playing records, minor league managerial experience, and coaching experience of all those who managed during the past 20 years. All but one (Ted Turner, a team owner) had some combination of the specified job-related experiences. We can thus conclude that these criteria are considered by owners when they hire managers. The amount of experience required as a player, minor league manager, or coach was different for Black, White, and Hispanic managers. Blacks and Hispanics had longer and more productive careers as players than did their White counterparts. Further, there were differences between the minority and White outfielders who became managers. A comparison of the playing careers of the minority and White outfielders who became managers revealed that the minority outfielder/managers outperformed the Whites in all offensive categories and had nearly an identical batting average. Minority managers tended to be outfielders, a position in which they are overrepresented but a position that has produced a limited number of managers. Black and Hispanic managers had less minor league managerial experience than did White managers and had similar experience as major league coaches. It would appear that major league baseball teams, although using appropriate job-related criteria in the hiring of managers, did not apply these criteria in an equitable manner.

Whereas this study focused on only those who became managers, further research should investigate the backgrounds of those who, although possessing the necessary qualifications, did not become managers. Further study of the exact nature of these prior job-related activities would also provide a clearer understanding of the relationship between these activities and a successful managerial career. For example, what types of coaches tend to become managers, and does managing at different levels in the minor or winter leagues make a difference in terms of job opportunities and eventual success? Hopefully with the continued expansion of major league baseball and the persistent hiring and firing of managers, more minorities will become managers and thus provide researchers with additional data to explore this issue.

Kenneth L. Shropshire, Diversity, Racism, and Professional Sports Franchise Ownership: Change Must Come from Within
67 University of Colorado Law Review 47 (1996)*

INTRODUCTION

....

Racism exists in the sports industry at both conscious and unconscious levels. Illustrative of openly expressed racism are the comments of Cincinnati Reds owner Marge Schott referring to two African American stars as "million-dollar niggers" and saying that she would "rather have a trained monkey working for

[her] than a nigger."[7] Regarding the existence of unconscious racism in all sectors of American society, the comments of Professor Charles Lawrence are representative of the critical race literature:

> Americans share a common historical and cultural heritage in which racism has played and still plays a dominant role. Because of this shared experience, we also inevitably share many ideas, attitudes, and beliefs that attach significance to an individual's race and induce negative feelings and opinions about nonwhites. To the extent that this cultural belief system has influenced all of us, we are all racists. At the same time, most of us are unaware of our racism. We do not recognize the ways in which our cultural experience has influenced our beliefs about race or the occasions on which those beliefs affect our actions. In other words, a large part of the behavior that produces racial discrimination is influenced by unconscious racial motivation.[8]

One possible path for decreasing actual or perceived racism against African Americans in any business setting is to increase African American ownership. The broad assumption underlying the advocacy of this remedy is that increased diversity in the ownership of an industry will decrease occurrences of discrimination.

. . . .

This article is largely and intentionally bipolar in its examination of sports as a black and white issue. The historical treatment, and now dominance, of African Americans on the field of play in the three most popular American sports separates African Americans from the role that other minorities play in sports. African Americans were historically expelled from professional sports, while other minorities, such as Hispanics and Native Americans, were accepted on the field of play. One of the earliest black athletes, frustrated in his attempts to play in the white world of organized sports, said at the time: "If I had not been quite so black, I might have caught on as a Spaniard or something of that kind.... My skin is against me."[15]

. . . .

I. PROBLEM: LACK OF DIVERSITY IN PROFESSIONAL SPORTS OWNERSHIP

Paralleling society's efforts to end racism, attempts to end all but the most rigid and institutionalized racial inequalities in the business of sports generally have been unsuccessful. African Americans remain woefully underrepresented at the management and ownership levels.

Although African Americans comprise a little over twelve percent of the population of the United States, minorities in general, and African Americans in particular, have been small players in professional sports franchise ownership. African Americans constitute less than three percent of ownership, and all minorities constitute less than five percent of the key management positions in professional sports.

. . . .

These numbers are especially striking as African Americans constitute such a large percentage of the participants in the leagues owned by this group of primar-

---

7. *Winking at Baseball's Racism*, N.Y. TIMES, Feb. 5, 1993, at A26.

8. Charles Lawrence, *The Id, the Ego, and Equal Protection: Reckoning with Unconscious Racism*, 39 STAN. L. REV. 317, 322 (1987).

15. GEOFFREY C. WARD & KEN BURNS, BASEBALL: AN ILLUSTRATED HISTORY, 40-41 (1994).

ily white men. In 1994 African Americans constituted eighty percent of the players in the National Basketball Association ("NBA"), sixty-five percent of the
players in the National Football League ("NFL"), and eighteen percent of the
players in Major League Baseball. Taken together, the statistics show that African
Americans make up the majority of players in the three major American sports
leagues.

Despite that majority, diversity is absent from the ownership power centers of
professional sports, just as in other sectors of society. In 1994, . . . of the 275 individuals with ownership interests in the professional sports leagues of baseball, football,
and basketball, only seven of these owners were African Americans. None of the
seven holds or combines to hold a controlling interest in a franchise. Although some
argue that the on-the-field percentages are an indicator of equality, equal achievement has not occurred in terms of success at the highest and most controlling levels.

In years of debate over statistics in race discrimination cases, the courts have
determined that statistics alone, as staggering as they may be, are not enough
legally to prove the existence of discrimination. . . .

When the numbers of minorities are low in a particular occupation, the assumption of discrimination is reasonable but not self-validating. Thus, the existence of disparate representation has been correctly cited as the result of only two
broad possibilities: either the low numbers are due to discrimination or they are
not. Undoubtedly, statistics do not tell the whole story and, generally, do not
legally make the entire case. Regardless of the limits of the law, however, the vast
disparities that these percentages indicate clearly suggest that racism and discrimination permeate American sports management and ownership.

II. IDEAL STATE: VALUE OF DIVERSITY IN OWNERSHIP

A. General Benefits

What would be the primary benefits of greater African American ownership in
professional sports? Two of the major benefits would be (1) the social value of diversity and (2) the financial value of diversity. The social value of diversity consists of both the actual value that diversity can bring to an enterprise through the
presentation of different points of view and the perceived value that diversity may
have in improving the image of an almost all white ownership. The financial value
of diversity includes allowing minorities access to a piece of the lucrative sports
ownership pie and front office employment, expanding the individual franchise
revenues by attracting more fan support and attendance from minorities, and
bringing about equity in player salaries without regard to race.

. . . . [The author's discussion of the actual and perceived values of diversity is
omitted. — ed.].

C. Ownership Glass Ceilings and Differential Racism

Glass ceilings are present in much of American society. Part of the reason for the
existence of such ceilings is the discomfort that many white Americans feel with
African Americans in positions of power. African Americans may not be treated
dramatically differently by whites in the business setting until they seek a position
of powe — until they seek to break through the glass ceiling. This has been referred
to as a form of "differential racism." The best recent example of America's glass
ceilings may have been Colin Powell's contemplation of running for the presidency

of the United States. Although Powell undoubtedly held many of the traditional qualifications for the office, he hesitated and eventually decided not to run. Given the tremendous media attention paid to Powell's African American heritage, part of his thought process in deciding whether to run presumably included the role that his race plays in how people view him. The question Powell apparently heard many asking was whether a black man could really hold the top job in the world.

....

In the major sports leagues, integration came slowly. Once integration did occur, it was even longer before African Americans played the most authoritative positions on the field. The quarterback in football is illustrative. As author Phillip M. Hoose writes, "the nearer that a position is to where the ball usually is, the less likely it is that a black will occupy it ... [and] [t]he more responsibility or control involved in a position, the less likely it is that a black will play it."[116] Apart from the authority the position carries, Hoose points to another reason for the historical absence of African American quarterbacks in large numbers: "We reserve our shining reverence for the leader of the pack. The quarterback, the image of intelligence and maturity, sacrifice and command, is the figure in whom we hope our sons, watching with us, will recognize themselves."

Just as this glass ceiling, or differential racism, may be the reason for an absence of African Americans in top-level positions on the field in sports, in politics, in corporate America, and in the entertainment industry, glass ceilings that keep African Americans from acquiring ownership interests in sports franchises probably exist as well.

III. LEGAL RECOURSE: CAN THE LAW COMPEL DIVERSITY?

.... [O]ne may question whether existing law provides any possible causes of action or remedies by which to increase diversity and African American ownership of professional sports franchises. The conclusion is that present law can only play a limited role in bringing about increased African American ownership in professional sports.

A. Constitutionality of Possible State or Federal Affirmative-Action Legislation

Although no state or federal legislation currently regulates sports franchise ownership, given the considerations expressed in Parts I and II above, legislators may yet decide to become involved. Should either state or federal lawmakers attempt to institute an affirmative-action program in this area, however, serious questions as to the constitutionality of such a program would arise. In addition, beyond the constitutional questions, both state and federal legislators may be hesitant to become involved for policy reasons.

1. Limits on State Legislation According to Regents of the University of California v. Bakke and Richmond v. J.A. Croson Co.

State legislatures are not ideally suited to regulate sports franchise ownership because each state only has power to control what happens within its own borders. No individual state could control what happens in a national sports league as a whole. A state could, however, attempt to regulate any sports team operating

---

116. *Id.* at xix.

within its borders. The question would then arise as to whether such regulation would survive judicial scrutiny.

The courts have never had an opportunity to address this question directly because no such legislation has yet been attempted. Although analogous case law indicates that an affirmative-action program in this area would likely not survive constitutional scrutiny, it is not a foregone conclusion that legislation supportive of the value of diversity would be unconstitutional.

The Supreme Court emphasized the value of diversity in *Regents of the University of California v. Bakke*.[120] There, Justice Powell wrote that an affirmative-action program designed to attain a diverse student body by taking race into account as a factor in making admissions decisions would be justifiable in the face of an equal protection challenge. Applying the traditional strict-scrutiny test, Powell stated that the achievement of diversity in a student body is a compelling state interest. Powell specifically cited the benefits that diversity delivers by bringing diverse ideas to the classroom. Unfortunately, Powell was not joined in this part of the opinion by any other justice. Four other justices applied an intermediate level of scrutiny and found that the program was remedial in nature and, therefore, constitutional.

In *Richmond v. J.A. Croson Co.*,[126] although it did not directly overrule *Bakke*, the Court stated that any state or local governmental action that is explicitly based on race must meet the traditional requirements of strict scrutiny (i.e., the state action must be "necessary" to achieve a "compelling" governmental interest). Specifically, the Court held that a minority "set-aside" program for government construction contracts in Richmond was not narrowly tailored to achieve a compelling state interest.

It would appear, therefore, that any legislation passed by a state that is specifically designed to benefit a minority must meet the requirements of the Court's strict-scrutiny test. What is unclear is whether the goal of increasing diversity in a particular setting is enough to meet the compelling-state-interest requirement. Justice Powell apparently thought so in *Bakke*; however, no other justice joined him in that opinion. Nevertheless, *Croson* does not specifically delineate what a compelling state interest is, and the Court has not had occasion to decide whether diversity, in and of itself, qualifies.

Regarding *Bakke* and other similar cases, the argument certainly could be made that diversity in a university setting is more valuable than elsewhere. The university is where society expects ideas to be generated and discussed by people representing a wide variety of viewpoints. The same generation-of-ideas argument, however, is not ideally transferable to sports. *Bakke* is, therefore, not directly applicable to diversity in sports franchise ownership. The argument would have to be constructed by amplifying the existing role that the diverse images and ideas generated by sports have on society. Considering that *Bakke* itself may have been effectively overruled by the now explicit requirement of a compelling state interest, it seems unlikely that state legislation having the sole purpose of increasing diversity in sports franchise ownership would be upheld.

A state legislature may have more success if it bases the legislation on a finding of past discrimination in franchise sales or ownership. *Croson* stated that a gov-

---

120. 438 U.S. 265 (1978); *see also, e.g.*, Hopwood v. Texas, 861 F. Supp. 551 (W.D. Tex. 1994).

126. 488 U.S. 469 (1989).

ernmental interest in remedying past discrimination may be adequate if it is supported with appropriate evidence. Importantly, under *Croson*, if statistics are to be used in support of affirmative-action legislation, such statistics will need to compare the number of African American owners in the major sports leagues to the number of willing and able prospective African American owners, rather than simply to the general population of African Americans.

There may be another problem with analogies to *Bakke* and *Croson*. Courts may be more hesitant to find a statute constitutional if it seeks to increase diversity and/or remedy past discrimination via regulation of private entities rather than regulation of government conduct. Both *Bakke* and *Croson* involved state action regulating government programs....

Beyond the Equal Protection concerns raised by *Bakke* and *Croson*, the so-called "dormant Commerce Clause" may present a further hurdle to the constitutionality of state legislation. Because the major sports leagues are all national in scope, any state regulation affecting the leagues could be subject to preemption by the U.S. Congress's power under the Commerce Clause. The Supreme Court has stated that a state or local regulation that affects interstate commerce will be upheld if it "regulates even-handedly to effectuate a legitimate local public interest, and its effects on interstate commerce are only incidental . . . unless the burden imposed on such commerce is clearly excessive in relation to the putative local benefits."[141]

Although the goal of diversifying sports management would likely qualify as a "legitimate" public interest, it is unclear whether the effect of local regulation would be adjudged "incidental" or whether its burdens would outweigh its benefits. For example, California state courts have held that the benefits of applying state antitrust and eminent-domain laws to National Football League franchises were outweighed by the effects of such laws on the nationally uniform regulation of the league. Each court cited the interdependent nature of the NFL as the reason for its holding. Each team is dependent on the others for the success of the league, and varying state laws may compel all teams to comply with the laws of the strictest state.

Arguably, that rationale does not apply in this area because legislation would not necessarily affect the league as a whole, only the ownership of the team in a particular state. The court in *Oakland*, however, found that "each League franchise owner has an important interest in the identity, personality, financial stability, commitment, and good faith of each other owner."[145] The Commerce Clause, therefore, may present a serious challenge to state legislation in support of diversifying sports franchise ownership.

Finally, there is the policy question of whether a state would *want* to regulate the ownership of sports franchises within its borders. . . . Unless a large number of states agreed to some uniform law on affirmative action, an individual state may decrease its chances of gaining a professional sports franchise or retaining the franchises it has by constraining current ownership. For these reasons, if there ever is to be governmental regulation, it appears that the United States Congress is better suited to regulate franchise ownership.

---

141. Edgar v. Mite Corp., 457 U.S. 624, 640 (1982) (quoting Pike v. Bruce Church, Inc., 397 U.S. 137, 142 (1970).

145. 220 Cal. Rptr. at 157.

2. Limits on Federal Legislation According to *Metro Broadcasting, Inc. v. FCC* and *Adarand Constructors v. Pena*

As discussed above, the Federal Congress may be better suited to regulate sports franchise ownership due to its nationwide powers. Until recently, federal programs that were facially based on racial classifications received more deference from the Court than their state-law counterparts. The Court has now made it clear, however, that strict scrutiny will be applied when reviewing federal statutes just as when reviewing state and local governmental actions.

. . . .

Adarand Constructors v. Pena[155] overruled much of *Metro Broadcasting*. In *Adarand*, the Court specifically held that the applicable standard of scrutiny by courts in reviewing any government affirmative-action program—whether local, state, or federally implemented—is strict scrutiny. *Adarand* involved congressionally mandated preferences for minority-owned firms in awarding federal construction contracts. The Court remanded the case for a determination of whether the challenged regulations survive strict scrutiny. But the Court also stated that *Metro Broadcasting* was overruled only to the extent it is inconsistent with the level of scrutiny to be applied in cases where there is a governmental actor. . . .

. . . .

Thus, although *Adarand* applied a higher level of scrutiny to congressional action, it did not hold that diversity as a goal was constitutionally insufficient under a strict-scrutiny test. . . .

In addition, in order to apply the reasoning of *Metro Broadcasting* to the sports industry, one must view sports as a form of entertainment that has a societal impact similar to that of the broadcast industry. In order for the analogy to be accurate, the message that sports presents would have to derive some of the same benefits from diversity as does the programming presented by the broadcasting industry.

Certainly sporting events deliver many messages. The youth who sees only whites as owners, officials, and quarterbacks gains an understanding of who the leaders are in society as well as who the leaders are not. This reinforces both the conscious and unconscious beliefs regarding race held by all who watch. This message delivered by sports franchises—that is, the persons chosen to fill these leadership roles—is determined in large part by the owners. That is the same premise that was behind the congressional determination at issue in *Metro Broadcasting*—that minority owners will send out messages in broadcasting that are more sensitive to minority groups than would white owners.

The comparison between the "representative" messages that would be delivered by increasing diversity in sports franchises and the actual speech issues in *Metro Broadcasting*, however, seems tenuous. Moreover, no matter what the message sent by increased diversity in sports might be, that message probably does not constitute speech that is protected by the First Amendment, as in *Metro Broadcasting*. It would be difficult to argue that any message is delivered other than the outcome of the game. The message in sports is not like that of a miniseries, sitcom, or news-related program, but instead it is images on the field and the images of the people in charge of the hugely successful sports industry. Although much of the spirit of *Metro Broadcasting* regarding diversity is applicable

---

155. 115 S. Ct. 2097 (1995).

to the African American sports ownership discussion, the case, like *Bakke*, is not directly on point.

Thus, although the United States Congress may be better suited to regulate sports franchises than are state legislatures, after *Adarand*, federal affirmative-action programs no longer receive more judicial deference than their state-law counterparts. It is, therefore, just as unlikely that a federal affirmative-action program, regulating private parties such as franchise owners, would be adjudged constitutional.

Further, there is no indication that Congress will attempt to regulate in this area. In fact, affirmative action has recently seemed to fall from political favor. For example, one of the statutes involved in *Metro Broadcasting* was recently repealed. Consequently, although such action would not necessarily be unconstitutional, it does not appear that either federal or state affirmative-action legislation in the area of sports franchise ownership will be forthcoming soon.

B. *Title VII and Section 1981—Any Help?*

Even if Congress and the state legislatures do not decide to regulate sports franchise ownership directly, existing federal laws may provide some help.

Arguably, barring African Americans from franchise ownership is similar to those cases in which a person is denied partnership in a law firm based on race. The law most applicable in law firm-partnership cases is Title VII of the Civil Rights Act of 1964.[171] But Title VII is not applicable to the sports ownership scenario because it applies only to employer-employee relationships. In other words, that law is applicable only where there is a preexisting relationship, not where a relationship is being sought. Sports owners generally do not have preexisting employment relationships with the various leagues. Also, unlike law firms, there are no "associates" employed and waiting to be considered as "partners." Presumably, athletes playing in the various leagues would have difficulty making an argument that the move from player to owner is a mere promotion. In fact, such a transition seems to be the exception.

Another possible mechanism of legal recourse is the Civil Rights Act of 1870.[173] In its present form, the Civil Rights Act of 1870, as codified at 42 U.S.C. § 1981, provides: "All persons within the jurisdiction of the United States shall have the same right in every State and Territory *to make and enforce contracts . . .* as is enjoyed by white citizens. . . ."

Section 1981's scope of coverage is wider than that of Title VII; it applies to the making and enforcing of all contracts, not just employment contracts. The Supreme Court also has held that Section 1981 applies to both public and private discrimination. Consequently, Section 1981 may provide relief whenever an individual is denied admission to a partnership based on his race, because a partnership is a contractual agreement. If an individual is denied the opportunity to become a partner because of his race, he is denied the opportunity to make a contract in violation of Section 1981. Thus, if a plaintiff can prove he has been denied an ownership opportunity in a sports league because of his race, he may have a cause of action under Section 1981. However, to bring this type of action successfully, a plaintiff would have to establish racial motivation, not just the absence of African American ownership or other comparable statistics. Absent the

---

171. 42 U.S.C. § 2000(e)(1)-(17) (1988).
173. 42 U.S.C. § 1981 (1988).

unlikely event of owners publicizing that they have denied an individual a sports franchise based on race, the use of Section 1981 will not bring about change.

....

It cannot be disputed that trust and confidence among fellow owners of a sports league is desirable for the efficiency and success of the league. A bad choice can doom the partnership. There are thirty or fewer franchises in each of the professional leagues. Consequently, individuals who enter into a partnership or who expand their partnerships are very selective of whom they permit to join, and the courts are aware of this selectivity. The necessary trust and confidence will not exist if the partnership is compelled by force of law to admit an individual whom the partnership does not want. There will just be too much bad blood and distrust. Once a legal action is brought, the possibility that the petitioner and the partners could work together harmoniously is minimal. Moreover, such legal action could jeopardize the partnership. This is why reinstatement is a disfavored remedy for high-level employees, both in the employment and partnership contexts, and why a judicial mandate of minority sports franchise ownership is even more unlikely.

Thus, antidiscrimination law provides only limited protections to minorities seeking to own professional sports franchises. Title VII does not apply directly because there will normally not be an existing employer-employee relationship at stake; and Section 1981only prevents owners from flagrantly discriminating on the basis of race in choosing their co-owners.

C. Other Laws That May Affect Diversity

As it currently stands, the law is clear that the owners in a given league may sell or grant franchises to whomever they choose, and, provided nothing in their decision-making process violates any other laws (e.g., Section 1981), no legal action can force the existing owners to sell to a particular group. The plaintiffs in the following two cases based their actions on antitrust laws, arguing against the anti-competitive nature of a league not accepting them as franchise owners. Neither bidder was African American, and neither was successful.

In the first case, Irving Levin desired to purchase the NBA's Boston Celtics.[201] Although he was financially well-positioned to do so, the NBA owners voted against him. In that case, the concern of the other owners was that Levin would align with an owner with whom the majority of the other NBA owners disagreed. After Levin brought suit, the court stated that the owners had the right to choose their ownership partners and that they could reject ownership applications for any reason or for no reason at all, provided the reason was not illegal....

....

The court allowed the NBA to bar these prospective owners at least substantially for these personal reasons.

In the second case, *Mid-South Grizzlies v. NFL*,[205] the owners of the Memphis World Football League franchise.... sought to have their team taken in as an expansion franchise in the NFL. When the NFL owners refused, the owners of the franchise sued in federal court. The Grizzlies' owners lost based on the same prin-

---

201. Levin v. NBA, 385 F. Supp. 149, 150 (S.D.N.Y. 1974).
205. 720 F.2d 772 (3d Cir. 1983), *cert. denied*, 467 U.S. 1215 (1984).

ciples that were expressed in Levin—the decision to expand, and who receives an expansion franchise, is that of the existing owners alone. The court ruled that the NFL could not be compelled to expand into Memphis.

In both the existing franchise purchase and expansion areas, the choice as to which potential owners to bring on board is that of the respective league owners. Just as in any other business, courts are reluctant to compel business owners to take on new partners. So long as the reason for rejection is not illegal, courts are not likely to intervene.

.... [A discussion of the impact of litigation and litigation threats is omitted.— ed.]

IV. WILL IT HAPPEN?: NEED FOR VOLUNTARY EFFORTS

As the previous section indicates, courts are not likely to interpret existing law as a mandate to compel existing professional club owners to admit minority ownership into their league memberships without flagrant racism. Apart from an occasional racist statement by an owner or manager, the racism in sports franchise ownership is nowhere near as overt as it was in the Denny's case. What is likely to be much more effective—at least in the short term—is increased commitment from existing owners and players to recognize the important benefits that diverse ownership in sports can bring about.

....

V. CONCLUSION

There are many difficulties in breaking African Americans into the ownership ranks of professional sports. The greatest obstacles are not financial but structural. The owners themselves must somehow be compelled to desire change; however, they likely suffer from the same levels of conscious and unconscious racism as the rest of society. Indeed, the issues discussed in this article are applicable to businesses beyond sports.

The key barrier to change is the legally protected clubbiness of the owners. They have the nearly exclusive right to select their co-owners. There is no requirement, unless self-imposed, that the owners accept the best financial offer. As a group the owners of any league certainly could mandate that any multiowner group seeking a franchise must include African American investors. The NFL took a step in this regard with the new Jacksonville franchise, in which African American and former NFL player Deron Cherry has an ownership interest. Similarly, Charlotte African American businessman Bill Simms is part of the ownership group for the Charlotte franchise.

It will be difficult to use legal pressure to compel greater African American ownership. No current legislation on either the state or federal level regulates sports franchise ownership. Given the constitutional problems that would arise if such legislation were implemented and the recent public backlash against affirmative action in general, it does not appear that the lack of diversity in franchise ownership will be addressed by statute. In addition, although Section 1981 offers protection from flagrant discrimination, it is ineffective to put any real pressure on the owners to diversify their group.

The burden is thus on league leaders and the athletes to bring about such change.

2. Domestic Violence

Laurence Schoen, Note, Out of Bounds:
Professional Sports Leagues and Domestic Violence
109 Harvard Law Review 1048 (1996)*

. . . .

Recently, allegations of domestic abuse by athletes have generated increased public attention. . . . All four major professional sports leagues currently discipline players for off-the-field misconduct, including illegal substance abuse and gambling, but none has taken a similar stance toward domestic violence.

This Note explores the possibility of a professional sports league enacting a domestic violence policy similar to league antidrug policies. Part I outlines the arguments for and against a league-wide domestic violence policy and concludes that the arguments in favor are more persuasive. Part II then considers some of the legal challenges that might arise if a league were to adopt such a policy and concludes that a league could address this problem in several ways without risking judicial intervention.

I. POLICY ARGUMENTS

A. Arguments in Favor of Enacting a Domestic Violence Policy

1. Athletes May Have a Higher Propensity for Domestic Abuse. — There is a growing perception that athletes are more prone to domestic abuse than the rest of society. Indeed, "it has become a challenge to read any sports section for a week without finding a tale of domestic abuse involving an athlete." According to a study conducted by the Washington Post, fifty-six current and former professional football players and eighty-five college players were reported to the police for violent behavior toward women between January 1989 and November 1994.

Domestic violence experts, sports sociologists, and even former players have speculated on why athletes may be more likely to commit acts of domestic abuse. First, players trained to use violence and intimidation on the field may have difficulty preventing these lessons from carrying over into their personal relationships. Second, sports may cultivate a "macho sub-culture" that equates masculinity with violence, "denigrat[es] anything considered feminine," and thereby "set[s] the stage for violence against women." In the locker room, for example, boasting of physically and sexually aggressive behavior toward women is commonplace.

No matter how persuasive these theories, the current evidence is inconclusive regarding whether athletes are in fact more likely than nonathletes to batter their domestic partners, or if the media's intense scrutiny of sports figures simply creates this impression. Regardless of the answer to this question, however, there are several other reasons that a sports league might wish to discipline players for domestic abuse.

---

2. League Discipline of Athlete-Abusers May Be Necessary to Protect the Public Image of the Game. — Adoption of a domestic violence policy may be a matter of self-interest for the league. Both the owners and players have a stake in maintaining the public image of the game and have acknowledged in their collective bargaining agreements that misconduct by players off the field can be detrimental to the league's success. It is uncertain, however, whether negative publicity surrounding domestic abuse by athletes translates into financial losses. Although such misconduct clearly tarnishes the league's image in the eyes of the general public, it is possible that it has no effect on the consumption habits of those who actually watch the games.

3. League Discipline of Athlete-Abusers Is Desirable As a Matter of Public Policy. — The case for a domestic violence policy in professional sports can also be made on public policy grounds. Although the responsiveness of both law enforcement officials and the media to domestic violence has increased dramatically in recent years, many domestic assaults continue to be marginalized as "family disputes" — and therefore treated as if they were less reprehensible than other crimes. Some feminist theorists argue that because the "meaning of violent acts toward women is generated in a sociocultural context that fosters, shapes, and justifies the use of violence to maintain a male-dominated status quo," a national effort to combat domestic violence requires not only stronger law enforcement, but also the participation of all social institutions that contribute to the development and maintenance of male violence against women. In this view, the leaders of such institutions — including sports figures — must act to "increase the social costs of gender violence, create social norms that define violence against women as unacceptable, promote concepts of male self-control, responsibility, and accountability, and foster equitable, nonviolent relationships."

The need for professional sports leagues to combat domestic violence may be more compelling than for other social institutions. First, Mariah Burton Nelson argues that "manly sports" constitute the "dominant culture in America today," and that even watching these games on television can contribute to the formation of violent attitudes against women. Particularly in sports such as football and hockey, "[w]here assaults that would be illegal off the field become an accepted, even celebrated part" of the game, it is imperative that the league send a message that such conduct is inappropriate outside the confines of the game. Second — even if sports leagues do not play a disproportionate role in creating a culture in which violence against women is tolerated — because athletes are role models for children, action by the leagues to discipline athlete-abusers might still have a disproportionately positive impact and set an example for other social institutions.

Finally, there is some evidence that police, judges, and juries are more lenient when dealing with professional athletes. A sports league might address this problem by administering its own sanctions against domestic abusers. This rationale for a domestic violence policy is problematic, however, in that it essentially advocates private enforcement of criminal law.

B. Arguments Against Enacting a Domestic Violence Policy — and Why They Are Unpersuasive

1. Sports Leagues Should Not Usurp the Role of the Government. —....

....No constitution or statute confers upon such private associations the "police power" to justify "trying to supplement the criminal law or trying to enforce customary morality." Any action by a league to impose such extrajudicial sanctions on athlete-abusers might be construed as an attempt to usurp the role of the government.

Underlying this argument is the notion that a professional sports league constitutes what some commentators refer to as a "private government" or "ruling organization." The league "is not just one of many competitive businesses seeking to maximize the marketability of its product." Even though a player's relationship with the league is contractual in nature — "with the implied right of all parties involved not to agree to contracts they regard as injurious" — the league's near-monopsony status in the labor market for players' services affords it substantial power over its players. If an individual employer terminates a worker for off-duty misconduct, that worker may re-enter the labor market in search of other opportunities. By contrast, if a sports league imposes similar sanctions, the player is barred from playing not only for one particular team, but also for any other team in the league.

When a private entity performs governmental functions, it may compromise individual rights because a private association is not required to comply with the same due process requirements as is a state actor. Nevertheless, "private governments" do have a legitimate role in the ordering of social relationships in those spheres in which public government is "undesirable" — particularly when the private organization can "claim a particular right, based on special knowledge, to administer some aspect of human behavior." Since the National Basketball Association (NBA) Commissioner presumably knows more about basketball than does a district court judge or a legislator, he can legitimately promulgate and enforce rules concerning excessive violence on the court or off-the-court conduct that directly impacts the game on the playing floor, such as steroid use or players betting on games involving their own teams. By contrast, when the league seeks to enact rules in a realm in which it has no specialized knowledge and in which public government intervention *is* desirable — such as domestic violence — the legitimacy of such private action must be questioned.

There are several responses to this line of argument. First, although the Commissioner does not have any special competence vis-a-vis the courts in determining whether domestic abuse has occurred, he is in a better position to judge whether allowing a guilty player back on the field will harm the public image of the league. Second, because sports play a crucial role in shaping male attitudes toward women, league sanctions would have an impact that governmental action could not achieve alone. Third, league drug policies already intrude upon the domain of the criminal justice system.

2. Individual Teams Can Already Discipline Players. — Even if the imposition of sanctions against athlete-abusers is in the league's best interests, it does not necessarily follow that a league-wide domestic violence policy is necessary to accomplish this objective. In every major sport, individual teams already have the authority to discipline players for off-the-field misconduct. For example, the NFL collective bargaining agreement allows a team to fine a player one week's salary, suspend him for up to four weeks, or terminate his contract for engaging in "[c]onduct detrimental to [the] Club." In practice, however, teams have routinely allowed athlete-abusers to continue playing and have imposed little or no punishment — a result that is not surprising given the competitive structure of professional sports leagues.

First, management's short-term interest in winning constrains the disciplinary decisions of individual teams. If the expected decline in the team's performance from losing a player's skills on the field outweighs the short-term harm to the team's reputation from allowing him to play, it is unlikely that the team will suspend or ban that player for domestic abuse. Second, by definition, all of the teams in a league are somewhat interdependent; when an athlete-abuser is allowed to continue playing, the public image of the league as a whole may suffer. One team, however, bears almost the entire cost of suspending an athlete-abuser because it loses the benefit of his services on the playing field. As a result of this external diseconomy, owners may make decisions that, although optimal from their perspective, are inefficient for the league as a whole. Third, each owner faces a form of the prisoner's dilemma. Even if he wants to suspend or terminate an athlete-abuser to protect the image of his team and the league, he cannot be certain that other teams will impose discipline on their wayward players.

A league-wide disciplinary policy for domestic violence would both eliminate these inefficiencies and better maximize fairness. When discipline is left to the individual team, the coach or general manager is left to perform the roles of investigator, prosecutor, judge, and jury simultaneously. By contrast, leagues are more likely to have the institutional capacity and economies of scale to establish a system with adequate due process protections to adjudicate allegations of domestic violence. Furthermore, because an individual team's short-term interest in winning constrains its decisionmaking, it may have an incentive to impose sanctions on marginal players and to allow its better players to go unpunished. A neutral league official would have less of an incentive to discriminate in this manner.

3. *Problems of Implementation.* — Even assuming that a league-enforced domestic violence program would be desirable in theory, it might prove difficult to administer effectively. First, no objective mechanism like drug testing exists to determine whether a player has committed an act of domestic violence. A league could mitigate this problem, however, by requiring a criminal determination of guilt before imposing disciplinary sanctions against athlete-abusers. Although such an approach would not address cases in which the victim refuses to press charges, it would protect the league against claims that it is intervening in a realm where it lacks institutional competence and would avoid the legal challenges that would inevitably arise if a player was acquitted by a criminal court after being suspended by the league.

Second, although a league's policy might play an important role in changing societal attitudes toward domestic violence, it could also have undesirable side effects. Spouses of professional athletes may already be hesitant to press domestic abuse charges because they fear that a "court appearance could end up on the 6 o'clock news and ultimately destroy a career and comfortable lifestyle." The knowledge that the league will automatically discipline the abuser might create even more disincentive for the victim to follow through on her charges, thus rendering her vulnerable to continued abuse. As a result, any domestic violence policy enacted by the league should make an effort to provide financial and psychological support for the victims of disciplined players. Thus, on the whole, objections to a league-wide domestic violence policy are unpersuasive.

II. POTENTIAL LEGAL CHALLENGES TO A DOMESTIC VIOLENCE POLICY

This Part examines how sports leagues might go about enacting a domestic violence policy that minimizes the likelihood of legal challenges by disciplined players. Three approaches are discussed below.

A. Ad Hoc Use of Commissioners' "Integrity of the Game" Powers to Discipline Abusers

In lieu of adopting a formal domestic violence policy, a league commissioner might simply begin disciplining players implicated in domestic violence offenses. All four professional sports leagues have provisions in their constitutions and collective bargaining agreements granting their commissioners broad power to discipline players for off-the-field misconduct. For example, the "integrity of game" clause in the uniform NFL Player Contract "recognizes the detriment to the League and professional football that would result from impairment of public confidence in the honest and orderly conduct of NFL games or the integrity and good character of NFL players," and authorizes the Commissioner to fine, suspend for a definite or indefinite period, or terminate the contract of a player who engages in gambling-related activities, who uses performance-enhancing drugs, or who "is guilty of any other form of conduct reasonably judged by the League Commissioner to be detrimental to the League or professional football."

Despite the apparent breadth of these "integrity of the game" powers, their precise scope remains unclear. If interpreted literally, such a clause seemingly grants the Commissioner the power to discipline a player for any conduct that might "reasonably" be construed to be detrimental to the public image of the League, no matter how unreasonable the ensuing infringement on player privacy might be. In practice, however, sports commissioners have confined the exercise of this disciplinary authority primarily to cases — such as betting on league games or using illegal drugs — in which the player's off-the-field misconduct arguably compromises public perception of the quality of play on the field. Nevertheless, in some instances, commissioners have exercised this authority quite broadly. In 1990, for example, NFL Commissioner Paul Tagliabue refused to allow former Eagles lineman Kevin Allen to reenter the league after he completed a thirty-three month prison term for rape. In light of these cases, a formal decision to begin disciplining players for domestic abuse would hardly constitute an unprecedented expansion of the commissioners' powers.

The avenues of appeal open to a player disciplined for off-the-field misconduct vary by league. Under the NFL, NBA, and NHL collective bargaining agreements, a player has no right of recourse to an independent arbitrator. By contrast, baseball players can appeal any sanctions imposed by the Commissioner to the contract grievance arbitrator for a "just cause" review. Although this system allows the Commissioner to maintain a "reasonable range of discretion," the arbitrator evaluates whether the penalty imposed is "reasonably commensurate with the offense" and is "appropriate, given all the circumstances." Baseball's arbitrators have sometimes overturned or reduced penalties imposed by the Commissioner under the League's drug policy, most notably in the case of New York Yankees pitcher Steve Howe. However, the arbitrators have also acknowledged that player misconduct off the field is a legitimate grounds for discipline because of the negative publicity such behavior generates for the League.

Even if an appeal before an independent arbitrator is unavailable or unsuccessful, a player sanctioned for domestic abuse could still challenge a sports commissioner's decision in court. This challenge could plausibly take a number of forms. First, the player might argue that the commissioner exceeded his professional competence by imposing discipline for conduct unreasonably judged detrimental to the league. Such a claim is unlikely to succeed, however, because in accordance with private association law, courts have afforded sports commissioners "great deference in interpreting the scope of [their] jurisdiction in any context." As with other types of player improprieties, courts would have no reason to assume that they are in a better position than the league commissioner to determine whether a player's domestic abuse is detrimental to the league.

Second, the player might challenge the process by which the league commissioner reached the decision to impose discipline. In *Charles O. Finley & Co. v. Kuhn*,[74] the Seventh Circuit recognized two "narrow exceptions" to the common law doctrine that decisions of private associations are not subject to judicial review: first, when the action taken disregards the association's own rules and procedures or contravenes the "laws of the land"; or second, when the association fails "to follow the basic rudiments of due process of law." The second exception, of course, does not hold a private association to the same due process requirements as would apply to a state actor; in fact, the *Finley* court was reluctant to articulate any mandatory elements of due process for a private association, noting only that the "procedure must not be a sham." At a minimum, a commissioner must grant the player an opportunity to be heard "in a meaningful time and in a meaningful manner." A hearing is not considered meaningful if evidence indicates that the commissioner has prejudged the player's case or is otherwise biased. Substantial potential for bias exists when a disciplinary process vests the investigative, prosecutorial, and adjudicatory functions in one office. As a result, a commissioner who decides to discipline a player based on allegations of domestic abuse would be well- advised to divorce himself from the investigative process in the early stages of the case. Alternatively, the commissioner might lessen the need for judicial scrutiny of the league's procedures by disciplining only abusers who have already been convicted of a domestic violence offense.

Third, a player disciplined for domestic abuse might challenge the league's action as the equivalent of a group boycott in violation of section 1 of the Sherman Antitrust Act. When a sports league bans a player, no individual team in that league may hire him, regardless of its assessment of his skills or chances of overcoming his previous problems. Such an antitrust claim would probably fail, however. A league commissioner's "integrity of the game" authority is derived from the collective bargaining agreement and is in all likelihood shielded by the nonstatutory labor exemption to the antitrust laws. In *Mackey v. National Football League*,[84] the court made clear that the league, as well as the players' union, is entitled to invoke the exemption, provided that the particular restraint at issue "primarily affects only the parties to the collective bargaining" agreement, "concerns

---

74. 569 F.2D 527 (7th Cir.), *cert. denied*, 439 U.S. 976 (1978).
84. 543 F.2d 606 (8th Cir. 1976), *cert. dismissed*, 434 U.S. 801 (1977).

a mandatory subject of collective bargaining" under the National Labor Relations Act (NLRA), and is the result of "bona fide arm's-length bargaining." All of these conditions appear to be satisfied in the present context. First, even though the league's disciplinary rules affect players who were not in the league at the time of the agreement, the NLRA definition of "employee" encompasses potential employees such as college athletes. Second, the extent to which an employee is subject to discipline is a "term or condition" of employment. Third, the league commissioners' "integrity of the game" powers have consistently been the subject of intense dispute during collective bargaining sessions.

In all likelihood, league commissioners already have the legal capacity to begin spontaneously disciplining players for domestic abuse. The nonstatutory labor exemption should shield their decisions from antitrust challenge. Moreover, in accordance with private association law, courts will scrutinize the sanctions imposed by the league only if a commissioner violates the procedural safeguards outlined in the collective bargaining agreement, or if he prejudges the player's case. However, because a commissioner's powers are derived solely from those that the players cede to him by contract, a commissioner would be ill-advised to risk alienating the players by imposing sanctions for domestic violence without providing any notice of his intentions.

B. Use of Commissioner's Unilateral Rulemaking Authority

The "integrity of the game" provisions contained in each league's collective bargaining agreement authorize the league commissioners to promulgate and enforce rules that are necessary to promote public confidence in the game. Consequently, instead of beginning to discipline athlete-abusers retroactively, a commissioner might first promulgate a domestic violence policy with specific rules for player discipline. In 1990, NFL Commissioner Tagliabue took a similar approach to the issue of drunk driving and announced rules that would penalize players for alcohol-related convictions.

A disciplined player might contest a domestic violence policy enacted in this manner on several grounds. First, the player could file a labor claim with the contract grievance arbitrator challenging the process by which the policy was instituted. Because the extent to which a player is subject to discipline constitutes a term or condition of employment, the player could argue that the commissioner's rulemaking constituted a unilateral change in a mandatory subject of collective bargaining — a violation of the NLRA. However, the NFL grievance arbitrator has previously held that in those areas "where the Commissioner retain[s] certain historical integrity of the game" powers, players "cannot be heard to complain that the continued exercise of such authority violates the duty to bargain provisions" of the NLRA. Although a commissioner cannot enact a rule that directly contradicts another provision of the league's collective bargaining agreement, labor law does not otherwise impede the commissioner's rulemaking authority. Because sports leagues currently do not address the issue of domestic violence in their collective bargaining agreements, the commissioners should have the authority under existing labor law to enact a domestic violence policy.

Second, the player might attempt to challenge the manner in which the policy is administered. To minimize the likelihood of judicial intervention, the Commissioner should either consider a policy that restricts sanctions to players convicted of domestic abuse or else delegate his investigative and prosecutorial functions to an independent official.

Third, the player might bring an antitrust claim, arguing that if the promulgation of the domestic violence rules did not violate the league's duty to bargain, then the nonstatutory labor exemption does not apply. This reasoning is somewhat disingenuous, however. Although the domestic violence rules themselves would not be a mandatory subject of collective bargaining, they would have been enacted solely to clarify the commissioner's "integrity of the game authority," which *is* a mandatory subject of collective bargaining. Perverse incentives would result if the exemption applied when the commissioner exercises his powers on an ad hoc basis, but not when he articulates coherent rules.

Even if the nonstatutory labor exemption were found not to apply, it is unlikely that a court would overturn domestic violence regulations on antitrust grounds. Past decisions have held that the enactment of "reasonable" disciplinary rules by a professional sports league does not violate the Sherman Act. Although a league-wide disciplinary rule almost by definition restrains trade, like any private association, a league cannot survive if it cannot enact reasonable governing rules to "maintain the confidence of the public vital to its existence."

Unlike the use of a commissioner's "integrity of the game" powers to discipline players for domestic abuse on an ad hoc basis, the formal promulgation of a domestic violence policy by the commissioner would both provide players notice of his intentions and avoid creating the appearance that he is singling out a particular player when he imposes the first set of sanctions. However, the prolonged legal battles over the Commissioner's unilateral changes to the NFL's drug policy underscore the costs to a league of attempting to circumvent the union on player disciplinary issues.

C. The Cooperative Approach: Incorporation of Specific Rules into the Collective Bargaining Agreement

Another option for a sports league seeking to implement a domestic violence policy is to negotiate with the relevant players' association in order to establish a mutually acceptable set of rules to be incorporated into the collective bargaining agreement. Such a policy would be less susceptible to aggrieved players' claims of inadequate procedural safeguards and unambiguously shielded from potential antitrust challenge by the nonstatutory labor exemption.

It is conceivable that the players' associations would be receptive to the concept of a domestic violence policy. Even if athletes are more prone to domestic violence than nonathletes, it remains likely that the vast majority of players are not domestic abusers and thus share the owners' financial interest in maintaining the public image of the leagues. However, if the negative publicity stemming from player involvement in domestic violence only affects the leagues themselves over the long term, players would have less of a stake than the owners due to the short duration of the average playing career. In that event, players might attempt to use negotiations over a domestic violence policy to extract concessions from owners on other issues.

III. CONCLUSION

It is unclear whether athletes have a higher propensity for domestic abuse than the general population, but it is readily apparent that domestic violence is a significant problem among professional athletes and in society at large. Given the evidence that sport as an institution bears some responsibility for cultivating a culture in which violent acts against women are perpetrated, and the fact that sports leagues already discipline players for illegal substance abuse, there is little danger that action by the leagues to discipline domestic abusers would unduly infringe upon the domain of the criminal justice system. Furthermore, as long as the league provides adequate procedural safeguards to disciplined players, a court is unlikely to intervene in any decision by the league to impose sanctions.

Ultimately, the question whether a sports league should seek to discipline athlete-abusers comes down to how the league conceptualizes the relationship between sports and society. If one is to believe the lofty proclamations in the leagues' collective bargaining agreements stating that improper conduct by players off the field alienates fans and jeopardizes the future success of the league, the imposition of sanctions against domestic abusers is in the leagues' self-interest. Furthermore, if sports are more than just another business, but also a "public trust" — a claim frequently made by owners seeking public financing for new stadiums — the league has an obligation to further the public policy objective of combatting societal domestic violence.

Chapter 8

Broadcasting and Intellectual Property

Introduction

As the introductory excerpt to Chapter 3, *supra*, establishes, television is the key economic engine for professional sports. The largest network deals for the rights to broadcast league games have been worth billions of dollars. An ancillary source of revenues for sports industry participants are those generated by endorsements, licensing, sponsorships and the sale of other intellectual property rights. This chapter provides two articles illustrative of the scholarship that explores these topics.

The largest revenue stream for the most successful sports ventures has been television. From the beginning of televised sporting events, the various leagues have strategized on the level of broadcasting that would best serve the overall marketing goals of the sport. The primary concerns of these parties have been whether sports fans who can view games for free on television will also attend and the resulting impact on gate receipts if they fail to do. The law has played a pivotal role in supporting the various rules used by leagues to generate the greatest revenues possible from television contracts. For example, the right to "black-out" games in a city when a sellout has not been achieved a few days before the game is to be played is supported by federal law. The article by Alan Fecteau also examines the ability of these laws to regulate in new and emerging technologies.

Just as the sale of broadcast rights has generated revenues, so too has the sale of naming rights on sports facilities, official sponsorships of organizations and events and player endorsements of products. With respect to the law of intellectual property in the sports context, issues at the professional, collegiate, and amateur levels have ranged from protection of individual rights of publicity to the ownership interest in names such as the "Browns" and the "Colts."

The article by Professor Daryl Wilson examines patent, copyright, and trademark law and places a particular emphasis on the right of publicity. His focus is on existing and proposed intellectual property legislation and their potential impact on issues related to sports. Like Fecteau, he examines the impact of these laws in the midst of changing broadcast technologies.

Two other articles, not included herein, that examine licensing issues are: Sean H. Brogan, *Who are These "Colts?": The Likelihood of Confusion, Consumer Evidence and Trademark Abandonment in* Indianapolis Colts, Inc. Metropolitan Baltimore Football Club, Ltd., 7 MARQ. SPORTS L.J. 39 (1996); Julie Garcia, *The Future of Sports Merchandise Licensing*, 18 HASTINGS COMM. & ENT. L.J. 219 (1995); Lori L. Bean, *Ambush Marketing: Sports Sponsorship Confusion and the Lanham Act*, 75 B.U.L. Rev. 1099 (1995).

1. Broadcasting

Alan Fecteau, NFL Network Blackouts: Old Law Meets New Technology with the Advent of the Satellite Dish
5 Marquette Sports Law Journal 221 (1995)*

....

One can point to several factors that may be said to have contributed to the ongoing, staggering popularity of the NFL. But no factor has been more significant than the advent of national network-televised NFL games.

During the past forty years, the nationwide broadcast networks and the NFL have developed something of a symbiotic relationship. The NFL has provided the networks "up-close" adventure, with real people featured in a "which side are you on" conflict. The networks, in turn, have provided the NFL with national exposure, and substantial revenues from broadcast rights fees.[6]

Though the league and the networks have flourished together, the NFL has been forced to regularly deflect legal challenges related to its relationship with the television industry. One of the most regularly-challenged NFL policies has involved the league's historical propensity to impose a television "blackout"within a league member's "home territory."[8] As pro football gained wide popularity, annoyed fans and local media outlets began suing the NFL to have its blackout rule changed or eliminated.

In cases challenging NFL blackouts, courts have entertained issues under the Federal Sherman Act of 1890, the Federal Copyright Revision Act of 1976, the Federal Communications Act of 1934, and even the Constitution of the United States.

The league has historically asserted television blackouts are necessary to protect local ticket sales. League administrators have argued the NFL should not be required by the law to "give something away." Fans have countered, saying that the NFL has had it "both ways" to the extent that the NFL has received nationally-generated income from television, while at the same time the league has received locally-generated income from ticket sales. Fans have also relied upon studies questioning the validity of the assumption that local televising harms local ticket sales.

---

6. The NFL negotiated its first collective television rights package in 1962 for two years at $4.65 million dollars per year. By 1987, the league had signed television rights packages with three national broadcast television networks (CBS, NBC & ABC), and two nationwide cable television services (ESPN & TNT), totaling $1.438 billion. Garubo, *supra* note 3, at 371. The NFL continued to contract with the five national networks until 1994, when one of the nation's original and bulwark broadcast networks, CBS, found itself outbid by the emerging FOX Network. Landing a contract for NFL coverage has been widely perceived to have been a dramatic step toward FOX's gaining of credibility within the national broadcast television industry as a bona fide "fourth network," that could vigorously compete with the traditional "big three" broadcast networks (CBS, NBC & ABC).

8. The NFL defines a team's "home territory" as; "The city in which the club is located and for which it holds a franchise and plays its home games, and includes the surrounding territory to the extent of 75 *miles* in every direction from the exterior of the corporate limits of such city." NFL CONSTITUTION, art. IV, § 4.1 (1976) (emphasis added).

Legal issues regarding NFL television blackouts date back to the early days of television, and have persisted through the advent of cable television and the home earth station or satellite dish. Although constitutional issues raised by NFL blackouts appear to be something of a stretch, other claims regarding: (1) monopoly; (2) copyright; and (3) broadcast statutes, are more plausible.

This paper outlines development of the law regarding NFL blackouts in the three areas listed above, with some predictions for the future. The paper also analyzes how courts have broadly interpreted federal statutes, to the benefit of the NFL, throughout the technological changes characterizing the telecommunications industry during the last forty years.

I. MONOPOLY

A. Monopoly Challenges to NFL Blackouts

In different contexts, the National Football League has been sued for monopolizing professional football in the United States. However, most plaintiffs raising federal anti-trust claims against the NFL under the Sherman Act of 1890, have been unable to show a "causal link" between the NFL's monopoly status and injury,[19] or have been unable to show definitive damages to earn a significant jury award.[20]

1. Early Anti-Trust Challenge

In the early days of televised NFL games after World War II, the league's twelve clubs separately sold broadcast rights to local television stations at their discretion without much league interference. Fearful of lost ticket revenue, most teams refrained from selling television rights to home games. NFL rules also prevented teams from selling television rights where a game could be viewed in the home territory of another team.[21]

The practical impact of the league restraint resulted in a blackout of all NFL games when the local team played at home. It was only when the local team played away from home, that the game could be seen in that city.

In the early 1950s the NFL's policy seemed heavy-handed, as there were few television stations and some of the league's twelve franchises' home territories intersected. Two teams occupied Chicago, while both Washington and Baltimore had franchises.

NFL blackout rules began to impact league scheduling, which annoyed some franchises. Viewing choices became so limited that fans often found themselves with no game to watch, even though several games were being televised, simply because of league rules. After receiving complaints from fans and local television station operators, the Federal Justice Department challenged the NFL's blackout rules in 1953 as violating the Sherman Act of 1890.

---

19. *See* Kapp v. National Football League, 390 F. Supp. 73, (N.D. Cal. 1974), *aff 'd*, 586 F.2d 644 (9th Cir. 1978) (jury found no causal link between proven league "group boycott," otherwise violating the Sherman Act of 1890, and damage to plaintiff).

20. *See* United States Football League v. National Football League, 644 F. Supp. 1040 (S.D.N.Y. 1986) (jury awarded only nominal damages to plaintiff in absence of willingness to speculate as to actual damages, after plaintiff proved illegal monopoly, and harm caused to plaintiff).

21. United States v. National Football League, 116 F. Supp. 319, 322-27 (E.D. Pa. 1953).

A federal court in Philadelphia upheld the portion of the NFL's television scheme regarding blackouts of home territories for the purposes of *home games* — But struck the portion protecting home territories when the home team played *away* from home.

The league declined to appeal the decision, leaving itself subject to a court decree regarding any future league agreements with respect to television. The NFL likely did not contest the decision because, in the early 1950s, television revenue did not represent a substantial portion of the league's income. At that time, the NFL had little at stake. But soon, that changed.

....

B. The Sports Broadcasting Act of 1961

After battling through internal squabbles, and an adverse federal court ruling, Rozelle pushed the Sports Broadcasting Act of 1961 through Congress.[38] The Act allowed professional sports leagues to pool television rights, then sell them to a network in a fashion exactly as devised by the AFL.

The Act immunized the NFL from the above-mentioned adverse ruling, delivered from the same court that had reviewed NFL blackout rules in 1953. Since the NFL remained subject to that court's decree, the court had properly reviewed the NFL plan, and struck it down as violating the anti-trust laws. But when Congress passed the Sports Broadcasting Act, federal lawmakers effectively "overruled" the federal court.

1. Blackout Provision

The Act also contained an important provision regarding television blackouts. Under the provision, Congress *adopted* part of the federal court's 1953 ruling regarding the NFL. The Act banned protection of home territories from other sports league teams when a team played away from home, but allowed blackouts for the benefit of a team playing at home in the name of protecting ticket sales to the game.

It is important to note that under the Act, blackouts included *any type* of sports league-imposed blackout. So if the NFL wished to blackout *all other league games* from an area, to protect the local entry playing at home that day, it could legally do so.

....

C. Court Interpretation of the Sports Broadcasting Act of 1961

The first court to review league policy under the Sports Broadcasting Act of 1961 expanded its language for the benefit of the NFL. The court in *Blaich v. National Football League*, held that the NFL could legally blackout the otherwise sold out 1962 league championship game between the Green Bay Packers and the host New York Giants.[44]

The court held the Act's language could be easily read so that the statutory term "game at home" included a league championship game played at home. According to the court, it would be foolish to judicially amend the Act by interpreting the term to also mean "except for a championship game."

---

38. Pub. L. No. 87-331, 75 Stat. 732 (1961)(codified as amended at 15 U.S.C. §§ 1291-1295 (1988)).

44. *Blaich,* 212 F. Supp. at 319.

Although its statutory interpretation seemed sound enough, the *Blaich* court seemed to gloss over the key fact that the game had been sold out well ahead of time. Since the purpose of the statute had purportedly been to protect local ticket sales, a sold out contest would appear to obviate the need for statutory protection. In the case of a sellout, it would appear that there would be no local ticket sales left to protect.

The *Blaich* court relied on a dubious historical examination of the less-than-capacity crowds for NFL championship games, and concluded "[t]he fact that *this year's* game is a sellout does not overcome the demonstrated experience of recent years." The rationale is questionable because the examined years were *before* enactment of the Sports Broadcasting Act of 1961, which officially established the NFL's rationale as local ticket sale protection.

Although the NFL blackout prevailed in *Blaich*, arguably the seed had been planted for future change. How long could the NFL continue to blackout sold out home games, with the clear purpose of the immunizing Sports Broadcasting Act of 1961 — the protection of local ticket sales?

1. Congress Softens Blackout Policy

About ten years after *Blaich*, the NFL's historically poor Washington Redskins started winning games, and attracting new fans, including some who had been elected to Congress. When Congressional representatives experienced difficulty obtaining tickets to sold out Redskin home play-off games against the Green Bay Packers and Dallas Cowboys, the inevitable happened.

Before the next season started, Congress had amended the Communications Act of 1934,[51] requiring the NFL to lift any local blackout of a home game if the game is sold out at least seventy-two hours in advance of the scheduled starting time.

The NFL complained that local ticket sales would be lost because large numbers of local fans, who might otherwise have bought tickets in advance of the deadline, would delay a buying decision until the last moment — in anticipation of a ruling as to whether the game will be locally-televised. With that dubious argument, however, the league convinced Congress to write the law so as to allow it to expire on December 31, 1975.[55]

2. Instant Replay — Local Ticket Sales or National Exposure?

Since the statute expired, the NFL has voluntarily adhered to its terms with one exception. Interestingly, under current NFL rules, where a franchise sells all its tickets in time to allow for a local telecast, *no other* NFL game can be shown on the telecasting network's local affiliate that day. This is the case even where a game had been previously scheduled to be televised, and starting times for games *do not conflict*.

For example, imagine that the NFL's Atlanta Falcons play at home, starting at 1:00 p.m., Eastern time. The game would be blacked out on the Atlanta FOX- affiliated station. A later game would routinely be scheduled by FOX and the NFL for Atlanta, likely featuring a San Francisco 49ers or Arizona Cardinals home contest from the West.

---

51. 47 U.S.C. § 101 (1975).
55. 47 U.S.C. § 331 (1975).

When the Falcons' game sells out, the NFL lifts the local blackout on the early Falcons game. Strangely enough, however, the NFL goes one step further and also eliminates the later game from Atlanta FOX coverage. An old movie is dusted off and appears on the screen. The NFL's television "penalty" imposed upon localities for high ticket sales seems to undermine the purpose the NFL put forth in support of the Sports Broadcasting Act of 1961 — to protect such sales. If the NFL believes local ticket sales are important enough to warrant statutory protection, why would the league effectively penalize local viewers in NFL cities by reducing league television coverage, after other locals have filled the stadium?

Arguably, the answer can be found by examining who regularly purchases remaining tickets to sold out NFL games. Often a local network affiliate, which otherwise regularly televises the games of a given NFL franchise when the team is away from home, purchases the remaining tickets to that team's home contests in the interest of local goodwill. The NFL is, of course, powerless to stop the purchase and allows the local blackout to be lifted. Not wishing to give one network an edge in NFL exposure, simply because some local network affiliate is willing to buy remaining tickets, the league chooses to remove any further televised games from that network affiliate that day.

Still, the NFL's policy glibly assumes network affiliates — not fans — always buy remaining tickets.

3. Signal Penetration into Home Territories

A federal court in Florida, in like manner of the *Blaich* court, more recently loosely interpreted the Sports Broadcasting Act of 1961 for the benefit of NFL blackout rules.[58]

Since passage of the Act, the NFL has interpreted the statute's section regarding television blackouts of home territories to include television stations with studios and transmitters outside the seventy-five-mile limit, but with signal penetration inside the protected zone. According to the league, the NFL could blackout home games from telecast on such stations.

The studios and transmitter of television station WTWV in south Florida were located beyond the seventy-five-mile barrier defining the Miami Dolphins' home territory, but the station signal easily penetrated the blackout zone so WTWV tested the NFL's interpreration of the Act in court.[60]

The court held for the NFL based upon the view that the purpose of the Act — to protect local ticket sales — would be undermined if the plaintiff were allowed to beam Dolphin home games inside the seventy-five-mile NFL radius.

The legislative history surrounding the language of the Sports Broadcasting Act of 1961 is inconclusive. But clearly, Congress seemed to codify part of the 1953 case *United States v. National Football League* as part of the Act.[63] Testimony in that case by then NFL commissioner Bert Bell defined a league's home territory as not inclusive of television stations and transmitters located beyond the seventy-five-mile circle.

The impact of a signal penetration definition for the NFL's federally endorsed home territory is to greatly enlarge the territory for the purposes of television

---

58. *WTWV*, 678 F.2d 142.

60. *WTWV*, 678 F.2d at 142.

63. *Id.* at 883–886.

blackouts. Because a station's signal may be seen within the seventy-five-mile zone, viewers residing outside the zone are effectively pulled into the zone for the purposes of the blackout.

4. Interpreting the Sports Broadcasting Act — Language or Purpose?

In *Blaich*, the court strictly interpreted the language of the Sports Broadcasting Act of 1961, giving little weight to a key fact striking at the purpose of the Act. However, in *WTWV*, the court relied upon the purpose of the Act as the basis of its decision. It appears the only judicial consistency evidenced between *Blaich* and *WTWV* is that the court ruled for the NFL both times.

5. Dish Owners Emerge: Old Statutes v. New Technology

Courts backed the NFL's right to blackout telecasts throughout the emergence of nationally-televised professional football. Bouncing games across the continent required use of specialized equipment to send and receive signals, to include home earth stations or satellite dishes. For years, professional broadcasters monopolized this sort of historically expensive hardware. Consumers simply could not afford to outfit themselves with satellite dishes and other such high-tech communications equipment.

In recent years, of course, that has changed. The satellite dish has become increasingly available and affordable to consumers and small businesses alike. With respect to NFL blackouts, the result of the advent of the satellite dish has been predictable, and is generally described in Part Two and Part Three of this article. Satellite dish owners have by-passed NFL blackouts with the new competing technology. The league quickly sought courtroom protection for broadcasts from unauthorized reception. Since courts have been forced to apply dated legislation to consumer use of modern equipment, the results have not been without strained reasoning.

II. COPYRIGHT LAW: NFL 1, DISH OWNERS 0

To date, there has been one challenge by a home earth station owner to the NFL television blackout policy under the Federal Copyright Revision Act of 1976.[65]

In St. Louis, several bar owners imported the "dirty feed"[66] of blacked-out St. Louis Cardinals home games with a satellite dish they had purchased and placed atop their buildings. The bar owners freely admitted pirating the plaintiff NFL's dirty feed, but the bar owners claimed protection from the NFL's reliance upon the Act under an exemption in the Act. The exemption allowed retransmitting otherwise copyrighted material with "apparatus of a kind commonly used in private homes."[67]

Enacted before satellite dishes were generally available to consumers, Congress passed the exemption to protect small businesses from liability for using audiovisual equipment to retransmit otherwise copyrighted material.

---

65. 17 U.S.C. § 101 (1988).

66. Signals sent from event to network headquarters. The "clean feed" contains no commercial advertising. Advertisements are added by the network at its headquarters to create the "dirty feed," which is then transmitted back to the broadcast area. Roberts, *supra* note 14, at 365–66.

67. 17 U.S.C. § 110(5) (1988).

Two lower federal courts and the Eighth Circuit held against the bar owners as they were not yet prepared to conclude that satellite dishes amounted to audiovisual equipment "commonly used in private homes" for the purposes of the statute.[69]

Interestingly, however, the circuit court left itself open to the proposition that some day satellite dishes would be commonplace in private homes, and thereby might fall within the Act's exemption.[70] In so doing, the circuit court in *National Football League v. McBee & Bruno's* [71] properly sent out a warning signal to the NFL and Congress that an amendment to the Copyright Revision Act of 1976 may be in order if satellite dish use by consumers expands.

III. COMMUNICATIONS LAW: NFL 2, DISH OWNERS 0

To date, there has been one challenge to the NFL blackout rules by a home earth station under the Federal Communications Act of 1934.[72]

Like the bar owners in *McBee & Bruno's*, the owners of The Alley, Inc., in Miami, freely admitted pirating otherwise locally-blacked-out NFL games featuring the Miami Dolphins. Unlike the St. Louis bar owners, the defendants in *National Football League v. The Alley*,[73] claimed protection under the Communications Act of 1934, not the Federal Copyright Revision Act of 1976.[74]

The principal legislation regulating broadcasting in the United States, the Communications Act, prohibits unauthorized interception of "communication by wire or radio."[75] However, the same section of the Act contains a proviso, allowing unauthorized interception where the communication is transmitted "for the use of the general public."

In its defense, The Alley, Inc. argued that the NFL's "dirty feed" had been broadcast "for the use of the general public," and so was covered by the proviso. In a brief opinion, without much discussion, the court in *The Alley* declared that the NFL's satellite communications were not intended for public use.

There can be little doubt that the court correctly found that the NFL's satellite feed was not intended for public use, at least insofar as the otherwise blacked-out Miami area is concerned. As discussed in Part One above, the Sports Broadcasting Act of 1961[79] allows local blackouts. As such, the court's holding is well-grounded. Still, the court's rationale appears to be wanting. According to the court, "[T]he necessity of *special and expensive receiving equipment* not in common household use demonstrates that the satellite transmissions *cannot have been intended* for use by the general public."

According to the court, because satellite dishes were expensive at the time of its ruling, the NFL could not have intended to use them to transmit information for public use. By this rationale, the court seems to have tied the NFL's communicative intent to the cost and availability of a product. This rationale is strained, es-

---

69. National Football League v. Cousin Hugo's, 600 F. Supp. 84 (E.D. Mo. 1984); *McBee & Bruno's*, 621 F. Supp. 880 *aff'd*, 792 F.2d 726.

70. *McBee & Bruno's*, 621 F. Supp. at 885.

71. *Id.*

72. 47 U.S.C. § 101.

73. *The Alley*, 624 F. Supp. 6.

74. 17 U.S.C. § 101.

75. 47 U.S.C. § 605(a) (1975).

79. 15 U.S.C. § 1292 (1988).

pecially when one considers that satellite dish prices have declined in recent years, making them more available to consumers. As stated by the court in *McBee & Bruno's*, satellite dishes may some day be much more commonplace.

In its own way, therefore, the court in *The Alley* has left an opening under the Communications Act of 1934 similar to the opening left by *McBee & Bruno's* under the Copyright Act of 1976. If and when satellite dish use becomes less expensive, the NFL's intent to communicate for the use of the general public will change accordingly. As such, unauthorized interception under the Communications Act of 1934's proviso may well be permissible.

CONCLUSION

The NFL and television have flourished together during the past forty years. Despite challenges under federal law, the NFL has generally been allowed to protect local ticket revenue with television blackouts, while also commanding large rights fees from national television networks.

NFL policies created soon after passage of the Sports Broadcasting Act of 1961, however, seem to indicate that national television exposure is more important to the league than local ticket sales.

During the several years it competed with a rival league, the NFL chose not to take advantage of its statutory authority, so as to better compete for valuable television exposure. Since its merger with the AFL, the NFL has taken full advantage of its authority, and even enacted blackout policies that punish localities for high ticket sales.

Since the advent of consumer and small business use of satellite dishes, the NFL has successfully sued to stop pirating under both the Copyright Act of 1976 and the Communications Act of 1934. With respect to dish use, however, both acts are dated and do not provide the league complete protection if dishes become more commonplace consumer items. As a result, the NFL may conclude that it must lobby Congress for updated legislation. The better view is that Congress should not commit to updating the acts to regulate satellite dish use.

But, the emergence of new communications technology, like the satellite dish, should not be stunted by heavy-handed government involvement. Instead, the NFL would appear to be in the best position to alleviate pirating by working with the networks to encrypt, or "scramble," its broadcasts to prevent unauthorized reception. Along these lines, the NFL Sunday Ticket plan may be viewed as a very positive step, because it allows dish owners to lawfully take fuller advantage of a new technology.

Subscribers to NFL Sunday Ticket should thank members of the United Sports Fans of America (USFA) who were sympathetic characters — fans and small businessmen out to please customers. USFA members led the league out of the darkness, and showed that dish-owning fans and business operators might indeed be willing to pay the NFL to become authorized recipients of NFL broadcasts.

The satellite dish will only become more commonplace in the years ahead. The NFL would do well to adjust accordingly, and work with dish users to form other such equitable arrangements — rather than insisting upon protectionist legislation.

2. Intellectual Property

Darryl C. Wilson, The Legal Ramifications of Saving Face: An Integrated Analysis of Intellectual Property and Sport
4 Villanova Sports & Entertainment Law Journal 227 (1997)[*]

I. INTRODUCTION

. . . .

A review of intellectual property as it pertains to sports serves a dual purpose. First, it illustrates the basics of a legal area of great significance while highlighting the easy access available for practitioners of sports law. Second, this review provides an opportunity for speculation on how two new intellectual property developments may be treated by the sports law community: a proposed Model Privacy and Publicity Act and the new Federal Dilution Act. Additionally, publicity and dilution rights have special significance for athletes since these areas involve the ability of celebrities to protect their images beyond the boundaries of traditional intellectual property.

. . . . [A discussion that offers a historical perspective on the development of sport and intellectual property law is omitted. — ed.].

III. THE UNION OF INTELLECTUAL PROPERTY AND SPORT

. . . .

A. The Spectrum of Patentable Sports Items: Utility Patents

. . . .

Patents are exclusively regulated by the Federal Patent Act.[75] The Act includes processes, machines, manufactures and compositions of matter as patentable subject matter. These items are generally classified as utility patents. Even within this grouping, it is common to characterize machines, manufactures and compositions of matter together as "products," to allow delineation between these types of claims and those involving "processes."

1. *Mechanical Inventions*

The mechanical invention belies connotations of "products" with standard moving parts such as springs, wires, nuts and bolts. For these types of inventions, one of the primary concerns is whether the basic requirements for patentability are met. The threshold test for patentability is fairly constant, regardless of the subject matter for which a patent is being sought. Nevertheless, basic patentability is one of the more highly emphasized aspects of utility patent litigation.

An instructive series of sports cases involves an invention for assisting individuals in weightlifting. In *Universal Athletic Sales Co. v. American Gym, Recreational & Athletic Equipment Corp.*,[81] the court surveyed the most common concerns raised by the average utility patent. . . .

---

75. 35 U.S.C.§§ 1-376 (1995).
81. 397 F. Supp. 1063 (W.D. Pa. 1975).

The plaintiff essentially claimed a machine for simulating the chest press exercise. The invention involved the interaction of a frame and lever wherein the weights could be mounted to the machine in a manner that allowed for flexibility in the amount of resistance the user wished to encounter. The defendant claimed that the machine failed to meet the statutory requirements of novelty and nonobviousness.

To properly evaluate the patent the court was forced to evaluate the prior art. The prior art dated back to 1871 with the most relevant apparatus being very similar to Zinkin's machine. The evaluation of the operative principles entailed both an examination of the invention as a whole and a more particularized review of the separate parts. The court concluded that despite the usefulness of the machine, the sum of the individual parts were of no greater value when ultimately combined. Quoting from an opinion on basic patentability, the *Universal* court noted that the machine is one about which it might be said, "[t]wo and two have been added together, and still they make only four."[93]

The appellate court disagreed with the district court's evaluation of the evidence. The court noted that the pertinent prior art evaluated by the lower court was limited and called for review by qualified experts in the field. The variance between the prior art and challenged claims was especially significant since the differences related to the design and use of the various machines. The court said that, at least for purposes of non-obviousness, the lower court failed to select the proper prior art. Thus the original patent was restored.

The *Universal* opinions illustrate the basic requirements for securing a utility patent, as well as the posturing of the vast majority of reported patent disputes. In *Universal*, the allegedly infringing defendant claimed that the plaintiff's invention was improperly granted a patent. This triggered a review of the patent holder's compliance with the basic statutory and judicial requirements. If the defendant sees that such a ploy will be unsuccessful, he or she will alternatively seek to differentiate his or her invention from the plaintiff's.

One of the more controversial attempts at differentiation involves a defendant's assertion that the claims do not in fact "read on" the disputed invention. In other words, the alleged infringer's application does not make the identical literal claims to invention that the plaintiff does. A plaintiff then responds that the offending invention remains guilty of infringement under the "doctrine of equivalents." Under this doctrine, an infringement occurs if it performs in substantially the same way to reach the same basic result of the patented device, despite variations in explanatory verbiage. Thus the claims of the patented device are constructively expanded to encompass those of the defendant, despite the lack of direct infringement. Variations on the attempted use of the doctrine have figured prominently in the area of sports.

In the recent litigation of *Nike, Inc. v. Wolverine World Wide, Inc.*,[101] Nike was unable to successfully use the doctrine. The *Nike* case involved a shoe which, among its many parts, included a sole with a sealed inner member inflated with a gaseous medium. Nike sued Wolverine for infringement based on a Wolverine shoe which included a "heel insert containing 80-90% viscous silicone liquid and [10-20%] air at ambient pressure." The court applied a basic two-step analysis to

---

93. *Id.* (Quoting Great Atl. & Pac. Tea Co. v. Supermarket Equip. Corp., 340 U.S. 147, 152 (1950)).

101. 43 F.3d 644 (Fed. Cir. 1994).

the question of infringement first construing the relevant claim of the invention to determine its scope and meaning, and secondly, comparing the claim as properly construed to the alleged infringing product. The court concluded that the Wolverine shoe did not infringe.

The court noted that the term "inflated" did not include air which was merely contained or trapped. The Wolverine shoe was not "inflated" with air or any other gas but instead simply contained air at ambient pressure. Due to the failure of Nike's claim to exactly read on the Wolverine shoe, no literal infringement was present. Only through a more expansive interpretation of the claims would infringement be found. To succeed, Nike would have to argue that Wolverine's product was the equivalent of the Nike shoe and persuade the court to read the claim language as broad enough to cover trapped air. Nike was unable to meet these requirements.

. . . .

2. Nonmechanical Goods

Product patents include machines, manufactures and compositions of matter. Each of these subgroups can be further defined to arguably encompass every item, save those not literally "made by man." The protection of compositions of matter contemplates the mixture of two or more ingredients with properties which the ingredients singularly fail to possess. Thus, chemical compounds, alloys and mechanical or physical mixtures resulting in gases, powders, liquids and solids fall within this category.

The composition of matter category is of vast importance in the sports world. It is under this subgrouping that companies involved in drugs and nutrition seek protection. . . .

B. Copyright Law Tries to Keep Pace

. . . .

The Copyright Act provides that original works of authorship fixed in any tangible medium of expression now known, or later developed, are protected.[128] The Act lists items contemplated for protection.

Unlike patent law, the legal requirements to secure copyright protection are relatively simplistic. Protection is automatically bestowed on the author of the qualified expression at the moment of its creation. While direct copying of the work of another is expressly prohibited, there is no penalty associated with protecting a duplicate work as long as it is independently developed. It follows that if protection is available for works that are identical, those having a very subtle difference are even easier to protect. . . .

1. Expressive Designs

An exemplary case involving the basic requirements of copyright law in the sports context is *John Muller & Co. v. New York Arrows Soccer Team*.[134] In that case, the artist responsible for designing the team logo sought copyright protection once a dispute arose between the two parties. Since there were no factual issues in controversy, the court was free to make a determination premised on the

---

128. 17 U.S.C. § 102 (1995).
134. 802 F.2d 989 (8th Cir. 1986).

normal legal standards involved in a basic copyright case. The court noted that copyright protection is available only for works that show a minimum level of creativity and originality.

The court stated that the designer had failed to grasp the important distinction between the two areas and determined that the logo lacked creativity. The court did however, recognize the lack of any defining standard for determining the existence of an adequate level of creativity.

2. *The Prohibition Against Calculated Expressions*

Copyright findings against designs, descriptions and discussions of sporting rules have presented the sports aficionado with a dilemma in a closely related area; that is, whether sports statistics presented in a creative fashion are protectable. The case of *Kregos v. Associated Press*[141] addressed this issue. The plaintiff developed a form for statistical references on the efficiency of certain baseball pitchers. The form was published in newspapers throughout the country. To Kregos' dismay, the Associated Press began running a nearly identical form shortly thereafter. When Kregos sued for infringement of the copyright that he originally received for his stat sheet, the court denied him protection because "[a]ny curtailing of the right to use [the statistical] categories would exact a substantial limitation on competition."

Thus, the prohibition was nearly complete where copyright of game related material was concerned. There was no protection for charts, instructions, rules or other writings concerning sports. Ironically, it was sport, and not the game itself which was deemed unworthy. Items associated with play, such as toys and games, were very likely to receive coverage. This remains true today.

3. *Broadcast Technology's Less Than Immaculate Reception*

The print media, rather than television or radio, initially gave fans a face-to-face feeling of sports interaction during the earliest stages of organized sport. In addition to written descriptions of events, artists used to include their own renditions of the games. Black and white photography soon came of age, but was quickly followed by the perfection of the movie camera, which its inventor, Thomas Edison, used to film a boxing match. It was, however, the advent of live broadcast technology that facilitated the exponential involvement of the masses with the games.

.... Federal regulations were deemed necessary to keep broadcasters in line and cases immediately arose to test the boundaries of the new law.[150] For instance, in *Pittsburgh Athletic Co. v. KQV Broadcasting Co.*,[151] the plaintiff owners of the Pittsburgh Pirates baseball team sued to enjoin the defendants, a local media outlet, from broadcasting its games. The Pirates claimed that KQV, despite knowledge of contracts between the Pirates and other broadcasting entities, broadcast Pirates games to public. The court said the radio station's behavior violated established rules of intellectual property and the Communications Act.

....

---

141. 731 F. Supp. 113 (S.D. N.Y. 1990), *aff'd in part, rev'd in part*, 937 F.2d 700 (2d Cir. 1991).

150. *See* The communications Act of 1934, Pub. L. No. 416, 48 Stat. 1064 (1934). The Act has been amended several times and is in the midst of reformation even at this time.

151. 24 F. Supp. 490 (W.D. Pa. 1938).

a. Basic Coverage

Baltimore Orioles, Inc. v. Major League Baseball Players Ass'n (MLBPA)[158] is the ultimate case attempting to legally save face. In *Baltimore Orioles*, the court was asked to determine whether ballplayers had ownership rights of their televised performances during their games.

The players said their performances were not the proper subject of copyright protection because they lacked artistic merit. Relying on the statutory construction technique *expressio unius est exclusio alterius*, the players implied that the expression of these rights excluded all broader copyrights the owners may have. The players, however, did not prevail because this argument conflicted with the plain meaning of their collective bargaining agreement with the baseball owners.

b. Cable Extends the Field

Cable television provides access to a wide variety of sports telecasts. While cable television is nearly as old as commercial television, programmers have only recently realized its value in the sports arena. This newfound exploitation has expanded the range of problems beyond those normally involved under standard broadcast copyright issues.

In some instances, disputes arise due to cable's ability to transform traditional television stations into superstations. The National Basketball Association (NBA) has recently been involved in an ongoing controversy in this regard. In *Chicago Professional Sports, Ltd. v. National Basketball Ass'n*,[167] the owners of the Chicago Bulls and WGN, the team's cable broadcaster, sued the NBA. The *Chicago Professional Sports* court found the league unlawfully suppressed competition. The court said that the league could not restrict the number of games a team could broadcast nationally through its cable operator.

While *Chicago Professional Sports* and the compulsory licensing provisions contained therein centered on cable television, this case alluded to problems created by satellite transmissions. Satellite dishes give the sports fan even greater access to athletic events, far beyond those accessible by normal broadcast television, cablevision and pay access television. Thus far, the satellite transmitters have been successful in maintaining their autonomy, but with the greater proliferation of satellite receivers among the populace and recent changes in the Communications Act, these victories may be short lived. This would once again empower entities including the National Football League, who desires control of their signal transmissions.

c. Identify Is the Key—That Trademark Swing

....

1. *Calling Names*

....

Often, a team or city will attempt to use another city or team's logo. This action of unfair competition is commonly called false advertising, palming off, deceit or misappropriation. Many common law protections remain viable today, which is important because not all teams have the means or desire to obtain a fed-

---

158. 805 F.2d 663 (7th Cir. 1986).
167. 754 F. Supp. 1336 (N.D. Ill. 1991).

erally registered trademark. While there are numerous examples of sports cases that have used the common law of unfair competition, plaintiff teams and cities often base their claims on existing statutes.

a. The Statue of Liberty Formation

The body of law concerning unfair competition has periodically experienced growth resulting in a shrinkage of its apparent coverage. Various federal and state laws have been passed to clarify the scope of several common law doctrines. When the circumstances outlined by the statutes are not present, however, plaintiffs are often left without remedies they may have enjoyed prior to the statutes' passing. Congress adopted the Federal Trade Commission Act (FTCA) to establish a comprehensive regulatory scheme for advertising.[180] Since the FTCA made no provision for state enforcement, separate laws commonly known as little FTC Acts were developed to augment the federal legislation.[181] Additionally, each state established its own trademark laws and related legislation to provide a broad safety net. The Federal Trademark Act does not expressly preempt these state laws. Thus, while federal legislation is fairly straightforward, state and common law have proven most likely to be abused by sporting concerns.

2. *Image Is Everything*

a. Blurring and Tarnishment

If image is everything, then it will not do to have it tarnished or diluted. In an effort to protect their citizens from this potential harm, states have responded with anti-dilution statutes. Anti- dilution statutes extend the coverage of normal trademark laws, despite the lack of competition between the original and the offender, by making actionable certain references to recognized goods.

For instance, in *Dallas Cowboys Cheerleaders, Inc. v. Pussycat Cinema, Ltd.*,[186] the plaintiffs asserted that their protected mark was infringed and diluted by the defendant's advertisement and exhibition of the film "Debbie Does Dallas." Although the defendant asserted that the public did not believe that the Dallas Cowboys football team or its cheerleaders produced the movie, the court found the statute was satisfied if it can be implied that the offending item was sponsored or approved by the plaintiffs. The fact that the plaintiff held no registered trademark in the items complained of did not fail to bar recovery.

The Second Circuit's decision in *Dallas Cowboys* sets the stage for a concurrent reading of the federal unfair competition clause of the Lanham Act and various state laws, in a manner that substantially broadens the claims of entities with officially protected status. If the recognition is strong enough, a team can now simply argue that a new product's advertising may be bad for the team's image and seek to enjoin the marketing of the new product, regardless of how remote the goods or services are from those of the plaintiff.

In *Jaguar Cars, Ltd. v. National Football League*,[191] a car maker sought to enjoin one of the new expansion franchises in the National Football League (NFL),

---

180. *See* 15 U.S.C. §§ 41-58 (1995).

181. *See, e.g.*, Deceptive and Unfair Trade Practices Act, FLA. REV. STAT. §§ 501.81 to 501.213 (1995).

186. 604 F.2d 200 (2d Cir. 1979).

from using the name "Jacksonville Jaguars." The case was settled after the team agreed to change its mark to an enlarged jaguar head instead of a partially pouncing jaguar that the car company felt was too close to their own bounding feline logo. *Jaguar Cars* is illustrative of the blurring subgroup in dilution law. No general guidelines, however, have been created such as those available to test standard trademark claims.

Indeed, the likelihood of confusion standard has been rejected as a hindrance to assuring that the coverage intended by the dilution laws is extensive enough. Broad unspecifically defined limitations on words, marks and similar subjects naturally heighten the risks of conflicting with constitutionally guaranteed principles of free speech. A consistent response to the constitutional issue has yet to evolve; however, there are numerous hurdles that have been erected to try to block litigants before they reach this point.

Dallas and *Jaguar* highlight the ineffectiveness of the blocking scheme even though the posture of the respective cases is opposite. The normal inquiry in instances involving dilution is an analysis of the strength of the plaintiff's trademark. If the mark is not very distinct, there can be no dilution. Thus, many claims are dismissed after this initial investigation. The nature of sport in society reduces that line of inquiry to perfunctory at best, since it is taken as a given that, by virtue of the mark's use in professional sports, society is at least aware of the mark.

b. The Right of Publicity

Another area of trademark-related law in which sports take center stage involves the right of publicity. While not as old as the dilution theory, it shares dilution's goal of providing protection beyond that accorded by conventional trademark coverage. The term "right of publicity" arose from a 1953 New York sports case, *Haelan Laboratories, Inc. v. Topps Chewing Gum, Inc.*[199] In *Haelan*, rival chewing gum manufacturers fought over the right to use photographs of leading baseball players on cards which were packaged with the gum.

Prior to *Haelan*, courts analyzed disputes of this type under traditional concepts of privacy. The *Haelan* court, however, coined the phrase "right of publicity" as being far more descriptive of the matter at issue. The *Haelan* court had substantial precedent directly on point both statutorily and at common law to support its finding under principles of unfair competition. Yet the court took an activist role in identifying a new right due to the sporting nature of the suit.

IV. UPON FURTHER REVIEW, NO FACE GUARDING

....

To understand the few advantages and many disadvantages associated with the development of dilution and publicity rights, one must first realize that the variegated pattern of laws for both these subjects has been uniformly criticized. The perpetual critiques have led to a variety of responses suggesting federalization or some like standardized approach as the key to complete acceptability of these laws.

---

191. 886 F. Supp. 335 (S.D. N.Y. 1995).
199. 202 F.2d 866 (2d Cir. 1953).

A. Proposals for Standardization

1. *Dilution*

On January 16, 1996, the latest version of the Federal Trademark Dilution Act (FTDA) was signed into law.[206] This version, which does not differ greatly from similar proposals dating back almost a decade, amends the present trademark law. Thus, the Trademark Office or courts making findings regarding trademark infringement are bound by the traditional standard of likelihood of confusion, but may also use the dilution statute as a federally-oriented basis for trademark actions.

Those who oppose the federal measure generally agree that it simply attempts to codify, without clarification, the indefiniteness associated with common concepts of fame and distinction. Due to the synergetic workings of the law of trademarks and unfair competition, opponents assert that knowingly going beyond the customs of the former implies an endorsement for ignoring the limitations of the latter. One engages in unfair competition by providing a method for enjoining other competitors attempting to enter the market on the basis of the expanded view of trademark protection. It follows that a wholesale embrace of these circumstances can have a deleterious effect on society since the principles of competitive fairness are the underpinnings of our free enterprise economy. This subtle restraint on prospective competitors moves instead toward an oligopoly of the powerful. As other goods are prevented from entry, the few established companies can then fill the void with products of their own.

Supporters feel that the concerns of the opposition have been adequately addressed by the adoption of a factor approach to potential violation that somewhat mimics the accepted formula for determining conventional trademark issues. Traditional protections center on the concept of whether the public is likely to be confused by the alleged offender. Since normal trademark disputes are largely resolved on an ad-hoc basis, supporters believe it will be no stretch to ask a factfinder to go one step further in its analysis to make the dilution decision.

Almost all cases have linked a prayer for relief on dilution with the more standard claims of infringement. This has certainly been true in sports. For instance, in *Augusta National, Inc. v. Northwest Mutual Life Insurance Co.*,[210] the plaintiffs were able to prevent the defendants from establishing an outing known as the "Ladies Masters at Moss Green Plantation" on the basis of likelihood of confusion and a loss in value and distinctiveness of the championship. The court awarded permanent injunctive relief pursuant to the Federal Trademark Act and the state anti-dilution statute.

In sports cases, as previously noted, it is easy for the complainant to dodge the dilution inquiry on the distinctiveness of the mark. It is as if there is judicial notice that sport marks are inherently strong. Sport marks' ability to race between dilution and Lanham Act standards seeking the most favorable remedy, is not cause for alarm since the remedies are consolidated. There is, however, nothing to prevent a party from seeking the remedies of the trademark statute and additional remedies under a more beneficial dilution statute.

---

206. *See* Pub. L. No. 104-98, 109 Stat. 985 (1996).
210. 193 U.S.P.Q. 210 (S.D. Ga. 1976).

....

2. *The Right of Publicity*

A Model Right of Privacy and Publicity Statute (Model Act) has recently been drafted to serve as an example for state statutory reform.[215] This reform can take the form of amendments to current acts or could be adopted in conjunction with a scheme involving the Commission on Uniform State Laws.

The Model Act draws heavily on a combination of different state laws, as well as the mix of the formal areas of trademark and copyright law. The states chosen as primary resources for the model were California and New York which are recognized as the entertainment centers of the United States. One of the shared characteristics of both jurisdictions is that the impetus for development of the right was the result of cases involving sports figures.

For instance, in *Ali v. Playgirl, Inc.*,[218] professional boxer Muhammad Ali was successful in an action against Playgirl, despite there being no showing of his face or any other recognizable body parts. An image of a nude African-American man in a boxing ring corner, captioned "the Greatest" and alternatively "Mystery Man" gave rise to a finding of liability due to the plaintiff's fame and the media's regular reference to him as "the Greatest." Alternatively, a half-time performer during a televised football game, was denied the remedy he sought for commercialization of his routine on the grounds that he was part of the whole football spectacle which was public in nature and entitled to be broadcast. Likewise, another fully recognizable individual pictured at a Pittsburgh Steelers football game was denied recovery in an action against SPORTS ILLUSTRATED when the magazine did an article on fans. Yet a shadow of a car with a silhouetted individual gave rise to a successful claim against a tobacco company by a racing car driver.

Courts are more comfortable with protecting less ephemeral imagery and look to established privacy principles to do so; hence the suggested combination of privacy and publicity in the Model Act. A visual overview of the features of the new act compared with the laws of some equally viable states highlight some of the more important aspects at issue. Especially relevant to sports are the provisions for "face in the crowd" exceptions and the First Amendment considerations. The former provision seeks to prevent an opening of the proverbial floodgates by restricting suit when crowd shots are taken without any focus on a particular individual. The latter prevents actions of the right for publicity in the face of particularly newsworthy events. Thus, sports broadcasts or similar written commentary will almost always fall within the provision, making it, theoretically at least, more difficult for the athlete being pictured or broadcast for noncommercial purposes to file suit. Likewise, individuals singled out during photos of team activities are most likely to be deemed a face in the crowd and therefore are without standing to proceed on a "model" cause of action.

Whether the Model Act will ultimately be adopted as law in the same manner as the federal dilution rules is a question that can only be answered in time. Unless the implementation of the Model Act, or even the continued use of state acts, show marked improvement in remedying the losses of the common man, the op-

---

215. *See* A.B.A., SECTION OF INTELLECTUAL PROPERTY LAW: ANNUAL REPORT 212 (1994-95).

218. 447 F. Supp. 723 (S.D.N.Y. 1978).

position to these types of statutes is sure to remain. The Model Act has yet to be tested, but there is nothing in it that seems to explicitly assure that it will not also be a tool primarily available for the rich and famous, including athletes, since it is based on California and New York statutes.

....

Part III

Intercollegiate Athletics

Chapter 9

Governance and Reform of Intercollegiate Athletics

Introduction

Since the early stages of intercollegiate athletics, numerous commentators and social scientists have warned of the threat that intercollegiate athletics pose, if left unchecked, to the overall well-being of institutions of higher education. This chapter presents a representative sampling of such works. In a 1929 study sponsored by the Carnegie Foundation, Howard Savage sought "to present a summary of American college athletics, their merits and their defects, together with such suggestions looking to their improvement." The report discussed, among other things, the evolution of college athletics into an integral and formal part of institutions of higher education. According to Savage, this transformation of college athletics threatened to shift its fundamental purpose from the development of various constituencies within the university to the fostering of financial and commercial interests. The excerpt included herein focuses on what Savage characterized as the fundamental causes of the defects in American college athletics: commercialism and negligent attitudes toward educational opportunity.

Written in 1929, the Savage report was described by Professor John Thelin as in the "vanguard of reform initiatives." Thelin also characterized the report as a manifesto against commercialism. Indeed Savage's commentary on the threats posed by the commercialization of intercollegiate athletics has been heralded by other commentators and studies. In 1987, the Executive Committee of the American Council on Education authorized the appointment of a Special Committee on Athletics to examine the role of faculty in the governance of intercollegiate athletic programs. The resulting report of this study stressed the primacy of faculty governance of intercollegiate athletics and outlined the general principles that underlie faculty responsibility. The report argued that adequate faculty representation and responsibility in the governance of intercollegiate athletics would ensure the integrity of the student-athlete's educational experience, first and foremost. The report also recommended that each institution develop avenues through which faculty input could be transmitted, received, and applied to the governance of intercollegiate athletics. Moreover, faculty should play a direct and central role in decisions relating to financial disbursements, student-athlete curricula and policy matters affecting college athletics.

Following two years of study, the Knight Foundation Commission reported that the importance of intercollegiate athletics to college life created a dilemma: unless kept in perspective, intercollegiate athletics threatened to overwhelm and undermine the integrity of institutions of higher education. The Commission

215

openly acknowledged that college sports had encroached upon the fundamental mission of colleges, leading to problems so pervasive as to be deemed systemic. The need to curb this encroachment led the Knight Commission to propose a model of reform which combined presidential control with three interrelated principles: academic integrity, financial integrity, and independent certification of intercollegiate athletics programs. Professor John Thelin proposes that the primary contribution of the Knight Foundation Commission's report was to bring together college presidents to confront the major issues involving intercollegiate athletics. The key components of the Knight Commission report are presented in this chapter.

The Commentary section of this chapter includes analysis of and proposals regarding the governance of intercollegiate athletics. In the *Games Colleges Play*, Professor John Thelin examines the historic relations between intercollegiate athletics and the academic policies of American universities. As a part of his analysis, Professor Thelin examines the major initiatives undertaken to reform intercollegiate athletics including the 1929 Carnegie Foundation Report, the ACE Report of 1987 and the Knight Foundation Commission Report of 1991. He concludes that despite a pattern of abuse in intercollegiate athletics, reform efforts have achieved only limited success. This paradox is attributable in large measure to college athletics, the "peculiar institution" within American higher education, which is a "perennial source of opportunity and temptation." The excerpt provides insight into the reasoning that underlies his characterization of college athletics as a peculiar institution and his assessment of major efforts to reform college athletics.

Articles by Rodney Smith and Robert Davis analyze the effectiveness of NCAA initiated reforms. According to Smith, past NCAA reform efforts have fallen short due to lack of a coherent focus on academic values. In discussing the values to which the NCAA purportedly adheres in regulating college athletics, Professor Smith also considers whether the benefits derived from participation in intercollegiate athletics support the educational mission of colleges and universities. Reaching an affirmative conclusion in this regard, he proposes that in order to be effective, substantive and structural reforms of intercollegiate athletics must be premised on values that reside within the educational principle rather than values that inhere in amateurism and competitive equity.

The 1991 NCAA Convention was touted as the reform convention. Based upon his analysis of legislation enacted at the convention, the excerpt authored by Professor Davis concludes that reform was more illusory than real. Specifically he asserts that the NCAA missed an opportunity to enact systematic reform by passing measures that constituted superficial efforts at reform and failing to develop unequivocal policies relating to academics, commercialism and the student-athlete/university relationship.

The protection and enhancement of the educational value represents a consistent theme in articles not included herein that examine the effectiveness of institutional governance and NCAA initiated reforms. Of these articles, the following are particularly noteworthy. In *Rule-Making Accuracy in the NCAA and Its Member Institutions: Do Their Decisional Structure and Processes Promote Educational Primacy for the Student-Athlete*, 44 U. KAN. L. REV. 1 (1995), Professor John Allison examines the impact on student-athletes and educational primacy of NCAA processes, structures and substantive rules. As a part of his analysis, Allison persuasively argues that meaningful reform of intercollegiate athletics must not overlook the fundamental premise that the ultimate responsibility for the regulation of athletic programs resides with individual institutions. He suggests that this is true notwithstanding the considerable authority that institutions may delegate over the control of their intercollegiate programs to the NCAA or to the conferences to which they belong. Emphasizing the notion of local governance of intercollegiate athletics, Professor Allison concludes that a system of governance that treats institutions as self-regulating entities is the "only workable system" by which to govern intercollegiate athletics. *Id.* at 16.

The primacy of institutional governance in promoting educational primacy serves as a critical assumption that underlies Professor Timothy Davis' proposed model of governance that is designed to limit the extent to which intercollegiate athletics interferes with the educational mission of colleges and universities. In *A Model for Institutional Governance for Intercollegiate Athletics*, 1995 WIS. L. REV. 669, he offers a model of governance based on three concepts: "intercollegiate athletics is a subsidiary of post-secondary education; [s]econd, a formalized system of checks and balances, structural and substantive, is necessary to ensure a proper balance between athletics and academics; and [f]inally, the nature of the relationship between student-athletes and their institutions, as well as the commercialism of college sports, justifies and requires external mechanisms for holding colleges and universities accountable." *Id.* at 599-600. As it relates to institutional control, he argues that the model rests on the assumption that institutional governance will act in conjunction with uniform national standards, promulgated by a body such as the NCAA. Thus the NCAA creates rules and articulates the fundamental policies to which institutions must adhere. *Id.* at 600.

The final article of note, which is not included in this anthology, is written by Professor David Skeel. In examining the role of the NCAA in the governance of intercollegiate athletics, he notes the necessity of incorporating within models of governance mechanisms of accountability. David A. Skeel, Jr., *Some Corporate and Securities Law Perspectives on Student-Athletes and the NCAA*, 1995 WIS. L. REV. 669. Borrowing from principles extant in securities law, Skeel proposes imposing a fiduciary obligation on the NCAA (or at least on its member institutions) as a means of forcing it to conduct its oversight responsibilities in a way that protects the interests of student-athletes.

As an introduction to the discussion of the governance of intercollegiate athletics, articles by Professors Davenport and Shropshire provide useful background information regarding the history of college sports and the amateurism principle.

1. History of Intercollegiate Athletics and the Amateurism Principle

J. Davenport, "From Crew to Commercialism— The Paradox of Sport in Higher Education"

in Sport and Higher Education edited by D. Chu, J. Segrave, and B. Becker (Champaign, IL: Human Kinetics, 1985), 6-13*

. . . .

IN THE BEGINNING

The faculties and administrators in early colleges and universities never planned anything as frivolous as sports and games as part of the curriculum. The concentration was solely on academics. Yet, as we all know, times changed and students were soon engaging in recreational activities which college authorities viewed as a method for students to release pent-up energies.

As the recreational pursuits became more organized, it was natural that a group from one college wished to test its ability against a corresponding team from another institution. Keep in mind that all this activity was done outside the jurisdiction of the university and was completely organized and managed by the students. The historic year for the beginning of intercollegiate sport was 1852 when a crew race was organized between Harvard and Yale (Scott, 1951, p.16). It soon became apparent to many college authorities that the news about the crew races was helping to publicize the college and, thus, aiding admissions.

The next intercollegiate sport was baseball, and the first contest was in 1859 between Amherst and Williams. But it was 10 years later in 1869 that the real watershed occurred in the saga of intercollegiate athletics. On November 6, 1869, the first game of intercollegiate football was held between Rutgers and Princeton. No other sport, especially in the big universities, was received with such enthusiasm, created more controversy, or caused more meetings. This has brought us to the original question—the place of athletics in higher education.

As football was played by more and more colleges, it soon became an important part of campus life but still was without the official sanction of the colleges and universities. Students raised the necessary monies from loyal alumni and faithful followers. Eventually, the sport that raised the most money (football) was categorized as major, and the sports with less money were labeled minor.

Colleges and universities discovered that football increased the prestige of the institution. This publicity, especially if the teams were winning, increased alumni donations, attracted prospective students, and "in the case of state-supported colleges, increased appropriations from the state legislature." (Eitzen & Sage, 1978, p. 52). Nevertheless, the administrators viewed the intercollegiate situation as outside the main purview of higher education.

---

* Reprinted by permission from Davenport, J., 1985, "From Crew to Commercialism— The Paradox of Sport in Higher Education" in *Sport and Higher Education*, edited by D. Chu, J. Segrave, and B. Becker (Champaign, IL: Human Kinetics), 6-13.

By the 1890s sports were becoming small business enterprises on college campuses, the situation aptly described by these remarks:

> The 1890s were a critical time for American collegiate sports. Big name universities were determined to win at any cost and were committing bigger and bigger excesses to do so. Professional baseball pitchers were becoming campus stars. Coaches were inserting non-students for football games and putting themselves in their own line ups. Jam packed college grandstands went wild rooting for 'heroes' who attended school only during baseball and football seasons. Street brawls between players and townspeople often followed hotly-contested games. Collegiate sports were at a critical crossroads and might have been set back many years—or even abolished—had it not been for the urgent and historic meeting in Chicago on January 11, 1895. (Wilson & Brondfield, 1967)

This meeting was the beginning of "The Intercollegiate Conference of Faculty Representatives," better known as The Big Ten. This conference became one of the first to have regulations regarding students' eligibility and participation; many of The Big Ten rules were copied by other parts of the country. An important concept in the formation of The Big Ten was that the control of intercollegiate athletics would be in the hands of faculty, not athletic personnel.

Thus, rules and regulations were formulated, but the situation in football by 1905 was climactic when it was reported that during that year, 18 had been killed and 143 seriously injured while playing the game. President Roosevelt met with representatives from Harvard, Yale, and Princeton and urged them to do something about the appalling reports he was received about football. Consequently, a meeting was held in New York in December 1905 with about 30 institutional representatives present. Even though the reason for the meeting was football, the Intercollegiate Athletic Association of the United States was formed (its name changed to the NCAA in 1910), and its purpose was to oversee all sports, as thus defined in the original constitution:

> Its object shall be the regulation and supervision of college athletics throughout the United States, in order that the athletic activities in the colleges and universities of the United States may be maintained on an ethical plane in keeping with the dignity and high purpose of education. (Applin, 1979)

A few paradoxes emerge here as well. The institutions were to have their own autonomy with this new NCAA, and yet, they relied on an outside agency for regulations. Furthermore, the early NCAA did not have regulatory control or an enforcement mechanism. In essence, it was a sports rule-making advisory body and a good forum for discussion of concerns at the National NCAA meeting each year. The NCAA did promote the growth of conferences, and these conferences helped bring member institutions "in to line." Is it not amazing that these original student-organized sports were still not formally in the educational mainstream at any individual college or university but were publically prominent enough to cause the formation of a national body? However, an attempt had been made for control and though problems existed, sports continued to grow.

BY THE 1920s

The 1920s saw "The Golden Age of College Sports." As one author stated, "There came new freedoms, new drives, new searchings for emotional and physical outlets; and sports seemed to provide the one big national denominator." (Wilson, 1967, p. 109)

Finally, in the 1920s institutions of higher education formally recognized intercollegiate athletics as part of education and, for the most part, placed them in the physical education departments. It was also recommended that coaches be faculty members and that they be given appointments in the physical education department. This change was viewed with some alarm by many physical educators who had strived and secured academic respectability for the profession of physical education. Furthermore, the importance of physical education was recognized by the faculty and administration; in addition, almost all institution of higher education in the 1920s had a requirement in physical education which did much to enhance its importance to the academic community. There was justifiable concern from the physical education viewpoint that the hired coach who was also to teach physical education would neglect his teaching duties in favor of his first love, coaching. Many people did both jobs very conscientiously, but the reverse was also true.

Now that athletics was part of the educational program, intercollegiates received institutional funds which allowed sports to grow even further. Thus, the commercialization of collegiate sports increased, especially in football. The game was making big money and, hence, critics attacked it as being big business. It is important not to forget some of the outgrowths of these financial gains on our college campuses....

The tennis courts, the golf courses, the ice rinks, and so forth, that grace many campuses were a concomitant outgrowth of the big revenue producing game of football, especially in the 1920s. Even though it is perpetual fiction at some institutions, it is truth at others that the majority of the other sports in which colleges participate are financed by the monies made from football and basketball.

During the Golden Age of Sports, there were also an increase of alumni associations, identifying with the college through sport. This situation was reinforced by the discovery of how important a publicity office and, more currently, sports information office could be to the school. The alumni were kept informed about their school through news about the teams. The importance of sport to the alumni is described in the book, *The Development and Scope of Higher Education in the United States* (Hofstadler & Hardy, 1952):

> Athletics, because they are a symbolic link between the alumnus and his youth, are also the strongest link between the alumnus and his school. In some, yet undefined because no social psychologist has yet made a study of the alumnus— renewed contact with intercollegiate athletics revives his youth as no other experience could. He returns to the stadium with a sense of expectation that he could not think of getting from a visit with a former teacher or a visit to the library.... The alumnus is important to the university: He is a major source of direct support...he joins the undergraduate in underwriting commercialized athletics. (p.114)

Intramurals, too, became popular programs on college campuses in the twenties as more students wished to engage in sporting activities. One important aspect about the intramural movement in the 1920s, rarely present today, was its close relationship to the intercollegiate program, undoubtedly due to the fact that freshmen were ineligible for the varsity teams. Mitchell (1939) in his book *Intramural Sports* indicated that one of the objectives of intramurals was to have students learn skills so they would be proficient enough for the intercollegiate teams (p.20). The famous Carnegie Report of 1929 (Savage, 1929) extensively comments on the dichotomy of the intramural programs at some institutions and states that "another negative tendency is the intimate connection of intramural athletics with intercollegiate athletics under personnel that is interested primarily or exclusively in intercollegiate contests (p.84)."

Even though the twenties was boom time, the old problems had not gone away and in some respects had increased due to the commercialism and popularity of winning teams. In 1925, the following was written about sport and higher education:

> In the eyes of the general public, a college...stands high or low in the public estimation largely on the basis of the performance of its athletic teams; specifically its football...teams...The fame and value of a university have come to be measured by the space it occupies in the sporting pages of newspapers, and the size of the crowds that gather in its million-dollar stadium. As things now stand, the only thing that college athletics advertises is—athletics. The whole business has got out of proportion and out of hand. What is needed is not a general housecleaning but a revolution. (Gavit, 1925, 143-144)

The twenties ended with the Crash of '29 and the release of the famous Carnegie Report entitled *American College Athletics* (Savage, 1929). The publication was the compilation of the findings of a 3-year investigation including visitations to campuses on the whole issue of athletics in the colleges and universities. It described all the abuses in college sport and urged the college administrators to take charge and to clean up the situation. As can be expected, most of the allegations or wrongdoings were involved with football. Obviously, the report was not well received, and most people involved in athletics claimed that the bad practices mentioned were not going on at their institution but somewhere else. Consequently, nothing much changed, but the report itself is a treasure trove of facts and figures about intercollegiate athletics....

....

THE GREAT DEPRESSION

The great Depression, which affected all facets of our society, certainly had an impact on higher education and concomitantly, intercollegiate athletics. Budgets were drastically slashed; gate receipts went down; teachers and coaches were released; and athletic contests were scheduled with opponents in closer proximity to reduce travel costs. Yet, even though sports programs were faced with financial changes, there seemed to be no changes in the problems regarding illegal inducements and recruiting. The NCAA attempted to address the situation in 1933 by appointing a special committee to study recruitment and subsidization. In 1934 the traditional Round Table meetings at the annual convention discussed the findings of the committee who presented a code of legal and illegal acts. The chairman of the committee, Z.G. Clevenger of Indiana University, opened the Round Table with these remarks:

> There isn't a man in this room who believes that this recruiting and subsidizing problem can be solved completely here today, or next year, or the year after... all I think we can do is to approach as nearly as we can to a set of ideals that the most of us at least can agree upon, and then try to see if we cannot approx-

imate those ideals in the way we carry out the programs.... and of course, that
will depend to a great extent upon the integrity of those of those handling the
athletic programs.... and the integrity of those having charge of the various
colleges and universities. (NCAA, 1934, pp. 101-102)

The delegate from Georgia commented that the real problem was that there was
no clear-cut definition of subsidization. The NCAA president stated in closing the
Round Table that the NCAA "has never assumed the responsibility of trying to be
a governing body.... These are local problems. Perhaps, all that the NCAA can do
is in an educational way to try to state standards, or ideals" (NCAA, 1934, p. 115).

In 1937 the Round Table discussions centered on the conduct and control of
intercollegiate sports. The two dominant themes in that Round Table were presented in the form of questions that continue today: Is it high time that colleges
and universities take charge? And is the athletic program a part of the educational
program? (NCAA, 1937, pp. 19, 21).

WORLD WAR II

The advent of World War II caused a hiatus in the growth of intercollegiate sports
as the nation's energies were channeled into the war effort. There were some suggestions to eliminate athletic schedules, but athletic programs were maintained at
reduced levels. Due to decreasing enrollments eligibility restrictions were relaxed,
allowing freshmen and first-year transfers to play on the varsity teams.

When the war ended in 1945, intercollegiate sports started anew on over-emphasis, and at some institutions the game of basketball was becoming as big time
as football.

THE 1950s AND 1960s

An indication that sports were becoming more commercial was the move in the
late 50s and early 60s to separate athletics from physical education departments.
In many colleges and universities athletics not only split administratively but were
housed in different facilities. Furthermore, there was a return to the status of
years ago where coaches were full-time coaches and were not given faculty rank.
The move certainly raised the question once again—the role of athletics in higher
education.

Intercollegiate athletics were moving rapidly to even a bigger business operation where money and winning were the overriding factors. To win meant good
recruiting, and stories were abundant of abuses and irregularities, both financial
and academic. Presidents and faculties were unable at this juncture to exert control, and the fortunes of the athletic program often determined the fate of the
chief executive officer....

....

With the popularity of television, a new commercial dimension and a new challenge faced college sports in the early 50s. At first, the NCAA and conferences did
not wish to have football games televised, believing it would hurt ticket sales for
the games. Then, as the monetary aspect became apparent, being on TV assumed
another big business aspect to collegiate sport. Its importance is certainly illustrated by the litigation now going on between the NCAA and the College Football Association as to who controls the rights to negotiate TV contracts for institutions' contest.

Abuses in intercollegiate sports reached a peak in the early fifties with the basketball scandals; thus it was time for the NCAA to change from an advisory body to a governing body with full power to police and penalize. An initial attempt at control had been a Sanity Code of Ethical Practices with expulsion of violators from the NCAA, but it proved ineffective and was dropped within a few years. Thus, Walter Byers was made executive director of the NCAA and the constitution was revised, whereby the Committee on Infractions had the power to censure institutions in violations of NCAA rules. Now there was no doubt that control for the most part was in an outside agency, not at a respective institution.

However, the new regulatory body did not stop the illegalities, and irregularities in collegiate sports and reports of violators poured in to the NCAA office. To try and combat some of the unethical conduct, more and more rules were adopted as evidenced by the present day NCAA Rule Book.

The 1950s at the time may have appeared traumatic with the growing commercialism, scandals, and illegal operations but historically was the calm before the storm of the 1960s and 1970s. The student protests on campus in the 1960s and early 70s had a major impact on all higher education and intercollegiate athletics. On some campuses students voted to divert those funds usually specified for athletics to ghetto projects or social action causes. The demands of athletes to determine their own dress and to wear long hair and beards was constant challenge to the coaches. Racial discrimination was brought out into the open and there was a demand for parity and more black coaches. The emergence of the drug culture was another component that challenged all of higher education and athletics.

.... [Professor Davenport's discussion of the impact of Title IX is omitted. — ed.].

Kenneth L. Shropshire, Legislation for the Glory of Sport: Amateurism and Compensation
1 Seton Hall Journal of Sport Law 7 (1991)*

....

I. AMATEURISM

....

B. *Origin of the Rules Against Compensation*

1. Ancient Greeks

A common misconception held by many people today is that the foundation of collegiate amateurism had its genesis in the Olympic model of the ancient Greeks.... The "myth" of ancient amateurism held that there was some society, presumably the Greeks, that took part in sport solely for the associated glory while receiving no compensation for either participating or winning. In his book,

---

The Olympic Myth of Greek Amateur Athletics, classicist David C. Young reported finding "no mention of amateurism in Greek sources, no reference to amateur athletes, [and] no evidence that the concept of 'amateurism' was even known in antiquity. The truth is that 'amateur' is one thing for which the ancient Greeks never even had a word."[12] Young further traces the various levels of compensation that were awarded in these ancient times including a monstrous prize in one event that was the equivalent of ten years worth of wages.

The absence of compensation was not an essential element of Greek athletics. Specifically, the ancient Greeks "had no known restrictions on granting awards to athletes."[15] Many athletes were generously rewarded. Professor Young asserts that the only real disagreement among classical scholars is not whether payments were made to the athletes but only when such payments began.

The myth concerning ancient Greek athletics was apparently developed and perpetuated by the very same individuals that would ultimately benefit from the implementation of such a system. The scholars most often cited for espousing these views of Greek amateurism were those who sought to promote an athletic system they supported as being derived from ancient precedent. In his work, Professor Young systematically proves these theories false by countering with direct evidence and an analysis of the motivation for presenting inaccurate information. Similar faults by other scholars led to the inevitable development of fallacious cross-citations with each relying upon the other for authority. One scholar is believed to have actually created a detailed account of an ancient Greek athlete which Professor Young concluded was a "sham" and "outright historical fiction."[19] The reasoning behind such deliberate falsehoods was apparently designed to serve as "a moral lesson to modern man."

In simplest terms, these scholars were part of a justification process for an elite British athletic system destined to find its way into American collegiate athletics. "They represent examples of a far-flung and amazingly successful deception, a kind of historical hoax, in which scholar[s] joined hands with sportsm[e]n and administrator[s] so as to mislead the public and influence modern sporting life." With amateurism widely proclaimed by the scholars of the day, the natural tendency was for non-scholars to join in and heed the cry as well.

The leading voice in the United States espousing the strict segregation of pay and amateurism was Avery Brundage, former President of both the United States Olympic Committee (USOC) and the International Olympic Committee (IOC). Brundage believed that the ancient Olympic games, which for centuries blossomed as amateur competition, eventually degenerated as excesses and abuses developed attributable to professionalism. "What was originally fun, recreation, a diversion, and a pastime became a business.... The Games...lost their purity and high idealism, and were finally abolished....[S]port must be for sport's sake...."[24]

Professor Young and other like-minded scholars contend that the development of the present day system of collegiate amateurism is not modeled after the ancient Greeks. Rather, today's amateurism is a direct descendant of the Avery

---

12. *Id.*
15. E. GLADER, AMATEURISM AND ATHLETICS 54 (1978).
19. *Id.* at 12, 13.
24. *Id.*

Brundages of the world and is actually much more reflective of the practices developed in Victorian England than those originated in ancient Greece.

2. England

In 1866, the Amateur Athletic Club of England published a definition of the term "amateur." Although the term had been in use for many years, this was, perhaps, the first official definition of the word. The definition which was provided by that particular sports organization required an amateur to be one who had never engaged in open competition for money or prizes, never taught athletics as a profession, and one who was not a "mechanic, artisan or laborer."[27]

The Amateur Athletic Club of England was established to give English gentlemen the opportunity to compete against each other without having to involve and compete against professionals. However, the term "professional" in Victorian England did not merely connote one who engaged in athletics for profit, but was primarily indicative of one's social class. It was the dominant view in the latter half of the nineteenth century that not only were those who competed for money basically inferior in nature, but that they were "also a person of questionable character." The social distinction of amateurism, attributable to the prevailing aristocratic attitude at the time, provided the incentive for victory. "When an amateur lost a contest to a working man he lost more than the race...[h]e lost his identity...his life's premise disappeared; namely that he was innately superior to the working man in all ways."[31] Thus, concepts of British amateurism developed along class lines, were reinforced by the "mechanics clauses" that existed in amateur definitions. These clauses typically prevented mechanics, artisans and laborers from participation in amateur sport. The reasoning behind the "mechanics clause" was the belief that the use of muscles as part of one's employment offered an unfair competitive advantage. Eventually, under the guise of bringing order to athletic competition, private athletic clubs were formed that effectively restricted competition "on the basis of ability and social position" and not on the basis of money. Over the years this distinction has been used to identify those athletes who are ineligible for amateur competition because their ability to support themselves based solely on their athletic prowess has given them a special competitive advantage. It is from these antiquated rules that the modern eligibility rules of the NCAA evolved. Any remaining negative connotations regarding professionalism owe their continued existence to these distinctions.

3. United States

The amateur/professional dilemma confronting today's American universities is based on the presumption that if a college competes at a purely amateur level it will lose prestige and revenue, as it loses contests. However, open acknowledgment of the adoption of professional athleticism would result in a loss of respectability for the university as a bastion of academia. The present solution to this dilemma has been for collegiate athletic departments to "claim amateurism to the world, while in fact accepting a professional mode of operation."[35]

Two sports, baseball and rowing, were the first to entertain the questions of professionalism versus amateurism in the United States. Initially, the norm for or-

---

27. *Id.* at 100.
31. Young, *supra* note 1, at 18 n.17.
35. SMITH, *supra* note 32, at 166.

ganized sports in this country was professionalism. Baseball was played at semi-professional levels as early as 1860 and the first professional team, the Cincinnati Red Stockings, was formed in 1868. The first amateur organization, the New York Athletic Club, was established in the United States in 1868.

In 1909, the NCAA (which had successfully evolved from the Intercollegiate Athletic Association established in 1905) recommended the creation of particular amateur/professional distinctions. With the subsequent adoption of these proposals, England's Victorian amateur and professional delineations were incorporated into American intercollegiate athletics.

Prior to the adoption of the NCAA proposals, "professionalism" abounded. For example, in the 1850's Harvard University students rowed in a meet offering a $100 first prize purse and a decade later they raced for as much as $500. Amateurism, at least as historically conceived, was largely absent from college sports in the beginning of the twentieth century. Competition for cash and prizes, collection of gate revenue, provisions for recruiting, training and tutoring of athletes, as well as the payment of athletes and hiring of professional coaches had invaded the arena of intercollegiate athletics. Professionalism had infiltrated collegiate sports and had perverted amateurism as it was understood in the nineteenth century.

The sheer number of competing American educational institutions was, in itself, a major reason that athletics in the United States developed far beyond the amateurism still displayed at the learned British counterparts. In England, an upper level education meant one of two places, either Oxford or Cambridge. With each institution policing the other, the odds of breaching the established standards of amateurism were not high. In the United States, while the Ivy League schools competed strongly amongst themselves, there was also the rapid emergence of many fine public colleges and universities. Freedom of opportunity, a pervasive factor in the genesis of American collegiate athletics, made it increasingly more difficult for the Harvards and Yales to maintain themselves as both the athletic and the intellectual elite within the United States.

According to some scholars, the English system of amateurism, "loosely" derived from the Greeks, simply did not have a chance of success in the United States. As noted above, one factor contributing to its demise was increased competition among a larger number of institutions. Another was the difference in egalitarian beliefs between the two nations:

> The English amateur system, based upon participation by the social and economic elite...would never gain a foothold in American college athletics. There was too much competition, too strong a belief in merit over heredity, too abundant an ideology of freedom of opportunity for the amateur ideal to succeed....
> It may be that amateur athletics at a high level of expertise can only exist in a society dominated by upper-class elitists.[44]

In spite of the ideological conflicts, the early post-formative years of the NCAA were spent attempting to enforce the various amateur standards....[Professor Shropshire's historical discussion of NCAA efforts to promote amateurism is omitted.—ed.].

---

44. *Id.* at 174.

------

2. Governance and Reform of Intercollegiate Athletics

(a) Major Studies

Howard J. Savage,
American College Athletics 291–311 (1929)*

CHAPTER XII

...

IV. THE CAUSES OF THE PRESENT DEFECTS IN AMERICAN COLLEGE ATHLETICS

The fundamental causes of the defects of American college athletics are two: commercialism, and a negligent attitude toward the educational opportunity for which the college exists. To one, and generally to both, of these inter-acting causes, every shortcoming of college sport can be traced. Both may be abated, even if neither, in view of the imperfectibility of human nature, can ever be absolutely eliminated.

A. COMMERCIALISM

We have defined commercialism as that condition which exists when the monetary and material returns from sport are more highly valued than the returns in play, recreation, and bodily and moral well-being. Through the medium of self-interest it affects every person whom it touches: college officers, teachers, undergraduates, and alumni, the press, and the public. Because some of its results are desirable, as many other material things are desirable, it is frequently argued that commercialism can be beneficent as well as harmful. This argument neglects the influence of time, which in its passage withers the beneficent aspects of commercialism into evils that are the more difficult to eradicate because of the depth of their roots.

Commercialism has made possible the erection of fine academic buildings and the increase of equipment from the profits of college athletics, but those profits have been gained because colleges have permitted the youths entrusted to their care to be openly exploited. At such colleges and universities the primary emphasis has been transferred from the things of the spirit or the mind to the material.

In general, university trustees are relatively innocent of commercialism by formal or tacit delegation of their responsibilities. Yet they have profited by it; the task of finding money for new equipment and buildings has been lightened. As for members of faculties, commercialism has added to their numbers through providing from athletic profits a part of the salaries of certain teachers. Rising gate receipts have brought them enlarged facilities. But the college teacher finds also that

------

commercialism has complicated the instructional task through the admission of the unfit, the lowering of academic standards for the sake of gain, and the pressure exerted from various sources at a great number of points not be "unfair" to athletes. Through commercialism the coach or director of physical education has received very great increases in salary, luxurious trappings, and sometimes the means and the opportunity to attract and subsidize athletes of unusual skill.

. . . .

It is the undergraduates who have suffered most and will continue most to suffer from commercialism and its results. . . . Commercialism motivates the recruiting and subsidizing of players, and the commercial attitude has enable many young men to acquire college educations at the cost of honesty and sincerity. More than any other force, it has tended to distort the values of college life and to increase its emphasis upon the material and the monetary. Indeed, at no point in the educational process has commercialism in college athletics wrought more mischief than in its effect upon the American undergraduate. And the distressing fact is that the college, the Fostering Mother, has permitted and even encouraged it to do these things in the name of education.

The argument that commercialism in college athletics is merely a reflection of the commercialism of modern life is specious. It is not the affair of the college or the university to reflect modern life. If the university is to be a socializing agency worthy of the name, it must endeavor to ameliorate the conditions of existence, spiritual as well as physical, and to train the men and women who shall lead the nations out of the bondage of those conditions. To neither of these missions does commercialism in college athletics soundly contribute.

B. NEGLIGENCE RESPECTING EDUCATIONAL OPPORTUNITY

At a time when higher education in the United States is being much scrutinized, it is fitting that enquiry should be directed as well at its informal as at its formal aspects. In an agency primarily intellectual, athletics may take their place among the devices of informal education and recreation. In a socializing agency, the functions of athletics become more formal and more closely associated with the activities of the curriculum. But if at their best they are to be made to contribute indirectly or directly to the education of youth, their essential nature as sport must be preserved.

. . . .

We turn now to three respects in which the college has been negligent in its relating of athletics to college education. To characterize them thus implies no lack of discussion or theory; it does imply a certain poverty of lasting good results from action, ascribable principally to the workings of commercialism.

1. The Lack of Intellectual Challenge

It has been recently pointed out that a fundamental defect in the American college is its lack of intellectual challenge to the young and alert mind. If this is true respecting its academic aspects, it is doubly true of college athletics as they are at present conducted. Their governance has been delivered utterly into the hands of older persons, whose decisions are made with little reference to the benefits that the reasoning processes involved might confer upon younger minds. Most intercollegiate contests entail little independence of judgment on the part of players, whether in preparation or in actual participation. At every turn, our college athletics are mechanized into automatism, and our athletes and managers are puppets pulled by older hands. What intellectual challenge intercollegiate sport might afford has given way before the forces of commercialism. Fortunately for the future, intramural athletics have not succumbed to the deadening touch; but they are even now dependent for their existence upon the profits from intercollegiate football. If the spiritual and intellectual challenge of intramural sport can in time rejuvenate intercollegiate athletics, no man should withhold his hand from the task.

2. Control through Formula; Imitation

The problems of college athletics, like other problems in human relationships, are not to be completely solved by formula, however much they may be temporarily changed. As in the case of single branches of competitive athletics, standards and rules form the conventions of sport, and so long, as sport exists, it will have its conventions. But conventions are not formulas. It is often assumed that if college athletics, as distinct from school athletics, are to contribute to education, they must be controlled (that is, restricted and curbed) through the direct action of faculties. This formula has failed at two points: If, on the one hand, it means delivering college athletics into the hands of men whose chief professional interest and means of livelihood they are, the result is not to check but to propagate commercialism. If, on the other hand, academic teachers on college faculties are placed in control, such men, being specialists, only in comparatively rare instances can and do give to the governance of college athletics that concentrated attention and devotion which they bestow upon their chosen fields of teaching and scholarship. Probably more than any other single factor, the operation of faculty control, even at its best, has tended to deprive the undergraduate of that opportunity of maturing under progressively increasing responsibility which an enlightened policy of guidance affords.

Imitation in the control of college athletics has wrought an equal havoc. To assume that the athletic policies and regulations that appear to work well at one university or in one section of the land can without modification be taken over successfully into another is fallacious. A clear understanding of the functions of athletics in their relation to the educational process, however that process be conceived, a sincere and uniform recognition of the principles of human conduct that athletics involve, and an honorable adherence to the spirit as well as the letter of the conventions of sport, have wrought vastly beneficial changes in college athletics wherever they have been effectuated with due reference to specific phases of local sentiment. The solution of the problem of control is not imitation but adaption, not repression but guidance by college presidents, deans, teachers, directors of physical education, or alumni who understand the implications of the term "sport," whose generosity prompts the gift of many hours without compensation, and whose honesty is beyond self-interest or commercialism.

3. Morals and Conduct

In the field of conduct and morals, vociferous proponents of college athletics have claimed for participants far greater benefits than athletics can probably ever yield, and, in attempting to evaluate these supposed benefits, have hailed the shadow as the substance. The workings of commercialism have almost obliterated the non-material aspects of athletics. And yet such qualities as loyalty, self-reliance, modesty, cooperation, self-sacrifice, courage, and, above all, honesty, can be more readily and directly cultivated through the activities and habits of the playing field than in almost any other phase of college life. What, therefore, is needed is not one set of moral and ethical standards for sports and games, and another for all other phases of college life, but a single set of standards so sincerely valued that by taking thought they can be made operative in life's every aspect. The transfer or spread of training implied is as much the affair of the academic teacher as of the coach or the director of physical education. It must begin with a diminished emphasis upon the material benefits of college athletics and a sincere resolution to substitute other and more lasting values for those that now are prized.

CONCLUSION

The prime needs of our college athletics are two, — one particular and one general. The first is a change of values in a field that is sodden with the commercial and the material and the vested interests that these forces have created. Commercialism in college athletics must be diminished and college sport must rise to a point where it is esteemed primarily and sincerely for the opportunities it affords to mature youth under responsibility, to exercise at once the body and the mind, and to foster habits both of bodily health and of those high qualities of character which, until they are revealed in action, we accept on faith.

The second need is more fundamental. The American college must renew within itself the force that will challenge the best intellectual capabilities of the undergraduate. Happily, this task is now engaging the attention of numerous college officers and teachers. Better still, the fact is becoming recognized that the granting of opportunity for the fulfillment of intellectual promise need not impair the socializing qualities of college sport. It is not necessary to "include athletics in the curriculum" of the undergraduate or to legislate out of them their life and spirit in order to extract what educational values they promise in terms of courage, independent thinking, cooperation, initiative, habits of bodily activity, and, above all, honesty in dealings between man and man. Whichever conception of the function of the American college, intellectual or socializing agency, be adopted, let only the chosen ideal be followed with sincerity and clear vision, and in the course of years our college sport will largely take care of itself.

––––––––––

The Special Committee on Athletics, The Role of Faculty in the Governance of College Athletics
Academe 43 (Jan. – Feb. 1990)*

College athletics in this county is in continuing crisis. Even after several years of proposals and discussions of reform, the gains achieved are quite modest.

. . . .

It is not surprising that the crisis in intercollegiate sports continues. The fact of the matter is that the economic environment that produced academic and financial improprieties in the past has not substantially changed. The teams that win the most continue to earn the most in college sports. Adherence to rigorous ad-

––––––––––

* Copyright 1990 American Association of University Professors, Academe. Reprinted with permission. All rights reserved.

missions and academic standards is an impediment to winning, and a college that seeks to provide its athletes with a serious academic endeavor runs the risk that its competitors will not. The commercial rewards of athletic success continue to be juxtaposed to rigorous academic pursuits.

The time has come to recognize that intercollegiate athletics poses a major governance problem for American colleges and universities. Athletics is no longer merely an interesting extracurricular activity that occupies the campus on Saturday afternoon. In major programs, athletics often functions as an auxiliary enterprise that generates its own substantial revenues. On many campuses this has led to a suggestion that the intercollegiate athletic program should not be subject to the same governance structure as are more traditional educational endeavors. Moreover, policymaking in athletics is greatly affected by decisions that are made far from campus. These include decisions made in the National Collegiate Athletic Association (NCAA), by competing institutions, and by the broadcasters that are providing the revenues that have financed the recent expansion of college sports.

Recent experience has shown that the athletic department should not be allowed to function as a separate entity. Such an arrangement ignores the important implications that athletics has for the college's educational program, including the potential for skewing the allocation of institutional resources and impeding the educational development of athletes.... The goal of structural reform in the governance of college sports should be more fully to integrate athletics into the educational mission of the institution.

The policy statement that follows addresses the general allocation of authority in the governance of athletics.

. . . .

The statement emphasizes the obligation of faculty in ensuring academic primacy in an institution's athletics programs. An essential message is that the faculty has primary responsibility for ensuring the educational integrity of the student's academic experience. In addition, the faculty has a vital role to play in assessing the educational and budgetary implications of decisions concerning the scope of the athletic program. This statement addresses how responsibility for policy-making on athletics should be allocated between the faculty and other components of the university.

I. GENERAL PRINCIPLES

The basic framework for defining faculty responsibility in the governance of athletics is found in an earlier statement of Association policy. The 1966 *Statement on Government of Colleges and Universities*...underscores the need for joint participation in governance by the various constituencies within the university....

The *Statement on Government* recognizes that the faculty has primary responsibility with respect to fundamental areas of educational policy and that the faculty, along with other components, should participate in the exchange of information that accompanies long-range planning.

The derivative 1972 *Statement on the Role of the Faculty in Budgetary and Salary Matters* elaborates on the faculty's joint participation in a university's internal budgetary process. An important premise of that statement is that budgetary matters are an appropriate faculty concern.

. . . .

Both statements provide that the authority for final decision making is to be allocated among the governing boards, the president, and the faculty consistent with the responsibility that each component appropriately claims within the overall governance structure....

A. *The Importance of Full Disclosure of Information About the Athletic Program*

In the past, the governance of athletics has been made more difficult because administrators and others have treated information about the athletic program as highly secret.

. . . .

For the future, the presumption must be that all aspects of the operation of the athletic department, including the education of athletes and the finances of booster clubs, are open to scrutiny with the university community. A special effort should be made to ensure the confidentiality of information where that is needed to protect the privacy of individual athletes and employees. In general, however, policies with respect to athletics should be subject to the same openness of debate that attends other financial and educational issues within the academic community.

B. *The Primacy of Faculty Responsibility for the Athlete's Educational Experience*

The faculty has primary responsibility for those aspects of an athlete's experience that involve education. Thus, it is the faculty's duty to ensure that the athlete has a full opportunity to participate in the educational process and that a proper balance is achieved between athletic and educational experiences. Especially in the present era of intensive, highly commercialized college sports, there are often pressures within the athletic program that draw athletes away from the type of preparation, review, and class attendance that are fundamental to a meaningful education. The faculty has the primary obligation to ensure that pressures are tempered and that athletes have adequate opportunity to pursue educational goals....

C. *The Faculty's Role in Policy-Making in Other Aspects of the Athletic Program*

A variety of other issues involving athletic policy have a substantial administrative component and thus come within the range of authority of other units of the university.... Among the matters warranting attention are questions such as the level of competition at which the university will participate and more specific questions concerning length of playing seasons and policies with respect to team travel. A decision to move to a higher level of competition, for example, will often mean that athletes face increased pressures on their academic schedules. In the same vein, long playing seasons present a significant barrier to regular class attendance. Because of their mixed educational and administrative character, such issues of athletic policy will call for joint participation by faculty, administration, and, where appropriate, other components of the university.

. . . .

Faculty input is particularly important with respect to the budgetary deliberations undertaken in connection with the athletic program, even with the understanding that ultimate budgetary authority may reside in another body. The allocation of money to and within the athletic program can be a direct determinant of the level of competition that is pursued and hence greatly influences the degree of nonacademic pressures that participants experience.... A mechanism should exist for sufficient faculty participation in the budgetary decisions that determine the overall size and scope of the athletic program.

D. *The Institutions's Relationship with Outside Regulatory Bodies*

Outside regulatory bodies, such as the NCAA and athletic conferences, play an important role in establishing policies that affect the internal functioning of a university's athletic programs. . . . The coordination and execution of a university's participation is properly a function of the president or chancellor. On the other hand, the legislative deliberations of the outside body will frequently affect areas over which the faculty has primary internal responsibility.

Each institution should develop mechanisms that recognize the role of the chief executive officer in speaking for the institution, but which also afford an opportunity for faculty participation in the formulation of the institution's response. . . .

II. THE MECHANISMS FOR FACULTY PARTICIPATION

A. *Oversight of the Educational Experiences of Athletes*

. . . .

The faculty must reassert its primary responsibility in monitoring the educational experiences of athletes. The candid goal of this endeavor should be to counterbalance the pressures in college sports that would subvert the athlete's educational effort. Such balance can be achieved only by removing all decision making that relates to academic matters from the commercial incentives that otherwise affect the daily functioning of the athletic department.

Several specific areas warrant faculty attention. These include admissions standards for athletes, where the goal should be to ensure that the educational talents of athletes meet the requirement of the general student body. In addition, programs for tutoring and instruction in study skills should be the same as those offered to non-athletes. Whatever attention may be given to the special needs of athletes, the goal should be to promote the athlete's fuller integration into the student body.

The faculty should also give special attention to ensuring that the athlete's individual curriculum has coherency and reflects normal progress through a recognized degree program. The temptation to elevate maintenance of the athlete's eligibility over substantive academic achievement should specifically be resisted. Because of the uncertainty and changes that can attend any student's movement through the university, ensuring that there is substance to the athletes's educational program will be a particular challenge. However, the goal of the faculty's endeavor in this area is clear: to temper the effects of athletic participation on the student's educational choices.

The mechanisms for faculty monitoring are already in place in many institutions. These take the form of committees and offices that set general academic policy and provide oversight. The issues raised are often of importance to the administration, and it is appropriate that the faculty's primary responsibility in this area be carried out through a structure that utilizes existing administrative entities and involves appropriate administrative participation. . . .

. . . .

Coordination of the faculty's role in these endeavors can appropriately be the responsibility of the representative faculty senate or assembly. To the extent that there is a need for a distinctive faculty voice on such educational issues, the faculty senate or assembly is the appropriate body to provide it.

. . . .

B. *Institutional Policy-Making on Athletics*

An internal forum should be available in which the various components of the university, including the faculty, jointly deliberate the formulation of athletic policy. A university-level athletic committee with representation from those with applicable governance authority would be appropriate. Because of the high degree of faculty responsibility for many of the issues presented, the faculty representation on such a body should be substantial.

. . . The selection [of faculty] should be undertaken with a view to ensuring the independence of the faculty voice and thus direct election by the general faculty or its elected governing body is preferable. Such direct election will also serve to define lines of responsibility within the faculty.

. . . .

A broad range of matters would be expected to come before such a body. The degree of finality to be accorded to such joint deliberations will be determined by the allocation of responsibility among the various governing components. . . . In these instances, its deliberations should carry a presumption of finality.

C. *Policy-Making by Outside Bodies*

Because of the significant internal effects of rule-making by external associations, a university should take steps to ensure that its voice is heard in whatever deliberations accompany the external decision making. Once the institution has formulated its positions on important issues, the president or chancellor or other designated representatives should be able to present the institution's position as a unified one.

A structure should be established to allow participation by internal components, including faculty, so that the institution's positions are carefully and thoroughly developed before they are advocated to the external body. As with internal governance, the degree of faculty responsibility will vary depending on the nature of the policy in question. The faculty's responsibility, and hence its interest, will be highest with respect to those regulations that have the most significant implications for the educational experiences of athletes. The faculty perspective is also important for issues that have major budgetary implications and those that define the level of importance assigned to athletics within the institution. The same university-level committee that decides internal athletics policy may prove the appropriate vehicle for faculty participation. On matters of significant educational importance, full deliberation by the elected faculty senate or assembly may be necessary.

. . . .

III. CONCLUSION

The faculty authority to establish and maintain general academic standards entails faculty responsibility to assure specific application of these standards in the education of student athletes.

The faculty is responsible for reviewing academic programs for student athletes. The faculty must assure the primacy of academic concerns in athletics as well as other student programs. Protection of academic integrity against misplaced internal priorities or external demands in athletics programs, as in other matters, is the essential reason for the faculty's role in institutional governance.

The overriding principle...is that responsibility for the academic welfare of student athletes is not an extra-curricular or departmental obligation of a few faculty members and administrators; it is a fundamental responsibility of the faculty as a whole.

....

A Dissenting Opinion

....

It is unlikely that faculty members on individual campuses would or could have a great deal of influence, until the basic system changes. Under this system, costs are high. Not every college can win, and losing on the field causes financial losses. These losses are in one way or another absorbed out of funds that might have served academic purposes. As long as a losing season brings huge financial losses, administrative offices are pressured to go along with or wink at what will win. Frequently, winning policies are dishonest academically and in other ways as well.

....

The Association should appoint a committee to prepare suggestions for fundamental reform. Among the measures considered should be ineligibility for freshmen, shorter practices and seasons, an end to recruiting, to athletic scholarships, and to lower admissions standards for athletes. We should explore what can be done to further the establishment of professional minor leagues, which would afford athletes who lack academic interests or talents an alternative route to an athletic career. The new committee should also be asked to take a close look at the financial implications of the current system, investigating whether college sports do "make money," and if so, where and for whom and for what.

Finally, the new committee should address the issue of whether, under cover of giving a few black athletes a "chance at college they would not otherwise have," the current athletics system covers up the lag in bringing to campus disadvantaged black students who are interested in an education and could benefit from it....

[The shortcomings of institutional control were examined by the Knight Commission on Intercollegiate Athletics in a series of three reports. The excerpt included herein is taken from the Knight Commission's first report which was published in March 1991. In this report, the Commission concluded that the problems affecting intercollegiate athletics were so "deep-rooted" as to be systemic. According to the Commission, the pervasiveness of the problems required a new structure if intercollegiate athletics were to be restored to their proper place in colleges and universities. The new structure suggested by the Knight Commission was characterized as a one-plus-three model which attempted to reinforce the idea that college presidents should control athletic programs. The key elements of the one-plu-three model are set forth below. The Commission's second release titled *A Solid Start: A Report on Reforms of Intercollegiate Athletics* (March, 1992) reported on the progress that had been made in reforming intercollegiate athletics since the release of its initial report. The Commission's concluding report, *A New Beginning for A New Century: Intercollegiate Athletics in the United States* (March, 1993), heralded reform efforts such as the NCAA's certification process and the enhanced role of university presidents in the governance of intercollegiate athletics and identified future challenges such as costs containment and gender equity. A January 23, 1996 New York Times' editorial emphasized that the NCAA's major overhaul of its governance structure was premised on the recommendations of the Knight Commission. The three reports prepared by the Commission are combined and published in the Reports of the Knight Foundation Commission on Intercollegiate Athletics (March 1991–March 1993).—ed.].

Knight Foundation Commission, Report of Knight Foundation Commission on Intercollegiate Athletics, Keeping the Faith with the Student-Athlete: A New Model for Intercollegiate Athletics (March, 1991)*

....

The Need For Reform

As our nation approaches a new century, the demand for reform of intercollegiate athletics has escalated dramatically. Educational and athletics leaders face the challenge of controlling costs, restraining recruiting, limiting time demands, and restoring credibility and dignity to the term "student-athlete." In the midst of these pressures, it is easy to lose sight of the achievements of intercollegiate sports and easier still to lose sight of why these games are played.

....

Games and sports are educational in the best sense of that word because they teach the participant and the observer new truths about testing oneself and others, about the enduring values of challenge and response, about teamwork, discipline and perseverance. Above all, intercollegiate contests—at any level of skill—drive home a fundamental lesson: Goals worth achieving will be attained only through effort, hard work and sacrifice, and sometimes even these will not be enough to overcome the obstacles life places in our path.

....

All of the positive contributions that sports make to higher education, however, are threatened by disturbing patterns of abuse, particularly in some big-time programs. These patterns are grounded in institutional indifference, presidential neglect, and the growing commercialization of sport combined with the urge to win at all costs. The sad truth is that on too many campuses big-time revenue sports are out of control.

....

A New Model: "One-Plus-Three"

Individual institutions and the NCAA have consistently dealt with problems in athletics by defining most issues as immediate ones: curbing particular abuses, developing nationally uniform standards, or creating a "level playing field" overseen by athletics administrators.

But the real problem is not one of curbing particular abuses. It is a more central need to have academic administrators define the terms under which athletics will be conducted in the university's name. The basic concern is not nationally uniform standards. It is a more fundamental issue of grounding the regulatory process in the primacy of academic values. The root difficulty is not creating a "level playing field." It is insuring that those on the field are students as well as athletes.

We reject the argument that the only realistic solution to the problem is to drop the student-athlete concept, put athletes on the payroll, and reduce or even eliminate their responsibilities as students.

Such a scheme has nothing to do with education, the purpose for which colleges and universities exist. Scholarship athletes are already paid in the most meaningful way possible: with a free education. The idea of intercollegiate athletics is that the teams represent their institutions as true members of the student body, not as hired hands. Surely American higher education has the ability to devise a better solution to the problems of intercollegiate athletics than making professionals out of the players, which is no solution at all but rather an unacceptable surrender to despair.

It is clear to the Commission that a realistic solution will not be found without a serious and persistent commitment to a fundamental concept: intercollegiate athletics must reflect the values of the university. Where the realities of intercollegiate competition challenge those values, the university must prevail.

The reform we seek takes shape around what the Commission calls the "one-plus-three" model. It consists of the "one"—presidential control—directed toward the "three"—academic integrity, financial integrity and accountability through certification. This model is fully consistent with the university as a context for vigorous and exciting intercollegiate competition. It also serves to bond athletics to the purposes of the university in a way that provides a new framework for their conduct.

The three sides of the reform triangle reinforce each other. Each strengthens the other two. At the same time, the three principles can only be realized through presidential leadership. The coach can only do so much to advance academic values. The athletics director can only go so far to guarantee financial integrity. The athletics department cannot certify itself. But the president, with a transcendent responsibility for every aspect of the university, can give shape and focus to all three.

With such a foundation in place, higher education can renew its authentic claim on public confidence in the integrity of college sports. All of the subordinate issues and problems of intercollegiate athletics — athletic dorms, freshman eligibility, the length of playing seasons and recruitment policies — can be resolved responsibly within this model. Without such a base, athletics reform is doomed to continue in fits and starts, its energy rising and falling with each new headline, its focus shifting to respond to each new manifestation of the underlying problems. It is the underlying problems, not their symptoms, that need to be attacked. The "one-plus-three" model is the foundation on which those who care about higher education and student-athletes can build permanent reform.

THE "ONE": PRESIDENTIAL CONTROL

Presidents are accountable for the major elements in the university's life. The burden of leadership falls on them for the conduct of the institution, whether in the classroom or on the playing field. The president cannot be a figurehead whose leadership applies elsewhere in the university but not in the athletics department.

The following recommendations are designed to advance presidential control:

1. **Trustees should explicitly endorse and reaffirm presidential authority in all matters of athletic governance**. The basis of presidential authority on campus is the governing board. If presidential action is to be effective, it must have the backing of the board of trustees. We recommend that governing boards:

- Delegate to the president administrative authority over financial matters in the athletics program.
- Work with the president to develop common principles for hiring, evaluating and evaluating and terminating all athletics administrators, and affirm the president's role and ultimate authority in this central aspect of university administration.
- Advise each new president of its expectations about athletics administration and annually review the athletics program.
- Work with the president to define the faculty's role, which should be focused on academic issues in athletics.

2. **Presidents should act on their obligation to control conferences**. We believe that presidents of institutions affiliated with athletics conferences should exercise effective voting control of these organizations....

3. **Presidents should control the NCAA**. The Knight Commission believes hands-on presidential involvement in NCAA decision-making is imperative....

....

4. **Presidents should commit their institutions to equity in all aspects of intercollegiate athletics**. The Commission emphasizes that continued inattention to the requirements of Title IX (mandating equitable treatment of women in educational programs) represents a major stain on institutional integrity. It is essential that presidents take the lead in this area.

5. **Presidents should control their institution's involvement with commercial television**....In the Commission's view it is crucial that presidents, working through appropriate conference and NCAA channels, immediately and critically review contractual relationships with networks. It is time that institutions clearly prescribe the policies, terms and conditions of the televising of intercollegiate athletics events. Greater care must be given to the needs and obligations of the student-athlete and the primacy of the academic calendar over the scheduling, requirements of the networks.

THE "THREE": ACADEMIC INTEGRITY

The first consideration on a university campus must be academic integrity. The fundamental premise must be that athletes are students as well. They should not be considered for enrollment at a college or university unless they give reasonable promise of being successful at that institution in a course of study leading to an academic degree. Student-athletes should undertake the same courses of study offered to other students and graduate in the same proportion as those who spend comparable time as full-time students. Their academic performance should be measured by the same criteria applied to other students.

....

The Commission's recommendations on academic integrity can be encapsulated in a very simple concept — "No Pass, No Play." That concept, first developed for high school athletics eligibility in Texas, is even more apt for institutions

of higher education. It applies to admissions, to academic progress and to graduation rates.

The following recommendations are designed to advance academic integrity:

1. **The NCAA should strengthen initial eligibility requirements.** Proposition 48
has served intercollegiate athletics well. It has helped insure that more student-
athletes are prepared for the rigors of undergraduate study It is time to build on
and extend its success. We recommend that:

- By 1995 prospective student-athletes should present 15 units of high
  school academic work in order to be eligible to play in their first year.
- A high school student-athlete should be *ineligible* for reimbursed campus
  visits or for signing a letter of intent until the admissions office indicates he
  or she shows reasonable promise of being able to meet the requirements
  for a degree.
- Student-athletes transferring from junior colleges should meet the admissions requirements applied to other junior college students. Moreover, junior college transfers who did not meet NCAA Proposition 48 requirements when they graduated from high school should be required to sit out
  a year of competition after transfer.
- Finally, we propose an NCAA study of the conditions under which colleges
  and universities admit athletes. This study should be designed to see if it is
  feasible to put in place admissions requirements to insure that the range of
  academic ability for incoming athletes, by sport, would approximate the
  range of abilities for the institution's freshman class.

2. **The letter of intent should serve the student as well as the athletics department.** Incoming freshmen who have signed a letter of intent to attend a particular
institution should be released from that obligation if the head coach who recruited them leaves the institution, or if the institution is put on probation by the
NCAA, before they enroll. Such incoming student-athletes should be automatically eligible to apply to any other college or university, except the head or assistant coach's new home, and to participate in intercollegiate athletics....

3. **Athletics scholarships should be offered for a five-year period.** In light of
the time demands of athletics competition, we believe that eligibility should
continue to be limited to a period of four years, but athletics scholarship assistance routinely should cover the time required to complete a degree, up to a
maximum of five years. Moreover, the initial offer to the student-athlete should
be for the length of time required to earn a degree up to five years, not the single
year now mandated by NCAA rules. The only athletics condition under which
the five-year commitment could be broken would be if the student refused to
participate in the sport for which the grant-in-aid was offered. Otherwise, aid
should continue as long as the student-athlete remains in good standing at the
institution.

4. **Athletics eligibility should depend on progress toward a degree.** In order to
retain eligibility, enrolled athletes should be able to graduate within five years and
to demonstrate progress toward that goal each semester....

5. **Graduation rates of athletes should be a criterion for NCAA certification.** ...

THE "THREE": FINANCIAL INTEGRITY

An institution of higher education has an abiding obligation to be a responsible steward of all the resources that support its activities — whether in the form of taxpayers' dollars, the hard-earned payments of students and their parents, the contributions of alumni, or the revenue stream generated by athletics programs. In this respect, the responsibility of presidents and trustees is singular.

. . . .

The Commission therefore recommends that:

1. **Athletics costs must be reduced.** . . .

2. **Athletics grants-in-aid should cover the full cost of attendance for the very needy** . . . . [W]e recommend that grants-in-aid for low-income athletes be expanded to the "full cost of attendance," including personal and miscellaneous expenses, as determined by federal guidelines.

3. **The independence of athletics foundations and booster clubs must be curbed.** . . . All funds raised for athletics should be channeled into the university's financial system and subjected to the same budgeting procedures applied to similarly structured departments and programs.

4. **The NCAA formula for sharing television revenue from the national basketball championship must be reviewed by university presidents.** . . . The Commission recommends that the [revenue-sharing plan for distributing television and championship dollars] be reviewed annually by the Presidents Commission during the seven-year life of the current television contract and adjusted as warranted by experience.

5. **All athletics-related coaches' income should be reviewed and approved by the university.** . . . As part of the effort to bring athletics-related income into the university, we recommend that the NCAA ban shoe and equipment contracts with individual coaches. If a company is eager to have an institution's athletes using its product, it should approach the institution not the coach.

6. **Coaches should be offered long-term contracts**. Academic tenure is not appropriate for most coaches, unless they are *bona fide* members of the faculty. But greater security in an insecure field is clearly reasonable. . . .

7. **Institutional support should be available for intercollegiate athletics.** The Commission starts from the premise that properly administered intercollegiate athletics programs have legitimate standing in the university community. In that light, general funds can appropriately be used when needed to reduce the pressure on revenue sports to support the entire athletics program. . . .

THE "THREE": CERTIFICATION

The third leg of our triangle calls for independent authentication by an outside body of the integrity of each institution's athletics program. . . .

The academic and financial integrity of college athletics is in such low repute that authentication by an outside agency is essential. Periodic independent assessments of a program can go a long way toward guaranteeing that the athletics culture on campus responds to academic direction, that expenditures are routinely reviewed, that the president's authority is respected by the board of trustees, and that the trustees stand for academic values when push comes to shove in the athletics department.

Regarding independent certification, the Commission therefore recommends:

1. **The NCAA should extend the certification process to all institutions granting athletics aid....**

2. **Universities should undertake comprehensive, annual policy audits of their athletics program.** We urge extending the annual financial audit now required by the NCAA to incorporate academic issues and athletics governance. The new annual review should student-athletes' admissions records, academic progress and graduation rates, as well as the athletics department's management and budget. This activity should serve as preventive maintenance to insure institutional integrity and can provide the annual raw data to make the certification process effective.

3. **The certification program should include the major themes put forth in this document.** If the new certification program is to be effective and institutions are to meet its challenge.... This document concludes with ten principles that, in the form of a restatement of the Commission's implementing recommendations, can serve as a vehicle for such self-examination. We urge the NCAA to incorporate these principles into the certification process.

....

PRINCIPLES FOR ACTION

It is clear that this nationwide effort must grow from our campuses. We have reduced the essence of our concerns to the "one-plus-three" model. We have expanded this model through the implementing recommendations that form the core of Chapter II. But the question remains, where to begin?

We believe that any institution wishing to take seriously the "one-plus-three" model would do well to start with the following statement of principles which recasts this report's main themes. We urge presidents to make this statement the vehicle for serious discussions within their institutions and, in particular, with the members of the governing board. Each principle is significant. Each deserves a separate conversation. Together they can define what the university expects, and how it hopes to realize its expectations.

A STATEMENT OF PRINCIPLES

...This institution is committed to a philosophy of firm institutional control of athletics, to the unquestioned academic and financial integrity of our athletics program, and to the accountability of the athletics department to the values and goals befitting higher education. In support of that commitment, the board, officers, faculty and staff of this institution have examined and agreed to the following general principles as a guide to our participation in intercollegiate athletics:

I.   The educational values, practices and mission of this institution determine the standards by which we conduct our intercollegiate athletics program.

II.   The responsibility and authority for the administration of the athletics department, including all basic policies, personnel and finances, are vested in the president.

III. The welfare, health and safety of student-athletes are primary concerns of athletics administration on this campus. This institution will provide student-athletes with the opportunity for academic experiences as close as possible to the experiences of their classmates,

IV.   Every student-athlete — male and female, majority and minority, in all sports — will receive equitable and fair treatment.

V.   The admission of student-athletes — including junior college transfers — will be based on their showing reasonable promise of being successful in a course of study leading to an academic decree. That judgment will be made by admissions officials.

VI. Continuing eligibility to participate in intercollegiate athletics will be based on students being able to demonstrate each academic term that they will graduate within five years of their enrolling. Students who do not pass this test will not play.

VII. Student-athletes, in each sport, will be graduated in at least the same proportion as non-athletes who have spent comparable time as full-time students.

VIII. All funds raised and spent in connection with intercollegiate athletics programs will be channeled through the institution's general treasury, not through independent groups, whether internal or external. The athletics department budget will be developed and monitored in accordance with general budgeting procedures on campus.

IX. All athletics-related income from non-university sources for coaches and athletics administrators will be reviewed and approved by the university. In cases where the income involves the university's functions, facilities or name, contracts will be negotiated with the institution.

X.   We will conduct annual academic and fiscal audits of the athletics program. Moreover, we intend to seek NCAA certification that our athletics program complies with the principles herein. We will promptly correct any deficiencies and will conduct our athletics program in a manner worthy of this distinction.

We believe these ten principles represent a statement around which our institutions and the NCAA can rally. It is our hope that this statement of principles will be incorporated into the Association's developing certification program. The Commission believes that the success of the NCAA certification program must be judged on the degree to which it advances these principles as the fundamental ends of intercollegiate programs. Ideally, institutions will agree to schedule only those colleges and universities that have passed all aspects of the certification process: Institutions that refuse to correct deficiencies will find themselves isolated by the vast majority of athletics administrators who support intercollegiate athletics as an honorable tradition in college life.

The members of the Knight Foundation Commission are convinced, as we know most members of the public and of the athletic and academic worlds are convinced, that changes are clearly required in intercollegiate athletics. Making these changes will require courage, determination and perseverance on the part of us all. That courage, determination and perseverance must be summoned. Without them, we cannot move forward. But with them and the "one-plus-three" model we cannot be held back. The combination makes it possible to keep faith with our student-athletes, with our institutions, and with the public that wants the best for them both.

(b) Commentary

John R. Thelin, Games Colleges Play: Scandal and Reform in Intercollegiate Athletics 1–3, 197–99 (1994)*

INTRODUCTION

American Higher Education's "Peculiar Institution"

Intercollegiate athletics are American higher education's "peculiar institution." Their presence is pervasive, yet their proper balance with academics remains puzzling. A visit to a typical large American university indicates the remarkable prominence of varsity sports: a football stadium seating sixty thousand, a basketball arena for fifteen thousand, an indoor football practice complex, and perhaps a dormitory complex or training center reserved for varsity athletes are all facilities virtually unknown at universities in other countries yet taken for granted in the United States. A glance at a university budget shows that annual operation of a large varsity sports program costs about the same as running a professional school in engineering, law, or even medicine. It is standard practice for a head football or basketball coach to be paid at least as much as an academic dean. Today at some American universities, the varsity football coach draws a base salary that exceeds that of the president—an arrangement that, although unusual, is not deemed inappropriate by some boards of trustees.

For all this prominence, the place of intercollegiate athletics in the priorities of the university remains unclear. In contrast to the publicity generated by winning teams, a detailed budget for an intercollegiate athletics program remains one of the most inaccessible documents. Even though sports information directors readily provide press guides with detailed statistics on basketball players' field goal percentages or teams' victories from past and present, athletic directors claim they do not have sufficient staff to compile the annual graduation rates of student-athletes. A check of institutional accreditation self-studies, mission statements, and annual reports suggests that an American university seldom discusses intercollegiate athletics as part of its primary purposes of teaching, research, and service. The irony of this silence is that, for many universities, big-time athletics stand out as a central activity, a program likely to be protected and promoted.

This blurred identity also characterizes the place of college sports in institutional governance. Athletic directors often report directly to university presidents, which indicates an access to leadership and decision making that far exceeds the privileges of an academic dean. At some universities, a head coach (usually of football or men's basketball) may also serve as athletic director, creating a strange reporting arrangement conducive to self-dealing and relatively unchecked concentration of administrative power within a department. Foundations, associations, and fund-raising groups incorporated for the special purpose of supporting a university's sports program often become fiefdoms that gain leverage from their affiliation with the campus and use of the name and logo of the university, but with only limited accountability to the host institution. These special sports foundations and associations typically have their own board of directors, staff, and pay-

---

roll and often marginal requirements for reporting to the university's administration or board. Meanwhile, in formal reports about institutional mission and structure, universities usually bury intercollegiate athletics among extracurricular activities or auxiliary enterprises, masking their actual importance.

How do we explain such peculiar arrangements? What is the place of intercollegiate athletics in terms of the governance and organization of the American university? How do colleges and universities characterize intercollegiate athletics in relation to educational purposes? How does the funding of intercollegiate athletics compare with financial arrangements for other institutional departments and activities? And, to each of these queries, we need to add an important historical dimension: How, over time, have intercollegiate athletics come to occupy their distinctive, peculiar place within the American campus?

University officials historically have shown a tendency to avoid reconciling their commitment to and investment in intercollegiate athletics with the educational mission of the institution. There is a slippery quality that characterizes the justifications that university presidents and athletic directors invoke when they are asked to explain the connection between college sports and higher education. At one time, college sports are described as an educational activity, often praised for their power to "build character"; at another time, intercollegiate athletics are conveniently endorsed for having contributed to institutional publicity and prestige, or they are depicted as helpful to university fund raising, with benefits supposedly accruing to the entire institution. On closer inspection, these separate, shifting claims constitute a liturgy, not substantiated conclusions. The rationales are not wholly convincing because they are untested claims and, if taken together, are often inconsistent, even conflicting.

A corollary is that although avoiding scrutiny of college sports as part of higher education may allow campus presidents, deans, and trustees to avoid hard questions over the short run, it is a reprieve that ultimately weakens the institution. It has potential to dilute the administrative credibility of a university president and diverts resources and attention from educational priorities. I have no wish to dictate a single formula for the proper balance of academics and athletics. American higher education is sufficiently diverse to allow for variation and institutional self-determination. Nor is raising these questions to be mistaken for an abolitionist tract. To think of the American campus *without* intercollegiate athletics would be difficult, even undesirable. Rather, my concern is that within American higher education, most institutions have been reluctant to study and accurately state what their own policies, practices, and priorities involving intercollegiate athletics are—while at the same time they have resisted public review, external scrutiny, or oversight.

. . . .

EPILOGUE

An American Dilemma: Balancing Academics and Athletics

Four national reports—the 1929 Carnegie Foundation study, the 1952 Presidents' Report for the American Council on Education, George Hanford's 1974 study for the American Council on Education, and the 1991 Knight Foundation Commission study—are significant events in attempts to reform intercollegiate athletics over the past six decades. The four reports displayed remarkable similarities of theme and vocabulary: commitment to the idea of the student-athlete; acknowledgment that varsity athletics were important to the college experience; and praise for the role of the coach as teacher. All four emphasized that college and university presidents must be centrally involved if athletic programs were to be an appropriate, accountable part of higher education. They warned against commercialization of college sports and its imbalanced dependence on media and constituencies outside the campus. Finally, the reports portrayed the excesses of recruitment, athletic scholarships, and special privileges as corruption of the student-athlete ideal.

This liturgy suggests that college sports have achieved continuity in twentieth-century American life as a distinctive part of both higher education and popular culture, an activity whose importance has also made it a source of perennial problems. The recurrence of the same language and motifs in the national studies every two decades or so leaves a perplexing question: if the reform reports were consequential, why have the same problems persisted without solutions over more than a half century? What reforms have taken root?

One explanation is that invocation of the same themes and words by each generation of sports reformers has tended to obscure an unfortunate drift. The vocabulary has remained the same, but the expectations have changed almost beyond recognition. For example, in both 1930 and 1990 one could talk about the "student-athlete" while overlooking the social fact that the meanings were markedly different. To read the four reports without attention to the specific conditions at the time each was published reinforces the impression that amateurism and academic control endured as the "right thing" for colleges to pursue. When one looks at the debates and proposals that followed publication of each report, it also becomes evident that an equally durable legacy has been the capacity of athletic departments and their supporters to defer publicly to the rhetoric of reform while simultaneously diluting the intent of the new policies and proposals. "Reform" all too often took the form of capitulation to and accommodation of professionalism. To argue that this has been a pragmatic and realistic adaptation to America's commercial and competitive culture conveniently explains away the right and the obligation of a college or university to offer a distinctive experience, including that of the genuine student-athlete.

Certainly there have been substantial changes in the organization and control of college sports since 1929. Intercollegiate athletics, once a chaotic, unregulated activity, have become one of the most sophisticated and codified enterprises in American life. However, the gestures toward codification and control have often represented the ironies of reform; that is, they have perfected and perpetuated some of the very practices they were intended to correct. The student-athlete came to be the athlete-student. The organizational revolution has been the assent of the incorporated athletic association, a structure that has allowed athletic directors and boosters to create, basically on their own terms, a privileged entity attached to the university. The ability of the NCAA to organize, promote, and control college sports has been an equally awesome success story. Such accomplishments have not necessarily involved sound educational reforms.

Another interesting legacy of the four reports is that in each episode organized intercollegiate athletics has tended to resist systematic analysis, often because many of the favorable characteristics attributed to high-powered college sports programs have been either untestable or exaggerated. This siege mentality has perpetuated the erroneous stereotype that those who have studied the condition and character of college sports were by definition a lunatic fringe intent on abolishing varsity sports. It is important to keep in mind that, historically, most charges of corruption have been family feuds within the ranks of major conferences in which one coach or athletic official has made accusations about another. . . .

A watchword of the four reform reports has been to balance, not abolish, intercollegiate athletics. To advocate that college sports ought to be fused with scholarly programs has left the historical puzzle that in each era it was not clear how that fusion should take place. Once in a while, the two spheres of high-powered academics and athletics have coincided, but even this has not always been a panacea. For example, in September 1991 an article in the *Washington Post* reported that the University of Michigan used federal research grant money to cover entertainment expenses for the Rose Bowl game, an incident that led to an investigation by a House of Representatives subcommittee. So, although the university had achieved a "balance" and an "integration" of sorts, it had not convincingly fulfilled the more subtle task of maintaining a proper balance of academics and athletics. It also was a reminder that academic leaders, not only athletic officials, have often been involved in the activities of college sports that lead to the dubious games colleges play.

Robert N. Davis, Athletic Reform: Missing the Bases in University Athletics
20 Capital University Law Review 597 (1991)*

. . . .

INTRODUCTION

. . . .

The 85th annual convention of the National Collegiate Athletic Association (NCAA), held in Nashville, Tennessee in January, 1991, has been much touted as the "Reform Convention. . . ."

The Reform Convention completed its business with what many of its delegates view as significant changes in the direction of intercollegiate athletics. In baseball parlance, these delegates believe that they have hit a home run based on the reform measures passed. . . .

The convention delegates may have hit a home run, but, in my view, they have missed the bases by failing to address some of the critical problems facing college sports. Allow, if you will, each base to symbolize one of these fundamental problems. First base represents the need for stressing the importance of academics. Second base represents the need to remove commercialism from intercollegiate athletics. Third base represents the need to more clearly define the relationship that exists between our institutions of higher learning and student-athletes. Finally, home plate represents the need for the NCAA to adopt clear policies on the

---

three preceding subjects. When the NCAA succeeds in implementing these policies in their proper order, it will have touched upon all the bases, and the result will be a legitimate home run. At present, however, the NCAA must either go back and touch the bases it has missed or risk being tagged out.

I. REFORM MEASURES PASSED AT THE 1991 NCAA CONVENTION

. . . .

A. *First Base: Academic Reform*

The January, 1991 NCAA convention has been referred to as the convention with the "most extensive package of major legislative proposals at any single convention in NCAA history," and potentially "one of the most significant meetings in the organization's history."[17] Yet the membership postponed any major academic reform proposals until next year. Granted, it is important to study the area so that the proposals developed adequately address the concerns of the academic and athletic community. Nevertheless, I am troubled by the reluctance of the NCAA delegates to take the intercollegiate athletics bull by the horns and directly address the problem of academic quality.

The reform necessary in intercollegiate athletics cannot be expected to occur overnight. Still, progress will undoubtedly be severely impeded if those areas needing the most attention are not addressed first. Ideally, I would have preferred to see the 1991 convention focus on academic integrity and commercialism. Instead, the 1991 convention delegates directed their efforts to cost-containment proposals—ways of marginally reducing athletic department costs. Although cost containment is a worthwhile end in itself, in this instance it merely diverted attention from more important problems encountered in intercollegiate athletics.

The 1991 Convention delegates did succeed in passing Proposal No. 58, which operates under NCAA Bylaw 14 governing academic and general requirements. Proposal No. 58 directs the Academic Requirements Committee to develop proposed legislation for the 1992 convention that would strengthen the NCAA requirements for initial and continuing eligibility.

Proposal No. 81 was also passed. This proposal requires Division I institutions to define their own satisfactory progress rules. At a minimum, however, each institution must define satisfactory progress to include successful completion by student-athletes of fifty percent of the course requirements in their respective majors before the beginning of their fourth year.

These are the only academic reform measures adopted at the so called "Reform Convention." A cursory examination reveals that, in and of themselves, these measures are not reforms at all. They are simply promises to look at the problem, again, in the future. Thus, in my view, the NCAA missed first base by not devoting more of this year's reform agenda to academic proposals.

B. *Second Base: Commercialism Reform*

A review of the convention voting summary in the NCAA News reveals not one proposal relating to the removal of commercialism from intercollegiate ath-

---

17. Robert N. Davis, *Academics and Athletics on a Collision Course*, 66 N.D. L. Rev. 239, 266 (1990)[hereinafter Davis].

letics. Noticeably absent from any of the proposed reform legislation is any attempt by the NCAA to more equitably distribute its basketball championship
television revenues among all of its member schools.

Ironically, the one proposal passed by the delegates involving commercialism is
Proposal No. 72, involving conference promotional activities under NCAA Bylaw
12 on amateurism. Proposal No. 72 grants permission to a conference to "use a
student-athlete's name, picture or appearance to support its *charitable or educational activities or activities considered incidental to the student-athlete's participation in college athletics*, [emphasis added] as is now permissible for a member
institution...."[24] Thus, while the delegates seem unable to mount an effective
campaign against increasing commercialism in intercollegiate sports, when a hot
student-athlete can attract big crowds and sell tickets, the delegates are very quick
to capitalize on advertising such stars under the guise of promoting the institutions' "charitable and educational activities...."

What has the NCAA done to stem the flow of commercialism? Regrettably, it
has not done much. Prior to the 1991 convention, the NCAA adopted a revenue
distribution plan for the $1 billion television package in which CBS acquired the
right to broadcast the men's NCAA basketball tournament....

....I think that the wrong message is being sent by the NCAA. Rather than discouraging commercialism and encouraging the academic development of student-
athletes, winning is financially rewarded and academic progress is awarded a
mere pittance. Second base remains untouched.

C. *Third Base: Athlete-Institution Relationship Reform (Wages, Hours, and
Working Conditions)*

Missing third base by the NCAA delegates is one of the most disturbing omis-
sions. It is disturbing because the omission demonstrates a reluctance to address a
very fundamental question regarding the nature of the relationship between the
institution and the student-athlete, which is the NCAA's *raison d'etre*.

The measures passed at the convention specifically applicable to the well-being
of the student-athlete resemble those terms and conditions of employment that
are normally contained in a collective bargaining agreement. In my opinion, it
would be better if the NCAA explicitly recognized the relationship which it now
tacitly fosters and treated the student-athletes as employees. If this is ever done,
however, I believe that the same rigorous academic requirements should be applied to these student-athlete-employees as are applied to the general student
body. I also believe that, under these circumstances, the student-athlete should be
provided with the benefits and protections that are legally required of an employment relationship. If both halves of this essentially dual relationship were thus
properly recognized, each could be properly addressed. The student-athlete-employees could then be treated fairly, both as students attaining an education and
as athletes providing a service to the university.

The following proposals regarding the relationship between the university and
the student-athlete were passed during the January, 1991 convention. Again, these
measures bear a great resemblance to those often seen in collective bargaining
agreements pertaining to employer-employee labor relations matters.

---

24. *Id.*

Under NCAA Bylaw 16, which governs awards, benefits, and expenses for student-athletes, Proposal No. 30 was passed. This proposal requires that there be no more wings, floors, or residence halls devoted exclusively to athletes; it is to be implemented within a five-year period. The purpose of this rule is to better integrate the student-athlete into the general university community. However, the new rule presents problems for some coaches; it reduces the ability of coaches to keep track of student-athletes, who may be spread throughout university residence halls. Controlling athletes plays a very important part in a team's overall performance.

Proposal No. 31 prohibits a Division I institution from providing more than one training-table meal a day when other university dining facilities are open. This measure is part of the cost-containment initiative, but it also aims to better integrate student-athletes into the general student body.

Proposal No. 32 requires that a team or individual must leave no earlier than forty-eight hours prior to game time and must depart within thirty-six hours after the competition has concluded. Limited exceptions apply to travel involving Alaska and Hawaii. While this measure has the obvious financial benefit of reducing expenses, it represents yet another example of the extensive controls being placed on student-athletes and the institutions for whom they play. Proposal No. 32-1 permits an exception to these time limitations for NCAA championship competitions.

Proposal No. 64 allows student-athletes participating in NCAA championships to receive awards without limitation on their value. Proposal No. 87 allows athletes to request financial assistance if they have special needs. These funds were established through part of the revenue-distribution plan.

NCAA Bylaw 17 governs playing and practice seasons and includes Proposal No. 38, which was passed to reduce time demands on student-athletes by limiting playing and practice seasons. One part of this rule change (38-D) reduces the playing season by four weeks, from twenty-six weeks to twenty-two weeks, for team sports. Football and basketball are excluded. Proposal 38-E mandates that both team and individual sports establish working hours. Specifically, this rule requires Division I and II institutions to limit the number of hours during the day and week spent on "athletically related activities." It also requires that athletes be given one day off each week during the season.

. . . . [After listing and critiquing additional legislative initiatives, Professor Davis concludes as follows. — ed.].

Again, the need for such detailed controls on the demands placed upon student-athletes by institutions is a very strong signal that something is terribly amiss. The NCAA, however, continues to avoid tackling the real problem of adequately defining the institution and student-athlete relationship. The NCAA manual, ideally, should be a clear set of guidelines and principles for intercollegiate sports competition. In lieu of this, the NCAA delegates have passed measures that cause the NCAA manual to resemble a specific labor code. Third base has yet to be tagged.

D. *Other Reform Proposals*

I register my disappointment with the 1991 NCAA Reform Convention because my expectations for reform were very high. After several years of turmoil in intercollegiate athletics, it finally appeared that great strides would be made. Unfortunately, as the aforementioned reform measures demonstrate, the "Reform

Convention" is a misnomer. To more accurately reflect the work that was accomplished, the 1991 Convention should be referred to as the "Tinkering Convention," or the "Labor Code Convention."

. . . .

The 1991 Convention also passed a great number of proposals that do not fall under the "labor code" description. These proposals address a wide variety of subjects and lend to the appearance that the Convention enacted significant reform. Indeed, some of these measures are not unimportant and, certainly, their cumulative effect is more than trivial. . . .

. . . . [Discussion of these proposals is omitted. — ed.].

Again, these rule changes enacted by the 1991 Convention do more to tinker with the workings of the system as it already exists than they do to implement fundamental, systemic reform. I do not mean to sound as though nothing the NCAA does is enough. The proposals that were adopted last year do, in fact, go much further than the convention delegates were willing to go in the past. Yet, many of these rule changes are superficial when compared with the magnitude of the problems in intercollegiate sports. The NCAA needs to do more, for example, than reduce the permissible number of basketball games from twenty-eight to twenty-seven. That is why I maintain that the NCAA missed the bases in its last attempt at bat. The "home run" hit by the 1991 Convention delegates is illusory. They did not safely touch home plate because they failed even to develop clear, unequivocal policies on academics, commercialism, and the student-athlete and institution relationship, much less to implement such policies.

. . . .

CONCLUSION

I do not mean to be entirely negative in my analysis of the efforts of others who have taken on a formidable task. The 1991 NCAA Convention and the Knight Commission do, at least, represent an effort to begin making some very difficult choices. While the bases for meaningful systemic reform were missed, the base runner has not yet been tagged out. The NCAA has an opportunity to return to the playing field and touch the bases before it is tagged out of intercollegiate athletic reform. At least in this turn at bat the NCAA managed to hit the ball, which it was unable to do in many previous attempts. The NCAA has had many opportunities at bat, but it has consistently failed to touch the bases when the ball was hit. Perhaps we should allow a pinch hitter to step in for the NCAA. I do not believe that the pinch hitter should be Congress or the states. Perhaps an independent regulatory body, one that is not comprised of the same membership that is being regulated, could take to the base paths and touch the bases. . . .

―――――――――――

Rodney K. Smith, An Academic Game Plan for Reforming Big-Time Intercollegiate Athletics
67 Denver University Law Review 213 (1990)

I. INTRODUCTION

. . . .

....I contend in this article that reform must combine elements of arguments made by both schools. Structural changes are necessary. Any substantive reform efforts must be supported by structures that are designed to strengthen the voice of those who support reforms of an academic nature. Additionally, structural reforms must be accompanied by substantive reforms. In both structural and substantive areas, the focus must be on academic values. Indeed, one of the major problems with reform efforts to date is that they have lacked a coherent and unified focus, a focus that must be centered on academic values. To date, the NCAA has purported to rely on various purposes and principles in its efforts to govern intercollegiate athletics. While the educational value is one of those principles, perhaps even the principal value adhered to by the NCAA in its efforts to regulate big-time intercollegiate athletics, the NCAA has never adequately focused its reforms on that value. The NCAA has never had a coherent and unified game plan based on academic values; rather, it has simply moved from play to play, reform to reform, without any sense of unified academic purpose. The NCAA has also lacked focus in its reform efforts because it has continued to adhere to values, such as amateurism, that have little to do with the realities of big-time intercollegiate athletics.

In this article, therefore, after explicating the values the NCAA purports to adhere to in regulating intercollegiate athletics, I begin by arguing that the NCAA should jettison the amateurism principle, at least in the governance of the big-time, revenue-producing sports. By ceasing to adhere to the amateurism value, the NCAA and others in a position to influence the reform of intercollegiate athletics can assure that the reform focuses on academic values and can avoid the dissonance and disillusionment related to the sense that NCAA is inherently suspect because it indulges in hypocrisy when it asserts amateurism on the one hand and signs a $1 billion television contract for televising big-time basketball on the other hand. In addition to jettisoning the amateurism value, the NCAA must create or refine governance structures that will aid in the development of a unified package of reforms. The NCAA needs an academic game plan, not a sporadic effort at piecemeal reform. The NCAA should design a long-range plan for reform based on academic values.

....

II. AN EXAMINATION OF THE VALUES THAT OUGHT TO SERVE AS THE FOUNDATION FOR BIG-TIME INTERCOLLEGIATE ATHLETICS (AND THOSE THAT SHOULD NOT)

In Article 1 of the NCAA Constitution, the fundamental policy or basic purpose of the Association is set forth:

> The competitive athletics programs of member institutions are designed to be a vital part of the educational system. A basic purpose of this Association is to maintain intercollegiate athletics as an integral part of the educational program and the athlete as an integral part of the student body and, by so doing, retain a clear line of demarcation between intercollegiate athletics and professional sports.[16]

---

16. NCAA Const. art. I, § 1.3.1. *reprinted in* NATIONAL COLLEGIATE ATHLETIC ASS'N. 1989-90 NCAA MANUAL 1 (1989) [hereinafter NCAA MANUAL].

Actually, this policy states two basic values or purposes: (1) the educational value, maintaining intercollegiate athletics as an integral part of the educational program, and (2) the amateurism value, retaining a clear line of demarcation between intercollegiate athletics and professional sports. These two values or purposes may be complementary in some instances, but, as will be argued in this article, they are separable. For example, an athletic event can be amateur in nature without being an integral part of an educational program, and as I argue in the following section, an athletic program may be commercialized without necessarily compromising its role as an integral part of an educational enterprise.

Thirteen principles for the conduct of intercollegiate athletics by members of the NCAA are delineated in Article 2 of the NCAA Constitution. Those principles can largely be grouped under either the educational value, the amateurism value, or the value of equal competition. This third value of equal competition often is referred to as the need for a "level playing field," and is designed to ensure that no school is given benefits that are not also made available under the NCAA rules to other similarly situated institutions. . . .

A. *The Educational Value*

As previously noted, the educational value is set forth in Section 1.3.1 of Article 1 of the NCAA Constitution. Arguably, it received further support and definition in Sections 2.2 and 2.4 of Article 2 of the Constitution. Respectively, those provisions provide as follows:

> 2.2. THE PRINCIPLE OF STUDENT-ATHLETE WELFARE.
> Intercollegiate athletics programs shall be conducted in a manner designed to protect and enhance the physical and educational welfare of student-athletes.[18]
> 2.4. THE PRINCIPLE OF SOUND ACADEMIC STANDARDS. Intercollegiate athletics programs shall be maintained as a vital component of the educational program and student-athletes shall be an integral part of the student body. The admission, academic standing and academic progress of student-athletes shall be consistent with the policies and standards adopted by the institution for the student body in general.[19]

Together with Section 1.3.1 of Article 1, these sections make it clear that the NCAA professes to adhere closely to academic or educational values in the governance of intercollegiate athletics, including big-time, revenue-producing sports at the collegiate level. Most commentators favor tying the regulation and reform of big-time intercollegiate athletics to educational values or principles, although some recent advocates of major reform in intercollegiate athletics believe that big-time, commercialized athletics at the collegiate level cannot be tied to academic or educational values. The skeptics, however, claim that in order to avoid hypocrisy, institutions ought to recognize that their commercialized athletics programs cannot be effectively tied to pristine educational values.

    . . . .

. . . [E]ven proponents of reforms that would divorce much of big-time athletics from the academic world argue that they do so in order to strengthen educational values. Thus, significant unanimity remains among the disputants regarding the

---

18. *Id.* at 3.
19. *Id.*

issue of maintaining academic or educational values and standards in intercollegiate athletics. Nevertheless, little attention has been brought to bear on the issue of what educational or academic values inhere directly or indirectly in intercollegiate athletics. This unwillingness to focus on those issues in a thoughtful way is exacerbated by the reaction of academics who assert that big-time athletics is not a "critical ingredient" of the academic life of the university. Thus, whether as a matter of academic hostility to athletics, which may itself be based on some lingering class bias, or simply a lack of analytical focus due to inattention to detail, the interplay between big-time athletics and education has been woefully underscrutinized....

....[A] very important part of any effort to assess reform proposals from an academic vantage point, or in terms of educational values, preliminarily must deal with the issue of whether big-time intercollegiate athletics are educational or can be operated to further educational values.

Donna Lopiano, associate athletic director at the University of Texas, has argued that:

> Athletics, like music, art and drama is performing art. The athletic contest is no different than the theater or the symphony, albeit the audience appears to be more rabid...Athletics and theater must be, at their heart, laboratory settings where the exceptionally talented student maximizes his or her potential.[32]

In her remarks, Lopiano added that, "[i]t is only when we define athletics as an educational program very closely comparable to an academic entity that we finally possess the litmus paper with which we can test the legislative and other answers to problems in athletics, which have evaded resolution for close to 80 years." Thus, at least in one sense, it can argued that participation in athletics is comparable to participation in the orchestra or drama and can provide a litmus test for assessing reform efforts. In this regard, it would also seem that big-time athletics should be supported as part of the academic enterprise, because such athletic opportunities give the athlete the opportunity to refine and develop his or her skill in the crucible of the best competition available. However, despite the appeal of such an argument for those who would argue that athletics are educational, it is not clear why activities such as drama, dance and orchestra are themselves educational, thereby rendering athletics derivatively educational so long as athletics can be related to other performing arts.

....

....[I]n addition to the assertion that participation in athletics is as much a part of the educational enterprise as are drama, dance and other performing arts, it can be argued that big-time athletics, like research, play an important role in serving societal interests. In both instances, however, I remain troubled that we still may be begging the question by merely arguing that by analogy to other practices that are accepted to be a part of the educational enterprise, athletics should be declared to be an apt part of the collegiate academic enterprise. Those other practices — performing arts and research — must themselves be tied to

---

32. NATIONAL COLLEGIATE ATHLETIC ASSOCIATION, SIXTH SPECIAL CONVENTION PROCEEDINGS 72 (1987), cited in Smith, *Reforming Intercollegiate Athletics: A Critique of the Presidents Commission's Role in the NCAA's Sixth Special Convention*, 64 N. DAK. L. REV. 423, 450 (1988) [hereinafter Smith, *Sixth Special Convention*].

some educational theory, and then athletics could be assessed in light of that theory, not only by analogy to the practices that purportedly comply with the underlying theory. Furthermore, stating that athletics, like research, perform a service function, without further explication of the nature of that service is to indulge in incomplete analysis. One must examine the nature of the service arising out of big-time intercollegiate athletics in order to support athletics as academics on such grounds.

President Gordon Gee of the University of Colorado recently argued for a third sense in which athletics can be considered to be an integral part of the educational enterprise. He noted that, "[c]ollegiate athletic competition had its origins in the Greek ideal of education. Apart from intellectual and aesthetic development, physical education and competition were essential to molding character...."

Big-time intercollegiate athletics may support the educational enterprise in other direct ways. Allen Guttman has noted that, "[i]n sport we can discover the euphoric sense of wholeness, autonomy, and potency which is often denied us in the dreary rounds of routinized work that are the fate of most men and women."

....

As each of the preceding arguments for the tie between athletics and the educational enterprise indicate, it can be argued with some force that athletics is and should be an integral part of collegiate education....

Care must be taken to protect both the micro interest of the student-athlete and the macro interests of the educational institution itself in analyzing any reform package demonstrated by the interplay between Section 2.2 of Article II of the NCAA Constitution, calling for the protection of the physical and educational welfare of student-athletes, and Section 2.4, requiring that intercollegiate athletic programs be maintained "as a vital component of the educational program." For the sake of its own institutional integrity, an institution must evaluate the role that athletics plays at the institution generally. Additionally, for the sake of its ethical and educational duty to its individual students, the institution and other entities involved in governing intercollegiate athletics must be attentive to the educational needs of the student-athletes. Indeed, care must be taken to ensure that structural and substantive reforms address the need to protect the student-athlete's interest, particularly given the student-athlete's relative lack of power in the decisionmaking process related to the governance of intercollegiate athletics.

As such, I assert that every reform package, my own included, must be evaluated to ascertain whether or not it directly furthers educational purposes both at the institutional and the student-athlete levels. If those questions are not raised and analyzed, then decisions will necessarily be suspect....

B. *The Amateurism Value*

As previously noted, both Sections 1.3.1 and 2.6 of Articles I and II, respectively, of the NCAA Constitution require that attention be given to the principle of amateurism, in evaluating NCAA regulations. In particular, Section 2.6 provides that, "[s]tudent-athletes shall be amateurs in an intercollegiate sport.... Student participation in intercollegiate athletics is an avocation, and student-athletes should be protected from exploitation by professional and commercial enterprises."[46]

---

46. NCAA CONST. art II § 2.6 *reprinted in* NCAA MANUAL, *supra* note 16, at 4.

There is less consensus among commentators regarding the utility of the amateurism value, particulary as relates to the heavily commercialized, revenue-producing sports of Division I-A football and Division I basketball that largely make up big-time intercollegiate athletics. For example, in his recent book assailing big-time intercollegiate football, Rick Telander argued that the concept of amateurism is "corrupt." [47] Relatedly, it has been argued that it is questionable to assert that student-athletes should be protected "from exploitation by... commercial enterprises" when the NCAA has just signed a $1 billion television contract for big-time basketball. Nevertheless, it remains conceivable that amateurism may nevertheless be defended, as it relates to the role of the student-athlete, despite the fact that Division I institutions are on a commercial fast-track. As was the case with academic or educational values, the interests of the student-athlete might be separated from those of the institution. As such, amateurism might need to retain some vitality to protect the student-athlete from exploitation, but not necessarily to eliminate all commercialization of intercollegiate athletics.

It does not take great insight to recognize that assertion of the amateurism value has a certain self-serving allure for the institution, in that it might justify institutional refusals to share the income generated from such athletic events with the athlete who helped to earn it. However, even before assailing the amateurism value on the ground that it is self-serving, it would be worthwhile to examine the value itself as it relates to big-time athletics in the intercollegiate context. To begin with, like "education," amateurism is difficult to define. Professor Ronald Smith has pointed out that we have never come up with "a successful, workable definition of amateurism." [50] In fact, if amateurism means that an athlete does not receive anything of economic value for his or her participation in intercollegiate athletics, it is recognized more in the breach than in reality in both Divisions I and II, because athletes receive scholarships for their participation in many intercollegiate sports at those levels.

. . . .

For a number of reasons, I do not believe that amateurism should continue to be a significant litmus test, except where it can be asserted to protect a student-athlete from actual exploitation. First, amateurism in big-time intercollegiate athletics is anachronistic and may even be reflective of some class bias. It is at best anachronistic and clearly is hypocritical because institutions are generating substantial revenues from their major athletic programs and because intercollegiate athletics have been prone to some degree of professionalism from their very inception. Athletes have been paid; sometimes quite well. However, at least with the rise of the NCAA and its professed allegiance to amateurism, payments beyond those enumerated in the preceding paragraph have been forced underground or under the table. . . .

In addition to being hypocritical, anachronistic and perhaps even biased, the invocation of amateurism as a value critical to the operation of big-time intercollegiate athletics, may inhibit the necessary focus on the educational value. Indeed, amateurism seems to be of utility only to the extent that it furthers educational or academic values. The value of amateurism as a principle related to the governance of big-time intercollegiate athletics seems to be related to its capacity to focus on

---

47. TELANDER, *supra* note 7, at 48.
50. *Id.* at 50, (citing R. SMITH, SPORTS AND FREEDOM (1988)).

exploitation that may result from too much attention to economic and commercial matters and too little attention to educational ones. As such, nothing would be lost by focusing solely on the educational value and jettisoning the amateurism value, as applied to big-time intercollegiate athletics. In fact, much might be gained. In particular, enforcing amateurism values may detract from the educational benefits made available to the student-athlete.

Finally, in a related sense, by focusing on the academic needs of student-athletes involved in prominent sports, rather than amateurism, savings might be generated in other areas, including the savings gained by eliminating non-need-based scholarships for minor sports. Indeed, amateurism may have some utility at that level, because if the assertion that there is subtle class bias in the amateurism value applied across the board, to revenue-producing and non-revenue-producing sports, is accurate, then it might be applied to non-revenue-producing sports in an even purer form without raising objections of class bias....

....

C. *The Principle of Competitive Equity*

The principle of competitive equity provides that, "[t]he structure and programs of the Association and the activities of its members shall promote opportunity for equity in competition to assure that individual student-athletes and institutions will not be prevented unfairly from achieving the benefits inherent in participation in intercollegiate athletics."[61] Additionally, this principle is further defined in Article II Section 2.13 of the NCAA Constitution.... Like amateurism, the principle of competitive equity can and should be subsumed in the academic value.

....

Both efficiency and cost-containment are secondary values, in that one must always ask why efficiency and/or cost-containment are important. It is important to save money, but the real importance of such saving relates to what the money saved will be used to produce or acquire. In Section 2.13, of its Constitution, the NCAA seemingly recognizes this when it asserts that such fiscal and related cost-containment practices are necessary to provide "student-athletes with adequate opportunities for athletics competition as an integral part of quality educational experience." Efficiency and cost-containment are important to further the educational value, both in terms of athletic participation as an educational value in itself and in its terms of the indirect benefits accruing to the student-athlete from the efficient operation of intercollegiate athletics. As such, the primary focus should remain on academic or educational values; efficiency and cost-containment should not be permitted to become ultimate ends in themselves. If they were to become ends in themselves, they might be used to temper or dilute the educational value, particularly as it relates to student-athletes involved in big-time intercollegiate athletics....

D. *Summary*

In this Part of my article, I have argued that the educational value, both institutionally and as applied to the particular student-athletes involved in big-time intercollegiate athletics, should be retained and should become the focal point of all efforts to reform the regulation of intercollegiate athletics. Other values espoused by the NCAA, including amateurism, efficiency and cost-containment, are at best secondary, in that they should be used to enhance the educational value, as related to big-time intercollegiate athletics. When those values become ends in themselves, however, they may actually be invoked in manner detrimental to academic values.

Chapter 10
Institutional Relationships

Introduction

This chapter examines the legal and social implications of the relationships existing between the principal participants in intercollegiate athletics: student-athletes, coaches, and institutions. Understanding the legal relationships extant in intercollegiate athletics, however, requires familiarity with broader themes that serve as a backdrop against which the principles, derived from public and private sources, governing college sport have developed. Accordingly, Section (1) includes articles by Timothy Davis and Alfred Mathewson that attempt to provide a broader context within which to examine the legal relationships in intercollegiate athletics. Professor Davis' perspective speaks to the substantial impact of commercial realities on the amateurism and education principles that not only undergird the NCAA regulatory scheme, but influence the propriety of public intervention (judicial and legislative) into college athletics. The author suggests a model that provides an alternative way of defining legal relationships in intercollegiate sports. In proposing a common law for intercollegiate athletics, Professor Mathewson argues that the principal legal rights assigned to collaborators in intercollegiate athletics relate to their right to associate. He suggests that judicial failure adequately to balance rights between student-athletes and their institutions is due, in part, to non-recognition of this fundamental aspect of the relationship. Professor Mathewson's proposed common law or code of intercollegiate athletics would reassign legal rights between the major participants in intercollegiate athletics.

With rare exception, courts and scholars recognize the contractual nature of student-athletes' relationships with their institutions. This contractual relationship is premised principally on the Letter of Intent and the Statement of Financial Assistance. The former is the document pursuant to which the student-athlete promises to attend a particular college and to participate in the institution's intercollegiate athletics program. The validity of the Letter of Intent is conditioned, among other things, on the institution's written commitment to provide financial aid, which is typically expressed in a form document. Timothy Davis, *Absence of Good Faith: Defining A University's Obligation to Student-Athletes*, 28 Hous. L. Rev. 743, 770-71 (1991).

The contractual relationship is the point of departure for understanding the legal relationship between student-athletes and their institutions. Given the pre-eminence of contract in setting the contours of this relationship, it seems appropriate to begin Section (2) with Michael Cozzillio's detailed exploration of the components of this express contractual undertaking.

Although scholars acknowledge the contractual underpinnings of the student-athlete/university relationship, they also argue that the economic and social realities of big-time intercollegiate athletes warrant viewing this relationship from per-spectives that extend beyond its contractual roots. Consistent with this perspec-tive, the next series of articles offers perspectives on reformulating the student-athlete/university relationship. Although suggestions vary, a common theme surfaces—the need for increased judicial scrutiny and thus public ordering of the student-athlete/university relationship. In this regard, the Hilborn article discusses legal mechanisms for imposing duties on institutions, such as an obligation to provide student-athletes with an educational opportunity, that arguably arise from the purported special relationship between these contracting parties. The ar-ticle by Hilborn also argues that the realities of modern day intercollegiate athlet-ics are such that athletic scholarships should represent taxable income under the principal tests applied by courts. Professor Peter Goplerud closes-out Subsection (2) with his proposal for a major reordering of the student-athlete/university rela-tionship—compensating student-athletes. His article examines the range of legal consequences, including tax, labor and antitrust, that could conceivably result from paying student-athletes a stipend for their athletic participation.

---

1. Models of Intercollegiate Athletics

Timothy Davis, Intercollegiate Athletics:
Competing Models and Conflicting Realities
25 Rutgers Law Journal 269 (1994)*

I. INTRODUCTION

Two competing models of intercollegiate athletics emerge from judicial deci-sions and scholarly discourse. Although these models share common elements, they nevertheless reflect sharply contrasting visions of intercollegiate athletics. One model, the amateur/education model, has assumed a position of prominence. Assumptions underlying this model have historically been invoked to influence ju-dicial decisionmaking on matters ranging from student-athlete entitlements to worker's compensation benefits to antitrust challenges to NCAA regulations. Under the prevailing amateur/education model, college sports are an avocation, engaged in by student-athletes to reap the educational, physical, mental, and so-cial benefits presumably derived from athletic competition.

The competing paradigm, the commercial/education model, recognizes the dy-namic influence which commercialism exerts over intercollegiate athletics. The commercial/education model, more closely reflective of the modern day economic realities of college sports, can thus be contrasted with the competing amateur/ed-ucation model, premised on illusory assumptions which fail to acknowledge com-mercialism as the driving force in college athletics.

Dissonance between the amateur/education conceptualization and the present day realities of college sports casts doubt on the legitimacy of employing the principles and values of the amateur education model in judicial decisionmaking. A reexamination of judicial decisions premised on the amateur/education model, in light of the alternative conceptual scheme, demonstrates the need to restructure the rights and responsibilities of participants in college sports. Understanding the assumptions underlying the commercial/education model also elucidates the true reasons for promotion of the amateurism principle.

This Article argues that the values of the amateur/education model no longer adequately function as a basis for analyzing legal issues arising in college sports. Costs ensue from resort to this model for the parameters of analysis: judicial refusal to explicitly recognize the commercial/education model precludes an honest evaluation of the competing interests at work in disputes between a student-athlete and his university.

At the same time, however, affording wider legitimacy to the commercial/education model tacitly accepts the move toward professionalism in college sports. This, in turn, increases the potential liability exposure of colleges and universities with regard to athletic activities. Therefore, practical, social, and economic concerns demonstrate that wholesale adoption of the commercial/education model is far from a cure-all for the complexities of contemporary intercollegiate athletics.

Nonetheless, meaningful opposition to implementation of the commercial/education model in judicial decisionmaking will require conscious deliberation over what intercollegiate athletics should entail, since this model is a true reflection of the forces which currently influence relationships and choices made in intercollegiate athletics. Because the suitability of this or any other vision of intercollegiate athletics cannot be determined until the prevalent models are identified and evaluated, this Article undertakes such a task...

....

II. COMPETING MODELS OF INTERCOLLEGIATE ATHLETICS

A. *The Amateur/Education Model*

1. The Amateur Value

Under the amateur/education model, the student-athlete is viewed as an amateur, and college athletics is considered an integral part of the educational purpose of universities. The NCAA articulates the amateurism principle as follows: "Student-athletes shall be amateurs in an intercollegiate sport.... Student participation in intercollegiate athletics is an avocation, and student-athletes should be protected from exploitation by professional and commercial enterprises."[17]

The principle of amateurism reflects more than a line of demarcation between professional and amateur sports: the student-athlete under the amateur/education model occupies an idealized status, and embodies altruistic values of selflessness, devotion, sacrifice, and purity. The overinflated importance of college and professional sports in American society and the enormous societal expectations which accompany this position makes this ideal all but unobtainable.

---

17. NCAA Const. art. 2, § 2.7, *supra* note 11, at 4.

. . . .

Amateurism in its purest sense means that an athlete is given nothing of pecuniary value in exchange for participating in college sports. In other words, a quid pro quo is absent. Yet, because financial assistance and other tangible benefits accrue to student-athletes, college athletics has spawned a hybrid form of amateurism. Professor Rush refers to this hybrid form of amateurism as "scholarship amateurism."

2. The Education Value

The education principle provides the other prominent feature of the amateur/education conceptual scheme. The education value embodies the notion that college athletics is an integral part of the educational process. Several arguments have been asserted to support this view of college athletics.

Some commentators assert that, like students who participate in performing arts such as orchestra or dance, participants in intercollegiate athletics have an opportunity to define and develop useful skills. Others suggest that because of the physical conditioning and competitiveness inherent in sports, athletics assist in developing the character of student-athletes. Finally, it is thought that college sports provide a sense of community and create healthy diversions for students, and are therefore educational in nature.

The rules and regulations which govern intercollegiate sports also reflect educational values. For example, educational values are protected by Proposition 48, limitations on the number of hours a student-athlete can practice, and minimum academic eligibility requirements. Through its rules and regulations, the "NCAA professes to adhere closely to academic or educational values in the governance of intercollegiate athletics, including big-time, revenue-producing sports at the collegiate level."[33] Indeed, enhancement of the educational value in big-time intercollegiate athletics is the subject of intense debate in, and the goal of, proposed reforms.

3. Evaluating the Amateur/Education Model

The amateur/education model of intercollegiate athletics fails to acknowledge the forces and interests at play within modern day college sports. This model's disregard for a university's financial motive in promoting the success of its athletes and of its programs generally is simply one illustration. Related to this shortcoming is the model's failure to openly address essential features of the student-athlete's relationship with his university.

Moreover, the amateur/education model is premised on values, particularly amateurism, which are themselves anachronistic. Tracing the concept of amateurism to its Greek roots, the amateurism value historically reflected social class bias: only members of the upper and middle classes possessed the resources necessary for travel, equipment and other expenses which an amateur athlete incurred. "[Amateurism] may be anachronistic, in that it is a throwback to an era when only the leisure classes had the time and wherewithal and were permitted to participate in athletics."[39]

---

33. Smith, *supra* note 7, at 217. It should be noted that this article focuses on "big-time intercollegiate sports" which is typically defined as consisting of Division I-A football and Division I basketball, the primary revenue-producing sports.

39. Smith, *supra* note 7, at 225 n.54.

B. *The Commercial/Education Model*

1. Commercialism in College Sports

The commercial/education model of intercollegiate athletics is the competing model which materializes from a review of cases and scholarly literature. This model assumes that college sports is a commercial enterprise subject to the same economic considerations as any other industry. Under this model, economics displaces the principle of amateurism as the controlling force in college sports.

Thus, the commercial/education model envisions college sports as a form of entertainment which derives revenues from gate receipts, radio and television contracts, and alumni contributions. The visibility, pride, and prestige which a winning team or athlete brings to the institution, though less tangible benefits, are other earmarks of the commercialization of college athletics. Thus, a predominant characteristic of this model is that college athletics is a commodity: it is marketed, advertised, and sold like any other product in order to capitalize on the potential benefits of a successful athletic program.

In sum, this model postulates that the desire to enhance revenues and realize other benefits leads to increased pressures on colleges to recruit the best athletes and to field winning teams. Indeed, commercialism and the concomitant pressure to win results in a compromise of the other feature of this model, the educational value.

2. The Education Value

Despite the considerable impact of economic factors on college sports under this model, education remains a component of the commercial/education conceptualization of intercollegiate athletics. The financial aid given to student-athletes provides many educational opportunities that otherwise would not be available. In addition, the desire to retain an academic focus in intercollegiate athletics has precipitated reforms such as Proposition 48's freshman academic requirements, requiring institutions to publish student-athlete graduation rates, limits on the amount of time student-athletes can devote to practice, and minimum grade point average requirements. Finally, the educational component of this conceptual scheme appears in the form of a university's contractual obligation to its student-athlete to provide him with an educational opportunity free from conduct obstructing this pursuit.

The apparent commonality between the models notwithstanding, the educational component of these models are differently situated. The underlying values of the amateur/education model, amateurism and education, are compatible. In contrast, under the commercial/education model, the economic and educational components represent the ever-present tension between commercial and academic interests in college sports.

In sum, the commercial/education model emerges as an alternative conceptual scheme for analyzing the legal issues confronting college sports. Indeed, review of the cases reveals that these two competing models provide the conceptual framework for judicial decisionmaking in this arena. Judicial decisions resolving whether student-athletes are properly considered employees for worker's compensation purposes demonstrate this proposition. As will be seen, legal doctrine and the conceptual model selected converge to dictate the resolution of such issues....

III. DOCTRINAL PARAMETERS

....[A detailed discussion of the purpose of workers' compensation and the tests generally employed to determine entitlement thereto is omitted. — ed.]

C. *Worker's Compensation Decisions Concerning the Rights of Student-Athletes*

Courts are sharply divided over the question of whether a student-athlete on scholarship falls within the scope of worker's compensation statutes. In the first reported decision to address this issue, *University of Denver v. Nemeth*,[85] a student-athlete sought worker's compensation benefits for a back injury sustained during football practice. Nemeth alleged that he was entitled to receive worker's compensation benefits because he was employed to play football for the university and because his injury arose in the course of his employment. The Colorado Supreme Court agreed with Nemeth, and held that Nemeth was an employee injured in the course of his employment. While the court did not specifically rely on either the control or relative nature of the work standards, its recognition of a contractual relationship between Nemeth and the university nevertheless emerged from a sound application of the principles of employment law.

In 1963, a California Appellate Court followed *Nemeth* in recognizing a student-athlete as an employee. *Van Horn v. Industrial Accident Commission*[90] was an action for the worker's compensation death benefits of a student-athlete killed in a plane crash which occurred en route from an intercollegiate football game.

The *Van Horn* court directly confronted the dispositive issue of whether a student-athlete in receipt of an athletic scholarship was an employee of the institution for worker's compensation purposes. Applying employment law principles, the court determined that the student-athlete was an employee, and rejected the institution's attempt to characterize the scholarship as a grant-in-aid rather than payment for services. Simply stated, the court recognized that the essence of the student-athlete/university relationship is a contract of hire in which a scholarship is awarded in exchange for athletic services.

Contrary to *Nemeth* and *Van Horn*, other courts have declined to recognize the existence of a contract of hire between a scholarship student-athlete and his institution. The court in *Rensing v. Indiana State University Board of Trustees*[96] acknowledged the contractual nature of a student-athlete's relationship with his university, but nevertheless concluded that the contractual arrangement did not create a contract of hire. The court reasoned that the absence of an express or implied intent to enter into an employment agreement negated the existence of an employer-employee relationship. The court also noted that Rensing had failed to establish another element of an employment agreement, the performance of services for pay. Siding with the University's contention, the court characterized the scholarship as a grant-in-aid rather than payment for services rendered.

The Michigan Court of Appeals in *Coleman v. Western Michigan University*[103] applied employment law in denying a student-athlete worker's compensation

---

85. 257 P.2d 423 (Colo. 1953).
90. 33 Cal. Rptr. 169 (Ct. App. 1963).
96. 444 N.E.2d 1170 (Ind. 1983).
103. 336 N.W.2d 224 (Mich. Ct. App. 1983).

claim. Unlike *Rensing*, the *Coleman* court applied common law factors of the economic reality test in declining Coleman's claim for benefits.

Coleman appealed the Michigan Worker's Compensation Authority Board's denial of his claim for compensation benefits for injuries sustained during a football game. The claimant was the recipient of an annual renewable scholarship which covered tuition, room, board, and books. He played football and was awarded a scholarship for two years.

Since the Michigan Compensation Act defines employee broadly, the court resorted to common law principles, specifically the economic reality test, to determine whether the board erred in refusing to define Coleman as an employee for worker's compensation purposes. The court focused on two considerations: (1) the extent of the university's right to control and discipline the activities of the student-athlete; and (2) the extent to which plaintiff's sports participation was an integral part of the university's business. With regard to the school's right of control over Coleman, the court adopted the compensation commission's finding that "[p]laintiff's scholarship did not subject him to any extraordinary degree of control over his academic activities. The degree of defendant's control over this aspect of plaintiff's activities was no greater than that over any other student."[110] The court emphasized the irrevocability of the scholarship during the football season as additional support for the finding that the university lacked extraordinary control over Coleman.

The court next addressed the issue of whether the student-athlete's participation in sports constituted an integral part of the university's business. In finding that it did not, the court noted that the university could effectively carry out its business, education and research, in the absence of an intercollegiate football program. Significantly, the court so held despite finding that the scholarship conferred a measurable economic gain upon Coleman: the financial aid essentially constituted wages awarded by the university in exchange for Coleman's commitment to participate in sports.

Therefore, though the *Coleman* court recognized the contractual nature of the relationship between Coleman and the university, it held that, in light of the economic realities, this contract did not give rise to an employer/employee relationship.

D. *Significance of Model Selection*

The decisions rendered in *Rensing* and *Coleman* on the one hand, and *Van Horn* and *Nemeth* on the other, are significant for their demonstration of how the preconceptions concerning intercollegiate athletics sway the legal determination of the relationship between an athlete and his university.

That the *Rensing* court viewed college sports from the perspective of amateurism and educational values is evident from the court's liberal reference to NCAA regulations to "establish...that college athletics is a non-business activity and merely an extension of the educational process."[115] For instance, the court focused on the NCAA's fundamental policy and purpose of maintaining the line of demarcation between college sports and professional sports. Consistent with the amateur/education model of intercollegiate sports, the court opined that the primary purpose of scholarships is to allow student-athletes to pursue educational

---

110. *Coleman*, 336 N.W.2d at 226.
115. Rafferty, *supra* note 84, at 99.

opportunities. Thus, the notion that a student-athlete is "first and foremost a student" guided the court down a path from which legal recognition of an employer/employee relationship would have seemed illogical and legally unsupportable. Without question, invocation of these values compelled the court to characterize financial aid as a gratuity as opposed to compensation for services performed, the bargained-for-exchange elements of the relationship notwithstanding.

Similarly, the findings in *Coleman* regarding the University's lack of control over the student-athlete were shaped by the amateur/education conceptualization of intercollegiate athletics. The *Coleman* court summarized its perception of intercollegiate athletics with the following:

> Plaintiff's scholarship did not subject him to any extraordinary degree of control over his academic activities. The degree of defendant's control over this aspect of plaintiff's activities was no greater than that over any other student. Moreover, the record suggests that the parties contemplated a primary role for plaintiff's academic activities and only a secondary role for plaintiff's activities as a football player. Plaintiff recognized that "you are a student first, athlete second."[120]

Consistent with the amateur/education model, the *Coleman* court viewed amateurism and academia as the essence of a student- athlete's relationship with his university. However, the *Coleman* court's conclusion regarding a lack of control is incompatible with the substantial degree to which universities, through their athletic departments and coaches, actually control the student-athlete's life, particularly the details of his sports participation. "The coach must establish authority over the athlete off the field so that during competition, nothing impedes a top performance by everyone on the team. When the coach tells the quarterback to run a certain play, the quarterback knows that he must run that specific play."

The *Coleman* court's conclusion that playing football was not an integral part of the university's business of education also reveals its adoption of the assumptions incorporated in the amateur/education model. The court downplayed the commercial benefits accruing to universities as a result of successful athletic programs, noting the irrelevance of such payments to the successful operation of a university.

Though resting on faulty assumptions embodied in the amateur/education model, it is not surprising that the *Coleman* and *Rensing* courts adopted the prevailing societal view of intercollegiate athletics. While this naive view of college sports is partly attributable to an ignorance of the inner workings of college athletics, the amateur/education model also incorporates pragmatic considerations.

Contrary to *Coleman* and *Rensing*, the *Nemeth* and *Van Horn* courts acknowledged the economic and sociological realities of intercollegiate athletics as set out in the commercial/education model. For example, the *Van Horn* court recognized the educational aspect of this model when it stipulated that not every scholarship athlete is an employee. According to the court, employee status is only achieved where the evidence establishes the existence of a contract of employment. The court reasoned that one who participates for compensation as a member of an athletic team may be an employee for worker's compensation purposes in spite of the fact that academic credit is also awarded for such participation.

---

120. Coleman v. Western Mich. Univ., 336 N.W.2d 224, 226 (Mich. Ct. App. 1983).

The foregoing reflects the court's understanding that more than academics is at work in a student-athlete's participation in sports; the *Van Horn* court explicitly noted that a student-athlete may operate in the dual capacity of a student and an employee. The dispositive question is whether the student-athlete receives financial assistance in exchange for his sports participation. By rejecting the university's argument that the student-athlete's participation in football was voluntary and that the scholarship was a gift, the court refused to assume that amateurism forms the basis of the relationship.

Similarly, the *Nemeth* court's reasoning is consistent with the economic realities reflected in the commercial/education model. The court's conclusion that the student's job was conditioned on his sports participation recognized the relationship as a bargained-for-exchange in which both parties received benefits and suffer detriments. Significantly, the *Nemeth* court acknowledged that the provision of services for financial aid is the essence of the student athlete's relationship with his college. Therefore, in accordance with the commercial/education model, the court implicitly recognized that the student-athlete's true value resides in his ability to successfully compete on behalf of his institution.

In summary, legal doctrine and philosophical visions of college athletics combine to shape the judicial response to a student-athlete's status as an employee for worker's compensation purposes. Courts declining to define student-athletes as employees adopt the views of intercollegiate athletics embodied in the amateur/education model of college sports. The judiciary in these cases perceives college sports as serving an academic function where intercollegiate athletics are simply an avocation of the student.

Juxtaposed with these decisions are cases in which the judiciary recognizes the impact of commercialism on college sports and on the student-athlete's relationship with his university. Here, the duality of the student-athlete's role, as a student on the one hand and an employee on the other, provides the framework from which the relevant issues are analyzed. Employment status stems from the quid pro quo which earmarks the contractual obligations between a student-athlete and his institution. Nevertheless, these cases recognize that the student-athlete is still a student, hence creating an educational component to college sports.

The student-athlete worker's compensation decisions also illustrate the significant extent to which a court's reliance on a particular conceptual model influences the ultimate disposition of the case. Recognizing these judicial tendencies, parties to disputes arising within intercollegiate athletics construct their policy and legal arguments upon these two competing conceptual schemes.

IV. WALDREP V. TEXAS WORKERS' COMPENSATION COMMISSION

.... [Professor Davis' discussion of *Waldrep v. Texas Workers' Compensation Commission* as a recent illustration of the impact of model selection on a student-athlete's right to workers compensation is omitted. With respect to *Waldrep*, Davis concludes that the amateur/education model and the commercial/education model served as foundations for the university's, Texas Christian University, and former student-athlete's, Kent Waldrep, respective positions on the latter's entitlement to workers' compensation benefits.—ed.]

....

Reliance on the amateur/education and the commercial/education model as bases for judicial decisionmaking is not limited to student-athletes' attempts to obtain worker's compensation benefits. The pattern of decisional law emerging from intercollegiate sports suggests that courts have applied the amateur/education model in resolving any dispute that originates there. In notable instances, however, courts have shifted toward acceptance of the commercial/education paradigm. Perpetuation of the traditional trend in the context of antitrust challenges with noteworthy deviations is next examined.

V. BASES FOR MODEL SELECTION

A. *Antitrust Challenges: Adherence to Pattern*?

Student-athlete challenges of NCAA amateurism rules illustrate the extent to which the amateur/education conceptualization of college athletics influences judicial decisionmaking. NCAA amateurism rules impose the sanction of ineligibility on student-athletes who receive compensation beyond tuition and room and board in exchange for participation in a particular sport. Amateur status, and consequently eligibility to participate in a particular sport, is also sacrificed when a student-athlete either registers to participate in a professional sports league draft or consults with an agent.

Courts have uniformly rejected student-athletes' claims that the "no-draft," "no agent," and "limited compensation" rules violate the Sherman Antitrust Act. Some courts reason that the noncommercial nature of NCAA amateurism rules remove them from the purview of antitrust regulation. Applying a rule of reason analysis, other courts conclude that NCAA amateurism rules are reasonable since they advance and maintain the amateurism value. Regardless of the particular rationale used in upholding NCAA regulations, the amateur/education model's conception of intercollegiate athletics provides indispensable support for the validation of these rules.

The outcome in *Banks v. NCAA*[184] demonstrates this phenomenon. In *Banks*, a student-athlete playing football for Notre Dame registered for the National Football League draft and consulted with an agent. The NCAA declared Banks ineligible to play football in his remaining year at Notre Dame. Banks sought to permanently enjoin the NCAA and Notre Dame from enforcing the no-draft and no-agent rules, asserting that both rules violated section 1 of the Sherman Act.

The Seventh Circuit affirmed the district court's holding that Banks had failed to establish that the no-draft and no-agent rules had an anti-competitive effect on trade. The language of the court's opinion, and its allusion to the NCAA's stated purpose in particular, revealed the court's perception of college sports as resting on the amateur ideal:

> Because the no-draft rule represents a desirable and legitimate attempt "to keep university athletics from becoming professionalized to the extent that profit making objectives would overshadow educational objectives," the no-draft rule and other like NCAA regulations preserve the bright line of demarcation between college and "play for pay" football. . . . We consider college football players as student-athletes simultaneously pursuing academic degrees that will prepare them to enter the employment market in non-athletic occupations, and hold that the regulations of the NCAA are designed to preserve the honesty and

---

184. 977 F.2d 1081 (7th Cir. 1992).

integrity of intercollegiate athletics and foster fair competition among the participating amateur college students.[190]

The foregoing vision contrasts sharply with that expressed in the *Banks* dissent, which criticized the majority for adopting an outmoded view of college sports. The dissent emphasized that college sports are no longer merely about "spirit, competition, camaraderie, sportsmanship, [and] hard work," but are instead a commercial enterprise which generates monetary and non-monetary benefits for both student-athletes and their institutions. The dissent maintained that only by recognizing these realities could a fair assessment be made of the extent to which the NCAA amateurism rules represent an illegal restraint on trade.

In contrast to *Banks* and other decisions focusing on the ideals of amateurism are those which demonstrate a shift toward acceptance of the assumptions underlying the commercial/education model of college sports. *NCAA v. Board of Regents*,[197] a case which challenged NCAA control over television coverage of football games, manifests this shift. The NCAA's plan limited the total number of games which could be televised and the number of games which any single member institution could televise. Applying a rule of reason analysis, the Supreme Court agreed with the plaintiffs in holding that the NCAA's television plan violated the Sherman Act.

In dicta, the Court distinguished between cases challenging NCAA amateurism rules from those regulating NCAA television contracts on the ground that the former regulates noncommercial matters while the latter regulates commercial activity. In acknowledging this distinction, the Court conveyed that college sports should be viewed as a business. However, it stopped short of fully adopting a commercial/education model of intercollegiate athletics by intimating the applicability of the amateur/education model in all cases arising within intercollegiate athletics except those of a blatantly commercial nature.

Thus, courts have recognized two categories of NCAA rules. The first group, rules governing commercial activities such as television rights, are subject to antitrust laws. The second group, rules governing noncommercial activities such as no-draft and no-agent rules, evade scrutiny. Noting this dichotomy in the context of *Gaines v. NCAA*,[203] where a student-athlete challenged the validity of the no-draft and no-agent regulations, one commentator concluded:

> The [*Gaines*] court concludes that the NCAA's regulation of noncommercial activities are exempt from antitrust scrutiny. The court distinguishes rules pursuing economic objectives from those preserving amateurism. The antitrust laws apply to commercial objectives such as the broadcast and promotion of college football. However, the NCAA's second primary goal is preserving amateurism as an integral part of the educational process. The NCAA achieves this goal by preventing the commercialization of the college athlete through the 'no-draft' and 'no-agent' rules. Since the rules have noncommercial objectives, the Sherman Act does not apply to them.[204]

In summary, courts have relied on principles and values which undergird the amateur/education model of college sports to uphold NCAA rules unless the chal-

---

190. *Banks*, 977 F.2d at 1090 (citation omitted).
197. 468 U.S. 85 (1984).
203. 746 F. Supp. 738 (M.D. Tenn. 1990).
204. McCarthy & Kettle, *supra* note 180, at 302.

lenged provisions regulate commercial matters. Despite the inherently commercial aspect of the 'no-draft' and 'no-agent' rules, courts have deferred to the amateurism principle as articulated in the NCAA rules to conclude that such rules fail to constitute unlawful restraints on trade. Unfortunately, judicial reliance on principles of amateurism preclude courts from evaluating the true extent to which NCAA amateurism rules are noncommercial. An occasional and limited shift toward recognition of the commercial/education model notwithstanding, the amateur/education model is the dominant influence in the resolution of antitrust challenges arising in the context of college sports.

B. *Contractual Nature of Relationship*

Courts and commentators overwhelmingly acknowledge that the award of an athletic scholarship is an inducement for a student-athlete's commitment to an institution to compete in intercollegiate athletics. Consequently, a contract between the student and college is formed....

....Analysis of the documents creating the student-athlete's relationship with his institution and the parties' respective expectations support the contract characterization.

The Letter of Intent, the Statement of Financial Assistance, and various university publications such as bulletins and catalogues, create the express contract from which the student-athlete's and institution's respective obligations arise....

Moreover, economic realities support a contractual characterization of the relationship. In the realm of intercollegiate athletics, the student-athlete's value lies in his ability to compete successfully for a team, and he receives financial aid in exchange for this value. Hence, a quid pro quo is the essence of the relationship between the athlete and his university.

The dependence of financial aid on athletic performance not only distinguishes student athletes from other students but places them in "a unique and increasingly significant relationship with the university."[218] Thus, a contractual view of the relationship has a two-fold significance. It recognizes the evolution, spawned by the increased commercialism of college sports, of the student-athlete's relationship with his university. In addition, it represents a tacit shift towards adoption of assumptions which underlie the commercial/education model of college sports.

Well reasoned analyses and the modern realities of intercollegiate athletics notwithstanding, the commercial/education model has not been fully embraced. Professors Weistart and Lowell, noteworthy skeptics of the contract characterization, criticize the failure of courts and commentators to characterize the athletic scholarship as an educational grant. They posit that if the student-athlete/university relationship is viewed from an academic rather than a contractual premise, the obligations imposed on the student-athlete are nothing more than a condition to the receipt of a gift. Under the grant-in-aid conceptualization, Professors Weistart and Lowell analogize scholarship athletes to music students who receive financial aid with the understanding that they will perform in public as a part of their academic program.

These commentators' preference seems partially derived from perceived problems with the alternative conceptual scheme of intercollegiate athletics. Still,

---

218. Nestel, *supra* note 36, at 1401.

Weistart and Lowell concede that where the pertinent documents and a university's policy evidence an exchange of financial assistance for athletic participation, a contractual characterization is the only accurate interpretation of the relationship.

This skepticism has not persuaded courts to adopt the grant-in-aid characterization of athletic scholarships. Despite judicial caution in defining this relationship as contractual, such a characterization marks a shift away from an idyllic conception of college sports and toward a vision which more closely mirrors reality.

C. *The Existence of a Special Relationship Between a Student-Athlete and the University: Complete Paradigm Shift?*

.... [The author next discusses *Kleinknecht v. Gettysburg College,* 989 F.2d 1360 (3rd Cir. 1993), in which the Third Circuit Court of Appeals found that a special relationship exists between an intercollegiate athlete and his college. He proposes that the enduring significance of *Kleinknecht* may inhere in the court's recognition and incorporation of the modern reality of the student-athlete/university relationship into its reasoning and its echoing the values contained within the commercial/education conceptualization of college sports. — ed.].

VI. MODEL SELECTION

A. *Societal Expectations*

The prominence of the amateur/education conceptual theme in judicial decisionmaking is based on beliefs associated with the role of college sports in society and pragmatic considerations. A model of intercollegiate athletics which would eradicate the myths of this model threatens the lofty societal expectations of intercollegiate athletics and its participants. The judiciary's adherence to the amateur/education model of college sports evinces its reluctance to make this tradeoff, and reveals the judicial perception that intercollegiate athletics plays a social role within universities.

Judicial affinity for the amateur/education model also stems from concern that abandonment of the amateurism ideal will shatter the image of college sports organizations as establishments dedicated to academic pursuits. The conflict between the professionalism of college sports and educational goals legitimates this apprehension. Hence, NCAA regulations represent "desirable and legitimate attempt[s] to 'keep university athletics from becoming professionalized to the extent that profit making objectives would overshadow educational objectives.'"[244]

However, ignoring the commercialization of intercollegiate athletics will not enhance the educational experience of its participants. Only honest consideration and recognition of the conflict between commercialism and educational values can preserve the latter: ...

B. *Pragmatic Considerations*

Judicial reticence to adopt the commercial/education model also reflects the concern that the commercial/education model would increase a university's liabil-

---

244. NCAA v. Board of Regents, 468 U.S. 85, 123 (1984) (White, J. dissenting) (quoting Kupec v. Atlantic Coast Conference, 399 F. Supp. 1377, 1380 (M.D.N.C. 1975).).

ity exposure for personal injury and educational malpractice claims. Consequently, recognition of the realities of the commercial/education model is likely to encourage litigation that will expend scarce judicial resources. Adherence to the value of amateurism reflected in the amateur/education model provides a convenient means of forestalling these consequences.

Moreover, the economic aspects of the commercial/education paradigm blur the line of demarcation between college and professional sports. Amateurism and educational values shield institutional interests from perceived harms to which the university would fall victim under the alternative scheme. However, recognition of the commercial aspects of college sports would facilitate professional treatment of intercollegiate athletic activities for other legal purposes.

For example, employee characterization of scholarship athletes, indicating a shift to the commercial/education paradigm, increases the likelihood that scholarships will be taxable as gross income. Currently, courts employ a "quid pro quo test" in determining whether a scholarship award is excludable from gross income under section 117 of the Internal Revenue Code. Scholarships given in exchange for services rendered are not excluded from gross income under this test.

This characterization also has important tax implications for universities which are tax-exempt institutions. Revenue generated by athletic programs are considered attributable to the institution's educational purpose and therefore are specifically exempt under section 501(a) of the Internal Revenue Code. The NCAA's definition of the student-athlete is consistent with the Code's view that participation in athletic competition is predominantly educational.

Adoption of a commercial/education model, in contrast, increases the likelihood that income from intercollegiate sports will be taxable as unrelated business income because this model recognizes the business component of college sports.

. . . .

A characterization of college sports which blurs the distinction between amateurism and professionalism also holds consequences for labor law issues.

> A conclusion that the student-athlete is an employee would have significant consequences. For example, if the student-athlete qualified as an employee under the National Labor Relations Act, 29 U.S.C. 151-169 (1982), he theoretically could unionize and engage in protected concerted activity, such as strikes and collective bargaining. The finding of an employer-employee relationship would necessitate a dramatic reevaluation of the university/student-athlete relationship in terms of fair labor standards, occupational safety and health, equal employment, and labor management relations as a whole.[259]

It is uncertain whether affording student-athletes employee status will wreak the disastrous consequences some fear. Nevertheless, application of the commercial/education paradigm at least clouds the NCAA's carefully drawn line between college and professional sports.

VII. CONCLUSION

The values and principles of the amateur/education model have historically shaped the boundaries of judicial determination of the rights and responsibilities within the arena of intercollegiate athletics. These values, illusory and out of step

---

259. Cozzillio, *supra* note 42, at 1299 n.95 (citation omitted).

with the contemporary realities of college athletics, do not accurately describe the relationship between a scholarship athlete and his university. Though greater recognition of the commercial/education model is not a magic solution to the many legal and social issues confronting contemporary intercollegiate athletics, this scheme is at least the proper starting point for constructive debate. The commercial/education model will compel educators, administrators, and athletic officials to directly confront the reality of commercialism in college athletics, with an honest balancing of interests and responsibilities replacing the current disingenuous subterfuge. Similarly, it will force us to contemplate what role intercollegiate athletics should play in society if we deem the commercialism that currently exists unacceptable.

The decisions in *Waldrep* and *Kleinknecht,* together with the nearly universal recognition of the contractual nature of the student-athlete/university relationship, represent a gradual shift toward the commercial/education model of intercollegiate athletics. Whether this slight shift toward the commercial/education model will gain momentum is questionable since resistance to this change by educators, coaches, the courts, and society at-large reflects deeply rooted societal values and is furthermore driven by self- interest. At present, the hypocrisy resulting from the disregard of commercialism as the reigning force within intercollegiate athletics is not sufficiently offensive to discredit society's idyllic vision of college sports.

Alfred Dennis Mathewson, Intercollegiate Athletics and the Assignment of Legal Rights
35 St. Louis University Law Journal 39 (1990)*

I. INTRODUCTION

All is not right in the world of intercollegiate athletics. Thousands of young men and women, primarily between the ages of eighteen and twenty-four, participate in public exhibitions of athletic contests on behalf of the universities and colleges in which they matriculate. All revenues derived from the staging of these exhibitions, including gate receipts and proceeds from the sale of television rights, are retained by the universities and the associations formed by them to regulate such exhibitions. The students may participate only if they receive no share of these revenues or accept compensation, except for scholarships and other permissible but nominal amounts. Furthermore, they may not accept compensation or pecuniary reward from any source for their athletic skill.

The nomenclature for this system, in which all persons collaborating in the production, sale, and delivery of athletic contests to the public, except the athletes, share in the immediate commercial rewards generated, is "amateurism." Amateur intercollegiate athletics as such is mandated neither by natural law nor the legislative enactment of state legislatures or Congress. Rather, the prohibition against the sharing of the spoils with athletes, as well as other matters relating to player eligibility, for whom students may play and the consequences of violations, are es-

---

tablished by agreements among universities and colleges. Through these agreements, which I call "first-tier" agreements, universities and colleges form associations to govern intercollegiate athletics and establish the terms and conditions by which the members will produce, sell, and deliver exhibitions to the public. The principal governing association in the United States and the subject of much discussion in this Article is the National Collegiate Athletic Association (NCAA).

Student athletes, the ultimate subjects of a vast number of the terms and conditions of first-tier agreements, are not members of these associations or otherwise parties to such agreements. Instead, student athletes enter into what I refer to as "second-tier" agreements directly with universities, which by their own terms are subject to first-tier agreements. Saddled with terms and conditions of first-tier agreements that they believe are unfair, more and more student athletes are redressing adverse university or governing association actions in the courts. These forays into the judiciary have been largely unsuccessful. Over the years, several commentators have railed against the treatment of student athletes in intercollegiate athletics and cried for more legal accountability on the part of the NCAA with respect to its regulation of student athletes. Although the nature and scope of the advocated accountability remains unclear, implicit in their cries for accountability through the judicial system is the existence of enforceable private legal rights for student athletes.

. . . .

To examine the assignment of legal rights between universities in intercollegiate athletics, I reviewed more than forty reported cases in which a student sued a university or governing association or a university sued a governing association in connection with its intercollegiate athletics program. Each case was examined for several factual variables: (1) university, (2) student, (3) governing association or university rule violated, (4) sport, (5) legal grounds on which the actions of a university or governing association were challenged, (6) legal relief or remedy sought, (7) disposition at trial level involving the procedural matter or determination of merits, (8) state or federal court, and (9) who won.

Studying the cases for these variables was very revealing. Perhaps the most startling observation was that students and universities rarely asked the courts to mandate systemic reform. Although the majority of cases concern the so-called revenue producing sports of football and basketball, other sports such as hockey, soccer, and tennis generated a significant number of cases. Regardless of the sport involved, the most frequently sought remedy was the right to participate as students or their university surrogates asked the court to enjoin the university or governing association from restricting their right to participate in intercollegiate competition. Several plaintiffs sought damages, but no case was found in which an athlete claiming that he or she was underpaid asked for quantum meruit damages for the fair market value of services rendered less the scholarship. The most common measure of damages identified in the cases was the speculative compensation lost at the professional level.

The cases confirmed my long held suspicion that there is not a unique body of sports law, and that the legal rules applicable to intercollegiate athletics, and sports in general, developed through the application of legal rules from established bodies of law. In each case the student athlete, or a university on his or her behalf, urged the court that the student possessed private legal rights under principles of an established body of law under which the NCAA or the university could be held accountable in a court of law. They argued that these principles applied to defined strings of events that occurred in the context of intercollegiate athletics. Thus, the plaintiffs advanced causes of action arising under the fourteenth amendment, federal or state antitrust laws, contract law, tort law, worker's compensation laws, federal statutes such as Title IX of the Educational Amendments of 1972, and other similar laws.

. . . .

My journey took a decided twist upon observing student athletes in case after case asking the courts to award participation rights as a remedy to their grievances. Why did student athletes want to participate in a system that so obviously exploited them? While I pondered this mystery, I read Cheung, *The Contractual Nature of the Firm.* Cheung reminded me of the fundamental economic proposition that people enter into an exchange because they perceive that they will gain from the transaction. Student athletes thus evaluate entry into the system of intercollegiate athletics relative to their other options. The contribution of Cheung's work to my analysis was not that it solved a mystery for me but that it inspired me to view the university and student as collaborators in the production, sale, and delivery of intercollegiate athletic competition to the public. This viewpoint led me to conclude that the principal legal rights assigned under current American law to collaborators in intercollegiate athletics relate to the right to associate.

. . . .

II. THE ASSIGNMENT OF LEGAL RIGHTS TO ASSOCIATE AND NOT TO ASSOCIATE

The Coase Theorem, as commonly articulated, rests upon the premise that a legal order somehow assigns legal rights or entitlements to those persons who are subject to that legal order. I have always found this fundamental premise as intriguing as the relationship of transaction costs and legal rights to economic efficiency. How are legal rights assigned? By whom and to whom are they assigned? And what are legal rights anyway? I suppose the latter is the most interesting of the three questions, for law students learn early in their study of the law that legal rules, whether rooted in common law or promulgated by legislatures, establish the benefits or burdens that society will confer, exact, or impose on people as they interact with one another. Thus, legal rights are assigned to persons through legal rules by legal rulemakers, i.e., courts and legislatures. When a legal rule confers benefits and imposes burdens — and a legal rule necessarily accomplishes both — it may be said to effectuate an assignment of legal rights to those persons affected by it. However, Coase appears to have been concerned only with the right to control or influence the allocation of resources under certain circumstances in preference to others. In this section, I shall discuss the specific delimitation of legal rights among universities, governing associations, and student athletes and how those rights establish the right to control or influence the allocation of resources in the industry of intercollegiate athletics.

The assignment of legal rights among collaborators involved in the production, sale, and delivery of intercollegiate athletic competition to the public flows from the confluence of three sets of similar legal rules, respectively applicable to three distinct factual contexts in which the courts have historically abstained from resolving disputes. These contexts are (a) sports, (b) the relationship between students and the university and (c) voluntary associations. In cases involving each of these contexts separately, courts have articulated rules requiring judicial restraint except to the extent necessary to enforce legally binding agreements made by the parties, including, but not limited to, any implied contractual rights arising under the law of voluntary nonprofit associations. When these contexts are combined in the intercollegiate athletics setting, the courts will honor rights obtained under the terms of legally binding agreements reached or accepted by the collaborators, but will not dictate terms upon colleges, universities, and students staging sports contests.

Whether the relationships among collaborators arise out of individual contracts or out of membership in voluntary unincorporated associations, legal rights are assigned based upon the association of collaborators with each other. The collaborators obtain the basic right to associate voluntarily with any other collaborators who are willing to associate with them, as well as other legal rights that might be obtained through the exercise of that right. Implicit in the right to associate, and equally important, is the right to refuse to associate. The exercise of this right is the principal sanction used by governing associations in intercollegiate athletics. .... [A discussion of judicial abstention in the sports, student/university and voluntary association contexts is omitted. — ed.].

D. *The Intercollegiate Athletics Context*

Legal rights governing the second-tier relationship between the student athlete and the university are such that each has the right to associate or to refuse to associate prior to their association. They have whatever other rights they subsequently agree upon in legally binding agreements. The student athlete customarily agrees, as a part of those agreements, to associate or collaborate with other universities with whom the student's university has entered into first-tier relationships for the production, sale, and delivery of intercollegiate athletic competitions. As the student athlete further agrees to be bound by the first-tier agreements, the various governing associations also obtain legal rights.

The operation of this assignment of legal rights may be demonstrated by examining four components of the second-tier relationship between a university and a student athlete: formation, nature and quality of the right to participate, the duration of the period of collaboration and its termination, and transfers of student athletes from one university to another.

Formation occurs upon the decision of a university and a student athlete to associate together in the production of intercollegiate athletics. The agreement to associate is evidenced by a letter of intent, scholarship, or grant-in-aid, but these documents do not necessarily contain the entire agreement between the parties. No university may compel the formation of this relationship with a student athlete if the student does not choose to do so. And in general, a student athlete may not compel a university to associate with him or her unless it so chooses. A university's ability to associate with a student athlete may be restricted, however, by virtue of its first-tier agreements — the most notable being requirements that athletes meet minimal academic entrance standards, become a student at the university, and qualify as an amateur. Thus, a university not only may, but must, refuse to associate with athletes lacking these characteristics.

The nature and quality of the student athlete's right to participate is fixed by the agreement of the parties. The student athlete ordinarily obtains the right to participate in practice sessions, conditioning programs, games with other universities, and post-season and television appearances when merited. In most cases, the student athlete receives a scholarship in exchange for participation. The ability of a university to deliver some or all of the participation agreed upon may be restricted by virtue of its first-tier agreements. For example, if the university violates its first-tier agreements it may be banned from television and post-season appearances even though it promised, perhaps only implicitly, such appearances to the student athlete.

The duration of the period of association will extend for as long as the parties agree. But again, the period of association to which the university may agree is restricted by first-tier agreements. The university will associate for a maximum period of five years, but the student athlete may participate for no more than four of the five years. Furthermore, the first-tier arrangements of the university preclude second-tier arrangements greater than one year at a time. Thus, at the end of any academic year a university may refuse to associate further with a student athlete. Moreover, the university must terminate its association with the student athlete if the student commits a disqualifying act or fails to measure up to academic requirements. Other member universities of the same governing association often agree to refuse to associate in intercollegiate athletics if a university does not terminate its association with a disqualified student athlete.

The student athlete is free at any time to partially or entirely cease his association with university intercollegiate athletics. The student athlete may choose to associate with another university after ceasing his association with one university, but such a decision is discouraged by the impact of first-tier agreements on available alternatives. First-tier arrangements permit but discourage a member university from associating with a student athlete who previously associated with another university. Such subsequent associations are discouraged by requiring the new university to withhold the transferred student athlete from full participation for a period of one academic year. In addition, the new university may not provide the transfer student athlete with financial aid for a period of one academic year unless the original university consents. A student athlete who wishes to transfer without suffering this transfer tax must engage in the costly process of seeking changes in the first-tier agreements or refuse to associate.

Under such a regime of associational rights, the persons or institutions with control or possession of resources will direct the use thereof unless they relinquish the right through contract. Many readers, no doubt, are familiar with the playground spectacle in which a lesser talented kid of means threatens to take his or her ball unless he or she can play in the game. In the intercollegiate athletics context, universities control the equivalent of the playground ball — resources. Not only are they able to withhold the ball unless they can play, they can insist on the right to select the other players in the game with the blessing of the law.

It is true that universities necessarily must relinquish some of the right to control resources through first- and second-tier agreements. As will be demonstrated herein, universities bind themselves in first-tier agreements in order to relinquish little control to student athletes in second-tier agreements. The allocation of the right to control essential resources to universities reflects the legal system's notion that universities will direct those resources into activities providing the greatest societal benefit.

III. THE SEARCH FOR RESTRICTIONS ON THE RIGHTS TO ASSOCIATE AND NOT TO ASSOCIATE

No legal rule in Anglo-American jurisprudence, whether statutory or common law based, explicitly provides for an assignment of legal rights based upon the unique circumstances of intercollegiate athletics. The courts apply rules that identify specific factual variables that occur in the context of intercollegiate athletics, such as voluntary associations. The application of these rules has the effect of assigning participants only those rights that they have agreed upon in addition to the right to refuse to associate. Accordingly, aggrieved student athletes have been forced to search, like the Federal Baseball Club, for other legal rules that identify any of the factual variables in the string of events occurring in the context of intercollegiate athletics: rules that place restrictions on the permissible terms and conditions on which the collaborators may associate or on the right to refuse to associate, rules that limit the right of universities to direct the use of resources contrary to the interests of student athletes.

The result has been claims that a student athlete was deprived of his right to participate in intercollegiate athletics without due process, that eligibility rules were a denial of equal protection of the laws, that the actions of a university constituted a breach of contract, that imposition of penalties amounted to a tortious interference with contractual rights, that the actions violated antitrust laws, and that student athletes were entitled to compensation under workmen's compensation laws. Other types of cases have been brought but they fall into isolated categories. The cases generally fall into four classes corresponding to the four components of second-tier agreements described in the preceding section: Formation, Nature and Quality, Termination, and Transfer cases. In Formation cases, the university should not have formed or entered into a collaborative relationship with a student athlete. Typical Formation cases occur when a student does not meet academic entry standards or is no longer eligible because of participation in a foreign country.

Nature and Quality cases are those in which a university has been subjected to sanctions that infringe upon the nature and quality of the student athlete's right to participate in intercollegiate athletics, such as bans on television and post-season appearances.

In Termination cases, the university has terminated its relationship with a student athlete and refused to further associate in intercollegiate athletics with that student athlete. An example might be when a student has committed a disqualifying act and the NCAA or other governing association determined that the student athlete was permanently or temporarily ineligible for athletic participation. Frequently, cases involving the termination of a relationship for failure to satisfy academic entry standards arise only after a relationship has been formed, but for organizational purposes those cases are included with the Formation cases.

Transfer cases include those instances when a university has complied with first-tier restrictions on participation by a student athlete who has transferred from another university.

The classification of the cases as Formation, Nature and Quality, Termination, and Transfer is a necessary step in their analysis. Nonetheless, I have chosen to organize my discussion in terms of the usual causes of action used to challenge the action of the governing association or university rather than these four categories. I shall examine the use of due process, equal protection, antitrust, and contract-related rules by student athletes and universities on their behalf.

....[A detailed discussion of the judicial determination of claims that fall within these four categories cases is omitted.—ed.]

IV. THE DEFECTS IN THE ASSIGNMENT OF LEGAL RIGHTS

The preceding section may be summarized as follows: Student athletes bring legal actions to challenge two principal defects in the relationships among student athletes, their universities, and governing associations resulting from the assignment of legal rights among them. They use due process, equal protection, and antitrust laws to influence the substantive terms of first-tier provisions and they use contract-based actions to hold universities accountable for second-tier promises in spite of first-tier agreements. Professor Weistart refers to the lack of influence on substantive terms and lack of accountability for second-tier promises as "structural deficiencies."[156] It seems clear that the litigation by student athletes constitutes an effort to correct these structural deficiencies by bargaining over first-tier provisions and university accountability after the formation of second-tier agreements.

This section of the Article demonstrates that the optimum assignment of legal rights between student athletes and universities is not obtainable in intercollegiate athletics through bargaining because transaction costs preclude such bargaining in the formation stage of second-tier relationships. Instead, such bargaining does not occur until student athletes embark on a course of litigation when their eligibility or right to participate in intercollegiate athletics is in jeopardy....

A. Impact of Transaction Costs at Formation

....

From the university's perspective, the transaction costs of bargaining with each individual student over every term would render the production if intercollegiate athletic competitions impossible.... Some bargaining over second-tier agreement terms does occur, more so over the parol portions of the agreement, and only over terms that do not render production of the product unfeasible....

Transaction costs also motivate students not to exercise their right to refuse to associate if the university will not separately bargain over the incorporation clause. Students lack information about the future and have great difficulty evaluating the right to participate offered by the university. Moreover, no student has the leverage to force a university to negotiate individually. On the other hand, collective action would only add virtually prohibitive transaction costs for incoming freshmen. After all, how would one find out who all the other potential freshmen are and how much would it cost in time and money to communicate with them? Moreover, who would bear the initial outlays to organize such collective action?

B. Impact of Transactions Costs When Eligibility is Threatened

Transaction costs do not vanish when the eligibility of student athletes is threatened. Because of the nature of the exchange between student athletes and universities, if an "exchange" is an appropriate characterization, the perceived value of participation differs once a student athlete enters the system....

....

...[S]tudent athletes are willing to litigate when eligibility is threatened because all opportunity to realize the value that they expect to receive from the professional expectancy will be lost. It is no coincidence that most of the cases involve sports for which professional careers exist. Student athletes litigate when television and postseason appearances are banned because they perceive, with some justification, that the value of the professional expectancy is a function of those items. Is it not true

---

156. Weistart, *supra* note 5, at 169-71.

that a star athlete at a prestigious university with a major athletic program has a better chance of winning the Heisman Trophy than a star athlete at a less prestigious university? In fact, a student athlete who has a choice between those schools may choose the more prestigious university because of that higher expected value. In any event, the student athletes who litigate must perceive that the value which will be lost is greater than the cost of proceeding with the litigation. Moreover, their loss will include their investment in that expectancy. It would not be reasonable to expect student athletes to simply treat the loss as another of life's experiences.

C. *The Resulting Inefficient Industry*

The occurrence of structural deficiencies should not surprise anyone because they result from a deliberate assignment of the right to control the allocation of essential resources to universities. The assignment of legal rights may be unfair to student athletes adversely affected by them and many have so argued. But perhaps the most severe defects lie in the removal of student athletes as a force capable of balancing the discretion of universities and compelling the universities to pay the full cost of the activity of intercollegiate athletics.

Courts have acknowledged that inefficiencies occur in amateur intercollegiate athletics, but they are of the opinion that the benefits of amateurism to society clearly outweigh the inefficiencies. As indicated elsewhere in this Article, the courts seem to take judicial notice of this proposition without requiring evidentiary proof. Judicial attitudes thus not only reflect the notion that universities are better repositories of the control of resources in intercollegiate athletics, they also reflect a sense that student athletes generally are not suitable repositories. In acting on these attitudes, courts lose sight of the need for balance in the control of the allocation of resources. Without checks on those who have been assigned the right to control, activities will not necessarily bear the costs they engender and resources will not be efficiently allocated. As shown in Part II, universities do not have a legal obligation to pay the costs of the compensation promised to student athletes and student athletes are unable to obtain accountability for such items through bargaining during the formation stage. Without a legal obligation to pay them, universities in many instances do not. Economic theory predicts that universities acting to further their self-interest will exploit this circumstance. Consequently, young people lured by the prospect of success in the industry of athletics choose to develop their athletic skills over their academic and job skills.

. . . .

V. THE SOLUTION : A COMMON LAW OR CODE OF INTERCOLLEGIATE ATHLETICS

In the preceding pages, I have argued that the system which produces, sells, and delivers intercollegiate athletics is inefficient. This inefficiency is due in large part to the assignment of legal rights among student athletes and universities. A logical path to improve efficiency is clearly reassignment of these legal rights. Legal rights should be reassigned so that the intercollegiate athletics industry does not lose the counter-balance of self-interested student athletes. This new assignment of rights should be accomplished by restricting universities' right to refuse to associate and by limiting the range of permissible terms and conditions to which the parties may agree when they choose to associate, or which otherwise flow through associational law. In this section, I will suggest the substance of possible restrictions and the methods by which their imposition may be effected. An appropriate regime may be created through the promulgation of a uniform code of intercollegiate athletics enacted by Congress or state legislatures or through the development of common law rules recognizing the unique relationship among student athletes, universities, and governing associations.

A code of intercollegiate athletics would function as a device, similar to state corporation codes, capable of reducing the high transaction costs of bargaining among student athletes, universities, and governing associations. Promulgation of a code offers several advantages, including a wider range of solutions, and the checks and balances of the political process. But the principal advantage is uniformity. The interstate nature of intercollegiate athletics and the need for uniformity suggest that congressional promulgation is preferable. However, uniformity could be obtained through a uniform code adopted by states in the manner of the Uniform Commercial Code and other uniform statutes.

Recognition of a common law relationship among the collaborators engaged in the production and delivery of intercollegiate athletics and a related set of rules to govern these relationships would also substitute for more costly and inefficient bargaining. Such an approach would be similar to the way fiduciary principles govern the relationship between fiduciaries and beneficiaries. A common law approach requires continued litigation and its results may be less uniform than the statutory approach. The common law approach, however, does allow the rules to develop gradually whereas the statutory approach will require guessing.

A. *A Code of Intercollegiate Athletics*

.... The right of universities to refuse to associate ought to be restricted by limiting the right of universities to define and enforce amateurism, and by conferring specific substantive rights on student athletes with respect to the educational obligations of universities.

1. Amateurism and Its Enforcement

Any meaningful code of intercollegiate athletics must address amateurism. Framers of a code must decide whether to prohibit amateurism through first-tier agreements or to simply regulate its imposition. Choosing the former would allow an individual university to restrict its association with student athletes by limiting compensation to specific items without regard to other universities' policies. More important, little more would be required in such a code as market discipline would remedy many of the problems described in this Article, including structural deficiencies. But I question whether universities and legislatures are ready to toss aside in one broad stroke the brand of amateur intercollegiate athletics so revered by the Supreme Court and the rest of the judiciary.

Accordingly, I suggest a code of intercollegiate athletics that accepts amateurism, but regulates it. I am mindful that altering the status quo will result in a different evolutionary pathway and may lead to the eventual extinction of amateur intercollegiate athletics, at least as it is now known.

....

a. *Definition of Amateurism*

The first two prongs of the NCAA's amateurism policy constitute the core of the definition of amateurism at the collegiate level. Universities may not compensate student athletes for athletic skill except as permitted, and student athletes may not receive compensation for athletic skill from any source. Some of the litigation brought by student athletes, as well as some violations of NCAA rules by student athletes, is motivated by resentment against the fundamental concept in the first prong that focuses on the compensation received by the athletes but not on compensation of other collaborators. . . .

. . . .

A code of intercollegiate athletics could address both the resentment and the underinclusiveness of the definition of amateurism. It need not abolish amateurism but it should disavow the broad brush approach of the NCAA and broaden the scope of the amateur characterization.

b. *Abolition of Automatic Permanent Ineligibility*

Closely related to concerns about the scope of amateurism are the penalties for its violations. A major concern of the university tribunal in *NCAA v. Regents of the University of Minnesota* was the mandatory penalty of permanent ineligibility for minor infractions of amateurism. The NCAA does not disagree that minor violations should not receive the ultimate penalty but uses an *"Alice in Wonderland"* approach; first it sentences, then it holds a hearing to determine if the sentence should be reduced. The purpose of this approach is to deter universities from willful violations. If a university must constantly fear the imposition of the maximum penalty, it reduces the temptation to cut corners. Yet this approach means that neither the university nor student athletes know what the real penalties will be for a violation and there is no guarantee that like offenses will receive like treatment.

A code of intercollegiate athletics should replace this system with one that reverses the present approach. It should establish a system in which offenses and penalties are established in advance rather than on an ad hoc basis and penalties are proportionate to offenses

c. *Greater Role in the Process*

. . . .

A code of intercollegiate athletics should require that student athletes have a greater role in the processes of governing associations when decisions will be made directly affecting student athletes. They should have a right, independent of the university, to appeal their loss of eligibility. Student athletes should be allowed to participate in hearings to appeal sanctions against their university even if it is only to plead for leniency. Moreover, they should have the right to appeal sanctions if the university chooses not to do so. Such a right would be similar to a shareholder's right to bring derivative actions. Finally, student athletes ought to have a formal role in rulemaking decisions that affect student athletes. They should be permitted to present their positions on proposed rules prior to adoption.

d. *Uniform Minimum Academic Standards*

A student athlete has unfettered discretion in deciding whether to associate with a university. A university has broad discretion in deciding whether to associate with a student athlete. In general, student athletes should expect that a university may use that discretion to refuse to associate with student athletes based upon their prior academic and athletic performance. The choice of academic standards is usually a prerogative of the autonomy of a university. Thus, a student athlete may be acceptable to one university but not acceptable to another.

Uniform minimum academic standards infringe upon this autonomy. There is only one plausible justification for an infringement on the academic autonomy of universities when intercollegiate athletics are concerned but not in other academic programs: that is the elimination of competitive advantages on the playing field for universities willing to admit gifted student athletes who have dubious academic potential under uniform criteria relative to universities that will not.

Proponents of uniform standards argue that such standards are necessary to prevent the exploitation of minority student athletes, thereby acknowledging that the issue of uniformity has principal meaning only to minority student athletes. They overlook the significance of university autonomy in fulfilling the aspirations of minority students to obtain a college education. It is noteworthy that the principal culprit in *Parish v. NCAA* was the governing association and its uniform standard rather than the university. University autonomy is not only desirable in the area of minority access to higher education, it is essential. Given the differences in performance under most standardized criteria along racial lines, universities necessarily must take a closer look at minority applicants, and this can not be done under rigid adherence to uniform standards. A university must have a free hand in setting the range of credentials acceptable to it if it is to provide access for larger numbers of minority applicants, including student athletes.

No university can determine at the outset which of these students with credentials that deviate from the norm will succeed; it can only know that some of them will. The question ought not to be whether universities can admit such students. If a university wants to devote resources and bear the costs of saving a handful, why prevent it from doing so? Rather than subject universities to a uniform academic standard, a code of intercollegiate athletics should focus on the programs available to a student athlete once he matriculates, not on the admissions process.

e. *Less Inclusive Transfer Rule*

The articulated purpose for rules discouraging transfers between universities is to prevent raiding by competing universities. The fear is that unrestrained transfers could transform intercollegiate athletics into professional sports through continuous bidding for the services of student athletes after they enter the system.

. . . .

A blanket transfer rule imposes additional costs on a student athlete for making an error in his original valuation. He may desire to transfer because of personality clashes with a coach or teammates, homesickness, dissatisfaction with the academic program, or disappointment in playing time. Not every student athlete desires to transfer because of improper inducements. In fact, the reported cases involve transfers for other reasons.

A code of intercollegiate athletics should seek to balance the concerns relating to the disruption of the athletic programs of universities with legitimate attempts on the part of student athletes to correct erroneous valuation decisions. Student athletes who desire to transfer for reasons other than improper inducements ought to be able to transfer without additional costs. Perhaps every student athlete should be entitled to transfer at least once without penalty. Or perhaps governing associations should establish an arbitrational system pursuant to which a student athlete could petition a tribunal who would determine if it is a legitimate transfer request. If so, the student athlete could transfer without penalty.

2. Substantive Right to an Education

. . . .

As matters now stand, the university is obligated only to provide an opportunity to receive an education. As I have suggested elsewhere in this Article, the promise to provide this opportunity resembles a lottery ticket. The opportunity would have more substance if the university were required to do more than merely let student athletes enroll and take courses.

. . . .

A code of intercollegiate athletics should extend the obligation of universities, and in addition to lengthening the period of commitment, it should require minimum levels of support programs. It is unrealistic to expect that student athletes can take full advantage of the opportunity to obtain an education without assistance. The necessity for academic support increases as a university admits student athletes with academic credentials substantially deviating from those of its typical students. Imposing a more substantive obligation to provide an education does not mean that universities should guarantee a degree. It simply means that the university will be required to take specific measures to enhance the likelihood that a student athlete receives one. Such results would also be relevant in evaluating academic enhancement programs used by universities.

B. *A Common Law of Intercollegiate Athletics*

Realistically, promulgation of a code may take several years. Seeking relief through the common law provides an alternative evolutionary pathway that the framers of a code could build upon. The development of a common law of intercollegiate athletics, although accomplishable, faces several obstacles. Courts must be asked to cast aside their reverence for intercollegiate amateurism. Uniformity among jurisdictions is not guaranteed. Solutions crafted through legislative compromise are not available because of considerations of judicial restraint. A proponent of common law rules must be willing to bear the costs of advocating advances in the law. Finally, its development will depend upon the serendipitous occasions of actual disputes.

A common law of intercollegiate athletics will have to address two basic issues. It must define the relationships that are covered and determine the substantive rights based upon those relationships in specific circumstances. The first issue poses little difficulty. I have devoted substantial space in this Article to the first- and second-tier relationships among student athletes, universities, and governing associations in connection with the production, sale, and delivery of intercollegiate athletics. Most courts and commentators deem the second-tier relationship between a student athlete and his university as contractual, but conspicuously have not determined the class of contract. The first-tier relationships creating governing associations are deemed to be matters of voluntary associations law. Although some light has been shed on first- and second-tier relationships, the relationship between student athletes and governing associations remains obscured. A common law of intercollegiate athletics must recognize the existence of this relationship and allocate rights directly between student athletes and governing associations.

The second issue is more problematic. The nature of common law development requires actual cases with concrete circumstances. Some of the cases and circumstances discussed previously lend themselves to common law development more so than others. The types of cases best suited for this approach are perhaps cases involving contract-based issues, Termination cases involving due process issues, cases in any category in which a court may be asked to narrow the scope of amateurism or provide standards for setting penalties, and Transfer cases in which the court may be asked to narrow the scope of the blanket rule covering all transfers.

. . . . [Professor Mathewson's discussion of how contract-based and termination cases will facilitate the development of a common law of intercollegiate athletics is omitted. — ed.].

VI. CONCLUSION

This Article presents a starting point for the debate over the future of intercollegiate athletics. It does not call for the end of amateurism, only the end of its enshrinement by law. We must determine if amateurism can exist without express legal protection or we may discover that we have a system that is a dinosaur that refused to evolve. I suspect that until the aggrieved student athlete has power in the system of checks and balances in the industry of intercollegiate athletics, the industry will continue to evolve inefficiently, capable of survival only through legal subsidization. I propose to save this system with an idea as old as the law itself; I ask that we provide legal rights to student athletes, sufficient to enable them to receive adequate consideration for their efforts, or at least, what they have been promised.

---

2. Student-Athlete/University Relationship

Michael Cozzillio, The Athletic Scholarship and the College National Letter of Intent: A Contract by Any Other Name
35 Wayne Law Review 1275 (1989)*

. . . .

This Article argues that the typical National Letter of Intent (NLOI) explicitly contains both language and broad institutional policy which makes it impossible to construe the resulting relationship between the university and the student-athlete as anything but contractual. The Letter of Intent discredits the tenuous argument that the financial aid arrangement is part of a "gentlemen's agreement" or a gratuitous grant of scholarship monies. Notwithstanding its noncommittal title, the Letter of Intent is not an "agreement to agree" or a similar hybrid formation that historically has been discounted by the courts as a nonbinding gossamer.

Rather, it is, alone or in conjunction with the university's financial aid package, a bilateral contract enforceable through traditional contract machinery.

Many courts have acknowledged that the university-student partnership is contractual in nature, particularly when financial aid has induced a student's commitment to attend the institution. However, the courts have never fully explicated the nuances of this contractual relationship and the parameters of each party's rights and duties. This Article attempts to fill that gap by dissecting the contract between a university and a student-athlete from the pre-contractual negotiation phase through the ultimate performance or nonperformance of the agreement.

. . . .

II. HISTORY OF THE NATIONAL LETTER OF INTENT PROGRAM

The National Letter of Intent Program (NLIP) was spawned by concerns for both the participating institutions and the student-athletes they recruited. In the early stages of intercollegiate athletics, recruiting efforts were circumscribed to high schools geographically proximate to the university. Advances in transportation, communications, and technology had not yet shrunk the country to the point where transcontinental recruiting would become a way of life. The typical high school student did not contemplate up-rooting and relocating to another part of the country. The universities could not justify the higher costs of recruiting beyond a small area because intercollegiate athletics had not evolved into the huge revenue producing industry that it is today.

After World War II, returning veterans ballooned college enrollments and injected new vitality into languishing athletic programs. This factor, together with the increased popularity of television, spurred college athletics' rise to national and international prominence. School administrators quickly saw college sports as big business and perceived the development of their athletic programs as mealtickets. Success on the gridiron was viewed as a critical revenue source— rather than a financial windfall. Thus, aggressive recruiting was sometimes rationalized as the first step in the refinement of an athletic program that would eventually fund the universities' laboratories, computer rooms, and related facilities. It is no mystery that recruiting became a monster that soon began to gorge itself on its creator.

Fierce recruiting for the best athletes presented difficulties for universities, students, parents, and high school faculties. A coaching staff commonly began its recruiting crusade searching for the next year's holy grail while the current athletic campaign was still in progress. On the receiving end, the student-athlete was constantly besieged with a "hard sell"' by an athletic department's most persuasive salespeople. Sales pitches varied from sincere coach-to-mother conversations about the student-athlete's education and general well-being to slick self-promotion of a university's glorious athletic history and the perquisites that such success had engendered. Pressure on the student-athlete and his parents, high school coaches, friends, and teammates was overwhelming. The student-athlete's schedule, already crowded with studies, practice, games and post-season tournaments, was disrupted to the breaking point. The economic exigencies, especially for small institutions, reached prohibitive proportions as competition for quality student-athletes intensified.

The need for some solution was indisputable. The seminal concept for a Letter of Intent germinated on a conference by conference basis at the end of World War

II. In the early 1960s, momentum gathered for a more formal, national Letter of Intent structure. However, initial NCAA suggestions of a compulsory system were met with vigorous dissent. Accordingly, the current voluntary program was adopted in 1964. Thirty-five conferences and seventy-nine independent institutions now participate in the NLIP. The group comprises almost every four year undergraduate institution in the country.

Under the NLIP, an athletic director of the university typically will, in writing, offer the prospective student-athlete a scholarship in exchange for the student-athlete's commitment to attend the institution and participate in intercollegiate athletics. The manifestation of commitment is contained in the National Letter of Intent (NLOI), which must be executed first by the athletic director, then by the student and the student's parent or guardian. The university must file the executed Letter with the appropriate conference commissioners within twenty-one days. A prospective student-athlete can sign only one Letter. The Letter is valid only if the student-athlete has received an "award or recommendation for athletic financial aid"' (when pertinent) at the time the Letter is to be executed. The financial aid representation must list the terms and conditions of the award, as well as its amount and duration. The student-athlete who signs the Letter of Intent agrees to enroll at that institution and waives the right to participate in any intercollegiate athletics with another NLIP member institution. This contractual injunction is effective for two calendar years. The "renegade" athlete, regardless of the date of his transfer, will be eligible for only two years of intercollegiate activity in any sport. Although the deadlines for signing and submitting the Letter of Intent vary from sport to sport, the Letter is a commitment to the university generally, as evidenced by the student-athlete's statement, "I understand that I have signed this Letter with the *institution* and not for a particular sport."[55] The scholarship commitment on the university's part is normally characterized as a yearly obligation renewable on an annual basis up to four years, or five years in certain circumstances.

The Letter of Intent and its restrictions are rendered nugatory if the student-athlete does not meet the admission requirements, financial aid eligibility requirements, or NCAA prerequisites to admission or scholarship assistance. Other actions that nullify the commitment include: attendance and graduation from a junior college after signing the Letter during high school or in the first year of junior college; service on active duty for eighteen months in the armed forces or as a religious missionary; discontinuation of the student-athlete's sport by the institution; failure to attend any institution for one year, and subsequent denial of an athletic scholarship by the institution to whom a Letter of Intent was originally addressed. Other circumstances, such as incapacity or duress, may render voidable obligations incurred under the Letter of Intent. A material breach of a promise or a failure to comply strictly with express conditions may also warrant discharge of the parties' commitments.

The NLIP was designed to be a measure that would accommodate the concerns of *all* parties. Most commentators agree that the program has been a qualified success. The recruitment process has been improved to the point where it is only moderately maddening to all participants. If nothing else, the university recruit-

---

55. Letter of Intent, *infra* Appendix A, at para. 4 (emphasis in original).

ment methods have been streamlined and the incidence of continued overtures after the student-athlete reaches a decision has been considerably ameliorated.

III. CONTRACT FORMATION

....[A thorough discussion of contract formation and letters of intent in general is omitted.—ed.]

C. *Formation of the Scholarship/Letter of Intent Contract*

1. *The Scholarship As Offer*

The typical scholarship proposal tendered by a university to a student constitutes an offer in traditional contract terms. The necessary language of commitment is present in the scholarship proposal. Standard scholarship letters illustrate the university's overall commitment to provide financial aid to the prospective student-athlete. In fact, the recruit is generally instructed to refrain from signing the Letter of Intent without a scholarship proposal in hand. Further, the proposal is addressed to the recipient of the scholarship, and the scholarship terms are delineated in great detail. In virtually all respects, the requisite language and detail satisfies the requirements of the traditional "offer." Thus, at first blush the scholarship proposal, as conveyed to the student-athlete and embraced in the Letter of Intent, invites a response that would seemingly form a contract.

Yet, it may be too sanguine to assume that the scholarship proposal is an "offer" susceptible to immediate contract formation by a proper student-athlete acceptance. Two problems arise that cloud the issue: first, does the person tendering the scholarship offer have authority to bind the university; and second, does the qualifying language in paragraph two of the Letter negate the crucial "language of commitment" factor.

....

The scholarship offer could be attacked as unenforceable on the grounds that the athletic director or other university representative lacked the requisite authority. However, this suggestion is tenuous, given the nature of college athletic scholarships and the well-established role of the athletic directors and coaching staffs. If these personnel do not have the requisite authority to bind an institution, then a similar argument could be made with respect to admissions directors, registrars, and others, wreaking havoc upon a university-student relationship that already is fraught with uncertainty....

The second problem is not so readily resolved. The indefiniteness of the offering-the vague or "open" language-does not appear in the offer itself. Rather, paragraph two of the Letter qualifies or modifies the university's commitment:

> I MUST RECEIVE IN WRITING AN AWARD OR RECOMMENDATION FOR <u>ATHLETIC FINANCIAL AID</u> FROM THE INSTITUTION AT THE TIME OF MY SIGNING FOR THIS LETTER TO BE VALID. The offer or recommendation shall list the terms and conditions of the award, including the amount and duration of the financial aid. If such recommended financial aid is not approved within the institution's normal time period for awarding financial aid, this letter shall be invalid.[149]

---

149. Letter of Intent, *infra* appendix A, at para. 2.

Arguably, the rider language is a manifestation to the reasonable person that the university has not made a bona fide offer. Although the entire tone of the document, especially the mandate that the Letter not be signed without a scholarship commitment, compels a contrary conclusion, paragraph two may be construed as a clause akin to standard commercial language conditioning an entire transaction upon "home office approval." If so, there are several plausible interpretations of the clause's impact upon the formation question.

On one hand, the initial scholarship offer and execution of the Letter of Intent may comprise the entire agreement, with approval of the recommendation constituting pro forma terminology of no legal consequence. Under this interpretation, the approval of the recommendation is a foregone conclusion, rendering the initial transaction a binding offer and acceptance. This suggestion is eminently plausible because over ninety-nine percent of all scholarship commitments tendered at the initial stage are eventually approved. In a related sense, paragraph two may be a condition precedent to the effective performance of the agreement; technically not a modification or corruption of the offer, but rather a provision similar to a financing contingency in real estate contracts, or a typical condition of satisfaction. This type of proviso serves as a prerequisite to the agreement's enforceability— but does not preclude the agreement's formation. A contract would exist, but the conditional duty would not be triggered until the qualifying condition was either met or excused.

On the other hand, paragraph two may suggest that the initial scholarship "offer" is nothing but a form of preliminary negotiations or an invitation for offers. The Letter of Intent would, thus, become the offer, and the acceptance would be the university's approval of the scholarship recommendation. This would create the unusual, though not unique, phenomenon of the offeree setting the terms of the offer....

  . . . .

...The overall tenor of the Letter of Intent supports the conclusion that the university is the offeror and the student-athlete the offeree. The Letter itself requires a scholarship offer before the student-athlete's acceptance is effective. Throughout the entire process, the university is the suitor, laying financial incentives at the feet of the *object d'amour*. A reasonable person could only believe that, at the time of the signing of the Letter, all other would-be suitors are precluded from negotiating with or extending an offer to the student-athlete. A contrary conclusion does violence to the rationale underlying the Letter of Intent program. There is also no language in the Letter of Intent suggesting that the student-athlete's "commitment" is a revocable offer until receipt of the scholarship approval. Couching the student-athlete's Letter as the first step in the offer/acceptance scenario is theoretically possible, but practically unthinkable. Neither the law nor the "industry" should indulge this interpretation and its consequences upon the actors.

2. The Letter of Intent As Acceptance

Assuming arguendo that the scholarship presentation in the Letter of Intent exchange is an offer, the next step in formation is to determine whether an adequate acceptance has been tendered. It has been suggested that offers similar in form to the typical university scholarship pledge do not provide a clear signal as to the desired method of acceptance. If so, the arguably ambiguous nature of the scholarship offer could invite several types of acceptance. While the doubtful offer traditionally was viewed as inviting an acceptance by promise, the better view suggests that, when the offer is unclear or invites either type of acceptance, the offeree may choose the mode of acceptance. In either event, the Letter of Intent is a promissory acceptance—a wholly appropriate response to the scholarship offer. The Letter, signed by the student and his parents or guardian, satisfies the concluding stage in the bilateral contract pattern.

Some might argue that the student-athlete has promised nothing by executing the Letter of Intent and that the university has presented an offer that seeks performance. Under this argument, the Letter merely manifests the student-athlete's intention to perform. The Letter provides formal notice suggesting future performance in response to a unilateral contract offer. The student-athlete's performance would only be a condition precedent to the university's duty to provide the scholarship. He would have no duty to perform, and his refusal to attend school or participate in intercollegiate athletics would constitute nonsatisfaction of the condition. Thus, the university would be excused from paying—tempered, of course, by pertinent NCAA regulations. Under the unilateral contract model, the student-athlete would have no duty to perform and would be immune from damages for breach of contract stemming from his nonperformance.

Despite the unilateral contract's reassuring features to those who cringe at the thought of a defendant student-athlete, the approach is intellectually infirm. The Letter of Intent is the consummation of a binding, executory pact between the university and the student. There is little to indicate that the university has bargained for the individual's performance without any prior commitment, nor is there any evidence that the scholarship pledge can be abbreviated at will. The university does intend to secure a promise from the student. This intent is evidenced by the various types of preparations and decisions made depending upon the athletes who have accepted Letters of Intent, and also by the fact that universities are permitted to offer a limited number of scholarships. With the exception of the scholarship approval language addressed above, it would be difficult for a student to argue that the Letter of Intent package expressly allows the student to reserve the right to revoke or rescind his commitment. Nothing in the Letter suggests that the student has secured an option on the scholarship while preserving his right to attend, or at least barter with, another institution. Moreover, even if the manifestations of the parties reflect no clear indication of a bilateral contract, courts have historically favored a presumption of bilaterality. This presumption is derived from the belief that a party to be advantaged by a performance will generally desire assurances that such performance is forthcoming. Therefore, the Letter of Intent is most logically characterized as an acceptance of a bilateral contract offer, manifested through the student-athlete's promise to attend.

. . . .

3. The Duration of the Agreement Between University and Student-Athlete

The final subissue is whether the contract establishes a precise length of time for performance and, if not, whether a period can be judicially supplied. NCAA regulations provide that the standard scholarship commitment is renewable on a yearly basis, and most scholarship commitment letters indicate that the duration of the financial aid package is one year. This annual scholarship is exchanged for the student-athlete's pledge to attend and play.

If the scholarship is a yearly proposition, then the university can argue that each year it may withhold offering a scholarship. The common parlance suggesting that a student-athlete's scholarship has been "revoked" may be a mischaracterization because a new offer eventuates each year. Accordingly, the bilateral contract configuration describing the initial Scholarship/Letter of Intent arrangement would exist only for the student-athlete's freshman year. Absent a promissory equivalent to the Letter of Intent, the university's scholarship proposal for subsequent years would be a unilateral contract offer, accepted by the student-athlete's performance. This offer/acceptance by performance process would continue until the student-athlete had graduated or exhausted all eligibility. Further, if the continuing scholarship offer is unilateral, then the student-athlete would have no duty to perform. It would be necessary to evaluate the impact of the student-athlete's partial performance, and the extent to which it created additional duties, or compromised the university's ability to revoke, during that academic year.

An alternative interpretation is that the initial scholarship is an offer to a four year contract that calls for a series of one year performances. Many scholarship letters intimate that the one year scholarship is renewable each year up to four years, provided the student meets the university's requirements. Because most students consider their scholarship to be a four year ride, the parties' actions may reflect an intent to be bound for four years.

There is, however, no concrete manifestation of a student promise to attend an institution beyond the initial commitment of one year. Even if the university's scholarship commitment is construed as a four year pledge, it is unlikely that the student-athlete's transfer prerogative has been compromised. If a four year bilateral contract scenario is assumed, the only plausible conclusion is that the student has an option to cancel at the conclusion of the first year—or "at will" any time after the first year. This interpretation supports the four year framework suggested by the scholarship pledge as it is normally conveyed to student-athletes and their parents, and remains true to one of the purposes of the Letter of Intent, which is to impose a binding obligation for at least one year. In this sense, the arrangement would be similar to a contract between a professional sports club and a player with a nonguaranteed contract. The player commits for a designated period of time, but the club reserves the right to terminate his services at its discretion. The key distinction is that here the service provider, the student-athlete, possesses the power to terminate the relationship.

. . . .

. . . . [Professor Cozzillio's substantial discussion of theories pursuant to which the student-athlete/university contract can be voided is omitted.—ed.]

IV. VALIDATION

. . . . [A general discussion of the consideration doctrine is omitted.—ed.].

B. *Consideration and the Letter of Intent*

The promises in the NLOI appear to meet the three part consideration test advanced by Professors Calamari and Perillo as applied to the university and the student-athlete. The first element requires the promisee, the university in this sequence, to suffer legal detriment; i.e., to do something it is not legally obligated to do, or refrain from doing what it is legally privileged to do. In the NLOI, the university suffers legal detriment in at least two ways. First, the university is under no legal compulsion to offer financial aid to the student-athlete. The university simply offers it in an effort to attract the student to that institution. The university is doing what it is otherwise not legally obligated to do. Second, because the university is limited by the NCAA in both the amount of financial aid and the number of awards that it may provide, giving financial aid to one student forecloses the university from extending that financial aid to another student. Thus, the university is refraining from doing what it is legally privileged to do.

The next element of the consideration test requires that the detriment induce the promise, or, that the promisor make the promise because he wishes to exchange it for detriment suffered by the promisee. This second element is present in the NLOI because the promisor, the student-athlete, extends his promise to attend in exchange for the university's providing financial aid and offering an education....

The third element of the test requires the promise to induce the detriment. Generally, this element is satisfied if the promisee "knows of the offer and intends to accept it."[245] In the NLOI, the university, the promisee, knows that the student-athlete promises to attend the school and participate in the athletic program. When the athletic director signs the Letter of Intent on behalf of the university, he expressly signifies its response to that promise.

The consideration supporting the student-athlete's promise is the legal detriment suffered by the university. Consideration must also support the university's promise to provide the student with financial aid. The consideration in this exchange is represented by the student-athlete's promise to attend that university as evidenced by the executed Letter of Intent.

Given the bilateral nature of the Letter of Intent arrangement, the consideration issue must now be addressed from the standpoint of the student as promisee. The first element of the three part consideration test requires that the student suffer legal detriment. Prior to the time the student-athlete signs the Letter of Intent, he is under no legal obligation to attend any university. By signing the Letter, the student-athlete has obligated himself to attend a university with which he otherwise had no legal relationship. The promisee can also suffer legal detriment by refraining from doing what he is otherwise legally able to do—attend a different university and participate in that university's athletic program....

The second element of the consideration test requires the student-athlete's detriment to induce the university's promise. The university must have promised to provide financial aid to the student in exchange for the student's detriment. The university has committed scholarship funding to the student-athlete because it wishes to attract him to the university in the hope that his athletic skills will enhance the university's athletic program. Therefore, the student-athlete's detriment has induced the promise by the university, satisfying the second component of the consideration regime.

Third, the promise must induce the detriment; the promisee must know of the offer and intend to accept. Paragraph two of the Letter of Intent mandates that the student-athlete receive the university's financial aid award or recommendation when he signs the Letter. This representation must be in writing and contain the "terms and conditions of the award, including the amount and duration of the fi-

---

245. J. Calamari & J. Perillo, *supra* note 7, § 4-2, at 188.

nancial aid."[249] When the student signs the Letter of Intent, thereby providing the detriment, he has before him the full terms of the offer made by the promisor university. The student-athlete knows of the offer and manifests an intent to accept the offer by signing the Letter of Intent. This procedure satisfies the third element of the consideration test.

Thus, on the surface, the student-athlete's promise to attend the university and the university's promise to provide financial aid are each supported by consideration. However, the Letter of Intent is not without potential escape hatches, illusory-like promises, and other infirmities that may raise doubts about the document's "validity" or "substance." . . .

C. Illusory Promises and the Letter of Intent

. . . . [Professor Cozzillio's discussion of the potential illusory nature of the agreement is omitted. —ed.]

In sum, several potential questions arise under a traditional consideration analysis. However, it is unlikely that the Letter of Intent arrangement would fail for lack of consideration. If the Letter of Intent were found to be invalid on consideration grounds, the now panaceic doctrine of promissory estoppel waits in the wings to rescue the victim of the putative breach.

V. PROMISSORY ESTOPPEL

. . . .

B. Promissory Estoppel and the NLOI

The importance of promissory estoppel to enforcement of promises contained in the NLOI cannot be overstated. The Letter of Intent is by no means immune from attack for lack of consideration or fatal indefiniteness. Various other potential difficulties that plague the agreement may prevent relief under contract theory. Thus, promissory estoppel could be the last refuge of a party who, believing that the agreement is binding, finds that it fails to satisfy the minimum criteria of a "contract." The characterization of promissory estoppel as an independent concept, or merely as a remedy for reliance upon wholly gratuitous, unbargained-for promises, will dictate the extent to which the parties are left without effective redress if the Letter of Intent fails to satisfy contractual thresholds.

Promissory estoppel could become operative in several respects in the Scholarship/Letter of Intent exchange. First, the agreement could be compared to a social obligation, educational grant, or similar arrangement that lacks the crucial intent to be bound or anticipation of legal consequences. It is unlikely that promissory estoppel in its most pristine form would be invoked in these situations given the unmistakable pretense of bargain in the NLOI. . . .

Second, promissory estoppel may be activated if the promises made by either party are construed to be illusory, or if the requisite validating exchange is found lacking. In this sense, promissory estoppel would again serve as a consideration substitute in a transaction that plainly contemplated or consummated a bargain. . . .

Notwithstanding surveys reporting judicial disregard for the reliance component, even the more progressive applications of the doctrine seemingly would still

---

249. *Id.*

require the university or the student-athlete to prove justifiable and detrimental reliance. A university jilted by a student-athlete probably must show that it offered one of its limited scholarships in reliance upon the student-athlete's Letter of Intent and commitment to attend. The reliance may assume several forms. For example, the university's anticipation of a high-school standout's attendance may have been manifested by large-scale publicity campaigns, hiring special coaches or tutors tailored to the student's particular needs, or even expanding existing seating and playing facilities. The university may simply have bypassed or forfeited another student-athlete with similar athletic abilities, or perhaps may have wasted the scholarship commitment because it was too late to secure another quality applicant at the time of the student-athlete's recantation.

Potential reliance-based recovery is by no means limited to the university. The student-athlete may have ample evidence of reliance upon a university's representations of financial aid. A university's eleventh hour decision to withdraw the promised financial aid could leave the student-athlete without any options to attend other schools. The student may have expended significant time and expense in anticipation of attendance at a particular institution, including taking certain courses suited to the pledged university, purchasing an automobile or clothing, or taking similar steps designed to accommodate the peculiar needs of the university.

A collateral question arises when a student attends a particular school because of an affinity for its head coach. If the student has exacted a promise from the university to maintain the coaching staff, or if such a promise could be inferred, then promissory estoppel may serve as a suitable basis for relief if the university permits that coach to abdicate his responsibilities by accepting a coaching position elsewhere. Of course, as discussed below, if the representation pertaining to the coaching staff is a condition precedent, then it may only be a trigger to the student-athlete's duty to attend. The student-athlete may walk away from the contract because strict compliance with the condition was not achieved, but the student-athlete will not have a cause of action because no promise has been breached.

. . . .

VI. PERFORMANCE

. . . . [A discussion of performance obligations in general is omitted. — ed.]

B. *Performance Obligations Under the Letter of Intent: The Qualifiers*

In order to assess the duties of the parties under the Letter of Intent it is necessary to identify the promises made and any conditions, either express or constructive, upon which they depend. Having already established that the arrangement between the university and the student-athlete is bilateral, the remaining task is to ascertain the promises advanced and any express or constructive conditions upon which the promises depend.

At the threshold, the university has promised to provide the student-athlete with financial aid in exchange for the student-athlete's promise to attend that university and play a college sport. Several provisions in the Letter of Intent expressly condition the respective performances. First, the student-athlete must meet the requirements for admission to the university, its academic requirements for scholarship funding, and the NCAA requirements for freshman financial aid. Second, most scholarship commitments require the student-athlete to observe all academic rules of the institution, maintain satisfactory grades, and comply with rules and regulations established by coaching staffs. Finally, the student-athlete must comply with pertinent conference and NCAA rules and regulations incorporated by reference into the agreement. In addition to these three provisions, which actually seem to be conditions inserted as promise modifiers, there are two other qualifiers that merit brief attention: the twenty-one day filing requirement of paragraph nine, and the approval of the financial aid recommendation of paragraph two. All five provisions are collateral to the exchange at the heart of the contract—scholarship money for athletic participation....

....

C. The Duty to Pay and the Duty to Play: The Parties' Rights and Responsibilities Under the Scholarship/Letter of Intent Scheme

To this point, the Article has posited that the Scholarship/Letter of Intent configuration is a bilateral contract containing an exchange of promises the performance of which is contingent upon the satisfaction of various express and constructive conditions. Collateral conditions that may affect the parties' duties to perform have also been addressed. The remaining issue centers upon the constructive conditions created by the promises to pay and play, and the definition of performance or substantial performance under this scenario. Because the university's duty is fairly well defined as a commitment to provide a financial aid package to the student-athlete, and to provide an opportunity to secure an education and participate in the university's athletic program, this section will primarily address the student-athlete's responsibilities and the difficulties encountered in attempting to establish the parameters of satisfactory performance.

Of course, this does not suggest that the university's performance obligations are so clearly delineated as to preclude controversy. Various performance issues may arise when the university, for example, refuses to give the student-athlete a starting position on the team, provide him with the playing time that he desires, or otherwise neglects to fulfill promises that it may have expressly or impliedly made to the student-athlete, such as maintaining the existing coaching staff. Basic coaching prerogatives such as game strategy and substitutions are probably not subject to challenge by the affected players—absent clear and unequivocal representations from the coaching staff or other agents of the university. Thus, such matters as playing time, guarantees of a starting position, and dispensation from practice sessions are seldom actionable.

However, the student's right to challenge wholesale changes in the coaching hierarchy is much more significant, particularly because many schools "sell" the coach as the key incentive for the student-athlete's commitment. A university that explicitly, or even tacitly, promises to maintain its current coaching staff should make every effort to honor that covenant—or risk legal reprisals. Actions for breach in this context may very well lie if evidence exists to establish that the university has undertaken such a duty. On the facts presented herein, however, the primary basis upon which a student-athlete could terminate the agreement without prejudice or sue for breach is the university's failure to provide the requisite financial aid. Thus, the arrangement again parallels the traditional contract between a professional sports team and its players, in which the principal predicate for the athlete's termination of the agreement is the club's failure or refusal to pay monies owed.

Focusing upon the student-athlete's duties, the predominant question that has recurred without resolution throughout personal services litigation in the sports and entertainment arenas centers upon a determination of what constitutes "satis-factory performance." Does the professional basketball player who averages 25 points per game rather than his customary 30 violate his agreement to play? Like-wise, if a student-athlete fails to approach his potential as a college performer, is the university, as a matter of contract law, justified in pulling his scholarship? De-rivatively, is the student-athlete vulnerable to a breach of contract suit because he has failed to perform as expected?

While the parameters of an entertainer's performance obligations are not read-ily drawn, it is safe to say that the foregoing questions must be answered in the negative. A contrary response would render professional athletes subject to law-suits whenever they failed to measure up to the previous years' statistics, and, as applied to the student-athlete, would demean a higher education system already viewed in a dim light. Yet, to suggest that there are no guidelines either to assess an athlete's compliance with his promise to compete or to evaluate his "em-ployer's" ability to terminate the relationship would destroy the very fabric of the bilateral contract model.

....

2. The Parameters of Substantial Performance

The line between full performance and substantial performance is quite thin in any personal services contract in the sports or entertainment fields. Substantial performance could equal full performance in terms of playing skill, where the ul-timate performance of the promise has no upper limit. Thus, if a major league pitcher hurls a "perfect game," he has undeniably "performed;" but if he pitches a two-hit shutout in the following game, he most certainly has not breached the contract, nor has he merely "substantially performed." Applying this reasoning, a university claim of an immaterial breach for a student-athlete's lackluster perfor-mance would be an aberration. The student-athlete's promise to perform amounts to a promise to try, or to do his best. The student-athlete would breach this promise only by obvious failure to make an honest effort, a constructive refusal to perform.

Under this analysis, an interesting problem arises with respect to the student-athlete who refuses to perform altogether. Consider a scenario in which eight out of twelve athletes on a college basketball team refuse to play, requiring surrender of the game and possible forfeiture of any revenues that had been collected in ad-vance. The athletes could also refuse to participate during an entire season. In large-scale college athletics, this eventuality could result in the loss of hundreds of thousands of dollars, and a large amount of goodwill and public confidence. It is arguable, then, that the university would have an action in breach, the materiality depending upon the significance of the nonperformance vis-a-vis the total perfor-mance due, in addition to possible suspension of scholarship benefits. If the stu-dent-athletes have violated their agreement to participate in intercollegiate athlet-ics for the university, they could be held accountable in an action for damages for a refusal to perform. If the breach is deemed material, the university would have the option to continue or withdraw the scholarship, and sue for damages. The university could also treat the breach as immaterial, and proceed with its own performance, reserving its right to pursue a damages action post hoc. Any other conclusion ignores the fact that the parties have entered into a binding, bilateral contract.

The possible hysteria resulting from any conclusion that a student-athlete could be sued for breach of promise might prompt a resurrection of the unilateral contract theory—the university promises scholarship money in exchange for performance, and such performance rests at the behest of the athlete, with the only "sanction" for a refusal to perform being the discharge of the university's duty to pay scholarship monies. However, this conclusion is merely a placebo. A unilateral contract configuration does not resolve the problem of an athlete who, after enjoying nearly a year of scholarship benefits, such as a baseball player who might not have to perform until the spring, refuses to participate. In that case, the university could probably still sue to recover the monies advanced. Further, the unilateral contract model would require strict compliance with the condition precedent to payment, and any failure on the part of the athlete to perform would justify withholding scholarship funds. Thus, the unilateral contract analysis does not necessarily mitigate the potentially harsh consequences upon the nonperforming athlete. Although the athlete may be immune from breach, he may also be foreclosed from arguing that he has substantially performed the condition precedent to the university's duty to pay. The student-athlete scholarship could be withdrawn for the slightest noncompliance—qualified by pertinent NCAA regulations.

. . . .

VII. CONCLUSION

The arrangement between a university and a student-athlete represents a binding bilateral contract, at least during the first year of matriculation. It would be a grave mistake to describe the relationship in noncontractual terms simply to avoid the complex and difficult conceptual problems attending a conclusion that a contract exists. It is what it is, and no manner of judicial contrivance or scholarly legerdemain will alter the true intent of the parties. The agreement is well suited to "administration" under traditional contract machinery, although the idiosyncracies of the academic setting necessitate some fine tuning.

The university and the student-athlete must recognize that their commitments harbor profound consequences in light of the other party's expectations and reliance, and in terms of their own integrity. The Letter of Intent program has been established partially to provide a mechanism for the university and the student-athlete to extract promises from one another beyond an informal, precatory exchange. The sense of commitment that it conjures just may spill over into other areas of intercollegiate athletics, which could use a facelift in many respects. The legal system should not bypass this issue, and should not be unavailable as recourse to a victim of a breach simply because it takes place in an academic setting. A simple look at the annual recruiting budget and income from the athletic program of an average university emphatically negates any suggestion that the student-university relationship is mere child's play. These arrangements must be given legal significance in order to provide both the universities and student-athletes proper credit for integrity, intelligence, and maturity. The author hopes that couching this somewhat unique relationship in traditional terms will demonstrate that its peculiarities only warrant special attention in the application of contract law—but under no circumstances do they justify exclusion from traditional contract enforcement machinery.

Harold B. Hilborn, Comment, Student-Athletes and Judicial Inconsistency: Establishing a Duty to Educate as a Means of Fostering Meaningful Reform of Intercollegiate Athletics
89 Northwestern University Law Review 741 (1995)*

. . . . .

I. INTRODUCTION

Intercollegiate sports have become a multi-million dollar entertainment industry. . . .

Despite this reality, the NCAA Constitution mandates that member institutions
should maintain sports programs as a vital component of the educational program and that the admission, academic standing, and academic progress of student-athletes should be consistent with the policies and standards adopted by the
institution for the student body in general. Moreover, the NCAA has also adopted
a principle of amateurism whereby student-athletes should be motivated primarily by education and by the opportunity for development of character afforded by
participation in intercollegiate athletics: amateur athletes should view their participation in sports as an "avocation" rather than as a profession. As a result, universities and athletes must guard against exploitation by professional and commercial enterprises. Finally, the NCAA Constitution mandates that universities
regulate the time required of student-athletes for participation in intercollegiate
athletics to minimize interference with their opportunities for acquiring a quality
education.

Doubts of the coexistence of big-business intercollegiate athletics and the
ivory-tower principles of American higher education embodied in the NCAA
Constitution have sparked much debate. That is, how compatible are the NCAA's
guiding principles with the reality of college sports? Despite the NCAA's lofty
goals, the commercialization of intercollegiate sports has marred the NCAA's
stated educational objectives. Since substantial funding of athletic programs flows
from outside the institutions, universities feel pressured to emphasize income-pro-
ducing spectator sports to ensure sponsors a return on their investments. This extensive commercialization inevitably causes many colleges to fail to educate student-athletes. Thus, not surprisingly, graduation rates in the revenue-producing
sports of basketball and football lag behind the rates for other athletes and
nonathletes alike. After five years, only thirty-two percent of Division I-A basketball players and forty-seven percent of Division I-A football players receiving
scholarships graduated. For all students, the rate is forty-eight percent, and for all
student-athletes, the figure is a somewhat higher fifty-six percent. (The inclusion
in the study of women and Ivy League athletes may skew the figures for all student-athletes upwards). At one-third of colleges and universities with a major basketball program, fewer than one in five players ever graduates. These trends are
even more disturbing in light of evidence that student-athletes enter not only with
dreams of athletic excellence, but also with legitimate expectations of a quality

---

* Copyright 1995 by Northwestern University School of Law. Used with permission. All
rights reserved.

college education. Survey data show that seventy-three percent of freshman and sophomore college football and basketball players believe, at the time of matriculation, that earning a degree is important.

Abysmal graduation rates underscore just one symptom of the unhealthy relationship between education and college sports. These statistics say nothing of the quality of education, the student-athletes' fields of study, the means by which the few passed their courses, or admission standards. In revenue-producing sports, admissions officers lump student athletes into a special pool of applicants, emphasizing height, speed, and program need over academics. Under intense pressure from alumni and coaches to field better teams, schools consistently accept athletes who score lower than nonathletes on standardized tests. In addition, too many enter college with insufficient academic skills. At the 1991 Nike summer basketball camp, a showcase for the best high school athletes, about half of the 123 players attending tested below grade level in reading, and one-fifth read between third and fifth grade levels. To help these marginal students remain eligible for athletics, universities provide them with academic advisers (many of whom are employed by the athletic department rather than by academic units), who do everything from making certain that a star linebacker attends an early-morning class to arranging for tutoring.

. . . .

This Comment attempts to reconcile the commercial reality of intercollegiate athletics with its ideological underpinnings by proposing that courts subject colleges and universities to liability when they fail to educate student-athletes. . . .

II. THE CONTRACTUAL RELATIONSHIP

. . . . [Discussion of general contract principles and the contractual nature of the student's relationship with his or her university is omitted. — ed.].

C. The Student-Athlete's Contract: Procedure

. . . . [Discussion of the National Letter of Intent is omitted. A detailed discussion of this topic is contained in the Cozzillio article that appears *supra* in this Subsection. — ed.].

. . . [U]nder the current application of contract law to athletic scholarships, student-athletes find no legal remedies for breach by the university. Although express terms seem to protect student-athletes, courts have deferred to universities' "reasonable" interpretations of implied contract terms to validate a school's breach. Yet where a student-athlete breaches an express term of the contract with the legitimate goal of fulfilling an implied term, courts have still held for defendant universities. As a result, the judicial procedure for interpreting these contracts makes it difficult for student-athletes to claim that universities have a duty to educate them.

D. The Scope of Substantive Implied Duties to Students

1. In General.— The relationship between students and schools is unique and special. Historically, the common-law doctrine of *in loco parentis* embodied the most comprehensive interpretation of that relationship. As to mental training, moral and physical discipline, and welfare of students, college authorities stood in place of parents and had the discretion, with few exceptions, to make any regulation or policy they deemed necessary so long as it did not violate the law. Where there was such a special relationship between the university and the student, the

former had a duty to protect the latter from harm. In essence, the student's dependence upon the university may create a special relationship.

However, beginning with *Brown v. Board of Education*,[89] the application of *in
loco parentis* began to wane. Although the decline has resulted in increased freedom for students on college campuses, it also loosened the special relationship between students and universities. In *Baldwin v. Zoradi*,[93] for example, the court
noted that imposing tort liability on a university for injuries sustained by a student as a result of another student's intoxication would create a duty for the university to control alcoholic intake by others. In establishing the reasonableness of
such a duty, the court looked at several factors, including the university's moral
blame, the need for deterrence, and the ability of the university to insure itself financially. The court decided that such duties would be overwhelming given the
probable impact on students' civil liberties. As a result, the decline of *in loco parentis* effectively removed schools' moral obligations to prevent drinking, despite
the potential harm that this behavior poses to students.

However, courts must carefully distinguish legal contractual obligations from
moral duties. Where terms in a university handbook create specific policies and
procedures for implementing the policies, the contract may supersede *in loco parentis*. For example, if a university promulgates an explicit policy on sexual harassment that includes a requirement to investigate and discipline those who violate
it, the university has a legal duty to enforce that policy in good faith. But the link
between the duty to protect and the duty to educate may be somewhat tenuous
because the primacy of education at a university is seldom an express part of the
contract. However, the decision in *Wilson v. Continental Insurance Cos.*[99] indicates that a school may have an implied contractual duty to pay special attention
to vulnerable segments of its population even in absence of the *in loco parentis*
doctrine.

In *Wilson*, students alleged that the Marquette University Law School negligently
encouraged them to enroll in an extracurricular course in "mind control" to improve their study habits. The law school virtually required minority students to participate in tutoring and additional courses such as the mind control class, and the
school did so because many minority students entered law school under lower admission standards than white students. The plaintiff alleged that, as a result of the
course, his mental health deteriorated, causing him to withdraw from the school.

In holding for the university, the court reasoned that it could not find a legal
duty unless there was a foreseeable harm, and a school can foresee a detrimental
psychological impact only if it has required psychological evaluations for its students prior to matriculation. Moreover, imposing a duty to select curriculum in a
manner that protects the mental health of each student would subject schools to
constant harassment in the courts, which might in turn cause irreparable harm to
public and private education. In essence, the court acknowledged that a special relationship may exist between universities and marginal students and that, theoretically, there is a duty to guarantee education. However, fear of the administrative
impact has prevented courts from imposing upon universities contractual duties
to take extra care in educating marginal students.

---

89. 347 U.S. 483 (1954).
93. 176 Cal. Rptr. 809 (Cal. Ct. App. 1981).
99. 274 N.W.2d 679 (Wis. 1979).

2. *Educational Malpractice and Nonathletes.*—Courts have responded with hostility to tort claims of educational malpractice for similar reasons. In *Peter W. v. San Francisco Unified School District,*[107] the seminal educational malpractice case, the plaintiff graduated from one of the district's public secondary schools, yet he alleged that he still lacked adequate academic skills. The court declined to consider his substantive claims of negligence, focusing instead upon the facts that had a bearing on the existence of a duty of care. The court expressed its fear that the establishment of a duty would leave the definition of standard of care to juries that would lack guidance on the standard against which the school's conduct could be measured. " '[D]uty' is not sacrosanct in itself, but only an expression of the sum total of...considerations of policy...,"[111] wrote the court. The court added that "[t]he ultimate consequences, in terms of public time and money, would burden [schools]—and society—beyond calculation."

Courts also frown on claims of educational malpractice even where unique fact patterns severely restrict the pool of potential litigants. In *Hoffman v. Board of Education,*[113] for example, the New York Court of Appeals held that a school district that employed a certified clinical psychologist to examine a student prior to entering kindergarten, placed the student in a class for children with retarded mental development, kept the student in that class for ten years, and subsequently discovered that he was not retarded could not be subject to liability for educational malpractice. The court based its holding on "the principle that courts ought not interfere with the professional judgment of those charged by the Constitution and by statute with the responsibility for the administration of the schools...."

Thus, the court based its animosity toward educational malpractice on some concept other than duty; instead, the animosity arose out of the court's unwillingness to substitute its own judgment for the professional judgment of school boards. The court suggested that disgruntled students may best resolve their disputes with schools through administrative processes provided by statute.

Although courts have recognized breach of contract as a cause of action in cases involving the education provided by universities, few cases have challenged the quality of higher education. In the two cases that have presented this challenge, the courts cited remarkably similar policy reasons for denying claims of breach of the duty to educate. In the first case, the Idaho Supreme Court stated:

> The legislature has established educational boards and agencies governing the quality of education in both public and private institutions in this state. It is through those administrative channels that the plaintiffs should pursue their redress for their allegedly inadequate education at North Idaho College, and not through the court system.... [120]

In the second case, *Cavaliere v. Duff 's Business Institute,*[121] the court invoked the same policy, noting that unless an institution of higher education purports to in-

---

107. 131 Cal. Rptr. 854 (Cal. Ct. App. 1976).
111. *Id.* at 860 (quoting Dillon v. Legg, 69 Cal. Rptr. 72, 76 (Cal. 1968) (internal quotations omitted)).
113. 400 N.E.2d 317 (N.Y. 1979).
120. *Wickstrom,* 725 P.2d at 161-62 (Donaldson, C.J., dissenting).
121. 605 A.2d 397 (Pa. Super. Ct. 1992).

volve a specific contractual undertaking, "in the student handbook and catalog or otherwise," judges and juries may not review the quality of education.

  3. *The Duty to Student-Athletes.*—Even though courts have decided only a limited number of cases on the issue of whether a university has a duty to educate student-athletes, generally the courts have been unwilling to impose this duty. In *Jones v. Williams,*[124] for example, the court structured its decision to avoid a consideration of the duty question altogether. In *Jackson v. Drake University,*[125] a student claimed that by actively recruiting him to play intercollegiate basketball and subjecting him to numerous regulations, the university undertook to provide an atmosphere conducive to academic achievement. Holding for the school, the court reasoned that it could not find a duty to educate where there was no clear standard of care by which to measure the university's conduct. The court justified its refusal to recognize this duty on the basis of judicial inexperience in defining the standard of care. However, it appears that the court based the existence of this inexperience upon earlier holdings by courts that there is no general duty to educate. The court further defended its refusal to establish a duty to educate by articulating its fear that the finding of a duty might result in an enormous amount of litigation involving college athletic programs and that courts would be forced to pass judgment on the manner by which universities operate their athletic programs.

  Despite these results, a few courts have found that contract law can provide student-athletes with a cause of action. In *Ross v. Creighton University,*[131] for example, the court held that where a university makes identifiable contractual promises to a student-athlete, there may be a breach of contract action if the school has not made a good faith effort to perform on its promises. Still, the court's construction severely constricts breach of contract claims because it requires student-athletes to bargain for the specific terms of their scholarships, a prospect that is highly unlikely given the prevalence of standard-form scholarship contracts, the widespread use of the National Letter of Intent, and foremost and implicitly, the imbalance of bargaining power between high school students and universities during the recruiting process. Moreover, as long as courts employ a biased procedure for interpreting implied terms of scholarship agreements and embrace amorphous notions of "public policy" and "administration" to reject claims of breach of the duty to educate, student-athletes will likely never succeed in breach of contract claims. As a result, the contract doctrine as interpreted by most courts only perpetuates the subversion of academics to athletics.

III. THE ABSENCE OF AN EMPLOYER-EMPLOYEE RELATIONSHIP

  . . . .

A. *Taxation of Scholarships*

  By exempting scholarships from federal income tax, the Internal Revenue Service (I.R.S.) has given courts a primary justification for holding that students who receive financial aid are not university employees. The Internal Revenue Code begins with the premise that all income is taxable. However, the government gener-

---

124. 431 N.W.2d 419 (Mich. Ct. App. 1988).
125. 778 F. Supp. 1490 (S.D. Iowa 1991).
131. 740 F. Supp. 1319 (N.D. Ill. 1990), *aff'd*, 957 F.2d 410 (7th Cir. 1992).

ally exempts scholarships from taxation on the ground that recipients are students rather than employees. Litigation has arisen frequently over the taxation of graduate student teaching assistants who receive tuition waivers while providing services of immeasurable benefit to universities. In determining whether teaching assistantships are taxable, courts employ either a primary benefits test or a quid pro quo test. Under the primary benefits test, the court inquires whether the scholarship primarily benefits the grantor or the grantee; if the grantor is the primary beneficiary, the court holds that the scholarship is taxable and deems the recipient an employee. The quid pro quo test involves an assessment of whether the grant results from a bargained-for relationship; if there has not been a bargain between the student and the university, the court holds that the scholarship is not taxable and that the student is not an employee.

While the court must make a fact-specific determination under either of the tests, the outcomes might not necessarily be consistent. For example, in *Kopecky v. Commissioner*,[141] the court used the primary benefits test to determine that even though all scholarship recipients similarly situated to the petitioner had to perform services for the university as teaching assistants, the I.R.S. could tax the student's scholarship since the university treated him as an employee for administrative purposes. The court held that, for all intents and purposes, the scholarship recipients were employees and that the university did nothing to mask this fact.

In contrast, the court in *Steiman v. Commissioner*,[143] applying the same test and reasoning that all degree candidates had to perform teaching duties as part of their training, exempted a graduate student's scholarship even though the candidate provided valuable services to the university. Because the university's purpose in awarding the scholarship was not to fill teaching positions, but rather to provide degree candidates with the opportunity to enhance their own knowledge by enlightening others, the court would not consider scholarship recipients to be employees subject to federal income taxes.

Courts have also decided subsequent cases using the quid pro quo test. In *Taylor v. Commissioner*,[145] the court focused on whether the petitioner, a graduate student, fit the general, common-law definition of an employee. The court held that: "Generally speaking, an EMPLOYEE is a person who renders service to another usually for wages, salary, or other financial consideration, and who in the performance of such service is entirely subject to the direction and control of the other, such being the EMPLOYER." A student who performs services purely incidental to the goal of education has not bargained for wages. When determining whether a scholarship recipient has bargained for wages, courts prefer not to compare the student to members of the faculty. The fact that a student does not have to pay social security taxes and does not receive the benefits of a university health or retirement plan does not prove the lack of a bargained-for relationship; administrative treatment alone will not determine whether the scholarship recipient is an employee.

Thus, under the quid pro quo test, courts normally examine whether schools require teaching, research, or other services of all candidates for a particular degree as a condition to receiving the degree irrespective of the grantor's motives or the actual benefits received by the grantee. In reaching its decision that the gradu-

---

141. 27 T.C.M. (CCH) 1061 (T.C. 1968).
143. 56 T.C. 1350 (1971).
145. 71 T.C. 124 (1978).

ate student should not be treated as an employee for tax purposes, the court in *Taylor* focused on this control issue. The court found that the plaintiff's responsibilities to the university as a graduate student were only incidental to his ability to receive a degree and that the plaintiff was not compensated for his services.

These decisions leave the status of the student-athlete who receives a scholarship in a state of flux. If a court were to apply the primary benefits test from *Kopecky*, it may determine that because student-athletes do not receive paychecks or employee benefits, and thus do not look like employees, their scholarships should not be taxable, and they should not be considered employees.

But if a court looked at the same circumstances under the analysis made by the court in *Steiman*, it might reach the opposite result. The court could have reasoned that because universities do not offer degrees in intercollegiate athletics, the primary purpose of college sports is not to provide education for those with special talents, and thus an athlete should be considered an employee since he provides a valuable service to the university and is compensated through his scholarship.

Under the *Taylor* quid pro quo test, courts could very well employ the same reasoning as the court in *Steiman* and reach the opposite result. Because participation in sports is purely incidental to the direct transfer of funds from the athletic department to the student-athlete's university account, the court may conclude that the student-athlete has not bargained for tuition payments, is not controlled by the university, and therefore is not an employee.

Despite the ambiguities these cases expose, the I.R.S. has never challenged the tax exemption of a student-athlete's scholarship benefits. It has, however, issued a revenue ruling that student-athletes are only exempt to the extent that their scholarships do not exceed expenses for tuition, fees, room, board, and necessary supplies. The I.R.S. recognizes this exemption only if the university expects (but does not require) the student to participate in a particular sport, requires no particular activity in lieu of participation, and does not cancel the scholarship if the student cannot participate. In short, the I.R.S. has determined that athletic scholarships exist primarily to aid recipients in pursuing academic studies. It has reached this conclusion even though parties have raised valid factual questions under the primary benefits and quid pro quo tests as to whether student-athletes are employees.

.... [Discussion of the workers compensation implications of judicial refusal to recognize student-athletes as employees of their colleges and universities is omitted. The workers' compensation issue is addressed in the Davis article which appears earlier in this chapter. — ed.].

IV. PROPOSALS FOR REFORM

....

A. The Implied Contractual Duty to Educate

If universities are permitted to benefit from their contention that their primary goal is to provide education to student-athletes, even though they continue to simultaneously use the student-athletes to create a unique entertainment product as an externality, they should also be required to take some legal responsibility for failing to educate these student-athletes. The exploitative nature of the relationship between student-athletes and the universities they attend will not fade until courts hold colleges and universities accountable for the academic performance of

their student-athletes. This subpart analyzes the implied contractual duty to educate student-athletes and illustrates that the duty is consistent with many of the
policy factors that comprise the duty equation.

The claims that a school has an educational duty to its students and that it
breaches this duty by failing to provide the level of education appropriate to a
particular student underlie the educational malpractice cause of action. Breach of
contract, on the other hand, involves an analysis of the terms of the contract, either express or implied. When a contractual term is implied, courts consider public policy ramifications to verify the scope of the contract. Thus, tort and contract
considerations mirror each other; whether a defendant owes a duty of care to a
plaintiff is a question of law for the judge to determine.

The nature of the relationship between the parties assists courts in answering
this question. They will often employ a comprehensive balancing test to determine the scope of a duty. First, courts might consider the administrative factor;
that is, they will not impose a duty if the attempt to do so would unduly burden
the judicial system. Therefore, the possibility of a flood of litigation or the reversal of a strong precedent may inhibit the imposition of a duty. Second, courts may
also impose duties based on moral or ethical considerations. Sometimes, though,
this does not reflect "liability based on fault" and is thus too subjective.

Other judges premise duty on economic efficiency; a defendant may be liable if
its cost of preventing harm to a plaintiff is less than the latter's avoidance cost.
Moreover, the need to deter other potential litigants from engaging in similar conduct may also be a consideration. Finally, broad and amorphous notions of "justice" may impact the imposition of legal duties. In the name of justice, judges may
give attention to the parties before them, placing loss where it will be felt the least
and can best be borne. Theoretically, courts may apply these malleable concepts
of public policy to hold that a duty exists in virtually any situation.

Although the decline of *in loco parentis* has removed from universities many of
the burdens associated with controlling student conduct, application of this reasoning to the universities' duty to student-athletes should not apply given the extensive control of universities over student-athletes. The distinction between students and athletes eliminates the principal criticism of the imposition of duty: that
courts will encounter an unmanageable flood of litigation from disgruntled students, thereby burdening universities with unlimited liability. Courts may limit
their docket by hearing only those cases that assert that the student and the school
have a special relationship. Therefore, courts should not fear that the consequences
of imposing a contractual duty to educate would reach nonathlete students.

Courts have begun to recognize the existence of a special relationship between
student-athletes and the universities they attend. As a result, courts should impose
on universities an implied contractual duty to educate student-athletes that does
not necessarily exist for students in general. In *Kleinknecht v. Gettysburg College*,[198] for example, the Third Circuit considered the scope of a college's medical
duty to its intercollegiate lacrosse athletes. The student died of cardiac arrest during a practice session. Although the university employed athletic trainers, it sta-
tioned none at the practice field on the day of the athlete's death. The nearest telephone was at least two hundred yards away, beyond an eight-foot-high fence. The

---

198. 989 F.2d 1360 (3rd Cir. 1993).

court did not focus on the standard of care, the appropriateness of the school's decision to have athletic trainers elsewhere; rather, it limited its inquiry to a preliminary analysis of whether the relationship between the parties could justify the articulation of any standard of care. In doing so, it looked at the existence of a special relationship, general foreseeability, and public policy.

The court found that the school's active recruitment of the student-athlete created a special relationship between the parties. The court noted that:

> There is a distinction between a student injured while participating as an intercollegiate athlete in a sport for which he was recruited and a student injured at a college while pursuing his private interests, scholastic or otherwise. This distinction serves to limit the class of students to whom a college owes the duty of care that arises here.[202]

The court also recognized that it was not imposing an unjust financial or administrative burden upon the university that would potentially outweigh the public policy of protecting student-athletes.[203]

In addition, Congress has distinguished the relationship between student-athletes and universities from that between students in general and schools by requiring that universities exercise greater care in the recruitment of student-athletes. Colleges and universities have a statutory duty to disclose certain information to the Secretary of the United States Department of Education and to prospective student-athletes.[204] The mandatory disclosures include the number of students (broken down by race, sex, and sport) who received athletics-related student aid, the number of students at the institution (broken down by race and sex), the completion or graduation rate for students who received athletic-related student aid (broken down by race, sex, and sport), the completion or graduation rate for all students at the institution (broken down by race and sex), the average completion or graduation rate for the four most recent completing or graduating classes (broken down by race and sex), and the average completion or graduation rate for the four most recent completing or graduating classes of students who received athletics-related aid (broken down by race, sex, and sport). Ostensibly, the legislation aims to ensure that high school athletes may make an informed choice of schools by comparing the various relationships between athletics and academics; such legislation should prevent some exploitation of student-athletes.

Educators exhibit the deepest recognition of the differences between student-athletes and students in general, arguing that student-athletes need more than disclosure requirements; they need contractual protection to distinguish them from nonathlete students. The treatment of student-athletes smacks of injustice. For example, they spend an average of thirty hours per week on sports, and sometimes they devote as many as fifty hours; in contrast, students who receive federal work-study aid cannot work more than twenty hours per week. As a result, athletes live in a constant state of exhaustion during the season, making studying difficult. Moreover, athletic requirements implicitly affect academic choices, particularly where competition and practice schedules may conflict with classes. Said one commentator:

---

202. *Id.* at 1368 (distinguishing Alumni Ass'n v. Sullivan, 572 A.2d 1209 (Pa. 1990)).
203. *Id.*
204. 20 U.S.C. § 1092(e) (Supp. V 1993).

[W]hen a student-athlete is required to reach his or her highest possible level of academic [and athletic] achievement without regard to whether the individual has time or energy to meet only minimum academic requirements to maintain eligibility, the institution is demonstrating a lack of regard not only for the welfare of student-athletes but also for the centrality of education in its mission.[210]

Often, universities create a special relationship that seems even more blatant. College recruiters may promise parents that the university will "take care" of the student-athlete by providing "special dormitories, special food, [and] carefully chosen courses." At many schools, assistant coaches register student-athletes for classes, sometimes without even consulting the students as to which courses they would like to take. At nearly all others, student-athletes receive academic and support services to which other students do not have equal access. Finally, universities create a special relationship with student-athletes when they matriculate students who may not otherwise be qualified to enter the university. Schools with the most successful athletic programs admit their student-athletes based on the NCAA's minimum standards of eligibility. By the measure of typical college students, these standards are abysmally low, and they do not prohibit schools from admitting athletes under even lower standards and simply waiting until the next year to have them compete.

The special relationship between colleges and student-athletes creates implied contractual terms that courts should consider as strongly as the express terms of scholarship contracts. The reality of the relationship between colleges and student-athletes provides more of a compelling moral justification for imposing an implied duty to educate than do express, identifiable contractual promises. As a result, a case such as *Taylor*[217] would turn out differently; it would be unconscionable for the express terms of the contract to make it impossible for a student-athlete to fulfill his educational requirements. Moreover, recognizing implied contractual terms eschewing education would render *Taylor* more consistent with *Begley*.[218] Courts could continue to hold that parties must consider the meaning of their express scholarship agreements within the framework of the NCAA's academic requirements and the circumstances under which universities create a special relationship with student-athletes.

The imposition of a contractual duty to educate would not pose undue burdens on the courts or on schools, even if one fears that the pool of student-athlete litigants is still too large. Although the lack of a clearly articulated standard of care might pose some initial problems for courts, this is not a valid concern; it only reflects the same judicial inexperience that preceded the creation of causes of action for other forms of professional misconduct.

Furthermore, universities panicked over their egregious athletic programs will not be automatically subject to voluminous damages by the imposition of a duty and liability alone; plaintiff student-athletes will still have to prove causation and actual damages resulting from alleged breaches of duty. The student-athlete must show that the university's conduct, as opposed to some conduct or condition of

---

210. BAILEY & LITTLETON, *supra* note 16, at 89.

217. 191 S.E.2d 379 (N.C. Ct. App. 1972) (holding that the express terms of a student-athlete's scholarship contract requiring him to play football outweighed the implied educational terms that might have allowed him to stop playing to concentrate on his studies).

218. 367 F. Supp. 908 (E.D. Tenn. 1973).

his own, more likely than not created the harm. In addition, he will have to show some actual damage as a result. In a case such as *Ross v. Creighton University*,[223] where the student proved severe and measurable mental harms, this would not be difficult. However, athletes who can complain only of lost wages for the years in which they went to college instead of working would have a difficulty proving harm, especially when courts consider that they received room and board (not to mention at least a scintilla of an opportunity to become educated); this value will certainly approximate the rather low wages of a high school graduate. The cost of contractual liability to universities will thus be marginal given that many student-athletes will be unable to fulfill their substantial burden of proof.

And where courts now dismiss such cases for lack of a duty, they may still discard the most frivolous cases under the doctrine of *de minimus non curat lex*—the law does not concern itself with trifles. Furthermore, there is no evidence that imposing a duty to educate would result in objectionable pre-enrollment screening of student-athletes. Rather, universities could simply subject them to the same requirements as other students.

Finally, establishing a contractual duty to educate does not infringe upon the rights of universities, educational boards, and agencies to set standards governing the quality of education in public and private institutions. If courts accept the proposition that implied contractual terms are equally or more important than express contractual terms, the *Cavaliere* exception must apply: a contractual undertaking on the part of universities enables, and may in fact require, the trier of fact to review the quality of education. Thus, it would be inaccurate to conclude that imposing contractual liability on universities would subject them to any, let alone "constant," harassment in the courts.

In sum, imposing liability on universities is consistent with the notions of "justice" that some judges use to solve the duty equation. Universities purport to be on a mission to educate student-athletes, so they should make greater strides toward achieving their lofty goals. The special relationship between universities and student-athletes is not only morally compelling, but it is also practical; it ensures that the duty to educate does not become so broad as to threaten a flood of litigation from disenchanted nonathlete students. Moreover, requirements of causation and actual damages will minimize universities' economic burdens of liability and limit the number of cases that courts must hear.

. . . .

V. CONCLUSION

Unfortunately, the realities of college sports do not comport with the NCAA's ideology of amateurism embodied in its constitution. The relationships between student-athletes and universities are contractual, much like the relationships between universities and students in general. However, courts have refused to interpret scholarship contracts as imposing on universities a duty to educate student-athletes. At the same time, they have been unwilling to recognize the connection between college athletes and universities as an employer-employee relationship. These decisions seem contradictory; while courts espouse the primacy of educa-

---

223. Ross v. Creighton Univ., 740 F. Supp. 1319 (N.D. Ill. 1990), *aff'd*, 957 F.2d 410 (7th Cir. 1992).

tion in college sports in rejecting the notion that student-athletes are employees, they seem to forget education when students seek to hold universities to their academic representations.

As the result, courts should acknowledge that universities have a duty to educate student-athletes based on the special relationship between the parties that distinguishes athletes from students in general. The imposition of such a duty would unduly burden neither universities nor the judicial system. Alternatively, courts may interpret the special relationship between the parties as one of employment. If they continue to defer to notions of amateurism, courts should prefer the first option. Nonetheless, either alternative would benefit student-athletes by inducing reform of the college sports system in a manner otherwise unachievable. Universities that choose to adopt truly amateur policies would no longer wrongfully exploit those with much athletic prowess and little academic talent; rather, they would treat athletes as they treat all other students. Those that choose the professional path could cease to pretend that athletes are students and instead provide them with the benefits of employment without being branded as corrupt by the NCAA.

C. Peter Goplerud III, Pay for Play for College Athletes: Now, More Than Ever
38 South Texas Law Review 1081 (1997)*

. . . .

II. INTERCOLLEGIATE ATHLETICS AND COMMERCIALISM

A. *Overview of the NCAA and Relevant Regulations*

. . . .

Prior to the 1997 convention, the athlete in Division I on full scholarship was limited to receiving tuition, fees, room, board, and books. The athlete could not work during the school year if she was on full scholarship. The athlete could not receive any money or gifts from boosters. The athlete could not receive "pay" for anything connected with his athletic ability or talents. The athlete could receive a Pell grant of up to $2400 and the NCAA established an emergency fund to allow athletes to receive money from its special assistance fund where a hardship created a need for clothing or health care. In May 1996 the NCAA made some changes with regard to the special assistance fund. It is now available to all student athletes, including those on partial scholarships who have unmet needs. The association estimates that the pool of athletes eligible for this assistance is now about 61,000. Athletes may use money from the fund, which is administered by the member conferences, for such things as clothing and other "essential expenses," excluding entertainment; up to $500 for Pell Grant eligible athletes and those on full scholarships who have unmet needs; certain academic course supplies; medical and dental expenses not covered by student insurance; and family emergencies. The funds may not be used to finance needs that could have been

---

covered by a scholarship. In addition, non-qualifiers may not use the funds during their first academic year. The fund may not be used for entertainment purposes. Nor may it be used to purchase disability or other insurance aimed at protecting against loss of future professional sports earnings. Finally, it may not be used for administrative purposes by a member institution.

The NCAA has long been concerned that athletes are tempted to accept gifts from boosters and sports agents because of financial hardships created by the above restrictions. In the time period since the previous article was published, agents have not cleaned up their act. Indeed, several players have been suspended by the NCAA for taking largess from agents and the association itself has formed a special task force to deal with the agent situation. For this reason, as opposed to general concerns about exploitation of the athletes, the NCAA Council proposed legislation to allow for athletes' employment during the school year in order to let them make enough money to cover cost of attendance. Proposals to allow unlimited compensation from outside employment and to allow loans to be taken out based on future professional earnings for certain superstar athletes were defeated. Passage of the limited improvements was credited to a dose of reality and an increased voice for the student athletes themselves.

The new legislation, however, does not go anywhere near far enough and may be counter to many of the NCAA's restrictions on practice time, number of games, and length of season. It is also not without controversy, with coaches and athletic directors expressing concern over policing of the new rule. The focus on ways to curb abuses by sports agents also misses the bigger point which is the major premise of this presentation. The focus should not primarily be on the star athlete who is likely to attract the attention of sports agents and professional prospects who is exploited under the current system. Rather, concern should also be present for the starting offensive lineman who will never play professional football, but who is an integral part of a successful team, or the point guard who will never play in the NBA but is vital to a team's appearance in the NCAA Basketball Tournament.

B. *Commercialism in Collegiate Athletics*

Collegiate sports clearly are big business. Television revenues and gate receipts are enormous at most of the top Division I schools; the lesser schools do not receive huge amounts, but it does significantly help run the program at most places. Division I schools reported sports revenues of approximately $1.8 billion for 1995–1996. It is clear that it is the athletes who are responsible for filling the stands for Michigan football and Kentucky basketball, but all they may legally receive is room, board, tuition, fees, and books.

Licensed products bearing university logos are an increasingly significant source of revenue for most of the top Division I schools and even the lesser recognized schools in Division I. This revenue is produced through fan recognition of certain jersey numbers worn by star players. For example, the University of Michigan collected approximately $4.9 million in royalties from the sale of licensed products bearing the school's athletic logos. This revenue comes from the sale of products with a retail value of $132 million. Michigan officials readily concede that these figures were inflated by the high visibility of its "Fab Five" basketball team of the early 1990s. This may be the highest figure for any college, but it is not the only one in seven figures. Nebraska, North Carolina, Kentucky, and Penn State each received in excess of $2 million during 1996. Much of this money came from the sale of jerseys or other items bearing the numbers of outstanding athletes. The sales occur because of the popularity and prowess of the athlete. The athlete, of course, receives nothing from the sale of his or her jersey in the campus bookstore.

Agreements by coaches or schools with shoe companies are now multi-million dollar sources of revenue. Other corporate sponsorships of schools' athletic programs are now beginning to be significant sources of revenue. Coaches also have other outside sources of revenue which in some cases bring their coaching related income to nearly one million dollars....

....

C. *The Proposal*

It is time to give more serious consideration than ever before to stipends for collegiate athletes. As noted above, the proposal developed a year ago has flaws, mostly legal, which require modification. A market component must be inserted in the stipend, but the proposal must also provide for a certain amount of restraint and competitive balance in keeping with the NCAA's long-standing concerns for both factors within collegiate athletics. Therefore, the NCAA should develop legislation providing for stipends for athletes in major revenue producing sports at the Division I level. The stipends should be available to men in football and basketball, and women in basketball, volleyball, and other sports in sufficient numbers to satisfy gender equity requirements. The exact amount of the stipend to an individual athlete would be within the discretion of the individual school. However, the schools should have a limit on the total amount of money allocated to student-athletes. This "salary cap" would be set at an average of $300 per month per scholarship athlete, with half of the money going into a trust fund to be paid to those athletes receiving degrees within five years of matriculation. Those schools with football programs would calculate their football amounts separately with the total amount varying depending upon whether a school is Division I-A or I-AA. These athletes would also be able to work, as under the new rule, with the stipend not counting against the cost of attendance. Schools may, of course, spend less than the cap or may choose not to pay the stipend to any athletes. In addition, scholarship athletes in the non-revenue sports would be allowed to be employed during the school year, even in campus settings, and would have no cap on their earnings. The only stipulation would be that the jobs must be available to non-athlete students as well as athletes.

III. LEGAL ISSUES WHICH ARISE FROM PROPOSAL

A. *Antitrust Questions*

An issue which could arise should the association choose to enact legislation allowing for the payment of players would be a question of price-fixing. The proposal made a year ago is flawed in this respect. It is quite believable that an athlete in a revenue producing sport would become disgruntled with only receiving $150 per month while competing, and find a resourceful attorney willing to bring an action under the antitrust laws. For reasons discussed below, it is likely that such an action would be successful. Thus, the more prudent legislative action would be the salary cap approach which allows for individual decision-making based upon market determinations developed by the member institutions.

The NCAA has found itself as a defendant in antitrust actions on numerous occasions, with mixed results. Section 1 of the Sherman Antitrust Act provides that: "[e]very contract, combination in the form of trust or otherwise, or conspiracy, in restraint of trade or commerce among the several States, or with foreign nations, is hereby declared to be illegal."[31] The Supreme Court has long held that only unreasonable restraints of trade are proscribed by the act. Some restraints on economic activity are viewed by the Court as so inherently anti-competitive that they are deemed per se illegal. Examples of this type of conduct would be group boycotts, market divisions, tying arrangements, and price-fixing.

It is arguable that most of the regulatory activity in which the NCAA engages is per se illegal. Actions such as the establishment of limits on the type and amount of financial aid appears to be price-fixing. Certainly a fixed stipend such as proposed previously appears to be price-fixing. However, in the context of intercollegiate athletics the Supreme Court has recognized that certain types of restrictive activity by the NCAA may, under appropriate circumstances, be allowed under the act. The very nature of competitive sports is such that in order to promote competition, some actions which would normally be viewed as restraints will be allowed to exist. The Court has said that "[w]hat the NCAA and its member institutions market...is competition itself—contests between competing institutions" and thus, it is "an industry in which horizontal restraints on competition are essential if the product is to be available at all."[35] Any number of rules relating to the size of playing fields, squad size, length of seasons, number of scholarships, academic standards, and the like must be agreed upon in order to market a product, collegiate sports, which might not otherwise be available. The Court, therefore, in reviewing a challenge to the NCAA's actions in entering into a television contract for football, did not apply the per se rule, instead choosing to use a "rule of reason" analysis. The rule of reason analysis has been utilized in all recent antitrust cases involving the NCAA as well.

The rule of reason analysis requires the court to determine if the harm from the restraint on competition outweighs the restraint's pro-competitive impact. The plaintiff bears the initial burden of showing the restraint causes significant anti-competitive effects in a relevant market. If this burden is met, the defendant must then produce evidence of the restraint's pro-competitive effects. If this is done, the plaintiff must finally show that any legitimate objectives of the restraint can be met through less restrictive means.

To date, the courts have also been consistent in upholding, against antitrust challenge, every regulatory action of the NCAA which has directly impacted athletes. The Supreme Court has, on the one occasion noted above, ruled against the NCAA in an antitrust action involving its proprietary action in entering into contracts for the televising of football games. There is, perhaps, reason to believe that even some of the NCAA's regulatory activities may now be suspect under the Sherman Act.

In a recent case, *Law v. NCAA*, a federal district judge in Kansas ruled against the NCAA in an antitrust challenge to an action limiting coaching salaries for "restricted earnings" coaches.[43] In *Law*, the court analyzed the action of the association in setting salaries for so-called restricted earnings coaches. The rule was es-

---

31. Sherman Act, 15 U.S.C. § 1 (1990).
35. *Id*. at 101.
43. 902 F. Supp. 1394 (D. Kan. 1995).

tablished as a cost-cutting measure for Division I basketball. It limited the coaches to $12,000 in salary during the school year and an additional $4000 during the summer months. Each program was allowed one restricted earnings coach, in addition to the head coach and two assistants. A challenge was brought to this rule by several restricted earnings coaches, with the central claim being that the rule constituted price fixing contrary to the Sherman Act. The court agreed, finding no pro-competitive basis for the rule. The court noted that while cost control could be a valid consideration and provide an equalizer among programs, this rule did not accomplish anything concrete in terms of cost containment. There were no limitations placed on the salaries of the remainder of the coaching staffs at member institutions. The court, likewise, gave short shrift to the NCAA's argument that the victims of the price-fixing could simply go to another market where the price is not fixed. Finally, the court was not impressed that the restriction could actually be pro-competitive in that it would save the NCAA from financial disaster, thus continuing the competition the association fosters. Ultimately, the court found there was no legitimate pro-competitive purpose for the rule and permanently enjoined its enforcement.

This case and language in other NCAA antitrust cases lend support for the notion that the limit on scholarships and even a dollar specific stipend would violate the antitrust laws. Today there can be no doubt that the NCAA is actively involved in commercial activities, no matter whether it is engaged in regulatory or proprietary functions. The courts have recognized this, and certainly the commentators have recognized it as well. In conducting collegiate sporting events, the NCAA is promoting a certain brand of sports, which it continues to label amateur. As noted above, it is big business, particularly football and men's and women's basketball. Everyone, from administrators to coaches and trainers, is paid, and some make enormous sums of money. Of course, the players are the only ones who are not paid. And, it is they who are the suppliers of labor for this endeavor called collegiate sports.

The NCAA's limitations on scholarships, in so far as they prohibit stipends, are part of its regulatory program. The association would no doubt contend that these are noncommercial and, therefore, out of the purview of the Sherman Act. One jurist has labeled a similar assertion in regard to the NCAA's rules on eligibility and the professional football draft "incredulous."[57] It is quite clear that the rules act as a restraint on a relevant market, the labor market for collegiate athletes. They are obviously an attempt to perpetuate the amateur nature of collegiate athletics. But, this overlooks the key to the NCAA and collegiate athletics:

> Intercollegiate athletics programs shall be maintained as a vital component of the educational program, and student-athletes shall be an integral part of the student body. The admission, academic standing and academic progress of student-athletes shall be consistent with the policies and standards adopted by the institution for the student body in general.[58]

Amateurism has certainly been a significant part of the NCAA's programs, but there have been and continue to be exceptions to this requirement. As recently as the 1960s, the NCAA allowed schools to provide athletes on scholarship with

---

57. *Banks*, 977 F.2d 1098 (Flaum, J., concurring in part and dissenting in part).
58. NCAA MANUAL, *supra* note 7, at § 2.5.

"laundry money." And, the NCAA has long allowed athletes who are clearly professionals, to continue to compete in collegiate athletics in other sports. The only restriction is that they may not receive financial aid from the school. Collegiate athletics could survive if stipends were paid to the athletes. The strong allegiances to individual schools and traditions would survive if the athletes in certain sports received a stipend in addition to their tuition and room and board. The athletes would still be required to be full-time students. The stipend would not change the competition on the field, only the nature of the competition for players.

The present system is clearly a restraint. Many athletes do not have the funds to buy clothing, cannot fly home without going to the special assistance fund (except in an emergency), and often struggle to meet ordinary financial requirements of life. The restrictions are not necessary to maintain collegiate athletics; as noted there is already precedent for chipping away at the amateur nature of the venture. And, a stipend, coupled with a "salary cap," is a less restrictive means of promoting collegiate athletics and maintaining competitive balance. It would not be possible under this proposal for a school to offer unlimited amounts of money and, in effect, act like a professional sports team during free agent signing periods.

B. *Workers' Compensation Issues*

If the proposal is adopted, even in some modified form, by the NCAA, it is likely that in most jurisdictions the athletes receiving stipends would then be covered by the workers' compensation laws of those states. Coverage brings with it legal and financial considerations for the athletic departments impacted.

....

The majority of the state statutes do not explicitly address coverage of scholarship collegiate athletes.... Thus, the major hurdle facing a collegiate athlete seeking to receive benefits under a workers' compensation scheme, including one receiving the proposed stipend, would be the necessity of finding an employment relationship.

Little comfort can be found in the case law developed to date on the issue of an employment relationship. It is true that several older cases support the position of the athlete's eligibility for workers' compensation coverage. And, several commentators have argued that the scholarship athlete should be considered an employee under the workers' compensation laws. But the more recent judicial trend is to deny the collegiate athlete coverage. The courts have generally held that collegiate athletes on scholarship, under current NCAA rules, are not employees as that term is defined in workers' compensation statutes. The reasoning has generally focused on the supposed amateur nature of intercollegiate athletics and the NCAA's basic principles describing athletics as an avocation, not a vocation.

.... [A discussion of key cases in which courts have addressed student-athletes' entitlement to workers compensation is omitted. These cases are discussed in the article by Professor Davis that appears *supra* in this section. — ed.].

Under most state statutes, if the NCAA adopts a stipend provision the athletes on scholarship would probably fall within existing definitions of "employee." The stipend appears to be a wage paid for services rendered. Intent would, of course, be an issue in that a court would look to whether the stipend was any more tied to services rendered than the rest of the scholarship package. The analysis in *Rensing* focused on the amateur nature of collegiate athletics and the NCAA's prohibition on payment of players. Such reasoning would no longer be available to a court. It is conceivable that even the Michigan court would look at the economic reality test differently if a stipend provision was in place. As noted, collegiate athletics is big business. If additional money is paid to players it is likely that the school will attempt to exercise more control over them. Control, of course, is a factor used in determining whether an employment relationship exists. Arguably, a college scholarship which includes a stipend begins to look more like a professional sports contract that happens to include tuition, fees, room, board, and books as well as a cash component. Under most definitions a recipient of this type of "scholarship" would be an employee.

The best comparison would be to graduate assistants or teaching assistants on college campuses. The comparison is a valid one in that a graduate assistant in an English department or engineering college will often receive a tuition scholarship plus a stipend. The stipend and the scholarship are awarded in exchange for the student's serving as a teacher for a set number of classes or laboratory sessions. In the athletic setting, the scholarship and the proposed stipend would be awarded in exchange for the student's participation in the school's athletic program....

C. Other Legal Issues Arising From the Proposal

1. Gender Equity

Gender equity measures must be taken into account when adopting the proposal. Title IX requires not only equal opportunities for participation, but equal treatment and benefits for athletes with intercollegiate programs. Violations of the law will produce actions for injunctive relief and even for monetary damages. It is quite clear that schools providing stipends under the proposal would have to provide the stipends for a proportionate number of women athletes. Any disparities will wave red flags and likely subject the school to sanctions under the law.

2. Labor Law Issues

Another question which arises in the context of consideration of stipends for collegiate athletes is whether the athletes would then be employees for purposes of the National Labor Relations Act. The act essentially gives employees of businesses engaging in interstate commerce the right to organize and engage in concerted activity for the purpose of collective bargaining or other mutual aid. The act further defines "employee" to mean any employee unless otherwise excluded by the act. The courts have construed the act to give the National Labor Relations Board great latitude in determining who is an employee under the act. In analyzing the question with regard to collegiate athletes receiving stipends along with their scholarships, one would have to look at the conditions of that scholarship.

Scholarships for collegiate athletes typically require enrollment as a full-time student, compliance with NCAA rules, compliance with athletic department rules, and requirements established by the coaches of the particular sport. The athlete does receive some benefits similar to those of a traditional employee. If the local definition of "employee" required additional benefits to be paid to an athlete, the stipend proposed would be added support for the determination that the athlete is an employee for federal labor law purposes. Certainly the "tools of the trade" are supplied by the athletic department and the university provides the place and time of work. No athlete could be viewed as an independent contractor.

The only issue is whether this stipend is for services rendered or simply a part of the scholarship. Consistent with the position taken above, the stipend must be viewed as being paid for services rendered, just as would be the case for a traditional employee. The athlete in a Division I revenue producing sport is at her institution to participate in sports, and, oh, by the way, get an education. Again, the comparison to a graduate assistant in an academic department is instructive. The stipend paid to the graduate assistant appears to trigger tax consequences and workers' compensation consequences similar to a traditional employee. It should also trigger labor law consequences, should the athletes desire to take advantage of them.

It is not hard to imagine the reaction throughout the world of collegiate sports should a court determine that college athletes have the right to form unions. What would be the bargaining unit? Would the linebackers be a separate unit or would they have to organize with the rest of the defensive squad? Again, one would expect significant efforts to influence Congress with regard to specific exclusions for intercollegiate athletics.

3. *Taxation Issues*

Currently, athletic scholarships are not taxable to the athlete. Based upon experience with graduate assistants, it is clear that if the stipend is added, at least that portion of the scholarship would constitute taxable income to the athlete. This would also add the burden of withholding for income tax as well as for social security and Medicare. It might further provide fuel for those who advocate the general removal of the tax-exempt status of collegiate athletics. Providing the stipend could have an impact on evaluations of unrelated business income for NCAA member institutions.

IV. PRACTICAL FINANCIAL CONCERNS AND WHY IT WON'T HAPPEN OVERNIGHT

Assume for the moment that the legal issues raised above do not deter the membership's consideration of the proposal. There are nonetheless several serious political and practical concerns. The history and culture of the NCAA has for decades revolved around the concept of amateurism and the notion of the "student-athlete." Athletics are an integral part of the educational experience. Further professionalizing the programs, the argument goes, destroys this concept. The purists argue that any denigration of the amateurism concept is a giant step towards the destruction of intercollegiate athletics....

There are, however, some very respected coaches who believe it is time to support the concept of paying stipends to athletes. Tom Osborne of the University of Nebraska has argued for many years that players should be able to receive money for living expenses. Hayden Fry of the University of Iowa is another advocate for the stipend, noting that "[t]icket prices have gone up and revenues from bowl games and TV have increased,...[b]ut nothing has gone to benefit the athlete."[110] However, even many who conceptually support the proposal acknowledge the enormous practical and financial difficulties presented. The financial impact is such that the proposal probably has no chance for passage this century.

---

110. Maly, *supra* note 61, at Big Peach 4.

There are sources of revenue or ideas for revenue redistribution which could support the proposal. As noted, the NCAA budget is $239 million for 1996-97. That figure will go up in the coming years. The bowl games following the 1996 college season paid out over $100 million to participating schools and their conferences. Estimates are that licensed products generate over $2 billion annually in sales, providing generous royalties for colleges and universities. Corporate sponsorship agreements with individual schools provide additional funds. The NCAA Basketball Championship generates in excess of $50 million annually for the member schools; and, if the NCAA ever approves a national football championship playoff system, an additional $100 million or more will be available for distribution to the schools. Finally, there are television contracts and gate receipts that add to the revenues of most of the Division I schools.

The other side of the equation begins with the reality that many of the Division I schools lose money on their athletic programs. Even those making money argue they have very little flexibility in their budgets, particularly those with gender equity pressures. The proposal as structured above would cost approximately $29 million annually, with the impact as high as $400,000 for Division I-A football schools.

While there is no doubt that absorbing these costs would be difficult for most schools, there are sources of revenue which could support the proposal. It will require athletic administrators to be creative and to look for ways to cut costs in existing programs without cutting quality and equality. It is arguable that many, if not most, Division I athletic programs have unnecessary extravagance and duplication. It may also be time to suggest to the professional sports leagues that direct subsidies are due their "minor leagues," the college athletic programs. Corporate sponsors such as McDonald's or Nike should be considered as potential benefactors of this program. For the present, however, these outside sources are not available in any meaningful way. Therefore, existing funding would have to be utilized to implement the proposal for stipends for athletes.

The cost of the stipend is not the only cost presented. If the athlete is viewed as an employee in a given state for workers' compensation purposes the schools may have to purchase insurance coverage. There may also be additional insurance or fringe benefit costs associated with a determination of employee status. If the program begins to look more professional than amateur, there may be tax consequences to the schools with very significant price tags. If athletes had success with either the potential claims under the Sherman Act or those under Title IX, costs would escalate. Then there is the possibility of added leverage through unionization and collective bargaining. This too would have additional costs.

It is difficult to be sympathetic to concerns for the loss of amateurism in collegiate sports as a result of consideration for stipends. When a school makes an estimated $4 million in revenues directly traceable to the participation of one basketball player, concerns over the loss of amateurism are difficult to swallow. Intercollegiate athletics revolves around big money. Winning brings more money to programs and, thus, coaches are under pressure to produce. Those who do produce at the Division I level can expect six and seven figure annual incomes. Athletes spend twelve months a year playing, practicing, and training for their particular sport. For approximately eight months per year they are also students. The athletes are primarily responsible for the generation of the revenues used to pay the aforementioned coaches and programs. In return, they receive, relatively speaking, incredibly poor compensation. The days of sports at the collegiate level, at least in Division I programs, being "just a game" are long gone. Sports have a way of putting educational institutions on the map. How many people would know of the College of Charleston without basketball?

Finally, it is suggested that amateurism in and of itself is not the reason most fans watch collegiate sports. Loyalties to educational institutions and to tradition are very important. Ticket prices for collegiate events are more affordable than for professional events, and a modest stipend for athletes will not alter that situation. Rivalries and the national championships sanctioned by the NCAA are a natural attraction. A retreat from pure amateurism will not detract from this attraction.

More attention must be paid to athletes' welfare. The relaxation of the work restrictions is well-intentioned, but is misdirected. It is counter to the association's own concerns over the amount of time the athletes have in a day for sports, school, and life. It throws one more factor into the mix, which is a mistake. There are, of course, natural concerns over athletes having jobs under this rule which pay good wages for little or no work. Policing will be a nightmare.

It is time for collegiate athletes to receive monthly stipends as part of their scholarship package.... We are no longer in an age of innocence where there is no commercialism in college athletics. It is big business and those most responsible for the product put on the field, the players, should be compensated.

Chapter 11

Constitutional and Statutory Dimensions

Introduction

The articles in this chapter highlight the increasingly significant role of public law as a source for establishing the principles that govern relationships in intercollegiate athletics. The extent of the common law's displacement by statutory law and constitutional principles has traditionally been less prevalent in intercollegiate athletics than in the professional setting. For example in professional sports, regulation of the terms and conditions of the employment of players has shifted over time from contract law, to antitrust law to labor law. In contrast, the private law of contract, rather than public law doctrine, continues to set the legal parameters for defining the student-athlete's relationship with his or her institution. As the articles in this chapter that address antitrust issues suggest, the displacement of common law values by public law principles and accompanying law is impacted severely by the perceived, if not, real differences between professional sports and intercollegiate. For example, the George Kokkines article—examining the application of antitrust laws to invalidate NCAA amateurism rules—concludes that student-athletes, in contrast to their professional counterparts, have found antitrust law less receptive to a host of claims. These include claims alleging NCAA regulations improperly restrain player mobility, compensation and eligibility. Nevertheless, as Professor Roberts points out in addressing the broader implications of *Law v. NCAA*, the case may represent a shift toward increased antitrust scrutiny of NCAA regulatory provisions in the not too distant future.

Similarly, other articles in this chapter demonstrate the increasing extent of the public regulation of intercollegiate athletics. For example, federal legislation as manifested in the Americans with Disabilities Act ("ADA") and the Rehabilitation Act (articles pertaining to other important federal legislation, Title IX, are located in the section that follows) hold the potential for radically changing college athletics. Articles by Katie Burroughs and Professor Matthew Mitten examine the two contexts within which Rehabilitation Act and ADA challenges are likely to arise in intercollegiate athletics: actions by learning-disabled student-athletes challenging NCAA academic eligibility rules, and actions involving institutional decisions to preclude athletic participation by student-athletes with physical impairments that expose them to increased risk of injury or death. The Burroughs' article critically evaluates NCAA and judicial approaches to learning disabled students-athletes by focusing, in part, on *Ganden v. NCAA* and other cases that critically evaluate judicial approaches to learning disability. This article is followed by the NCAA-Justice Department Consent Decree that was entered into after the Justice Department announced that NCAA eligibility rules failed effectively to accommodate the needs of learning disabled students such as Ganden. The Mitten excerpt examines the second of these issues largely in the context of *Knapp v. Northwestern University*. Apart from discussing legal analysis, this article includes an important discussion of who is the most appropriate party to make decisions regarding a student-athlete's participation in athletic competition notwithstanding an increased risk of physical harm.

In addition to resorting to statutory based remedies, such as antitrust law or the ADA, athletes and others involved in intercollegiate athletics have invoked constitutional law doctrine to address an array of grievances ranging from assertions by student-athletes of deprivations of their rights to participate in intercollegiate competition due to unconstitutional NCAA eligibility rules, to assertions that mandatory drug testing programs violate first and fourth amendment rights. (Articles regarding drug testing appear in Part V *infra*). Brian Porto's article considers the larger issue of whether student-athletes have a property interest in eligibility. His important discussion provides a useful point of departure from which to consider articles that follow which explore the constitutional dimensions of a student-athlete's right to participate in athletic competition. For instance, Professor Shropshire examines this issue in the context of the constitutionality of NCAA initial eligibility rules, particularly given their potential for denying access of African-American student-athletes to educational opportunities.

This chapter leads off, however, with articles that explore the constitutional dimensions of intercollegiate athletics based upon issues that arose in Jerry Tarkanian's saga against the NCAA. In her important article, Professor Sherry Young discusses abuses in the NCAA regulatory process that prompted athletes and others to challenge the constitutionality of NCAA enforcement procedures. She also examines the critical issue, decided by the Supreme Court in *NCAA v. Tarkanian*, of whether NCAA enforcement procedures can properly be subjected to due process analysis. In this regard, she specifically addresses whether the NCAA is a state actor—a critical requirement in determining whether NCAA rules can survive due process scrutiny. The article that follows by James Thompson explores another important issue spawned by Tarkanian's dispute with the NCAA— whether states can enact legislation that affords participants in intercollegiate athletics with due process protections that exceed those granted by NCAA rules and regulations. Following his analysis of the leading case in this regard, *NCAA v. Miller*, Thompson concludes that the *Miller* court's reliance on the Commerce Clause in invalidating state due process legislation was appropriate. Thompson adopts a view that differs from that espoused in Young's article *Is Due Process Unconstitutional? The NCAA Wins Round One in its Fight Against Regulation of its Enforcement Proceedings*, 25 Ariz. St. L.J. 841 (1993). Although length considerations precluded us from including Young's article, we highly recommend it to our readers.

Other noteworthy articles include: John Kitchin, *The NCAA and Due Process,* 5-SPG Kan. J.L. & Publ Pol'y 71 (1996); Sherry Young, *Is Due Process Unconstitutional? The NCAA Wins Round One in its Fight Against Regulation of its Enforcement Proceedings*, 25 Ariz. St. L.J. 841 (1993); Christopher L. Chin, *Illegal Procedures: The NCAA's Unlawful Restraint of the Student-Athlete,* 26 Loy. L.A. L. Rev. 1213 (1993); C. Peter Goplerud III, *NCAA Enforcement Process: A Call for Procedural Fairness,* 20 Cap. U.L. Rev. 543 (1991); Leroy Pernell, A Commentary on Professor Goplerud's Article, *"NCAA Enforcement Process: A*

Call for Procedural Fairness", 20 Cap. U.L. Rev. 561 (1991); Ethan Lock, *Unreasonable NCAA Eligibility Rules Send Braxston Banks Truckin'*, 20 Cap. U.L. Rev. 643 (1991); Lee Goldman, *Sports and Antitrust: Should College Students be Paid to Play?*, 65 Notre Dame L. Rev. 206 (1990).

---

1. Due Process

Sherry Young, The NCAA Enforcement Program and Due Process: The Case for Internal Reform
43 Syracuse Law Review 747 (1992)[1]

INTRODUCTION

. . . .

Even though the NCAA insists that its procedures comport with due process, it has expended great effort to obtain judicial approval of its second (or perhaps more appropriately, its first) line of defense — that it has no obligation to provide due process in the enforcement of its rules. The NCAA argued throughout the 1970s and 1980s that its enforcement activities neither constituted state action for purposes of constitutional analysis nor were actions taken under color of state law subject to the federal and state civil rights statutes. That issue was ultimately resolved in favor of the NCAA in *National Collegiate Athletic Ass'n v. Tarkanian.*[19] Prior to *Tarkanian*, however, there were conflicting lower court decisions. Therefore, the NCAA also argued, again with mixed success, that even if it was a state actor it did not have to provide due process because there is no constitutionally protected liberty or property interest in participation in intercollegiate athletics. *Tarkanian*, however, made the existence of a protected interest a moot issue. Because the NCAA was not a state actor, it was free to deprive individuals and institutions of even protected interests without any pretense of providing due process, and without any fear of judicial limits on Association procedures.

After its hard-won victory in *Tarkanian*, the NCAA made no attempt to cut back on the procedural protections voluntarily provided to participants in the infractions process. Instead, the Association continued to revise the process in the direction of providing ever more satisfactory procedures. However, critics of the system were not appeased. Stymied in their efforts to obtain either judicial review or internal reform that went as far as they would like, critics turned to state and federal legislatures. The NCAA has opposed state due process legislation on the ground that the existence of multiple standards of due process would severely limit its ability to enforce its rules in a fair and consistent manner. While federal due process legislation would eliminate the problem of multiple standards in the various jurisdictions, the NCAA has opposed federal legislation as well.

---

19. 488 U.S. 179.

....

I. ALLEGATIONS OF ENFORCEMENT ABUSES: AGING BUT NOT FORGOTTEN

Much of the recent due process legislation can be traced to allegations of procedural deficiencies that have long since been corrected by the NCAA. The NCAA has done a poor job of educating the legislators about the internal reforms that have already taken place. Therefore, a brief discussion of some of the early complaints and recommendations for reform will shed light on the current popularity of due process legislation.

A. *Early Allegations of Abuse*

Many of the complaints about inadequate procedures can be traced to the 1978 Congressional hearings on the NCAA enforcement program. Criticisms were leveled at every stage of the proceedings. At the investigation stage, witnesses alleged that there were no internal standards controlling the initiation of investigations. One school might be investigated after receipt of only a few allegations, or even without any allegations being received at all, while others might not be investigated no matter how many charges were received. It was also alleged that the enforcement program was used to retaliate against institutions and individuals for taking positions with which the enforcement staff disagreed. Several witnesses expressed reluctance to testify, and did so only under subpoena, because they were afraid of retaliation. The charges of selective enforcement were bolstered by claims that the NCAA's substantive rules were so byzantine that given six weeks an investigator could put any school in the country on probation. NCAA investigators were accused of misrepresenting their identity to the people they interviewed, and of evading policy so that players could be interviewed alone and then engaging in threats, intimidation, and vulgarity to encourage the witness to make damaging statements. One student testified that he was told by the investigator that the NCAA was not interested in punishing him for his own misconduct, but merely just wanted to find out what was going on at the institution. The student ultimately lost his eligibility based on an admission he made during that interview. Witnesses also testified that the investigators breached their duty of confidentiality by telling witnesses and prospective recruits that a university was under investigation, and by leaking information to the press.

At the charging stage, the Association was accused of overwhelming the institution with the number of allegations, including some allegations that were trivial and others for which the staff had no basis at all. The enforcement staff was accused of failure to cooperate with the institution under investigation, even though under NCAA policy the investigation is supposed to be a cooperative endeavor. Failure to cooperate was exemplified by refusal to identify the sources of allegations or share the whereabouts of witnesses, refusal to reveal the content of statements that had been made to investigators, and refusal to provide the institution with investigatory guidelines prepared by the NCAA. More general criticisms included the complete lack of discovery of evidence that the staff intended to rely upon in presenting its case, and complaints that the pre-hearing role of the Committee on Infractions and its Chair created at the very least the appearance that the case had been prejudged.

Claimed deficiencies at the hearing stage were even more egregious. Institutions alleged that they were given no notice of the rules and procedures that would be observed at the hearing. An inappropriate camaraderie existed between the Committee on Infractions and the enforcement staff, and the stated burden of proof was not properly applied. Individuals, notably students, former students and former coaches, had no right to appear even though their interests could be adversely affected. Such individuals could appear, if the institution so desired, as "institutional representatives." However, the university could not provide a student with transportation to the site of the hearing, or pay an attorney to represent him.

A major source of complaints was the use of investigator summaries of witness interviews rather than producing the witnesses for confrontation and cross-examination. In conjunction with the refusal to provide witness statements to the institution prior to the hearing, the use of summaries forced the institution to react on the spot to surprise testimony, precluded effective challenges to the accuracy of the investigator's characterization of the alleged statement, and deprived the Committee of the opportunity to weigh credibility in cases of conflicting evidence. Finally, witnesses argued that the record of the hearing was totally inadequate. The only record of the proceedings was a tape recording made on equipment controlled by the enforcement staff. Witnesses alleged that the resulting tape often failed to register remarks made by staff to Committee members, and contained gaps and inaudible sections. It was often difficult to tell just who made particular statements.

Further, the NCAA would not provide the parties with a transcript of the tape, nor would it permit the parties to provide a court reporter at their own expense. The only way a party could review the record of the hearing in preparation for an appeal was to travel to NCAA headquarters in Mission, Kansas at its own expense. Once there, they would be permitted to review the tape, under the supervision of an enforcement staff member. The representative of the institution could take notes, but the notes could not constitute a verbatim copy of the tape or any portion thereof. If the party seeking review of the record was someone other than the member institution, they could only review portions of the tape determined by the staff to be relevant to that individual.

After the Committee on Infractions found that the institution was guilty, the staff advised the Committee as to the penalties that had been imposed in comparable cases. If the institution chose to appeal, the proceedings before Council were *de novo*. The Council undertook, in a very limited time, to retry the facts as well as evaluate the propriety of the penalty. As at the hearing before the Committee on Infractions, an inappropriate camaraderie was alleged to exist between the fact-finder and the enforcement staff. The Council was at liberty to find additional violations and impose greater penalties. Again, individuals were not entitled to appear except as institutional representatives, and the extra benefits rule applied to the appearance of students. As discussed in Part II *infra,* only limited judicial review of NCAA decisions was available.

B. *Congressional Recommendations for Reform*

After considering all of the problems outlined above, the Congressional Subcommittee recommended a number of changes in the NCAA enforcement program. To eliminate the difficulty of disproving stale allegations, reduce the impact of the "cloud" that hangs over a program under investigation, and eliminate the worst aspects of selective enforcement, the Subcommittee recommended that time limits be created for each stage of the proceeding. The Subcommittee concluded that there should be less contact, especially *ex parte* contact, between the enforcement staff and the Committee on Infractions. Therefore, it recommended that the staff not be directly supervised by the Committee, that the Committee not be involved in approving official inquiries, and that the staff should no longer be involved in the consideration of penalties or the preparation of the infractions report.

To make the investigation truly cooperative, the Subcommittee recommended that the institution be informed of all accusations and the sources of the accusations as part of the notice of official inquiry. All evidence to be used at the hearing should be discoverable by all parties in interest. Witnesses should be allowed to have counsel present, and should be so informed where their interests could be adversely affected. Interviews of witnesses should be conducted jointly, and information obtained during *ex parte* interviews would be excluded at the hearing.

All parties in interest should have the right to appear at the hearing and be represented by counsel. Institutions should be allowed to provide travel expenses and attorneys fees to student-athletes. All parties should have access to a complete transcript of the hearing. The Subcommittee further recommended that the substantive rules of the Association be simplified, that the NCAA make direct determinations of ineligibility, and that no new sanctions be imposed on member institutions for complying with a valid court order.

C. NCAA Response

The NCAA did not immediately concur with Congress as to the advisability of several of the above reforms. Most importantly, the Association was unwilling to concede that the imperatives of the Due Process Clauses of the United States and various state constitutions applied to the activities of a private association. In the absence of either internal reform by the NCAA or any congressional intervention in enforcement activities more emphatic than "recommendations", parties that were aggrieved by the existing enforcement procedures had no alternative but to appeal to the courts.

II. JUDICIAL REVIEW OF DUE PROCESS CHALLENGES TO NCAA ENFORCEMENT PROCEDURES

The NCAA has long argued that, as a private association, its rules and procedures should not be subject to judicial review....

....

In order to obtain judicial review of NCAA enforcement proceedings, the aggrieved party must be able to demonstrate some impairment of a legally protected interest. The most common approach has been to argue that the NCAA has violated the plaintiff's constitutional rights without due process of law, or has deprived the plaintiff of rights secured by the Constitution and laws of the United States "under color of any statute, ordinance, regulation, custom or usage, of any state or Territory...."[91] The analysis under either cause of action is essentially the same. To establish an entitlement to due process, the plaintiff must demonstrate both state action and the existence and impairment of a protected interest. Only then will the court turn to the issue of how much process is due.

---

91. 42 U.S.C. § 1983 (1988).

A. *State Action*

I. The Early Cases

The protection provided by the Fourteenth Amendment and section 1983 does not extend to private conduct abridging individual rights, no matter how unfair that conduct may be. Therefore, in order to secure judicial review of NCAA determinations, the plaintiff must first establish that the NCAA is a state actor or acted under color of state law. In the first reported case to examine the issue, *Buckton v. National Collegiate Athletic Ass'n*,[96] the court concluded that there was a substantial likelihood that the NCAA would be found to engage in conduct that is subject to constitutional scrutiny. The court first noted that private conduct is not subject to such scrutiny. However, "[c]onduct that is formally "private" may become so entwined with governmental policies or so impregnated with a governmental character as to become subject to the constitutional limitations placed upon state action."[98] The court then held that in supervising intercollegiate athletics the NCAA "performs a public function, sovereign in nature, that subjects it to constitutional scrutiny."[99]

Further, the court noted that accepting state support can inject state action into the conduct of a private association, and that, "state universities make up one-half of the membership of the NCAA; that these public institutions pay dues to the NCAA; and that state involvement in the NCAA includes the support, control and regulation of member institutions as well as the provision of state facilities for NCAA contests." On the basis of the foregoing factors, the court concluded that the plaintiffs had demonstrated a substantial likelihood of success on the merits.

Prior to 1982, virtually every court that considered the issue concluded that the NCAA engaged in state action, although often on slightly different grounds than the *Buckton* court. In *Howard University v. National Collegiate Athletic Ass'n*,[104] the court noted that if only state institutions belonged to the NCAA, the actions of the Association would clearly constitute state action. Where there is a mixture of public and private institutions, "[d]rawing the line as to the requisite quantum of public participation to invoke fourteenth amendment protection is a difficult task indeed." However, the court concluded that in the case of the NCAA there was no need to draw that line since the "degree of public participation and entanglement...is substantial and pervasive."[106] In reaching that conclusion, the court considered the extent to which public institutions contributed to the membership, financing and leadership of the NCAA. In *Parish v. National Collegiate Athletic Ass'n*,[109] the Fifth Circuit held that the substantial role played by state institutions and officers, the state financial support of the NCAA and the state's traditional governmental interest in all aspects of the educational system led to the conclusion that, in overseeing college athletics, the NCAA was "performing a traditional governmental function...."[110]

---

96. 366 F. Supp. 1152 (D. Mass. 1973).
98. *Id*. at 1156 (quoting Evans v. Newton, 382 U.S. 296, 299 (1966)).
99. *Id*. (*citing* Curtis v. NCAA, C-71 2088 ACW (N.D. Cal. Feb. 1, 1972) (unreported)).
104. 510 F.2d 213 (D.C. Cir. 1975).
106. *Id*.
109. 506 F.2d 1028 (5th Cir. 1975).
110. *Parish*, 506 F.2d at 1032-33.

. . . .

Only one early decision accepted the NCAA's contention that it did not engage in state action. In *McDonald v. National Collegiate Athletic Ass'n*,[111] as in many of the cases discussed above, the action was initiated by student athletes seeking to enjoin the NCAA and their university from declaring them ineligible and excluding them from participation in athletic contests. The NCAA argued that it did not declare the students ineligible, the university did. The court concurred. It held that the action of the university did constitute state action, and that any contractual obligations the university might have to the NCAA did not absolve the university of its duty to provide due process to its students. . . .

McDonald was overruled by implication when the Ninth Circuit held that the NCAA's enforcement activities were "state action" in *Associated Students v. National Collegiate Athletic Ass'n*.[112]

2. *The Tide Turns*

In 1982, the United States Supreme Court handed down three "state action" decisions that were to have a significant impact on the way lower courts subsequently analyzed the issue of whether the NCAA engages in state action. In *Lugar v. Edmondson Oil Co.*,[113] the Court first noted that the purpose of the state action doctrine is to limit judicial review of private conduct, holding that:

> Careful adherence to the "state action" requirement preserves an area of individual freedom by limiting the reach of federal law and federal judicial power. It also avoids imposing on the State, its agencies or officials, responsibility for conduct for which they cannot fairly be blamed. A major consequence is to require the courts to respect the limits of their own power as directed against state governments and private interests. Whether this is good or bad policy, it is a fundamental fact of our political order.

The court then set forth a two-part test for when conduct is "fairly attributable to the State."[119]

> First, the deprivation must be caused by the exercise of some right or privilege created by the State, or by a rule of conduct imposed by the state or by a person for whom the State is responsible. . . . Second, the party charged with the deprivation must be a person who may fairly be said to be a state actor. This may be because he is a state official, because he has acted together with or has obtained significant aid from state officials, or because his conduct is otherwise chargeable to the State.[120]

In *Blum v. Yaretsky*,[121] decided the same day, the Court elaborated on that test. First, the Court held that extensive state regulation of otherwise private conduct does not establish a sufficiently close nexus between the state and the conduct of the regulated entity to allow the conduct to be considered that of the state itself. Second,

---

111. 370 F. Supp. 625 (C.D. Calif. 1974).
112. *Associated Students*, 493 F.2d at 1254.
113. *McDonald*, 370 F. Supp. at 626.
119. *Id*. at 937.
120. *Id*.
121. 457 U.S. 991 (1982).

a State normally can be held responsible for a private decision only when it has exercised coercive power or has provided such significant encouragement, either overt or covert, that the choice must in law be deemed to be that of the State. Mere approval of or acquiescence in the initiatives of a private party is not sufficient to justify holding the State responsible for those initiatives under the terms of the Fourteenth Amendment.[122]

Third, "the required nexus may be present if the private entity has exercised powers that are 'traditionally the *exclusive* prerogative of the State'."[123]

The third state action case handed down that day, *Rendell-Baker v. Kohn*,[124] illustrated how the court intended to apply the foregoing tests. As in *Lugar* and *Blum*, the court concluded that there was no state action and therefore no right to judicial review of the conduct of the private entity that injured the plaintiffs. The defendant, a private school, had discharged plaintiffs, allegedly for exercising their First Amendment rights. Although the school received over ninety percent of its funding and virtually all of its students from the state, and was subject to extensive state regulation, the court held that the acts of private contractors do not become acts of the state "by reason of their significant or even total engagement in performing public contracts." The fact that a private entity serves the public does not make its activity "state action."

The court also rejected the claim that state action was present because the private entity was performing the traditional public function of education, because the education of maladjusted students has not been traditionally the *exclusive* function of the state. Finally, the court rejected the claim that there was a "symbiotic relationship" between the state and the school, holding that "the school's fiscal relationship with the State is not different from that of many contractors performing services for the government." Because the decision to discharge the plaintiffs was not "compelled or even influenced by any state regulation,"[130] the terminations were not the product of state action.

After *Lugar*, *Blum*, and *Rendell-Baker*, most courts began to reconsider the then-prevailing position that the NCAA was a state actor. In *Arlosoroff v. National Collegiate Athletic Ass'n*,[131] the Fourth Circuit began by acknowledging that most courts had concluded that the NCAA was subject to the limitations of the Fourteenth Amendment. However, "[t]hese earlier cases rested upon the notion that indirect involvement of state governments could convert what otherwise would be considered private conduct into state action. That notion has now been rejected by the Supreme Court, however, and its decisions require a different conclusion."[133] In concluding that the NCAA had not engaged in state action, the court first noted that the regulation of intercollegiate athletics is not a function that has traditionally been exclusively reserved to the state. Further, although

---

122. *Id.* at 1004-05 (citing Flagg Bros., Inc. v. Brooks, 436 U.S. 149, 164-65 (1978) and Jackson v. Metropolitan Edison Co., 419 U.S. 345, 357 (1974)).

123. *Id.* at 1005 (emphasis added) (quoting Jackson v. Metropolitan Edison, 419 U.S. 345, 357 (1974)).

124. 457 U.S. 830 (1982).

130. *Rendell-Baker*, 457 U.S. at 841.

131. 746 F.2d 1019 (4th Cir. 1984).

133. *Arlosoroff*, 746 F.2d at 1021 (citing Rendell-Baker v. Kohn, 457 U.S. 830 and Blum v. Yaretsky, 457 U.S. 991 (1982)).

about half of the NCAA's member institutions are state schools, and those state schools provide more than half of the NCAA's revenues, there was no indication that the public institutions caused the adoption of the bylaw at issue. "It is not enough that an institution is highly regulated and subsidized by a state. If the state in its regulatory or subsidizing function does not order or cause the action complained of, and the function is not one traditionally reserved to the state, there is no state action." Other courts quickly adopted the reasoning of *Arlosoroff*.

3. National Collegiate Athletic Ass'n v. Tarkanian:[138] *The Final Word*

. . . .

On November 28, 1972, UNLV received a notice of preliminary inquiry into alleged violations of NCAA rules. That notice did not specify which rules UNLV. had violated, which individuals were allegedly involved in the violations, or who had made the allegations. After receipt of the preliminary inquiry, UNLV replaced the head basketball coach and the athletic director resigned. Tarkanian was hired as head basketball coach in the spring of 1973. Although the President of UNLV repeatedly inquired about the status of the investigation, he got no information until February 1976, when UNLV received an official inquiry requiring it to investigate over 70 alleged violations.

The Nevada Attorney General's office conducted the investigation on behalf of UNLV. The NCAA staff declined to cooperate with UNLV's investigation, refusing to provide investigative leads or even a copy of the NCAA's policies, procedures and guidelines for conducting such investigations. UNLV alleged that the NCAA investigators engaged in a wide variety of misconduct during the investigation — repeatedly questioning individuals who reported no wrongdoing, threatening witnesses, breaching the rule of confidentiality by telling recruits that UNLV was under investigation, and demonstrating bias by telling witnesses that they would "get Tarkanian."

At the hearing before the Committee on Infractions, the NCAA's evidence against UNLV consisted exclusively of the investigators' summaries of witness interviews. No representative of UNLV was present at those interviews. The witnesses were not informed that they could be represented by counsel. The witnesses were not permitted to tape the interview or make any verbatim record of the questions and answers. The investigators were not permitted to tape the interview. The witnesses allegedly were not given the opportunity to review and correct the investigators' memorandum of the interview. The witnesses were not allowed to attend the hearing, and were consequently unable to challenge the investigators' account of what they had said.

UNLV was not advised of the identity of the witnesses upon whom the investigators intended to rely until the day of the hearing, making it impossible for the university to ask the witnesses what they had told the NCAA investigators. The NCAA did not disclose the content of witness statements to UNLV until during the hearing. In several instances, the university found itself in the embarrassing position of offering a conflicting statement from the same witness, with no way to reconcile the discrepancy, challenge the competing version, or allow the Committee to assess the credibility of the witness in person.

---

138. 488 U.S. 179 (1988).

In addition to the challenge of having to combat surprise testimony consisting exclusively of hearsay presentations by the "prosecution," UNLV had to deal with evidentiary standards that were not disclosed to it prior to the hearing, and are not easy to sort out after the fact. The burden of proof is supposed to be on the enforcement staff. Further, two members of the Committee testified before Congress that, although there was no written policy on the matter, it was their understanding that where there is directly conflicting testimony with no corroborating evidence for either side, and no opportunity to examine the demeanor of the witnesses, the staff will not have carried their burden and the infraction will not be found.

A single example of the evidence accepted in support of a finding of infraction will demonstrate how the process actually operated in this case. One of the most serious allegations against Tarkanian was that he had arranged with a UNLV professor for a player to get a "B" for a course without having to attend class or do the required work. The evidence of this infraction was the report of the investigator who claimed that the professor had volunteered this information to him. The report had not been reviewed or signed by the professor. UNLV denied that the infraction had occurred. UNLV provided the Committee with an affidavit from the professor stating: that he had not made the statement to the investigator, that he had not made any arrangements with Tarkanian or anyone else for that student or any student to receive special treatment or grades, that the student-athlete had turned in his term paper, and that the "B" the student-athlete received was actually below the class average.

UNLV also provided the Committee with an affidavit from the student-athlete stating that there had been no special arrangement and that he had attended the class and done the required work. Finally, UNLV provided the Committee with affidavits from other students in the class stating that the student-athlete had attended the class, and from the student who had typed his term paper for him and who had been present in the class when the student-athlete did the required oral presentation. The Committee nevertheless found that the infraction had occurred. On appeal to Council, UNLV presented polygraph and voice analyses tests supporting the truth of the professor's testimony that the event had not occurred. The Council affirmed the finding of infraction.

Ultimately, the NCAA found UNLV guilty of thirty-eight infractions, including ten that involved Tarkanian. The Committee proposed sanctions including a two-year probation, and ordered UNLV to show cause why additional sanctions should not be imposed if UNLV did not remove Tarkanian from the university's athletic program during the probationary period. On appeal, the NCAA Council adopted all of the Committee's recommendations.

UNLV held a hearing for Tarkanian. While the university remained convinced that no wrongdoing had been established, it concluded that it had no choice but to accept the NCAA's findings. Tarkanian was notified that he was to be removed from his coaching position during the probation. Tarkanian then filed suit in Nevada state court for an order enjoining UNLV from suspending him. The injunction was granted, and the trial court ultimately held that the NCAA was a state actor and that Tarkanian had been denied procedural and substantive due process.

The Nevada Supreme Court affirmed the decision of the trial court. The court noted that the early cases had concluded that the NCAA engaged in state action and was subject to the requirements of due process, and that more recent cases had reconsidered that position in light of *Lugar, Blum* and *Rendell-Baker*. However, the court held that the *Blum* trilogy did not require a finding in favor of the NCAA. Applying the tests set forth by the Supreme Court, the Nevada court noted that UNLV was a state university and Tarkanian was a state employee. It concluded that "the right to discipline public employees is traditionally the exclusive preroga-tive of the state"[172] and that the effect of UNLV's acquiescence in the NCAA's find-ings and sanctions was to delegate authority to the NCAA over those personnel de-cisions. Therefore, the NCAA was required to provide due process to Tarkanian before depriving him of the benefits of his employment contract, and the proce-dures employed by the NCAA did not meet the minimum requirements of due process.

In reviewing that decision, the United States Supreme Court stated that this case presented the "mirror image" of the typical state action case. In the usual case, the decisive act is done by a private party, and the issue is whether the state was sufficiently involved in that conduct to make it state action. Here, the deci-sive act (the decision to suspend Tarkanian from coaching) was done by the state actor (UNLV) and the question is "whether UNLV's actions in compliance with the NCAA rules and recommendations turned the NCAA's conduct into state ac-tion."[178] The Court expressly rejected the Nevada court's finding that the NCAA and UNLV had jointly imposed the penalty on Tarkanian, or that UNLV had del-egated the authority to sanction public employees to the NCAA, stating that "[t]hese contentions fundamentally misconstrue the facts of this case."[179]

The Court held that the NCAA did not and could not directly discipline Tarkan-ian or any other state employee, and that the university had delegated no such power to the NCAA. "The commitment by UNLV to adhere to NCAA enforce-ment procedures was enforceable only by sanctions that the NCAA might impose on UNLV itself."[182] "Neither UNLV's decision to adopt the NCAA's standards nor its minor role in their formulation is a sufficient reason for concluding that the NCAA was acting under color of Nevada law when it promulgated standards gov-erning athlete recruitment, eligibility and academic performance."[183] Further,

> [i]t would be ironic indeed to conclude that the NCAA's imposition of sanctions against UNLV — sanctions that UNLV and its counsel, including the Attorney General of Nevada, steadfastly opposed during protracted adversary proceed-ings — is fairly attributable to the State of Nevada. It would be more appropri-ate to conclude that UNLV has conducted its athletic program under color of the policies adopted by the NCAA, rather than that those policies were devel-oped and enforced under color of Nevada law.[184]

Having determined the absence of state action on the part of the NCAA, the Court reversed the decision of the Nevada Supreme Court without considering whether Tarkanian had a protected interest and whether or not the procedures of the NCAA satisfy the minimum requirements of procedural due process. While

---

172. *Id.* at 337; 741 P.2d at 1348.
178. *Tarkanian*, 488 U.S. at 193.
179. *Id.* at 192.
182. *Id.* at 196.
183. *Tarkanian*, 488 U.S. at 195.
184. *Id.* at 199.

the dissent remained unconvinced by the Court's reasoning, the *Tarkanian* decision makes it unlikely that any lower court will hold that the NCAA engages in state action in the course of its enforcement program.

B. *Protected Interest*

Even if a litigant could surmount the state action barrier, he would still have to demonstrate that the NCAA's action had deprived him of some protected interest. The issue is complicated by the variety of interests that could be asserted. The student-athlete's interest could be characterized as a property interest in athletic participation as a component of the student's education, in an opportunity to develop skills marketable to professional teams, or in exposure that could result in professional opportunities. It is also possible to assert a property interest in an athletic scholarship, assuming that the scholarship is rescinded when the player is ruled ineligible. Another possibility is some variety of liberty interest in participation. The equities are especially strong where the student is innocent of any wrongdoing, but loses the opportunity to participate because of sanctions imposed on his institution for the misconduct of others.

The interest of coaches and other athletic department personnel in continued employment almost certainly qualifies as a property interest, although the interest in continuing to serve in a particular capacity is more problematic. Coaches might also argue in favor of a liberty interest. Boosters could argue for a property right in preferential access to institutional facilities, especially if they can demonstrate that such access was granted in return for services rendered to the athletic department. Boosters might also allege a liberty interest in their right to associate with current and prospective athletes. Many of the arguably protected interests have yet to be presented to the courts. To date, courts have not arrived at any consensus as to the status of the interests that have been litigated.

.... [Discussion of cases addressing the issue of the existence of a protected property interest is omitted. A detailed discussion of property interests can be found in the Porto articles which appears *infra*. - ed.]

C. *What Process Is Due*

"Once it is determined that due process applies, the remaining question is what process is due."[226] Due process rules are designed to protect the individual from *mistaken* or *unjustified* deprivations of liberty or property. In deciding what process is due in a particular situation, a court must consider the importance of the private interest, the risk of erroneous deprivation posed by the procedures used, the probable value of additional safeguards, and the impact of fiscal and administrative burdens created by the proposed safeguards on the legitimate interests of the defendant. The purpose of requiring procedural safeguards is to "minimize substantively unfair or mistaken deprivations...by enabling" the person who would be deprived to effectively contest the basis of the deprivation.[229]

The question of whether NCAA enforcement procedures meet the requirements of due process has been litigated in several jurisdictions, and is the subject of continuing scholarly commentary. Most courts examining the issue have con-

---

226. Morrissey v. Brewer, 408 U.S. 471, 481 (1972).
229. Carey v. Piphus, 435 U.S. 247, 259-60 (1978).

cluded that the NCAA does provide all of the process that is due. In *Howard University*,[232] the court held that the NCAA had complied with its due process obligations by providing the member institution and student-athletes with notice of the charges, an opportunity to participate in the hearing, and the right to appeal an adverse determination. The court of appeals did not comment on the trial court's reliance on the absence of a factual dispute, or its statement that the lack of access to investigative reports and inability to confront and cross-examine witnesses might have been problematic if the facts had been disputed. Other courts have concluded that NCAA procedures are constitutionally sound.

A continuing source of controversy is the NCAA's requirement that member institutions declare student-athletes ineligible once the NCAA has determined the existence of an infraction, even though the institution may not agree that the student is in fact ineligible. The situation is complicated by the fact that, unlike the NCAA itself, state universities are clearly obligated to provide students with due process. In *Regents of the University of Minnesota v. National Collegiate Athletic Ass'n.*,[237] the NCAA determined that three Minnesota basketball players had violated Association rules and should be declared ineligible. The University provided due process hearings for the players, and the trier of fact found that the three did not violate the rules and should not be declared ineligible.[238]

The NCAA then applied coercive sanctions to the University in an ultimately successful attempt to force the University to declare the students ineligible. The University sought an injunction to block the threatened sanctions. The NCAA contended that the institution was contractually obligated to observe Association rules and declare the students ineligible. The trial court held that both the University and the NCAA were bound by the results of the campus due process hearings. "Minnesota...could not later disavow the findings made by its committees in order to comply with its NCAA membership obligation to abide by NCAA rules and decisions. That would...make a mockery of due process."[243] The President of the University of Minnesota was even more emphatic in his criticism of the NCAA's "due process" hearings in eligibility determinations:

> Thus, we had a duty to provide objective and impartial hearings but, at the same time, we were told that if such hearings did not lead to the desired results — as predetermined by the NCAA — then we were in contempt of the association's rules.... [D]ue process hearings under these circumstances are nothing short of a sham.... Any system of justice that allows only one verdict is fundamentally flawed.[244]

The court of appeals reversed,[245] rejecting the contention that there was a conflict between the University's duty to provide due process to its students and its contractual obligation to nevertheless declare them ineligible. The court did not find it necessary to address the issue of whether a hearing with predetermined re-

---

232. 510 F.2d 213 (D.C. Cir. 1975).

237. *Regents of Univ. of Minn.*, 422 F. Supp. at 1158.

238. *Id.* at 1159.

243. *Id.* at 1162.

244. *NCAA Hearings Part I*, 1978, *supra* note 9, at 251 (testimony of Dr. C. Peter McGrath, President, University of Minnesota).

245. *Regents of Univ. of Minn.*, 560 F.2d 352.

sults is consistent with the notion of due process, because it found as fact that the University committees had confirmed that the students had committed the acts that constituted the violations. The court found no infirmity in the NCAA's practice of reserving to the Association the right to consider mitigating factors, and limiting the role of the institution to a determination of whether the violation occurred. The issue of how the impasse between the NCAA and the member institution should be resolved in the event that the institutional hearing results in a finding that no infraction occurred remains unsettled.

In three cases, NCAA or athletic conference enforcement procedures have been held inadequate under a due process analysis. In *Behagen*,[249] the Big Ten suspended basketball players from competition and practice. Although conference rules provided for notice and an opportunity to be heard at the hearing, the players were not notified and did not appear. The court first held that "action beyond the scope of a body's own procedural regulations is a violation of due process of law."[251] For the guidance of the parties, the court then clarified what it considered to be the rudimentary requirements of due process in this situation.

> Plaintiffs should be given a written notice of the time and place of the hearing at least two days in advance. Accompanying such notice should be a specification of the charges against each, and the grounds which, if proven, would justify imposition of a penalty. The hearing should be such that the Directors of Athletics have an opportunity to hear both sides of the story. This does not require a full-dress judicial hearing, with the right to cross-examine witnesses. However, it should include the presentation of direct testimony in the form of statements by each of those directly involved relating their versions of the incident. Plaintiffs should be given a list of all witnesses who will appear, and should be allowed to hear all testimony. Plaintiffs should be given a written report specifying the Directors' findings of fact, and if there is to be any punishment the basis for such punishment. The proceedings should be recorded, and the tapes should be made available to plaintiffs in the event they wish to appeal...as is their right....If these minimal standards are followed in cases of this nature, it is this Court's opinion that the requirements of due process will have been met.[253]

In *Stanley*,[254] the court enjoined a conference enforcement proceeding that it held defective under a due process analysis. The major defect in the procedure was the use of hearsay evidence submitted in the form of an investigator's report. The court was concerned about the potential for biased presentations of the witness's testimony, as well as the inherent unreliability of hearsay and double hearsay evidence. Further:

> As stated in *Goldberg v. Kelly*,..."[i]n almost every setting where important decisions turn on questions of fact, due process requires an opportunity to confront and cross-examine adverse witnesses."...The individual is entitled to an opportunity to refute the allegations which are based on testimony of persons

---

249. *Behagen*, 346 F. Supp. 602.
251. *Id*. at 606.
253. *Id*. at 608.
254. *Stanley*, 463 F. Supp. 920.

whose memory might be faulty or who, in fact, might be perjurers or persons motivated by malice, vindictiveness, intolerance, prejudice, or jealousy.[257]

The court noted the practical problems with requiring live testimony, including the conference's lack of a subpoena power and the expense involved. However, the court held that if the conference cannot produce the witnesses for cross-examination it should, at the very least, provide written statements signed by the witness.

In *Tarkanian*,[260] the Nevada Supreme Court was equally troubled by the NCAA's use of investigator's summaries of witness statements. The court found *Stanley* persuasive, and concluded that "basing findings of fact upon pre-digested information creates serious due process problems."[261] The court was especially concerned about the potential for summaries that are inaccurate where, as here, the summaries were often prepared from memory long after the interview. The court concluded that alternative procedures were available, and that "[a]t a minimum the NCAA should be required to produce written affidavits of persons interviewed by the enforcement staff."[263] In summary, should NCAA enforcement procedures ever be subjected to judicial review for compliance with the minimum requirements of due process, it is likely that the current procedures would be found adequate. The only aspect of the current process that has generated any significant judicial criticism is the use of investigator's summaries of witness statements. However, even the most critical courts have stopped short of requiring live presentation of testimony and full rights of cross-examination, indicating that they would be satisfied with the presentation of signed witness statements. Because current policy calls for the acquisition of such statements "where possible," no radical change in Association policy is required to accommodate prevailing judicial opinion on the amount of process that is due.

D. *The Continued Vitality of Due Process Jurisprudence*

Given the above conclusions that NCAA enforcement procedures are not subject to judicial review for compliance with due process standards because the NCAA does not engage in state action, that the existence of a protected interest in athletic participation is problematic, and that the NCAA procedures probably already comport with the requirements of due process, why does the due process jurisprudence matter at all? The due process case law matters because it establishes the standard by which the conduct of many member institutions, public schools that are clearly state actors, will be judged. The NCAA must avoid imposing membership obligations which are inconsistent with the legal duties of member institutions.

Further, several states have passed legislation requiring the NCAA to provide due process to participants in its enforcement proceedings, and similar federal legislation has been proposed. To the extent that those statutes do not specify particular minimum requirements, there will undoubtedly be litigation to establish the amount of process that is due. The pre-*Tarkanian* due process cases are the most clearly applicable precedent. Finally, the NCAA can and should provide more

---

257. *Id.* [citations omitted].
260. Tarkanian, 741 P.2d 1345.
261. *Id.* at 1351.
263. *Id.*

process than the courts are likely to require, and must make very sure that it provides no less....

....[A thorough discussion of the NCAA enforcement program in effect in 1991-92 and state legislative initiatives mandating that NCAA procedures comport with minimum standards of due process are omitted. Also omitted is a discussion of NCAA internal proposals for reform and reforms adopted by the NCAA. - ed.].

Ronald J. Thompson, Comment, Due Process and the National Collegiate Athletic Association: Are There Any Constitutional Standards
41 UCLA Law Review 1651 (1994)*

....

I. THE SEARCH FOR DUE PROCESS PROTECTION IN NCAA ENFORCEMENT PROCEEDINGS

....

C. Legislative Efforts to Reform the NCAA Enforcement Program

....

Since the Supreme Court's *Tarkanian* decision, four state legislatures[91] have reacted to the finding that the NCAA is not subject to the Fourteenth Amendment's due process requirements by enacting NCAA regulatory legislation. Each of these state laws purports to require that NCAA enforcement program proceedings meet certain procedural due process requirements.

The Nevada legislature, for example, enacted its law in 1991. The Nevada law requires that the NCAA provide reasonable notice of a hearing to any party against whom it may impose sanctions. Further, the party is entitled to be represented by counsel, to confront and respond to all witnesses and evidence related to the allegations against him, to call witnesses on his own behalf, and to have access to the evidence to be offered against him at the proceeding. A record of the proceedings and a transcript of oral statements made at the proceedings are also required. The evidence to be used at such proceedings must not be "[i]rrelevant, immaterial or unduly repetitious" and may be "admitted if it is of the type commonly relied upon by reasonable, prudent men in the conduct of their affairs."[96] The laws of Nevada relating to privilege apply, and objections to evidentiary matters must be noted in the record of the proceeding. The person presiding over a proceeding must be impartial and shall not communicate with any party to the proceeding concerning issues of fact or law except upon notice to all parties. De-

---

91. FLA. STAT. chs. 240.5338-.5349 (1993); ILL. ANN. STAT. ch. 110, Act 25 (Smith-Hurd 1994); NEB. REV. STAT. §§ 85-1201 to -1210 (1991); NEV. REV. STAT. §§ 398.155-.255 (1991). In addition, the legislatures of Kansas, Ohio, Missouri, South Carolina, and Kentucky are considering similar legislation.

96. *Id.* § 398.185.

cisions of the proceeding "must be based on substantial evidence in the record, and must be supported by a preponderance of such evidence."[99] Finally, parties aggrieved by the decision in a proceeding are entitled to judicial review in the district courts.

. . . .

II. *NCAA v. MILLER*: THE NEVADA STATE LAW REGULATING THE NCAA'S ENFORCEMENT PROCEEDINGS IS UNCONSTITUTIONAL

A. The Case of Jerry Tarkanian Revisited

By the time the Nevada state legislature passed its law on April 8, 1991, the NCAA had begun another investigation of alleged rules violations at UNLV. Again, Coach Tarkanian was suspected of violating several recruiting rules, many of which stemmed from the school's dealings with New York City high school basketball star Lloyd Daniels, who was arrested on drug charges in Las Vegas in February 1987.

The NCAA enforcement staff investigated the alleged rules violations, UNLV filed its response to the allegations with the NCAA, and the Committee on Infractions scheduled an official hearing to review the alleged infractions for September 27-29, 1991. Before the Committee could hold the hearing, however, Tarkanian and several other UNLV employees accused of wrongdoing filed written demands that the NCAA comply with the newly enacted Nevada state law requiring due process standards in NCAA enforcement proceedings. Tarkanian and the other UNLV employees refused to appear before the NCAA Committee on Infractions until they were guaranteed the protections afforded them by the Nevada state law.

Rather than comply with Tarkanian's demand, the NCAA elected to file an action for declaratory and injunctive relief in the United States District Court for the District of Nevada. The NCAA sought a declaratory judgment that the Nevada state law regulating the NCAA enforcement proceedings was unconstitutional because the law imposes a direct burden on interstate commerce, substantially impairs existing contractual obligations, deprives the NCAA and its member institutions of the right to freely associate with each other and to maintain their intercollegiate athletic programs, and is impermissibly vague. The NCAA also sought an order enjoining application of the Nevada law.

The district court agreed with the NCAA and struck down the Nevada law as impermissibly burdening interstate commerce and impairing the obligation of contract. Judge McKibben, in a memorandum decision, also ordered Tarkanian and the other defendants to refrain from taking action to enforce or seek protection under the provisions of the Nevada NCAA regulation law.

B. Violation of the Interstate Commerce Clause

The Interstate Commerce Clause provides Congress with the power "[t]o regulate Commerce...among the several states."[117] Although the Constitution empowers the Congress with this regulatory power, the Supreme Court has long recognized that "the Commerce Clause even without implementing legislation by Congress is a limitation upon the power of the States."[118] Thus, this "dormant"

---

99. *Id.* § 398.205.
117. U.S. CONST. art. 1, § 8, cl. 3.
118. Freeman v. Hewit, 329 U.S. 249, 252 (1946).

aspect of the Commerce Clause limits state regulation of interstate commerce, even if Congress has failed to enact legislation in the specific area addressed by the challenged state statute.

The court first concluded that the product marketed by the NCAA — intercollegiate competition — and the regulation of intercollegiate athletics involved interstate commerce. The court reasoned that the NCAA's product would be completely ineffective if there were no agreed-upon rules to keep each competitor on equal footing with its rivals.

The court then cited recent Supreme Court precedent for testing whether state legislation impermissibly impinges Congress' power to regulate interstate commerce. In *Brown-Forman Distillers Corp. v. New York State Liquor Authority*,[123] the Supreme Court stated:

> This Court has adopted what amounts to a two-tiered approach to analyzing state economic regulation under the Commerce Clause. When a state statute directly regulates or discriminates against interstate commerce, or when its effect is to favor in-state economic interests over out-of-state interests, we have generally struck down the statute without further inquiry.... When, however, a statute has only indirect effects on interstate commerce and regulates evenhandedly, we have examined whether the State's interest is legitimate and whether the burden on interstate commerce clearly exceeds the local benefits.[124]

The court first concluded that the Nevada state law regulating the NCAA enforcement program was not invalid per se under the Commerce Clause because it did not overtly block the flow of interstate commerce at the Nevada border. Further, the challenged state statute did not discriminate against out-of-state interests, nor did it "sound of economic protectionism."

The court then applied the second part of the two-tiered approach articulated in *Brown-Forman Distillers*: balancing the local benefits of the state legislation and the burden on interstate commerce imposed by the regulation. Under this prong, the state's interests must be identified, analyzed to determine their legitimacy, and then weighed against the burden on interstate commerce resulting from the state legislation.

The court identified the Nevada state interests as ensuring that basic due process safeguards protect the careers and reputations of student-athletes, university employees, and fans of Nevada intercollegiate sports. The court recognized these objectives as being legitimate local public interests.

The Nevada NCAA regulatory law failed constitutional muster, however, because the legitimate public interests served by the law did not justify the burden imposed on interstate commerce. In order to successfully market its product of interstate intercollegiate athletics, the NCAA enforcement program must operate even-handedly and uniformly on all member institutions. The Nevada law would have the effect of making the NCAA establish a different set of rules in its enforcement procedures with respect to Nevada institutions. Further, because each state would be free to pass its own NCAA regulatory law, the end result would be that the NCAA, in order to ensure a "level playing field," would be constrained to the standards of the most stringent state law among the fifty states.

---

123. 476 U.S. 573 (1986).
124. *Id*. at 578-79 (citations omitted).

The court specifically noted three procedural due process safeguards mandated by the Nevada law that impermissibly burdened the NCAA's enforcement program. First, the Nevada statute provides that a party to an NCAA proceeding is "entitled to confront and respond to all witnesses and evidence related to the allegation against him."[132] However, the court noted, the NCAA lacks subpoena power and thus could not practicably comply with the Nevada law. Two other requirements of the Nevada law would also have mandated significant changes in the NCAA rules approved by its member institutions at national NCAA conventions. These requirements, in the court's view, were too significant a burden on the NCAA and its interstate business of intercollegiate athletics.

The court stated that the extraterritorial effect of the Nevada statute was substantial, as it severely restricted the NCAA from establishing uniform rules in presiding over the intercollegiate athletic programs of its member institutions. Because a statute's effect beyond the enacting state's borders and its practical effect on the regulated entity are proper concerns for the court in evaluating a statute's constitutionality, the court ruled that the Nevada law impermissibly burdened interstate commerce.

C. Violation of the Contract Clause

The court concluded that the Nevada law was also unconstitutional because it violated the Contract Clause. The Constitution provides that "[n]o state shall... pass any...Law impairing the Obligation of Contracts."[137] An application of the Contract Clause takes into account the degree of contract impairment as weighed against the state's interest served by the challenged state law. The court concluded that a contractual relationship existed between UNLV and the NCAA and that the modification to that contract affected by the challenged law significantly impaired the pre-existing contractual obligation.

Because UNLV, a state-funded university, was a party to the contract affected by the challenged state law, the state had the burden of showing that contractual impairment was "reasonable and necessary to serve an important public purpose." [140] The court found, however, that the Nevada Legislature's stated purpose of specifically targeting the NCAA's enforcement program for reform was too narrow to qualify as a broad public goal. A challenged law is less likely to survive constitutional challenge if its purpose is merely to alter the obligations of contracting parties. The court commented that the state was merely attempting to adjust its obligations under a contractual relationship that it had voluntarily entered and was still free to leave.

D. Summary of the Result of the Ruling

The district court did not rule that the NCAA was beyond the reach of the Nevada state legislature, but instead merely ruled that the challenged law went too far. However, the decision did qualify the command of earlier judicial decisions regarding obtaining procedural due process safeguards in NCAA enforcement proceedings: Definitive public goals and legislative action were not enough.

---

132. NEV. REV. STAT. § 398.155(2) (1991).

137. U.S. CONST. art. I, § 10.

140. State of Nev. Employees Ass'n v. Keating, 903 F.2d 1223, 1228 (9th Cir. 1990) (quoting United States Trust Co. v. New Jersey, 431 U.S. 1, 25 (1977)).

Congressional action would be necessary, or alternatively, state legislation must only minimally impact the NCAA.

III. A REVIEW OF RULINGS ON STATE REGULATION AFFECTING INTERSTATE COMMERCE

This Section is not intended to be a complete review of the principles underlying Supreme Court decisions on a state's ability, or the limits on that ability, to impact interstate commerce through its own legislation. Rather, this Section presents some principles and cases that are helpful in guiding a discussion on a state legislature's ability to legislatively regulate the NCAA's enforcement program.

When a state statute is challenged as violative of the Commerce Clause, and Congress has elected not to enact legislation in the area addressed by the state statute, the judiciary is expected to decide whether the state legislature has encroached upon Congress' constitutional powers. The courts are called upon to interpret the significance of Congress' silence in a particular area. As Professor Powell explained: "Now Congress has a wonderful power that only judges and lawyers know about. Congress has a power to keep silent. Congress can regulate interstate commerce just by not doing anything about it.... [W]hen Congress keeps silent, it takes an expert to know what it means."[144] Judges are, of course, the designated experts.

In deciding the validity of state statutes, the judicial branch is guided by the purposes of the Commerce Clause as stated by the framers of the Constitution. An important goal of the Commerce Clause is to create and foster a common economic market among the states. Courts often strike down state laws that deter interstate trade. There are a variety of different ways that a state law can tend to damage the economic union of states, some of which are instructive in considering legislation regulating the NCAA.

A. Legislation Discriminating Against Politically Unrepresented Interests

When a challenged state statute is designed such that its burdens are borne primarily by out-of-state interests, active judicial review is likely. Because the disadvantaged parties had no voice in the enacting state legislature, the state's own internal political process provided no impedance to the passage of the challenged state law. This political representation theory of judicial activism explains many of the Supreme Court's decisions regarding the dormant commerce clause.

Two cases demonstrate the importance this concept has in predicting a state law's constitutional validity. In *Southern Pacific Co. v. Arizona*,[148] a state law limited the length of trains operating within Arizona. The statute was enacted to promote public safety by reducing the risk of railroad accidents. This state law imposed a considerable burden on the interstate railroad company, as it was forced to either break up long trains at the state border or comply with the stricter Arizona law in neighboring states as well. The Court, questioning the actual safety value of the law, found the statute unconstitutional because it impermissibly burdened interstate commerce, even though Congress had not passed any legislation concerning the permissible length of trains.

---

144. Thomas R. Powell, *Business Taxation and Interstate Commerce*, 1937 NAT'L TAX ASS'N PROC. 337, 338.

148. 325 U.S. 761 (1945).

Conversely, in *South Carolina State Highway Department v. Barnwell Brothers, Inc.*,[150] the Court, in a unanimous decision, sustained another state statute that limited the width of trucks operated on South Carolina's highways. The South Carolina law had the effect of forcing out-of-state truckers to either comply with the stricter South Carolina law in other states in which they operated or change trucks at the state border — burdens similar to those at issue in *Southern Pacific*. The Court, in its ruling in *Southern Pacific*, distinguished *Barnwell* by stating that a state's powers over "its" highways are "more extensive" than its control over railroads.

Although arguments over which of the two example state laws actually burden interstate commerce more can be made, and the actual safety gain of one law might be more than the other, it is instructive to note that the political representation theory probably applies more in *Barnwell* than *Southern Pacific*. The *Southern Pacific* prohibitions probably burden the long-haul shipper more than the short-haul shipper. The long-haul shipper is more likely to be interstate and the short-haul trucker is more likely to be intrastate. The intrastate shippers presumably were represented in the state legislature and could thus be deemed to be willing to bear the burden of the regulation; the truck regulation seems more likely to withstand constitutional scrutiny. The interstate railroad, however, had little voice in the Arizona legislature, and therefore, less ability to exert political pressure to defeat the state law.

B. Legislation Isolating State Industries from Interstate Competition

State legislation that has the practical effect of economic protectionism is also subject to severe judicial review. If the statutory effect or purpose is to insulate state producers from interstate competition, thereby augmenting the economic security of the local market, the local legislation is likely to be found unconstitutional.

In the case of *Baldwin v. G.A.F. Seelig, Inc.*,[156] a New York law regulating the minimum price paid by milk dealers to milk producers was ruled unconstitutional, notwithstanding earlier cases upholding state minimum price laws. The law required the dealers to pay a minimum amount to milk producers located within the state. Naturally, the dealers would be encouraged to acquire their milk out of state, so the law provided that a milk dealer could not be licensed to sell milk in New York unless he paid the mandated minimum price to out-of-state producers as well. Justice Cardozo, in ruling the law unconstitutional, stated:

> Such a power, if exerted, will set a barrier to traffic between one state and another as effective as if customs duties, equal to the price differential, had been laid upon the thing transported. . . . If New York, in order to promote the economic welfare of her farmers, may guard them against competition with the cheaper prices of Vermont, the door has been opened to rivalries and reprisals that were meant to be averted by subjecting commerce between the states to the power of the nation.[159]

At first glance, it would appear that the burdened parties in *Baldwin* were the milk dealers, as they were being forced to pay higher prices to the producers.

---

150. 303 U.S. 177 (1938).
156. 294 U.S. 511 (1935).
159. Baldwin v. G.A.F. Seelig, Inc., 294 U.S. at 521-22 (citations omitted).

Therefore, as the dealers were politically represented in the New York legislature, the political representation concept would lead one to expect the state law to survive constitutional challenge because of the theoretical representation of the parties bearing the cost of the local legislation. However, the Vermont milk producers were also burdened by the New York legislation because the cost of exporting milk to a sister state was made artificially high. Another equally plausible argument, however, is that the ultimate bearers of the burden of the New York minimum price law were the milk consumers of the state. Thus, the state law could also be sustained under the political representation concept as well.

C. Legislation Failing to Use the Least Restrictive Means Available to Achieve the Legitimate State Goals

Other state statutes have been drafted to more directly serve public health and safety. The Court, when reviewing these statutes, has embraced a stricter, more active review when such statutes fail to employ a method that imposes the least possible burden on interstate commerce.

In *Dean Milk Co. v. City of Madison*,[161] the challenged local statute forbade the sale of milk advertised as pasteurized unless the milk had been processed and bottled within five miles from the central square of Madison, Wisconsin. The Court found the statute to be unconstitutional, even though it affected Wisconsin milk as well as out-of-state milk. The city had other means available to ensure the safety of the milk sold in the local market short of creating an economically restricted zone that milk producers from other areas could not penetrate.

D. Legislation Affecting Interstate Commerce and the Right to Privacy

If a local government can show that its legislation provides a local benefit that outweighs the detriments of the restraints imposed on interstate commerce, the Court is likely to sustain the legislation absent a contrary congressional intent. In *Breard v. Alexandria*,[164] the Court upheld a municipal ordinance forbidding door-to-door solicitation. The Court found that the local benefit of protecting a homeowner's privacy outweighed the burden imposed on interstate commerce. Legislation protecting a privacy right was thus given greater judicial deference than similarly burdensome legislation attempting to aid the local economy.

IV. WHY WOULD A STATE LEGISLATURE SEEK TO REGULATE THE NCAA?

....

A. Can a State Constitutionally Regulate the NCAA?

The *Miller* court struck down the Nevada NCAA regulatory act as violative of the Commerce Clause. A revised state statute must, therefore, be drafted in keeping with the overall goal of the Commerce Clause: preserving economic unity among the states. The Nevada state law as written meets some of the indicators of a state statute properly serving that goal, but resembles other regulations found unconstitutional in past decisions in more important ways.

---

161. 340 U.S. 349 (1951).
164. 341 U.S. 622 (1951).

The Nevada law was not motivated by economic goals. The legislature had no intention of protecting local economies or markets at the expense of out-of-state economic interests. The legislature was only trying to protect its citizens from perceived deprivation of procedural due process rights. This fact makes the Nevada law less like the economic protectionist cases—*Baldwin* and *Dean Milk*—in which state legislatures were attempting to preserve local markets at the expense of out-of-state competitors.

The legislative goal of protecting individual rights also makes the Nevada law similar to the privacy case involving interstate commerce, *Breard*. Greater judicial deference is appropriate if the local interest is protection of individual rights and not economic protectionism. However, the NCAA is not represented politically in the Nevada legislature. An argument that the university or the people of Nevada are the ultimate bearers of the burden because the NCAA could withdraw from operation in Nevada or that the university could withdraw from the NCAA is doomed by the provisions of the state law itself. The state law forbids the NCAA to impair the rights or privileges of membership within the association as a consequence of the state law. Thus, the NCAA is precluded from exercising the option of severing its contractual relationship with Nevada institutions. As a result of the NCAA's lack of political representation, there was arguably no political check within the legislature to the passage of the law, and therefore the bearer of the burden imposed by the law has no theoretical voice in whether the burden is too severe. This feature of the state NCAA regulatory acts, similar to the feature that distinguished *Barnwell* from *Southern Pacific*, is a serious defect inherent in any state legislature's attempt to regulate the NCAA enforcement procedures.

The Nevada law also fails to impose the least restrictive burden on interstate commerce as necessary to achieve the proffered state goal. For example, the law requires that defendants in NCAA enforcement hearings be given the right to confront hostile witnesses, a provision that the NCAA cannot comply with because it lacks subpoena power. Further, the NCAA regulatory law requires that all NCAA enforcement hearings be conducted by an impartial hearing officer and prohibits the NCAA from expelling institutions that fail to comply with NCAA regulations conflicting with the state statute. The district court deemed these burdens on the NCAA enforcement program too severe. Thus, a state legislature must find less restrictive ways to accomplish its goal of achieving fairness in NCAA hearings.

Perhaps most importantly, any state legislation purporting to regulate the NCAA will have a significant extra-territorial effect. The NCAA, if forced to comply with each state legislature's regulation, would probably select the most stringent state regulatory law and enforce it evenly against all of its member institutions. This course of action would ensure equal competition among member institutions without violating any single state regulatory law. Thus, one state legislature could impose its will on unrepresented interests beyond its own borders—similar to the state actions examined in *Southern Pacific* and *Dean Milk*.

An examination of the four statutes passed to date is useful in illustrating this point. The Illinois and Florida laws, nearly identical, differ from the Nevada law in only one substantial way. The Illinois and Florida legislatures detail findings of the legislature, presumably to bolster the argument that the state interests served by the regulation are legitimate and important. It is likely that this is a distinction without a difference, as the district court acknowledged that the state interests served were a legitimate public concern, even though the Nevada law has a less complete listing of public goals served by the local legislation.

The Nebraska law, however, only requires that the NCAA comply with the due process standards of the Nebraska Constitution when enforcing rules violations penalties against Nebraska residents and institutions. The exact standards required by that state's constitution are irrelevant in understanding the extra-territorial nature of state NCAA regulations. If the Nebraska Constitution requires more stringent standards than those required by the Nevada state law, and the NCAA does enforce the most stringent state law against all member institutions to assure a level playing field, then the Nebraska NCAA regulatory act will become the law of Nevada. Conversely, if the Nebraska Constitution is less demanding than the Nevada (or any other state) statute, the Nebraska legislature will have accomplished nothing with its enactment, as the law of some other state will already be controlling NCAA activities within Nebraska's borders.

As discussed earlier, the district court did not preclude any state action, but merely ruled that the current Nevada law went too far. But given the nearly impossible task facing a draftsperson of such a state law—constitutional regulation of an interstate private organization that is unrepresented in any state legislature with attendant extra-territorial effect—it is quite likely that any state statute would be found impermissibly burdensome on national economic unity.

. . . .

CONCLUSION

The NCAA has near total power over the professional lives of coaches and student-athletes. The district court's opinion allows the NCAA to continue its autonomous rule over intercollegiate athletics secure from state governmental intrusion. Like the society it serves, the judiciary might be overestimating the value of sports at the expense of the individual.

The encouraging point to remember in this story is that acceptable middle ground undoubtedly exists. The states want to protect the citizens from unfair administrative decisions. Citizens desire protection from being unfairly deprived of an occupation. The NCAA seeks fair competition in intercollegiate sports. In a sense, all of the parties are in search of the same goal: fairness.

2. Property Interest and Right to Participate

(a) Defining the Student-Athlete's Property Interest

Brian L. Porto, Note, Balancing Due Process and Academic
Integrity in Intercollegiate Athletics: The Scholarship
Athlete's Limited Property Interest in Eligibility
62 Indiana Law Journal 1151 (1987)*

INTRODUCTION

In approximately a dozen lawsuits litigated during the 1970's and 1980's, athletic scholarship recipients who had been declared ineligible for varsity competition asserted that the due process clause of the fourteenth amendment encompassed a property right to continued athletic eligibility. The plaintiffs claimed that as a result of this property right, student athletes are entitled to due process prior to being deprived of eligibility for athletic competition. Each plaintiff presented one of four rationales which, arguably, were available as potential bases for a property interest in athletic eligibility. The respective rationales were that: (1) athletic scholarship recipients possess significant economic interests in preparing for careers in professional sports; (2) continued athletic participation is an important part of the student athlete's pursuit of an education and that pursuit is a protected property right; (3) the material benefits of athletic scholarships create property interests in continued athletic eligibility; and (4) athletic scholarships are contracts whose provisions create property interests in the material benefits of the awards and in the awardees' expectations to compete.

The plaintiffs asserted that the National Collegiate Athletic Association (NCAA), which promulgates requirements for continued eligibility, is a "'state actor" and that the Association employed enforcement procedures which failed to satisfy even minimal standards of due process. The NCAA, a private, voluntary association of approximately 900 member schools, conferences and organizations, is responsible for the administration of intercollegiate athletics in all of its phases. The NCAA's avowed purpose is to preserve intercollegiate athletics as the domain of the amateur. Amateur is defined as "one who engages in a particular sport for the educational, physical, mental and social benefits he derives therefrom and to whom participation in that sport is an avocation."[8]

The charges of lack of due process for student athletes have been supported by scholarly commentaries which have maintained that during its disciplinary proceedings, the NCAA refuses to permit the student athletes' interest, restoration of eligibility, to be presented independently of the universities' interest, namely, paying their penalties and regaining access to television and post-season competition. The NCAA has responded that: (1) it is not a "state actor,"' and hence it is not bound by constitutional standards of due process; (2) student athletes are not en-

---

    8. Note, *supra* note 7, at 598-99.

titled to due process because the Constitution does not recognize a property right to continued athletic eligibility; and (3) NCAA disciplinary proceedings provide due process to student athletes even in the absence of a constitutional mandate.

Only one federal court has recognized a property right to athletic eligibility, yet student athletes continue to assert the right and commentators continue to comment on the merits of upholding it. This issue is part of a larger debate regarding the way in which the law should define that relationship between scholarship awardees and their universities. Two federal courts concluded during the 1970's that athletic scholarships are contracts, the terms of which are binding upon both the student athletes and their universities.[14] These decisions departed from the traditional view, still espoused by the NCAA, that athletic scholarships are educational grants or gifts which lack the exchange of enforceable promises necessary for a contract. One state court concluded in the 1980's that athletic scholarships are contracts of employment under which recipients who are permanently disabled as a result of an injury sustained during practice or in competition are entitled to collect benefits from a state workers' compensation fund.[17] That decision was vacated on appeal, as the appellate court adhered to the view that athletic scholarships are educational grants, not employment contracts.

This debate underscores the need to reexamine the property right issue. A reexamination must address the question of whether a property right to continued eligibility is protected by the Constitution and, if so, what process is due college athletes who successfully assert that right. The determination of what process is due will follow an assessment of whether any of the four proffered rationales for the property right can promote due process for student athletes without hindering the capacity of the universities to demand satisfactory academic performances from those student athletes. Another important question for reexamination is whether the athletes who are declared ineligible as a result of academic deficiencies are entitled to the same measure of due process as the athletes who are declared ineligible as a result of misconduct. To accord both groups of student athletes the same measure of due process appears to contravene the decision of the United States Supreme Court in *Board of Curators of the University of Missouri v. Horowitz*,[19] and to reduce the power of universities to enforce their academic standards with respect to the athletes. Perhaps, identical measures of due process in both academic and misconduct cases are necessary, however, because of the considerable benefits which scholarship athletes will lose if declared ineligible.

This Note contends that the Constitution recognizes a property right to continued athletic eligibility which is derived from the contractual nature of athletic scholarships. The scholarship contracts confer upon the awardees an entitlement to educational and financial benefits; the entitlement creates the property interest. Only this contractual rationale can balance due process protection for the student

---

14. Begley v. Corp. of Mercer Univ., 367 F. Supp. 908 (E.D. Tenn. 1973); Taylor v. Wake Forest Univ., 16 N.C. App. 117, 191 S.E.2d 370 (N.C. App. 1972), *cert. denied*, 282 N.C. 307, 192 S.E.2d 197 (1972).

17. *Rensing*, 437 N.E.2d 78.

19. 435 U.S. 78 (1978). Here the Supreme Court ruled that less stringent procedural requirements are necessary when a student is dismissed from school for academic deficiencies; a higher standard of due process is required, in the Court's view, when the dismissal results from charges of misconduct.

athletes with academic integrity for the universities. The Note also asserts that in order to achieve this balance, the process which is due the student athletes should be more substantial when ineligibility results from a violation of a coach's training rules or of an NCAA prohibition than when it results from academic failure.

II. THE SCHOLARSHIP ATHLETE'S PROPERTY INTEREST IN ELIGIBILITY

.... [Discussion of the state action requirement is omitted. - ed.].

B. *Four Rationales for the Property Right: Economic, Educational, Scholarship Per Se, and Contractual*

.... Courts have consistently expressed doubts about the existence of a property right, refused to resolve that issue in the case at hand, and then proceeded to the next step in due process analysis by affirmatively stating that the NCAA's procedures in that instance were sufficient to afford the plaintiff due process.[60] The challenge for student athletes is to demonstrate an entitlement to eligibility and the withdrawal of that eligibility without due process. The Supreme Court ruled in *Board of Regents v. Roth*[61] that: "To have a property interest in a benefit, a person clearly must have more than an abstract need or desire for it. He must have more than a unilateral expectation of it. He must, instead, have a legitimate claim of entitlement to it."[62] That claim of entitlement, in order to be legitimate, must be based upon a source independent of the beneficiary's own expectations, such as a state law or an institutional rule. Courts have divided over whether scholarship athletes have an entitlement to the benefits of athletic scholarships, with the majority either sidestepping the issue or denying the existence of an entitlement. Courts have heard four alternative rationales for the existence of a property right to continued eligibility.

The economic rationale views intercollegiate athletics as a training ground for professional sports and argues that the property right is derived from the collegians' economic interests in uninterrupted preparation for lucrative careers as professional athletes. Although the economic rationale has been accepted by the District of Minnesota,[66] it has failed when presented outside of that jurisdiction.[67] The majority view of this argument, expressed in *Colorado Seminary v. NCAA*,[68] is that because so few former college athletes ever sign a professional contract, the college athletes' economic interests in professional sports opportunities are "speculative and not of constitutional dimensions."[69] One commentator has written: "In the absence of settled state law on point, eligibility which may lead to a professional contract is clearly a unilateral expectation of a benefit without a legitimate claim of entitlement based on an independent source."[70]

The educational rationale views participation in college athletics as an integral facet of the student athlete's educational experience. As a substantial element of

---

60. *See* Comment, *supra* note 13, at 494.
61. 408 U.S. 564.
62. *Id.* at 577.
66. *See Hall*, 530 F. Supp. 104; *Regents of Univ. of Minn.*, 422 F. Supp. 1158; *Behagen*, 346 F. Supp. 602
67. *See Howard Univ.*, 510 F.2d 213; *Parish*, 506 F.2d 1028, *Justice*, 577 F. Supp. 356; *Colorado Seminary*, 417 F. Supp. 885; NCAA v. Gillard, 352 So. 2d 1072 (Miss. 1977).
68. *Colorado Seminary*, 417 F. Supp. 885.
69. *Id.* at 895.
70. Note, *supra* note 3, at 343.

the educational process, athletic eligibility should not be permitted to be sacrificed in the absence of due process. This reasoning is premised upon the longstanding recognition that the opportunity to pursue an education is a sufficiently important interest that it cannot be impaired without due process.

The scholarship per se rationale claims that the loss of an athletic scholarship per se is a denial of a property interest in athletic eligibility. The athletes who suffer such losses are likely to incur financial hardships which may cut off the opportunity to continue attending college and to earn a degree. The deprivation of the scholarships then, is also a deprivation of benefits to which the athletes were entitled according to the terms of their awards; the continued receipt of those benefits is a property interest which cannot be denied without due process. This argument has been unsuccessful because courts have concluded that since no school has yet revoked an athletic scholarship as a result of a declaration of ineligibility, no student athlete has been denied benefits which create a property interest.

The contractual rationale maintains that a property right to athletic eligibility is created by the contractual provisions of the athletic scholarships. The scholarships are contracts which have conferred upon the athletes certain benefits, including the right to participate in intercollegiate athletics, which cannot be denied without due process. The contractual argument has had a mixed reception in court. In *Colorado Seminary*, a federal district court in Colorado held that although the scholarships are contracts, they do not confer upon the recipients the entitlement to benefits which is necessary to create a property interest. The scholarship athletes have a unilateral expectation of participation, not a right to compete. The court said: "The athlete on scholarship has no more 'right' to play than the athlete who 'walks on.'"[83]

The contractual rationale was accepted, however, in *Hunt v. NCAA*.[84] A federal district court in Michigan concluded that the plaintiffs possessed a property interest derived from the scholarship agreements which they had signed, wherein each student athlete had been granted a package of benefits constituting a football scholarship. Since those scholarships had been conferred according to established NCAA rules and procedures and were understood by the awardees and their schools to bestow certain benefits, the plaintiffs had satisfied the entitlement requirement for a property interest. Unlike the *Colorado Seminary* court, which saw no legal difference between scholarship recipients and walk-ons, the *Hunt* court viewed the former as not merely expecting to participate, but as being entitled to participate.

C. Critique: Serious Flaws Plague Economic, Educational, Scholarship Per Se Rationales But Contractual Rationale Supports Property Interest in Eligibility

1. The Economic Rationale

This rationale views college athletics not as a component of university life, but as a means of acquiring the specialized qualifications for a profession. Just as courts have held that the rights of individuals to pursue professional training in law, dentistry or medicine cannot be denied without due process, so courts should rule that the rights of college students to pursue professional training in athletics

---

83. *Id.*
84. No. 676-370, slip op. (W.D. Mich. Sept. 10, 1976).

cannot be denied without due process. The economic rationale, however, possesses adverse policy implications of major proportions for intercollegiate athletics and higher education. It therefore must be rejected if there is to be a meaningful distinction between intercollegiate and professional athletics.

Acceptance of the economic rationale means acceptance of the notion that scholarship athletes are not students engaged in extracurricular activities, but apprentice entertainers who are training to be professional entertainers. At first glance, this notion appears perceptive and realistic, but a careful examination reveals that apprentice entertainers who are declared academically ineligible for athletics could understandably regard that declaration as a denial of due process and challenge it on either substantive or procedural grounds.

A suit on substantive due process grounds would contend that the legislative scheme being challenged, either the academic eligibility rules of the NCAA or the academic regulations of the defendant university, is arbitrary and capricious and is unrelated to a legitimate governmental interest, in this instance, a college athlete's preparation for a professional career. Such a suit would be likely if the economic rationale, as articulated by one recent student note, were adopted. This note argues: "The college athlete needs the opportunity to develop skills, and to avoid arbitrarily imposed disciplinary measures that restrict the development of skills, just as any other student who attends a university with the hopes of moving into a specified career."[91] This statement suggests that requirements for continued matriculation and graduation are, in light of the college athlete's specialized career goals, "arbitrarily imposed disciplinary measures that restrict the development of skills," namely, athletic skills.[92]

This challenge could be answered by pointing out that, as long as college athletes are amateurs and are enrolled in full-time courses of study, it is reasonable for the NCAA and universities to impose academic requirements upon them. A court which accepted the economically-based property interest in eligibility could nonetheless respond that academic strictures, which are reasonable when applied to students of history, chemistry or journalism, are unreasonable when applied to defensive backs and point guards training for careers in professional sports. Even if a substantive due process challenge failed, academically ineligible athletes could file suit on procedural due process grounds. It is commonplace for universities to recruit promising athletes despite substandard high school transcripts and a lack of basic academic skills, and to encourage those athletes to view the collegiate experience as an opportunity to train for a career in professional sports. The athletes who are recruited in this fashion and subsequently declared academically ineligible could claim a deprivation of a property interest in intercollegiate competition without procedural due process, namely, that they lacked notice of university and NCAA academic requirements.

The economic rationale for the property interest could thus expand due process in academic ineligibility cases to a point where athletes were exempted from academic requirements. While such exemptions may prove necessary in order for big-time college athletics to operate honestly, the choice of whether or not to abandon the student athlete concept is a major policy choice in higher edu-

---

91. See Comment, *supra* note 13, at 501.
92. *Id.*

cation which should be made directly by educators, not indirectly by judges. To abandon the notion of the student athlete is to announce that the training of individuals for careers in professional athletics has joined teaching, research and community service as a major mission of our universities. That momentous announcement should come as a result of careful deliberation within the educational community and not as an arguably unintended implication of a judicial response to a particular fact pattern.

2. The Educational Rationale

The idea that student athletes' property interest in intercollegiate competition derives from the fact that athletics are an integral component of undergraduate education also fails on policy grounds because it ignores the realities of big-time college sports. Participation in big-time intercollegiate athletics requires such substantial portions of the athletes' time and energy that the athletes often have very little time or energy to devote to studies. A federal district court in Minnesota has observed:

> The exceptionally talented student athlete is led to perceive the basketball, football and other athletic programs as farm teams and proving grounds for professional sports leagues. It may well be true that a good academic program for the athlete is made virtually impossible by the demands of their sport at the college level.[97]

Participation in intercollegiate athletics therefore is not an integral component of undergraduate education; indeed, such participation is frequently a detriment to the completion of an undergraduate degree. To argue, as the district court did in *Regents of the Univ. of Minnesota*,[98] that the student athletes' property interest in continued eligibility is derived from an intimate relationship between college athletics and the aims of higher education is to misread the realities of collegiate sport and the aims of higher education. The district court observed in Regents that "[t]he concepts of winning, losing and doing your best, while made somewhat trite by modern media, are nonetheless important to everyone's development."[100] The court thus views the undergraduate experience as merely a socialization mechanism, ignoring its at least equally important role as an instrument of intellectual growth. To assert that athletic participation is an integral component of a college education is to define a college education much too narrowly.

The educational rationale also encounters a serious doctrinal barrier through a misreading of *Goss v. Lopez*.[102] In Goss, the Supreme Court recognized a property interest in education entitling a student who had been suspended from school for ten days or less to notice and a hearing. It based that recognition upon requirements under Ohio law that (1) localities provide free elementary and secondary education to all residents between ages five and twenty-one and that (2) all residents between ages five and eighteen attend school for at least thirty-two weeks each year. Those regulations gave Ohio public school students an entitlement to an education, based on state law, which in turn created a property interest in continued attendance protectable by the due process clause of the four-

---

97. *Hall*, 530 F. Supp. at 109.
98. *Regents of Univ. of Minn.*, 422 F. Supp. 1158.
100. *Regents of Univ. of Minn.*, 422 F. Supp. at 1161.
102. 419 U.S. 565 (1975).

teenth amendment. Justice White, writing for the majority, concluded that "[h]aving chosen to extend the right to an education to people of appellees' class generally, Ohio may not withdraw that right on grounds of misconduct, absent fundamentally fair procedures to determine whether the misconduct has occurred."[105]

It is a mistake to conclude, as the district court did in *Regents*, that the property interest in education announced in *Goss* can be extended to the collegiate context and used to protect an athlete who has been declared ineligible. Although high school students may possess a property interest in education which is derived from state requirements that localities provide free public education to all children and that those children must attend school, the colleges and college students are not bound by any such attendance requirements, hence, no entitlement accrues to the collegians.

Participation in high school or collegiate athletics in and of itself is not a constitutionally protected right. *Goss* does not apply to athletic ineligibility because athletic competition is merely one component of the educational process. In the words of the Tenth Circuit Court of Appeals, "*Goss* [does not] establish a property interest subject to constitutional protection in each of these separate components."[108]

3. The Scholarship Per Se Rationale

The scholarship per se rationale, which claims that the student athlete's property interest lies in the benefits provided by athletic scholarships, is easily rebutted by the NCAA or a defendant university. As long as athletic scholarships are not revoked when their holders are declared ineligible, the student athlete plaintiffs are not deprived of any benefits which might constitute a property interest. Since NCAA rules permit, but do not require, universities to revoke athletic scholarships if their recipients become ineligible, courts are likely to continue ruling that no benefits to which the student athletes were entitled have been rescinded.

NCAA regulations provide that athletic scholarships are renewable annually, an arrangement which gives considerable discretion to coaches and athletic directors regarding the continuation of their student athletes' financial aid. A court could therefore uphold revocations by universities of athletic scholarships at the conclusion of an academic year, where the schools' ostensible reason for revocation is poor performance or insubordination, but their real reason is the former awardees' ineligibility for part or all of the next season. The NCAA requires that scholarships be subject to annual renewal but does not require that the scholarships of ineligible players be continued beyond the academic year in which the declaration of ineligibility occurred. The school which revoked a scholarship because of a player's prospective ineligibility would be able to successfully defend itself, therefore, against a claim that the revocation deprived the plaintiff athlete of benefits which created a property interest in the scholarship. As long as a university does not revoke an athletic scholarship during the academic year in which the beneficiary is rendered ineligible, that university need not fear that its decision will be reversed in court on the grounds that the ineligible athlete is entitled to the proceeds of the award.

---

105. *Id.* at 574.
108. *Id.* at 985.

4. The Contractual Rationale

The only line of reasoning which can support a property interest in continued eligibility views athletic scholarships as contracts which entitle student athletes to a package of benefits in exchange for fulfillment of an obligation to compete for the contracting university. This rationale satisfies the requirement that the claimant of a property interest possess an entitlement which is predicated upon a source independent of the claimant's expectations. It also can foster due process for college athletes without blurring the distinction between intercollegiate and professional athletics or forcing judges to announce a major change in higher education policy. The contractual argument is distinguishable from the scholarship per se rationale because, in the contractual view, the student athletes' property interest includes not just money, but also the expectation that, assuming health and skill, the awardees will participate in intercollegiate sports.

These scholarship athletes indeed do not merely expect to play, but rather, are obligated to do so by the terms of their scholarship agreements. One commentator has observed: "The student athlete has more than an abstract need or desire to participate in intercollegiate athletics: he is contractually obligated to do so. The expectancy of his participation is not unilateral: it belongs to the institution as well as to the individual."[117]

The benefits which student athletes seek to retain have a source independent of the athletes' expectations. That source is the scholarship agreements, which clearly express the athletes' obligations to the institution. The athletes' obligations exceed those imposed upon non-athletes. NCAA rules require that before signing letters of intent to enroll at particular schools, the athletes possess written statements from those schools which list the terms and conditions of the financial assistance offered, including its amount and duration. The athletes must agree to abide by the rules of their universities, the athletic conferences to which their schools belong, the NCAA, and their coaches in order to maintain eligibility. The universities frequently reserve the right to retract scholarships if the recipients fail to meet any obligations specified in the agreement. The prospective college athletes also sign letters of intent, which identify the schools at which these athletes will enroll. Each athlete may sign only one letter, which will be invalid unless it is signed by the recipient, the recipient's legal guardians and the preferred school's director of athletics. If the athlete reneges on this agreement and enrolls at a school other than the one indicated on the letter of intent, that athlete forfeits the initial year of athletic eligibility at the second school.

Courts have recognized that athletic scholarships impose obligations upon student athletes as well as upon the institutions which confer the awards. In *Taylor v. Wake Forest University,*[123] a football player who had been declared academically ineligible during his freshman year refused to resume competing even after improving his grades sufficiently to regain eligibility, but still sought to recover the financial aid which he had forfeited as a result of that refusal. The court observed that by signing the scholarship agreement, Taylor had agreed to maintain both the academic and physical aspects of his eligibility. As long as his grade-point average equalled or exceeded Wake Forest's requirements, he was scholastically eligible

---

117. *Id.* at 348.
123. 16 N.C. App. 117, 191 S.E.2d 379 (1972).

and was required to participate in practice sessions, unless injured, in order to satisfy the physical eligibility rules of the scholarship agreement. By refusing to practice or compete after his freshman season, Taylor failed to satisfy those physical eligibility rules, thereby breaching his contractual obligations to Wake Forest.

A federal district court in Tennessee found that a contract existed in *Begley v. Corporation of Mercer University*,[128] in which a prospective student athlete who was mistakenly awarded an athletic scholarship for the upcoming academic year sued the university for breach of contract after it revoked the award. The revocation resulted from a discovery that Begley's 2.9 high school grade-point average was based on a scale of 8.0 instead of the customary 4.0. As a result, Begley's grade-point average was below the minimum necessary for freshman eligibility under NCAA rules. The court agreed with Begley that he and Mercer University had signed a contract, but concluded that since Begley was unable, due to academic ineligibility, to perform his duties under that contract, he could not expect Mercer to perform its duties under the agreement.

The reasoning of the court in *Colorado Seminary* that scholarship recipients are no more entitled to participate than athletes who try out without scholarships is seriously flawed because the scholarship recipients are obliged by their scholarships to participate. The non-scholarship athletes, or walk-ons, have merely a "unilateral expectation of a benefit," namely, the hope of participation. The walk-ons cannot claim a property interest in eligibility. The scholarship players, in contrast, have a contractual duty to play. One commentator has written:

> The possession of an athletic scholarship ensures the student-athlete of a place on the team and of a right to compete for a position on the first string. The walk-on has no rights: the coach may prohibit him from trying out altogether and cut him from the team any time thereafter. The position of a walk-on thus is in no way analogous to that of a matriculated recruit.[136]

Even if a court did not agree that an athletic scholarship is an explicit contract which confers a property interest upon an awardee, that court could agree that where an athlete is recruited by a university and both parties anticipate the athlete's participation in athletics, an implied contract has been formed, creating a property interest in continued eligibility. The latter conclusion would be analogous to the holding of the Supreme Court in *Perry v. Sinderman*,[138] that a nontenured professor had a property interest in continued employment because the college which employed him operated a de facto tenure system. Since the college, in effect, awarded tenure to professors who had been working for it for seven years, and since the plaintiff had been working for the college for ten years, the parties had a mutual understanding sufficient to give the plaintiff a property interest in continued employment.

The understandings which exist between universities and athletic scholarship recipients are comparable to the understanding which existed between the university and the professor in *Perry*. Implied contracts exist where the schools and the student athletes anticipate the latter's participation in the athletic program, just as

---

128. 367 F. Supp. 908.
136. *Id.*
138. 408 U.S. 593 (1972).

an implied contract existed in *Perry* where, as a result of a de facto tenure system, both parties anticipated the plaintiff's continued employment. In college athletics, intense recruiting battles among schools for the services of highly skilled athletes are commonplace. These battles indicate that the combatant universities anticipate that the scholarship athletes who enroll at each institution will represent that institution in athletic competition. The scholarship agreement is the sort of "mutually explicit understanding," required in *Perry*, which supports a claim of entitlement to participate in intercollegiate athletics.

The contractual rationale is the foundation of a strong argument that student athletes who hold athletic scholarships possess a constitutionally protected property interest in athletic eligibility. The contractually-based argument is a logical extension of prior decisions in the case law of intercollegiate athletics and is the most effective means for promoting both due process and academic integrity in college sports.

. . . .

. . . . [A detailed discussion of NCAA enforcement proceeding is omitted. - ed.].

CONCLUSION

This Note has demonstrated that scholarship athletes possess a constitutionally protected property right to continued eligibility which derives from the contractual nature of an athletic scholarship. The recognition of a property right would cause judges to exercise an important role in guaranteeing procedural fairness by the NCAA in its relations with student athletes and their universities. Judges would nevertheless be confined to a sphere in which their expertise is well-established, namely, the identification of rights and of suitable procedures for enforcing those rights. Judicial power would be further limited if the educators who manage the universities which participate in intercollegiate athletics would revamp NCAA disciplinary procedures in the manner suggested by this Note.

Investigatory and adjudicatory procedures would be managed by separate entities. Student athletes whose eligibility is in jeopardy would be guaranteed on-campus hearings which do not have pre-determined outcomes. Student athletes would be entitled to appeal unfavorable decisions in on-campus hearings to the Presidents' Commission and to receive hearing transcripts to assist them in the preparation of appeals. The NCAA's Committee on Infractions would be limited to imposing punishment upon athletes found culpable. Any punishment meted out by the Committee would be based upon the recommendations of the Presidents' Commission.

College athletes would receive due process in disciplinary proceedings arising out of allegations of misconduct, yet universities would retain control over the promulgation of academic requirements for all students.

(b) Academic Eligibility

Kenneth L. Shropshire, Colorblind Propositions: Race, The SAT & The NCAA
8 Stanford Law & Policy Review 141 (1997)*

....

I. INTRODUCTION

This article focuses on the colorblind creation and revision of National Collegiate Athletic Association (NCAA) initial eligibility requirements for prospective student-athletes....

The key question is whether the present initial eligibility rules, and the frequently proposed changes to those rules, provide a basis for maintaining high academic standards in our colleges and universities without drastically and unnecessarily reducing the number of African-Americans who are eligible to attend these institutions with athletic scholarships. Revising the initial eligibility standards is almost an annual topic at NCAA Conventions. In August of 1996, new standards are scheduled to take effect yet again. What is the impact of these rules? An NCAA study shows that since the implementation of Proposition 48 in 1986, the percentage of scholarships allocated to black freshmen has dropped from 27.6% to 23.2%.

....

This article's critique of the NCAA's initial eligibility rules employs many of the principles of Critical Race Theory (CRT). One key goal of CRT is to challenge the dominant views and interpretations of race, racism, and the use of the law. Another key component of CRT is the belief that color-consciousness is necessary in the absence of a fully *colorblind* society. The dominant view in the college sports context is that stiffer standardized test requirements are justified because they are a necessary means of increasing the academic quality of student-athletes. Such a conclusion can only be drawn by viewing the initial eligibility issues in a *colorblind* manner, one which does not recognize the disproportionate negative impact of the rules on African-Americans. This article concludes that such a colorblind analysis is inappropriate.

....

My analysis also incorporates a traditional doctrinal legal analysis. And in the end, an appropriately framed action based on Title VI of the Civil Rights Act may be the appropriate vehicle to allow the excluded voices to be heard. No court action will be successful, however, unless this criticism from the bottom is fully heard by the courts and the leaders of college athletics.

II. REASONS FOR CONCERN ABOUT INITIAL ELIGIBILITY RULES

A. The Value of College Sports Participation

Participation in college athletics frequently provides substantial training for top-level coaching and sports-management positions. Participation in collegiate sports may lead to professional play as well as opportunities in the sports administrative business ladder. College players may be appointed to graduate assistant positions, potentially leading to college coaching positions or positions in professional leagues. Although this type of progression is certainly the exception, college players are the most likely beneficiaries of such opportunities....

More importantly, many student-athletes have used the opportunity that athletic scholarships provide to obtain a quality education and excel in other, non-sports-related fields. Were it not for the athletic scholarship, a university education and the student-athlete experience might have been unattainable for these students. These experiences underscore the importance of broadening rather than narrowing opportunities for anyone to attend the best possible college. It is the narrowing of opportunities which anyone focusing on these initial eligibility rules must not overlook.

B. The Purpose of Initial Eligibility Rules

. . . .

In 1965, the NCAA shifted away from its traditional "home rule" policy of admissions and adopted minimum initial eligibility standards for all NCAA student-athletes. The home rule policy had allowed schools to determine a student-athlete's eligibility based solely on the eligibility rules for that individual institution. The 1965 rule required students to have a high school record and standardized test scores sufficient to "predict" a college grade point average of 1.6, which is in the traditional C-/D+ range. The prediction was made by a formula using high school grades or high school rank and the student's score on the Scholastic Aptitude (later "Assessment") Test (SAT) or the American College Test (ACT). Students who failed to meet these requirements were not eligible to compete in NCAA-sanctioned events.

The 1.6 rule was repealed in 1973, and student-athletes were required only to attain a minimum grade point average of 2.0 for eligibility. But the varied grading policies across the country concerned the NCAA reformers. Was an "A" in rural Oklahoma the same as an "A" in a New York City public high school? Had the star athlete in Tucson been given a passing grade by a faculty member who was a basketball fan? The standardized tests, SAT and ACT, loomed in the eyes of reformers as the easiest route to establish a uniform measure of academic capability.

Critics did not raise the issue of racism in eligibility rules and the process used to develop such rules until the 1983 NCAA rule changes. The questions of whether the rules have a harsher impact on African-Americans and whether there is some intent to discriminate against African-American student-athletes have only increased over the years.

C. Proposition 48

As initially enacted, Proposition 48, officially NCAA Bylaw 14.3, required student-athletes to attain a 2.0 grade point average in an eleven-course core curriculum which mandated courses in math, English, natural sciences and social sciences. Additionally, students were required to achieve a minimum combined score of 700 out of 1600 on the SAT or 15 out of 36 on the ACT. Star college athletes such as Chris Washburn and John "Hot Rod" Williams were the types of athletes that caused the NCAA to adopt this sort of rule. Both had a combined score of 470 on the SAT, and under the old rules both were athletically eligible as freshmen. Both athletes were recruited by over 100 schools. Washburn initially enrolled at North Carolina State University, where the average SAT score was 1020; at Tulane University, where Williams enrolled, it was 1120.

Members of the African-American community have strongly criticized Proposition 48 from its inception. Criticism focused not only on the projected negative impact on African-American enrollment, but also on the lack of African-Americans involved in the original creation of the rule. There were no African-Americans on the American Council on Education's (ACE) ad hoc committee which drew up the original Proposition 48 document that was presented at the NCAA Convention in 1983. This absence led to vehement objection by African-American leaders. ACE attempted to calm this situation by appointing the president of Delaware State University, an historically black institution, to the committee a mere week prior to the 1983 Convention. By that point the committee's work was largely completed, so African-American educators and leaders considered the move a token gesture, and maintained their criticisms about not being consulted in the formulation of Proposition 48. Jesse Stone, a former Louisiana Supreme Court Judge and Dean of the Southern Law School in Baton Rouge, Louisiana, called the new standards "patently racist." This hostile mood surrounded the creation of rules that the NCAA stated were designed to "assert the supremacy of academic values" in college sports and to "preserve the integrity of the NCAA and of our [college] institutions."[40] The absence of African-American participation in the process by which Proposition 48 was drafted is a stark, clear example of the absence of voices from the bottom.

The freshman class of 1986-87 was the first "Proposition 48" class. The class entered their respective colleges and universities by satisfying Proposition 48's eligibility requirements. The graduation rate of student-athletes entering college in 1986 was 57%, an increase of 6% over the pre-Proposition 48 classes of 1983, 1984, and 1985. The average graduation rate overall for the freshman class of 1986-87 was 55%. Even more dramatic than the 6 percent overall increase in athlete graduation rates, supporters maintained, was an 8% increase in the graduation rate for black student-athletes.

This apparent success has made Proposition 48 a prime candidate for further tinkering in the past, and most likely will continue to do so in the future. Despite this continued experimentation, the increase in graduation rates has plateaued in recent years. The graduation rate of student-athletes entering college in both 1988 and 1989 was 58%, while the average graduation rate for all students was 57% in each year. Nonetheless, the NCAA membership voted to make Proposition 48 standards even more restrictive in 1992. At the 1992 NCAA Convention the members voted to increase the number of core courses required from eleven to thirteen. A sliding scale was also introduced to correlate the GPA with the stan-

---

40. See Greene, *supra* note 33, at 104 (citing Letter from Derek C. Bok, President of Harvard University and Chairman of the Ad Hoc Committee, & J.W. Peltason, President of ACE, to NCAA Division I members (undated)).

dardized test score. These revisions received final approval at the 1996 NCAA Convention and were put into effect on August 1, 1996. Prior to recentering, an athlete with a 2.0 GPA was required to score 900 on the SAT to be eligible to play as a freshman, compared with the previously required score of 700.

A statistic that has not received as much attention as the post-Proposition 48 increase in graduation rates is the number of would-be student-athletes harmed by the standard. How many students who do not meet the Proposition 48 standards might have graduated from college in spite of a low high school grade point average or standardized test score? According to Richard Lapchick of the Center for the Study of Sport in Society:

> [I]f Prop 48 had been in use in 1981, 69% of all black males entering college on athletic scholarships would have been ineligible. But 54% of those athletes eventually graduated (a rate that compares well with the graduation rate for all students, which was in the mid-50s throughout the mid-1980s). Clearly they had the skills all along, they just had to be developed.[53]

Had it been in force in 1981, Proposition 48 may have deprived that group of African-Americans of an opportunity to earn a college degree. Not only would it have denied 69% of all black males the opportunity to showcase their athletic talents, but it also would have stigmatized those student-athletes and denied most of them exposure to high-caliber academic opportunities.

Today, those athletes who would graduate from college were it not for their failure to satisfy initial eligibility requirements are among those commonly referred to as "Proposition 48 casualties." Failing to meet the requirements of Proposition 48 not only renders the athlete ineligible to compete, and under various past proposals, ineligible for financial aid during the freshman year, but also pegs the athlete with the stigma of labels such as "casualty" or "Prop 48 kid." At the very least this unnecessarily helps to perpetuate long-standing stereotypes of athletes, particularly African-American athletes, as "dumb jocks...."

....

In addition to stigmatizing students who fail to meet its requirements, Proposition 48 and related measures deny many of those students the opportunity to obtain a four-year college degree. In January of 1989, Proposition 42, a major rule change designed to strengthen Proposition 48, was ratified at the annual NCAA Convention. Proposition 42, which relied heavily on the SAT, was designed to redefine the focus of high school and collegiate student-athletes by denying athletes who failed to meet the initial eligibility requirements *all* financial aid during the freshman year of college. Proposition 42 was modified in 1990 to allow partial qualifiers to receive non-athletic, need-based institutional financial aid during the freshman year; non-qualifiers were still ineligible for *any* type of financial aid. Because of Proposition 42, non-qualifiers are unlikely to enroll in NCAA member institutions.

....

The harm to African-American Proposition 48 casualties is ironic because the college game—even though harsh and stereotypical treatment of blacks existed—was historically more accessible to African-American athletes than the pros. A number of African-Americans participated in early collegiate team sports. Propo-

---

53. William Oscar Johnson, *How Far Have We Come*, SPORTS ILLUSTRATED, Aug. 5, 1991, at 38, 51.

sition 48 is a rule which diminishes the role of African-Americans in sports. More importantly, the rule decreases the number of African-Americans eligible to attend college with the aid of athletic scholarships.

There are valid arguments in support of Proposition 48-type rules. The principles of academic values and integrity set forth by the NCAA are undeniably admirable and commendable. With 10,000 to 1 odds of a high school athlete becoming a professional athlete, steps must be taken to insure that there is an appropriate focus by these individuals, and the educational institutions they attend, on education. Efforts must continually be made to insure that the term "student-athlete" does not become an oxymoron in the next century.

As laudable as the NCAA's intent may be, a barrier to entry into college, whether through the actual denial of admission or by disallowing financial aid awards, should not be based on a standardized examination. Any comprehensive analysis of revisions to the initial eligibility rules cannot overlook the historical and current problems that arise when standardized tests are used as a qualification for entry. Only colorblind rulemakers could give standardized tests such an important role in the future of young student-athletes, and only stereotyped beliefs in the inferiority of the intelligence of African-American athletes could provide comfort in applying rules which disproportionately impact this group.

Although credit for increasing graduation rates has routinely been given to these tighter initial eligibility standards, there have been other academic improvements which may bear more responsibility for the increase. In response to greater scrutiny, many schools have improved their academic support programs. The NCAA has also instituted rules reducing the number of hours college athletes may practice per week. According to Pamela Zappardino, the executive director of the National Center for Fair & Open Testing (FairTest), the SAT-based initial eligibility requirement receives so much credit because it "looks objective, looks scientific, but Prop 48 and all that followed from it is an abuse of standardized testing."[71] Not surprisingly, the SAT, as well as the manner in which it is used by the NCAA, are key elements in the initial eligibility debate.

D. The Scholastic Assessment Test

The average SAT score for African-Americans in the 1980s and 1990s has hovered around 730, while the average for whites during this same period of time has remained about 200 points higher at approximately 930. Some allege that the disparity in scores is the result of cultural and/or racial bias in the exam. Others point to the difference in the quality of schools in the respective black and white communities. Still others claim that African-American students are not aware of or cannot afford courses that prepare students for these exams. Experts have supported and disputed all sides of this debate. Whatever explanation is presented for this disparity, the average scores show the facts. Only a colorblind analysis could completely ignore this factual racial disparity in exam scores.

. . . .

---

71. Pamela Zappardino, Speech at the National Rainbow Coalition Conference for Fairness in Athletics (June 23, 1995).

The NCAA's use of a standardized exam to determine one's eligibility is misguided. The SAT is meant only to help predict how well students will do academically in the first year of college. George Hanford, then-president of the College Board, wrote of Proposition 48:

> Such use of the SAT in the process of selecting students for admission to college would be contrary to the guidelines for test use published by the College Board.... [T]est scores should never be used alone in determining admission to college. The NCAA's action violates that principle.... In summary, under the NCAA rule, the SAT would be used for a purpose which it was neither intended nor designed to serve—determining athletic eligibility rather than college admissions; and... the way SAT scores are being used in establishing athletic eligibility is contrary to the College Board's guidelines with respect to the use of test scores in making college admissions decisions.[81]

Even with this background, many member institutions of the NCAA pushed for Proposition 42 in 1989, which maintained that if a student-athlete did not have minimums of a 700 on the SAT or a comparable score on the ACT and a 2.0 grade point average, he or she could not receive financial aid of *any* type from an NCAA member institution.... After extensive criticism, Proposition 42 was modified at the 1990 NCAA Convention. Under the revamped version partial qualifiers were able to receive need-based, non-athletic university financial aid; non-qualifiers were still ineligible for any type of financial aid.

Beginning in 1989, the NCAA employed the Data Analysis Working Group to analyze data regarding Proposition 48 and its effect on minority students. The Group's Conclusions, which looked favorably upon continued use of standardized tests, served as the basis for Proposition 16. However, an independent group of academics, the Scientific Conference on Re-examination of the Academic Performance Study, reviewed the Working Group's statistics and found that those statistics did not "serve as a very reliable basis" for the Working Group's conclusion. One member of the Scientific Conference said that the SAT helped "rotate out qualified blacks" while more whites were rotated in. Moreover, the Working Group's review may have been affected by racial bias. A research assistant assigned to work with the Working Group accused one member of the group of racial insensitivity and possible association with "Beyondism," a movement which has views on eugenics and favors selective breeding....

In 1995 the NCAA membership voted to retain the SAT and ACT in its initial eligibility standards. Effective August 1, 1996, students with a 2.0 grade point average in 13 core courses must score at least 900 on the SAT or 21 on the ACT. For each ten-point drop in SAT scores, students must have a corresponding .025 increase in grade point average.

....

III. STANDARDIZED TEST LITIGATION

A. *Sharif v. New York State Education Department*

New York state courts have agreed with the position that the SAT should not be the sole indicator to determine which students receive scholarships. *Sharif v.*

---

81. D. Chu et al., Sports and Higher Education 362 (1985).

New York State Education Department involved the state education department's use of SAT scores alone to determine the recipients of New York State Regents Scholarships and Empire State Scholarships.[98] On average, girls were receiving lower average SAT scores than boys, and thus fewer scholarships. The case was settled when the New York State Education Department agreed to use both the students' grades and SAT scores to determine the recipients.

. . . .

Proposition 16 allows the SAT to be the sole factor in deciding whether a student-athlete can receive a scholarship and athletic financial aid. The athlete's entire application package, including grade point average, is irrelevant if the minimum score is not met. But *Sharif* is probably applicable to the NCAA only by analogy because the NCAA is not subject to the same level of judicial scrutiny as is a governmental entity like the New York State Education Department. The Supreme Court has held that the NCAA is not a state actor.

B. *Groves v. Alabama State Board of Educators*

Another court reached a similar conclusion on the use of standardized tests in *Groves v. Alabama State Board of Education* in 1991.[106] The test involved was the ACT. The Alabama State Board of Education required college sophomores desiring to enter the state teacher training programs to obtain a minimum score on the ACT exam. The plaintiffs brought an action under Title VI of the Civil Rights Act of 1964, arguing that the minimum score requirement discriminated against African-Americans on the basis of race. The plaintiffs alleged that the ACT requirement constituted both disparate impact and disparate treatment; they succeeded on their disparate impact claim.

The Board of Education had incorporated the ACT in its qualifications for much the same reason as the NCAA. They were concerned that grades alone would not provide a uniform measure by which to evaluate applicants. The court found that "the State Board did not oversee grading practices, and the committee [evaluating the system] shared a perception held by much of the public that certain institutions awarded passing marks to students regardless of ability or achievement."[111] The ACT was chosen without much deliberation because it was a nationally standardized test, and it was taken on a routine basis by Alabama college-bound students.

However, the ACT score in *Groves* was not used as a predictor, but primarily as a public relations vehicle. The committee that determined the appropriate minimum score ignored the data they had on the racial disparities in ACT scores....

Groves was a class action Title VI lawsuit which included all past, present, and future black students denied admission into teacher education programs in Alabama based solely on failing to attain an ACT score of 16. Title VI specifically provides that "[n]o person in the United States shall, on the ground of race...be excluded from participation in, be denied the benefits of, or be subjected to discrimination under any program or activity receiving Federal financial assistance."[118] Proof of discriminatory intent is not required for a successful pri-

---

98. 709 F.Supp. 345 (S.D. N.Y. 1989).

106. 776 F.Supp. 1518 (M.D. Ala. 1991).

111. Groves, 776 F.Supp. at 1520.

118. 42 U.S.C. § 2000d.

vate action. A facially neutral rule cannot have "an unjustifiable disparate impact on minorities." A 1978 study showed that 85% of white Alabama students achieved a score of 16 or above, while 21% of African-Americans scored at that level. This disparity remained substantially the same over the years.

The court in *Groves* noted that there is no rigid mathematical standard for finding an adverse impact. The court, however, stated that:

> The Supreme Court's "formulations...have consistently stressed that statistical disparities must be sufficiently substantial that they raise...an inference of causation" —in other words, adequate to "show that the practice in question has caused the exclusion of applicants for jobs or promotions because of their membership in a protected group." However, the Supreme Court and lower courts have adopted various formulas to measure the degree of disparate impact in a particular case. The Equal Employment Opportunity Commission generally infers adverse racial impact where the members of a particular racial group are selected at a rate that is less than four-fifths, or 80%, of the rate at which the group with the highest rate is selected.[123]

The court in *Groves* concluded that a sufficiently substantial statistical disparity existed and that the ACT test was not justified as a screening method for qualified teacher training candidates. The court looked at both the selection of the test as the measure of ability as well as the selection of the cutoff point; it found them to be "homemade methodologies" to sort out unqualified teacher candidates.

Together, *Sharif* and *Groves* provide an example of the scrutiny that an institution's use of a standardized test should undergo. The disparity in average scores between African-Americans and whites makes this an area where it is inappropriate and arguably illegal to use "homemade methodologies" for predicting who the successful students will be. The NCAA may soon face federal litigation brought by student-athletes adversely affected by Proposition 48 because of a deficient standardized test score. The suit likely would be based on Title VI and argued in a manner similar to *Sharif,* with Proposition 48 challenged as a form of invidious racial discrimination....

IV. NEEDED REFORMS OF INITIAL ELIGIBILITY STANDARDS

Initial eligibility requirements are generally supported as a means of enhancing the academic quality of student athletes and increasing the academic integrity of NCAA member institutions. There are other, non-discriminatory means available to further these objectives. Below are my recommendations for revising the NCAA eligibility rules in a manner which accomplishes the objectives of Propositions 42 and 48 without having a racially disparate impact.

A. Retain Partial Qualifier Opportunities

The partial qualifier system may give the poor test taker the opportunity to show that he or she can handle the rigors of college academics in spite of a standardized test score below the qualifying minimum. Partial qualifiers are allowed, under current rules effectuated August 1, 1996, to enroll in an NCAA member institution and receive both athletic and non-athletic-based financial aid. They may

---

123. *Id.* at 1526 (citations omitted).

practice but not play with the athletic team for the first year. If a student-athlete's test score and grade point average are not high enough to partially qualify, he or she is a non-qualifier. Where a partial qualifier may receive athletics-based financial aid, a non- qualifier may only receive non-athletic institutional financial aid based upon need and institutional guidelines.

The harsh consequences of Proposition 42-type initial eligibility requirements are not necessary. Of those students who failed to meet the minimum standards in the academic years 1986-1987 and 1987-1988, the partial qualifiers, a full 79% of Proposition 48 victims, were in good academic standing once given the opportunity to succeed. This percentage is equal to the academic progress of students that met the initial Proposition 48 standard. As Lapchick says, "the predictions of disaster for athletes who were asked to do more proved false. The players produced."[134]

. . . .

The NCAA has a duty to encourage its member institutions to strive for higher academic success. A minimum grade point average should continue to be required. The NCAA, however, should not rely on a standardized test in making a determination that will affect the rest of a student-athlete's life when that test is used in a manner which is questioned even by the test's writers and administrators, and when statistics show the test to be a poor predictor of academic performance. Incentives that should be included are those that all student-athletes have the equal opportunity to attain. Future reforms of Proposition 48 should continue to reduce the role of the SAT and ACT.

B. Eliminate Freshman Eligibility

Freshmen should be ineligible to participate in varsity sports. Eliminating freshman eligibility would serve two purposes. First, it gives our institutions of higher learning the opportunity to assist students with any academic deficiencies. At the same time, it requires all academic institutions to invest in the academic career of student-athletes. Perhaps even more importantly, eliminating freshman eligibility would send a serious message to entering students: Universities are, first and foremost, places for learning. . . .

The issue was also introduced in the 1995 NCAA Convention. It was voted down after one of the most heated debates of the convention.

C. Add A Fifth Year of Eligibility

The five-year scholarship would provide student-athletes with adequate time and funds to receive their undergraduate degrees. The fifth year could be used at any time, including following the completion of a professional sports career. Like freshman eligibility, the issue of an additional year of eligibility was raised at the 1995 convention. After much debate and a call for reconsideration of the matter after it was first voted down, the proposal failed.

. . . .

D. Drop the Use of Standardized Test Scores Completely

Several institutions have dropped the use of standardized tests in their admissions decisions. Bates and Bowdoin colleges both have made submission of SAT

---

134. *Id.*

scores an optional part of the admissions process. In addition, Harvard Business School and Johns Hopkins Medical School no longer require standardized admissions tests. Both Bates and Bowdoin studied the academic performance of students following the optional use of the exam and found no negative impact....

....

E. Improve Education Prior to College

    ....

...It is before the student reaches college, before the student takes the SAT, and before the high school GPA is calculated, that academic deficiencies develop. The primary responsibility to form academic standards lies with the public education system. That is where educators and reformers should focus their efforts, not on screening out those without a minimum grade point average or test score. Those who advocate tightening the eligibility rules argue that doing so will in turn force the public schools to improve their effort. The problem of inadequate primary and secondary education can be dealt with more effectively if efforts are directed at the problem itself, rather than creating eligibility standards which create hardships for the very persons most disadvantaged by the inadequacies of our public education system.

V. CONCLUSION

The initial eligibility rules should not rely on standardized examinations. Unanswered questions regarding both the SAT's racial bias and its value as a predictor of academic success must be balanced against the initial eligibility requirements' effects on all students, especially African-Americans. Furthermore, in the absence of voices from the bottom, the NCAA leadership unfortunately chose to use a methodology which implicitly accepts long-standing stereotypes of African-American athletes in the student-athlete context. While academic integrity needs to remain a high priority, the standardized exam is not essential to, and perhaps does not even facilitate, its attainment. Much work remains to be done, but efforts to improve scholastic performance should not be made in a colorblind and stereotype-blind vacuum.

---

3. Disability Issues

(a) Academic Eligibility

Katie M. Burroughs, Learning Disabled Student Athletes: A Sporting Chance Under the ADA?
14 Journal of Contemporary Health Law & Policy 57 (1997)*

    ....

The issue of the eligibility of learning disabled students to participate in interscholastic and intercollegiate athletics arises in two distinct situations. First, stu-

---

dents diagnosed as learning disabled often repeat one or more grades in elementary school. As a result, these students may begin their senior year of high school at age nineteen, as opposed to the average age of eighteen. Such a student is ineligible to compete in interscholastic activities because most school systems deny participation to high school students who turn nineteen before the start of the school year. Second, special education courses offered at the high school level to accommodate learning disabled students, pursuant to federal legislation, often do not meet the National College Athletic Association ("NCAA") requirements for participation. Furthermore, these students may not qualify for athletic scholarships because special education courses are taught at a slower pace than mainstream classes. Such courses do not meet core eligibility requirements established by organizations such as the NCAA. Therefore, the NCAA may bar students enrolled in such courses from participating in NCAA-sanctioned, college-level athletic competitions.

This Article will focus on the application of the ADA to learning disabled student athletes denied participation in interscholastic or intercollegiate athletics....

....

I. UNDERSTANDING LEARNING DISABILITIES

....

According to federal regulations, "learning disability" is a broad term with vague parameters, encompassing a variety of causes, symptoms, treatments, and outcomes. Despite this lack of clarity, three established categories of learning disabilities exist: (1) developmental speech and language disorders; (2) academic skills disorders; and, (3) "other," a catch-all category including certain coordination disorders and learning handicaps not covered by the other terms. Each of these categories includes a number of specific learning disorders.

Developmental speech and language disorders reflect a difficulty in producing speech sounds, using spoken language to communicate, or understanding what other people say. The specific diagnosis may include a developmental articulation disorder, developmental expressive language disorder, or developmental receptive language disorder. Academic skills disorders result in a child being years behind his or her peers in developing reading, writing, and arithmetic skills. Here, the possible diagnoses include developmental reading disorder (or dyslexia), developmental writing disorder, or developmental arithmetic disorder. "Other" learning disabilities include categories such as motor skills disorders and various developmental disorders that do not meet the criteria for a specific learning disability. This category includes coordination disorders that can lead to poor penmanship, as well as certain spelling and memory disorders.

Learning disabilities also affect a child's or adult's emotional and social development. Although all children experience successes and failures in academic and social situations, learning disabled children are more sensitive and aware of their differences from others. Children with learning disabilities assimilate what is said about them and "may define themselves in light of their disabilities, as 'behind,' 'slow,' or 'different.'" To overcome these feelings of anxiety and low self-esteem resulting from negative feedback, the learning disabled child must be presented with structured experiences that provide a positive reality of success and accomplishment. Some researchers have suggested that learning disabled children benefit from participation in sports and extracurricular activities because it helps them to cope with threats to their self-esteem and anticipated loss of control that stems from the learning disability. According to these researchers, organized athletics can provide a structured environment in which the child can succeed. Moreover, the comprehensive physical education and recreational programming provided by team sports enhances the child's development and provides important skills, such as teamwork, which can be used and developed throughout life. Furthermore, research has found that a significant relationship exists between physical well-being and receptiveness to classroom learning.

II. THE AMERICANS WITH DISABILITIES ACT

President George Bush signed the ADA[51] into law on July 26, 1990. The ADA provided for "a clear and comprehensive national mandate for the elimination of discrimination against individuals with disabilities..."[52]

. . . .

A. What Is Covered Under the ADA?

The Rehabilitation Act prohibits discrimination against the disabled by governmental agencies receiving federal financial assistance. The ADA prohibits discrimination in the previously unregulated private sector. The ADA further prohibits discrimination against the disabled in all elements of society, including private schools, universities, restaurants, transportation services, telecommunications services, private employers, and landlords.

. . . .

B. Defining Disability

Congress intended Title II of the ADA to be interpreted consistently with prior interpretations of section 504 of the Rehabilitation Act. Much of the ADA's language is identical to that of the Rehabilitation Act because Congress intended to extend the application of the Rehabilitation Act to entities that do not receive federal financial assistance....

1. The Rehabilitation Act of 1973

Section 504 of the Rehabilitation Act provides in pertinent part:

> No otherwise qualified individual with handicaps in the United States, as defined in section 706(8) of this title, shall, solely by reason of her or his handicap, be excluded from the participation in, be denied the benefits of, or be subjected to discrimination under any program or activity receiving Federal financial assistance.[81]

Regulations promulgated under the Rehabilitation Act by the Department of Education and the Department of Health and Human Services prohibit colleges and high schools from discriminating against qualified handicapped athletes. The regulations provide that qualified handicapped athletes must be given "an equal opportunity for participation" in interscholastic and intercollegiate activities. To prevail under the Rehabilitation Act, a learning disabled athlete must show that (1) he is handicapped within the meaning of the Rehabilitation Act; (2) he is "oth-

---

51. 42 U.S.C. §§ 12101-12213.
52. *Id.* at § 12101(b)(1).
81. 29 U.S.C. § 794(a) (1994).

erwise qualified" for the services sought; (3) he was excluded from the services sought "solely by reason of his handicap;" and, (4) the program in question receives federal financial assistance.

2. Disability Under the ADA

A "disability" under the ADA, as well as under the Rehabilitation Act, is "(A) a physical or mental impairment that substantially limits one or more of the major life activities of such individual; (B) a record of such impairment; or (C) being regarded as having such an impairment."[88] The Report of the Senate Committee on Labor and Human Resources notes that this language is comparable to the regulatory definitions promulgated pursuant to section 504 of the Rehabilitation Act. While many disabilities are included within the ADA's definition of "disability," this Article focuses on the first definition of disability—physical or mental impairment—which includes learning disabilities within its parameters.

Under the implementing regulations of the ADA, "physical or mental impairment" means "(B) any psychological disorder or condition..., such as... specific learning disabilities."[91] A physical or mental impairment, though, is not a protected disability under the ADA unless the disability substantially limits a major life activity. "Substantially limits" generally means unable to perform a major life activity that the average person in the general population can perform, or significantly restricted as to condition, manner, or duration of such performance compared to a member of the general population. Major life activities include, among other things, "learning." Thus, an individual diagnosed with a specific learning disability is "disabled" within the meaning of the ADA because a diagnosed learning disability limits one's ability to learn.

3. Qualified Individual With a Disability

The ADA, unlike the Rehabilitation Act, defines "qualified individual with a disability" as:

> [A]n individual with a disability who, with or without reasonable modifications to rules, policies, or practices, the removal of architectural, communication or transportation barriers, or the provisions of auxiliary aids and services, meets the essential eligibility requirements for the receipt of services or the participation in programs or activities provided by a public entity.[97]

The definition embodies the interpretations reached by courts in their struggle to define "otherwise qualified individual" under the Rehabilitation Act. Thus, courts interpreting the term "qualified individual with a disability" under the ADA use an analysis similar to the analysis adopted by courts under the Rehabilitation Act.

Interpreting the Rehabilitation Act, the United States Supreme Court, in its first case dealing with the application of the term "qualified individual," held in *Southeastern Community College v. Davis*,[100] that an institution is not required to

---

88. 42 U.S.C. §§ 12101, 12101(2) (1994 & Supp. II 1990, Supp. III 1991, Supp. IV 1992, Supp. V 1993).

91. 28 C.F.R. § 35.104 (1993); 29 C.F.R. § 1630.2(h) (1993).

97. 42 U.S.C. § 12131(2).

100. Southeastern Community College v. Davis, 442 U.S. at 397. Davis could not understand speech except through lip reading. A community college rejected her application to the

lower or modify standards to accommodate a disabled person. The Court concluded that an "otherwise qualified person" is "one who is able to meet all of the program's requirements in spite of his [disability]."[102]

. . . .

To determine if a disabled individual under the ADA is "a qualified individual," courts must first determine what the necessary eligibility requirements are for the activity in which the individual wants to participate. Next, the court must make a factual determination as to whether the individual meets these requirements. If the individual does not meet the necessary requirements, the court must next determine whether a "reasonable accommodation" exists that would allow the individual to successfully participate in the activity.

III. JUDICIAL VIEWS ON ATHLETIC PARTICIPATION BY THE LEARNING DISABLED STUDENT UNDER THE ADA

The central issue in lawsuits brought by learning disabled student athletes seeking to compete in competitive sports is whether the student athlete is a qualified individual with a disability who has been discriminated against by reason of such disability. One line of cases holds that student athletes with learning disabilities are not qualified individuals under the ADA because no "reasonable accommodations" are available. The other line of cases holds that student athletes are qualified under the ADA, and thus are able to participate in high school athletics.

A. Sandison v. Michigan High School Athletic Association

The leading case holding that learning disabled athletes are not to be excluded solely by reason of their disability, and that waiving eligibility requirements is not a reasonable modification under the ADA, is *Sandison v. Michigan High School Athletic Association*.[113] Ronald Sandison and Craig Stanley sought a preliminary injunction against the Michigan High School Athletic Association ("MHSAA"). The purpose of the injunction was to prevent the MHSAA from prohibiting Sandison and Stanley from running on the cross-country and track teams and to preclude the MHSAA from penalizing the high schools for permitting the two students to participate. The United States District Court for the Eastern District of Michigan granted the injunction, allowing the plaintiffs to compete on the teams despite their ineligibility based on the MHSAA's nineteen-year age limitation. The United States Court of Appeals for the Sixth Circuit, however, dismissed as moot the MHSAA's challenge to the preliminary injunction, and reversed the portion of the injunction that ordered the MHSAA to refrain from penalizing the high schools.

Both Sandison and Stanley were high school athletes who were held back early in their educational training because of learning disabilities. Sandison began first grade two years late. Four years later, at age eleven, doctors diagnosed Sandison with an auditory input disability. With special education support, Sandison did not experience any further delay in his education. He participated on the high school cross-

---

nursing program because it believed Davis' hearing disability would not allow her to safely participate in the program and to safely care for patients. *Id*. at 407.

102. *Id*. at 407.

113. Sandison v. Michigan High Sch. Athletic Ass'n, 64 F.3d 1026 (6th Cir. 1995), *rev'g in part*, 863 F. Supp. 483 (E.D. Mich. 1994).

country and track teams during the first three years of high school. In May of 1994, three months before he was to begin his senior year, Sandison turned nineteen.

Craig Stanley was diagnosed early in his educational career with a learning disability in mathematics. Due to his learning disability, Stanley repeated kindergarten and spent five years in a special education classroom. Stanley then entered a regular classroom in the fourth, rather than the fifth, grade. Like Sandison, Stanley also competed on the cross-country and track teams during his first three years of high school. Prior to beginning his senior year, Stanley turned nineteen.

The MHSAA oversees interscholastic athletic events. Most high schools in Michigan are members of the organization and adopt MHSAA's rules governing interscholastic sports. MHSAA regulations prohibit student athletes over nineteen years of age, without exception, from participating in interscholastic sports.

Sandison and Stanley argued that their exclusion from interscholastic sports constituted unlawful discrimination because of their learning disabilities, and violated both the Rehabilitation Act and the ADA. The United States Court of Appeals for the Sixth Circuit ruled in favor of the MHSAA. Reversing the second portion of the preliminary injunction, which barred the MHSAA from penalizing the high schools because an ineligible player competed on a high school team, the court determined that the plaintiffs were unlikely to succeed on the merits of their Rehabilitation Act and ADA claims.

According to the court of appeals, the primary issues were whether the student athletes with learning disabilities were excluded by reason of their disability, and whether a waiver of the age requirement was a reasonable modification. The court examined plaintiffs' claims under the Rehabilitation Act and the ADA, reaching the same result under both statutes. First, the court held that the plaintiffs were not excluded from participation in high school interscholastic athletics "solely by reason of" their learning disability. Rather, the court found that absent their respective learning disability, Sandison and Stanley failed to satisfy the MHSAA age requirement. Thus, the court concluded that the boys did not meet the age requirement because of their birth dates, not because of their learning disability.

Next, the court held that the student athletes were not "otherwise qualified" to participate in interscholastic cross-country and track competitions. Initially, the court found that the age limitation imposed by the MHSAA was a "necessary requirement of the program."[136] Adopting the conclusion of the district court, the court of appeals found that the age restriction prevents injury to other players and eliminates unfair competitive advantages that older and larger participants might provide; therefore, it was essential in maintaining the amateur character of the athletic program.

Relying on the record compiled by the trial court below, the court found that "older students are generally more physically mature than younger students." The court, however, found that the district court erred, finding that a waiver constituted a reasonable accommodation. First, the court stated that expanding the permissible age range for participation would fundamentally alter the nature of the interscholastic athletic program. The court asserted that by disregarding the age

---

136. *Id.* at 1037. Certain eligibility requirements are essential by nature. Pottgen v. Missouri High Sch. Activities Ass'n, 40 F.3d 926, 930-31 (8th Cir. 1994), *rev'g*, 857 F. Supp. 654 (E.D. Mo. 1994).

restriction, more physically mature students would be permitted to participate in athletics, thereby changing the nature of high school athletics.

Second, the court found that making a competitive fairness determination of each athlete requesting a waiver would place an "undue burden" on MHSAA. MHSAA asserted that there are five factors to weigh in deciding if an athlete had an unfair competitive advantage: chronological age, physical maturity, athletic experience, athletic skill level, and mental ability to process sports strategy. MHSAA would have to require high school coaches and physicians hired by MHSAA to make eligibility determinations. The court found that balancing these factors in relation to opposing teams, team members, and the team unit was nearly impossible; thus, it was unreasonable to call upon coaches and physicians for this purpose.

Finally, the Sixth Circuit found that while participating in athletics helped the students progress through school, the waiver of the age restriction would not help these students overcome their learning disabilities. A waiver "merely remove[d] the age ceiling as an obstacle," but did not alter the fact that the students have a learning disability. Thus, the court concluded that a waiver of the age restriction was not a "reasonable accommodation."

In making its determination in *Sandison*, the United States Court of Appeals for the Sixth Circuit adopted the two-step analysis of the United States Court of Appeals for the Eighth Circuit in *Pottgen v. Missouri State High School Activities Association*.[148] The Sixth Circuit first determined that the age requirement was essential for safety reasons. Then, it conducted an individualized inquiry to see if Stanley or Sandison satisfied the age requirement with or without reasonable accommodation. According to the court, a waiver of the age requirement for learning disabled athletes could not be reasonable. Therefore, the student athletes could not be considered "otherwise qualified" and were not covered by the Rehabilitation Act or the ADA.

B. Johnson v. Florida High School Activities Association

In *Johnson v. Florida High School Activities Association*, the United States District Court for the Middle District of Florida held that a waiver of the less than nineteen years of age eligibility requirement to participate in high school athletics *was* a reasonable modification under the ADA.[150] Dennis Johnson, a high school senior diagnosed with a learning disability, sought an injunction against the Florida High School Athletic Association ("FHSAA"). The FHSAA found Johnson ineligible to participate on both the high school football and wrestling teams because he was nineteen years of age. Relying on the decision of the district court in *Sandison*, the *Johnson* court granted an injunction, enjoining the FHSAA from enforcing its rules prohibiting Johnson from playing interscholastic athletics and penalizing the high school for allowing Johnson to play.

Because of a hearing impediment, Johnson began kindergarten a year late. He was held back a second time in first grade because of his inadequate reading and

---

148. Pottgen v. Missouri State High School Activities Association, 40 F.3d at 930-31 (applying a two-step analysis to determine, first, whether the eligibility requirements were essential and, then, whether Pottgen met those requirements with or without reasonable modification).

150. Johnson v. Florida High Sch. Activities Ass'n, 899 F. Supp. 579, 580 (M.D. Fla. 1995), *vacated*, 102 F.3d 1172 (11th Cir. 1997), *appeal after remand*, 103 F.3d 720 (1997).

language skills. Johnson played football and wrestled for the first three years of high school. However, he turned nineteen two months before he was to begin his senior year. According to the FHSAA, Johnson could not participate in inter-scholastic sports because he turned nineteen before the school year started. The FHSAA denied Johnson's request for a "hardship" exception because the FHSAA committee lacked the authority under its bylaws to "waive the age eligibility rule." Under FHSAA rules, the age eligibility requirement cannot be waived because it is considered an essential eligibility requirement by FHSAA.

After first determining that the FHSAA was a public entity, the district court determined that Johnson was a "qualified individual with a disability" under both the Rehabilitation Act and the ADA. Next, the district court assessed whether the age requirement was an essential eligibility requirement. According to the court, the purposes of the FHSAA's age requirement were (1) to promote safety; and (2) to create an even, fair playing field, preventing schools from "red shirting" their players to build a better program. Adopting the reasoning of the district court's remand decision in *Sandison* and the dissent in *Pottgen*, the *Johnson* court found that "the relationship between the age requirement and its purposes must be such that waiving the age requirement in the instant case would necessarily undermine the purposes of the requirement." The court rejected the argument that because the FHSAA deems the age requirement essential, it is in fact essential. Relying on the dissent in *Pottgen*, the court stated that "'if a rule can be modified without doing violence to its essential purposes... it 'cannot' be essential to the nature of the program or activity.'"[168]

Because he was not the largest football team member playing his position, he did not present any danger to other players. The court noted that Johnson was a mid-level football player, and no more experienced than other players because he only played organized sports for three years. Furthermore, the court found that weight divisions in wrestling eliminated any safety concerns. Thus, the court concluded that Johnson's participation on the field did not undermine the purposes of safety and fairness of the FHSAA regulations. However, the court stressed that its holding was individualized and limited to the facts of Johnson's case. Therefore, the court held the essential purposes of the age requirement were not undermined by allowing Johnson to participate on the team.

IV. PROBLEMS WITH OPPOSING VIEWS

The *Johnson* case, and other district court decisions granting similar injunctions, present an individualized analysis of each learning disabled student's circumstances in accordance with the ADA and its implementing regulations. The opposing analysis set forth in *Sandison*, however, lacks legislative and judicial support. Courts recognizing a cause of action by learning disabled student athletes under the ADA offer three different reasons to support the proposition that student athletes with learning disabilities are protected under the ADA. First, learning disabled student athletes who are prohibited from participation in athletics are being excluded "by reason of such disability." Second, the essential eligibility requirements established by such organizations should be reviewed on an individualized, case-by-case basis by the courts to determine if the student athlete is

---

168. *Id.* at 585 (quoting Pottgen v. Missouri State High Sch. Activities Ass'n, 40 F.3d 926, 932-33 n.7 (8th Cir. 1994)).

otherwise qualified. Third, reasonable accommodations, which do not alter the nature of the program or pose an undue burden, must be provided by the organization. If the organization asserts reasonable accommodations are not possible, substantial justification must be shown....

.... [A detailed analysis of each of these rationales is omitted. - ed.].

V. NCAA REGULATIONS IN VIOLATION OF THE ADA?

Learning disabled students who challenge their denial from participating in high school athletics face the same battle in qualifying for participation in collegiate athletics. In a case of first impression, a high school student is challenging the NCAA for violating the ADA.[229] Chad Ganden, a state champion in the 100-yard freestyle, filed suit against the NCAA in the United States District Court for the Northern District of Illinois because the NCAA denied him the privilege of being able to participate on, and benefit from, NCAA-sanctioned athletic competition. The lawsuit is premised on the fact that Ganden took special courses for the learning disabled during high school that the NCAA refused to accept because they did not meet NCAA academic guidelines for eligibility. Ganden asked the judge to "order that the NCAA...be permanently enjoined from preventing Ganden from participating athletically in intercollegiate events during his freshman year."[232]

Ganden was diagnosed with a learning disability in sixth grade. He has a decoding problem that makes it difficult to translate letters into spoken words, thus affecting Ganden's ability to read. As a result of his learning disability, Ganden took some fundamental, or basic, courses during his freshman and sophomore years of high school before transferring into regular courses.

A. NCAA Eligibility Requirements

According to NCAA Division I eligibility requirements, to receive a scholarship and compete in a Division I college sport, a student must meet a minimum score on the American College Test ("ACT") or Scholastic Assessment Test ("SAT") and a minimum grade point average ("GPA") in thirteen college prepatory courses.[239] A "partial qualifier" is deemed eligible to practice with a team and to receive an athletic scholarship during his first year at a Division I school. A "partial qualifier" does not have to meet the requirements for a qualifier, but is required to present an acceptable GPA and SAT or ACT scores based on a separate partial qualifier index scale.

The NCAA defines a "core course" as a "recognized academic course that offers fundamental instruction in a specific area of study."[242] For high school courses for the learning disabled or handicapped to count toward the core course requirement, the principal of the high school must submit a written letter to the NCAA. The letter must state that "students in such courses are expected to acquire the same knowledge as students in other core courses and that the same grading standards are employed."[243]

---

229. Ganden v. National Collegiate Athletic Ass'n, No. 96-C6953, 1996 U.S. Dist. LEXIS 17368, at *1 (N.D. Ill. Nov. 21, 1996).

232. *Id.* at *1.

239. STEPHEN A. MALLONEE, 1996-97 NCAA GUIDE FOR THE COLLEGE-BOUND STUDENT-ATHLETE 2 (Michael V. Earle ed., 1996).

242. *Id.*

B. *NCAA Eligibility Requirements Adverse to Learning Disabilities*

The NCAA's Initial Eligibility Clearinghouse declared Ganden ineligible both to receive an athletic scholarship as a freshman and to compete during his four seasons of eligibility. Michigan State University appealed, on behalf of Ganden, the Clearinghouse's ruling to the NCAA's Academic Requirements Committee. The Committee granted Ganden a partial waiver, allowing Ganden to practice with Michigan State and to accept a scholarship. Ganden could not, however, compete with the swim team in NCAA-sanctioned meets until the following academic year. In addition, Ganden would lose one season of eligibility. Michigan State appealed the partial waiver decision to the NCAA Council, the NCAA's highest decision-making body, which denied Ganden's appeal.

Ganden's waiver was the first waiver granted by the NCAA to a student athlete with a learning disability. Ganden met the GPA and standardized test requirements, but did not meet the core course requirements. In Ganden's junior year, 3.5 core course credits completed during his freshman and sophomore years of high school were deemed unacceptable by the NCAA. Thus, Ganden fell below the thirteen core course credit requirement.

Initially, the United States District Court for the Northern District of Illinois determined that it had subject matter jurisdiction over the NCAA under Title III of the ADA. Next, the court found that Ganden could establish a "causal link" between his learning disability and the NCAA's denial of his waiver application, and, therefore, was a "qualifier." The court rejected the NCAA's argument, which relied on *Sandison*, for the proposition that Ganden's learning disability did not prevent him from meeting the "core course" requirement. Next, the NCAA argued that Ganden's combined GPA and ACT scores fell below the established requirements. The *Ganden* court found evidence that Ganden failed to take the core courses because of his learning disability, which required him to take special education classes. Thus, Ganden would likely be able to establish a causal link between his learning disability and the NCAA's failure to grant a waiver.

Next, the court addressed whether the NCAA could make any reasonable modifications to accommodate Ganden. First, the court identified the minimum GPA requirement and the defined "core course" requirements as the necessary eligibility requirements. Then, the court identified that the purpose of these eligibility requirements is to "(1) insure that student-athletes are representative of the college community and not recruited solely for athletics; (2) insure that a student-athlete is academically prepared to succeed at college; and (3) preserve amateurism in intercollegiate sports." The court initially concluded that a waiver would not "fundamentally alter" the nature of the intercollegiate athletic program. The court distinguished the case before it from *Sandison* and *Pottgen*, where both the Sixth and Eighth Circuits concluded that a waiver of the age requirement in interscholastic high school athletic programs would pose an undue burden on the athletic associations to assess, individually, each student's competitive abilities. The *Ganden* court reasoned that the NCAA already has the Initial Eligibility Clearinghouse in place providing individual assessments of each student athlete applicant.

The *Ganden* court followed the *Johnson* district court decision by assessing each applicant's case. The court refused to accept the analysis advanced by *Sandi-*

---

243. *Id.* at 3.

son and *Pottgen* that questioned whether the eligibility requirements served an important interest of the program. The *Ganden* court criticized this analysis for ignoring the central issue under the ADA: "[whether] reasonable accommodations [are] possible in light of the disability."[265] The court concluded that the correct analysis was to address the underlying purposes of the eligibility criteria to determine whether a modification of the stated purposes would be undermined in the individual plaintiff's circumstances. The court found, however, that the underlying purpose of the NCAA eligibility requirements would be undermined in Ganden's individual circumstance.

The court in *Ganden* determined that Ganden's request for a waiver to be certified a "qualifier" would fundamentally alter the particular accommodation provided by the NCAA. The court found that the NCAA accommodated Ganden by providing him an individualized assessment through a subcommittee that considered Ganden's disability, his efforts to overcome it, and his academic success during his final two years of high school. In Ganden's case, the court determined that the evidence in the record before it demonstrated that the remedial courses taken by Ganden were not "remotely similar" to the NCAA's "core course" requirement. Furthermore, the court contended that it would be unreasonable to require the NCAA to lower the GPA requirement because it would undermine the NCAA's objective to assess a student's academic potential. According to the court, it was less drastic to modify the core course requirement.

Thus, the court concluded that the NCAA, after an individualized assessment, had made a reasonable modification for Ganden's particular circumstances by granting him "partial qualifier" status. Therefore, the court denied Ganden's request for a preliminary injunction because his claim under the ADA would likely fail due to his inability to prove discrimination under Title III.

VI. PRACTIONERS' GUIDE TO BRINGING A CLAIM ON BEHALF OF A LEARNING DISABLED STUDENT ATHLETE UNDER THE ADA

As noted above, to establish a prima facie case of disability discrimination under the ADA, a plaintiff must show that he was denied participation because of his disability. The burden then shifts to the entity charged with discrimination, which must show that the eligibility requirements are essential to the program and that the plaintiff cannot meet these requirements despite reasonable modifications. Thus, when a student athlete has been denied participation on either an interscholastic or intercollegiate athletic team, the first step in bringing a viable claim under the ADA is to establish that the discrimination is "by reason of [the learning] disability."[276]

The *Sandison* and *Pottgen* decisions held that the appropriate test under this part of the prima facie case was whether absent the disability the student athlete could meet the established eligibility requirements. In those cases, the courts found that absent the student athletes' respective learning disabilities, the students could not meet the age requirement for participation in interscholastic high school athletics because of their birth dates. In *Ganden*, however, the Illinois District Court adopted the "causal link" test used by the court in *Dennin v. Connecticut Interscholastic Athletic Conference, Inc.* Under the "causal link test," the

---

265. *Id.* (relying on *Johnson*, 899 F. Supp. at 584).

276. 42 U.S.C. §§ 12101-12213, § 12132, §§ 12301-12310 (1994 & Supp. II 1990, supp. III 1991, Supp. IV 1992, Supp. V 1993).

student athlete must demonstrate that, but for his diagnosed learning disability, he could not meet the established eligibility requirements.

The next step in establishing a prima facie case of disability discrimination under the ADA is to determine what the essential eligibility requirements of the program are, and the underlying purpose for such requirements. Both the Department of Justice regulations and the Supreme Court's holding in *Arline* state that an individual inquiry is necessary at this point to determine if the individual meets the established requirements. If the court determines that these eligibility requirements are in fact essential to the program, the challenged entity must show why modifications to these requirements would not be reasonable. Reasonableness is determined by asking whether the proposed modification would substantially or fundamentally alter the nature of the program or impose undue financial burdens.

To determine whether a modification to existing eligibility requirements is reasonable, the Sixth and Eighth Circuit courts look to see whether the eligibility requirements serve any important interests of the program. However, the district courts in *Johnson*, *Dennin*, and *Ganden*, applied a balancing test that weighed the interests of the student athlete against the interests of the association. The individualized assessment effectuates the purpose of the ADA because, as the court stated in *Ganden*, a "modification of a rule rationally tailored to the denied privilege would [always] be unreasonable." Thus, to eliminate discrimination against individuals, which is often the product of "thoughtlessness and indifference—of benign neglect," not invidious acts of discrimination,[289] an individual assessment is necessary.

VII. CONCLUSION

The *Johnson* district court decision, though a well-reasoned and logical analysis under the ADA, illustrates the confusion and uneven application of the ADA to learning disabled athletes who want to participate in interscholastic athletics. Furthermore, recent claims, similar to Chad Ganden's against the NCAA, demonstrate that interpretation issues under the ADA must be resolved to provide for just and uniform results. Without additional guidance from the Department of Justice, the vague terms encompassed in the statutory language of the ADA will continue to be interpreted differently by individual courts, thus obviating the purpose of the ADA: to protect the disabled from unintentional and indifferent means of discrimination.

. . . .

NCAA-DEPARTMENT OF JUSTICE CONSENT DECREE (1998)

CONSENT DECREE

Background

The United States filed concurrently with this Consent Decree a civil action to enforce title III of the Americans with Disabilities Act of 1990 (ADA), 42 U.S.C.

---

289. Alexander v. Choate, 469 U.S. 287, 295 n.12 (1985).

§§ 12181-12189, against the National Collegiate Athletic Association (NCAA). This matter was initiated by complaints filed by several individuals with the U.S. Department of Justice under title III of the ADA. The complaints alleged that the NCAA's initial-eligibility requirements discriminate against students with learning disabilities. The United States Department of Justice investigated these complaints pursuant to its statutory mandate to investigate alleged violations of title III of the ADA, 42 U.S.C. § 12188(b)(1)(A)(i).

Allegations

The Department of Justice determined that the NCAA's policies, practices and procedures discriminated against student-athletes with learning disabilities in violation of title III. First, NCAA regulations relating to the certification of high-school classes as "core courses" excluded many classes designed to accommodate students with learning disabilities,without regard for the content of the course. Second, the process for considering exceptions for individual students — the waiver process — placed students with learning disabilities at a significant disadvantage relative to their peers.

The Department of Justice received complaints from a number of individuals. These complaints included specific instances in which courses were not accepted as core courses primarily because they were labeled "remedial" or "special education" classes. Based upon these complaints and other evidence, the Department concluded that modifications in several NCAA policies were necessary, that reasonable modifications were available, and that these modifications would not fundamentally alter the nature of the NCAA's program.

The NCAA disputes the allegations contained in the complaints. The NCAA acknowledges shortcomings inherent in the evaluation of core courses primarily on the basis of course title; changes have been made to the process to look solely at the content of a course in evaluating whether it meets the standard for a core course.

Good Faith Negotiations

The NCAA has engaged in good faith negotiations with the United States in seeking to resolve this matter. In fact, the NCAA has already implemented several new policies discussed during the course of settlement negotiations so that students with learning disabilities can begin to take advantage of the new procedures even before a formal settlement has been reached. During the course of the investigation, the NCAA made several constructive revisions in its policies toward students with learning disabilities, including: accepting course work completed between the time of graduation from high school and full-time college enrollment; and allowing students with learning disabilities to initiate their own appeal for a waiver of the initial-eligibility requirements, revising the rule that the only avenue for such an appeal was through a member college or university.

Agreement

In an effort to resolve their remaining differences expeditiously and without the burden, expense and delay of litigation, the parties have agreed to enter into this Consent Decree. By entering into this Consent Decree, the parties acknowledge that the NCAA does not waive its position that it is not a place of public accommodation and therefore title III of the ADA does not apply to it, nor does the

NCAA admit liability under the ADA. This Consent Decree reflects the entire understanding between the parties in regard to the resolution of this matter and is intended to resolve all remaining disputes between the parties.

Accordingly, it is hereby agreed by the parties and ordered by the Court as follows:

1. The NCAA agrees to propose to the committees with the authority to enact legislative changes to the NCAA's bylaws that the following proposed rules be adopted:

A.   NCAA Bylaw 14.3.1.3 reads, in part: "Courses that are taught at a level below the high school's regular academic instructional level (e.g., remedial, special education or compensatory) shall not be considered core courses regardless of course content." The NCAA agrees to propose:

1. That the words "special education" be taken out of the bylaw.
2. That the following sentence be inserted immediately after the language quoted above: "The prohibition of 'remedial and compensatory' courses does not apply to courses designed for students with learning disabilities. See Bylaw 14.3.1.3.4 for the rules governing courses for students with learning disabilities."

B. NCAA Bylaw 14.3.1.3.4 , as newly adopted in 1998, reads: "Courses for Students with Disabilities. The Academics/Eligibility/Compliance Cabinet may approve the use of high-school courses for students with disabilities to fulfill the core-curriculum requirements, even if such courses are taught at a level below the high school's regular academic instructional level (e.g., special education courses), if the high-school principal submits a written statement to the NCAA indicating that courses are substantially comparable, quantitatively and qualitatively, to similar core-course offerings in that academic discipline. Students with disabilities still must complete the required core courses and achieve the minimum required grade-point average in this core curriculum." The NCAA agrees to propose:

1. An additional sentence be added to the bylaw: "The fact that the title of the course includes a designation such as 'remedial,' 'special education,' 'special needs,' or other similar titles sometimes used for courses designed for students with learning disabilities, does not by itself disqualify a course from meeting the core curriculum requirements."

2. The words "are taught" be changed to "appear to be taught."

C. The NCAA agrees to propose that an additional rule be added to its bylaws allowing students with learning disabilities who do not meet the initial-eligibility requirements to earn an additional year of athletics competition, under certain conditions. The bylaw the NCAA agrees to propose is set out under the heading "Proposal" in the document attached as Attachment A. The NCAA further agrees that its interpretation of this rule will be consistent with the guidance included in Attachment A, and it will publish and distribute materials consistent with that guidance.

2. The United States reserves the right in its sole discretion to withdraw agreement to this Consent Decree and proceed with litigation in this matter if any of the rules required to be proposed pursuant to Paragraph 1 are modified in any way prior to their enactment or implementation. The United States also reserves the right in its sole discretion to withdraw agreement to this Consent Decree and proceed with litigation of this matter if the NCAA fails to adopt those rules by

January 31, 1999, or takes other steps, either through legislation or through other means, before or after that date, such that those rules are adopted but are not given full force and effect.

3. The parties acknowledge that this Consent Decree does not prohibit future legislative action by the NCAA consistent with the provisions of this agreement. The parties also acknowledge that the NCAA voluntarily agrees that any further legislative action by the NCAA will comply with title III of the ADA.

4. The NCAA agrees to adopt Attachment B as its formal policy for evaluating applications for waivers of the initial-eligibility requirements that are filed by students with learning disabilities. Within 30 days after the date on which the Court enters this Consent Decree, Attachment B shall be distributed to all relevant NCAA staff and committee members involved in determining whether applications for waivers filed by students with learning disabilities are granted. The NCAA will also include Attachment B with all training materials provided in the future to people involved in determining whether applications for waivers filed by students with learning disabilities are granted.

5. The policy statement contained in Attachment B, or a document consistent with the policy statement, shall be distributed to any person inquiring about filing an application for a waiver for a student with learning disabilities, including students, parents and guardians, attorneys, high-school officials or officials of an NCAA member institution.

6. The NCAA agrees that the waiver committee in Division I responsible for hearing applications for waivers of the initial-eligibility requirements filed by students with learning disabilities will be comprised of people with expertise in the field of learning disabilities, and that the waiver committee in Division II responsible for hearing applications for waivers of the initial-eligibility requirements filed by students with learning disabilities will include people with expertise in the field of learning disabilities.

7. The NCAA agrees that within 30 days after the date on which the NCAA receives notice that Court has entered this Consent Decree, it will designate one or more employees at the NCAA as ADA Compliance Coordinator(s).

A. The ADA Compliance Coordinator(s) will serve as a resource to other employeesof the NCAA and the NCAA Clearinghouse regarding the ADA. The NCAA agrees that within 120 days of the date the ADA Compliance Coordinator(s) are designated, the ADA Compliance Coordinator(s) will attend a seminar that includes instruction concerning a private entity's obligations under title III. The NCAA agrees that the ADA Compliance Coordinator(s) will attend a similar educational seminar annually.

B. The ADA Compliance Coordinator(s) will serve as a liaison between students with learning disabilities and the NCAA and the NCAA Clearinghouse. The NCAA agrees that the names, addresses and telephone numbers of the ADA Compliance Coordinator(s) will be published as soon as practicable in materials mailed to students with learning disabilities, high-school officials, and member colleges and universities.

8. By September 30, 1998, the NCAA agrees to provide training to all relevant staff regarding its new policies concerning students with learning disabilities, the provisions of this Consent Decree, and the provisions of title III of the ADA generally. The NCAA agrees to conduct similar training in 1999 and 2000. The NCAA agrees specifically to:

A. Conduct training for relevant NCAA staff and NCAA Clearinghouse staff, with an emphasis on how students with learning disabilities are taught and how curriculum is developed for students with learning disabilities.

B. Conduct training for relevant NCAA staff and members of the committee(s) responsible for hearing applications for waivers of the initial-eligibility requirements filed by students with learning disabilities, with an emphasis on predicting academic success in college for students with learning disabilities.

C. Submit the proposed curriculum for the training programs conducted in 1998, 1999 and 2000 to the United States for its prior approval, and to offer the United States the option of participating in the training programs.

9. Within 60 days after the date on which the NCAA receives notice that the Court has entered this Consent Decree, the NCAA agrees to publicize the provisions of this Consent Decree. The NCAA specifically agrees to:

A. Publicize the revision of its policies regarding the certification of core course designed for students with learning disabilities, with the purpose of encouraging high schools to submit these courses for certification.

1. The NCAA agrees to mail an announcement of the new standards for courses designed for students with learning disabilities to all high schools, encouraging schools to include appropriate courses on the core-course submission forms.

2. The NCAA agrees to mail a similar announcement targeted specifically for private high schools designed for students with learning disabilities.

3. The NCAA agrees to include in the package of information given to students who, at the time they register with the Clearinghouse, indicate an interest in the NCAA's policies with regard to students with learning disabilities, a notice advising the students to encourage their school to submit courses designed for students with learning disabilities for certification as core courses.

4. The NCAA agrees to mail an announcement to associations dealing with learning disabilities to encourage their members to contact local schools about submitting courses designed for students with learning disabilities for certification as core courses.

B. The NCAA agrees to amend the language of all its materials relating to student-athletes with learning disabilities to reflect the revision of its policies regarding the certification of core courses designed for students with learning disabilities, including but not limited to the core-course review worksheets and the "Putting Dreams into Action" brochure.

C. The NCAA agrees to continue its efforts to publicize the fact that students with learning disabilities have the option of filing an application for a waiver of the initial-eligibility requirements if the student is not certified as eligible by the NCAA Clearinghouse.

D. The NCAA agrees to publicize the provisions of this Consent Decree among its member colleges and universities.

1. The NCAA agrees to publish an announcement regarding its new policies designed for students with learning disabilities to all member colleges and universities.

2. The NCAA agrees to include in the announcement a statement advising member colleges and universities that they should not refrain from recruiting student-athletes with learning disabilities because the new policies are designed to enable that population of students to have an equal opportunity to achieve eligibility as students without disabilities. The NCAA agrees to assure member col-

leges and universities that the waiver process can produce successful results for student-athletes with learning disabilities.

10. On May 1, 1999; May 1, 2000; and May 1, 2001, the NCAA agrees to file a report documenting its efforts to comply with this agreement and to comply voluntarily with title III of the ADA. The report shall include:

A. Statistics tracking the ability of students with learning disabilities to receive avorable certification reports issued by the NCAA Clearinghouse. The statistics must include: the number of students who identify themselves as having learning disabilities in their dealings with the NCAA Clearinghouse; the number of those students who complete the registration process; the number of those students who are certified as eligible by the NCAA Clearinghouse; and the number of those students who file applications for a waiver of the initial-eligibility requirements.

B. Statistics on the number of courses designated by high schools as designed for students with learning disabilities that are certified as core courses. The statistics must also include the number of such courses proposed as core courses by high schools, but rejected by the NCAA or the NCAA Clearinghouse.

C. Statistics concerning the decisions by the committee responsible for hearing applications for waivers of the initial-eligibility requirements filed by students with learning disabilities. The statistics must include: the number of waiver applications filed by students with learning disabilities; the number of waiver applications filed by all other students; the percentage of students without disabilities who receive full waivers, receive partial waivers, and are denied a waiver; and the percentage of students with learning disabilities who receive full waivers, receive partial waivers, and are denied a waiver.

D. Statistics on the number of students whose claims to have learning disabilities are rejected by the NCAA.

E. The United States may, upon review of the statistics provided in these reports and upon review of other evidence that is provided to it, in its sole discretion withdraw its agreement to this Consent Decree and proceed with litigation in this matter if it determines that the NCAA's policies, practices or procedures violate title III. If the United States believes that the NCAA's policies, practices or procedures are in violation of title III, it will give the NCAA written notice of the alleged violation and provide it with an opportunity to cure any alleged violation. The parties shall engage in good faith negotiations to resolve any dispute.

11. Within 60 days after the date on which the NCAA receives notice that the Court has entered this Consent Decree, the NCAA agrees to make payments totaling $35,000 to be distributed among four student-athletes, as agreed to between the NCAA, the United States and the individuals. The NCAA agrees to provide the United States with notice (a copy of the letter and the check sent to each individual) within 10 days of the date these payments are made.

12. The United States may review compliance with this Consent Decree at any time. If the United States believes that the NCAA has not complied with any provision of this Consent Decree, it agrees to attempt to seek an amicable resolution of the matter with the NCAA. If the parties are unable to reach an amicable resolution of the matter, the United States may seek appropriate relief from this Court. The United States' failure to seek enforcement of any provision of this Consent Decree shall not be construed as a waiver of its right to do so with regard to the same provision or other provisions of this Consent Decree.

13. This Consent Decree shall remain in effect until May 1, 2003. At that time, this Consent Decree shall terminate unless the United States moves for cause for an extension. This Court retains jurisdiction over this case for the purposes of enforcement of this Consent Decree. Any party may bring such issues before the Court by filing an appropriate motion.

14. The NCAA agrees that it will not discriminate or retaliate against any person because of his or her participation in this matter.

15. This Consent Decree does not propose to remedy any other potential violations of the ADA or any other law. This Consent Decree does not affect the NCAA's continuing responsibility to comply with other aspects of the ADA.

16. The individuals signing this Consent Decree represent that they are authorized to bind the parties to this Consent Decree.

17. Both parties shall bear their own attorneys fees, costs and expenses.

18. This Consent Decree constitutes the entire agreement between the parties relating to this civil action, and no other statement, promise or agreement, either written or oral, made by either party or agents of either party, that is not contained in this Consent Decree, shall be enforceable.

SO ORDERED this 27th day of May, 1998.

William B. Bryant

United States District Judge

ATTACHMENT A

Fourth Year of Competition

Proposal:

The Division I Academics/Eligibility/Compliance Cabinet Subcommittees on Initial and Continuing Eligibility Issues recommend that the following legislation be enacted:

Students with learning disabilities who enroll in a Division I institution and do not meet the initial-eligibility requirements, and are not granted a full waiver, are entitled to a fourth year of athletics eligibility if they complete at least 75 percent of their degree program by the beginning of their fifth year of full-time enrollment, or have received a waiver that permits them to maintain athletics eligibility while completing a lower percentage of course work in their degree program. See Bylaw 14.4.3. Students who are eligible to earn a fourth season of athletics eligibility under this bylaw are limited to those whose diagnosed learning disability is such that they will not progress at a rate to earn a baccalaureate degree by the beginning of their fifth academic year.

How the proposal works:

At any point following a student's freshman year, he/she would take:

(1)   a copy of his/her most recent report diagnosing his/her disability;

(2)   a copy of his/her college transcript; and

(3)   any other documents relevant to his/her educational achievement [such as the student's high-school Individual Education Program (IEP) or similar reports

prepared by the student's college advisors] to the professional staff on campus that evaluates and/or assists students with disabilities.

The on-campus professional would evaluate the student's diagnosed disability, in combination with other factors bearing on his/her educational achievement. The campus professional would answer the question: Will this student progress at a rate to earn a baccalaureate degree by the beginning of his/her fifth academic year? Relevant factors include (but are not limited to) the likelihood that a student will need to take a reduced course load at some stage of his/her college education, the type of major the student will need to take a reduced course load at some stage of his/her college education, the type of major the student wishes to pursue, and the types of accommodations offered in that department.

Re-testing the student to develop a new diagnosis of the disability is neither contemplated nor suggested by this rule; the campus professional should merely review the reports and documents already existing.

In the event that no such professional staff exists on campus, the student would be directed to the off-campus professionals normally used by the institution.

If the campus professional is satisfied that the student meets the criteria, he/she would send a letter to the athletics department and to the student confirming this fact. The athletics department is responsible for communicating this information to the NCAA. In the event that the NCAA does not have on file a copy of the most recent diagnosis of the student's learning disability, the athletics department must submit a copy to the NCAA with the signed letter from the professional staff.

In the event that the on-campus professional does not certify that a student meets the criteria to be eligible for a fourth season, the student may appeal to the NCAA Division I Satisfactory-Progress Waiver Committee for consideration.

ATTACHMENT B

Policy Regarding Factors to be Considered For Determining Whether to Grant an Application for a Waiver of the Initial-Eligibility Requirements Filed by or on Behalf of a Student with a Learning Disability

The NCAA Division I Initial-Eligibility Waiver Committee's role is to make a determination, based on a careful review of all documentation, whether a student is academically prepared to succeed in college while participating in athletics. Only those students who have not met NCAA initial-eligibility standards come before the subcommittee for review. Upon receiving a request for a waiver of the established academic criteria, the subcommittee must evaluate a student's overall academic record to assess a student's readiness to practice and compete as a student-athlete in his/her first year of enrollment at an NCAA Division I or II member college or university. In reviewing a waiver request, the subcommittee shall consider any extenuating circumstances that may have been present that prevented the student from meeting the established standards.

Students with learning disabilities who do not meet the standards may initiate a waiver application independently, or a member institution may submit a waiver in his or her behalf. A specific waiver subcommittee on disabilities, consisting of individuals from the NCAA membership with expertise in the area of learning disabilities, will review each waiver application submitted by either a student or a member institution on behalf of a student. The waiver subcommittee on disabilities will begin each review of a waiver request for a student with a disability from the perspective that: each case is unique; the reasons for not meeting the standards vary greatly; and in some instances, the disability itself may have contributed to the student's deficiency.

In considering whether to grant a full or partial waiver to a student with a disability, the subcommittee must take into account a number of factors, including but not limited to:

1. The extent to which the failure of the student to meet any criterion is attributable to a student-athlete's disability.

2. Whether non-core courses taken by a student had been specified on the student's Individualized Education Plan (IEP) and/or had been approved by a state or local government as satisfying graduation requirements for students with disabilities.

3. The student's overall academic record, which includes the grades earned by the student in his/her core curriculum established by the NCAA; the likelihood that non-core courses the student has taken will prepare him/her to successfully complete a planned course of study at a particular college or university; as well as the student's test scores achieved in the SAT and/or ACT, both overall composite scores and scores in specific subject areas.

4. Weight of standardized tests. Although the nonstandard administration of an SAT or ACT is intended to accommodate for a particular student's disability (so that the score achieved under a nonstandard administration reflects the student's ability, rather than his or her disability), there are certain disabilities (particularly decoding disabilities) that may make achieving the necessary test score — even under a nonstandard administration — more difficult.

There is no minimum qualifying standardized test score that is necessary for receiving a full or partial waiver. The subcommittee shall review the student's overall academic record in determining whether the student is prepared to succeed academically in college.

Moreover, the subcommittee shall not place undue emphasis on a student's low test scores (below the 820/68 minimum and the accompanying subscores) when evidence is presented elsewhere in a student's overall academic record that suggests preparedness for freshman year as a student-athlete. Conversely, the subcommittee shall not place undue emphasis on a student's test score that is above the 820/68 minimum when evidence is presented elsewhere in the student's overall academic record that suggests a lack of preparedness. The subcommittee will emphasize evidence related to the student's high-school preparation and performance (as reflected in high-school courses, grades in both the core courses and overall GPA, performance(s) on standardized tests, and the student's motivation and attitude toward learning). Demonstrated areas of improved performance through high school (e.g., the student took increasingly more challenging courses, or, the student's grades improved steadily throughout high school) are significant factors in assessing a student's readiness and motivation for being a successful student-athlete.

Finally, the subcommittee also shall not place undue emphasis on a particular subscore when the subscore is within the student's area of disability. For example, if a student has a reading disability, the subcommittee will not place undue emphasis on the English subscore of ACT or SAT.

5. The assessments of a school principal, guidance counselor and teachers as to whether a student with a learning disability is likely to succeed academically in col-

lege while participating in athletics, including any objective evidence on whether participating in athletics assists or hinders the student's academic performance.

6. Written or oral comments by the student that may reflect the level of knowledge thatthe student acquired in high school and may be helpful in predicting his/her preparedness to succeed in college.

7. The accommodations available at the high school for students with learning disabilities.

8. The accommodations for students with learning disabilities actually used by the student.

(b) The Right to Participate and Enhanced Risk

Matthew J. Mitten, Enhanced Risk of Harm to One's Self As a Justification for Exclusion from Athletics

8 Marquette Sports Law Journal 189 (1998)*

This article discusses an athlete's legal right to participate in sponsored athletic competition with a physical abnormality that exposes him or her to an enhanced risk of injury or death. For purposes of this discussion, I assume that the athlete has the necessary physical skills and abilities to successfully play the sport with a physical impairment (*e.g.*, a cardiovascular or spinal abnormality or a missing or non-functioning paired organ such as an eye or kidney) and that his or her participation does not create an increased risk of physical injury to others. However, the athlete may be exposed to a substantially enhanced risk of personal injury by participating in a sport. A lack of available scientific data and reliable clinical studies may cause sports medicine experts to disagree regarding whether this increased risk of harm, created by the athlete's physical abnormality, justifies medical disqualification from athletic competition.

Considering the uncertainties present in sports medicine and the impossibility of accurately predicting whether a physically impaired athlete will actually experience serious injury or death during sports participation as a result of his or her medical condition what is the appropriate judicial construction of federal laws prohibiting medically unjustified discrimination? Resolution of this issue requires proper delineation of the respective bounds of an impaired athlete's liberty interest in having an opportunity to participate in sports and a team's right (or that of a sports league or sponsoring organization) to establish reasonable minimum physical standards that must be satisfied by all participants. How we resolve this question implicates broader social values such as the limits of libertarianism and acceptable communitarian protection of others' health and safety, because sports is a microcosm of society in many respects.

....

I. PARTIES' RESPECTIVE LEGAL RIGHTS AND PROTECTED INTERESTS

A. *Athletes*
. . . .

Participation in amateur sports at any level of athletic competition generally is considered to be a privilege rather than a legally protected right. Although some courts hold that a high school student cannot be arbitrarily denied an opportunity to participate in interscholastic sports competition, that sports are an integral part of one's scholastic and social development, or that athletic competition is vital to obtaining a college education by means of an athletic scholarship, courts generally refuse to recognize a constitutional right to play interscholastic sports. Similarly, there is no constitutionally protected liberty or property interest in playing intercollegiate athletics. Although a college athletic scholarship is a contract between the student-athlete and his or her university, it does not guarantee either a position on the team or playing time. The national governing body for each Olympic sport has a contractual relationship with its member athletes, and the Amateur Sports Act of 1978 gives the organization the exclusive right to determine the membership of its national team for purposes of international competition, so there is no legal right to participate in Olympic sports. Thus, the relationship between an amateur athlete and the sponsoring educational institution or athletics organization is legally considered to be consensual in nature.

B. *Teams and Athletics-Event-Sponsoring Entities*

An athlete may be medically disqualified by the team physician, or event sponsor's medical personnel, if a physical abnormality exposes him or her to a medically unreasonable risk of injury. A sponsoring educational institution or athletic organization may be reluctant to permit a talented, but physically impaired athlete, to participate in a competitive sport without medical clearance. The organization may also be concerned about potential legal liability from allowing an impaired athlete to participate. Apart from legal liability, the team or event sponsor also may have a paternalistic desire to protect a physically impaired athlete's health and safety by refusing to allow potential exposure to a risk of serious harm during athletic competition. In addition, there may be concern about potential psychological harm to others participating in the game or event or the detrimental effects of adverse publicity on the team or event sponsor's reputation if a physically impaired athlete suffers serious injury or death.

Courts have held that both public educational institutions and private athletic governing bodies have a legitimate interest in protecting an athlete from injury during athletic competition. Although these cases involved federal or state constitutional challenges to mandatory drug testing (rather than Rehabilitation Act or ADA claims), they recognize that a team or athletic event sponsor has at least some inherent right to protect an athlete's health and safety. Moreover, outside the context of athletics, there are several judicially recognized social justifications for preventing people from engaging in potentially dangerous activities and harming themselves. For example, minimizing the public cost of injury treatment and disability; avoiding the loss of productive members of society; and preventing the loss of economic support and/or consortium to the injury victim's family are valid objectives.

Even if a team or sponsor of an athletic event has a general *legal right* to protect the health and safety of participating athletes, the extent of its *legal duty* to protect an athlete from a voluntarily assumed enhanced risk of injury is uncertain. In *Orr v. Brigham Young University*,[20] a federal district court refused to impose a legal duty on a university to prevent an adult athlete from continuing to play intercollegiate football to avoid aggravating a pre-existing injury....

Although the doctrines of express assumption of risk or sovereign immunity may immunize a team or event sponsor from tort liability for allowing a physically impaired athlete to participate, uncertainty concerning legal liability is a legitimate interest to a team or sponsor of an athletic event.

....

II. REHABILITATION ACT CASES DEFINING AMATEUR ATHLETES' PARTICIPATION RIGHTS

To prevail on a claim that exclusion from a sport or athletic event violates the Rehabilitation Act, an athlete must prove: 1) he or she is "disabled"; 2) he or she is "otherwise qualified" for the position or opportunity sought; 3) he or she has been excluded from the position solely because of his or her disability; and 4) the position or opportunity exists as part of a program or activity receiving federal financial assistance. It is not necessary that an entity's athletic program directly benefits from federal funds. A public or private elementary or secondary educational institution, as well as any other sponsor of an athletic event, is covered by the Rehabilitation Act if any aspect of it receives any form of federal funding.

A physically impaired athlete also could assert that his or her exclusion from a sport violates the ADA, although cases challenging such exclusion, because of increased risk of injury to one's self, thus far have only been brought under the Rehabilitation Act. Such a claim requires proof of essentially the same elements as a Rehabilitation Act claim except that, instead of showing that the defendant receives federal funds, the athlete must prove that the defendant is covered by the ADA's "public entity" or "public accommodation" provisions. A sponsor of an amateur athletic event that is not covered by the Rehabilitation Act because it does not receive federal funds may nevertheless be covered under the ADA's public entity or public accommodation sections. Unless otherwise noted, I will consider both laws together in addressing a physically impaired amateur athlete's legal right to participate in sports.

A person with a physical impairment which substantially limits one or more of his or her major life activities, or has a record of such impairment, or is regarded as having such an impairment, is considered to be "disabled" and covered by the Act. The first Rehabilitation Act suits were brought by high school or college athletes with either a missing or non-functioning eye or kidney who had been excluded from participating in a contact sport. Courts either assumed that these athletes satisfied the Act's definition of an individual with a "disability," or found this requirement satisfied without engaging in extensive analysis.

.... [A discussion of these initial cases is omitted. - ed.].

In 1987, the United States Supreme Court decided another important case under the [Rehabilitation] Act by considering when it is legally permissible to ex-

---

20. 960 F. Supp. 1522 (D. Utah 1994).

clude a physically impaired person from an activity or program to *prevent a risk of harm to others.* In *School Board of Nassau County, Fla. v Arline,*[65] the Court held that the Act does not prohibit disparate treatment of the handicapped necessary to avoid "exposing others to significant health and safety risks." The Court explained that "in determining whether an individual is 'otherwise qualified,' she or he is entitled to an opportunity to have [one's] condition evaluated in light of medical evidence."[66] The decision to exclude an individual from a particular program or activity must be based on "reasonable medical judgments given the state of medical knowledge."[67] The nature, duration, probability, and severity of harm likely to result from the handicapped individual's participation, and whether it can be effectively reduced by reasonable accommodation, are factors to be considered.

. . . .

Recent Rehabilitation Act cases brought by athletes challenging their medical disqualification from a sport, specifically consider whether an athlete is "disabled" under the statute, as well as whether he or she is "otherwise qualified" to participate. In *Pahulu v. University of Kansas,*[72] the court upheld a public university's decision not to allow Alani Pahulu to continue playing college football after being medically disqualified by the team physician. After experiencing transient quadriplegia while making a tackle during a scrimmage, he was found to have an abnormally narrow cervical canal. After consulting with a neurosurgeon, the team physician concluded that he was at extremely high risk for sustaining permanent, severe neurological injury, including permanent quadriplegia, if he resumed playing college football. The university agreed to honor his athletic scholarship, although he was not permitted to play football. Nevertheless, he wanted to continue playing because three other medical specialists concluded that his spinal abnormality did not expose him to a greater risk of permanent paralysis than any other player.

The court first considered the Act's requirement that the plaintiff have a physical impairment which substantially limits one or more of his major life activities. It found that his congenitally narrow cervical canal is a physical impairment, and applying a subjective standard, that intercollegiate football is a part of the student's major life activity of learning. However, the court held that he is not "disabled" under the Act because his exclusion from football does not substantially limit his opportunity to learn since he retained his athletic scholarship, which provided him with continued access to all academic services, and he was allowed to participate in the university's football program in a role other than as a player.

Without citing any of the foregoing cases, the court also held that the student is not "otherwise qualified" because he was not able to satisfy all of the football program's requirements in spite of his disability, namely, medical clearance from the university's team physician to play football. The court found that the team physician's "conservative" medical opinion is "reasonable and rational" and "supported by substantial competent evidence" for which it is "unwilling to substitute its judgment."[75]

---

65. 480 U.S. 273, 287 (1987).
66. *Id.* at 285.
67. *Id.* at 288 (citations omitted).
72. 897 F. Supp. 1387 (D. Kan. 1995).
75. *Id.* at 1394.

In *Knapp v. Northwestern University*,[76] the Seventh Circuit reversed the lower court's holding that Northwestern University violated the Rehabilitation Act in following its team physician's medical recommendation that an athlete with a heart condition known as idiopathic ventricular fibrillation not play intercollegiate basketball. As a high school senior, Nicholas Knapp suffered sudden cardiac arrest while playing recreational basketball, which required cardiopulmonary resuscitation and defibrillation to restart his heart. Thereafter, he had an internal cardioverter-defibrillator implanted in his abdomen. He subsequently played competitive recreational basketball without any incidents of cardiac arrest for two years and received medical clearance to play college basketball from three cardiologists who examined him.

Northwestern agreed to honor its commitment to provide Knapp with an athletic scholarship, although it adhered to its team physician's medical disqualification from intercollegiate basketball. This recommendation was based on Knapp's medical records and history, the 26th Bethesda Conference guidelines for athletic participation with cardiovascular abnormalities, and opinions from two consulting cardiologists who concluded that Knapp would expose himself to a significant risk of ventricular fibrillation or cardiac arrest during competitive athletics.

All medical experts agreed on the following facts: Knapp had suffered sudden cardiac death due to ventricular fibrillation; even with the internal defibrillator; playing college basketball placed Knapp at a higher risk for suffering another event of sudden cardiac death compared to other male college basketball players; the internal defibrillator has never been tested under the conditions of intercollegiate basketball; and no person currently plays or has ever played college or professional basketball after suffering sudden cardiac death and having a defibrillator implanted.

The lower court held that Knapp is "disabled" under the Act. The parties did not dispute that Knapp is perceived as having a permanent cardiovascular impairment, which is a physical impairment under the statute. The court found that intercollegiate basketball is a major life activity for Knapp, because it "is an important and integral part of [his] education and learning experience."[79] Because practicing with the team and competing in games is necessary for learning discipline, teamwork, and perseverance, the trial court concluded that Northwestern's refusal to allow Knapp to play substantially limits his ability to play college basketball.

The Seventh Circuit disagreed with the lower court's conclusion and held that Knapp is not "disabled" under the Act. The appellate court held that "[p]laying intercollegiate basketball obviously is not in and of itself a major life activity."[80] Finding that learning is the affected major life activity, the court concluded that playing intercollegiate basketball is "only one part of the education available to Knapp at Northwestern."[81] Consistent with *Pahulu*, the court observed that Knapp's "inability to play intercollegiate basketball at Northwestern forecloses only a small portion of his collegiate [learning] opportunities"[82] and does not substantially limit his college education because his athletic scholarship continues,

---

76. 101 F.3d 473 (7th Cir. 1996), *cert. denied*, 117 U.S. 2454 (1997).

79. Knapp v. Northwestern Univ., 942 F. Supp. 1191, 1195 (N.D. Ill. 1996).

80. *Knapp*, 101 F.3d at 480

81. *Id.* at 481.

82. *Id.* at 482.

thereby allowing him full access to all of the university's other programs and activities.

The parties agreed that Knapp is not "otherwise qualified" under the Act if there is a "genuine substantial risk" that he could be seriously injured while playing basketball at Northwestern. The lower court noted that all medical experts agreed on the underlying basic scientific and medical principles, but that, because no one had ever played college basketball with an implanted defibrillator, the risk that Knapp would suffer another incident of cardiac arrest while playing could not be objectively quantified. Medical experts disagreed whether the risk of injury to Knapp was substantial enough to medically justify his exclusion from intercollegiate basketball.

The lower court conceded that excluding Knapp from an "'unessential' activity," such as intercollegiate basketball, that creates an increased uncertain risk of serious personal injury "is clearly rational in the medical profession," given the absence of proven safety. However, the court concluded that the Act "require[s] a judicial decision on the substantiality of the risk" necessitating consideration of "the testimony of all the experts who testified and determin[ing] which are most persuasive."[86] After weighing the experts' testimony, the court found that the risk of injury to Knapp while playing college basketball is not medically substantial and that the implanted defibrillator most likely would restore his heart beat to normal if Knapp's heart rate became abnormal during strenuous physical exertion.

The Seventh Circuit again disagreed with the lower court and concluded that Knapp is not "otherwise qualified" to play basketball at Northwestern under the Act. Citing *Davis*, the appellate court held that a university legally may establish legitimate physical qualifications that an individual must satisfy in order to participate in its athletic program. Agreeing with the lower court and the parties that a "significant risk of personal physical injury" that cannot be eliminated justifies medical disqualification from an activity, the court framed the controlling issue as, "[W]ho should make such an assessment[?]"[89]

Holding that Knapp's exclusion from Northwestern's basketball team was legally justified, the Seventh Circuit explained:

> We disagree with the district court's legal determination that such decisions are to be made by the courts and believe instead that medical determinations of this sort are best left to team doctors and universities as long as they are made with reason and rationality and with full regard to possible and reasonable accommodations. In cases such as ours, where Northwestern has examined both Knapp and his medical records, and considered his medical history and the relation between his prior sudden cardiac death and the possibility of future occurrences, has considered the severity of the potential injury, and has rationally and reasonably reviewed consensus medical opinions or recommendations in the pertinent field — regardless whether conflicting medical opinions exist — the university has the right to determine that an individual is not otherwise medically qualified to play without violating the Rehabilitation Act. The place of the court in such cases is to make sure that the decision-maker has reasonably considered and relied upon sufficient evidence specific to the individual and the potential injury, not to determine on its own which evidence it believes is more persuasive.

---

86. *Id.* at 1196-97.
89. *Id.* at 483.

....

....What we say in this case is that if substantial evidence supports the decision-maker — here Northwestern — that decision must be respected.[90]

III. SYNTHESIS AND CRITIQUE OF REHABILITATION ACT PRECEDENT

Federal trial and appellate courts, thus far, have resolved claims brought by physically impaired amateur athletes on a case-by-case basis, without clear direction from Congress or explicit guidance from the Supreme Court. Neither the Rehabilitation Act nor its accompanying regulations specifically address whether exclusion of a skilled athlete, with a physical abnormality from a desired sport substantially limits a "major life activity." Moreover, the Act is silent regarding whether a risk of physical harm solely to one's self precludes an athlete from being "otherwise qualified," and the Supreme Court has not yet considered this issue.

In construing the Act's requirements that an athlete be both "disabled" and "otherwise qualified" to participate, it appears that courts are implicitly balancing the athlete's interest in playing a sport with the sponsoring institution's interest in protecting the health and safety of participants. The foregoing cases illustrate that courts recognize that athletic competition is a valued component of both high school and college education, but are divided regarding the importance of athletics in a student's learning experience. On the other hand, the judiciary considers the protection of an athlete's health to be a legitimate objective, regardless of whether an educational institution has an affirmative legal duty to prevent a student from harming one's self, but does not always consider this interest to be paramount. Courts usually struggle to weigh appropriately the parties' conflicting interests particularly when medical experts are divided in their participation recommendations.

A. *Exclusion From Amateur Athletics as Substantially Limiting a Major Life Activity*

In determining whether an individual athlete's exclusion from athletics substantially limits a major life activity, courts should accord greater weight to the importance of athletic competition in high school and college education. Although most students do not participate in intercollegiate or interscholastic sports, it is appropriate to apply a subjective test in resolving this issue because the Act references "such person's major life activities," thereby indicating the necessary individualized nature of this inquiry. Consistent with this language, some courts have held that athletics are sufficiently intertwined with education, such that they constitute a major life activity for particular individuals playing interscholastic or intercollegiate sports.

At the high school level, interscholastic athletics play an integral role in enabling participants to earn better grades and develop social skills by teaching discipline, teamwork, commitment, motivation, and hard work. The vast majority of people do not participate in structured competitive athletics beyond high school, and their last opportunity to take advantage of these important educational benefits occurs during this formative four-year period.

Intercollegiate athletics play a different role in the educational process for the relatively small number of college students participating in them, but they are an important part of a university's primary mission of helping an individual maxi-

---

90. *Id.* at 484-85 (emphasis in original).

mize one's learning and career potential — whether it be academic, physical, or artistic prowess or a combination of these talents. Moreover, in other contexts, courts have recognized that intercollegiate athletics are an integral component of American higher education and provide invaluable lessons that help further general life success and careers outside of professional sports.

Whether exclusion from intercollegiate or interscholastic athletics substantially limits one's opportunity to learn must necessarily be considered on an individualized basis. Even if there are other educational benefits available to excluded physically impaired athletes, they are being denied an equal opportunity to participate fully in all of an educational institution's programs and activities which are generally available to all persons with the requisite skills and abilities. If physically impaired high school and college athletes are not covered by the Act, such an athlete is deprived of his or her federal right to have one's medical condition individually evaluated as well as the full potential educational benefits of competitive athletics if he or she is found to be "otherwise qualified" under the Act. Accordingly, it would further the Act's objectives of prohibiting medically unjustified discrimination against physically impaired persons by ensuring that these athletes are protected by the Act.

B. "Otherwise Qualified" to Participate in Amateur Athletics

In *City of Cleburne v. Cleburne Living Center, Inc.,*[98] the United States Supreme Court ruled that handicapped persons are not a suspect or quasi-suspect class justifying heightened scrutiny of alleged discrimination. Under *Cleburne*, to successfully defend a denial of equal protection of the law claim, a public school can justify the exclusion of a physically impaired athlete from a sport if its decision is rationally related to a legitimate objective such as protecting his or her health and safety. However, unlike the federal Constitution, the Rehabilitation Act requires that a covered educational institution or entity have more than merely a rational basis for discriminating against a physically impaired athlete. Courts have struggled to formulate the appropriate legal standard justifying exclusion of a physically impaired athlete from a sport for medial reasons.

The *Larkin* court properly rejected the contention that the Act creates an absolute right for a physically impaired amateur athlete to participate in a sport, even if there is universal agreement among physicians that his or her medical condition creates a significant risk of serious personal injury or death. Absent clear legislative intent supporting such a position, it is extremely unlikely that Congress intended the Rehabilitation Act to be a means of forcing covered entities to enable amateur athletes to take potentially life-threatening risks in a sport that is merely an avocation. To the contrary, in *Davis*, the Supreme Court held that the Act does not prohibit an educational institution from requiring that its students possess "reasonable physical qualifications" in order to participate in its programs and activities.

In construing the Act's "otherwise qualified" requirement, as applied to athletics, some courts hold that an athlete with a physical abnormality may be excluded from a sport only if there is a "substantial justification" for doing so. Even if this specific terminology is not used, or the appropriate legal standard is phrased

---

98. 473 U.S. 432 (1985).

somewhat differently, courts generally agree that the Act permits an athlete to be medically disqualified, if necessary to prevent a significant risk of serious personal injury such as a permanently crippling injury or death. Courts have adopted a similar judicial standard regarding the legally permissible exclusion of handi-capped persons from covered employment opportunities under the Act.

Judicial formulation and acceptance of the "significant risk of serious injury" standard as a legal justification for excluding a physically impaired athlete from a sport does not, however, resolve the key issue in determining whether an athlete is "otherwise qualified" to participate. As the *Knapp* appellate court recognized, this issue is, "Who should make such an assessment"[105] when there is no defini-tive scientific evidence and medical experts conflict in their athletic participation recommendations? There are three theoretical models of decision-making that have been adopted by courts in construing the Act as it governs athletes which I will term as: 1) the judicial/medical fact-finding model; 2) the athlete informed consent model; and 3) the team physician medical judgment model.

1. Overview of Three Decision-Making Models

Under the judicial/medical fact-finding model, which was used by the *Knapp* trial court, a court resolves conflicting medical testimony regarding whether a dis-abled athlete's condition creates a significant risk of substantial injury while play-ing a sport. The *Knapp* trial court judge concluded: "Congress has required a ju-dicial decision on the substantiality of the risk" and "I must consider the testimony of all the experts who testified and determine which are most persua-sive."[106] This model requires a court to determine whether there is a valid basis for medically disqualifying an athlete from participation as a matter of fact.

The athlete informed consent model permits the athlete (and his or her parents or guardian if he or she is a minor) to decide whether to participate if respectable medical authority provides clearance to play the sport. Under this model, the ath-lete is allowed to participate even if he or she has been medically disqualified by the team physician if willing to waive any potential legal claims against the educa-tional institution or sports event sponsor for injury that occurs while playing with his or her physical impairment....

....

Under the team physician model, a school has a valid legal justification, as a matter of law, for excluding an athlete who has been medically disqualified by the team physician. The school is entitled to rely on its team physician's reasonable opinion that the athlete's disability exposes him or her to a significant risk of sub-stantial injury during athletic competition, even if other physicians have provided medical clearance....

....

Each of these three models has its respective pluses and minuses. The litmus test, however, is which model best furthers Congressional intent in formulating the Rehabilitation Act, accords with Supreme Court precedent construing the Act, and furthers public policy? For the following reasons, I believe the team physician model accomplishes these objectives better than the other two models.

---

105. *Knapp*, 101 F.3d at 483.
106. 942 F. Supp. at 1196-97.

2. Judicial/Medical Fact-finding Model

The judicial/medical fact-finding model is consistent with some other cases construing the Act outside of the athletics context. These cases hold that the trial court must make a *de novo* assessment of the risk of personal injury to a disabled person. This model enables the court to disregard a reasonably conservative medical opinion disqualifying a disabled athlete to protect his or her health in favor of a more liberal medical opinion that would permit participation, contrary to the school's legitimate safety interests. In determining whether there is a significant risk of substantial harm to a disabled athlete as a matter of fact, a court would not be bound by the team physician's medical opinion.

This model, however, conflicts with Supreme Court precedent under the Act. *Davis* holds that an educational institution legally may require that its students possess "reasonable physical qualifications" in order to participate in its programs and activities.[112] It also contravenes the *Arline* holding that physically impaired persons may be legally excluded from activities "based on reasoned and medically sound judgments."[113] According to the Court, the purpose of the Act is to protect a physically impaired person "from deprivations based on prejudice, stereotypes, or unfounded fear" and to provide an opportunity to have one's condition individually evaluated in light of medical evidence."[114] The Act should not be construed to require courts to exhaust scarce judicial resources attempting to resolve an issue of medical uncertainty on which there is no consensus among medical experts.

If Congress had actually intended to limit a school's legal ability to exclude an athlete from a sport, consistent with its team physician's medical judgment, it could have established an explicit statutory framework for this purpose....

. . . .

The judicial/medical fact-finding model allows a court to substitute its judgment on medical issues for that of the team physician, which may thereby adversely affect the quality of sports medicine care rendered to athletes. The law should not create an incentive for a team physician to place greater weight on legal rather than medical considerations when evaluating athletes' physical fitness. This model encourages athletes, motivated by economic or psychological reasons, to shop for favorable opinions in order to obtain medical clearance to play a sport and facilitates second-guessing of the team physician's medical judgment. The team physician/athlete relationship is based on a trust relationship that will be seriously compromised if a court interferes with the exercise of medical judgment exercised to protect an amateur athlete's health and safety.

3. Athlete Informed Consent Model

The athlete informed consent model is based on a strong libertarian philosophy that would enable a physically impaired athlete to voluntarily assume the risk of a potentially serious injury, which is not medically certain, or even likely, to occur. This philosophy promotes individual autonomy over communality and is espoused in John Stuart Mill's seminal work ON LIBERTY..... [125]

---

112. 442 U.S. at 414.
113. 480 U.S. at 285.
114. *Arline*, 480 U.S. at 287, 289.
125. JOHN STUART MILL, ON LIBERTY (1986).

. . . .

When I initially considered this issue, I adopted a libertarian position and argued that there is no legal justification under the Act for excluding a physically impaired athlete from intercollegiate or interscholastic athletics if competent physicians have conflicting participation recommendations based on an individualized examination of the athlete and a differing evaluation of the medical risks. I asserted that, when there is no definite scientific answer or consensus among medical experts, and there are different credible conclusions regarding the medical risks of participating, a physically impaired athlete (and parents or guardian if he or she is a minor) has a legal right to choose to participate in school-sponsored athletics. Arguably, the Act's "reasonable accommodation" requirement mandates that the team or athletic event sponsor allow the athlete to choose the physician(s) whose assessment of the medical risks controls. Court-ordered athletic participation under the Act should create an implied immunity absolving a school from tort liability if an athlete suffers injury relating to or caused by one's physical abnormality.

This model embodies the philosophy that the Act prohibits a school or sponsor of an athletic event from substituting its decision for that of a fully informed athlete who chooses to participate in athletics based on credible medical clearance. The physically impaired athlete has a right to exercise his or her individual autonomy and choose to accept an enhanced, but medically uncertain risk of injury, free of a school's paternalistic concerns.

The primary weakness of the athlete informed consent model is its de-emphasis of a school's legitimate interest in protecting a physically impaired athlete's health and safety. Courts have recognized that the relationship between an educational institution and its athletes is consensual in nature. Also, *Davis* holds that a school may legally establish reasonable physical qualifications to ensure the safety standards that must be satisfied in order to participate in its programs and activities. Nevertheless, this model provides a physically impaired athlete who has been medically disqualified by the team physician with a federal right to participate in a sport if he or she is able to obtain medical clearance from another physician.

Even if one accepts Mill's libertarian view that an individual should not be prevented from engaging in activities that may endanger one's health, this philosophy does not support a construction of the Act requiring a school to involuntarily permit a medically disqualified athlete to participate in its athletic program. Properly interpreted, Mill's philosophy supports a physically impaired athlete's right to refuse medical treatment and to individually engage in athletic activities that threaten his or her health, but it does not justify requiring the sponsor of an athletics event to involuntarily provide a playing field for endangering one's personal health. For example, a long distance runner with a potentially life-threatening cardiovascular abnormality that may be aggravated by strenuous exercise cannot be forced to undergo a recommended medical procedure or prevented from running on one's own. However, he or she should not have a legal right to participate on the university's cross country team even if physically able to do so, after being medically disqualified by the team physician. Properly considered, Mill's libertarian philosophy does not affirmatively support requiring the school to allow him to participate even if other physicians provide medical clearance. A team or sponsor of an amateur athletic event should not be legally required to provide the arena for an uncontrolled medical experiment that may have tragic consequences.

4. Team Physician Medical Judgment Model

All things considered, the team physician medical judgment model strikes the appropriate balance between an amateur athlete's interest in athletic participation and the team or athletic event sponsor's interest in protecting the health and safety of participants. Under this model, an athlete receives an individualized evaluation of his or her physical condition and may be legally excluded only "based on reasoned and medically sound judgments."[133] All medically relevant factors relating to the personal health risks created by the athlete's physical impairment such as the nature, duration, probability, and severity of harm, as well as whether reasonable accommodations will effectively eliminate or safely reduce the risk of injury are considered.

Exclusion is permissible only if the court finds the team physician has a reasonable medical basis for determining that athletic competition creates a significant risk of substantial harm to a physically impaired athlete. A court is much better equipped to evaluate whether there is a reasonable basis for medically disqualifying an impaired athlete than to resolve, as a matter of fact, a medical issue when physicians have conflicting opinions. This model creates a presumption favoring the team physician, but it does not establish an irrefutable presumption that the team physician's medical judgment is correct or require a court to defer to it. For example, there may be no reasoned medical basis for excluding athletes with a missing or non-functioning paired organ from a contact sport. In this situation an athlete has the same risk of injury in terms of the probability of personal harm to a paired organ as any other participant. Although the consequences of an injury to a single eye or kidney may be more severe, protective gear or padding probably will effectively reduce this risk. This is the same result that the *Poole*, *Wright*, and *Grube* courts reached while using the athlete informed consent model. Thus, under the team physician model, athletes have a legal right to participate under the Act if there is no valid medical basis for disqualifying them.

The team physician medical judgment model best furthers the legitimate goal of enhancing the quality of sports medicine care rendered to athletes. Although one of the team physician's objectives is to avoid the unnecessary restriction of athletic activity, his or her paramount legal and ethical responsibility is to protect an athlete's health. Judicial recognition of the team physician's legal authority to medically disqualify a physically impaired athlete, without fear of unnecessary second guessing, creates a strong incentive to render high quality care to athletes.

The *Knapp* appellate court held that a team physician may rely on consensus guidelines regarding the advisability of athletic participation when an athlete has physical abnormalities. Such guidelines are particularly helpful to a physician if the medical risks of playing a sport are uncertain. As the *Knapp* appellate court explained, "[S]uch guidelines should not substitute for individualized assessment of an athlete's particular physical condition, [but] the consensus recommendations of several physicians in a certain field do carry weight" in judicial determination of whether there is a reasonable medical basis for disqualifying a physically impaired athlete.[142]

---

133. *Arline*, 480 U.S. at 285.
142. 101 F.3d at 485.

Although use of the team physician medical judgment model may preclude an athlete from engaging in competitive athletics at a particular school, it would not necessarily prevent an athlete from playing elsewhere. As the *Knapp* appellate court observed: "[On] the same facts, another team physician... might reasonably decide that Knapp met the physical qualifications for playing on an intercollegiate basketball team."[143] After losing his Rehabilitation Act suit against Northwestern University, Nick Knapp transferred to Northeastern Illinois University and received medical clearance to play college basketball.

The team physician medical judgment model places legitimate communitarian health and safety concerns above an athlete's libertarian personal autonomy interests. If all concerned parties — the athlete, team physician, and school — cannot agree on the acceptability of assuming an enhanced but medically uncertain risk on the playing field, it is better to err on the side of caution.

IV. PHYSICALLY IMPAIRED PROFESSIONAL ATHLETES' POTENTIAL CLAIMS

A disability discrimination claim brought by a professional athlete most likely would have to be asserted under the ADA because entities and organizations sponsoring professional sports generally do not receive federal funding. Depending upon the particular sport, the ADA's provisions relating to employers, public entities, or places of public accommodation, may apply. For example, a federal magistrate recently held that the Professional Golfers Association Tour is subject to the ADA in a suit brought by a physically impaired golfer seeking to ride in a golf cart in order to play professional golf.[150] Like similar claims brought by amateur athletes under the Rehabilitation Act, the key issues under the ADA are whether a professional athlete is "disabled" and whether exclusion solely because of an enhanced risk of physical harm to one's self is legally valid.

A. Exclusion from Professional Athletics as Substantially Limiting a Major Life Activity

To be protected by the ADA, a professional athlete must have a "disability," which requires proof that his or her physical impairment substantially limits a major life activity, has a record of such an impairment, or is regarded as having such an impairment. The ADA's regulations broadly define "physical impairment," which encompasses a permanent condition such as a missing or non-functioning paired organ (e.g., an eye or kidney), spinal stenosis, or a cardiovascular abnormality.[152] Although these regulations expressly list "working" as a major life activity, courts have held that the exclusion of a physically impaired person from only a particular job for a single employer or a narrow range of jobs does not substantially limit one's ability to work if he or she is eligible for other employment. For example, an individual with a physical abnormality which disqualifies him or her from a particular occupation such as a policeman, or fireman, but does not otherwise substantially limit another major life activity, is not "disabled" under the ADA.

The Equal Employment Opportunity Commission's (hereinafter "EEOC") interpretive guidelines, which accompany the ADA's regulations governing employ-

---

143. 101 F.3d at 485.
150. Martin v. PGA Tour, Inc., 984 F. Supp. 1320 (D. Or. 1998).
152. 29 C.F.R. § 1630.2 (h)(i) (1997).

ment, provide that an individual is not substantially limited in working if he or she "is unable to perform a specialized job or profession requiring extraordinary skill, prowess or talent."[156] An illustrative example is "a professional baseball pitcher who develops a bad elbow and can no longer throw a baseball."[157] The baseball player's physical impairment does not substantially limit his ability to engage in most other employment or other major life activities such as "caring for oneself, performing manual tasks, walking, seeing, hearing, speaking, breathing, [or] learning."[158] This illustration suggests that a physically impaired professional athlete is not "disabled" unless he or she proves that the impairment substantially limits a major life activity other than merely working as a professional athlete.

Strict application of the "substantially limits a major life activity" requirement can lead to the result that certain physically impaired professional athletes are covered by the ADA, whereas, others are not. For example, a blind or deaf athlete is "disabled" because either impairment substantially limits, respectively, the major life activity of either seeing or hearing. On the other hand, an athlete with spinal stenosis or a cardiovascular abnormality may not be able to prove that either medical condition substantially limits a major life activity. Yet the blind or deaf athletes are legally entitled to an individualized evaluation of their respective medical conditions, whereas, the other athletes are not. This is despite the fact that all of these athletes have the unique skills needed to play professional sports in spite of their physical impairment and are eligible for other non-athletic employment. There is no principled justification for protecting some physically impaired professional athletes under the ADA, but not others.

Even if a professional athlete's physical impairment does not actually substantially limit a major life activity, he or she should be able to show he or she is regarded as substantially limited in the major life activity of working, which is an alternative means of satisfying the ADA's definition of "disability."[160] In construing the same statutory language under the Rehabilitation Act, the Supreme Court observed that "[C]ongress acknowledged that society's accumulated myths and fears about disability and diseases are as handicapping as are the physical limitations that flow from actual impairment."[161] Therefore, the "disability" requirement is satisfied when a person is regarded as substantially limited in a major life activity, according to the Court, because "[s]uch an impairment might not diminish a person's physical or mental capabilities, but could nevertheless substantially limit that person's ability to work as a result of the negative reactions of others to the impairment."[162]

As a practical matter, a professional athlete is likely to assert an ADA claim only if the governing body for a professional sport, or all of the teams in a professional league, refuse to provide him or her with an opportunity to participate in a sport on the ground that his or her physical impairment is perceived as creating an undue risk of harm to him/herself. If a person is totally excluded from employment as a professional athlete, solely because of a fear that his or her physical im-

---

156. 29 C.F.R. § 1630, Appendix § 1630.2(j) (1997).
157. *Id.*
158. 29 C.F.R. § 1630 (i) (1997).
160. 42 U.S.C.A. § 12102(2) (1995).
161. *Arline*, 480 U.S. at 284.
162. *Id.* at 283.

pairment exposes him or her to an enhanced risk of personal injury, this effectively and substantially limits his or her ability to work because of all potential employers' negative reactions. Professional athletes train for many years to develop the specialized and unique skills necessary to earn their living. These long years of training and commitment constitute a major life activity for a professional athlete, and exclusion from a professional sport because of a perceived risk of harm to one's self substantially limits this major life activity.

The ADA's central purpose is to ensure that discrimination against a physically impaired person is medically justified based on an individualized evaluation of one's condition, rather than on an unfounded generalization or stereotype about the potential effects of a physical impairment. As a matter of policy, it is appropriate to treat all physically impaired professional athletes the same in determining whether they are protected by the ADA. Each of them should have "the opportunity to have [his or her] condition evaluated in light of medical evidence,"[166] and the federal right to participate in one's chosen profession, namely professional athletes, unless exclusion therefrom is medically justified.

B. "Otherwise Qualified" to Participate in Professional Athletics

The ADA expressly states that a "significant risk to the health and safety of others"[167] is a legitimate basis for excluding a disabled person from employment, but does not state whether a risk of harm to one's self justifies discrimination against a physically impaired employee. However, the EEOC's employment regulations interpreting the ADA provide that "a significant risk of substantial harm to the health or safety of the individual or others" justifies exclusion from employment. These regulations adopt the Supreme Court's *Arline* standard under the Rehabilitation Act, which requires an individualized medical assessment of a physically impaired person's condition in making this determination.

Courts are divided as to whether risk of harm to one's self is a legally valid basis for exclusion from employment or other activity under the ADA. In *Devlin v. Arizona Youth Soccer Association*,[171] a federal district court refused to strike a sports organization's affirmative defense that its exclusion of a youth soccer player is justified, because his participation "will pose a substantial risk of harm to him." The court allowed the soccer league to assert this defense and concluded, without elaboration, that there are unresolved issues of law and fact regarding this issue. However, in *Kohnke v Delta Airlines, Inc.*,[172] another federal district court ruled that "potential harm to a disabled person himself" is not a permissible justification for employment discrimination under the ADA. The court held that the EEOC regulation, recognizing this defense, is contrary to the ADA's express language and its legislative history.

A professional sports team or event sponsor has a legitimate interest in protecting the health and safety of all participating athletes. Absent very clear evidence that this furthers congressional intent, the ADA should not be construed to completely disregard this valid interest by refusing to recognize a defense based on a significant risk of substantial personal injury to a professional athlete. The ADA

---

166. *Arline*, 480 U.S. at 286.
167. 42 U.S.C.A. § 12113(b) and 42 U.S.C.A. § 12111(3) (1995).
171. 1996 WL 118445, at 4 (D. Ariz. 1996).
172. 932 F. Supp. 1110, 1113 (N.D. Ill. 1996).

should not be judicially construed to provide an absolute right for a professional athlete to participate in a sport, even if he or she is unable to obtain medical clearance from any competent physician, including the one(s) of his or her choosing.

Unlike an amateur athlete, however, a professional athlete should not be bound by the team physician's medical judgment, regarding whether the athlete's physical impairment creates exposure to a significant risk of substantial personal harm. A professional athlete has a greater interest in pursuing his or her livelihood, with its potential multi-million dollar earning potential, than an amateur athlete does in participating in sports as part of the educational process or for other personal objectives. Even though sponsors of amateur and professional sports both have a legitimate interest in protecting the health and safety of participants, a professional athlete's participation interests are entitled to more weight than those of an amateur athlete. Because exclusion from a professional sport has some significant adverse consequences to an athlete, he or she should be permitted to obtain second opinions regarding the medical risks of participation with his or her impairment.

I propose adopting the athlete informed consent model for professional athletes, which would enable a professional athlete to choose to participate, despite medical disqualification by the team physician, if other competent medical authority clears him or her to play. Under this model, a physically impaired professional athlete has a legal right to choose to participate in a sport only if there is respected medical authority clearing him or her to do so. A professional athlete would not be conclusively bound by the team physician's recommendation that he or she be medically disqualified, but rather may select the physician(s) whose determination of the medical risks of playing a sport with his or her physical impairment would be controlling. For example, although they were precluded from playing intercollegiate sports under the team physician medical judgment model, the ADA would provide Nicholas Knapp and Alani Pahulu with an opportunity to participate in professional sports, under the athlete informed consent model, because respected medical authority cleared them to participate.

Under my proposed athlete informed consent model, a court's role would be to ensure that there is a reasonable medical basis for clearing a physically impaired professional athlete to participate in a sport. The court should not resolve conflicting testimony by medical experts as a matter of fact, but should limit its judicial inquiry to whether medical clearance of a professional athlete is "individualized, reasonably made, and based upon competent evidence as a matter of law."[177] If so, a professional athlete is permitted to participate if he or she chooses to assume the risk of future personal injury resulting from his or her physical impairment while playing the sport. The team or sponsoring entity should be immunized from tort liability for allowing a physically impaired professional athlete to choose to participate under these circumstances.

V. CONCLUSION

Determining whether a physically impaired athlete has a legal right under the Rehabilitation Act or ADA, to participate in a sport or athletic event, despite an enhanced risk of personal harm requires consideration of both the athlete's liber-

---

177. This standard of review is the same as that used by the *Knapp* appellate court in applying the team physician medical judgment model. 101 F.3d at 485.

tarian autonomy interest in participating and the athletic event sponsor's communitarian interest in protecting the athlete from an unreasonable risk of injury. Each side's interests are legitimate, but neither side's rights are absolute. I believe that the team physician medical judgment model best balances these respective interests in the context of amateur athletics whereas, the athlete informed consent model most appropriately balances these interests in the context of professional athletics, because professional athletes have a more substantial interest in participating in sports than do amateur athletes.

4. Antitrust Challenges

James V. Koch, The Economic Realities of Amateur Sports Organization
61 Indiana Law Journal 9 (1985)*

....

I. INTERCOLLEGIATE ATHLETICS AS AN INDUSTRY

A rough, but usable, definition of an industry is that it is a collection of firms, each of which is supplying products that have considerable substitutability to the same potential buyers. The firms in the intercollegiate athletic industry are the individual colleges and universities that field athletic teams. From an economic standpoint, these "university-firms"' are primarily involved in the selling of athletic entertainment to potential fans and ticket purchasers. In addition, there exists the belief that the university-firms are supplying, via their athletic teams, intangibles such as pride and identification to alumni, legislators, and friends of the institution who might reward or support the institution. In addition, the university-firms in recent years have also been actively engaged in selling to radio and television networks the rights to broadcast or televise the intercollegiate athletic contests in which their teams compete.

Some of the inputs to this multiproduct productive process involve capital: stadiums, equipment, and the like. But the most crucial inputs to the production of intercollegiate athletics are people: the coaches, athletic directors and especially the student-athletes who play on the teams that the university-firms field. The key to understanding the development of modern intercollegiate athletics is an understanding of the competition for, and use of, inputs such as student-athletes. The development of the NCAA as the largest regulatory body in intercollegiate athletics has primarily come about because most university-firms have desired to limit competition between themselves concerning how they may hire and utilize their student-athlete inputs. The NCAA has written hundreds of detailed rules and regulations that circumscribe the conditions under which an individual university-firm may contact, visit, compete for, hire, and eventually use student-athlete inputs. The genesis of these rules has nearly always been a desire on the part of the

---

university-firms to restrict the competition for, and use of, student-athlete in-puts....

George Kokkines, Note, Sherman Act Invalidation of the NCAA Amateurism Rules
105 Harvard Law Review 1299 (1992)*

.... The NCAA regulates college sports by promulgating and enforcing bylaws that all member institutions and their athletes must obey.

Among the most important of these bylaws to student-athletes are the amateurism rules. College athletes who receive compensation beyond tuition and room and board for their participation in a particular sport lose college eligibility in that sport. In addition, an athlete loses eligibility in a sport if he submits his name for inclusion in that sport's professional league draft or if he consults an agent. Specifically, the "no-draft" rule provides that:

> An individual loses amateur status in a particular sport when the individual asks to be placed on the draft list or supplemental draft list of a professional league in that sport, even though: (a) The individual asks that his or her name be withdrawn from the draft list prior to the actual draft, (b) The individual's name remains on the list but he or she is not drafted, or (c) The individual is drafted but does not sign an agreement with any professional athletics team.[5]

The "no-agent" rule disqualifies an athlete in a particular sport if the athlete has ever "agreed (orally or in writing) to be represented by an agent for the purpose of marketing his or her athletics ability or reputation in that sport."

This Note argues that these amateurism rules violate section 1 of the Sherman Antitrust Act. Through the NCAA, colleges and universities have banded together to fix the amount of compensation they will pay college athletes and to boycott those athletes who attempt to ascertain the market value of their skills by consulting agents or entering professional league drafts. The NCAA's "limited compensation" rule denies student-athletes a fair share of the revenues they generate for their schools. The no-draft and no-agent rules restrain player mobility by discouraging athletes from testing the professional players' markets before their college eligibility expires.

The courts have refused to invalidate the no-draft, no-agent, and limited compensation rules. Some courts have ruled that, because the NCAA is a nonprofit organization and because it claims that its amateurism rules are not commercially motivated, antitrust law simply does not apply.[8] The majority of recent cases, however, have assumed that the amateurism rules are subject to antitrust scrutiny and have analyzed their reasonableness under the Sherman Act; in each of these

---

5. NCAA bylaw 12.2.4.2, *reprinted in* NCAA MANUAL, *supra* note 2, at 61.

8. *See* Gaines v. NCAA, 746 F. Supp. 738, 743-44 (M.D. Tenn. 1990) (holding that the Sherman Act does not apply to the NCAA's no-draft and no-agent rules because the rules are intended to preserve competition among student-athletes rather than to advance commercial goals).

cases, the NCAA's rules have been upheld.[9] Most significantly, the Supreme Court in *NCAA v. Board of Regents of the University of Oklahoma*[10] held that NCAA actions are subject to antitrust scrutiny and should be analyzed under the "rule of reason," which requires the Court to determine the restraint's "impact on competition." NCAA rules should be upheld if they increase economic marketplace competition by preserving the distinct product of college sports. In dicta, the Court indicated that the limited compensation bylaw enhances competition because it purportedly advances the noble tradition of amateurism — the notion that college athletes should participate in sports for the love of the game and not for compensation. The Court believed that this ideal is necessary to preserve intercollegiate athletics.

Lower federal courts have cited this dicta in upholding the no-draft, no-agent, and limited compensation rules.[14] These courts, however, have overlooked a vital point: the reality of college sports does not conform to the ideal of amateurism. This Note argues that, in practice, the defining characteristic of intercollegiate athletics is merely the college attendance of all its athletes. The requirements that college athletes not receive compensation or have contacts with agents or professional leagues are based on the outdated ideal of amateurism that is in no way necessary to the product of college sports. Courts should thus invalidate these rules as clear restraints of trade in the market for the skills of student-athletes.

. . . .

I. ANTITRUST CHALLENGES TO THE NCAA AMATEURISM RULES

Over the past three decades, college athletes have brought several suits challenging the no-draft, no-agent, and limited compensation bylaws as violations of the antitrust laws. Courts have rejected all of these challenges. A representative recent case is *Banks v. NCAA*,[16] in which a former college football player at the University of Notre Dame sought to invalidate the no-draft and no-agent rules. In 1990, with one year of college eligibility remaining, Braxston Banks entered the National Football League (NFL) player draft and hired an agent to assist him in his dealings with NFL teams. Although no professional team chose Banks in the draft and although he received no compensation from any team or agent except for travel expenses, the NCAA declared him ineligible to play college football. Banks sued for a preliminary injunction against both the NCAA and Notre Dame to prevent enforcement of the no-draft and no-agent rules.

Banks argued that the no-draft and no-agent rules violate section 1 of the Sherman Act because they constitute concerted boycotts of his football skills by NCAA institutions and restrict his mobility in the football players' market. In

---

9. *See* McCormack v. NCAA, 845 F.2d 1338, 1343-45 (5th Cir. 1988) (holding that NCAA restrictions on athlete compensation do not violated antitrust laws; *see also* Banks v. NCAA, 746 F. Supp. 850, 858-62 (N.D. Ind. 1990) (denying a plaintiff's motion for preliminary injunction on the grounds that the plaintiff, a college football player, had failed to demonstrate a reasonable likelihood of success on his claim that the no-draft and no-agent rules violate antitrust laws), *appeal docketed*, No. S91-1666 (7th Cir. Mar. 27, 1991).

10. 468 U.S. 85 (1984).

14. *See e.g.*, McCormack v. NCAA, 845 F.2d 1338, 1344 (5th Cir. 1988); Banks v. NCAA, 746 F. Supp. 850, 856-62 (N.D. Ind. 1990).

16. 746 F. Supp. 850 (N.D. Ind. 1990), *appeal docketed*, No. S91- 1666 (7th Cir. Mar. 27, 1991).

support of his claims, Banks argued that few players will enter the draft before their college eligibility expires for fear of not being chosen by a professional team and then not being allowed to return to college football. According to Banks' brief for his pending appeal, "if the NCAA's rules render [college athletes] ineligible, they will lose their lucrative athletic scholarships, and, in all probability, forfeit any chance to play professionally because they will have lost the necessary forum of intercollegiate athletics in which to exhibit their talents." In addition, he asserted that the no-agent rule prevents an athlete from obtaining the advice and information necessary to make an intelligent decision whether to enter a professional league draft.

The court found that Banks had not shown a likelihood of succeeding on his antitrust claim and denied his request for a preliminary injunction. Holding that the NCAA bylaws are subject to antitrust scrutiny, the court examined the no-draft and no-agent rules under the rule of reason, which requires a court to invalidate practices that decrease competition in the economic marketplace. Under rule of reason analysis, the extent of the defendant's market power — its "ability to raise prices above the competitive level by restricting output" — is a threshold issue. The court found no evidence that the bylaws at issue affected the salaries the NFL pays to incoming athletes or the value of scholarships that colleges award to student-athletes.

The court then held that, even assuming the NCAA had significant market power, Banks had failed to prove that the harmful effects of the no-draft and no-agent rules outweighed their beneficial effects on competition. Although the court agreed that the bylaws harmed Banks by excluding him from the college football market, it nonetheless accepted the NCAA's contention that the rules "have the procompetitive effect of promoting the integrity and quality of college football." The court concluded that the "concept of amateurism is no less central to the concept of amateur college football than are the modest propositions that an athlete must enroll in the college for which he wishes to play, attend classes, and maintain a minimal academic standing."

Similarly, the limited compensation bylaw was recently upheld against an attack under the Sherman Act in *McCormack v. NCAA*.[30] In that case, a lawyer-alumnus of Southern Methodist University (SMU) brought a class action suit on behalf of SMU alumni, football players, and cheerleaders against the NCAA for its suspension of SMU's football team from intercollegiate competition as punishment for the team's violations of NCAA restrictions on student-athlete compensation. The court rejected the plaintiffs' claims that the compensation restrictions constitute price fixing and that the suspension was an illegal boycott of SMU by the NCAA. The court assumed that the NCAA bylaws were subject to antitrust scrutiny, and held that the compensation restrictions were reasonable, and thus not in violation of the Sherman Act, because they create "the product [of college football] and allow its survival in the face of commercializing pressures."

II. THE NO-DRAFT, NO-AGENT, AND LIMITED COMPENSATION RULES VIOLATE SECTION 1 OF THE SHERMAN ACT

Contrary to these court decisions, the no-draft, no-agent, and limited compensation rules are unreasonable restraints of trade. This Part describes why antitrust

---

30. 845 F.2d 1338 (5th Cir. 1988).

law applies to the amateurism rules. It also analyzes the rule of reason framework the Supreme Court used in *Board of Regents* to determine the antitrust implications of NCAA action and argues that, under this framework, the courts have erred in upholding the no-draft, no-agent, and limited compensation rules. Specifically, the courts have failed to acknowledge the distinction between the ideal of amateurism and the reality of college athletics. Because the amateurism rules do not foster and promote the actual product of college sports, courts should invalidate them under section 1 of the Sherman Act.

Regardless of this Note's analysis, courts will probably continue to be wary of striking down the NCAA's amateurism regulations. According to one judge, "[i]t is not judicial business to tell a voluntary athletic association how best to formulate or enforce its rules."[35] Courts will be particularly hesitant to invalidate the limited compensation rule in the face of Supreme Court dicta describing the rule as essential to intercollegiate sports. Because the no-draft and no-agent rules are not as central to amateurism (the notion to which courts have paid homage) as the limited compensation bylaw, courts will presumably be less hesitant to strike down the no-draft and no-agent rules. This Part thus applies one approach to challenge the no-draft and no-agent bylaws, and a different approach to challenge the limited compensation rule. This will allow courts, if they so desire, to invalidate the former two rules while leaving the latter one intact.

A. *The Amateurism Rules Are Subject to Antitrust Scrutiny*

The NCAA's nonprofit status and the contention that the amateurism rules are unmotivated by commercial concerns do not shield the rules from antitrust scrutiny. For example, in *Goldfarb v. Virginia State Bar*,[38] the Court struck down a state bar association's rules that imposed minimum fee schedules for certain legal services on the grounds that "[t]he nature of an occupation, standing alone, does not provide sanctuary from the Sherman Act, nor is the public service aspect of professional practice controlling in determining whether § 1 includes professions." The Court rejected the bar association's argument that its conduct was exempt from antitrust scrutiny because of its nonprofit status or because of its focus on the noncommercial goal of regulating the ethics of the legal profession. Similarly, although the NCAA is a nonprofit organization, and although it may claim that its amateurism rules are not commercially motivated, its rules are nonetheless subject to antitrust law.

The Supreme Court's decision in *Board of Regents* confirms that the amateurism bylaws are subject to antitrust scrutiny. The *Board of Regents* Court found that NCAA restrictions regarding the number of football telecasts and the prices networks would pay the NCAA for the right to televise the games violated section 1 of the Sherman Act. In dicta, however, the Court indicated that some NCAA rules may be procompetitive. One court incorrectly understood this to mean that the amateurism rules are immune from antitrust scrutiny. However, instead of shielding the rules from the antitrust laws, the Court merely indicated that many NCAA actions might be procompetitive because they might be necessary to preserve the product of college sports. Therefore, instead of applying the per se rules against price fixing and boycotts, courts should analyze the various rules' effects in the marketplace

---

35. Shelton v. NCAA, 539 F.2d 1197, 1198 (9th Cir. 1976).
38. 421 U.S. 773 (1975).

under the rule of reason. The Court did not immunize any NCAA bylaws from antitrust analysis just because the rules purport to foster noncommercial goals.

B. *Defining the Rule of Reason in the Context of the NCAA Amateurism Rules*

Courts have analyzed the antitrust implications of the NCAA bylaws under the rule of reason. Under this rule, a court must determine the effects of the particular restraint in the relevant product market; if the restraint on balance increases economic competition, the court will uphold it. The Supreme Court applied this standard to NCAA action in *Board of Regents*, in which it held that it would be inappropriate to find the NCAA telecast rules per se illegal because college football is an "industry in which horizontal restraints on competition are essential if the product is to be available at all."[50] The Court stressed that "the NCAA plays a vital role in enabling college football to preserve its character, and as a result enables a product to be marketed which might otherwise be unavailable." Therefore, the Court examined the particular competitive effects of the telecast restrictions before finding that they violated the Sherman Act.

According to the rule of reason analysis propounded in *Board of Regents*, an NCAA rule is procompetitive if it is a "justifiable means of fostering competition among amateur athletic teams" and therefore "enhance[s] public interest in intercollegiate athletics." In other words, an NCAA bylaw will withstand antitrust attack if it is "tailored to the goal" of preserving the "product" of college sports in the economic marketplace. In suggesting that the limited compensation rule is procompetitive, the Court argued that:

> the NCAA seeks to market a particular brand of football — college football. The identification of this "product" with an academic tradition...makes it more popular than professional sports to which it might otherwise be comparable, such as, for example, minor league baseball. In order to preserve the character and quality of the "product," athletes must not be paid, must be required to attend class, and the like.[54]

The Court's analysis purports to look only at the marketplace effects of the challenged activity, and not at possible non-economic justifications for NCAA action.

The *Board of Regents* Court incorrectly deferred to the NCAA's self- interested definition of its product. As a result, rule of reason analyses of NCAA amateurism rules have become toothless. The Court's deference to the NCAA's description of college sports makes the product-promotion rationale circular — a defendant can call any of its activities procompetitive if it can argue that the activity in question is essential to the product which it defines. *Board of Regents* thus demonstrates the importance of the product definition. Working within the prevailing rule of reason formulation, the task is to define the *actual* attributes of the product of college sports and to determine whether the bylaws at issue preserve *those* attributes. The remainder of this Note attempts to do just that by defining the actual product of intercollegiate athletics. As this Note demonstrates, college sports in practice is distinct from amateurism, the ideal the NCAA uses to justify the no-draft, no-agent, and limited compensation bylaws.

---

50. *Board of Regents*, 468 U.S. at 101.
54. *Id*. at 101-02.

C. *The No-Draft, No-Agent, and Limited Compensation Rules Are Unreasonable Under the* Board of Regents *Test*

This section first argues that a plaintiff who challenges NCAA action satisfies the market power requirement of the rule of reason. It then argues that the no-draft and no-agent bylaws are not "tailored to the goal" of promoting the product of college sports, and on separate grounds, that the limited compensation bylaw is also not necessary to preserve intercollegiate athletics.

1. Market Power. — Many courts have required the plaintiff in cases applying the rule of reason to prove that the defendant has market power — the ability to affect the market price for the relevant product. In *Banks*, the court defined the NCAA's market power as the ability of the organization to affect the price its members or professional teams pay for the services of student-athletes. Although the court found no direct link between the market price for college athletes and the no-draft and no-agent bylaws, it presumed that the requisite amount of power existed: "the NCAA and its member institutions have near-total control of the market of college players; such control might be deemed to provide more than adequate market share to constitute market power."[59] Regardless of any discernible effect on market price, the NCAA has market power because it controls virtually all intercollegiate sports competition in the United States.

Furthermore, the amateurism bylaws *do* directly affect the market compensation of athletes. Because college athletes may lose their eligibility, the no-draft and no-agent rules deter them from determining their value to professional teams. These rules also affect the terms of contracts between professional teams and student-athletes who decide to forego eligibility and enter a professional league draft or consult an agent. An athlete who has foregone his eligibility, and must therefore either accept the professional team's offer or not play at all, has less bargaining leverage than an athlete who could threaten to return to college sports. Additionally, the limited compensation bylaw restricts competition among universities in their recruitment of student-athletes because it limits price competition; student-athletes receive less compensation for playing sports than if the limited compensation rule did not exist.

In any event, where the defendant's activity is a clear market restraint, courts have ruled that the plaintiff need not prove market power. According to *Board of Regents*, "when there is an agreement not to compete in terms of price or output, 'no elaborate industry analysis is required to demonstrate the anticompetitive character of such an agreement.'"[62] The television limitation plan at issue in *Board of Regents* was "inconsistent with the Sherman Act's command that price and supply be responsive to consumer preference"; in such a case the Supreme Court has "never required proof of market power." Similarly, the NCAA amateurism bylaws, by their nature, affect compensation paid to athletes. Courts should therefore permit plaintiffs to challenge the NCAA amateurism rules without explicitly proving market power.

2. The No-Draft and No-Agent Rules Do Not Promote the Product of College Sports. — Although the NCAA insists that its no-draft and no-agent bylaws are indispensable to the maintenance of its unique product of intercollegiate athletics,

---

59. *Id.* at 860.

62. *Board of Regents*, 468 U.S. at 109 (quoting National Soc'y of Professional Eng'rs v. United States, 435 U.S. 679, 692 (1978)).

because they prevent student-athlete contacts with agents and professional teams, other NCAA bylaws belie this argument. NCAA rules allow a college athlete to "inquire of a professional sports organization about eligibility for a professional-league player draft or request information about the individual's market value without affecting his or her amateur status."[65] Recently, the NCAA decided to allow student-athletes who have neither been drafted nor retained agents to negotiate with professional teams to determine their market values and still keep their NCAA eligibility as long as they do not sign with a professional team. NCAA rules also allow student-athletes to practice with professional teams as long as they do not play in professional games, accept payment, or sign professional contracts. Most importantly, if a professional league drafts any student without that student affirmatively requesting to be placed in the draft, the student remains eligible to play college sports. Both Major League Baseball and the National Hockey League allow their teams to draft college athletes without the athletes' explicit consent. Professional teams have thus drafted many college baseball and hockey players who continue to participate in college athletics. Given the range of contacts the NCAA permits student-athletes to have with agents and professional teams, the NCAA can hardly justify its no-draft and no-agent rules by claiming that such contacts somehow taint college athletes or destroy the NCAA's unique product in the economic marketplace.

Although the no-draft and no-agent rules do little to protect the viability of intercollegiate athletics, they do much to prevent college athletes from testing the professional players' market. The rules inhibit a student-athlete from entering a professional league draft and thereby determining professional teams' interest in his skills, for fear that he might not be drafted and then not be allowed to return to college sports. Likewise, the no-agent rule limits an athlete's ability to negotiate a fair deal with a professional team. Although other NCAA bylaws allow student-athlete contacts with professional teams, these bylaws are not broad enough to ensure that athletes can assess their own fair values in the professional markets.

The no-draft and no-agent rules also deserve little judicial deference from a policy standpoint because they mainly harm individual student-athletes who do not participate in the creation, implementation, or enforcement of the rules. The main benefactors of these rules are the NCAA member institutions, who employ the rules to prevent student-athletes from leaving college sports. Lack of student participation in rule formulation and enforcement is especially harmful because the NCAA controls virtually all intercollegiate athletics. Judicial invalidation of the no-draft and no-agent rules would help redress this imbalance of power between the NCAA and student-athletes and would vindicate the student's interest in retaining college eligibility.

3. The Limited Compensation Rule Does Not Promote the Product of College Sports. — The limited compensation rule is not tailored to the goal of promoting intercollegiate athletics because many NCAA institutions frequently violate the rule. The public knows these violations occur, but the product of college sports in the economic marketplace continues to increase in popularity. As one commentator has noted, "[i]t would be naive to suppose that simply the pretense of main-

---

65. NCAA bylaw 12.2.4.1, *reprinted in* NCAA Manual, *supra* note 2, at 61.

taining the amateur ideal is essential to continuing the current system."[75] In a recent example of college noncompliance with the limited compensation rule, a former football player at Auburn University claimed that his teammates had received frequent payments from university alumni and from the coaching staff. The NCAA uncovered similar violations by Southern Methodist University's football program during the 1980s. Over the past decade, at least 57% of the 106 NCAA Division I-A football teams—the "big-time" football programs — violated the limited compensation rule. Also, from 1952 to 1985, the NCAA imposed sanctions on thirty of thirty-three Division I national championship basketball programs for violating its amateurism rules.

Despite widespread violations of the NCAA's limited compensation rule, the NCAA's product continues to flourish in the economic marketplace. Consumer demand for college sports does not decline when violations of the rule are exposed. Rather, the quality of the sports programs and the athletes' affiliations with educational institutions appear to be the only two factors that affect consumer demand for college sports. In some instances in which the NCAA sanctioned universities for violating amateurism bylaws, popular demand and support for the particular sports programs actually increased.

Additionally, the limited compensation bylaw, like the no-draft and no-agent bylaws, does not promote college athletics because the NCAA bylaws themselves do not espouse a pure ethic of unpaid athletic participation. Universities compensate student-athletes who participate in intercollegiate sports with tuition and room and board payments. These in-kind benefits can be worth well over ten thousand dollars per year. A college athlete can also be a professional in one sport (and thus be paid to play that sport) and still retain college eligibility in another sport. In essence, the reality of college-athlete compensation undercuts the principle of amateurism.

General norms of fairness support this Note's conclusion that courts should invalidate the limited compensation bylaw under the rule of reason. This bylaw is in clear conflict with the NCAA's alleged purpose to protect college athletes from "exploitation by professional and commercial enterprises."[84] To the extent that member institutions comply with it, the limited compensation rule exploits many student-athletes by denying them a larger share of the revenues generated by their efforts. The NCAA estimates that sports revenues at Division IA schools exceed one billion dollars per year. Student-athletes would receive a much fairer share of the revenues in a system without the limited compensation rule than in a system with under-the-table payments and sometimes-enforced compensation restraints. The rule of reason analysis described above allows courts to reject the NCAA's self-interested definition of amateurism, to reveal the hypocrisy of the present system of frequent noncompliance, and to vindicate the student's interest in retaining eligibility.

III. POSSIBLE EFFECTS OF ELIMINATING THE NO-DRAFT, NO-AGENT, AND LIMITED COMPENSATION RULES

Elimination of the no-draft, no-agent, and limited compensation rules will decrease the exploitation of college athletes without inhibiting the NCAA's market-

---

75. Sharon E. Rush, *Touchdowns, Toddlers and Taboos: On Paying College Athletes and Surrogate Contract Mothers*, 31 ARIZ. L. REV. 549, 587 (1988).

84. NCAA CONST., art 2.6, *reprinted in* NCAA MANUAL, *supra* note 2, at 4.

ing of the product of college sports. If the specified NCAA bylaws were eliminated, universities could compete for the services of athletes by offering compensation packages. Student-athletes would be able to test the professional players' market. Moreover, the hypocrisy of the amateurism rules' existence within the billion dollar business of college sports would be eliminated. Proponents of the amateurism rules, however, have argued that paying athletes will lead to the elimination of academic requirements for student-athletes and harm non-revenue-producing sports. This Part responds to these concerns.

A. *Effect on NCAA Academic Eligibility Rules*

....

NCAA bylaws establishing minimum academic standards for athletes would likely withstand antitrust scrutiny because they are more closely related to the product of intercollegiate athletics than are the no-draft, no-agent, and limited compensation bylaws. Intercollegiate athletics appeal to consumers precisely because the athletes are students at a given school. To the extent that minimum academic standards ensure that athletes retain their student status, the rules promote the unique product of college sports. Courts could thus uphold these academic eligibility rules as serving procompetitive ends.

Courts that invalidate the limited compensation rule on the grounds that the rule does not promote college sports may, however, feel compelled to strike down the academic rules on the same grounds. Just as many universities violate the limited compensation rule, they frequently disregard NCAA academic bylaws. Courts could therefore conclude that neither rule is essential to the product of intercollegiate sports and simply invalidate both. Perhaps the only way a court could shield the academic rules from antitrust scrutiny while striking down the limited compensation rule would be to create an exemption for the academic standards based on a policy of fostering academic values in sports programs. Such an exemption would go beyond the product-promotion rationale of *Board of Regents*.

Assuming that the NCAA academic bylaws withstand antitrust attack, judicial invalidation of the amateurism principle may actually allow the NCAA to place more emphasis on academic values in its members' sports programs. Resources no longer spent policing infractions of the amateurism rules could instead be used to monitor and support athletes' academic progress....

B. *Effect On College Athletic Programs*

Elimination of the limited compensation rule will not mean that all colleges and universities will pay their athletes. Smaller colleges that do not compete with the prominent athletic programs, as well as colleges that cannot afford to compete for top players, would still be free to create programs that are amateur in nature. These colleges could form separate leagues. An increase in the number of athletic conferences would promote competition by increasing consumer choice.

If colleges do pay some revenue-producing athletes, they will have less money to fund the non-revenue-producing sports. Athletic compensation could be quite high, given that competitive bidding for high school athletes without the restraints of the amateurism rules may be intense. Colleges may eliminate scholarships to non-revenue producing-athletes or disband certain sports programs altogether. Elimination of non-revenue-producing sports would especially harm women because their sports fall disproportionately into the non-revenue category.

Invalidation of the limited compensation bylaw, however, need not have these adverse consequences. It is possible that universities, instead of eliminating non-revenue sports, will reduce the number of players receiving scholarships in revenue-producing sports, compensate only the star athletes, or cut salaries paid to coaching staffs. Thus, it is not certain that abolishing the limited compensation rule will automatically decrease the amount of money available to non-revenue-producing athletics. Moreover, the Civil Rights Restoration Act of 1987, which extended title IX protections against gender discrimination to all programs of an educational institution that receives federal aid, would presumably prohibit extreme disparities between women's and men's sports programs. The Office of Civil Rights, which is responsible for enforcing title IX, has indicated that equality requires equal opportunities for men and women, although not necessarily identical expenditures.

Regardless of the effects on non-revenue sports, the current redistribution from revenue-producing to non-revenue-producing sports exploits the athletes who bring in large sums of money for colleges and universities. As one commentator has argued,

> [t]here is no reason student-athletes should be the ones to provide the subsidies necessary to operate the non-revenue producing sports. Rather, the revenues should be raised by donations from those who are interested in the sport, alumni contributions, increases in tuition or taxpayer assessments.[101]

Thus, while elimination of some non-revenue sports would be unfortunate, it is more unfortunate to have them supported by profits unfairly extracted from the labor of other athletes.

IV. CONCLUSION

The no-draft, no-agent, and limited compensation rules are agreements among NCAA member institutions to prevent price competition for student-athletes and to boycott illegally athletes who attempt to pursue careers in professional sports before their eligibility expires. As a result of these rules, student-athletes are denied a fair share of the profits generated by their efforts and are inhibited from testing the professional players' market. Courts have wrongly deferred to the amateurism bylaws and to the NCAA's definition of the product of intercollegiate athletics. The NCAA's claim of the need to promote amateurism is merely a pretense; the NCAA bylaws themselves do not adhere to a pure notion of amateurism, and colleges and universities frequently violate the limited compensation bylaw. Under a meaningful rule of reason analysis, courts should invalidate these particular rules as unreasonable restraints of trade. An ideal that is not adhered to, either in the rules or in practice, cannot be necessary to promote the product of intercollegiate athletics.

---

101. Goldman, *supra* note 37, at 247.

Gary R. Roberts, The NCAA, Antitrust, and Consumer Welfare
70 Tulane Law Review 2631 (1996)*

I. INTRODUCTION

In May of 1995, a United States District Court in Kansas City held in *Law v. National Collegiate Athletic Ass'n*[1] that National Collegiate Athletic Association (NCAA) By-law 11.02.3 violated section 1 of the Sherman Act. By-law 11.02.3 had limited the salary that a restricted earnings coach (an REC) at an NCAA member institution could earn in a year to $16,000. This rule had been adopted by the NCAA membership at its January 1991 convention, pursuant to recommendations made by an ad-hoc Cost Containment Committee, as part of a larger overall effort to reduce the spiraling costs of intercollegiate athletics that was allegedly putting significant financial pressures on many member schools.

This decision is potentially very significant and deserves careful scrutiny because, unless it is regarded by future courts reviewing other NCAA rules as aberrational or narrowly limited to its facts, it could establish a precedent whose application threatens the entire structure of intercollegiate sports. And even if *Law* is narrowly applied in the future, it will surely be cause for the college sports power structure to pause and consider carefully its antitrust risks—not only in adopting rules that might be legally problematic themselves, but also in "restructuring" the NCAA in a way that will increase the apparent, if not actual, emphasis on commercialism in Division I intercollegiate athletics at the relative expense of amateur and academic ideals.

II. CHOOSING THE RULE OF REASON STANDARD

Because the REC salary rule fixed a maximum price that an NCAA Division I member could pay for its fourth basketball coach (men's and women's), the plaintiffs argued that the rule should be struck down as per se illegal price fixing under the authority of the Supreme Court's landmark decision in *United States v. Socony-Vacuum Oil Co.*[5] However, citing the Supreme Court's more recent decision in *NCAA v. Board of Regents*,[6] as well as *Broadcast Music, Inc. v. Columbia Broadcasting System, Inc.*,[7] Judge Vratil followed the judicial trend since the mid-1970s of eschewing per se invalidation, noting that due to the inherent need for NCAA members to establish some rules in order to achieve the organization's lawful goals, courts cannot conclude that any NCAA rule is of a type that would "'almost always tend to restrict competition.'"[8] In so ruling, the court quoted language from *Board of Regents* that is crucial for the NCAA's ability to defend its very existence: "'A myriad of rules affecting such matters as the size of the field, the number of players on a team, and the extent to which physical violence is to

---

* Originally published in 70 Tul. L. Rev. 2631-2674 (1996). Reprinted with permission of the Tulane Law Review Association, which holds the copyright. All rights reserved.
    1. 902 F. Supp. 1394 (D. Kan. 1995).
    5. 310 U.S. 150 (1940).
    6. 468 U.S. 85 (1984).
    7. 441 U.S. 1 (1979).
    8. Law v. NCAA, 902 F. Supp. 1394, 1402 (D. Kan. 1995) (quoting *Broadcast Music*, 441 U.S. at 19-20).

be encouraged or proscribed, all must be agreed upon, and all restrain the manner in which institutions compete.' "[9]

Of course, this observation is self-evident—that in order to have an "athletic competition" entertainment product, all of the participating teams must agree to the basic rules of the game on the field or court itself. It is unlikely that anyone would seriously allege that "agreements" by members of an athletic organization defining the shape and size of playing venues, the required equipment, or the rules for the conduct of the game itself would pose antitrust questions. But Judge Vratil then went on to quote further, less intuitively obvious dictum from *Board of Regents*:

> "Moreover, the NCAA seeks to market a particular brand of [sports]—college [sports]. The identification of this 'product' with an academic tradition differentiates college [sports] from and makes [them] more popular than professional sports to which [they] might otherwise be comparable.... In order to preserve the character and quality of the 'product,' athletes must not be paid, must be required to attend class, and the like. And the integrity of the 'product' cannot be preserved except by mutual agreement; if an institution adopted such restrictions unilaterally, its effectiveness as a competitor on the playing field might soon be destroyed. Thus, the NCAA plays a vital role in enabling college [sports] to preserve [their] character, and as a result enables a product to be marketed which might otherwise be unavailable."[11]

From this, it appears that the Supreme Court and Judge Vratil believe that most of the NCAA's incredibly large and complex network of rules is procompetitive, on balance, and thus justifiable under the rule of reason, because they preserve the features of amateurism and academic orientation that purportedly define the unique nature of the NCAA members' sports product. It is this premise that this Essay explores in Part IV. First, however, Part III reviews how Judge Vratil applied the rule of reason specifically to the salary cap placed on RECs.

III. RESTRICTED COACHES' EARNINGS AND THE RULE OF REASON

One useful aspect of Judge Vratil's opinion in *Law* is that it laid out very clearly the stages of and burdens involved in a proper rule of reason analysis. Despite her ritualistic incantation of the hopelessly overgeneralized and virtually meaningless statement of the rule of reason set forth in the *Chicago Board of Trade* decision,[14] Judge Vratil extracted her rule of reason directly from the Third Circuit's decision in *United States v. Brown University*,[15] which involves three stages. First, the plaintiff has the burden of establishing the prima facie case (*i.e.*, of proving that the restraint in question creates significant anticompetitive effects in one or more relevant markets). Second, once the prima facie case is made, the burden shifts to the defendant to establish significant procompetitive benefits flowing from the restraint on one or more related relevant markets (but not necessarily the same market(s) identified in the plaintiff's case)—a burden which if not arguably met may result in a judgment as a matter of law for the plaintiff. Third,

---

9. *Id.* at 1403 (quoting *Board of Regents*, 468 U.S. at 101).

11. 902 F. Supp. at 1403 (quoting *Board of Regents*, 468 U.S. at 101-02).

14. Board of Trade v. United States, 246 U.S. 231, 238 (1918).

15. 5 F.3d 658, 668-69 (3rd Cir. 1993).

if the defendant does establish evidence of sufficient procompetitive benefits, then the burden shifts back again to the plaintiff to show that comparable procompetitive benefits could be achieved through viable, less anticompetitive means.

While this statement of the rule of reason methodology is very general and leaves many important issues unanswered, it was sufficient to provide a framework for determining that the REC salary-cap rule was a violation of section 1 of the Sherman Act as a matter of law.

A. The Substantial Anticompetitive Effects

That the REC salary-cap rule has significant anticompetitive effects in the labor market in which basketball coaches sell their services is self-evident, and Judge Vratil essentially so found. The NCAA's contrary argument was that the anticompetitive effects were *de minimis* because RECs could avoid the effect of the rule by taking coaching jobs with basketball teams other than at Division I NCAA schools (*e.g.*, at high schools, Division II or III NCAA institutions, non-NCAA schools, or professional teams). In effect, this argument was that the restraint has little or no anticompetitive impact because the NCAA lacks market power over the hiring of basketball coaches.

The difficulty with the NCAA's "lack of market power" defense is that the very existence of the REC salary-cap rule *ipso facto* refutes it. The entire purpose of the rule was to hold down the prices that an NCAA member would have to pay for its fourth basketball coach, which necessarily implies that absent the rule, salaries of these coaches in an uncontrolled market would generally have been higher. Since its very purpose was to create REC salaries much lower than they would have been, *a fortiori* the rule causes a misallocation of society's economic resources that the Sherman Act was designed to prevent and flows from an exercise of collective market power.

Put another way, if the REC salary cap had no effect on the REC market because Division I members collectively have no market power, they would not have passed the rule. Each Division I school would have already achieved the same benefit of reducing expenditures without the rule by having unilaterally decided not to pay its fourth basketball coach more than $16,000 a year. That many schools had not done so on their own is compelling evidence that collectively the NCAA members exercise much greater market power than when they act individually in a competitive market.

Judge Vratil cited some unfortunate and often misunderstood dictum from *Board of Regents* for this proposition. There, the Supreme Court had rejected a similar NCAA argument that its rules restricting the number of times a school's football games could appear on television and the fees for each appearance were not anticompetitive because the NCAA lacked market power over the sale of television broadcast rights. In noting that the NCAA's claim was fallacious for both legal and factual reasons, Justice Stevens wrote for the majority that:

> [a]s a matter of law, the absence of proof of market power does not justify a naked restriction on price or output. To the contrary, when there is an agreement not to compete in terms of price or output, "no elaborate industry analysis is required to demonstrate the anticompetitive character of such an agreement." [The NCAA] does not quarrel with the District Court's finding that price and output are not responsive to demand. Thus the plan is inconsistent with the Sherman Act's command that price and supply be responsive to con-

sumer preference. We have never required *proof of market power* in such a case.[21]

This language, which applies squarely to the REC salary-cap rule as well, undoubtedly was not intended, and should not be interpreted, to mean that when horizontal competitors agree not to compete on price or to lower output, it is illegal even if the defendants do not possess market power. If there were no market power, there could be no injury to consumer welfare or the competitive process from an agreement not to compete because consumers or suppliers would simply shift their business to another source of or outlet for the good or service. Surely, antitrust law does not condemn commonplace price or output agreements among lawful partners or joint venturers when there is no adverse impact on consumer welfare (*i.e.*, they do not collectively have market power) because the agreed upon price or output level does not deviate from what the market would dictate if each partner/venturer acted independently at the same level of efficiency.

Thus, *Board of Regents* does not hold that a violation can occur even in the absence of market power. Rather, it stands for the proposition that, as Justice Stevens expressly says, in cases involving naked horizontal restraints on price or output—where the very purpose of the agreement is to fix price or output at a point that deviates from the market price or output—no " *proof of* market power" is required.[23] This simply means that when an agreement among otherwise horizontal competitors is designed to and has the effect of establishing a jointly set price and output level different from what each would separately charge and produce (in the aggregate) absent the agreement (assuming each could operate as efficiently), as was the case in *Board of Regents* and *Law*, then the conduct itself is sufficient evidence of the requisite market power. No elaborate industry analysis, market definitions, or complicated testimony of high-priced expert economists will be required to establish what the defendants' conduct already clearly proves.

Thus, when some Division I RECs were making as much as $60,000 to $70,000 a year in an unfettered market prior to the salary-cap rule being imposed, it is nonsense to argue that the NCAA members were not exercising market power when they voted to prohibit any member from paying an REC more than $16,000 a year. As Judge Vratil observed in a footnote, "Defendant's argument— essentially that price-fixing victims can simply go elsewhere and get a job in another part of the economy that is not fixed—is, of course, absurd and cannot carry the day for the NCAA in this litigation."[24]

B. *The Claimed Offsetting Procompetitive Benefits*

The NCAA's claimed procompetitive benefits that might be considered sufficient to overcome the clear anticompetitive effects of the REC salary cap were essentially of two types: (1) that the REC salary cap was one part of a larger effort to contain the rapid escalation of costs associated with operating a Division I athletic program, costs which if not controlled would cause many schools not to

---

21. NCAA v. Board of Regents, 468 U.S. 85, 109-110 (1984) (citing National Soc'y of Professional Eng'rs v. United States, 435 U.S. 679, 692 (1978)) (emphasis added) (footnotes omitted).

23. *Id.* at 110 (emphasis added).

24. Law v. NCAA, 902 F. Supp. 1394, 1405 n. 11 (D. Kan. 1995).

have a fourth basketball coach at all, and which might cause other schools to abandon Division I athletics altogether; and (2) the REC salary cap promoted on-court athletic competitive balance and the values of amateurism and scholar-ath-letes that define the very product that the NCAA members produce and sell to the public.

Judge Vratil quite properly rejected these "procompetitive" claims as legally un-recognizable, and thus entered summary judgment for the plaintiffs. However, her reasoning for doing so was unfocused, strained, and in significant respects wrong. Whether intentional or not, the effort to reject these NCAA claims on narrow and confusing grounds was probably rooted in large part in the judge's sense of need to distinguish the REC salary cap rule from the thousands of other rules the NCAA uses to standardize the conduct of its member schools, rules that *Board of Regents* said were probably lawful and that lower courts have found lawful under section 1. Much of Part IV of this Essay will look at whether the distinctions Judge Vratil and these other courts have made or implied are analytically sound.

1. Cutting Costs of Financially Desperate Members

Judge Vratil rejected the NCAA's cost containment argument initially on fac-tual grounds— that the NCAA offered "no compelling evidence" that in fact NCAA members were in as dire financial straits as it claimed or, even if they were, that fixing the maximum salaries of only the last and lowest paid coaches would have any meaningful impact on the problem. Without having studied the affi-davits and proffered evidence attached to the NCAA's brief opposing the sum-mary judgment motion, it is difficult to assess the validity of the judge's conclu-sion in this regard. It is sufficient for present purposes to note only that it is not appropriate for a court to grant summary judgment because the judge determined there was "no compelling evidence" to support a party's factual claim.

Judge Vratil, however, cited a second ground for rejecting the "cost contain-ment" defense; namely, that it failed as a matter of law because saving a member school's athletic program from shutting down due to financial problems suggests a procompetitive effect in a market other than the market in which the anticom-petitive effects were caused, which she asserted is impermissible to consider under the rule of reason.

> Procompetitive justifications for price-fixing must apply to the same market in which the restraint is found, not to some other market.... If price-fixing buyers were allowed to justify their actions by claiming procompetitive benefits in the product market, they would almost always be able to do so by arguing that the restraint was designed to reduce their costs and thereby make them collectively more competitive sellers. To permit such a justification would be to give busi-nesses a blanket exemption from the antitrust laws and a practically limitless li-cense to engage in horizontal price-fixing aimed at suppliers.[27]

This legal analysis is woefully superficial to the point of being simply wrong. In any organization of separate legal persons that pursues some lawful joint eco-nomic activity (*e.g.*, a trade association, a joint venture, a traditional partnership, or an organization created for industry self- regulation), the rules of that organi-zation will standardize its members' behavior in some respects; thus, by definition

---

27. *Law*, 902 F. Supp. at 1406 (citations omitted).

organizational rules restrain or eliminate unfettered competition among members. The conduct so restrained may involve the purchasing of inputs, the production of the product, or the marketing and selling of the product. But whatever the nature of the restrained conduct (*i.e.*, in whatever market the anticompetitive effects are felt), the only conceivable procompetitive justification for the restraint is that it allows the organization or its members to produce their products or services more efficiently and thus enhance consumer welfare in the organization's or its members' product market. Judge Vratil's statement of the rule of reason would effectively recreate a rule of per se illegality for all rules of a lawful joint organization that standardize the conduct of its members in any input market because that is not the market in which the procompetitive benefits are felt. This makes no sense.

In support of her incorrect legal position, Judge Vratil cited three prior court decisions, two of which were older Supreme Court opinions that have since been effectively overruled and the third was a recent First Circuit decision in an NFL antitrust case that she misquoted and misunderstood. But not only does Judge Vratil's legal position lack logical or precedential support, it is inconsistent with the analysis of several recent Supreme Court cases, including *Board of Regents*. The myriad of NCAA rules that restrain the competition of NCAA members in the market for employing student-athletes are, according to the Supreme Court, probably justified by the fact that the rules make possible a unique type of amateur athletic entertainment product that consumers would otherwise not be able to enjoy. Judge Vratil's rule, even if it were limited to cases involving the setting of price or salary levels, would make all NCAA rules restraining the compensation that student-athletes could be paid (*i.e.*, the amateurism rules) per se illegal because they are not procompetitive in the student-athlete market. Yet *Board of Regents* indicated these rules could be found reasonable for their procompetitive benefits in the product market.

Despite Judge Vratil's mistake in restricting the scope of the rule of reason inquiry, her conclusion that the NCAA's "cost containment" defense was deficient as a matter of law was right for the wrong reason. This defense was not illegitimate because the benefits of cost containment are felt in the product market, but because the defense itself improperly assumes that antitrust law should not apply to condemn the creation of market power in an input market. The exercise of market power by a group of buyers virtually always results in lower costs to the buyers—a consequence which arguably is beneficial to the members of the industry and ultimately their consumers. If holding down costs by the exercise of market power over suppliers, rather than just by increased efficiency, is a procompetitive effect justifying joint conduct, then section 1 can never apply to input markets or buyer cartels. That is not and cannot be the law.

By definition, *monopsony* power (*i.e.*, market power held by a buyer or buyers over suppliers of an input) allows the buyer(s) to force down the price paid or to restrict the quantity/quality of the input being purchased. While the cost savings to industry members who exercise such power may in part be passed through to consumers (the degree depending on the elasticity of demand for the industry's product) and may allow marginal members of the industry to remain in business when they would otherwise fail, monopsony power is still harmful overall to consumer welfare due to its effect of misallocating society's resources and thus diminishing consumer choice. Although the more subtle implications of monopsony power on consumer welfare has occasionally led courts to give it lower priority in antitrust enforcement, the law is clear that conspiracies to restrain competition in an input market are just as much a target of antitrust law as restraints in output markets.

Accordingly, it is not that the procompetitive benefits of the REC salary cap fall in the product market that makes the cost containment defense a loser. It loses because cost reduction through horizontal agreements that limit consumer choice and misallocate economic resources are simply not recognizably "procompetitive." Cost reductions that flow from creating efficiency are procompetitive, but those that flow from increasing and exercising market power over suppliers of inputs are not. It is on this basis that the cost containment defense should have been rejected as a matter of law.

2. Preserving Balanced Amateur Athletic Competition

Relying on the *Board of Regents* language saying that most NCAA rules are probably procompetitive, and thus lawful, because they allow the NCAA members to produce a unique amateur athletic product, the NCAA argued in *Law* that the REC salary cap resulted in this procompetitive benefit. While exploring the limits of this argument is the focus of Part III, it is sufficient here to note that Judge Vratil was able to dispose of it on the simple ground that the REC salary cap, like the restrictions of television appearances at issue in *Board of Regents,* had very little if any relationship to the maintenance of the amateur or scholar-athlete ideals that define the unique product of the NCAA's members. According to the judge, rules that define amateurism and impose academic requirements on the student-athletes "are qualitatively a far cry from a regulation limiting the amount of compensation a professional coach, or even a graduate student assistant coach, can earn as a livelihood."[34] Thus, the lack of direct connection between the REC salary cap and promoting the ideals of amateurism and the scholar-athlete meant that the NCAA's claim of procompetitive benefit here was invalid.

In effect, Judge Vratil held in *Law* that restraints on the markets in which NCAA members sell their athletic products (like the television rights market in *Board of Regents*) and in which they employ coaches and other administrators (like the labor market in *Law*) are too far removed from the ideals of amateurism and academic integrity to allow the "unique amateur athletic product" defense, but that this defense is available when NCAA members restrain the labor market for student-athletes. While this is surely a rational distinction, it is very questionable whether antitrust or public policy is served by, in effect, giving substantially greater economic "free market" protection to sports fans who watch NCAA sports and to coaches than to the young (and relatively politically powerless) athletes who produce these sports products. It is just this distinction that Part IV explores.

The court also rejected out of hand the NCAA's somewhat related argument that the REC salary cap was part of its effort to promote athletic competitive balance on the court/field, which would thereby make the entertainment product of its members of greater quality for consumers. While acknowledging that promoting product quality through rules that tend to increase athletic competitive balance (whatever that term might mean) is procompetitive, Judge Vratil rejected the claim here as a factual matter because:

---

34. Law v. NCAA, 902 F. Supp. 1394, 1408 (D. Kan. 1995).

[t]he NCAA has submitted no evidence to this Court that requiring schools to pay their fourth-ranked basketball coaches all the same low salary levels the playing field in any significant way, especially when there is no limit on how disparately the three more senior coaches may be paid by competitor schools.[35]

Indeed, the judge's point about no limits on other expenditures, including what head and assistant coaches earn, suggests that even if the NCAA had submitted affidavits of school officials positing that the REC salary cap promoted competitive balance, she would have rejected the claim anyway as counterintuitive.

Because the NCAA's claimed procompetitive benefits of the REC salary-cap rule (*i.e.*, cost containment and promoting a unique amateur athletic product) were deficient on their face, Judge Vratil determined that, like the television restraints in *Board of Regents*, the NCAA's rule could be struck down as a matter of law on summary judgment under the analytical procedure known as the "quick look rule of reason." Given the Supreme Court's mandate in various cases since the mid-1970s that the per se rules should not be used if there are plausible efficiency (*i.e.*, procompetitive) benefits that might flow from the challenged agreement, which suggests that some cursory evaluation of a defendant's claimed justifications is required even before applying a per se rule, it is not clear what the substantive difference is today between the use of per se categories and the quick-look rule of reason. Both require the court to evaluate at least superficially the defendant's claimed procompetitive benefits and, if they are facially lacking merit, to spare the court the burden of a lengthy rule of reason trial and to strike down the challenged agreement as a matter of law. Determining that the REC salary cap was not a per se violation because the NCAA is a unique type of organization, but then that the rule was nonetheless illegal as a matter of law under the quick-look rule of reason, is small comfort for the NCAA. The result is the same for essentially the same reason after essentially the same analytical process.

C. *Less Restrictive Alternatives*

Because Judge Vratil found that the NCAA's claimed procompetitive benefits were facially deficient, there was no need for her to evaluate whether the plaintiffs had met their burden as to the third part of the rule of reason test—that the restraint was "'reasonably necessary to achieve the legitimate objectives proffered by the defendant.'"[37] This spared the judge from having to attempt to give some substantive meaning to the mysterious "less restrictive alternatives" doctrine.

IV. APPLYING THE RULE OF REASON TO ALL NCAA RULES

....

Perhaps the most useful way to think about and analyze NCAA rules is to divide them into general categories based on the effect of each. This Essay utilizes six such categories:

1. *Structural/Operational*—those rules that establish and define the ways in which the NCAA is organized, governed, and operated;

---

35. *Id.* at 1410.

37. *Law*, 902 F. Supp. at 1401 (quoting United States v. Brown Univ., 5 F.3d 658, 678-79 (3rd Cir. 1993)).

2. *Amateurism*—those rules that restrict the compensation or things of value that student-athletes may receive or the ways by which they may earn compensation;

3. *Academic Eligibility*—those rules that define the levels of academic performance required from student athletes to have initial and continuing eligibility to participate in athletics;

4. *Staff Conduct*—those rules that restrict the conduct or business arrangements of the coaching or administrative staffs of members' athletic departments, including restrictions on gambling, drug use, academic fraud, outside income and activities, and the manner in which student-athletes are recruited;

5. *Production & Output*—those rules that regulate or limit the means by which each member may produce their athletic products and the quality or quantity of those products, including limits on the number of coaches, the number of games that can be played, the times that games or practices can be held, the way in which games are shown on television, and the football bowl games in which members can play (It is in this category that I would place the restrictions at issue in both *Board of Regents* and *Law*.); and

6. *Contest*—the rules that govern the actual conduct of athletic contests, including the size and shape of the venue, required equipment, employment and duties of game officials, and game rules themselves.

It would require an active imagination to claim that any of the rules in category 6 (Contest) violate the rule of reason. And one could make a rule of reason case that survives a laugh test against very few rules in category 1 (Structural/Operational). The same cannot be said, however, for many of the rules in each of the other categories, where significant anticompetitive effects can probably be identified which would then require significant procompetitive justifications that both clearly outweigh the anticompetitive harms and survive a less restrictive alternative analysis.

The purpose of Part IV is simply to explore how the rule of reason methodology outlined by Judge Vratil in Law, which was derived from the Supreme Court's analysis in *Board of Regents*, might apply to NCAA rules more generally. In order to do that in a short essay, the best approach is simply to focus on a few groups of rules that most dramatically illustrate the analytical issues presented inevitably in any case challenging an NCAA rule. The three rule groups chosen here for this purpose are the rules restricting the compensation student-athletes may receive from the university for their athletic services (from category 2), the rules limiting the number of games that a team in any given sport can play and when they can play them (from category 5), and the rules limiting the number of coaches a school can employ for each sport (from category 5).

A. *The Anticompetitive Effects*

1. Fixing Student-Athlete Compensation

The prima facie case for a plaintiff challenging a rule in one of the three rule groups is relatively easy to make. The rules restricting the compensation student-athletes can be given by their universities for athletic services is a blatant price (wage) fix. To tell the overwhelming majority of producers of an intercollegiate athletics product (well over 900 NCAA members who supply all but a tiny fraction of the intercollegiate athletics consumed by the public) that the only compensation they may give their athletes is a scholarship, room, and board is the establishment of a uniform maximum salary of exactly the same character as that set for RECs at issue in *Law*. And for many star athletes, there is no question that the value of this fixed maximum compensation is well below their free-market value (*i.e.*, their marginal revenue product).

One could argue in response that the goals of modern antitrust law, wealth transfers and resource misallocations, are not significantly undermined by paying all student-athletes a scholarship, room, and board. To the extent wealth transfers are a concern of antitrust law (a proposition which is not universally acknowledged), there are clearly such transfers in this system, although they are not the typical transfers from consumers to producers. The major beneficiaries of replacing a free-market-based bidding system with the NCAA's fixed compensation system include those student-athletes who would not have much if any market value yet still receive a scholarship, room, and board, that is, almost all athletes in the nonrevenue sports and "scholarship" athletes in the revenue sports whose talent is marginal. Likewise, coaches at schools whose programs generate large amounts of revenue are also undoubtedly beneficiaries of these wealth transfers. The losers are, of course, the very talented athletes in the revenue sports, especially at the largest revenue-generating programs. But the actual extent of these wealth transfers, and the number of winners and losers, not to mention the legitimacy of wealth transfers in the labor market as an antitrust goal in the first place, all make proving significant anticompetitive effects on this ground problematic.

Likewise, the extent to which fixing the "wages" of student-athletes distorts the allocation of society's resources would be hard to prove. Because at least in men's basketball and football few outstanding athletes coming out of high school have any alternative place to get further athletic training except in an NCAA program, it is unlikely that many athletes will chose some other "job" over college athletics due to the NCAA's fixed "wage." Furthermore, in the absence of any empirical studies on the issue, it seems that the best athletes (who would predictably have the highest market value) are already for the most part going to the most successful revenue-generating programs. These programs can use many of their revenues to provide attractive accouterments allowed by NCAA rules, such as beautiful facilities, first-class tutoring and coaching services, and the promise of great exposure on television and before large crowds. The extent to which a system of free-market bidding for players would thus reshuffle the allocation of players among colleges is hard to determine, and it would be even harder to ascertain the extent to which the reshuffled deck would provide a better quality product for consumers.

Nonetheless, despite the inherent difficulty of proving that antitrust goals are significantly harmed by the NCAA's fixed "salary" system, the sensitivity of antitrust law to price and the basic assumptions underlying antitrust policy suggest that the mere fact of the wage fix is sufficient to establish the requisite anticompetitive harm in a prima facie rule of reason case. While we cannot easily identify the manner and extent of the wealth transfers and resource misallocations, they surely are there. Were it not for the NCAA's unique structure and product (which is the essence of the procompetitive defenses it can raise), such a wage-fixing arrangement would undoubtedly be per se illegal without any inquiry into the extent to which the wage fix actually injured antitrust goals. That the NCAA may have legitimate procompetitive counterarguments that allow it to avoid the per se bullet should not also allow it to call into question the underlying assumptions about the anticompetitive nature of fixing a uniform wage, which is precisely what Judge Vratil concluded in *Law*.

2. Limiting the Number and Times of Games

The NCAA rules restricting the number of games a team in any given sport can play each year, and the period of time in which those games must be played, are on their face significantly anticompetitive. The two most obvious effects of market power are the ability to charge (or pay) a price higher (or lower) than the competitive price (which is why price fixing is manifestly anticompetitive) and the ability to restrict output. Limiting the number and times of games is a direct restriction on output that deprives consumers of the option to "consume" games that would be played but for the NCAA rules. Not only does this artificial restriction on output drive the price of those games that are played up (a wealth transfer from consumers to NCAA members), it misallocates resources away from producing something consumers want and would be willing to pay market prices for if it were available (a misallocation of resources). Thus, the anticompetitive effect of these rules is facially significant.

3. Limiting the Number of Coaches in Each Sport

Because the rule limiting the number of coaches a school can employ in each sport is neither a price restraint nor a limit on the quantity of output, its anticompetitive effects are a bit more subtle than those of the other two rules being considered. What this rule does is standardize one of the means by which each producer makes its product, thereby placing a limitation on the quality (not quantity) of each school's entertainment product in each sport. (This is the effect of virtually all of the category 5 rules except for those fixing the number and time of games.)

While restrictions on product quality, as opposed to price and output levels, are not considered among the most blatant types of anticompetitive conduct, they still generally have significant anticompetitive effects. By not allowing a school's football program to employ fifteen coaches (or to practice seven days a week for fifty-two weeks a year, or to give out 150 full scholarships to increase squad size), the NCAA essentially deprives each program of the opportunity to create a team that plays at a higher level of athletic performance. If it then follows that the NCAA places a limit on the quality of the product available for consumers, the anticompetitive harm— injury to consumer welfare—is arguably apparent.

While restricting an entertainment producer from performing better would normally *ipso facto* prove an anticompetitive effect, that is not necessarily the case here. Since the product is not produced by any one team, but rather is athletic contests between at least two teams on any given occasion, one team having a higher level of play would not necessarily make for a higher quality product. In fact, it might cause a lower quality product. If one team consistently defeated every other team eighty to nothing because its team were so relatively strong, the quality of the product when that team was involved would be very poor. Thus, the system needs some reasonable level of "competitive balance" among the teams to ensure a good quality product, a fact the Supreme Court acknowledged in *Board of Regents*.[52]

---

52. *See* 468 U.S. 85, 117 (1984).

However, creating some degree of competitive balance is usually regarded as a procompetitive benefit that should be considered in that context, even though in theory it also goes to the issue of whether a rule actually causes anticompetitive harm in the first place. Thus, this Essay considers competitive balance in Part IV.B.2, which deals with procompetitive benefits, keeping in mind that since this question implicates both the anticompetitive harms and procompetitive benefits issues, which party has the burden of proof is unclear.

For present purposes, it seems reasonable to assume that if the restrictions on the number of coaches (or any rule whose alleged anticompetitive effect would be primarily on product quality, not price or output level) were eliminated and these decisions were made individually by each school in a free market, the overall quality of intercollegiate athletics would increase. Some schools that would invest more to hire more coaches would clearly perform on the field or court at a higher level. Others not willing to invest in more coaches, presumably because their marginal revenue product would not be as great at those schools, would thus perform at relatively lower levels. Such disparities in product quality are inevitable in a free-market system, and, the unique competitive balance issue aside for the moment, having these disparities does not mean that consumers are worse off. Those teams that perform at a lower level would not attract as many fans and would have to charge much less for tickets and broadcast rights, but this is merely the free-market phenomenon of giving consumers a range of choices—higher quality at higher prices down to lower quality at lower prices. Consumer welfare is maximized only when the full range of choices that significant numbers of consumers might want is available.

Thus, limiting each team to a certain number of coaches (or players, or practices) in theory distorts the free market, diminishes consumer choices, and thus injures consumer welfare. Disregarding for now the possible validity of the competitive balance argument, these types of restrictions on product quality inherently have significant anticompetitive effects.

B. *The Procompetitive Benefits*

The alleged procompetitive benefits of virtually every NCAA rule, including those specifically explored in this Essay, are of two general types. First is the preservation of *amateurism*, which is procompetitive only because, as the Supreme Court noted in *Board of Regents*,[53] amateurism is the essence of the NCAA members' athletic competition product, and it distinguishes NCAA athletics from other types of entertainment products. Thus, promoting amateurism is important for making this different product available to consumers, and this is arguably procompetitive. Second is the promotion of *competitive balance* among the teams of the member schools, thereby enhancing the quality of the athletic competition product. This subpart explores the validity of these two alleged procompetitive benefits in the context of the three types of restraints explored above.

Before doing so, however, a preliminary observation is appropriate. It is not clear from the case law how procompetitive benefits (*i.e.*, gains for consumer welfare resulting from increased efficiencies of one kind or another) are to be weighed and balanced against anticompetitive harms (*i.e.*, losses for consumer welfare deriving from the creation or entrenchment of market power, and, arguably, wealth

---

53. *See id.* at 101-02.

transfers). Neither are qualitatively similar nor quantitatively measurable. All a factfinder could do is intuitively sense how "bad" or "good" an effect is and then subjectively decide whether his or her sense is that the "good" effects are greater than the "bad" based on his or her own life experiences and values.

In many if not most cases, one side or the other in the competitive balance will clearly overwhelm the other, making such cases good candidates for either invalidating the rule as a matter of law under a "quick-look" rule of reason approach or granting summary judgment for defendants. But the law is totally devoid of judicial guidance about how to deal with cases where there are significant competitive (i.e., consumer welfare) effects on both sides of the ledger. Should such cases simply be given to juries to resolve based on intuition? Should some system of presumptions or heavy burdens of proof be employed to guide juries? Or should we adopt presumptions and burdens that will allow courts to decide these cases as a matter of law?

A strong argument can be made for the proposition that because modern antitrust law exists to avoid concentrations of market power, when an agreement of competitors is shown significantly to enhance or entrench market power, it should be illegal unless the defendant can establish procompetitive benefits (i.e., efficiencies) that substantially outweigh the anticompetitive harms. One could argue that the unquantifiable procompetitive benefits must outweigh the unquantifiable anticompetitive harms in clear and convincing fashion, or even beyond a reasonable doubt, but the fact that antitrust policy specifically targets market power strongly suggests that in a rule of reason analysis the benefits of efficiencies generated must do more than simply roughly offset the harms from increases in market power. In short, before we tolerate significant increases in market power caused by agreements of otherwise horizontal competitors, there should be fairly compelling reasons for it.

In this regard, the Supreme Court's *Board of Regents* dictum suggesting that promoting amateurism and competitive balance probably justify most of the NCAA's rules seems a bit presumptuous. When the Court opined that "[i]t is reasonable to assume that most of the regulatory controls of the NCAA are justifiable means of fostering competition among amateur athletic teams and therefore procompetitive because they enhance public interest in intercollegiate athletics,"[57] and that "[t]here can be no question but...that the preservation of the student-athlete in higher education adds richness and diversity to intercollegiate athletics and is entirely consistent with the goals of the Sherman Act,"[58] it was in effect claiming that however pro-and anticompetitive effects are to be measured and balanced under the rule of reason, most of the NCAA's rules were presumably sufficiently more procompetitive than anticompetitive to satisfy the rule. But why? It seems unwarranted for a court to assume that the majority of NCAA rules would survive a rule of reason balance without any record evidence going to whether any particular rule or group of rules (other than the restrictions on football telecasting at issue) in fact caused the public to be more attracted to intercollegiate athletics, and without any discussion of how to weigh procompetitive effects against demonstrable significant anticompetitive effects. While one

---

57. *Board of Regents*, 468 U.S. at 117.
58. *Id.* at 120.

must be careful not to dismiss too lightly any Supreme Court dictum, no matter how ill-considered, this particular dictum should not be treated with "papal infallibility" since it does nothing but presume the outcome of factual inquiries that have never been made in the context of a legal test that has never been clearly articulated.

Beyond these observations, it is not the purpose of this Essay to explore how the rule of reason balance has been or should be accomplished in section 1 cases where demonstrable significant competitive effects exist on both sides of the balance. It is sufficient here to note that the law has provided precious little guidance on the matter.

.... [Professor Roberts' analysis of procompetitive benefits and anticompetitive aspects of the forgoing rules is omitted. — ed.].

2. Preserving Competitive Balance

Each of the three types of rules will arguably promote competitive balance for essentially the same reason—it prevents individual schools from utilizing some method to attract better athletes or to prepare their athletes to play at a higher level. Whether the method is paying athletes more compensation, playing more games, or hiring more coaches, a school could improve its on-field ability *vis-a-vis* other schools that do not utilize these methods for financial or academic reasons. To prevent this, NCAA rules standardize a wide range of behavior; for example, they fix athlete compensation, the number of games, and the number of coaches.

The Supreme Court, once again in *Board of Regents,* has indicated it assumes that promoting competitive balance is a procompetitive benefit that would justify many of the NCAA's rules.

> Petitioner argues that the interest in maintaining a competitive balance among amateur athletic teams is legitimate and important and that it justifies the regulations challenged in this case. We agree with the first part of the argument but not the second....
>
> ... It is reasonable to assume that most of the regulatory controls of the NCAA are justifiable means of fostering competition among amateur athletic teams and therefore procompetitive because they enhance public interest in intercollegiate athletics.[66]

Since the Court rejected procompetitive balance as a justification for the NCAA's television restrictions in *Board of Regents*, it would not be reasonable to interpret this dictum to mean that in future cases a court could simply assume or take judicial notice of the fact that most NCAA rules were procompetitive for this reason. For a court to find that an anticompetitive rule is lawful because it significantly promotes a procompetitive benefit of competitive balance, the NCAA would have to prove that in fact it did, notwithstanding Justice Stevens's musings in *Board of Regents* about what it is reasonable to assume. To establish that any of these rules produces a significant procompetitive benefit, the NCAA would have to prove both that barring individual schools from "competing" in the manner restrained to improve their athletic strength promotes "competitive balance" and, if so, that promoting competitive balance is procompetitive because it enhances the quality of the athletic competition product in the eyes of consumers.

---

66. *Id.*

Undertaking this analysis first requires an understanding of the meaning of "competitive balance." There are two distinct and very different concepts that are subsumed within the rubric of competitive balance. The first is that the term identifies the extent to which in any particular season, all of the teams playing at the same level are able to play close and exciting games (a "parity" definition). Alternatively, competitive balance may be defined in terms of the ability of teams over time to improve their athletic performance *vis-a-vis* other teams (a "potential to change" definition). Under this second definition, what is important is not how strong a team is in any given season, but rather, whether over a few years, a team is likely to change its relative ability to match up against other teams (*i.e.*, whether a bad team appears to have a reasonable chance over a short period to become one of the best teams, thereby keeping its fans' interest even during "down" years because of a hope of better things to come).

In evaluating the importance of NCAA rules for promoting competitive balance, it is initially worth noting that the totality of NCAA rules appear to do a very poor job of promoting either type of competitive balance. In Division I in basketball and Division IA in football, there is little parity at any given time. The best teams would, and often do, defeat lesser teams by huge margins in virtually every game. Likewise, NCAA rules seem to do a poor job of providing much opportunity for schools to significantly change their relative athletic ranking. Year after year, it is the same schools that field the top teams in each sport, with the only fluctuations being within a narrow range. While occasionally a team makes a significant movement up or down the pecking order, this is rare and almost never occurs in large increments. Thus, Northwestern University's amazing rise to the Big Ten football championship in 1995 was amazing precisely because of its rarity, and even then, Northwestern rose from being bad only in comparison to a small group of the most powerful teams.

a. Do NCAA Rules Promote Competitive Balance?

NCAA rules that require standard behavior by definition are designed to limit the ways that individual schools can attempt to improve the relative athletic strength of their teams. Schools are allowed to try to attract better athletes and prepare them to play better by hiring the best head coaches at top salaries, by providing the very best equipment and facilities, by serving the best food and providing the nicest housing, and by offering the best academic support. Schools may not, however, try to attract better athletes or prepare them to play better by increasing their athletes' compensation, playing more games, or hiring more coaches. The question thus is whether restricting the ways individual schools can "compete" to improve their relative athletic strength enhances either parity or the ability for relative change in rankings.

These are questions of fact that would have to be developed at trial. Nonetheless, some observations are appropriate here. Preventing individual schools from paying athletes, playing more games, or hiring more coaches in order to improve the quality of their play by definition tends to preserve the status quo and retard changing the current disparities between teams. There seems little doubt that allowing a free market to work (*i.e.*, letting every school do whatever it wanted and could afford to improve its teams) would create a more dynamic industry. Whether this would enhance or diminish parity depends on how the dynamic realignment would play itself out over any given period.

Because it is probable that the currently stronger teams would generally be more able to afford, both financially and academically, to pay athletes, play more games, and hire more coaches than currently weaker teams, it seems likely that a jury would find that in a free market there would be greater disparity in playing levels between the top tier and bottom tier of schools in Division I (IA in football). To that extent, it is likely that these NCAA rules do promote parity from numbers 1 to 105. But that tells us very little about whether competitive balance is enhanced.

Is competitive balance greater because Nebraska's football team would on average beat Bowling Green State by fifty points a game instead of seventy? Perhaps so if the relevant universe is all 105 Division IA schools, but why is that the relevant population? It may be that while the disparity between the very best and the very worst teams would be greater in a free-market system than under NCAA rules, that within various tiers of teams the competitive differentials might be less, and that within those tiers, or even among tiers, more relative movement over a short time might be possible. Given the inherent ambiguity of the term, it is not certain that a jury would be easily convinced that any one of the NCAA's rules, or even the rules as a whole, significantly enhance "competitive balance." That is particularly true given the large disparities in playing ability and little relative movement in rankings among NCAA members under the status quo, and the NCAA's seeming lack of concern over this apparent competitive imbalance today.

b. Is Competitive Balance a Procompetitive Benefit?

Even if a jury would find that under some reasonable definition of the term, competitive balance is enhanced by one or more of the NCAA rules, it does not necessarily follow that consumer welfare benefits by it. Is the present system with its substantial competitive differentials more procompetitive than a system in which each school would be allowed to improve its teams without constraint by NCAA rules?

Competitive balance is simply a description for a system in which most of the games in the short-and over the long term are likely to be close and exciting, or, put another way, in which the intercollegiate athletic product is of high quality. But since no team can or does play more than a small fraction of all the teams in its division, the quality of games should not be diminished just because the playing disparity between some teams increases. If the differential in playing abilities of the 105 Division IA football teams increased from top to bottom in a free-market system—one in which athletes were paid, and teams played as many games and hired as many coaches as they wished —every game could still be close and exciting if properly scheduled. Until the number of other schools that any one school's team can play against competitively becomes so few that it cannot put together an attractive schedule, consumer welfare need not be injured. The mere realignment of all 105 teams into narrower bands or tiers of competitive levels should not result in fewer close and exciting games, and might even produce more if it discouraged the scheduling of some obvious mismatches every year, as occurs today.

In sum, it is not clear how eliminating any particular NCAA rule would impact either the relative playing strengths of every team in Division I (IA in football) or the ability of teams to improve their relative position over time. While some dispersion at the very top and bottom would likely occur despite the enormous disparity that already exists, it is quite possible that some bunching at various levels would also occur, causing more competitiveness within certain ranges. And certainly having an unfettered market would enable teams to change their ranking within their respective tiers more quickly than they could in a tightly controlled market where competitive options are strictly limited by NCAA rule.

Furthermore, to the extent competitive balance is enhanced by any one or more current rules, it is not clear that this translates into a significant procompetitive benefit. Thus, while the claim that NCAA rules preserve competitive balance has a superficial rule of reason appeal to it (witness the dictum in *Board of Regents*), once carefully analyzed, the argument has less than compelling merit. As the Supreme Court noted in *Professional Engineers*, antitrust assumes that letting the free market operate results in optimal prices, output levels, and product quality.[71] Schools want to maximize revenue. The degree of consumer welfare generated by a product is reflected in the amount of revenue it generates. Thus, by allowing each school to make its own production decisions in the pursuit of maximum revenue, consumer welfare will be maximized. An industry claim that an artificial cap on employee salaries, output, or means of production enhances product quality and thus consumer welfare flies in the face of fundamental antitrust assumptions.

C. Less Restrictive Alternatives

Should the NCAA be able to persuade a jury that a challenged rule has procompetitive benefits that sufficiently outweigh its anticompetitive effects, it would still have to survive the less restrictive alternatives (LRA) analysis. Because the contours of the LRA doctrine are extraordinarily vague, it is hard to evaluate how it would apply to any particular NCAA rule. Potentially, however, it could present a virtually insurmountable hurdle for the NCAA.

The doctrine could mean that a challenged rule may be isolated from the rest of the NCAA's myriad of rules and then attacked on the ground that the claimed procompetitive benefits of the rule by itself could be achieved to virtually the same degree by a different rule that was less anticompetitive. Alternatively, the LRA doctrine might require a defendant to establish that the specific restraint is imposed at exactly the point where its marginal procompetitive benefit intersects its marginal anticompetitive effects —that there was not some alternative rule whose being substituted for the challenged rule would eliminate more anticompetitive harms than it would reduce procompetitive benefits. However, under either of these formulations, the LRA doctrine would likely be the death knell for virtually every NCAA rule.

To the extent that the rules limiting student-athlete compensation promote amateurism or competitive balance, a plaintiff could probably argue persuasively that giving schools the right to "pay" athletes a cash stipend on top of a scholarship, room, and board would not significantly undermine the procompetitive benefits but would be less anticompetitive. Likewise, allowing schools to play twelve football games each year, or thirteen, or fourteen, would not seriously undermine amateurism or competitive balance any more than playing eleven does. The same could be said for permitting ten, eleven, or twelve assistant football coaches instead of nine. Every NCAA rule would be subject to invalidation on the ground that it could be made "less restrictive" without seriously undermining whatever procompetitive benefits it might have.

---

71. 435 U.S. 679, 695 (1978).

This approach to the LRA doctrine is not desirable, despite its use in some cases challenging rules of professional sports leagues, because it would place an impossible burden on every type of joint organization whose rules are subject to the rule of reason—joint ventures, trade associations, industry self-regulating bodies, and so forth. But if the LRA doctrine does not allow plaintiffs to play this slippery-slope game of cherry-picking individual rules and hypothesizing less restrictive variations for each, it is unclear what meaningful or sensible role it might play.

The content of the LRA doctrine today is so hollow that it can be used in almost any case to strike down otherwise procompetitive rules. For example, it is not clear what exactly the doctrine allows or requires. Is it sufficient if the plaintiff suggests an alternative way that the defendants possibly might achieve a similar amount of consumer welfare benefits as the restraint does without causing the same degree of anticompetitive harm? Or, at the opposite extreme, must the plaintiff show that an alternative means having significantly less anticompetitive effects exists for achieving exactly the same procompetitive benefits that the restraint did? Or is the required showing somewhere in between? If a plaintiff throws out a dozen hypothetical alternative rules, how many of them must the jury find to be a plausible LRA before the challenged restraint is illegal—one, one-half, most, or all? And what must the likelihood be that an hypothesized LRA will produce the comparable procompetitive benefits or cause fewer anticompetitive harms? Also, must the proposed alternative be of the same nature as the challenged restraint, or can it be of a totally different character (*e.g.*, if the NCAA rules against paying athletes' salaries are found to create competitive balance, can a less restrictive alternative be to require greater revenue sharing among NCAA members or must it be limited to some way of compensating athletes)?

Until the courts are presented with some cases in which they are required to address these questions, we can only guess at how the LRA doctrine might affect a review of NCAA rules. However, given the vagueness of this doctrine and the tremendous latitude it thus gives courts to find a basis for condemning rules they do not like, the NCAA should never rest easy, lest it find itself in court with a judge whose favorite local university has just been severely sanctioned for violating a challenged rule.

....

Chapter 12

Social and Legal Restructuring

1. Racism in College Athletics

Introduction

Given the extent to which racism has impacted the experiences of ethnic minorities in sports, surprisingly little legal scholarship has examined race in the context of athletics. Recently, however, legal scholars have increasingly turned their attention toward the complex matrix woven by racism and athletics. Accordingly, the chapter begins with Professor Rodney Smith's explanation for the past failure of scholars to explore issues of race and sport. He suggests the marginalization of sport as an academic discipline may mask racial, cultural and gender bias.

This chapter provides a sampling of the increasing body of legal scholarship that addresses race and sport. The articles included in this anthology that address this topic tend to mirror the evolution of race and sports scholarship. Initially, scholarship focused on more discrete issues in which race was implicated. For example, Professor Linda Greene's classic article, *The New NCAA Rules of the Game: Academic Integrity or Racism?* 28 St. Louis U. L.J. 101 (1984), examined the disparate impact of NCAA initial eligibility rules on African American student-athletes. A recent article written by Professor Kenneth Shropshire, which is included in the Due Process Section, *supra*, builds upon Professor Greene's earlier work. He characterizes eligibility rules as a barrier to entry of African American athletes to Division I colleges and universities. Shropshire is particularly critical of the use of standardized tests as the primary component of barriers to entry to college sports given the underlying purpose of such tests.

In demonstrating a broadening of the inquiry into the role of racism in sport, articles by Professors Davis and Yarborough examine the intersection of the legal, social and economic dimensions of racism in athletics. As such, these articles reflect the extent to which racism in sports is a microcosm of society and therefore mirrors the plight of African Americans in the larger society. In the *Myth of the Superspade*, Timothy Davis traces the historical and present manifestations of racism in college athletics. Relying on an alternative analytical framework—critical race scholarship—he argues that, as is true in society generally, historically, overt racism limited participation opportunities for African Americans in collegiate sports. Although overt racism in sports has been significantly reduced, it has been displaced with a subtle form of racism that nevertheless results in harm to the interests of African Americans who participate in athletics. He also examines alternatives to traditional antidiscrimination norms as means of combating the deleterious consequences of racism in college athletics.

Resort to alternative analytical models is evidenced in the next article, which addresses the intersectionality of race, gender and sport. Also, drawing from themes developed in critical race scholarship, Professor Marilyn Yarborough proposes that African American women face unique challenges that create obstacles to participation and administrative opportunities in sports. These challenges are formidable given the dual subordinate status of African American women—they are neither white nor male. As a consequence of the invisibility of African American women, Professor Yarborough argues that the effect of race in sports has been defined in reference to its impact on African American men. Similarly, she proposes that efforts to end gender discrimination in sports have not effectively advanced the interests of African American women.

Additional noteworthy publications exploring racism in college athletics include: Paul M. Anderson, *Racism in Sports: A Question of Ethics*, 6 MARQ. SPORTS L.J. 357 (1996); Alfred Mathewson, *Black Women, Gender Equity and the Function at the Junction*, 6 MARQ. SPORTS L. J. 239 (1996); Marilyn V. Yarborough, *If You Let Me Play Sports*, 6 MARQ. SPORTS L.J. 229 (1996); Michael Oriard, *College Athletics as a Vehicle for Social Reform*, 22 J.C. & U.L. 77 (1995); Leroy Clark, *New Directions for the Civil Rights Movement*, 36 How. L. J. 259 (1993); Linda S. Greene, *The New NCAA Rules of the Game: Academic Integrity or Racism*, 28 ST. LOUIS U. L. REV. 101 (1984).

Rodney K. Smith, When Ignorance is Not Bliss: In Search of Racial and Gender Equity in Intercollegiate Athletics
61 Missouri Law Review 329 (1996)*

. . . .

II. SPORT AND ACADEMIC VALUES AT THE CULTURAL LEVEL

In a culture often preoccupied with sport, it is astounding, as noted by Professors Gorn and Oriard, "that athletics have remained so far beyond the boundary of intellectual discourse, [despite the fact that the] study of sport can take us to the very heart of critical issues in the study of culture and society."[12] Professor Hyland, a philosopher, agrees:

> There is a long tradition that calls on the academy, as one of its central tasks, to reflect on and analyze social phenomena that play an important role in a given culture. Thus, there are many varied considerations of the role of politics, religion, music, and the arts by the various disciplines in the academy, certainly including philosophy. Arguably, however, that social phenomenon in American life which has the biggest impact on our culture, yet which receives the least serious attention from our intellectual standard-bearers, is sport and athletics. There seems to be a long-standing prejudice that however popular a phenomenon sport may be, it is simply not serious' enough to be a legitimate subject of

---

12. Elliot J. Gorn & Michael Oriad, *Taking Sports Seriously,* THE CHRON. OF HIGHER EDUC., March 24, 1995, at A52.

intellectual inquiry. That has certainly been one of the long-standing prejudices of professional philosophy.[13]

This failure to study the role of sport in contemporary society may, as Hyland suggests, reflect some prejudice and may have adverse implications for racial and gender equity in athletics. For many academics, the study of sport or participation in athletics is considered to be so trivial as to be beneath serious consideration by the intellectually inclined.

This trivialization of athletics by the academic community, in turn, may further obscure the damage done by racial and gender inequities in athletics at all levels, and may make it more difficult to confront such inequity. If participation in athletics does involve academic skills and values, then the failure to recognize that fact may have significant racial and gender implications.

If we ignore the intellectual component of sport, we trivialize the significance of such participation. Athletes in our most popular, revenue-producing sports are recognized almost entirely for their physical and not for their intellectual prowess. Given that African-American male athletes have come to dominate in many athletic contexts, their participation may be particularly devalued in an intellectual sense. This devaluation may itself be a form of racial inequity.

The failure to recognize the academic dimension of participation in athletics may have significant gender-related ramifications as well. If there are educational skills and values that can be derived from participation in athletics, the fact that women participate in far fewer numbers has significant implications for women. In being denied equal opportunity to participate in athletics at all levels, women may be precluded from having the opportunity of mastering those educational skills and values that may be most effectively learned within the context of athletics. If, on the other hand, there is only limited educational content related to participation in athletics, the harm done to women, while important in the sense that they are precluded from full participation in a form of entertainment, would be less significant, at least in an educational sense.

It is necessary, therefore, to ascertain whether there are educational skills and values that are related to participation in athletics. Those who argue against supporting athletics on the ground that participation lacks significant educational or instructional content rarely offer clearly articulated reasons for their conclusions. For them, the nonacademic nature of participation in athletics appears to be a given, as a matter of implicit syllogistic reasoning.

There are, however, a number of educational skills and values directly related to participation in athletics. At the most direct level, some academics maintain that participation in competitive athletics is analogous to participation on the part of many students in a basic biology class, teaching the student memorization and basic analytical skills. Although it is unlikely that a student in the basic biology class will use what is learned in that class on a daily, or even a regular, basis in her employment, the course is nevertheless considered to be of academic worth. The same concept can be applied to a complex football playbook—the athlete learns to analyze how to respond to a unique set of complex situations by memorizing and applying an elaborate set of fundamental rules or plays that are de-

---

13. Drew A. Hyland, PHILOSOPHY OF SPORT xiii (1990).

signed to respond to certain situations as they arise. There is much that can be learned in other sports as well....

. . . .

Professor Hyland has noted that, "sport is a vivid and explicit combination of mental and physical activity. It thus offers a fascinating occasion for reflection on their interaction." He adds that, "through participation in athletics many of us are or can be led to a position on the [major philosophical issue of the relationship between mind and body] which rings true to our own lives, and so becomes itself a part of the self-knowledge which it is the office of philosophy to seek." This form of self-knowledge is significant and would be emphasized further in an educational sense, if we encouraged student-athletes to reflect on philosophical issues that arise in the sports context. Regrettably, however, present reluctance to characterize sport as an area of academic study apparently has negated the teaching of the philosophical insights that inhere in sport. Participation in athletics provides a largely untapped forum—a clinical opportunity—for the study of many perplexing philosophical, psychological and other issues. If athletic participation in the intercollegiate context were accorded academic weight or value, at least in a presumptive sense, such study might be legitimized and made a part of our educational process.

. . . .

Research clearly indicates that there are significant academic-related benefits that result from participation in a regular regimen of physical exercise. Although research indicates that regular exercise often enhances academic capacity, it does not necessarily support the same conclusion for highly competitive intercollegiate athletics, except insofar as participation at that level provides the student-athlete with a regular exercise regimen. Student-athletes are generally required to engage in regular exercise, however, both in-season and out-of-season and are, therefore, recipients of the academic benefits that attend an enforced regimen of regular exercise.

In addition to providing an inviting base for certain educational and related benefits and instruction in a variety of educational skills, participation in athletics may provide a forum for teaching certain values. Norma V. Cantu, assistant secretary for civil rights in the Justice Department, asserts that, "values we learn from participation in sports [include] teamwork, standards, leadership, discipline, work ethics, self-sacrifice, pride in accomplishment, [and] strength of character...."[35]

In addition to academic skills and values that may be learned through participation in athletics, athletics itself may contribute to the building of a sense of community. Ernest Boyer noted that, "big-time sport, collegiate and professional, is becoming the new civil authority in our culture. It draws pride and unifies the community the same way that great cathedrals did in earlier times." In our diverse culture, characterized by a wide variety of ethnic, religious, socio-economic and other groups, there may well be no other force quite like sport, in terms of bringing people of diverse backgrounds together in pursuit of a common purpose....

In conclusion, there is substantial evidence that there are academic benefits, skills, and values that are closely related to participation in athletics. The burden, therefore, shifts to academics who oppose this proposition to provide a more sub-

---

35. Norma V. Cantu, *Guest Editorial: Athletics Experience Vital to Both Sexes*, THE NCAA NEWS, April 26, 1995, at 4.

stantive response than they have provided to date. They must offer more support for their assertion that participation in athletics is of little or no academic value. Absent such a showing, evidence of racial and gender inequities in sport is all the more disquieting because those inequities may result in unacknowledged academic and career disadvantages.

....

Timothy Davis, The Myth of the Superspade: The Persistence of Racism in College Athletics
22 Fordham Urban Law Journal 615 (1995)*

....

The notion that racism plays a central role in college sport is not novel. For example, when examining the components of organized American sport, sociologists typically speak of the long-standing and pervasive presence of racism in college athletics. Notwithstanding what appears to be a presumption, legal scholars have devoted scant discourse to the legal ramifications of such racism. Particularly in this context, given accusations of discrimination against African-American participants, the failure of legal scholars to address the myriad issues related to racism in college athletics is as surprising as it is neglectful.

....

The reluctance...to discuss racism in sport is consistent with a general predilection not to explore the social conditions that influence sport in American society. Indeed, American society seems content to remain in blissful ignorance of the numerous factors, such as social class, race and gender, that influence college athletics....The comfort apparently arising from ignoring such issues does not, however, negate the reality of sport as a cultural practice that is not separate from the "social, economic, political, and cultural context in which it is situated."[22]

Reluctance to address directly the role of racism in college athletics also reflects differing perceptions. Unlike blacks, many white Americans refuse to acknowledge race as a factor that influences sport. The popular belief of athletics as a venue that provides a level playing field where athletic attainment prevails over bigoted, discriminatory attitudes and conduct contributes to this notion.

Given this background, a central purpose of this Article is to initiate and to lay the foundation for what I hope will be a continuing dialogue concerning the innumerable legal issues invoked by the continuing presence of racism in college sport....

I. HISTORICAL BACKGROUND

A. Early Years: Exclusion and Overt Discrimination

....

---

* Copyright 1995 by the Fordham Urban Law Journal. Used by permission. All rights reserved.

22. Sage, *supra* note 14, at 2.

Since the first intercollegiate competition in 1852, black athletes' involvement in college sport has been marked by racial discrimination and prejudice. The attitudes and assumptions that subordinated blacks in society in general fostered exclusionary conduct and blatant discrimination against black athletes during most of the history of college athletics.

1. *Formal Rules of Exclusion*

During the late Nineteenth and early Twentieth Centuries, legally countenanced segregation impacted virtually every aspect of social behavior and interaction, including sport. In college sport, a series of rules and customs limited black participation to historically black colleges and a few predominantly white colleges located in the northern United States.

In the South, prohibitions against blacks attending white colleges and universities effectively excluded the black athlete from playing for predominantly white southern institutions. Moreover, Jim Crow laws enacted to prohibit whites and blacks from social interaction extended to bar direct sporting competition between them. For example, a Texas Penal Code provision, enacted in 1933, prohibited "boxing, sparring or wrestling contest or exhibition between any person of the Caucasian or 'White' race and one of the African or 'Negro' race...."[39]

....

2. *Informal Rules of Discrimination*

During the late Nineteenth and early Twentieth Centuries, blacks played sports for a limited number of northern colleges such as Harvard, Amherst and Oberlin. Informal rules reinforced by social strictures, however, were as effective as legislation in limiting the opportunities available to black athletes to compete at predominantly white institutions outside of the South.

These informal limitations appeared in various guises. In some instances, they were manifested as a virtual prohibition of African-Americans from becoming student-athletes. For instance, few black students competed in sports for Catholic universities, because most such institutions excluded African-Americans students during this period. Often informal Jim Crow laws prohibited blacks from playing sports for the schools that did admit black students.

....

....Certain athletic conferences, such as the Missouri Athletic Conference (with the exception of Nebraska) systematically excluded black athletes pursuant to so-called "gentlemen's agreements" that prohibited blacks from participating in league contests. These "gentlemen's agreements" constituted a series of written rules or tacit understandings precluding black participation in organized sport.

The reach and impact of "gentlemen's agreements" extended beyond the walls of the institutions that relied on them to exclude black athletes....Prior to World War II, most northern teams with blacks on their rosters either did not schedule games against southern teams or would leave their African-American players at home when the team traveled south. It has also been suggested that a promise to withdraw voluntarily from games against southern schools was an element of the consideration that some northern institutions extracted from their black athletes.

---

39. Tex. Art. 614-11(f), Texas Penal Code (1933).

....

Northern institutions adopted other informal rules. These rules carried the weight of law and, thus, restricted the ability of black athletes to compete for white colleges and universities. Informal quotas typically restricted the slots open to black athletes to no more than one or two players on a team. In addition to numerical quotas, northern colleges imposed another requirement that limited the number of black student-athletes allowed to compete on their teams. Many of these institutions imposed a "superspade" requirement. In other words, the typical African-American student-athlete playing for a predominantly white college prior to the 1930s tended to be an exceptionally talented starter.

3. *The Black Athlete as an Outsider*

University policies also contributed to the plight of the black student-athlete. These policies operated to ensure that black student-athletes, competing for the few predominantly white colleges willing to admit them, were not spared the indignities of racism at their home institutions. A lack of institutional sensitivity and overt racism relegated the African-American student-athlete to outsider status.... Such attitudes resulted in the exclusion of the black athlete from the mainstream of campus social, academic and athletic life. Black student-athletes typically were not permitted to reside in campus housing or otherwise engage in campus social life. They encountered demeaning comments from coaches, teammates and other members of the university community, as well as the populace of the local communities in which those colleges were located. This sense of isolation was heightened by an absence of other black students, as well as black faculty, coaches or administrators.

....

B. The Post World War II Era: From Overt to Covert Racism

During the post-World War II era, the African-American student-athlete emerged as a force to be reckoned with at predominately white colleges and universities....

Factors both external and intrinsic to intercollegiate athletics contributed to the increased integration that began in the years following the war. Increased commercialization of college sport was one of the most significant intrinsic factors.... Commercialization enhanced the pressure on colleges to field winning teams. This, in turn, propelled colleges to recruit and obtain the services of the most talented student-athletes regardless of their color.[88]

While a moral desire to end segregation may have prompted many to seek the integration of organized collegiate sport, the economic interests of others may have been of primary importance. Despite the increased integration of college athletics, the emergence of the black athlete has been restricted primarily to the "revenue producing sports...."

....It appears that, in part, colleges set aside discriminatory practices in order to reap benefits. Such benefits came in the form of championship titles and recognition accrued from the contributions of African-American student-athletes. As noted by historian Adolph Grundman, the professionalization of college sport following World War II enticed colleges to recruit African-American student-ath-

---

88. Id.

letes. He posits that their recruitment served a dual purpose: it helped these schools strengthen their athletic programs, while at the same time it promoted the advancement of race relations.

Changes occurring in society at large also contributed to the desegregation of college athletics. During the period prior to *Brown v. Board of Education*, the laws of the nation were employed to perpetuate the segregation of college sport. Conversely, Supreme Court desegregation decisions, political decisions, and events occurring in professional sport helped to break down barriers for the African-American student-athlete....

....

II. STEREOTYPES AND COVERT RACISM IN COLLEGE SPORTS

A. Permanence of Racism in Intercollegiate Athletics

1. *Differing Perceptions*

The end of exclusionary practices and most other overt forms of discrimination in collegiate sport has increased the opportunities for African-American student-athletes to compete for predominantly white institutions. Increased access stemming from self-interest has not, however, resulted in a transformation of the underlying cultural attitudes and values that helped to produce overt discrimination against the African-American college athlete. As noted by one commentator, the cynical self-interest that contributed to opening doors for black athletes did not result in an overnight transformation of attitudes.[106] In short, racism persists in college sport.

In fact, distributive equality has been accompanied by new, more subtle manifestations of racism. Nevertheless, these manifestations derive from the racial stereotyping and insensitivity which has perpetually plagued American collegiate sport. The overall impact of these new forms of discriminatory conduct is a failure to integrate, in a meaningful way, African-American student-athletes into their university communities. As described below, these new forms of discrimination result in injury that is real and harmful not only to African-American student-athletes but to other African-Americans not involved in intercollegiate athletics.

(a) *The Egalitarian Ideal*

Despite its pervasiveness, many would still deny the continued presence of racism in college sport. This denial may be attributed, in large part, to the perception that sport itself transcends race. Sport in America is idealized as an endeavor in which one can be judged solely on the basis of ability and merit. One scholar expressed this desired, yet elusive, concept as follows:

> [I]n our culture sport is often presented as one area that is free from racism. It is presented as an activity in which hard work and talent are the primary contributors for success because the bottom line in the sporting world is winning and putting the best team or individuals into any competitive situation.[112]

The African-American is presumed to have an equal opportunity to share in the rewards that can arise from sports participation.

---

106. LAPCHICK, *supra* note 103, at 226.
112. Dewar, *supra* note 14, at 230.

.... The notion of race neutrality then becomes an inherent attribute of athletic competition in general, and of organized sport in particular. Yet, as will be discussed shortly, the experiences of black participants in college sport fall short of true egalitarianism.

(b) *Illusion of Equality*

Differences in the ways in which whites and blacks perceive the same events also influence the former's tendency to discount the impact of race in college sport. Many white Americans assume that the removal of barriers to access has eradicated all racial impediments in college sport; African-Americans by and large refuse to adopt this view. The perceptions of white Americans are formed against a backdrop of the high visibility of African-American athletes who compete in the three major sports, basketball, football and baseball. Such substantial visibility creates an illusion of integration and conveniently obscures the pervasiveness of racism in sport. The fallacy of this illusion is demonstrated in non-revenue producing sports (e.g., gymnastics, golf, swimming, tennis, soccer and volleyball), which provide few opportunities for African-Americans to compete. Such views also illustrate the superficiality of defining racism in terms of access and opportunities to participate in sport.

2. *The Influence of Race*

Considerations more fundamental than the skewed vision resulting from the illusion of black dominance in sport account for these differing perceptions. The endemic nature of racism masks its reality as well as its harmful consequences.

The explicit ideology of white superiority that prevailed during the Jim Crow era has been "submerged in popular consciousness." In fact, overt forms of racism are no longer considered acceptable. It is not so clear, however, whether or not the same moral culpability attaches to unconscious racism. Professor Bell states: "the very absence of visible signs of discrimination creates an atmosphere of racial neutrality and encourages whites to believe that racism is a thing of the past...."[129]

What emerges then is an unconscious norm of white dominance that provides the basis for assessing individual and group conduct. The manifestations of this norm, however, are difficult to define. Indeed, "[l]aw and much of our social discourse recognize racism only in the form of an overt expression of white racial superiority and deliberate efforts to denigrate, segregate, or deny opportunity on the basis of skin color."[132]

Despite the muted and elusive nature of its current manifestations, the prevailing ideology of white superiority remains a product of negative stereotypes and cultural beliefs adverse to people of color. Therefore, it continues to exert a substantial influence on the interests of people of color, causing them real injury.... In summary, just as racism has played a central role in America's "socio-historical experience" and continues to influence our attitudes, perceptions and inter-relationships, it also continues to influence college sport despite disparate perceptions. The persistence of racism in intercollegiate athletics is assured when there is incorporation (by the dominant culture) of stereotypes and notions concerning African-American athletes that undergirded the segregation of college sports prior to World War II.

---

129. Bell, *supra* note 28, at 574.
132. Brown, *supra* note 23, at 307-08.

B. The Influence of Racial Stereotypes

....

1. *The Mythical African-American Athlete*

....

(a) Historical Images

The virtual exclusion of African-Americans from organized collegiate sport during the Jim Crow era was rationalized by beliefs of inferiority and inhumanity. The ideology of race cast black males as possessing unique physical stamina and skills, yet lacking intellectual awareness and feelings. For instance, African-American athletes were "simply too spontaneous and impulsive in nature to participate within the structure of sports rules with the same degree of sophistication as whites."[151]

....

Just as stereotypes and myths incorporated into the ideology of race were relied on to exclude black athletes, they have also provided a convenient means of explaining the successes and failures of African-American athletes. Even though athletic success is dependent on multiple psychological, experiential and physical factors, black athletic accomplishments were defined in terms of "natural" ability and other stereotypes that belittled individual achievement.

As a consequence, the few blacks afforded the opportunity to compete during the Jim Crow era were characterized according to fraudulent stereotypes. For instance, the athletic feats of the "superspade" were attributed to characteristics supposedly indigenous only to African-Americans. These innate physiological and psychological skills, which predisposed black athletes to engage in certain types of physical activities, were used to explain their outstanding performances. As suggested above, the ultimate impact of perceptions based on stereotypes is to deprive individuals of their autonomy inasmuch as they are reduced to predictable objects.

(b) Modern Images

Today's African-American student-athlete has witnessed an end to most overt exclusionary practices and has gained access to certain opportunities. However, derogatory images and the "superspade" myth persist. As is generally true, today's expressions of race ideology in the sport context are more subtle because they often remain repressed within the white consciousness. Nevertheless, these expressions ultimately rest on beliefs that the success of black athletes results not from intellect, hard work and determination, but from innate physical skills. These stereotypes are crucial to the development of a consciousness of white superiority that reverberates within college sport today.

....

The perceived natural athletic ability of the black athlete detracts from the discipline and work ethic required to excel in competitive sport. Moreover, the attribution of success to innate traits reinforces the false belief that black athletes are slothful and obtuse. Conversely, the characterization of the representative white athlete, which is equally false, perpetuates the myth that whites excel in competi-

---

151. EDWARDS, *supra* note 88, at 38.

tive sport in spite of their physical inferiority. Such success is attributed to the intellectual resourcefulness of the white athlete who, according to this view, is forced to compensate for a lack of innate physical ability.

(c) Media Reinforcement of Stereotypes

The image described above finds frequent reinforcement in the popular media, which describes white and black athletes differently. References to white athletes will most often refer to their intellectual capabilities while references to blacks most often refer to their physical abilities. Given the limited contact between whites and blacks, it is the media, rather than individual contact, that serves as the primary source of information shaping the identities of each group. Unfortunately, the media's depiction is too infused with stereotypes to bridge the gap in understanding the true identities of whites and blacks. To the contrary, as Professor Adeno notes, the media assists in institutionalizing the social and information gap between whites and blacks.

. . . .

III. THE HARM CAUSED BY RACISM IN COLLEGE SPORT

. . . .

A. Manifestations of a Mindset of Superiority

The following analysis of the harm occasioned by unconscious racism in collegiate sport is undertaken to a considerable extent by examining the concerns raised by the Black Coaches Association (BCA). The BCA's grievances represent a useful laundry-list. They identify the two broad categories of harmful consequences caused by the persistence of racism in intercollegiate athletics: (i) denial of unqualified participation in the college sport infrastructure; and (ii) the adverse impact on the academic, social and psychological well-being of the African-American student-athlete.

. . . .

With respect to access for African-Americans to the NCAA infrastructure, the BCA demanded an examination of three concerns: the paucity of African-American executives within the NCAA administration, the need for more African-American college faculty and coaching staff and increased opportunities for female coaches. BCA concerns regarding African-American student-athletes include: alleged disparate impact and cultural bias of NCAA initial eligibility standards; reductions in scholarships, which allegedly reduce opportunities for prospective African-American student-athletes; decreases in the numbers of African-American student-athletes competing for Division I schools; legislation limiting the access of coaches to student-athletes and prospective recruits; restrictions on the amount of athletic activities of student athletes; and rules that restrict the money student-athletes are permitted to earn.

The foregoing concerns reflect societal beliefs that, despite the integration of college athletics, African-Americans remain partial participants in the various levels of college sport, such as administration and coaching. Indeed, the inequality of access for blacks to the administration of college athletics demonstrates the persistent influence of a particular racial stereotype: the black athlete as inferior to the white athlete regarding intellectual and leadership abilities.

. . . .

B. Racism's Impact on African-American Student-Athletes

Just as unconscious racism limits the opportunities available for African-American coaches and administrators, it also limits opportunities and otherwise harms to African-American student-athletes. From the black student-athlete's perspective, stereotypes that nurture unconscious racism cause a myriad of negative effects, including:

> subtle racism evidenced in different treatment during recruitment; poor academic advice; harsh discipline; positional segregation on the playing field and social segregation off it; blame for ills for which they are not responsible. Then there are the complaints of overt racism: racial abuse; blacks being benched in games more quickly than whites; marginal whites being kept on the bench while only blacks who play are retained; extra money for the white players; summer jobs for whites and good jobs for their wives.[222]

In short, the perpetuation of stereotypes, incorporated into a dominant ideology, continues to harm black student-athletes academically, athletically, economically, socially and psychologically.

Although the extent of the practice has decreased in recent years, the phenomenon of stacking illustrates the relationship between stereotypes and limited athletic opportunities for African-American student- athletes. Stacking involves the assignment of certain individuals to specific athletic positions based on race or ethnicity rather than ability. For African-Americans, stacking historically relegated them to positions requiring "speed, quickness, and jumping ability," and other physical abilities, instead of intellect. Thus, the "thinking" and control positions, such as pitcher in baseball and quarterback in football, were reserved for white players....

....

1. The Questionable Neutrality of NCAA Regulations

Another consequence of unconscious racism is the disparate impact of NCAA rules and regulations on African-American student-athletes. The NCAA's uniform rules and regulations are premised on a notion of colorblindness. Despite their assumed neutrality, the NCAA rules appear to impact black student- athletes disproportionately. Indeed, over the past ten years, considerable debate has revolved around the disparate impact of NCAA initial eligibility requirements on African-American student-athletes. However, eligibility rules provide but a single illustration of NCAA rules and regulations. Many believe that these rules as a whole operate to produce disproportionate injury to African-American student-athletes and their communities. Ultimately, the question posed is whether racial realities should be considered in assessing the need for and application of particular rules and regulations, especially those rules that concern limitations on player/coach contact, limitations on earned income, reductions in scholarships, sanctions for rules violations and academic eligibility standards.

.... [The issue of the neutrality of NCAA academic eligibility rules is discussed in detail in the article by Kenneth Shropshire that appears in the Due Process section of this anthology. — ed.].

---

222. LAPCHICK, *supra* note 103, at 236.

2. Academic Racism?

....

(a) Intellectual Marginalization

Several factors converge to produce neglect of the academic needs of African-American student-athletes. Principal among them is a mindset that all but disregards the educational interests of black student-athletes. As noted above, this mindset stems in large part from assumed beliefs nurtured by stereotypes of the intellectually inferior, yet athletically superior, black athlete....

The foregoing underscores what Professor Harry Edwards characterized as the three strikes that burden African-American student-athletes. First, they must contend with reverberations of the "dumb jock" caricature, which transcend racial boundaries. In addition, the African-American student-athlete must endure the racial implications of the myth of "innate black athletic superiority." Finally, there are the insidiously racist implications of the stereotype of the "'dumb Negro' condemned by racial heritage to intellectual inferiority."

Each of these "strikes" contribute to institutional tolerance of the devaluation of the academic needs of African-American student-athletes. Beyond their athletic skills, far too little is expected academically of the black student-athlete who becomes a commodity serving the financial interests of the institutions for which they compete. The product of this mindset is the exclusion of African-American student-athletes from the academic and social mainstream in many predominantly white colleges and universities.

(b) Racism and Higher Education

....

The unconscious racism within the existing American educational paradigm also contributes to the social isolation of African-American student-athletes. This isolation operates as another detrimental strike, rendering them particularly susceptible to academic and psychological injury. Additionally, as discussed above, the black athlete's isolation derives in part from the problems that confront all African-American students on predominantly white campuses. Social and academic isolation are, however, exacerbated in the case of the black student-athlete. The unconscious racism inherent in environments that fail sufficiently to nurture African-American students spawns deliberate actions that often relegate the black student-athlete to the status of a social and academic outsider.

By devoting greater efforts to recruiting African-American students who are athletes rather than those who are non-athletes, some commentators contend, universities contribute to the sense of isolation of black student-athletes....

....

The sense of isolation experienced by many black student-athletes is significant given that the quality of social interactions, including relationships with coaches and other students, contributes to the academic success of student-athletes. In short, all student-athletes are subjected to pressures that create an ongoing tension between their roles as students and athletes. Yet, the black student-athlete confronts the additional challenge of overcoming institutional barriers. For example, when barriers are perpetuated by unconscious racism, the athlete's ability to obtain requisite academic skills is impeded. This loss is damaging to the black student-athlete, as these skills are necessary for effectively addressing the myriad of situations they will encounter throughout life. Thus, the social marginalization experienced by today's black student-athletes adversely impacts their academic potential, just as exclusionary Jim Crow era practices were detrimental to the academic success of black athletes....

....

IV. REDRESSING THE HARM OF UNCONSCIOUS RACISM

....

A. A Race-Conscious Approach

....

As noted above, institutional environment is critical in determining the black student-athlete's potential for academic success at predominantly white institutions. As noted by the chief scientist of the Report of the American Institutes for Research, "What the report shows is just bringing [black student-athletes] on campus is not enough."[327] The something more that is required is the development of a supportive environment, one that would work to lessen the academic and social hostility black student-athletes encounter at predominantly white institutions.

The provision of an academically supportive environment may require increased hiring of African-American coaches and administrators who can provide the mentoring and design programs that will improve the academic, social and professional opportunities for black student-athletes. Concomitant with increases in the number of black coaches and administrators should be increased admission of non-athlete African-American students. More specifically, courts should require predominantly white colleges that recruit and employ student-athletes "to engage in race-conscious admissions and hiring policies to increase black student enrollment, faculty, and staff."[329]

Such efforts alone, however, are likely to prove inadequate. On account of the often deficient educational backgrounds of many black student-athletes, universities must implement academic support systems that "provide skill building opportunities along with tutorial services..."[330] As one sociologist noted, academic support programs must "shift their focus from the short term goal of eligibility to the long-term development of the black student-athlete."[334]

B. Contract-Based Remedies

The student-athlete's relationship with his or her college is widely acknowledged by courts and commentators as premised on an express contract... The existence of this contractual relationship brings into question the utility of contract to provide the basis for an antidiscrimination norm. It is relevant, therefore, to explore the extent to which statutory and common law contractually-based principles provide means for redressing the academic neglect of black student-athletes.

---

327. Rhoden, *supra* note 276, at A1.
329. Brown-Scott, *supra* note 285, at 53-54.
330. Sellers, *et al., supra* note 248, at 35.
334. Sellers, *et al., supra* note 248, at 35.

1. *Civil Rights Approach — Section 1981*

Section 1981 of the Civil Rights Act prohibits racial discrimination in the contracting process. In the institution's performance of its contractually-based educational obligation to its student-athletes, racism harms the latter's academic interests. Thus, racism resulting in harm during the performance stage of the contracting process invites inquiry into the availability of § 1981 as a means of redressing and thereby protecting the academic interests of black student-athletes.

In this regard, despite the contractual relationship, the utility of § 1981 is dubious. Section 1981, like most antidiscrimination statutes, proscribes only intentional acts of racial discrimination. Therefore, to sustain a § 1981 claim, the student-athlete would be required to show that the institution's conduct was motivated by race. Except in rare instances, however, the academic neglect of black student-athletes appears to result from unconscious rather than deliberately overt forms of racial discrimination....

2. *Common Law Contract as an Antidiscrimination Norm*

Common law contract principles may provide the theoretical foundation for developing an antidiscrimination norm to address the unconscious racism that confronts African-Americans engaged in collegiate athletics. As specifically described below, such principles can, in some instances, be employed to constrain discriminatory conduct that harms black student-athletes. In addition, these principles provide a basis for imposing affirmative obligations on universities and colleges to promote the academic interests of African-American student-athletes. The discussion that follows proposes that, of these principles, the duty of good faith and fair dealing holds the most utility for providing the basis for a common law antidiscrimination norm.

.... [A general discussion of the Good Faith Doctrine as an Antidiscrimination Norm is omitted. - ed.].

4. *Applying the Good Faith Antidiscrimination Norm*

A good faith performance doctrine premised on limiting discretion in order to promote reasonable expectations holds promise as a vehicle of redressing the unconscious racism that harms black student-athletes' academic interests. The propriety of applying the doctrine in this context stems from the discretion that institutions possess in determining the contours of their obligations to provide student-athletes with educational benefits. In addition, the parties' reasonable expectations justify the requirement that institutions provide their student-athletes a meaningful opportunity to benefit educationally.

The express contract between student-athletes and their institutions fails to define clearly the nature and scope of the latter's educational obligation to student-athletes. More precisely, the contract documents do not articulate the nature of institutions' contractual obligations to assist their student-athletes in achieving educational goals. The result of this failure is to imbue colleges and universities with considerable discretion in the performance of their educational obligation.

Under an impact theory of good faith, a broad contextual approach would be used to determine the reasonable expectations of the parties with regard to an institution's educational obligation to its student-athletes. This approach would conclude that a fundamental expectation that goes to the very heart of the student-athlete/university relationship is the expectation that student-athletes be afforded an opportunity to obtain a meaningful educational experience. Consequently, anything short of efforts directed toward integrating African-American student-athletes into the academic and social mainstream of campus life would deny them the full value of the contract into which they enter with the institution. "By diminishing the contract's value, the institution does not merely frustrate, but actually defeats the student-athlete's reasonable expectations."[407] Following such an analysis, consideration would be given to the impact of racism on this and other reasonable expectations inherent in the relationship. To the extent that overt or subtle forms of racism result in conduct that undermines these expectations, institutions would be held accountable pursuant to the good faith performance doctrine.

Under an impact theory, evidence such as the disparity between the graduation rates of African-American student-athletes and their white counterparts would suggest a breach of the good faith performance doctrine. Such a disparity would demonstrate that institutions, as parties to the contract, are exercising their discretion in performance in ways that obstruct the ability of African-American student-athletes to obtain educational benefits. For example, counseling an African-American student-athlete who entered college with low academic predictors to take courses aimed toward eligibility rather than skill-building would constitute an improper exercise of discretion. Such conduct would be "inconsistent with the parties'...purposes in contracting."[410]

Disparate graduation rates would also provide evidence that institutions exercised their discretion improperly by not doing or performing those things necessary to accomplish the purpose of the contract. Providing the requisite resources to afford African-American student-athletes with an ability to develop educationally may involve constructing academic assistance programs and counseling geared toward the long-term development of the student-athlete. Such programs would attempt to assist these students in developing skills, such as note-taking, writing, time management and reading comprehension. The required affirmative conduct on the part of institutions might also involve hiring black administrators to assist African-American student-athletes in making adjustments necessary to achieve academically.

VI. CONCLUSION

As noted at the beginning of this Article, the goal has not been to touch on all of the implications of racism in college sport. The more modest aim has been to begin a candid dialogue to address this issue. In this regard, certain key points are worthy of restatement if such a dialogue is to be meaningful.

First, as is true of society in general, untrue stereotypes underlie the subtle forms of racism prevalent in college sport. Despite its covert nature, persistent racism in college athletics inflicts real injury on its African-American participants. A particularly vulnerable group are African-American student-athletes. Their academic needs suffer as a result of misconceptions propelled by myths concerning their intellectual and athletic abilities.

---

407. Davis, *supra* note 261, at 778.
410. Centronics Corp. v. Genicom Corp., 562 A.2d 187, 193.

Secondly, long-term solutions to the harm inflicted upon student-athletes and other African-American participants in college sport will require honest and creative approaches that may transcend traditional doctrinal boundaries. In the short term, this Article has identified potential approaches for providing some modicum of relief for the harm caused by racism. Some of these theories suggest new ways of utilizing traditional doctrines. Whatever the mechanism employed, racial justice for African-American participants in college sport will remain elusive, absent recognition of the role of racism.

Marilyn V. Yarbrough, A Sporting Chance: The Intersection of Race and Gender
38 South Texas Law Review 1029 (1997)*

. . . .

III. "IF YOU LET ME PLAY SPORTS"

The jurisprudential "invisibility" of African-American women, residing as they do at the intersection of two subordinating factors, race and gender, is mirrored in other facets of their lives. Current debates and responses to claims of the disparate treatment of women in intercollegiate athletics is one such example. Efforts to raise participation rates for women, one of several ways to satisfy Title IX/gender equity compliance concerns, have relied on the so-called "country club" (golf, tennis, swimming) or "prep school" (lacrosse, field hockey) sports, or sports that depend on already enrolled students, the so-called "walk-on" sports. To the extent that educationally and economically disadvantaged women (categories to which a large percentage of African-American women and girls belong) lack any opportunity to participate in either category, reliance on these solutions to gender equity debates again contributes to their invisibility. Ironically, criticism of the demand for gender equity based on the potential negative impact on opportunities for "minority student-athletes," by its terms suggests that women (for whom equity is demanded) who are also members of minority groups are not included in the term "minority student-athletes," (for whom opportunity is potentially curtailed), additional evidence of the invisibility of women of color.

An earlier essay, *If You Let Me Play Sports*, was inspired by a Nike commercial. In the commercial, the voices and images of preadolescent girls blending into each other chant,

[I]f you let me play sports.
I will like myself more; I will have more self-confidence.
If you let me play sports. . . .
If you let me play, I will be 60 percent less likely to get breast cancer;
I will suffer less depression. If you let me play sports,
I will be more likely to leave a man who beats me.
If you let me play, I will be less likely to get pregnant before I want to.

I will learn what it means to be strong. If you let me play ... [16]

Among the research findings on which Nike relied were several that were not used in the ad that held special significance for women of color.

- A 45-year-old black woman is twice as likely to be overweight as a white woman the same age and 20% less likely to exercise regularly because exercise is viewed by many blacks as a luxury they don't have time for. Compared to white Americans, African-Americans under the age of 64 are 10% more likely to get heart disease, 30% more likely to have diabetes, and over 50% more likely to suffer from hypertension. [17]

- [G]irls derive as many benefits from sports as boys and ... Hispanic female athletes receive special benefits. They were more likely than their non-athletic peers to score well on achievement tests, stay in high school, attend college and make progress towards a Bachelor's degree. [18]

- African American women have not been represented proportionately among the increasing numbers of female athletes. By 1980, African American women represented only 6 to 8 percent of all women athletes; this was less than their proportion in the general population. Although African American women were over represented in certain sports such as basketball and track and field, they were almost completely absent from other sports such as tennis and swimming. [19]

...

As noted in my previous essay,

> Sports participation as savior is admittedly an optimistic and reductionist view whether claimed for men or women, whatever race.... [T]oo many variables—what sport, which race, which gender.... [In other words,] the individual circumstances of the participant play too big a part. Regardless, the effective denial of even those tentative and unpredictable benefits to a large segment of our population is unconscionable.
>
> Steps are being taken to insure that women and girls have equivalent opportunities to participate. My concern ... is whether African-American women [and girls] are receiving the benefits in equal numbers. [21]

That earlier critique, however, did not investigate or propose solutions for this dilemma except in its plea for less fragmentation in the pursuit of two extremely important and worthy goals: the elimination of race *and* sex discrimination in this aspect of society and the provision of equal educational opportunity for all student athletes. My purpose in this essay is to help us see this particular problem as a reflection of society's laws and values.

---

16. Text as reported in Eleanor Mallet, *Everywoman: Letting Girls Have a Sporting Chance*, THE PLAIN DEALER, Oct. 3, 1995, at E1.

17. WOMEN'S SPORTS FOUNDATION, WOMEN'S SPORTS FACTS 3 (Oct. 8, 1996) (citing Susanna Levin, "Walking Shorts: Leading the Way," *Walking*, Feb. 1993, at 9).

18. *Id.* (citing WOMEN'S SPORTS FOUNDATION, THE WOMEN'S SPORTS FOUNDATION REPORT: MINORITIES IN SPORTS 5 (1989)).

19. *Id.* (citing Rebertha Abney & Dorothy L. Richey, *Opportunities for Minority Women in Sports: The Impact of Title IX*, JOPERD: J. PHYSICAL EDUC., RECREATION & DANCE, Mar. 1992, at 56).

21. Yarbrough, *supra* note 15, at 231-32.

IV. THE INTERSECTION OF RACE AND GENDER

The anomalous situation of women of color in general equality jurisprudence bodes ill for similar debates about Title IX and gender equity that will inevitably arise. Although many authors have addressed this so-called "intersectionality" dilemma, few have proposed constitutional jurisprudential solutions that recognize the special problems of those who suffer discrimination because of their gender as well as their race. Professor Judy Scales-Trent, in one of the earliest law review articles on the subject, argues for strict scrutiny, the toughest level of review afforded in contemporary constitutional jurisprudence. The same year, Professor Kimberle Crenshaw... documented the disregard with which courts have treated statutory intersection issues that have come before them. As previously noted, the focus of this essay is a proposal that the courts adopt or adhere to a different way of looking at the levels of scrutiny and other treatment ostensibly accorded under the Equal Protection Clause, and Titles VI, VII, and IX, that will encompass not the strict scrutiny that Scales-Trent calls for, but instead, a balancing test based on the importance of the right or interest involved, the invidiousness of the classification, and other reasons for supporting or denying the differential treatment involved.

This proposal is not really new. Commentators freely discussed it in the late 1960s and in the 1970s. It is also not at all rare in equal protection jurisprudence. Several United States Supreme Court opinions contain language that either proposes something akin to this type of balancing test, or recognizes that for issues other than those related to athletics, indeed for those that have no relationship to race or gender, this type of balancing is indeed what is happening when the Court decides equal protection claims.

Before we explore these opinions, examples of the actual legal dilemmas caused by these intersection problems will likely provide context for the proposed balancing. As explained above in the discussion of gender equity and opportunities for minority student-athletes, those of us who are neither white nor male often experience *invisibility* as a result of our dual subordinate status. Professor Crenshaw describes three Title VII cases in which courts declared black women not to be representative of either African-American people or women, yet refused to recognize African-American women *qua* African-American women as a classification with recognizable rights to redress when they have suffered discrimination.

In *DeGraffenreid v. General Motors Assembly Division*,[27] the first case discussed in Crenshaw's article, the court stated that the lawsuit brought by black women who protested discriminatory hiring and layoff patterns against them were not subject to remediation, since no such discrimination existed against black men or white women. The court reasoned that:

> [T]his lawsuit must be examined to see if it states a cause of action for race discrimination, sex discrimination, or alternatively either, but not a combination of both....
> The legislative history surrounding Title VII does not indicate that the goal of the statute was to create a new classification of "black women" who would have greater standing than, for example, a black male. The prospect of the cre-

---

27. 413 F. Supp. 142 (E.D. Mo. 1976)

ation of new classes of protected minorities, governed only by the mathematical principles of permutation and combination, clearly raises the prospect of opening the hackneyed Pandora's box.[29]

As Crenshaw observed, "[t]he court's refusal...to acknowledge that Black women encounter combined race and sex discrimination implies that the boundaries of sex and race discrimination doctrine are defined respectively by white women's and Black men's experiences."[30]

In sports participation, the experience of the African-American woman has never been that of the white woman. Like the feminist movement in general, this is true whether we examine events that led to the passage of Title IX or the terms of its subsequent enforcement. As one sociologist has observed: "(a) Black women have been disproportionately located at the lower end of the economic hierarchy and, therefore, have been unable to afford private golf, swimming, or tennis lessons. (b) Overt racial discrimination prevented black women from gaining access to the sports participated in by white women."[33]

The newest scheme, touted by many as the saving grace for the achievement of gender equity or compliance with Title IX goals, is the addition of team sports for women, principally soccer and crew. The pendulum, earlier pointing toward soccer, given its popularity among young girls and boys, is now swinging toward crew, the ultimate walk-on sport, and the only presently existing team sport that can rival men's football in squad size. Conventional wisdom suggests that anyone with the least bit of athleticism can be trained to row in a relatively short period of time. Because the main thrust of proposed solutions to gender inequity and the lack of compliance with Title IX mandates has been the expansion of participation by women, through the addition of opportunities in the country club and prep school sports or those sports not traditionally accessible to black women, we lose yet again. Because it is a walk-on sport and because some student-athletes will find it difficult to attend college and thereby have an opportunity to walk-on without grants-in- aid, the opportunity for participation by women of color is an elusive one. This is a problem for poor women, whether African-American or not.

The thrust of the proposal that is the subject of this essay is that courts and legislators have begun to engage in a different analysis than the present one. With this constitutional flexibility, the treatment presently accorded under the various statutory and regulatory schemes could more effectively address their concerns. This would in turn provide guidance for institutions subject to Title IX or other gender equity mandates.

Shortly after *Craig v. Boren*,[36] the seminal opinion which provided for a third tier of scrutiny for classifications involving gender, a federal district court in Colorado examined the issue of gender discrimination in an interscholastic soccer program. In *Hoover v. Meiklejohn*, the court adopted a balancing test such as the one I propose today, citing judicial commentary from as early as 1970 criticizing the then two-tiered, later three- tiered, equal protection analysis. In the opinion of Judge Matsch in that case, the approach amounted to a *per se* test masquerading

---

29. *Id.* at 143, 145.
30. Crenshaw, *supra* note 23, at 142-43.
33. LEONARD, *supra* note 31, at 261.
36. 429 U.S. 190 (1976).

as critical analysis. Judge Matsch (later of Oklahoma City bombing trial fame) cites a dissent by Justice Marshall, an observation in dissent by Chief Justice Burger, a concurring opinion by Justice Stevens, and a concurring opinion by Justice Powell in noting public pronouncements critical of the three-tiered approach. Quoting Justice Stevens' concurring opinion in *Craig*, Judge Matsch stated:

> There is only one Equal Protection Clause. It requires every State to govern impartially. It does not direct the courts to apply one standard of review in some cases and a different standard in other cases. Whatever criticism may be levelled at a judicial opinion implying that there are at least three such standards applies with the same force to a double standard.
>
> I am inclined to believe that what has become known as the two-tiered analysis of equal protection claims does not describe a completely logical method of deciding cases, but rather is a method the Court has employed to explain decisions that actually apply a single standard in a reasonably consistent fashion. I also suspect that a careful explanation of the reasons motivating particular decisions may contribute more to an identification of that standard than an attempt to articulate it in all-encompassing terms.[44]

It is Justice Powell's formulation of an alternative, however, that Judge Matsch adopts in H*oover*. Judge Powell in turn credits...[an] article written...by then Professor, now Judge, J. Harvie Wilkinson III...As Professor Wilkinson explained,

> The constitutional inquiry to test governmental denials of equal opportunity ought to weigh and to balance carefully the following elements. (1) the importance of the opportunity being unequally burdened or denied; (2) the strength of the state interest served in denying it; and (3) the character of the groups whose opportunities are denied. (footnote omitted) The test is very different from the present suspect classification inquiry which focuses almost exclusively on the third element, purportedly ignores the first altogether if no suspect class is involved, and scrutinizes state interests only in two widely variant categories of rational and compelling.[46]

    ....

Judge Matsch went on to apply this analysis to Donna Hoover's claim, concluding,

> It is an inescapable conclusion that the complete denial of any opportunity to play interscholastic soccer is a violation of the plaintiff's right to equal protection of the law under the Fourteenth Amendment. This same conclusion would be required under even the minimal "rational relationship" standard of review applied to classifications which are not suspect and do not involve fundamental rights.

Before and after the use of such a balancing test in *Hoover*, several pronouncements in U.S. Supreme Court opinions and by lower courts have, if not advocating or recognizing the same reasoning, criticized the present three-tiered analysis.

Kenneth Karst's 1977 Harvard Law Review Foreword that reviewed the 1976 Supreme Court Term refers to Justice Marshall's and Justice Rehnquist's "discontent" with the Supreme Court's equal protection jurisprudence. He notes that

---

44. *Id.* (quoting *Craig*, 429 U.S. at 211-12 (Stevens, J. concurring)).

46. *Hoover*, 430 F. Supp. at 168-69 (citing J. Harvie Wilkinson, III, *The Supreme Court, the Equal Protection Clause, and the Three Faces of Constitutional Equality*, 61 Va. L. Rev. 945, 991 (1975)).

"coherent doctrine can be expected to lag behind...innovative decisions. In the case of current equal protection doctrine, however, the gap between results and articulated theory is unusually wide."[51]...He noted then that:

> The inadequacy of the two-tier approach, which had been remarked [on] before Rodriguez was decided, has since become even more conspicuous....It is now commonplace for an opinion of the Court in an equal protection case to be accompanied by an assortment of concurring and dissenting opinions, all staking out different ground. Surely we are near the point of maximum incoherence of equal protection doctrine.[54]

Several Supreme Court justices and a few commentators continue to suggest that although it is convenient to look at the Fourteenth Amendment Equal Protection Clause as having some fixed set of criteria, the description of the tiers and the tests is more than anything else a convenient way of explaining decisions after the fact....

....

V. CONCLUSION

Much of what appears in these opinions, and to some extent in the so-called "reverse discrimination" higher education cases such as *Hogan* and *Bakke*, and of course in Judge Matsch's opinion in *Hoover*, argues for an approach not *per se*, but more akin to the balance proposed in this essay. Under that approach, judges would be more reluctant to require proof of discrimination based on race *or* discrimination based on gender *or* the interests involved, and might in fact base their judgments on more balanced and rational considerations.

A woman of color would simply need to show that an official classification unduly burdened her in her pursuit of an important, or legitimate, or compelling— whatever the standard—benefit, in the case of opportunities for scholastic or intercollegiate sports participation, or equal educational opportunity. The invidiousness of the classifications would only add ballast to her claim of unreasonableness. In our other statutory paradigm, the workforce, the denial or recognition of claims of women of color who were not hired or not promoted or not given raises would likewise depend on a determination of the importance of that benefit and the invidious nature of the classification(s), and not on whether they fit a category that *per se* required strict or intermediate scrutiny. Equality, not based on artificial categories, would more resemble a continuum rather than three hurdles.

2. Gender Issues in Collegiate Sport

Introduction

In the introductory text to their chapter on gender equity, Professors Weiler and Roberts comment that "[n]o feature of college sports—perhaps of any part

---

51. *Id.*
54. Karst, *supra* note 8, at 3 (citation omitted).

of the sports world—has witnessed a greater impact from the law than the surge in athletics opportunities and resources for women student-athletes over the last quarter century."* The surge in athletic related opportunities for women athletes, due in large part to Title IX litigation, has resulted in the concomitant development of considerable scholarship regarding gender equity and Title IX. The voluminous nature of this literature led us to adopt a three-fold approach, the end result of which is the inclusion of articles that: address the significance of sports participation for women athletics; are doctrinally focused and thus summarize current judicial interpretations of Title IX; and offer differing perspectives on the complex and controversial web of issues generated by Title IX and efforts to achieve gender equity in intercollegiate athletics.

The article titled "Cheering on Women and Girls in Sport..." focuses on the value of sports participation for women and provides a helpful context within which to view the materials that follow. The author articulates the position that participation in sports by girls and women is instrumental in eroding stereotypes and in empowering women to develop the confidence essential to success in endeavors that transcend athletics.

This article is followed by excerpts that discuss the current state of judicial interpretation of Title IX standards. We encountered considerable difficulty in deciding on which articles to include herein inasmuch as we could have included any number of articles that provide in-depth analyses of Title IX case law. We opted, however, to include excerpts from two recent articles by Brake and Catlin and by Leahy that provide an overview of Title IX's legislative history and the current status of judicial interpretations of the statute.

The decision to limit to two, the articles that explore Title IX jurisprudence was influenced, in part, by our desire to include within this section two government publications: the Office of Civil Right's letters of clarification relating to standards for determining compliance with Title IX participation requirements and financial apportionment. We view these controversial documents as important components in the development of a Title IX/gender equity jurisprudence.

Articles by two advocates of gender equity in intercollegiate athletics, who urge caution in developing standards to achieve this goal, lead off the Commentary section. Professor John Weistart proposes that standards to achieve gender equity should take into account three realities of intercollegiate athletics: the budgetary structure of college sports that grants football and men's basketball preference over women's and other men's non-revenue sports in resource allocations; the evolving nature of sports, in general, and women's interest in athletic participation; and the need to avoid building new biases into intercollegiate athletics. Similarly, Professor Glenn George urges caution in using the proportionality standard as a substitute for actual student interest in attempting to achieve equity.

The Commentary section concludes with articles by Leahy and by Brake and Catlin that present sharply contrasting views on the adoption and implementation of standards for determining compliance with Title IX's requirement. These authors stake out conflicting positions on issues including: whether proportionality equals quota, reverse discrimination and the constitutionality of OCR and judicial interpretations of Title IX standards.

---

* Paul C. Weiler & Gary R. Roberts, Sports and the Law (2d ed. West 1998).

This chapter closes with an article that examines the issue of gender violence in collegiate sport. The authors, while advocating the use of Title IX as a means of holding colleges and universities accountable for acts of violence by student-athletes against women students, urge caution in developing policies premised upon stereotypical views of athletes.

(a) The Social Significance of Sport for Women

Cheering on Women and Girls in Sports:
Using Title IX to Fight Gender Role Oppression
110 Harv. L. Rev. 1627 (1997)*

. . . .

II. THE BEGINNING OF A THEORY OF EMPOWERMENT AND RESOCIALIZATION THROUGH SPORTS

The power of Title IX lies in its ability to change both women's and girls' everyday lives and the ways men and women interact in society. The backlash identified above, to the contrary, has the potential to preserve traditional gender roles and relations, thereby diffusing the power of Title IX. Feminist legal approaches to sports can help women and girls overcome this threat and reap the potential benefits of Title IX.

A. *Limits of Current Theoretical Approaches*

Current feminist legal approaches to Title IX, however, have not done enough to help women and girls reap the potential benefits of Title IX. Rather, those approaches based on a liberal feminist model have focused on changing women's and girls' everyday lives, to the exclusion of changing the ways men and women interact in society. Conversely, those approaches based on difference and dominance feminist models have focused on the latter, to the exclusion of the former. The limits of all of these approaches suggest that feminist legal theorists need to develop an integrated approach that includes the insights of each strand of feminist theory, yet transcends their artificial boundaries.

Advocates of the passage of Title IX were motivated in large part by liberal feminist theory. Indeed, Title IX was like almost all of the other feminist reforms of the 1960s and early 1970s, in that its goals were to provide access to traditionally male structures, and to provide equality of opportunity once inside. Proponents argued that, whenever schools and colleges offered boys' and men's sports, girls and women should have sports opportunities in proportion to their numbers. Further, proponents suggested that equal access requires that girls' and women's sports receive funding, facilities, coaching, and other support on a par with boys' and men's sports.

At the same time, though, the liberal feminist approach to sports, as embodied in the passage and enforcement of Title IX, provides little justification for why girls and women should play sports, beyond the fact that boys and men do. Indeed,

---

sports seemed valuable to the proponents of Title IX only because sports were a male preserve from which women were excluded. Liberal feminists have not explained why women and girls should want to participate in the structure of high school and college sports — a structure that had defined itself in part by excluding women and, for many years, people of color. Moreover, they have not considered that women and girls may experience sports differently from men and boys because of their historical exclusion and that, once inside, women and girls may simply perpetuate exclusionary practices against other groups as well as themselves.

Feminists who take either a difference or dominance feminist approach to sports have attempted to answer some of these questions. Many of their answers consist of critiques of liberal feminist legal approaches to sports. Both difference and dominance feminists argue that Title IX has done nothing to change the structures, practices, or policies of sports at the vast majority of high schools and colleges. Rather, they argue, Title IX simply lets women and girls join in.

Further, difference and dominance feminists argue that those who do join in are complicit in structures, practices, and policies that discriminate against women in at least three ways. First, Title IX benefits white women more than it does women of color, because white women attend college in much larger numbers than do women of color. Moreover, many colleges and universities have complied with Title IX by adding women's sports, such as golf, squash, and tennis, which are played predominantly by white women. Second, Title IX has squeezed out many female coaches and administrators by making the coaching and administration of women's sports more prestigious, and hence more attractive to male coaches and administrators. Finally, and most importantly, Title IX has done little to change an athletic culture that polarizes the sexes and perpetuates male domination. Athletic success is still equated with masculinity, and women and girls must "choose between being a successful girl and being a successful athlete."[71] When taken together, these facts suggest that Title IX has not dramatically altered the underlying sentiments that kept women and girls out of sports in the first place.

In addition to difference and dominance feminists' critique of the liberal feminist approach, difference feminists have posited affirmative reasons that women and girls *should* participate in sports, reasons beyond the mere fact that men and boys play sports. They argue that sports nurture and reinforce the cooperation and relationship skills that women already possess. If women are given opportunities to participate in sports on their own terms, as opposed to the male model that Title IX de facto adopted, they can exhibit these cooperation and relationship skills to the world and serve as models for an alternative social structure that is built on these qualities. Women can thereby transform the "ideology of meritocracy" that equates success, in sports and beyond, with masculine strength and domination.

However, the difference feminist approach does not address how sports can be valuable to *individual* women and girls. If sports only reinforce skills that women and girls already possess, they do not need to engage in sports to reap these benefits. Moreover, difference feminists do not believe that individual women benefit from the symbolism that often accompanies women's and girls' participation in

---

71. Mackinnon, *supra* note 7, at 120.

structures that previously excluded them. Indeed, unless women's and girls' participation can transform those structures, participation only taints the skills that women already possess. Therefore, the difference feminist approach does not provide any reason that individual girls can benefit from playing with or like the boys.

B. *Toward a Theory of Empowerment Through Sports*

Women and girls can in fact benefit from playing with and like men and boys. To some extent, women and girls can profit from breaking down stereotypes that continue to keep them out of sports. But even more directly, they can empower themselves by developing the confidence and self-esteem that they will need to succeed in school, the workplace, and the rest of their lives.

Sports help many women and girls gain more confidence in their everyday interactions. As most girls enter adolescence, they begin to believe that they are valued more for their relationships with others than for their intrinsic beings. Girls therefore learn to silence personal opinions and preferences in an effort to avoid conflict that could threaten their personal relationships. In the process, they come to define themselves in relation to others and to lose confidence in themselves as independent beings. Participation in sports can help girls overcome this disabling crisis in confidence. Sports can increase girls' feeling of self-worth by providing them a forum in which to learn how to assert themselves and, in team sports, to do so when others are relying on them. Moreover, sports can help girls realize and accept that, although some aspects of life are unavoidable, others are within their own control. Sports can therefore serve as an important means of survival in a society that attempts to define individual women and girls in relation to others.

Another way sports can increase the confidence of women and girls is by helping them develop better relationships with their bodies. Generally, men and women learn to experience their bodies differently. Most boys are socialized to play rough and take physical risks; girls, to play it safe and not hurt themselves. This mentality is rooted in the high value society places on women's, as opposed to men's, physical appearance. Girls are taught to maintain their appearance and to protect themselves from any activity that could mar it. As such, girls traditionally are discouraged from playing sports, and many girls lack the individual desire to play sports, especially once they reach adolescence. This lack of participation, in turn, leads to a vicious circle. Because women and girls see few of their peers playing sports, they assume that they are too weak and frail to play. Yet women and girls who actually play sports realize both that they are not weak and that they can survive any departures from bodily perfection. Sports can therefore help girls to value their bodies, and the power of their bodies, even when those bodies are not what they consider to be physically perfect.

C. *Toward a Theory of Resocialization Through Sports*

In addition to providing a source of individual survival strategies and empowerment, sports can also give women and girls the ability to transform existing social structures. First, by participating in sports, women and girls can learn valuable teamwork skills. This cooperative aspect of playing team sports can help women and girls work better with others, both in the classroom and in professional institutions generally.

Second, if more girls play sports with boys at an early age, boys and girls will necessarily view each other differently from the way they currently do. If girls always participate with the boys in youth soccer leagues and the like, men may come to see women's participation in professional institutions as a given. Girls may also learn to view boys as less intimidating, which would provide them with the confidence and skills necessary to succeed within professional institutions in later life. Moreover, this increased confidence will reinforce men's acceptance of women's participation. And once the people within these institutions have changed, the institutions themselves will be more susceptible to change. Hence, integrating sports at an early age has the potential to change the nature of gender hierarchy.

....

IV. CONCLUSION

Women and girls are playing sports in record numbers, calling into question traditional ideas about male and female activities. But these numbers are not enough to fight the gender role oppression that impedes true gender equality. Only if feminist legal theorists recognize and nurture the potential of sports to empower women and girls and to resocialize both men and women will these numbers lead to meaningful change. Feminist legal theorists can begin this process by encouraging the expansion of current approaches to Title IX litigation. With this start, women and girls and men and boys can look forward to the day when they can truly play as equals — both on the field and off.

(b) Title IX: Status of the Law

Deborah Brake & Elizabeth Catlin, The Path of Most Resistance: The Long Road Toward Gender Equity in Intercollegiate Athletics
3 Duke Journal of Gender Law & Policy 51 (1996)*

....

I. AN OVERVIEW OF TITLE IX

Title IX of the Education Amendments of 1972 is the federal law prohibiting discrimination on the basis of sex in education programs, including sports programs, by any school receiving federal financial assistance. Title IX has been the primary vehicle for asserting the right of women and girls to equal opportunity in high school and college athletics, and has played a vital role in opening competitive sports to female athletes over the last twenty-four years.

....

B. Title IX's Legal History

1. *Enactment of Title IX and the Emergence of Athletics as a Point of Controversy.* Title IX was passed in 1972 as a response to overwhelming evidence of

---

widespread discrimination against women at all levels of education. The language of Title IX, which provides that "No person in the United States shall, on the basis of sex, be excluded from participation in, be denied benefits of, or be subjected to discrimination under any education program or activity receiving federal financial assistance...,"[8] is modelled on the prohibitions against race and national origin discrimination contained in Title VI of the Civil Rights Act of 1964. Although Title IX was originally proposed as an amendment to Title VI that would have added the word "sex" to its prohibited forms of discrimination, the prevalence of discrimination in education resulted in a more narrowly tailored bill specifically aimed at educational programs.

While Title IX itself does not mention athletics, the issue of discrimination against women in sports programs was briefly addressed in the original debates on the legislation, reflecting an expectation that athletics would be covered. Soon after Title IX was enacted, prompted by strenuous lobbying by the National Collegiate Athletics Association (NCAA) which feared that Title IX signalled the demise of men's sports programs, several bills and amendments were introduced in Congress in an effort to exempt revenue-producing sports from coverage under Title IX. The debates that ensued over these efforts to limit the application of Title IX, as well as their subsequent defeat, reinforced the intent of Congress to end discrimination in college and high school sports.

In May of 1974, Senator John Tower (R-Tex.) made the first strike against Title IX in what became known as the Tower Amendment. Through this amendment, Senator Tower sought first to exempt all intercollegiate athletics, but then modified his amendment to exempt "intercollegiate athletic activity to the extent that such activity does or may provide gross receipts or donations to the institution necessary to support that activity."[14] His basic argument was that sports such as football provided a crucial revenue base for the entire athletic program of many schools, and that any interference with these teams in the name of gender equity would spell disaster for both the male athletes already playing and the female athletes who were seeking a chance to play. Senator Bayh, sponsor of the Title IX legislation, argued vociferously against the Tower Amendment, pointing out that it inappropriately "focused on the ability of certain intercollegiate sports to withstand the financial burdens imposed by the equal opportunity requirements of Title IX" rather than on discrimination against women. Nevertheless, arguments in favor of the amendment prevailed and the Tower Amendment was passed by the Senate.

When the Tower Amendment reached the conference committee on the Education Amendments of 1974, however, it was deleted in favor of a far different provision requiring the Department of Health, Education and Welfare (HEW) to promulgate interpretive regulations. This new provision, now known as the Javits Amendment, named after Senator Jacob Javits (R-N.Y.), instructed the Secretary of HEW to prepare regulations for implementing Title IX that included "with respect to intercollegiate athletics reasonable provisions considering the nature of particular sports."[18] This language confirmed that Congress intended Title IX to apply to athletic programs and acknowledged that certain sports may

---

8. 20 U.S.C. § 1681 (1994).

14. S. 1539, 93d Cong., 2d Sess. § 536 (1974).

18. Gender and Athletics Act, Pub. L. No. 93-380, § 844, 88 Stat. 612 (1974).

require greater expenditures to provide the same quality of competitive opportunities. The Javits Amendment became law in 1974, and remains controlling today.[19]

Several other attempts to limit Title IX's coverage were made after the Javits Amendment, but all were defeated. The continued resistance of Congress during the mid-1970's to restrict Title IX's protections provided further evidence of its commitment to end discrimination against women in college and high school athletic programs.

2. *Issuance and Adoption of Title IX's Regulations.* HEW issued its proposed Title IX regulations in June of 1974, followed by a lengthy period for public comment that produced almost 10,000 responses.[21] The proposed regulations included a requirement that institutions make affirmative efforts to accommodate the interests and abilities of women athletes — an indication of HEW's strong commitment to carrying out the objectives of Title IX. Unfortunately, this requirement was dropped in response to pressure from the NCAA and others who feared the impact of Title IX on men's athletic programs.

HEW issued final regulations early in the summer of 1975, incorporating many of the suggestions received during the comment period. Shortly thereafter, Congress held extensive hearings on the issue of the athletic regulations that included testimony from the sponsors of Title IX and many others who offered evidence of the pervasive discrimination against women in intercollegiate athletics and competitive sports generally....

After HEW issued the final regulations, Congress had forty-five days to disapprove them by concurrent resolution. During this period, bills were introduced seeking both disapproval of the regulations in their entirety and as they applied to athletics specifically. The impetus behind these bills was the continued lobbying of the NCAA, football interests, and those who feared that giving women equal opportunities would work too great a change on the athletic system that men had traditionally enjoyed as theirs alone. Recognizing that this was their last chance to formally derail Title IX as a vehicle for equal athletic opportunity, these groups fought especially hard to defeat HEW's regulations. Despite their concerted efforts, they did not succeed — none of the bills passed and the Title IX regulations went into effect on July 21, 1975.

3. *The Title IX Policy Interpretation.* The three year transition period for compliance with the regulations expired in July of 1978, and HEW's Office for Civil Rights (OCR) had received nearly one hundred complaints alleging discrimination in athletics programs by that date. Based on these comments, OCR determined the need for further guidance "so as to provide a framework within which complaints can be resolved and to provide institutions of higher education with additional guidance on the requirements of compliance with Title IX."[31] On December 11, 1978, OCR issued a proposed policy interpretation of the athletics regulations to assist schools in complying with Title IX.[32]

---

19. *Id.*
21. *Sex Discrimination Regulations: Hearings Before the Subcomm. on Postsecondary Education of the House Comm. on Education and Labor,* 94th Cong., 1st Sess. 436-42 (1975).
31. 44 Fed. Reg. 71,413, 71,413 (1979).
32. 43 Fed. Reg. 58,070-76 (1978).

As with the Title IX regulations, HEW received a large number of comments on the proposed Title IX athletics guidance. HEW staff also visited eight universities during the summer of 1979 to determine "how the proposed policy and other suggested alternatives would apply in actual practice."[34] Following the comment period, representatives of OCR met with interested groups, including women's groups, for additional discussions of the impact of Title IX guidance. After this extensive consideration, the final Policy Interpretation was issued in December of 1979. It provided a detailed set of "factors and standards" for determining whether a school had complied with Title IX in the area of intercollegiate athletics and also provided additional documentation of the historical and continuing discrimination against female college athletes.

While the Policy Interpretation does not have the force of law, it is the clearest statement of the enforcing agency's interpretation of the regulatory criteria for statutory compliance and therefore is accorded substantial deference by the courts. Thus, the 1979 Policy Interpretation has played a central role in the efforts of individual plaintiffs to force schools into compliance with Title IX.

4. *Title IX in the 1980's.* By the end of the 1970's, the struggles over Title IX appeared to be over. The law had survived numerous attempts to weaken its standards, the interpretive regulations had been implemented, the policy guidance was issued, and schools had been given three full years to comply with the regulation's athletic requirements. Title IX's promise of equal athletic opportunity for women and girls seemed on the brink of becoming a reality. The next decade, however, held a host of unpleasant surprises and battles for proponents of Title IX.

The first blow to the law came in a major Supreme Court decision, *Grove City College v. Bell*,[40] which resulted in the virtual cessation of Title IX athletics claims both in the courts and through the Department of Education's (DOE) Office of Civil Rights (OCR). In a second setback, DOE's OCR, taking direction from the conservative Reagan and Bush Administrations, made little effort to enforce Title IX through compliance reviews or complaint investigations. In response, major legislative campaigns had to be mounted to try to restore Title IX's muscle in the athletics area, requiring years of effort from advocates and legislators who supported Title IX's nondiscrimination objectives.

a. *The* Grove City *Decision.* In the early 1980's, courts divided over the question whether Title IX's language covered only those programs within an institution directly receiving federal funds or whether the receipt of funds in *any* program resulted in coverage for the entire institution. The *Grove City* decision resolved this question in favor of the more narrow interpretation of Title IX's reach, holding that the statute applied only to those programs or activities that actually received federal funds. In so doing, the Court effectively removed most college athletic programs, which rarely are direct recipients of federal funds, from Title IX's purview.

The impact of *Grove City* on efforts to eradicate discrimination in athletics programs was substantial. DOE's OCR immediately dropped or narrowed almost forty pending Title IX athletics investigations. For example, DOE's OCR had already found "discrimination in the accommodation of women athletes' interest

---

34. *Id.*
40. 465 U.S. 555 (1984).

and abilities as well as in travel allowances, per diems and support services in the athletics program at the University of Maryland."[47] One week after the *Grove City* decision, DOE's OCR (dropped the Title IX charges against the University because the program did not receive federal funds). *Grove City* also resulted in the suspension of cases where discrimination had been found and enforcement was being monitored by DOE's OCR. Furthermore, DOE's OCR simply disregarded the complaints of Title IX violations that continued to flood the office unless the athletic program at issue could be shown to be a direct recipient of federal funds.

Grove City also affected the first class action Title IX suit brought against a university for discriminating against women in all aspects of its athletics program. *Haffer v. Temple University*[50] was filed in 1981 as a Title IX action, but lawyers were forced to rely on the Equal Protection Clause of the Fourteenth Amendment and the state equal rights amendment to support their claims after the decision in *Grove City* removed Temple's athletic program from the reach of Title IX. Once the Civil Rights Restoration Act[53] was passed in 1988, the Court restored the application of Title IX claims to most athletic programs. Ultimately, *Haffer* settled in favor of the plaintiffs in 1988, eight years after a remedy for gross inequities in athletic opportunities had first been sought.

b. *Legislative Response to* Grove City. Congress acted immediately to correct the narrowing of Title IX that the *Grove City* decision had accomplished, recognizing that the limitation of Title IX coverage to programs directly receiving federal funds would severely impede its objective of eradicating sex discrimination in education. The Civil Rights Restoration Act of 1984, introduced in both the Senate and the House, sought to replace the statutory language "program or activity" with "recipient," thereby restoring coverage of athletic departments under Title IX.

After several years of debate, the Act was passed as the Civil Rights Restoration Act of 1987 and enacted over presidential veto in 1988.[56] Although the statutory language was modified over the course of debate, it served the purpose of overruling *Grove City*. As enacted, the Act broadened Title IX's definition of "program or activity" to include "all operations of a (institution)...any part of which is extended federal financial assistance...."[57] The Civil Rights Restoration Act therefore clarified that an entire institution is covered by Title IX if any of its programs or activities is a recipient of federal funds. Congress included specific findings indicating that the Act was intended to correct the limitations imposed by *Grove City* and to restore "an institution-wide application" of Title IX.

Unlike the debates surrounding Title IX regulations, the debates that occurred over the Civil Rights Restoration Act did not dispute whether or not intercollegiate athletic programs should come within the scope of Title IX. In fact, these debates revealed a consensus among lawmakers that discrimination against women

---

47. *See* S. REP. NO. 64, 100th Cong., 1st Sess. 11 (1987), *reprinted in* 1988 U.S.C.C.A.N. 3.

50. 524 F. Supp. 531 (E.D. Pa. 1981), *aff'd*, 688 F.2d 14 (3rd Cir. 1982) (per curiam), *modified*, 678 F. Supp. 517 (E.D. Pa. 1987).

53. Civil Rights Restoration Act of 1987, ch. 38, 102 Stat 28 (1988) (codified as amended at 20 U.S.C. § 1687 (1994).

56. 20 U.S.C. § 1687 (1994).

57. *Id.*

athletes is a significant civil rights problem deserving remedy under Title IX. A number of the members of Congress referred explicitly to the ongoing sex discrimination in competitive athletics as a compelling reason for restoring the broad application of civil rights laws. These statements serve as important evidence of the remedial objectives of Title IX and the intent of Congress that the statute's protections provide a strong guarantee of equality in the area of athletics.

. . . .

C. Recent Enforcement of Title IX

The passage of the Civil Rights Restoration Act and settlement of *Haffer* in 1988 appeared to herald a renaissance for Title IX enforcement. With the law's coverage of athletic programs restored, Title IX proponents had reason to feel optimistic that more schools would voluntarily come into compliance with Title IX in order to avoid being sued by private plaintiffs. This optimism changed to conviction after the 1992 decision by the Supreme Court in *Franklin v. Gwinett County Public Schools*.[63] In *Franklin*, the Court armed plaintiffs with the powerful weapon of the right to money damages for an intentional violation of Title IX. Until *Franklin*, plaintiffs bringing suit under Title IX could only seek compliance with the law, a remedy that often held little attraction for students who would graduate before any changes were made. Giving plaintiffs access to individual relief made the prospect of a contentious lawsuit more appealing both to plaintiffs and to the lawyers needed to represent them. The threat of having to pay out large damage awards also promised to operate as a powerful incentive for schools to bring their athletic programs, as well as their other educational programs, into compliance with Title IX. Perhaps even more importantly, the availability of damages avoided the problem of student-plaintiffs graduating from their respective schools and thereby making their legal claims moot. By including a claim for damages, plaintiffs would still have a justiciable Title IX claim even after graduation. Thus, *Franklin* represented a major step forward in Title IX enforcement.

The elimination of certain women's varsity teams ushered in by shrinking university budgets in the early 1990s has resulted in a surge of Title IX litigation in recent years. Without exception, the plaintiffs in these cases have won decisive victories against their schools and contributed to substantial progress toward equity in intercollegiate athletics. The courts' interpretation and legal analysis of Title IX in these cases has been remarkably consistent, providing Title IX proponents with a strong and uniform body of law upon which to rely.

1. *Major Court Decisions*. Since 1992, federal courts in the First, Third, Sixth, and Tenth Circuits have awarded victories to female student athletes in Title IX cases. Additionally, courts in the Seventh and Second Circuits have interpreted Title IX favorably for female athletes. Each of these decisions has focused on discrimination in the allocation of participation opportunities between male and female athletes, the primary area emphasized in recent Title IX athletics challenges. In analyzing participation opportunities, courts have adopted the three-prong test set out in the Title IX Policy Interpretation.[68] If a school can satisfy any one of the

---

63. 503 U.S. 60 (1992).

68. 44 Fed. Reg. 71,418. For a comprehensive discussion of why courts rely on the three-prong test, see *Cohen II*, 991 F.2d at 888.

test's three prongs, it is in compliance with Title IX's requirement to provide proportionate participation opportunities.

Under the first prong, the court examines whether athletic participation opportunities are provided to each sex in numbers substantially proportionate to their
enrollment. If a school cannot meet this prong, the court then determines whether
the school can demonstrate a history and continuing practice of program expansion for the underrepresented sex. If a school fails the second prong, the court finally asks whether the athletic interests and abilities of the underrepresented sex
have been fully and effectively accommodated by the school. If the plaintiffs can
show that the school also fails on this third prong, then the court must find the
school out of compliance with Title IX.

In applying this three-prong test, courts have arrived at the same conclusion:
that the schools that have been challenged to date have failed to provide adequate
opportunity to their female athletes and thereby are violating federal law.

a. Cohen v. Brown University.[69] In 1991, Brown University decided to cut two
women's teams and two men's teams from its athletics program, changing the status of these teams from varsity to club and removing all of their funding. Members of the women's teams brought a class action suit against Brown, claiming
that the demotion of the women's teams violated Title IX because the university
provided disproportionate participation opportunities to men and women. The
plaintiffs sought injunctive relief to reinstate the two dropped teams and to prevent Brown from eliminating any other women's varsity teams.

The district court granted the plaintiff a preliminary injunction, which Brown
immediately appealed to the court of appeals. In both courts, Brown argued that
Title IX compliance should be measured by comparing participation opportunities with the relative interests of male and female students, as measured by
Brown, rather than the percentage of each sex in the undergraduate enrollment.
In effect, Brown asked the courts to overlook the fewer opportunities it provided
to female athletes because neither men nor women are fully accommodated, even
though men enjoyed almost twice as many participation opportunities as women.

The First Circuit rejected Brown's arguments using the same legal analysis as
the district court. Applying the three-prong test outlined above and rejecting
Brown's attempts to rewrite Title IX policy, both courts reasoned that Brown
failed all three prongs and therefore did not effectively accommodate the interests
and abilities of its female athletes. The First Circuit labelled Brown's construction
of Title IX "myopic," stating that "the fact that the overrepresented gender is less
than fully accommodated will not, in and of itself, excuse a shortfall in the provision of opportunities for the underrepresented gender."[76]

At the subsequent trial on the merits, Brown lost again under the application of
the three-prong test. The creativity of Brown's arguments could not mask the fact
that it had neither substantially equivalent participation opportunities for men
and women nor a continuing history of program expansion for women, and the
school further could not demonstrate that the athletic interests and abilities of its
female students had been met. Brown has appealed the district court's decision.

---

69. 809 F. Supp. 978 (D.R.I. 1992) (*Cohen I*), *aff'd*, 991 F.2d 888 (1st Cir. 1993); 879 F.
Supp. 185 (D.R.I. 1995) (*Cohen III*) (collectively referred to as *Cohen*).

76. *Cohen II*, 991 F.2d at 899.

[The outcome of Brown's appeal is discussed in the Leahy excerpt that follows— ed.].

b. Roberts v. Colorado State University.[79] In 1992, Colorado State University (CSU) dropped its women's varsity softball team. Team members sued for reinstatement of their team and for compensatory damages, alleging CSU failed to provide equivalent participation opportunities to female athletes under Title IX. CSU argued that it had not violated Title IX because it had also dropped men's baseball when cutting the softball team, and that the cuts had had a larger negative impact on male athletes.

The district court did not accept CSU's argument, finding that the university failed each prong of the three-prong test. While most of its legal analysis followed the same path as that of the *Cohen* court, the district court in *Roberts* emphasized several important principles in Title IX jurisprudence. First, the court held that a school cannot satisfy the second prong, a history and continuing practice of program expansion for women, by simply pointing to an initial spurt of expansion in opportunities for women shortly after Title IX was enacted. It also cannot claim to have "expanded" women's share of opportunities by cutting more from its men's than its women's athletic programs. Second, the court held that a disparity of 10.6% between the percentage of female athletes and the percentage of female students did not meet the "substantially proportionate" standard of the first prong. Thus, while it remains unclear where the outer boundaries of the "substantially proportionate" measure lie, a disparity of 10% was too great for this court.

On appeal, the Tenth Circuit affirmed both the district court's use of the three-prong test as the appropriate measure of effective accommodation and its conclusion that CSU could satisfy none of the prongs.[85] The appeals court did overrule the district court on one point, agreeing with the First Circuit's ruling in *Cohen* that the plaintiffs bear the burden of proving a lack of accommodation of female athletes' interests and abilities under the test's third prong. Under this new standard, the Tenth Circuit found that plaintiffs had met their burden and therefore CSU failed the third prong as well as the first two and were not in compliance with Title IX.

c. Favia v. Indiana University of Pennsylvania.[88] Factually, the *Favia* case is very similar to *Cohen*. Indiana University of Pennsylvania (IUP) demoted two men's and two women's varsity teams to club status and cut off their funding. As in *Cohen*, the women's team members sued as a class for reinstatement of their teams.

Legally, the court had no difficulty in concluding that IUP was likely to be found in violation of Title IX because of failure to satisfy any of the prongs of the three-prong test. In a succinct opinion, the court found that IUP did not offer women athletic opportunities in substantial proportion to their enrollment, would not be likely to demonstrate a practice of continuing expansion of women's opportunities, and would not be able to show that the athletic interests and abilities of it female students had been fully and effectively accommodated. The court therefore granted

---

79. 814 F. Supp. 1507 (D. Colo. 1993) (*Roberts I*), *aff'd sub nom.* Roberts v. Colorado State Bd. Of Agric., 998 F.2d 824 (10th Cir. 1993) (*Roberts II*), *cert. denied*, 114 S. Ct. 580 (1993) (*Roberts III*) (collectively referred to as *Roberts*).

85. *Roberts II*, 998 F.2d at 829-32.

88. 812 F. Supp. 578 (W.D. Pa. 1992), *motion to modify denied*, 7 F.3d 332 (3d Cir. 1993).

a preliminary injunction to the plaintiffs restoring their two teams and preventing IUP from making any further cuts to women's varsity athletic opportunities.

Although IUP did not appeal the district court's decision, it later sought modification of the district court's order to replace one of the reinstated teams with a different women's sport. When the court denied the modification on procedural grounds, IUP appealed to the Third Circuit. Declining to alter the original injunction, the Third Circuit noted that substituting one team for the other did not "substantially ameliorate what the district court decided was likely to be a violation of Title IX."[93] The court of appeals also adopted the district court's application of the three-part test, citing *Cohen* approvingly.

d. Horner v. Kentucky High School Athletic Association.[95] In one of the few Title IX decisions involving high school athletes, twelve female softball players filed a Title IX discrimination suit when their state athletic association refused to sanction fast-pitch softball for girls despite sanctioning fewer sports for girls than for boys overall. After losing on summary judgment in the district court, the plaintiffs appealed to the Sixth Circuit.

Reversing the award of summary judgment, the Sixth Circuit first confirmed that Kentucky's high school programs came within reach of Title IX's protections because they received federal financial assistance. The court then looked to the three-prong test to analyze whether the state high schools had complied with Title IX's mandate of equal opportunity. Citing *Cohen* and *Roberts* for support, the court outlined the elements of the test and concluded that genuine issues existed as to whether the state provided equal athletic opportunity to its female students. The court therefore remanded the case to the district court. Although it is not a decision on the merits, *Horner* provides further support for the application of the three-prong test in evaluating participation opportunities and endorses the legal reasoning used by the First and Tenth Circuits in deciding such cases.

e. *Other Court Decisions*. Both the Second and the Seventh Circuits have also applied consistent standards for interpreting Title IX's requirements in recent cases. While these cases involve somewhat different legal analyses than the circuit cases described above, they further elucidate the approach of federal courts to Title IX in the area of nondiscriminatory participation opportunities.

In *Cook v. Colgate University*,[99] the plaintiffs went to court seeking elevation of the women's club ice hockey team to varsity status after the college had repeatedly denied their requests to do so. Pointing to the vast inequities between the women's club ice hockey team and the men's varsity ice hockey team, the plaintiffs argued that Title IX required the college to have a women's varsity team so as to provide equality of opportunity. Colgate argued in defense that Title IX did not mandate equality on a sport-by-sport basis, but rather required proportionality in the men's and women's programs as a whole.

The district court sided with the plaintiffs, finding that because there were gross inequities in the opportunities available to male and female hockey players, Colgate had violated Title IX. Although the district court's analysis stands alone in choosing to compare opportunities on a sport- specific level, its finding of discrimination was certainly merited. On a program-wide basis, Colgate clearly failed the

---

93. *Id*. at 343.
95. 43 F.3d 265 (6th Cir. 1994).
99. 802 F. Supp. 737 (N.D. N.Y. 1992), *vacated as moot*, 992 F.2d 17 (2nd Cir. 1993).

three-prong test in much the same way Brown University, Colorado State University and Indiana University at Pennsylvania had. It did not offer substantially proportionate athletic opportunities to women, did not have a continuing history of expansion, and had not fully and effectively accommodated its female athletes.[104]

The Seventh Circuit had occasion to interpret Title IX in *Kelley v. Board of Trustees of the University of Illinois.*[105] The reverse-discrimination case was brought by members of the men's varsity swimming team that had recently been eliminated at the University of Illinois. The plaintiffs claimed discrimination because the women's swimming team had not been cut in the institutional effort to reduce expenses. Applying the three-prong test, the district court did not find a Title IX violation because, even after the cuts, women continued to receive a lesser share of the school's athletic opportunities. On appeal, the Seventh Circuit affirmed the decision, once again deferring to the Policy Interpretation's three-part test for Title IX compliance in this area.[107]

2. *Major Settlements....*

In a Title IX challenge against the University of Texas at Austin, the plaintiffs obtained a landmark settlement requiring the university to greatly increase women's share of athletic opportunities at the institution. Female student athletes at UT-Austin filed a class action suit against the university seeking elevation of four club teams to varsity status. At the time, women represented 47% of the undergraduate enrollment and only 23% of the varsity athletes. The students alleged violations of Title IX based on discrimination in participation opportunities.

In July of 1993, the University settled with the plaintiffs, agreeing to bring the women's varsity participation rate up to 44% by the end of the 1995-96 school year and to maintain that rate thereafter.[109] The University also agreed to elevate two of the women's club teams, soccer and softball, to varsity status, and to review its program to gauge the necessity of adding other varsity teams. The settlement included a requirement that the percentage of athletic scholarships given female athletes be within two percentage points of their participation rate and a requirement that the facilities for women's teams be of the quality necessary to attract top athletes.

The *Sanders* settlement served as a model for the later settlement of a Title IX challenge to Virginia Polytechnical Institute. In March 1995, student athletes obtained a settlement in a class action challenge to the university's failure to provide sufficient varsity opportunities for women athletes. The university agreed to bring women's athletic participation rates within 3% of their enrollment rates by 1998 and to add lacrosse and softball as varsity women's sports. The school also agreed to bring the percentage of scholarship money flowing to female athletes to within 5% of their enrollment rates.[112]

....

---

104. *Cook,* 802 F. Supp. at 742-45.

105. 832 F. Supp. 237 (C.D. Ill. 1993), *aff'd,* 35 F.3d 265 (7th Cir. 1994), *cert. denied,* 115 S. Ct 938 (1995).

107. *Kelley,* 35 F.3d at 272-75.

109. Sanders v. University of Tex. at Austin, No. A-92-CA-405 (W.D. Tex. Oct. 25, 1993) (order approving settlement agreement).

112. James v. Virginia Polytechnic Inst., No. 94-0031-R (W.D. Va. Apr. 12, 1995) (order approving settlement agreement).

Crista D. Leahy, Note, The Title Bout:
A Critical Review of the Regulation and Enforcement
of Title IX in Intercollegiate Athletics
24 Journal of College and University Law 489 (1998)*

. . . .

4. The Appeal of the Trial On the Merits

a. The Majority Decision

Brown University did pursue an appeal. In April 1996, counsel for both parties revisited the First Circuit. As in the first appeal and the trial on the merits, Brown challenged the test the district court used to determine whether Brown's intercollegiate athletic program complied with Title IX on constitutional and statutory grounds. In addition to these arguments, Brown claimed error in certain evidentiary rulings made during the trial on the merits, as well as in the district court's order of specific relief in place of Brown's proposed compliance plan.[143]

The First Circuit, in a majority opinion authored by Judge Bownes, found no error in the district court's factual findings or with its interpretation and application of the law in determining that Brown had violated Title IX in the operation of its athletic programs. The court affirmed in all respects the district court's analysis and rulings on the issue of liability. However, the panel did find error with the district court's award of specific relief and remanded the case to the district court for reconsideration of the remedy.

The majority based the bulk of its decision on narrow procedural grounds, stating that "the law of the case doctrine precludes relitigation of the legal issues presented in successive stages of a single case once those issues have been decided."[144] Therefore, because the First Circuit, on appeal of the preliminary injunction, "squarely rejected Brown's constitutional and statutory challenges to the policy interpretation's three-[prong] test," those rulings of law controlled the disposition of the current appeal.[145]

While acknowledging exceptions to the law of the case doctrine—most notably, when the controlling authority has since made a contrary decision of law applicable to such issues—the majority rejected Brown's argument that the Supreme Court's decision in *Adarand Constructors v. Pena*[146] controlled the issues involved in Cohen. According to *Adarand*, federal remedial affirmative action programs must satisfy strict scrutiny, that is, such a program must seek to satisfy a compelling governmental interest and be narrowly tailored to achieve that goal. The First Circuit noted:

---

    143. *Cohen IV*, 101 F.3d 155, 162 (1996).
    144. *Id.* at 167 (1996).
    145. *Id.*
    146. 515 U.S. 200, 115 S. Ct. 2097 (1995).

> Title IX is not an affirmative action statute; it is an anti-discrimination statute....No aspect of the Title IX regime at issue in this case— inclusive of the statute, the relevant regulation, and the pertinent agency documents—mandates gender-based preferences or quotas, or specific timetables for implementing numerical goals.[147]

Consequently, the majority concluded that the Supreme Court's decision in *Adarand Constructors* was not relevant to the facts of *Cohen*, and did not warrant an exception to the law of the case doctrine. Therefore, the second three-judge panel was bound by the rulings of their colleagues two-and-one-half years earlier.

The majority did, however, find error with the district court's rejection of Brown's compliance plan and with the substitution of its own plan to "elevate and maintain women's gymnastics, women's water polo, women's skiing, and women's fencing to university-funded varsity status.'" The First Circuit ruled that, while expanding women's athletic opportunities in areas where there is proven ability and interest is the very purpose of Title IX, "Brown's proposal to cut men's teams [would be] a permissible means of effectuating compliance with the statute." Therefore, the court gave Brown an opportunity to submit another plan for compliance with Title IX. The court noted that two specific circumstances had changed since Brown submitted its initial plan: first, the substantive issues had been decided adversely to Brown. "Brown [was] no longer an appellant seeking a favorable result in the Court of Appeals." Second, the district court, in considering an appropriate remedy, did not labor under a time constraint so as to expedite an appeal.

b. The Dissent

Chief Judge Torruella, "not persuaded that the majority's view represents the state of the law today," respectfully dissented. Judge Torruella believed that the "law of the case" doctrine did not apply to this appeal because two decisions of the Supreme Court, which were rendered during the time between the two appeals, could not be reconciled with the decision on the first appeal. Specifically, Judge Torruella cited *Adarand Constructors v. Pena* and *United States v. Virginia*.[155] The Supreme Court in *Adarand*, Judge Torruella noted, applied strict scrutiny to all racial classifications, irrespective of whether they were benign or remedial. According to the dissent, the First Circuit "should now follow *Adarand's* lead and subject all gender-conscious government action to the same inquiry."[156]

Prior to the decision in *United States v. Virginia*, a gender-conscious governmental action was required to be substantially related to an important governmental objective. However, as Judge Torruella noted, the Supreme Court in *Virginia* "applied a more searching skeptical scrutiny," which requires that "parties who seek to defend gender-based government action must demonstrate an 'exceedingly persuasive justification' for that action."[157] Judge Torruella concluded that *Adarand* and *Virginia* could not be reconciled with the analysis in the initial

---

147. *Cohen IV*, 101 F.3d at 170.
155. 116 S. Ct. 2264 (1996).
156. *Cohen IV*, 101 F.3d at 190.
157. *Cohen IV*, 101 F.3d at 190 (citing United States v. Virginia, 116 S. Ct. 2264, 2274 (1996)).

appeal. Consequently, he believed that the first appeal is now unsound both "because it applies a lenient version of intermediate scrutiny that is impermissible following *Adarand*, and because it did not apply the 'exceedingly persuasive justification' test of *Virginia*."[158]

A second reason for reconsidering the merits of the appeal, according to Judge Torruella, was the fact that the first appeal was from a preliminary injunction. He noted that the standard for a preliminary injunction is different than those of a trial on merits. Moreover, during the first trial, all of the facts associated with the case were not yet available. The ruling was only preliminary, until a trial on the merits could be held. For all of these reasons, Chief Judge Torruella believed that a review of *Cohen v. Brown*, in terms of the three-prong test of the policy interpretation, was necessary.

Brown University filed a Petition for a Writ of Certiorari on February 20, 1997. The Supreme Court denied certiorari in April of 1997, and the saga of *Cohen v. Brown* came to an apparent end.[161]

. . . .

United States Department of Education — Office of Civil Rights, Clarification of Intercollegiate Athletics Policy Guidance: The Three-Part Test (May 16, 1996)

The Office for Civil Rights (OCR) enforces Title IX of the Education Amendments [sic] of 1972, 20 U S C S 1681 et seq (Title IX), which prohibits discrimination on the basis of sex in education programs and activities by recipients of federal funds. The regulation implementing Title IX, at 34 C.F.R. Part 106, effective July 21, 1975, contains specific provisions governing athletic programs, at 34 C.F.R. 106 41, and the awarding of athletic scholarships, at 34 C.F.R. 106 37(c). Further clarification of the Title IX regulatory requirements is provided by the Intercollegiate Athletics Policy Interpretation, issued December 11, 1979 (44 Fed Reg 71413 et seq (1979)).[1]

The Title IX regulation provides that if an institution sponsors an athletic program it must provide equal athletic opportunities for members of both sexes. Among other factors, the regulation requires that an institution must effectively accommodate the athletic interests and abilities of students of both sexes to the extent necessary to provide equal athletic opportunity.

The 1979 Policy Interpretation provides that as part of this determination OCR will apply the following three-part test to assess whether an institution is providing nondiscriminatory participation opportunities for individuals of both sexes:

---

158. *Id*. at 191.

161. Brown Univ. v. Cohen, 117 S. Ct. 1469 (1997).

1. The Policy Interpretation is designed for intercollegiate athletics. However, its general principles, and those of this Clarification, often will apply to elementary and secondary interscholastic athletic programs, which are also covered by the regulation. *See* 44 Fed Reg 71413.

1.   Whether intercollegiate level participation opportunities for male and fe-male students are provided in numbers substantially proportionate to their respective enrollments; or

2.   Where the members of one sex have been and are underrepresented among intercollegiate athletes, whether the institution can show a history and continuing practice of program expansion which is demonstrably respon-sive to the developing interests and abilities of the members of that sex; or

3.   Where the members of one sex are underrepresented among intercolle-giate athletes, and the institution cannot show a history and continuing practice of program expansion, as described above, whether it can be demonstrated that the interests and abilities of the members of that sex have been fully and effectively accommodated by the present program

44 Fed. Reg. at 71418

Thus, the three-part test furnishes an institution with three individual avenues to choose from when determining how it will provide individuals of each sex with nondiscriminatory opportunities to participate in intercollegiate athletics. If an in-stitution has met any part of the three-part test, OCR will determine that the in-stitution is meeting this requirement.

It is important to note that under the Policy Interpretation the requirement to provide nondiscriminatory participation opportunities is only one of many fac-tors that OCR examines to determine if an institution is in compliance with the athletics provision of Title IX. OCR also considers the quality of competition of-fered to members of both sexes in order to determine whether an institution effec-tively accommodates the interests and abilities of its students.

In addition, when an "overall determination of compliance" is made by OCR, 44 Fed Reg. 71417, 71418, OCR examines the institution's program as a whole. Thus, OCR considers the effective accommodation of interests and abilities in conjunction with equivalence in the availability, quality and kinds of other ath-letic benefits and opportunities provided male and female athletes to determine whether an institution provides equal athletic opportunity as required by Title IX. These other benefits include coaching, equipment, practice and competitive facili-ties, recruitment, scheduling of games, and publicity, among others. An institu-tion's failure to provide nondiscriminatory participation opportunities usually amounts to a denial of equal athletic opportunity because these opportunities provide access to all other athletic benefits, treatment, and services.

This Clarification provides specific factors that guide an analysis of each part of the three-part test. In addition, it provides examples to demonstrate, in con-crete terms, how these factors will be considered. These examples are intended to be illustrative, and the conclusions drawn in each example are based solely on the facts included in the example

THREE-PART TEST — Part One: Are Participation Opportunities Substantially Proportionate Enrollment?

Under part one of the three-part test (part one), where an institution provides intercollegiate level athletic participation opportunities for male and female stu-dents in numbers substantially proportionate to their respective full-time under-graduate enrollments, OCR will find that the institution is providing nondiscrimi-natory participation opportunities for individuals of both sexes.

OCR's analysis begins with a determination of the number of participation opportunities afforded to male and female athletes in the intercollegiate athletic program. The Policy Interpretation defines participants as those athletes:

a. Who are receiving the institutionally-sponsored support normally provided to athletes competing at the institution involved, e.g., coaching, equipment, medical and training room services, on a regular basis during a sport's season; and

b. Who are participating in organized practice sessions and other team meetings and activities on a regular basis during a sport's season; and

c. Who are listed on the eligibility or squad lists maintained for each sport, or

d. Who, because of injury, cannot meet a, b, or c above but continue to receive financial aid on the basis of athletic ability.

44 Fed. Reg. at 71415.

OCR uses this definition of participant to determine the number of participation opportunities provided by an institution for purposes of the three-part test.

Under this definition, OCR considers a sport's season to commence on the date of a team's first intercollegiate competitive event and to conclude on the date of the team's final intercollegiate competitive event. As a general rule, all athletes who are listed on a team's squad or eligibility list and are on the team as of the team's first competitive event are counted as participants by OCR. In determining the number of participation opportunities for the purposes of the interests and abilities analysis, an athlete who participates in more than one sport will be counted as a participant in each sport in which he or she participates.

In determining participation opportunities, OCR includes, among others, those athletes who do not receive scholarships (e.g., walk-ons), those athletes who compete on teams sponsored by the institution even though the team may be required to raise some or all of its operating funds, and those athletes who practice but may not compete. OCR's investigations reveal that these athletes receive numerous benefits and services, such as training and practice time, coaching, tutoring services, locker room facilities, and equipment, as well as important non-tangible benefits derived from being a member of an intercollegiate athletic team. Because these are significant benefits, and because receipt of these benefits does not depend on their cost to the institution whether the athlete competes, it is necessary to count all athletes who receive such benefits when determining the number of athletic opportunities provided to men and women.

OCR's analysis next determines whether athletic opportunities are substantially proportionate. The Title IX regulation allows institutions to operate separate athletic programs for men and women. Accordingly, the regulation allows an institution to control the respective number of participation opportunities offered men and women. Thus, it could be argued that to satisfy part one there should be no difference between the participation rate in an institution's intercollegiate athletic program and its full-time undergraduate student enrollment.

However, because in some circumstances it may be unreasonable to expect an institution to achieve exact proportionality—for instance, because of natural fluctuations in enrollment and participation rates or because it would be unreasonable to expect an institution to add athletic opportunities in light of the small number of students that would have to be accommodated to achieve exact proportionality—the Policy Interpretation examines whether participation opportunities are "substantially" proportionate to enrollment rates. Because this determination depends on the institution's specific circumstances and the size of its athletic program. OCR makes this determination on a case-by-case basis, rather than through use of a statistical test.

As an example of a determination under part one: If an institution's enrollment is 52 percent male and 48 percent female and 52 percent of the participants in the athletic program are male and 48 percent female, then the institution would clearly satisfy part one. However, OCR recognizes that natural fluctuations in an institution's enrollment and/or participation rates may affect the percentages in a subsequent year. For instance, if the institution's admissions the following year resulted in an enrollment rate of 51 percent males and 49 percent females, while the participation rates of males and females in the athletic program remained constant the institution would continue to satisfy part one because it would be unreasonable to expect the institution to fine tune its program in response to this change in enrollment.

As another example, over the past five years an institution has had a consistent enrollment rate for women of 50 percent. During this time period, it has been expanding its program for women in order to reach proportionality. In the year that the institution reaches its goal—i. e., 50 percent of the participants in its athletic program are female—its enrollment rate for women increases to 52 percent. Under these circumstances, the institution would satisfy part one.

OCR would also consider opportunities to be substantially proportionate when the number of opportunities that would be required to achieve proportionality would not be sufficient to sustain a viable team, i.e., a team for which there is a sufficient number of interested and able students and enough available competition to sustain an intercollegiate team. As a frame of reference in assessing this situation, OCR may consider the average size of teams offered for the underrepresented sex, a number which would vary by institution.

For instance, Institution A is a university with a total of 600 athletes. While women make up 52 percent of the university's enrollment, they only represent 47 percent of its athletes. If the university provided women with 52 percent of athletic opportunities, approximately 62 additional women would be able to participate. Because this is a significant number of unaccommodated women, it is likely that a viable sport could be added. If so, Institution A has not met part one.

As another example, at Institution B women also make up 52 percent of the university's enrollment and represent 47 percent of Institution B's athletes. Institution B's athletic program consists of only 60 participants. If the University provided women with 52 percent of athletic opportunities, approximately 6 additional women would be able to participate. Since 6 participants are unlikely to support a viable team, Institution B would meet part one.

THREE-PART TEST — Part Two: Is there a History and Continuing Practice of Program Expansion for the Underrepresented Sex?

Under part two of the three-part test (part two), an institution can show that it has a history and continuing practice of program expansion which is demonstrably responsive to the developing interests and abilities of the underrepresented sex. In effect, part two looks at an institution's past and continuing remedial efforts to provide nondiscriminatory participation opportunities through program expansion.[2]

OCR will review the entire history of the athletic program, focusing on the participation opportunities provided for the underrepresented sex. First, OCR will assess whether past actions of the institution have expanded participation opportunities for the underrepresented sex in a manner that was demonstrably responsive to their developing interests and abilities. Developing interests include interests that already exist at the institution.[3] There are no fixed intervals of time within which an institution must have added participation opportunities. Neither is a particular number of sports dispositive. Rather, the focus is on whether the program expansion was responsive to developing interests and abilities of the underrepresented sex. In addition, the institution must demonstrate a continuing (i.e., present) practice of program expansion as warranted by developing interests and abilities.

OCR will consider the following factors, among others, as evidence that may indicate a history of program expansion that is demonstrably responsive to the developing interests and abilities of the underrepresented sex.

- an institution's record of adding intercollegiate teams, or upgrading teams to intercollegiate status, for the underrepresented sex;
- an institution's record of increasing the numbers of participants in intercollegiate athletics who are members of the underrepresented sex; and
- an institution's affirmative responses to requests by students or others for addition or elevation of sports.

OCR will consider the following factors, among others, as evidence that may indicate a continuing practice of program expansion that is demonstrably responsive to the developing interests and abilities of the underrepresented sex:

- an institution's current implementation of a nondiscriminatory policy or procedure for requesting the addition of sports (including the elevation of club or intramural teams) and the effective communication of the policy or procedure to students; and
- an institution's current implementation of a plan of program expansion that is responsive to developing interests and abilities.

OCR would also find persuasive an institution's efforts to monitor developing interests and abilities of the underrepresented sex, for example, by conducting periodic nondiscriminatory assessments of developing interests and abilities and taking timely actions in response to the results.

---

2. Part two focuses on whether an institution has expanded the number of intercollegiate participation opportunities provided to the underrepresented sex. Improvements in the quality of competition, and of other athletic benefits, provided to women athletes, while not considered under the three-part test, can be considered by OCR in making an overall determination of compliance with the athletics provision of Title IX.

3. However, under this part of the test an institution is not required, as it is under part three, to accommodate all interests and abilities of the underrepresented sex. Moreover, under part two an institution has flexibility in choosing which teams it adds for the underrepresented sex, as long as it can show overall history and continuing practice of program expansion for members of that sex.

In the event that an institution eliminated any team for the underrepresented sex, OCR would evaluate the circumstances surrounding this action in assessing whether the institution could satisfy part two of the test. However, OCR will not find a history and continuing practice of program expansion where an institution increases the proportional participation opportunities for the underrepresented sex by reducing opportunities for the overrepresented sex alone or by reducing participation opportunities for the overrepresented sex to a proportionately greater degree than for the underrepresented sex. This is because part two considers an institution's good faith remedial efforts through actual program expansion. It is only necessary to examine part two if one sex is overrepresented in the athletic program. Cuts in the program for the underrepresented sex, even when coupled with cuts in the program for the overrepresented sex, cannot be considered remedial because they burden members of the sex already disadvantaged by the present program. However, an institution that has eliminated some participation opportunities for the underrepresented sex can still meet part two if, overall, it can show a history and continuing practice of program expansion for that sex.

In addition, OCR will not find that an institution satisfies part two where it established teams for the underrepresented sex only at the initiation of its program for the underrepresented sex or where it merely promises to expand its program for the underrepresented sex at some time in the future.

The following examples are intended to illustrate the principles discussed above.

At the inception of its women s program in the mid-1970s, Institution C established seven teams for women. In 1984 it added a women's varsity team at the request of students and coaches. In 1990 it upgraded a women's club sport to varsity team status based on a request by the club members and an NCAA survey that showed a significant increase in girls high school participation in that sport. Institution C is currently implementing a plan to add a varsity women's team in the spring of 1996 that has been identified by a regional study as an emerging women's sport in the region. The addition of these teams resulted in an increased percentage of women participating in varsity athletics at the institution. Based on these facts, OCR would find Institution C in compliance with part two because it has a history of program expansion and is continuing to expand its program for women in response to their enveloping interests and abilities.

By 1980, Institution D established even teams for women. Institution D added a women varsity team in 1983 based on the requests of students and coaches. In 1991 it added a women's varsity team after an NCAA survey showed a significant increase in girls' high school participation in that sport. In 1993 Institution D eliminated a viable women's team and a viable men's team in an effort to reduce its athletic budget. It has taken no action relating to the underrepresented sex since 1993. Based on these facts, OCR would not find Institution D in compliance with part two. Institution D cannot show a continuing practice of program expansion that is responsive to the developing interests and abilities of the underrepresented sex where its only action since 1991 with regard to the underrepresented sex was to eliminate a team for which there was interest, ability and available competition.

In the mid-1970s, Institution E established five teams for women. In 1979 it added a women's varsity team. In 1984 it upgraded a women's club sport with twenty-five participants to varsity team status. At that time it eliminated a women's varsity team that had eight members. In 1987 and 1989 Institution E added women's varsity teams that were identified by a significant number of its enrolled and incoming female students when surveyed regarding their athletic interests and abilities. During this time it also increased the size of an existing women's team to provide opportunities for women who expressed interest in playing that sport. Within the past year, it added a women's varsity team based on a nationwide survey of the most popular girls high school teams. Based on the addition of these teams, the percentage of women participating in varsity athletics at the institution has increased. Based on these facts, OCR would find Institution E in compliance with part two because it has a history of program expansion and the elimination of the team in 1984 took place within the context of continuing program expansion for the underrepresented sex that is responsive to their developing interests.

Institution F started its women's program in the early 1970s with four teams. It did not add to its women's program until 1987 when, based on requests of students and coaches, it upgraded a women's club sport to varsity team status and expanded the size of several existing women's teams to accommodate significant expressed interest by students. In 1990 it surveyed its enrolled and incoming female students; based on that survey and a survey of the most popular sports played by women in the region, Institution F agree to add three new women's teams by 1997. It added a women's team by 1991 and 1994. Institution F is implementing a plan to add a women's team by the spring of 1997. Based on these facts, OCR would find Institution F in compliance with part two. Institution F's program history since 1987 shows that it is committed to program expansion for the underrepresented sex and it is continuing to expand its women's program in light of women's developing interests and abilities.

THREE-PART TEST — Part Three: Is the Institution Fully and Effectively Accommodating the Interests and Abilities of the Underrepresented Sex?

Under part of the three-part test (part three) OCR determines whether an institution is fully and effectively accommodating the interests and abilities of its students who are members of the underrepresented sex—including students who are admitted to the institution though not yet enrolled. Title IX' provides that a recipient must provide equal athletic opportunity to its students. Accordingly, the Policy Interpretation does not require an institution to accommodate the interests and abilities of potential students.[4]

While disproportionately high athletic participation rates by an institution's students of the overrepresented sex (as compared to their enrollment rates) may indicate that an institution is not providing equal athletic opportunities to its students of the underrepresented sex an institution can satisfy part three where there is evidence that the imbalance does not reflect discrimination, i.e., where it can be demonstrated that, notwithstanding disproportionately low participation rates by the institution's students of the underrepresented sex, the interests and abilities of these students are, in fact, being fully and effectively accommodated.

In making this determination, OCR will consider whether there is (a) unmet interest in a particular sport; (b) sufficient ability to sustain a team in the sport; and

---

4. However, OCR does examine an institution's recruitment practices under another part of the Policy Interpretation. See 44 Fed Reg. 71417. Accordingly, where an institution recruits potential student athletes for its men's teams, it must ensure that women's teams are provided with substantially equal opportunities to recruit potential student athletes.

(c) a reasonable expectation of competition for the team. If all three conditions are present OCR will find that an institution has not fully and effectively accommodated the interests and abilities of the underrepresented sex.

If an institution has recently eliminated a viable team from the intercollegiate program, OCR will find that there is sufficient interest, ability, and available competition to sustain an intercollegiate team in that sport unless an institution can provide strong evidence that interest, ability, or available competition no longer exists.

a) Is there sufficient unmet interest to support an intercollegiate team?

OCR will determine whether there is sufficient unmet interest among the institution's students who are members of the underrepresented sex to sustain an intercollegiate team. OCR will look for interest by the underrepresented sex as expressed through the following indicators, among others:

- requests by students and admitted students that a particular sport be added;
- requests that an existing club sport be elevated to intercollegiate team status;
- participation in particular club or intramural sports;
- interviews with students, admitted students, coaches, administrators and others regarding interest in particular sports;
- results of questionnaires of students and admitted students regarding interests in particular sports; and
- participation in particular inter-scholastic sports by admitted students.

In addition, OCR will look at participation rates in sports in high schools amateur athletic associations, and community sports leagues that operate in areas from which the institution draws its students in order to ascertain likely interest and ability of its students and admitted students in particular sport(s).[5] For example, where OCR's investigation finds that a substantial number of high schools from the relevant region offer a particular sport which the institution does not offer for the underrepresented sex, OCR will ask the institution to provide a basis for any assertion that its students and admitted students are not interested in playing that sport. OCR may also interview students, admitted students, coaches and others regarding interest in that sport.

An institution may evaluate its athletic program to assess the athletic interest of its students of the underrepresented sex using nondiscriminatory methods of its choosing. Accordingly, institutions have flexibility in choosing a nondiscriminatory method of determining athletic interests and abilities provided they meet certain requirements. See 44 Fed Reg. at 71417. These assessments may use straightforward and inexpensive techniques, such as a student questionnaire or an open forum, to identify students' interests and abilities. Thus, while OCR expects that an institution's assessment should reach a wide audience of students and should be open-ended regarding the sports students can express interest in, OCR does not require elaborate scientific validation of assessment.

An institution's evaluation of interest should be done periodically so that the institution can identify in a timely and responsive manner any developing interests and abilities of the underrepresented sex. The evaluation should also take

---

5. While these indications of interest may be helpful to OCR in ascertaining likely interest on campus, particularly in the absence of more direct indications, institution is expected to meet the actual interests and abilities of its students.

into account sports played in the high schools and communities from which the institution draws its students both as an indication of possible interest on campus and to permit the institution to plan to meet the interests of admitted students of the underrepresented sex.

b) Is there sufficient ability to sustain an intercollegiate team?

Second, OCR will determine whether there is sufficient ability among interested students of the underrepresented sex to sustain an intercollegiate team OCR will examine indications of ability such as:

- the athletic experience and accomplishments—in inter-scholastic, club or intramural competition—of students and admitted students interested in playing the sport;
- opinions of coaches, administrators, and athletes at the institution regarding whether interested students and admitted students have the potential to sustain a varsity team; and
- if the team has previously competed at the club or intramural level whether the competitive experience of the team indicates that it has the potential to sustain an intercollegiate team.

Neither a poor competitive record nor the inability of interested students or admitted students to play at the same level of competition engaged in by the institution's other athletes is conclusive evidence of lack of ability. It is sufficient that interested students and admitted students have the potential to sustain an intercollegiate team.

(c) Is there a reasonable expectation of competition for the team?

Finally, OCR determines whether there is a reasonable expectation of intercollegiate competition for a particular sport in the institution's normal competitive region. In evaluating available competition, OCR will look at available competitive opportunities in the geographic area in which the institution's athletes primarily compete, including:

- competitive opportunities offered by other schools against which the institution compete; and
- competitive opportunities offered by other schools in the institution's geographic area, including those offered by schools against which the institution does not now compete.

Under the Policy Interpretation, the institution may also be required to actively encourage the development of intercollegiate competition for a sport for members of the underrepresented sex when overall athletic opportunities within its competitive region have been historically limited for members of that sex.

CONCLUSION

This discussion clarifies that institutions have three distinct ways to provide individuals of each sex with nondiscriminatory participation opportunities. The three-part test gives institutions flexibility and control over their athletics programs. For instance, the test allows institutions to respond to different levels of the interest by its male and female students. Moreover, nothing in the three-part test requires an institution to eliminate participation opportunities for men.

At the same time, this flexibility must be used by institutions consistent with Title IX's requirement that they not discriminate on the basis of sex. OCR recognizes that institutions face challenges in providing nondiscriminatory participation opportunities for their students and will continue to assist institutions in finding ways to meet these challenges.

OCR Home Page (Last updated August 28, 1997).

United States Department of Education — Office of Civil Rights, Letter Clarifying Apportionment of Financial Aid in Intercollegiate Athletics Programs (May 16, 1998)

Ms. Nancy S. Footer
General Counsel
Bowling Green State University
308 McFall Center
Bowling Green, Ohio 43403-0010

Dear Ms. Footer:

This is in response to your letter requesting guidance in meeting the requirements of Title IX specifically as it relates to the equitable apportionment of athletic financial aid. Please accept my apology for the delay in responding. As you know, the Office for Civil Rights (OCR) enforces Title IX of the Education Amendments of 1972, 20 U.S.C. § 1682, which prohibits discrimination on the basis of sex in education programs and activities. The regulation implementing Title IX and the Department's Intercollegiate Athletics Policy Interpretation published in 1979 — both of which followed publication for notice and the receipt, review, and consideration of extensive comments-specifically address intercollegiate athletics. You have asked us to provide clarification regarding how educational institutions can provide intercollegiate athletes with nondiscriminatory opportunities to receive athletic financial aid. Under the Policy Interpretation, the equitable apportioning of a college's intercollegiate athletics scholarship fund for the separate budgets of its men's and women's programs — which Title IX permits to be segregated — requires that the total amounts of scholarship aid made available to the two budgets are "substantially proportionate" to the participation rates of male and female athletes. 44 Fed. Reg. 71413, 71415 (1979)).

In responding, I wish (1) to clarify the coverage of Title IX and its regulations as they apply to both academic and athletic programs, and (2) to provide specific guidance about the existing standards that have guided the enforcement of Title IX in the area of athletic financial aid, particularly the Policy Interpretation's "substantially proportionate" provision as it relates to a college's funding of the athletic scholarships budgets for its men's and women's teams. At the outset, I want to clarify that, wholly apart from any obligation with respect to scholarships, an institution with an intercollegiate athletics program has an independent Title IX obligation to provide its students with nondiscriminatory athletic participation opportunities. The scope of that separate obligation is not addressed in this letter, but was addressed in a Clarification issued on January 16, 1996.

Title IX Coverage: Athletics versus Academic Programs

Title IX is an anti-discrimination statute that prohibits discrimination on the basis of sex in any education program or activity receiving federal financial assistance, including athletic programs. Thus, in both academics and athletics, Title IX guarantees that all students, regardless of gender, have equitable opportunities to participate, in the education program. This guarantee does not impose quotas based on gender, either in classrooms or in athletic programs. Indeed, the imposition of any such strict numerical requirement concerning students would be inconsistent with Title IX itself, which is designed to protect the rights of all students and to provide equitable opportunities for all students.

Additionally, Title IX recognizes the uniqueness of intercollegiate athletics by permitting a college or university to have separate athletic programs, and teams, for men and women. This allows colleges and universities to allocate athletic opportunities and benefits on the basis of sex. Because of this unique circumstance, arguments that OCR's athletics compliance standards create quotas are misplaced. In contrast to other antidiscriminatory statutes, Title IX compliance cannot be determined simply on the basis of whether an institution makes sex-specific decisions, because invariably they do. Accordingly, the statute instead requires institutions to provide equitable opportunities to both male and female athletes in all aspects of its two separate athletic programs. As the court in the Brown University case stated, "[i]n this unique context Title IX operates to ensure that the gender-segregated allocation of athletic opportunities does not disadvantage either gender. Rather than create a quota or preference, this unavoidable gender-conscious comparison merely provides for the allocation of athletic resources and participation opportunities between the sexes in a non-discriminatory manner," *Cohen v. Brown University*, 101 F.3d 155, 177 (1st Cir. 1996), *cert. denied*, 117 S. Ct. 1469 (1997). The remainder of this letter addresses the application of Title IX only to athletic scholarships.

Athletics: Scholarship Requirements

With regard to athletic financial assistance, the regulations promulgated under Title IX provide that, when a college or university awards athletic scholarships, these scholarship awards must be granted to "members of each sex in proportion to the number of students of each sex participating in ... intercollegiate athletics," 34 C.F.R. 106.37(c). Since 1979, OCR has interpreted this regulation in conformity with its published "Policy Interpretation: Title IX and Intercollegiate Athletics," 44 *Fed. Reg.* 71413 (December 11, 1979). The Policy Interpretation does not require colleges to grant the sane number of scholarships to men and women, nor does it require that individual scholarships be of equal value. What it does require is that, at a particular college or university, "the total amount of scholarship aid made available to men and women must be substantially proportionate to their [overall] participation rates" at that institution. *Id.* at 71415. It is important to note that the Policy Interpretation only applies to teams that regularly compete in varsity competiion. *Id.* at 71413 and n. 1.

Under the Policy Interpretation, OCR conducts a "financial comparison to determine whether proportionately equal amounts of financial assistance (scholarship aid) are available to men's and women's athletic programs," *Id*. The Policy Interpretation goes on to state that "[i]nstitutions may be found in compliance if this comparison results in substantially equal amounts or if a disparity can be explained by adjustments to take into account legitimate nondiscriminatory factors." *Id*.

A "disparity" in awarding athletic, financial assistance refers tothe difference between the aggregate amount of money athletes of one sex received in one year, and the amount they would have received if their share of the entire annual budget for athletic scholarships had been awarded in proportion to their participation rates. Thus, for example, if men account for 60% of a school's intercollegiate athletes, the Policy Interpretation presumes that — absent legitimate nondiscriminat factors that may cause a disparity — the men's athletic program will receive approximately 60% of the entire annual scholarship budget and the women's athletic program will receive approximately 40% of those funds. This presumption reflects the fact that colleges typically allocate scholarship funds among their athletic teams, and that such teams are expressly segregated by sex. Colleges' allocation of the scholarship budget among teams, therefore, is invariably sex-based, in the sense that an allocation to a particular team necessarily benefits one sex to the exclusion of the other. *See Brown*, 101 F.3d at 177. Where, as here, disparate treatment is inevitable and a college's allocation of scholarship funds is "at the discretion of the institution," *Brown* 101 F-3d at 177, the statute nondiscrimination requirements obliges colleges to ensure that men's and women's *separate* activities receive equitable treatment. Cf. United States v. Virginia, 518 U.S. 515, 554 (1996).

Nevertheless, in keeping with the Policy Interpretation allowance for disparities from "substantially proportionate" awards to the men's and women's programs based on legitimate nondiscriminatory factors, OCR judges each matter on a case-by-case basis with due regard for the unique factual situation presented by each case. For example, OCR recognizes that disparities may be explained by actions taken to promote athletic program development, and by differences between in-state and out-of-state tuition at public colleges, 44 Fed. Reg, at 71415. Disparities might also be explained, for example by legitimate efforts undertaken to comply with Title IX requirements, such as participation requirements. *See e.g. Gonyo v. Drake Univ.* 879 F. Supp . 1000, 1005-06 (S D. Iowa 1995). Similarly, disparities may be explained by unexpected fluctuations in the participation rates of males and females. For example, a disparity may be explained if an athlete who had accepted an athletic scholarship decided at the last minute to enroll at another school. It is important to note it is not enough for a college or university merely to assert a nondiscriminatory justification. Instead, it will be required to demonstrate that its asserted rationale is in fact reasonable and does not reflect underlying discrimination. For instance, if a college, consistently awards a greater number of out-of-state scholarships to men, it may be required to demonstrate that this does not reflect discriminatory recruitment practices. Similarly, if a university asserts the phase-in of scholarships for a new team as a justification for a disparity, the university may be required to demonstrate that the time frame for phasing-in of scholarships is reasonable in light of college sports practices to aggressively recruit athletes to build start-up teams quickly.

In order to ensure equity for athletes of both sexes, the test for determining whether the two scholarship budgets are "substantially proportionate" to the respective participation rates of athletes of each sex necessarily has a high threshold. The Policy Interpretation does not, however, require colleges to achieve exact proportionality down to the last dollar. The "substantially proportionate" test permits a small variance from exact proportionality. OCR recognizes that, in practice, some leeway is necessary to avoid requiring colleges to unreasonably fine-tune their scholarship budgets.

When evaluating each scholarship program an a case-by-case basis, OCR's first step will be to adjust any disparity to take into account all the legitimate nondiscriminatory reasons provided by the college, such as the extra costs for out-of-state tuition discussed earlier. If any unexplained disparity in the scholarship budget for athletes of either gender is 1% or less for the entire budget for athletic scholarships, there will be a strong presumption that such a disparity is reasonable and based on legitimate and nondiscriminatory factors. Conversely, there will be a strong presumption that an unexplained disparity of more than 1% is in violation of the "substantially proportionate" requirements.

Thus, for example, if man are 60% of the athletes, OCR would expect that the men's athletic scholarship budget would be within 59%-61% of the total budget for athletic scholarships for all athletes, after accounting for legitimate nondiscriminatory reasons for any larger disparity. Of course, OCR will continue to judge each case in terms of its particular facts. For example, at those colleges where 1% of the entire athletic scholarship budget is less than the value of one full scholarship, OCR will presume that a disparity of up to the value of one full scholarship is equitable and nondiscriminatory. On the other hand, even if an institution consistently has less than a 1% disparity, the presumption of compliance with Title IX might still be rebutted if, for example, there is direct evidence of discriminatory intent.

OCR recognizes that there has been some confusion in the past with respect to the Title IX compliance standards for scholarships. OCR's 1990 Title IX Investigator's Manual correctly stated that one would expect proportionality in the awarding of scholarships, absent a legitimate, nondiscriminatory justification. But that Manual also indicated that compliance with the "substantially proportionate" test could depend, in part, upon certain statistical tests. In some cases, application of such a statistical test would result in a determination of compliance despite the existence of a disparity as large as 3-5%.

We would like to clarify that use of such statistical tests is not appropriate in these circumstances. Those tests, which are used in some other discrimination contexts to determine whether the disparities in the allocation of benefits to different groups are the result of chance, are inapposite in the athletic scholarship context because a college has direct control over its allocation of financial aid to men's and women's teams, and because such decisions necessarily are sex-based in the sense that an allocation to a particular team will affect only one sex. *See Brown* 101 F.3d at 176-78 (explaining why college athletics "presents a distinctly different situation from admissions and employment," and why athletics requires a different analysis than that used "in such other contexts "in order to determine the existence vel non of discrimination"). In the typical case where aid is expressly allocated among sex-segregated teams, chance simply is not a possible explanation for disproportionate aid to one sex. Where a college does not make a substantially proportionate allocation to sex-segregated teams, the burden should be on the college to provide legitimate, nondiscriminatory reasons for the disproportionate allocation. Therefore, the use of statistical tests will not be helpful in determining whether a disparity in the allocations for the two separate athletic scholarship budgets is nondiscriminatory.

While a statistical test is not relevant in determining discrimination, the confusion caused by the manual's inclusion of a statistical test resulted in misunderstandings. Therefore, OCR is providing this clarification regarding the substantial proportionality provision found in the 1979 Policy Interpretation to confirm the substance of a longstanding standard. In order to ensure full understanding, OCR will apply the presumptions and case-by-case analysis described in this letter for the 1998-99 academic year. OCR strongly encourages recipients to award athletic financial assistance to women athletes in the 1997-98 academic year consistent with this policy clarification, both as a matter of fairness and in order to ensure that they are moving towards the policy clarification stated in this letter.

I trust that this letter responds to the questions the University has regarding the "substantially proportionate" provision of the Policy interpretation in the context of the funding for an institution's two separate athletic scholarship budgets for male and female athletes. I am sending a copy of this letter as technical assistance to the complainants and the other 24 recipients also currently involved with OCR on the issue of awarding athletic financial assistance. We will be in contact with you shortly to continue to work with the University regarding this matter and to discuss other points raised in your letter. If you have any questions regarding this letter, please contact me at (312) 886-8387.

Sincerely yours,

Dr. Mary Frances O'Shea
National Coordinator for Title IX Athletics

(c) Title IX Commentary

John C. Weistart, Can Gender Equity Find a Place in Commercialized College Sports?
3 Duke Journal of Gender Law & Policy 191 (1996)*

....

I. THE STRUCTURE OF ATHLETIC DECISION-MAKING

....

B. Budgetary Structure and Gender Equity

....

2. *The Implications of Present Budgetary Arrangements of Major Athletic Programs.* The budgetary structure of major athletic programs has rather ominous implications for women's sports. Indeed, the interaction of the policy of rough self-sufficiency and the pressures to meet competitors' expenditures may go a long way in explaining why progress toward gender equity has been so slow. It may

---

also explain the intensity of the anger towards women's sports, especially that expressed by football partisans. The traditional budgetary arrangement inevitably relegates non-revenue sports to a secondary, contingent position. The position of these sports is secondary in the sense that the needs of football and basketball will come first. Indeed, the explanation for the primacy of these sports is nearly tautological: football and basketball must be preferred ahead of other sports because if they are not preferred there might not be any other sports. A weakening of the commitment to keep football and basketball competitive would affect the income stream upon which other sports depend and thus threaten their very existence. Thus, the revenue sports must be supported and they are supported at a level at which they are "competitive," a condition that is largely defined by many factors not within the immediate control of the school's budget makers.

The Padilla-Baumer study confirms these observations. Major athletic programs spend large amounts of money and receive significant financial returns. Only a small portion of that money is used to fund non-revenue sports, however. The authors' analysis suggests that "for every additional $1 spent on athletic programs, between three and seven cents were spent on nonrevenue sports."[76] Thus, if an additional $1 million becomes available because the revenue sports win on the field, only about $50,000 of this will be spent on non-revenue sports.

This disparity explains why coaches and athletic directors can say, presumably with a straight face, that women's sports are expensive. Two hundred thousand dollars spent to establish a new women's team at a Big Time school does not look like much compared to the $10 million spent on football. On the other hand, in the perspective of the athletic director, if an increased expenditure of $50,000 is regarded as "appropriate," then the prospect of spending $200,000 for a new women's sport is likely to be viewed as extraordinary. Stated another way, if one has been trained to think of non-revenue sports as nonessential and secondary, then any request beyond some very low minimum may seem like an unreasonable demand, even though in the larger perspective of the budget, it is quite modest.

Implicit in the budgetary structure is the further assumption that the claims of non-revenue sports will necessarily be contingent. They will be fully and generously funded only if the fortunes of the revenue sports prove bountiful. If revenues are not what was expected, then other sports should expect less. And in the event of a true crisis in one of the revenue sports, non-revenue sports should expect severe consequences. Their existence, after all, is derivative, and if truly significant adjustments have to be made, the contingency that underlies non-revenue sports will have to be realized — in the form of severe budgetary cuts.

This secondary, contingent status that is described here extends to all non-revenue sports, men's and women's. It should be clear, though, that in the present environment, women's sports are going to be more severely affected than men's. Men's non-revenue sports are already established and presumably have assumed a place that presents no threat to the existing balance that clearly prefers the two expensive men's sports. The claims of equality for women's sports represent a new and potentially quite damaging demand. The money that would go to women's sports is a new expenditure and one that is potentially quite large if women's

---

76. Padilla & Baumer, *supra* note 18, at 139.

sports were funded at the levels of parity that Title IX demands. A school that unilaterally decided to divert significant sums of money to women's sports would be laying the seeds of its rather immediate self-destruction in the race for broadcast and attendance revenues. Thus, the incentives to step up and be the first to establish a well- supported women's program are few. Indeed, a path of quiet collective resistance to a full-scale implementation of Title IX will do the most to preserve the existing balance of power among major schools and seems to explain why progress under Title IX has been so limited.

. . . .

Some might argue that Title IX was intended to accept the traditional mechanisms for athletic funding and thus also accept that the advancement of non-revenue sports is dependent upon the availability of sufficient receipts from revenue sports. Under this view, the speed of the movement toward gender equity would accelerate or slow down depending on the flow of money from the on-the-field successes of football and men's basketball. After all, there is no evidence that Title IX was intended to mandate that schools spend more money on athletics, a policy choice that is highly dubious because of its potential drain on academic programs.

The suggestion that the hierarchial structure of athletic spending was intended to be approved by Title IX is refuted by both the statute and its legislative history. The language of the statute mandates gender-blind equal opportunity. No qualification is made based on the availability of funding. Thus, any suggestion that funds from a particular source were understood as a prerequisite to compliance finds no hint of plausibility in the text. The correctness of this conclusion would appear to be fully confirmed by Congress's refusal to adopt the Tower Amendment, a measure that would have exempted revenue sports from the coverage of the statute. One of the arguments made for exempting revenue sports was that they needed special protection because they were the source of funding for other sports. Rejection of the Tower Amendment rather strongly implies that Congress did not embrace the notion that women's sports were entitled to *only* a contingent status. With the proposed amendment defeated, the statutory commitment to equal opportunity remained unqualified.

3. Budgetary Arrangements in Other Competitive Programs. . . .

. . . .

The revenue-generating potential of football reinforces its ability to command first attention in budgetary decisions. The revenues from football are both very welcome and somewhat fickle. A scaled-down version of the Arms Race will occur, for the question will be constantly presented whether hiring a better, but more expensive, coach or improving the locker room or spending more on recruiting will significantly improve the revenue picture. Similarly, on-the-field reversals — losing too many games — hold a real prospect for upsetting budget projections, an event which will ensure that the football program receives careful attention.

What is said about football is also true to a lesser extent for men's basketball. The revenues from basketball are attractive and are thus likely to be nurtured. Women's basketball is also a significant expense item, a fact that will ensure that it receives due attention in departmental decision-making. While it does not generate significant revenues in the budget presented here, there has been a rapid ascendancy in the popularity of women's basketball generally, and the dynamic forces that influence decision-making for the preferred men's sports may soon be seen in this women's counterpart.

The point of the above analysis is to underscore again that the predominant positions of football and basketball are likely to sway decision-making within the department, even in less competitive leagues. The numbers here serve to confirm that these sports command a level of attention that is not equaled by most women's sports. And in the face of the deficits already present, it is unlikely that not-yet-offered women's sports will command a high priority. The reality of this budget is that no sport pays for itself, and some sports, especially football, represent a significant budgetary risk. In this environment, there is no strong internal incentive to add additional sports. Absent such an incentive, a firm external control is necessary if gender equity is to be achieved.

A third perspective on athletic spending can be drawn from the factual record in *Cohen v. Brown University*.[92] The case has produced selected data about the relative cost of sports at that school. . . .

When unrelated events prompted a trimming of the overall athletic budget, the department chose to eliminate two men's sports and two women's sports. This decision was made at a time when women were underrepresented among the school's athletes. The amount the University saved by eliminating the two women's sports was only $62,000. There is no evidence of a significant redirection in the more than $1.9 million allocated to the three expensive men's sports.

. . . . Not only do these sports have a long tradition at the school, they also have greater public appeal than other offerings. While the revenue potential of these sports is not enough to cover their costs, the fact that money can be generated at all by these endeavors is thought to warrant their special treatment.

II. THE STANDARD FOR REVIEWING ATHLETIC DEPARTMENT DECISION-MAKING

. . . .

A. The Demands of the Present Sports Context

We will eventually turn to the issue of whether this three-part test is appropriate for the task of securing compliance with Title IX. Before addressing that question, we must examine more closely the particular realities that any compliance measure will face in the modern sports context. A successful compliance standard must be sensitive to these. Three elements warrant particular attention. One is the apparent bias in favor of men's sports that is embedded in the present decision-making structure. A second is the reality that there can be no absolutes in predicting the extent of women's eventual interest in sports and in judging the relative appeal of men's and women's sports in the future. A particular effort must be made to avoid building new biases into the statute, whether in favor of particular sports or in the form of assumptions about the degree of women's interests. Third, any set of rules used in the present context should be seen as transitional. A major goal for such rules will be to guide the massive transition between a prior state of affairs that was almost exclusively male to a future in which the only certainty is uncertainty. Thus, a delicate balance must be achieved

---

92. 809 F. Supp. 978 (D.R.I. 1992), *aff'd*, 991 F.2d 888 (1st Cir. 1993).

between firm prompting — necessary to achieve movement — and flexibility, which is necessary to deal with the uncertainty inherent in the future development of men's and women's sports.

1. *Responding to the Structural Bias of Athletic Decision-Making.* The first section of this paper discussing the structure of athletic decision-making supports a conclusion that has very important implications for Title IX enforcement. The conclusion to be reached is that the commercial realities of college sports create a very strong bias against women's sports. Because of the financing arrangement that has been selected, revenue sports, particularly football and men's basketball, are strongly favored in budgetary allocations. Indeed, not to favor them would be to opt out of the most financially lucrative opportunities that are available, a choice that few schools are prepared to make.

This financial environment creates a strong incentive to give women's sports a very low priority in budgetary decision-making. Those sports are a net drain on the budget and, in the near term, hold a limited prospect of new revenues. In short, the demand for new women's sports creates a direct challenge to the primacy of the preferred men's sports. The nurturing of these latter sports requires flexibility. Adding women's sports has the potential of severely limiting a school's capacity to meet enhancements by competitors that may yield an athletic advantage.

The implication of this budgetary structure for Title IX is apparent: Title IX is not self-enforcing; a strong external mandate is needed to achieve the statute's goal. The task confronted by any regulation in this area will be to overcome the weak to non-existent internal incentives that a department has to expand women's offerings. This lack of internal incentives suggests that wide deference to internal decision-making is inappropriate. Rather, the emphasis of any regulation should be on clarity and directness. Phrasing that invites softened enforcement will be readily embraced and, thus, opportunities for avoidance should be carefully circumscribed.

The perspective developed here may provide some insight into the strong and vitriolic attacks on Title IX that have come from football partisans. When they suggest that Title IX represents a direct assault on football, there is a sense in which they are correct. The athletic financial pie is limited, and thus there cannot be both new expenditures for women's sports and a continuing commitment to match competitors' spending. Implementation of the former has undeniable implications for the latter. But the statute, and especially the rejection of the Tower Amendment, answers the question of which is to have priority. Title IX's commitment to women's sports is not qualified, by competitive needs or otherwise. It does not follow, however, that a full embrace of Title IX necessarily makes college football significantly less competitive or less attractive. To the extent that is the critics' fear, it is misdirected. There are mechanisms for accommodation of both interests, but these involve financing arrangements different from those now used by schools. A profitable alternative outlet for the energy of the critics of Title IX is to begin working on financial structures that permit effective and durable limits on program expenditures. A later section examines that question more fully.

2. *Challenging What We Think We Know About Women's Sports.* The public discussion of Title IX reveals a surprising tendency toward firm statements about what women do and do not want in sports, and what they will and will not achieve. For example, one fan interviewed by the *Los Angeles Times* confidently surmised that "[i]t is unrealistic to believe that under any circumstance the number of women interested in participating in a sports program in high school or

college will ever approach the percentage of males that are doing so."[112] This comment was specifically intended as a refutation of the wisdom of a legal standard that requires substantial proportionality between women athletes and women in the student body. A columnist in the *Chicago Tribune* was certain that the court in the *Brown University* case was wrong in approving the substantial proportionality test. In his view, the real reason why women were underrepresented in athletics at Brown was clear: "[f]or better or worse, young women are generally less interested in sports than young men."[113]

Another set of "inherent truths" concerns the continuing primacy of football and men's basketball. Some people believe that these two sports will always be the most popular sports at the college level because they have professional counterparts. Or because men play sports better than women play theirs. Or just because these men's sports are more interesting.

A careful look at the developing landscape reveals why such assertions are much more confident than they should be. For example, in recent years, the women's basketball teams at Stanford University and the University of Colorado have outdrawn their men's counterparts in attendance. In addition, the 1995-96 basketball season saw a surge in the televised coverage of women's games, a decent gauge of whether fan interest is evolving. Moreover, the raw numbers on women's participation in sports can hardly leave one confident that we already know all that we can know. In 1971, before there was any significant activity under Title IX, approximately 290,000 girls were participating in high school sports. In just six years, the number rose to more than 2 million. Participation rates have been greatly affected by budgetary changes and shifts in total enrollment, but the number today is still 2.1 million. The obvious unanswered question is what this number would be after a couple of decades of adequate funding and vigorous enforcement of Title IX. Sobering implications can be found in the experience of one independent school in the Southeast. Several years ago it made a commitment to fund, and to find appropriate competition for, any group of students interested in forming any interscholastic team. For the last several years, 80 percent of the girls, as well as a similar percentage of the boys, have chosen to participate in interscholastic sports.

Those who contend that there never will be enough interest among women make another fatal analytical error as far as college athletics is concerned. The standard of substantial proportionality does not require, for example, that 50 percent of an evenly balanced student body actually participate in athletics. The number of women athletes needed to meet this standard is quite small at most schools. To take one example, at the University of Illinois, a school with a student body of 25,000, only 325 women athletes would be needed to meet the proportionality standard. And since the assumption at schools such as the University of Illinois is that athletes will be recruited, and not drawn from students who have independently decided to attend the school, women athletes will in fact be drawn from a pool that is much larger than 25,000. Hence, with an appropriate commitment from the school administration to encourage recruiting and to support women's teams, a sufficient number of athletes most likely can be found.

---

112. Bob Rohwer, *An Even Field?*, L.A. TIMES, Nov. 1, 1994, at V1 (quoting Arlyn F. Obert).

113. Stephen Chapman, *Opinions: Title IX Debate Is a Matter of Interest*, NCAA NEWS, May 10, 1995, at 4.

Another common assumption is that we already know what sports interest women and how relatively popular they will be. Again, however, recent history has taught us that we ought not to embrace any conventional wisdom. A few years ago, only a couple of thousand fans attended the women's Final Four basketball tournament. Last year the event sold out at over 18,000 fans. Fourteen cities vied to host the event in 1999 and 2000. Similar errors in judging popularity have been made with respect to sports other than basketball. For many years, it was assumed that soccer was mainly a men's sport. Indeed, in 1972 only about 300 women played collegiate soccer. But in 1992, there were over 8,000 participants in soccer at the three levels of NCAA competition.

A further reason for reserving judgment about the long-term future of women's sports is the potential for major changes in the Big Time football and basketball markets. At their highest level of competition, these sports are heavily commercialized. Many, if not most, of the successful programs operate at a significant distance from the notions of amateurism and academic primacy that were their origins. For example, graduation rates at many schools continue to be low, despite much publicized "reforms" promulgated by the NCAA. In recent years, the basketball programs at Kentucky, Arizona, Syracuse, and Oklahoma State had graduation rates of 20 percent, 20 percent, 21 percent, and 17 percent, respectively. For African-American basketball players at Kansas, Massachusetts, and Missouri, the graduation rates were 17 percent, 0 percent, and 0 percent. Results are not significantly more encouraging for Big Time football programs. A national publication recently proposed that the University of Miami should shut down its highly successful football program because of a long series of academic, NCAA, and civil infractions. The athletic products of the top programs are extremely popular on television, and the flow of large broadcast dollars is not necessarily dependent on these sports having a university affiliation. Although there is no purely commercial alternative on the immediate horizon, it is not inconceivable that market forces will coalesce to give rise to new versions of pre-professional sports that are delinked from the present requirements for a four-year degree. Part-time enrollment of athletes or a loose or non-existent affiliation with colleges may eventually be seen as creating a larger labor pool and a more interesting product.

Such a development would be something of a mixed blessing for women's sports. A major source of funding would be adversely affected. On the other hand, a lessening of the role of Big Time sports would allow for a reorientation of college sports toward less commercialized versions. The notion that the only good sports are those that have a professional counterpart may lose its present hold and permit a new emphasis on broader scale participation, albeit at less glamorous levels. In this environment, the relative acceptance of women's sports would likely increase, perhaps significantly so.

The basic point again is that any legal standard should accept the dynamic nature of women's sports at the college level. Our knowledge of women's sports at present is roughly at the level that our understanding of men's sports was in 1920. It clearly would have been a mistake to have frozen our assumptions about men's offerings at that point in time. We would probably still have college boxing programs and a curiously awkward version of basketball. Independent forces, including the desire to protect the preferred men's sports, create pressures to keep women's sports at their current levels. One function of the standard for legal review, therefore, should be to both allow for and encourage further development of women's sports. Sensitivity to this goal will accept that judges and administrative agencies will have to make decisions in the face of a good deal of uncertainty. Thus, remedies to expand women's opportunities should not be judged against a standard of scientific certainty as to future viability. A more suitable measure is one that asks whether there are plausible grounds to support an expansion that would further the broad goals of Title IX.

3. *The Special Pressures of a Transitional Rule.* As suggested, any legal standard used to judge compliance with Title IX in college sports should be sensitive to the fact that is an area of endeavor that is very much in transition. Whatever the legal standard, it should not be defined by firm assumptions about what women's sports will look like in forty or fifty years. Indeed, a strong case can be made that whatever test for compliance we have now should not be the rule that applies several decades from now. The base of knowledge about the progress of women's sports will most likely be quite different at that future point. Perhaps we can eventually embrace a rule that assumes that athletic administrators will make neutral budgetary allocations. As previously suggested, however, there is presently little reason to be confident on that score. For now, our legal standard must deal with the known of the departmental resistance to the expansion of women's sports and the unknown of what women's sports will look like in the future.

A transitional rule should accept the fact that the historical context of college sports has been very male oriented. Clearly the adoption of Title IX was intended to change this. An effective transitional rule should have a significant element of urging and prompting built into it, as excessive deference to existing methods of decision-making is not likely to yield meaningful results. Given the continuing pervasive effects of the historical bias, a firm and clear method of judging progress may be necessary.

On the other hand, a transitional rule should avoid any specific direction as to the type of sports to be offered or the levels of funding to be provided. In a very concrete sense, the most useful rule for the present will be one that accepts a level of experimentation in women's athletics. New sports should not be rejected because they have no track record or an unproven one, nor should they be rejected because they might eventually fail. While universities should not be required to spend money foolishly, by the same token, schools cannot demand that new women's sports irrefutably prove their viability. Because women's sports are in transition, there cannot be exquisite certainty that all choices made now will become permanent. In short, transitional rules should embrace a procedure for change and resist any effort to codify a particular model for women's sports.

.... [Professor Weistart's Analysis of the Department of Education's three-part test to determine whether a school is effectively accommodating the interests of men and women in athletics is omitted. — ed.].

IV. CONCLUSION

In a very real sense, the present state of affairs of gender integration in college sports is not satisfactory. Supporters of expanded women's sports can properly claim that progress toward gender equity has been slow. Indeed, the fact that the equalization of sports programs lags well behind advances in other aspects of higher education understandably raises suspicions about the sincerity of the efforts that have been made to date. On the other hand, advocates for men's sports feel deeply wronged. After several instances in which schools have dropped men's non-revenue sports and explained their actions on the basis of the need to shift money to women's sports, questions have been raised about the fairness of an interpretation of Title IX that advances the interest of one group by denying opportunities to another. Adding to the debate are the proponents of men's revenue sports, especially football, who believe that Title IX requires the dismantling of their commercially successful ventures. Indeed, what may be most remarkable about the present Title IX debate is the absence of any voice that suggests that the existing trends are acceptable.

A number of different futures for Title IX and college sports can be foreseen. It is quite possible that the recent history of acrimony and slow progress will continue for some time. The present course is particularly subject to the uncertainties of outside forces. Changes in the political trends in the federal government will speed or retard forward movement as the then-current perception of ideological advantage dictates. By the same token, as long as women's sports are kept in a secondary, contingent relationship with men's revenue sports, a variety of other, seemingly distant events will move the fortunes of women's teams forward or backwards. These include changes in television viewing habits with respect to football and basketball, the development of new forms of non-sports entertainment products, and the revelation of evermore dismaying scandals in Big Time sports.

To the extent that colleges continue to use a model of economic competition to dictate funding levels in men's revenue sports, the present atmosphere of suspicion and political maneuvering will be encouraged. Moreover, there will be a continuing need for strong external enforcement of Title IX. The economic competition model creates a selfishness in men's revenue sports and offers negative incentives for gender integration. Firm outside regulation is thus necessary to correct the distortions that are created.

While the present state of gender integration is not satisfactory, it is important to note that it is not inevitable either. Just as the existing tensions between genders in sports are the product of choice, they can be unchosen. There is an obvious decision that lies ahead and that is whether the economic engine that drives revenue sports will be restrained. The reasons for doing so are immensely attractive. A long-standing source of budgetary distress will be tempered, if not quieted. The attractiveness and variety of sports opportunities will be increased, with relatively little change in the versions that are presently popular. The intensity of external oversight will be reduced. And most importantly, a source of long simmering distrust will be removed. It may even be that universities are able to fulfill their educational function in a more effective way.

B. Glenn George, Who Plays and Who Pays:
Defining Equality in Intercollegiate Athletics
1995 Wisconsin Law Review 647*

. . . .

II. WHO PLAYS AND WHO PAYS?

. . . .

A. *Equitable Accommodation: Equality as Proportionality*

Much of the litigation under Title IX has focused on OCR's first and simplest method of satisfying the Policy Interpretation's definition of equitable accommodation: ensuring that the number of male and female athletes proportionately reflects the number of men and women in the student body. The proportionality rule is appealing on several levels. Its simplicity alone is a significant advantage. Neither the schools nor the courts need engage in complex calculations, studies, fact-finding, or discussions. Determining the percentage of women in the student body determines the number of women athletes needed for Title IX compliance.

In fact, proportionality has become the only realistic means of satisfying OCR's definition of equitable accommodation. The second option, demonstrating "a history and continuing practice of program expansion," is not a viable alternative for most institutions. The common pattern following Title IX's enactment was an expansion of women's sports in the 1970s, with few additions since that time. Brown University, sued in 1991 for eliminating women's gymnastics and volleyball (along with men's golf and water polo), is a typical example. With one exception, all of the women's teams were added between 1971 and 1977. The program remained stable until Brown's 1991 decision to downsize both men's and women's athletics. Examining this sequence of events in *Cohen v. Brown University*, the First Circuit concluded, "The very length of this hiatus suggests something far short of a *continuing* practice of program expansion."[33]

OCR's third alternative, a demonstration that the "interests and abilities of the members of that sex have been fully and effectively accommodated," has been interpreted in such a way that it essentially is mooted by a lawsuit. Because these cases are usually filed by women athletes seeking reinstatement of eliminated teams or elevation of club/intramural teams, the courts reason, obviously there are interests not being accommodated.

The proportionality rule perhaps begs the question, however. We would never seriously contemplate a rule requiring that enrollment in every class or every major reflect the gender proportions of the student body. We demand instead that all courses and majors be equally *available* to men and women students. We might be concerned about a relatively small percentage of women in certain majors (the sciences, for example). We might examine the program to ensure there are no overt or subtle barriers which discriminate against or discourage members of either gender. We might consider programs to encourage more significant involvement of women. But ratios would never be mandated.

The proportionality model is a very rough equivalent to mandatory affirmative action, but it is implemented in a vastly different context. For example, we have the option of offering a biology course to all and waiting to see which students actually register for the class. Absent any gender-related barriers, we can be reasonably comfortable in concluding that registration reflects student interest by gender and that the interest of both sexes is being equitably satisfied. With an intercolle-

---

33. *Cohen*, 991 F.2d at 903; *see also* Roberts v. Colorado State Univ., 814 F. Supp. 1507, 1514 (D. Colo. 1993) (no new women's intercollegiate teams added since the 1970s).

giate sports program, waiting for the students to sign up before deciding what sports will be offered for each gender is simply not an option. By definition, the institution must predetermine (consistent with NCAA regulations) both the number of sports offered and the slots available for men and women students.

In the employment context, the courts have had thirty years of experience in defining the concept of "sex discrimination." Most cases have focused on the elimination of sex as a criterion or consideration in employment decisions—sometimes referred to as "gender-blind" decisionmaking. Affirmative action plans based on gender have also received judicial approval, but typically in the context of a voluntarily adopted plan that is "carefully tailored" to the purposes of Title VII. The challenge for those faced with implementing Title IX is to define a comparable measure of equality in the context of a program in which participation cannot be determined by an open application process.

Even if one accepts the basic premise of proportionality as the appropriate measure for equality under Title IX, one might reasonably question the group of comparison. The proportion of male and female students at the institution may be unrelated to the number of students at the institution or in the high school population with the requisite skills to play at the intercollegiate level. The problem is similar to the issue that arises in employment cases when the plaintiff attempts to support his or her claim of impact discrimination by comparing the employer's hiring pool to the number of protected class members available for the job. The courts have consistently required a comparison to the pool of individuals with the necessary qualifications rather than to the general population.

Of course, looking just at the skilled athletes in the student body is unsatisfactory as well. Student-athletes are rarely recruited from the student body at large. They are specifically targeted and recruited as high school students by the appropriate coach and then admitted to the institution, sometimes under special (i.e., lower) admissions standards. If these talented high school athletes represent the pool from which the college athletes are selected, then the recruiting pool may be the proper basis for the proportionality measure. The number of men and women athletes available depends not on the student body at large but on the eligible number of high school athletes.

Regardless of the gender composition of any of the possible "pools" that might be used for comparison, an institution might reasonably make the choice to promote the development of certain women's sports at the high school level by offering competition opportunities at the college level. But should this be a choice of policy or legal mandate? What does the obligation of nondiscrimination require?

B. *Reexamining Equal Opportunity in Sports*

The proportionality issue raises yet another threshold question. If we are using student body proportions as a substitute or shorthand for student interest, then the courts and OCR should be prepared to accept evidence of actual student interest if and when that information is available — just as we accept as "equitable" unequal gender enrollments in our courses and majors that are available to all students. This assumes, of course, that we can find reliable measures of interest, a problem discussed below. This reasoning also suggests that OCR's third alternative for satisfying Title IX, a demonstration "that the interests and abilities of the members of [the underrepresented] sex have been fully and effectively accommodated," requires a more sophisticated analysis.

The issue cannot reasonably be framed as whether the interests of all potential women student-athletes are being satisfied; given limited resources, the question should be whether the satisfaction and/or frustration levels of men and women are equitable. Title IX requires no particular program size; indeed, Title IX does not require a sports program at all. A school could choose to eliminate its sports program altogether or limit it to a track team for men and a track team for women. Either choice would comply with Title IX, although hundreds of men and women who had hoped to play football, basketball, volleyball, or soccer might be disappointed.

Student interest cannot serve as a substitute for the proportionality model unless interest can be reliably measured. Measurement options might include a review of the participation rates in a school's intramural and club sports programs. Much like a biology class or an engineering major, these opportunities are typically available to all students. A significant and consistent disparity in gender participation rates over time could be evidence of disparate interest levels for intercollegiate sports as well. Furthermore, OCR is now requesting institutions to conduct sports interest surveys as part of its compliance reviews.

Measuring student interest involves an inherent problem, however. Surveying incoming students suggests that we allow students to select the college of their choice consistent with their credentials, and then field our sports teams from the matriculated pool. For big-time sports programs, this has little to do with reality. Most athletes are specifically recruited to play, and those athletes often select schools on the basis of their competition opportunities.

The University of Colorado recently agreed to conduct a sports interest survey as part of its Title IX compliance agreement with OCR. The survey was distributed to all freshmen and transfer students during orientation sessions. It listed forty-five sports and asked the respondent to indicate both past participation at the high school level and interest in participating at the university. Men's level of interest in participating at the intercollegiate level was almost twice that of female respondents; the interest levels were fifteen percent and eight percent, respectively. Thus, of the eleven percent who indicated an interest in playing intercollegiate athletics, sixty-eight percent were male and thirty-two percent were female. This correlates with the current group of student-athletes, which is sixty-four percent male and thirty-six percent female. The undergraduate body at large is approximately forty-seven percent female.

A review of participation in other sports programs available to all students at the University of Colorado indicated similar gender disparities. Over 10,000 students at the university participated in the intramural program in 1993-94; only about twenty-three percent of those participants were women. In club sports, however, forty-two percent of the 1993-94 participants were women. The Athletic Department sponsors a unique "Ski Club," which serves in part as a "feeder" for the university's intercollegiate ski team. Participants are provided coaching and competition opportunities. The Ski Club is open to all students willing to pay the required fee, yet participation rates are approximately seventy percent male and thirty percent female. Although some of this data may be flawed and its meaning debatable, the numbers should at least give one pause. According to three of four possible "interest measures," the University is currently more than equitably satisfying the interest level of its women students.

Assuming these numbers have some validity and might be considered as evidence of disparate interest, it is still possible to be troubled by the source of that disparity. Are women the victims of socialization which brands sports as "unlady-like"? Perhaps, but interestingly enough, the University of Colorado survey indicated that the high school participation rates by gender were very similar and significantly higher than the interest in intercollegiate athletics. Although only eight percent of the women respondents expressed an interest in playing at the intercollegiate level, sixty-one percent reported participation on a high school team. Of the male respondents, fifteen percent expressed interest in intercollegiate competition while sixty-seven percent reported high school participation.

Interest levels at the intercollegiate level may also reflect the knowledge of limited opportunities. Perhaps fewer women express an interest because they are already aware that available slots are scarce. Offering more slots might create more demand, thus encouraging higher women's participation. This reasoning would not explain the comparable disparity of interest in sports at the intramural and club levels, however, as indicated by actual participation.

Lack of significant television exposure might play into the calculus as well. Boys who grow up watching college sports competitions on television may be attracted to the "fame" associated with football and men's basketball. If so, one might expect the increasing television exposure given women's basketball to generate additional interest in the sport.

Another possibility is a difference in focus, perhaps resulting from the almost nonexistent professional sports opportunities for women. No doubt, many men pursue intercollegiate athletics in part because they hope to attain the wealth and fame of professional athletes. At least some women athletes may examine their options, consider the vast number of hours associated with playing at the intercollegiate level, and conclude that their time is better spent on classes and obtaining a degree. This is pure speculation, but if such choices are being made, I would be reluctant to encourage the choice of sports over studying.

On the other hand, the proportionality measure may not be merely an easy substitute for student interest. Perhaps it is a statement of policy irrespective of actual student interest (assuming a reasonable measure of such interest could be found and might, in fact, demonstrate a difference between the interest levels of men and women students). In other words, even if a larger percentage of male students are interested in competing at the intercollegiate level, perhaps we should reject whatever factors may have created that unequal demand. We might insist that women students receive this benefit/resource in equal proportions, particularly given that slots on intercollegiate sports teams are limited resources for which the demand is likely to be greater than the supply.

We assume, and not unreasonably, that offering intercollegiate competition opportunities for women will generate their interest. This may be a laudable goal. It may be the right answer, and it certainly should be within an institution's prerogative to make that decision voluntarily as a policy statement. But is this what is meant by Title IX's prohibition of sex discrimination? Such an interpretation also raises the problem of "reverse discrimination." If the interest level of men is higher, does the proportionality model unfairly frustrate a higher proportion of potential male athletes?

III. THE STRUGGLE OF THE NCAA

The recent efforts of the NCAA to overcome its historical resistance to Title IX are notable and represent a significant change of position. The NCAA Executive

Director speculated shortly after Title IX was passed that it would mean "the possible doom of [men's] intercollegiate sports."[48] The NCAA lobbied for the exclusion of intercollegiate athletics from Title IX, and then supported the Tower Amendment, which would have exempted revenue-producing sports from the statute's coverage. When those efforts failed, the NCAA filed a lawsuit to invalidate the OCR regulations. In light of such a beginning, it is little wonder that supporters of women's sports eye the Title IX enforcement efforts of the NCAA with some caution and skepticism.

Recent events, however, demonstrate a serious attempt by the NCAA to address the Title IX problem. In 1992, the NCAA released the results of a national survey of its members that attempted to measure the status of women's programs. The study of Division I programs revealed that, although women comprise roughly half of the students at these institutions, women represent only thirty-one percent of the student-athletes and receive an even lower percentage of the scholarship dollars and recruiting expenditures.

The NCAA responded to the Gender-Equity Study by appointing a sixteen-member task force to study the issue. This body issued its Final Report in July of 1993, making a variety of recommendations to the NCAA and its committees.[54] The Report defines gender equity in broad terms as "fair and equitable distribution of overall athletics opportunities." Reminiscent of Solomon, the Report describes an equitable program as one in which "the participants in both the men's and women's sports programs would accept as fair and equitable the overall program of the other gender."[55] Yet the Task Force ultimately defers to OCR and the courts when it reaches the specifics. In its Guidelines to Promote Gender Equity, the Report states, "The ultimate goal for each institution should be that the numbers of male and female athletes are substantially proportionate to their numbers in the institution's undergraduate student population."[56]

Even before the completion of the Task Force Report, the 1993 NCAA Convention adopted a new certification program that requires its members to develop a gender equity plan and to conduct periodic self-studies, which must include an evaluation of the school's commitment to the fair and equitable treatment of its men and women athletes. The 1994 NCAA Convention, in direct response the Task Force Report, passed legislation adopting the Task Force's recommendation that gender equity be added to the NCAA Manual under "Principles for Conduct in Intercollegiate Athletics." Proposals presented at the 1995 NCAA Convention would have increased the number of women athletes permitted in certain sports, as a means of achieving proportionality without adding new sports. These proposals were effectively tabled, however, pending further discussion and review scheduled for the 1996 Convention.

At least two conferences and some individual institutions have moved ahead with compliance plans of their own. The Big Ten is requiring its members to reach a 60:40 male to female student-athlete ratio by 1997 (although the student

---

48. Bart Barnes & Nancy Scannel, *No Sporting Chance: The Girls in the Locker Room,* WASH. POST, May 12, 1974, at A1, A14.

54. FINAL REPORT OF THE NCAA GENDER EQUITY TASK FORCE (July 26, 1993).

55. *Id.* at § 2. The goal of the definition may be laudable but it provides little practical guidance.

56. *Id.* at § 3.

body ratio for the Big Ten schools is much closer to 50:50). The Southeastern Conference is requiring its members to offer at least two more women's sports than men's sports by 1995. Neither of these plans necessarily achieves gender equity as defined by OCR, the courts, or the NCAA Gender-Equity Task Force, however, since neither makes student-body ratios a part of the equation. The University of Iowa, also a member of the Big Ten, has opted for a more aggressive approach. It has committed to reach student body proportionality by August 1997.

IV. LOOKING FOR ANSWERS

The answers to the questions surrounding implementation of Title IX are not obvious, and I am troubled by the possible criticism that even raising questions suggests my opposition to the progress being made for women in intercollegiate athletics. Nonetheless, I would propose several approaches for consideration.

A. *Reinterpreting the Legal Premises*

In the absence of a statutory amendment or even a significant change in OCR's long-standing Policy Interpretation, one view of "equality" might require a closer look at the alternative of accommodating student interest. The proportionality model would remain a "safe harbor" for those institutions which might adopt such an approach as a policy matter and/or are unwilling to attempt serious measures to define the respective levels of student interest. For schools choosing to respond to student interest, that alternative would be allowed and would be defined as something more than a group of women who wish to play a particular sport. The possible measures being examined at the University of Colorado might be a good starting place; no doubt the combination of several measures is better than reliance on a single survey or set of participation statistics. Ideally, OCR could assist this effort by providing examples of the kinds of measures it will consider for compliance purposes.

Allowing institutions more flexibility in determining the number of women athletes in their athletics programs might also accelerate our focus on many other aspects of gender equity. Once we are satisfied that we have the "right number" of women athletes, we can begin to examine more closely their support and treatment within an athletic program.

A second alternative accepts the proportionality model but with a different focus and rationale than is commonly associated with this model. One might describe the proportionality model as a "micro" solution directed at a "macro" problem. Big-time sports programs at most Division I-A schools have long been detached from their respective educational institutions. These programs have developed large and powerful lives of their own virtually unrelated to the fundamental mission of higher education. Demanding that women participate in athletics proportionately to their numbers in the student body may be a way to reassert that connection. Although it would likely be difficult to justify this rationale as based on original congressional intent, perhaps broader concerns may be used to support an expansive reading, just as affirmative action plans permitting "discrimination" are allowed in spite of the explicit prohibitions of Title VII.

Sports provide a valuable experience for those with the talent and commitment to compete at the intercollegiate level, yet athletics should remain (or return to) an *extracurricular* activity. Although some students (perhaps many or most in men's football and basketball) may perceive the experience as a training camp for professional sports, statistics prove most of those students wrong. The substantial majority who will never have the opportunity to use their athletic talents for their livelihood are done a great disservice if we have not provided an education as part of the package. Our athletic programs should be designed with those students, not the handful who may play professionally, in mind.

Demanding an infusion of women athletes—a group for which there are virtually no professional sports opportunities—may be a step in that direction. Recruiting should focus on those with the talents to compete both athletically and academically at the institution in question. And tying the numbers back to the student body (rather than to the pool of interested or skilled students) conveys precisely the right message: the athletics program is a part of the institution and thus should reflect the broader student body whose education is the institution's primary goal and mission.

The benefit for the student-athlete is obvious. The best thing we can do for any student-athlete is to ensure a degree at the end of the playing field. We currently admit many student-athletes whose qualifications are well below those of their average fellow students, and then ask them to keep up academically while devoting hundreds of hours a year to practice, training, traveling, and competing. Even the few student-athletes who continue to play at the professional level are entering a career that is, by definition, risky and short-lived at best. When we allow intercollegiate athletics programs to become training grounds for professional sports with only tenuous connections to educational institutions, we jeopardize our student-athletes' futures with only the crassest of justifications.

B. *NCAA Initiatives*

The question of student interest versus proportionality apparently is an issue the NCAA either has not fully addressed or has resolved in favor of proportionality. The Gender-Equity Task Force touts proportionality as the "ultimate goal," perhaps an indication that the Task Force recommends proportionality as the "right" or "ethical" result for NCAA members, irrespective of legal mandates. Perhaps, but it is doubtful.

The hard numbers proportionality demands, if student interest is relevant and measurable, only add to the type of resistance initially demonstrated by the NCAA and now by at least some of its individual members. We have no commonly accepted definition of "fairness" in this context. Without a broader discussion, it seems unlikely that the resistance can be fully overcome. Some of the resistance may simply result from dated beliefs about women's athletics that we can dismiss as "discrimination." To the extent the legal mandates (as opposed to our policy goals) raise real issues, however, those issues deserve the attention of all the relevant parties.

The NCAA has a variety of resources at its disposal to aid in a fuller understanding of and ultimate compliance with the mandates of Title IX. Given the NCAA's historical opposition to Title IX, however, its advocacy of an interest model as an alternative to proportionality may be viewed as just another tactic to undermine the goals of gender equity. To avoid having these efforts dismissed as those of self-serving Title IX opponents, any attempts by the NCAA to explore the interest model should be packaged with a much broader set of initiatives to demonstrate its commitment. I would suggest the following components.

First, the NCAA could begin a discussion with OCR of the interest model as an alternative to proportionality. Although the NCAA has no power to alter judicial interpretations of Title IX, its dominance of intercollegiate athletics would likely be sufficient to spur OCR to explore more fully the options under Title IX.

Second, the NCAA could provide its members the framework for evaluating the interest model as an alternative to proportionality. For those members considering an interest model, the NCAA could provide a resource and clearinghouse to assist in designing a variety of measures for student interest. Neither OCR nor the courts are likely to adopt such an approach absent serious and reliable attempts to measure interest levels. Sharing information on conducting student surveys, for example, would facilitate the development of better and more credible measures of interest. Even without OCR's blessing, NCAA members facing Title IX litigation would be in a far better position to argue the interest model to the courts.

Third, once the NCAA has reached a conclusion as to what constitutes Title IX compliance, the NCAA should ground its commitment to Title IX by the imposition of serious sanctions. Assume, for example, that the NCAA concluded Title IX compliance could be achieved either through proportionality or the equitable satisfaction of student interest determined by a variety of possible measures. Having reached that decision, the NCAA's commitment to Title IX would be demonstrated by sanctioning any member unable to establish its compliance with one of those alternatives. Adherence to Title IX surely would be swift and universal if made a condition of NCAA competition (or bowl game participation or sharing in television revenues). At least in theory, compliance with federal law should be as important as the kinds of infractions for which such sanctions are currently used.

Fourth, if the student interest measures used by NCAA members turn out to demonstrate the kinds of disparities between men and women found at the University of Colorado, the NCAA should initiate its own research to explain and understand those disparities. If women are less interested in sports than men, we should know what lies behind that disinterest so that we can knowledgeably consider how the NCAA and its members should respond.

Finally, in conjunction with studies attempting to explain any gender disparity in interest levels, the NCAA should continue to examine ways in which women's athletics can be supported and encouraged. Requirements like proportionality seem to create antagonism, or "polarization," as one commentator has labeled it. Other suggestions, such as capping men's teams while encouraging female walk-ons, are likely to generate a similar reaction. The problem with such alternatives is that they look like anything but equality as long as the male and female athletes and teams are subject to different rules. More carrots are needed to go with the sticks.

One promising possibility is to expand the NCAA's current approach to skiing championships. In skiing competitions, the scores of the men's and women's teams are combined to determine the rankings. Regardless of how good the men's team might be at a particular school, the championship will not be a realistic possibility without a competitive women's team. This inevitably creates incentives for the institution and the skiers to support and promote both the male and female teams. Ignoring the team of either gender is simply self-defeating. A similar system could govern a variety of other sports. In track, for example, the men's and women's teams already compete at the same times and locations. Creating a school championship based on the performances of both teams would promote equality in a way that may be far more practical (and acceptable to all concerned) than any solutions a court could possibly devise.

A combined championship will not work for every sport, and, obviously, does not address the "problem" of football. Nonetheless, a mutually supportive and cooperative atmosphere among the men's and women's sports teams may create a climate that will spread to the athletics program as a whole.

V. CONCLUSION

My principal goal in this Article is to raise some questions concerning what appears to be a developing consensus on the meaning of and obligations imposed by Title IX in the intercollegiate sports arena. The most troubling aspect of my inquiries is the suggestion that we should back away from the current momentum that is pushing the NCAA and its member institutions to examine seriously their Title IX duties. Intercollegiate athletics faces a number of challenges in the coming years, many of them related to budget constraints. Title IX must remain a critical concern in meeting each of these challenges.

But defining the parameters of Title IX is only a piece of the puzzle, and it raises additional questions about why women choose or fail to choose athletic pursuits. When we better understand the needs of both men and women student-athletes, we can begin to fashion programs which are more satisfactory to all concerned.

Crista D. Leahy, Note, The Title Bout: A Critical Review of the Regulation and Enforcement of Title IX in Intercollegiate Athletics
24 Journal of College and University Law 489 (1998)*

....

III. TAKING A SHOT AT THE TITLE[203]

The guidelines outlining equal opportunity set forth in the Department of Education's policy interpretation have become the target of attack in the debates surrounding Title IX, with the proportionality test at the center of the controversy. Instead of increasing opportunities for women, many colleges and universities, in an attempt to comply with the policy interpretation, are cutting opportunities for men. Reducing male opportunities has led to allegations that the participation test is a form of affirmative action that establishes a quota for female participation in athletics. These charges stem from the view that recent decisions such as *Cohen* and *Kelley* effectively have elevated the proportionality test to a level above the other two benchmarks of compliance, resulting in a reliance upon statistical parity

---

203. Donal C. Mahoney, *Taking a Shot at the Title: A Critical Review of Judicial and Administrative Interpretations of Title IX as Applied to Intercollegiate Athletic Programs*, 27 CONN. L. REV. 943 (1995).

to demonstrate equal opportunity. Consequently, Title IX—a statute that forbids discrimination—allegedly has been transformed into a statute that mandates it.

A. *The View of the Courts*

The District Court in *Cohen I* and *Cohen III*, and the Court of Appeals for the First Circuit in *Cohen II* and *Cohen IV*, accorded the Department of Education's Policy Interpretation substantial deference. Although treated as only a tangential issue during the appeal of the injunction, the court did note that, because the policy interpretation is a "considered interpretation" of the regulation, it should receive substantial deference. During the trial on the merits, Brown University raised a more strenuous objection to the deference the court gave the policy interpretation than the university raised during the proceeding leading to the injunction. However, Judge Pettine adopted the view of the First Circuit in *Cohen II*, holding that the policy interpretation should be given "substantial weight."[205] In support of this view, Judge Pettine advanced three arguments. First, because the policy interpretation is a "considered" document—that is, because the original draft was published for public comment and because the agency staff visited colleges and universities to evaluate how the interpretation could be applied—it warranted substantial deference. Second, Judge Pettine contended that, because Congress has had the opportunity to disapprove of the policy interpretation, and chose to reaffirm the agency's intent to broadly construe Title IX's prohibition against discrimination, it should be inferred that legislative intent was correctly expressed in the policy interpretation. Finally, he argued that institutions are not compelled to demonstrate statistical parity; rather, the proportionality test simply provides a "safe harbor" that allows universities to demonstrate compliance. The First Circuit, in *Cohen IV*, endorsed Judge Pettine's decision and his view of the role of the policy interpretation. Therefore, the policy interpretation has been given substantial deference in all significant cases involving Title IX and intercollegiate athletics. More specifically, the three-prong test measuring equal opportunity has been systematically applied as the yardstick for compliance.

.... Upon analysis of these criteria, it appears that both the *Cohen* and the *Kelley* courts have awarded this policy statement a higher degree of deference than it deserves.

B. *The Reliance On Statistical Parity in the Second and Third Benchmarks*

1. Program Expansion

An examination of the application of the second and third prongs of the equal opportunity test in light of *Cohen* and *Kelley* supports the argument that statistical parity has, indeed, become a necessary component of compliance. In *Cohen III*, the court found that, although Brown University had an impressive history of program expansion, the University had failed to maintain a "continuing practice" of intercollegiate program expansion for women.[211] Thus, the fact that Brown had created eighteen teams for women during the 1970s in an attempt to comply with Title IX was irrelevant in the 1990s. The court failed, however, to discuss whether

---

205. *Cohen III*, 879 F. Supp. 185, 198 (D.R.I. 1995) (quoting *Cohen II*, 991 F.2d at 896-97).

211. *Cohen III*, 879 F. Supp. at 211.

Brown might have complied with the mandate of Title IX by adding women's sports gradually, perhaps one every two or three years over the decades, in order to comply with the "continuing practice" of expansion of the second prong. Rather, it appears that the court effectively penalized Brown for having made efforts in the 1970s to accommodate the growing interests and abilities of women in intercollegiate athletics. On its face and in practice, the program expansion benchmark seems to penalize institutions that added teams in the 1970s and 1980s, while rewarding institutions that failed to follow Title IX's mandate until recently.

The question this apparent inconsistency raises is, when can a college or university stop expanding its program? Surely institutions are not expected to expand opportunities forever. When is program expansion enough? The answer from the current case law now seems to be as follows: when the proportion of male and female athletes is substantially proportionate to the make-up of the undergraduate student body. If Brown officials had continued to add teams for women during the 1980s, they certainly would have been allowed to stop upon reaching a figure that closely resembled substantial proportionality. Therefore, it appears that the goal of the program-expansion component of compliance is substantial proportionality. Upon reaching statistical parity, a college or university could stop adding opportunities for the underrepresented gender. That is, not only is the proportionality test a safe harbor for universities, it is also the "finish line" for the program expansion component of compliance as well.

2. Full and Effective Accommodation of Interest and Ability

Moving to the third prong of the opportunity test, full and effective accommodation of interest and ability, it appears that the same reliance upon statistical parity exists. Suppose there is a university with an undergraduate student body which is 50% male and 50% female, and an athletic participation ratio of 65% male and 35% female. And at this fictitious institution, suppose that there are more women than men who are interested and capable of competing in varsity athletics. In order to move towards compliance with Title IX, does the school have to accommodate the interests of its women "fully," even if it means supporting an athletic department that is 60% female and 40% male? No, the university need only satisfy the interests of its female athletes to such an extent that female participation in athletics will be substantially proportionate to the number of women in the student body. As long as half of the athletic department is men and the other half women, the university is presumed to be effectively accommodating the interests and abilities of the underrepresented sex, regardless of the measured interest at the particular school, and the institution can find shelter under the "safe harbor" of the first benchmark. Here again we see that statistical parity is at the heart of the interests and abilities benchmark of compliance as well.

The First Circuit in *Cohen II* found that Brown was not satisfying the third prong of the equal opportunity test because the plaintiffs demonstrated that there was unmet interest and ability to compete at the varsity level among women's club teams. It maintained that Brown read the "full" out of the duty to accommodate "fully" and "effectively," and thus, the court rejected Brown's proposal that a university satisfactorily accommodates female athletes if it allocates athletic opportunities to the same proportion of interested and able women as it does to interested and able men, regardless of the number of non-participating women or the percentage of the student body that women comprise. However, what if

Brown were the fictitious university mentioned above? What if achieving statistical parity still did not achieve "full" accommodation? According to the aforementioned language of the First Circuit, "full" may be read out of "full and effective accommodation," as long as proportionality exists.

C. Relevance Of A Numerical Target

The foregoing analysis illustrates that, at the heart of each benchmark included in the Policy Interpretation, is the vague notion of substantial proportionality. This reliance on statistical parity effectively elevates the first benchmark to a higher significance than the second and third, and it undermines the argument that universities can travel any one of three distinct paths to compliance. Moreover, the proportional-to-enrollment test has emerged as the only possible means of Title IX compliance when a university is cutting back its sports offerings. By definition, a college or university cannot be demonstrating program expansion or accommodating interest and ability if it is cutting back. In a time when a majority of schools are faced with budget cutbacks and limited funding, the proportionality test appears to be the only means of compliance. What is more, if schools like the University of Illinois continue to cut men's sports in an effort to comply with the proportionality test of Title IX, women may be afforded opportunity based solely on their gender, but men will be denied opportunity for exactly the same reason.

Proportionality with student body enrollment is the functional equivalent of imposing employment quotas on employers based on aggregate population statistics—a principle the Supreme Court has expressly rejected. In *Richmond v. J.A. Croson Co.*,[218] the city of Richmond defended its 30% minority subcontracting requirement on the premise that this number was halfway between .067% (the percentage of city contracts awarded to African-Americans during the years 1978-83) and 50% (the percentage of African-American in the city of Richmond). The Court rejected this justification and demanded that numerical figures, in essence, quotas, must bear a statistical relationship to the pool of *qualified* minorities. Thus, in the Supreme Court's judgment, the 30% minority subcontracting requirement was tied to the African-American population of Richmond, and as such, rested on the unsupported and faulty assumption that minorities, in absence of discrimination, will choose a particular trade "in lockstep proportion to their representation in the local population."[220]

In Title IX and gender equity, the mandate of the first benchmark measuring equivalence of opportunity is based upon the same unrealistic and faulty assumption—that is, that in the absence of discriminatory policies women (or men) will choose to participate in intercollegiate athletics in proportion to their representation in the college or university. Although the gender balance in the undergraduate student population can be accurately measured, it is not necessarily the case that disproportionately lower involvement by women in athletics proves discrimination in a college or university's athletic departments. Because special qualifications are required to participate in intercollegiate athletics, comparison of the participation rates to the undergraduate enrollment, rather than to the pool of able and interested athletes, has little probative value. According to Walter B. Con-

---

218. 488 U.S. 469, 109 S. Ct. 706 (1989).
220. *Id.* at 471, 109 S. Ct. at 710 (citation omitted).

nolly, Jr., and Jeffery D. Adelman, the relevant population used in determining the pool of able and interested athletes should be high-school-aged athletes who are interested in participating in intercollegiate sports, because varsity teams recruit almost exclusively high school athletes and not students currently at the university (enrolled students are almost never recruited, and typically, if one of these students happens makes a varsity team, he or she does so as a "walk-on"). The enrollment population should only be relevant for club and intramural teams, *i.e.*, teams that do not recruit. Although it is nearly impossible to measure the number of high school athletes who are actually interested in playing in college, one can easily measure the aggregate number of female high school athletes. As will be discussed below, the percentage of high school female athletes is substantially proportionate to the percentage of intercollegiate female athletes. Consequently, maybe women's interests are accommodated fully and effectively even in the absence of statistical proportionality.

D. *The Proportionality Test Establishes A Quota*

The proportionality test relies upon the unsupported notion that the proportion of men and women interested in varsity athletic competition is equal to the proportion of men and women who have expressed an interest in earning a college degree by enrolling at an institution. And while this idea is alluring, it is *not* the mandate of Title IX—to eradicate discrimination in varsity athletics. Without having a basis from which to establish actual student interests and abilities, "the addition and subtraction of opportunities to achieve statistical parity is not only arbitrary, but is in itself discriminatory and contrary to the intent of Title IX."[226] Reducing scholarship opportunities for one gender in order to benefit members of the other gender contradicts how Title IX was supposed to operate: decisions should not be made "on the basis of sex" and that neither gender should be preferred over the other in order to remedy the effects of past discrimination.

Colleges and universities, hoping to achieve substantial proportionality, necessarily must create positions for women students, sometimes irrespective of their athletic interest or ability. Because this system requires that opportunities be granted based solely on one characteristic, gender, without regard for other qualifications, this system obviously creates a quota. An institution is left asking how many athletic opportunities it has for one gender, and whether it is enough to satisfy substantial proportionality. Adding varsity positions for women until the percentage of women varsity athletes equals the percentage of women students is a form of affirmative action that is strictly prohibited by the statute itself. Section 901(b) of the statute bemoans this result:

> [n]othing contained in subsection (a) of this section shall be interpreted to require any educational institution to grant preferential or disparate treatment to members of one sex on account of an imbalance which may exist with respect to the total number or percentage of persons of that sex participating in or receiving the benefits of any federally supported program or activity, in comparison with the total number or percentage of persons of that sex in any community, State, section or other area....[229]

---

226. *Id.* at 30.
229. 20 U.S.C. § 1681(b) (1994).

This plain language of the statute unmistakably dictates that Title IX is not an affirmative action statute and that it should not be used to create a quota system.

1. Proportionality Is Manifestly Contrary to the Statute

Although the legislative history is ambiguous as to whether Title IX was intended to be program-specific or was intended to apply to all programs of a school receiving federal financial assistance, the legislative history contains no such ambiguity on the issue of the use of quotas as a means of compliance. Senator Birch Bayh, (D. Ind.) the principal Senate sponsor, addressed the dangers of interpreting Title IX to require quotas....

....

What is more, the Court stated in *Cannon* that "the drafters of Title IX explicitly assumed that it would be interpreted and applied as Title VI [of the Civil Rights Act of 1964] had been...."[230] In Title VI litigation, the Court has rejected setasides and quotas without regard to ability or qualifications. In *Regents of the University of California v. Bakke*,[231] Justice Powell opined,

> [i]f petitioner's purpose is to assure within its student body some specified percentage of a particular group merely because of its race or ethnic origin, such a preferential purpose must be rejected not as insubstantial but as facially invalid. Preferring members of any one group for no other reason than race or ethnic origin is discrimination for its own sake.[232]

By applying this reasoning to the enforcement of Title IX, it is evident that the statistical parity mandated by the proportionality test is also "discrimination for its own sake."

Appellate courts have rejected the § 901 defense, asserting that the first benchmark is but one available means of compliance. However, accepting the assertion that the second and third prongs are based on substantial proportionality, then the § 901 defense appears to be a valid one.

2. Proportionality Equals Affirmative Action

An examination of the percentages of female participation in high school and college athletics demonstrates further how the enforcement of Title IX has been transformed into an affirmative action program. According to an ongoing project being conducted by Dr. Christine Grant at the University of Iowa, during the 1993-94 school year girls represented 37.8% of high school athletes, while women represented 35.7% of college athletes in the NCAA. According to these national statistics, it would appear that colleges and universities collectively are accommodating the interests of capable female athletes. Statistically speaking, if women constitute practically the same percentage of athletes in high school and college, it follows that substantial proportionality exists between the pool of interested and capable women and the pool of female collegiate athletes. While it may be that gender discrimination at the interscholastic level is the cause of lower participation rates for girls, to expect women to constitute nearly 50% of colle-

---

230. Cannon v. University of Chicago, 441 U.S. 677, 696, 99 S. Ct. 1946, 1956 (1979).
231. 438 U.S. 265, 98 S. Ct. 2733 (1978).
232. Davidson & Kerr, *supra* note 203, at 46-47 (quoting *Bakke*, 438 U.S. at 306, 98 S. Ct. at 2757).

giate athletes when they constitute less than 40% of high school athletes certainly would require a system of affirmative action. However, decisions like *Cohen* have forced this quota upon athletic departments across the country. This quota is based "upon the 'completely unrealistic' assumption" that women will choose to participate in athletics in "lockstep proportion to their representation" in the undergraduate population, despite their representation among secondary- school athletes.

E. Constitutionality of Title IX Enforcement

Although both the *Cohen* and *Kelley* courts rejected the notion that OCR's policy interpretation violated the Equal Protection Clause of the Constitution, a recent Supreme Court decision makes that argument worth reviewing. To defend the constitutionality of Title IX and its applicable regulations, the First and Seventh Circuits specifically relied on *Metro Broadcasting v. FCC*,[241] which stated that Congress has broad remedial powers under the Due Process Clause of the Fifth Amendment to remedy past discrimination. The Seventh Circuit, in *Kelley*, noted, "[w]hile the effect of Title IX and the relevant regulation and policy interpretation is that institutions will sometimes consider gender when decreasing their athletic offerings, this limited consideration does not violate the Constitution" because of the broad remedial powers enumerated in *Metro Broadcasting*.[243] However, subsequent to both decisions, *Metro Broadcasting* has been overruled by the Supreme Court in *Adarand*.[244] The Court ruled in *Adarand* that federal remedial affirmative action programs are held to the same standard of strict scrutiny—viz., strict scrutiny—as state programs have been held to since *Richmond v. J.A. Croson Co.* Thus, the Supreme Court's holding in *Adarand* significantly limited the remedial powers of Congress under the Fifth Amendment, the same powers that both the First and Seventh Circuits used to justify the gender considerations when decreasing male athletic opportunities. That is, it undermined both the *Cohen* and *Kelley* courts' understanding of the constitutionality of Title IX's applicable regulations.

Even absent a specific finding that discrimination has occurred, remedial measures based on gender are permissible to the extent that they serve important governmental objectives and are substantially related to the achievement of those ends. As for the important governmental objective, the Seventh Circuit, in *Kelley*, noted that Title IX prohibits educational institutions from discriminating on the basis of gender and does not ensure an increase in athletic participation by women. "There is no doubt but that removing the legacy of sexual discrimination...from our nation's educational institutions is an important governmental objective."[248] However, the relationship between this objective and the mandate of substantial proportionality between rates of athletic participation and undergraduate enrollment is dubious at best. Moreover, as has already been discussed, the denominator of undergraduate student enrollment, although easily calculated, is not substantially related to ensuring equal opportunity. In equal employment cases, the denominator is the qualified female labor force, rather than the popula-

---

241. 497 U.S. 547, 110 S. Ct. 2997 (1990).
243. Kelley v. Board of Trustees of the Univ. of Ill., 35 F.3d 265, 272 (7th Cir. 1994).
244. Adarand Constructors v. Pena, 515 U.S. 200, 115 S. Ct. 2097 (1995).
248. *Id.*

tion in general, because the latter group is not substantially related to providing equal opportunity for women. Therefore, although it is certain that Title IX's mandate that gender discrimination in education be eliminated is an important objective; the meaningfulness of its relationship to the current methods of regulation and enforcement is much less certain.

.... [Discussion of the propriety of judicial deference to OCR regulations is omitted—ed.].

CONCLUSION

The future of Title IX appears to be as ambiguous and divisive as its past. Since its enactment in 1972, uncertainty and debate have followed every move. Title IX, a direct attempt to protect the rights of women by eliminating sexual discrimination in the field of education, has become synonymous with mandating gender equity in athletics.

Analyzing the case law surrounding Title IX has demonstrated that regulation and enforcement of the statute have resulted in certain unintended consequences that have ignited an explosion of both political and social debate. Both the *Cohen* and *Kelley* decisions illustrate OCR's current enforcement policy and the courts' overwhelming reliance on the policy interpretation as the yardstick for measuring Title IX compliance. In the wake of these decisions, OCR's Title IX enforcement has led to gridlock and has caused rancorous political and social fallout. A critical analysis of OCR's regulation and enforcement of Title IX demonstrates the vulnerability of the current means of enforcement. Not only is the policy interpretation on shaky legal footing, but the three-prong test it outlines can be attacked successfully on constitutional grounds as well.

....

Considering the public controversy surrounding *Cohen v. Brown*..., the future of Title IX still appears hazy and uncertain. Predicting the outcome of future cases or the success of NCAA tactics is simply a guessing game. The answer to one question, however, could provide insight into what lies ahead for the issue of gender equity in athletics, that is: What is the purpose of intercollegiate athletics?

Two different models exist concerning the purpose of intercollegiate athletics. Under the prevailing amateur-education model, student-athletes participate in intercollegiate sports to to gain educational, physical, emotional and social benefits. Amateurism essentially means that a student-athlete receives nothing in pecuniary value for participating in college sports. Since, however, student-athletes receive financial assistance and other tangible benefits, college athletics has created, according to Professor Sharon Rush, a different form of amateurism: "scholarship amateurism."[287] The educational component of amateurism is that participating in intercollegiate athletics can be educational.

There is one major flaw associated with the amateur-education model of intercollegiate athletics—its underlying reliance on values, particularly amateurism, which are anachronistic. The principle of amateurism has long since been undermined by sneaker contracts and television....

....

---

287. *Id.* at 275(citing Sharon E. Rush, *Touchdowns, Toddlers, and Taboos: On Paying College Athletes and Surrogate Contract Mothers*, 31 ARIZ. L. REV. 549, 581 (1989).

Because many agree that the principle of amateurism has vanished in intercollegiate athletics, a new model has emerged. Under the commercial-education model of intercollegiate athletics, "college sports are a commercial enterprise subject to the same economic considerations as any other industry."[288] The economics of intercollegiate sports replaces the principle of amateurism as the "controlling force in college sports."[289] The education model continues to embody the notion that college athletics is an integral part of the educational process.

The future of Title IX depends largely upon which model of intercollegiate sports the athletic infrastructure—from the NCAA down to individual institutions—endorses. Reconciling the tenets of Title IX with those of the amateur-education model seems possible. Equality and fairness seem to be interwoven with the principle of amateurism. Mandating gender equity in a commercial enterprise, however, represents a much more difficult task.

If the commercial model is realized, then sports like football and men's basketball will continue to occupy the intercollegiate athletics spotlight. Sneaker contracts, commercial endorsements, and television coverage will supersede any notion of gender equity or fairness. In fact, men's minor sports will lose out just as much as women's teams. Just as Title IX has had a diminishing effect on sports like wrestling, men's swimming and men's gymnastics, the realization of the economic model will generate the same results. Because television and commercial endorsements display little demand for women's sports and men's minor sports, and because the economic model relies on the theory of supply and demand, opportunities will continue to diminish for female athletes and participants in men's minor sports. Only those sports that are in high demand by external, commercial factors will survive. Football and men's basketball, along with an occasional soccer and baseball team, will swallow up all of their counterparts. Gender equity will be pushed aside because money will occupy the bottom line.

On the other hand, if the amateur model prevails, Title IX's future seems much brighter. Women's sports and men's minor sports will have a fighting chance at surviving in an environment that is not completely controlled by commercialism. Governing bodies will have the autonomy needed to level the playing field. While economics and the theory of supply and demand will never be totally displaced in college athletics, if the amateur model survives, the general benefits of athletic participation, including the lessons associated with hard work, commitment, and teamwork could potentially outweigh the tenets of commercialism.

. . . .

---

288. Davis, *supra* note 286, at 279.
289. *Id.*

Deborah Brake & Elizabeth Catlin, The Path of Most Resistance: The Long Road Toward Gender Equity in Intercollegiate Athletics
3 Duke Journal of Gender Law & Policy 51 (1996)*

....

II. THE BACKLASH AGAINST TITLE IX

....

B. Myth Meets Backlash: Quotas, Reverse Discrimination and Special Treatment for Football

....

1. *The "Quota" Argument and the Myth of Reverse Discrimination.* In a cynical effort to benefit from the affirmative action debate in Congress and across the country, the leaders of the backlash against gender equity in sports are arguing that Title IX, as it has been applied by the courts and DOE's OCR, mandates reverse discrimination against men because the three-part test does not take into account men's relatively greater interest in sports than women's. The primary strategy of the Title IX opponents has been to emphasize proportionality as the single or the most important test applied by the courts and DOE's OCR, and then equate "substantially proportionate" with "quotas".

a. *The Misplaced Focus on Substantial Proportionality.* The emphasis on the substantial proportionality test is not borne out by the facts. In actuality, all three parts of the test count equally both in the courts and in DOE's OCR enforcement actions. Every single court decision to address the equal accommodation of athletic interest and ability has equally applied all three parts of the Policy Interpretation's three-part test. Universities have lost these cases not because the courts have only looked at proportionality, but because they have failed to prevail on any one of the three parts of the test. DOE's OCR also looks at all three parts of the test, as is demonstrated by the fact that some universities have been found in compliance under prongs two and three even when they do not meet proportionality.

A variation on the Title IX opponents' emphasis on proportionality as the primary measure of compliance is the assertion that, regardless of whether DOE's OCR and the courts currently apply all three prongs of the test, institutions which choose to comply with prongs two or three will eventually be forced to reach proportionality. This would occur, the argument continues, because prongs two and three require an institution to continually add programs to keep pace with women's athletic interest. Only when a school reaches proportionality will it be free from its obligation to add new women's opportunities. However, if the underlying assumption of this argument is true—that women's interest will continue to outpace existing opportunities—it is difficult to see how the three-part test works an injustice because the very intent of Title IX was to open up opportunities for women as their interest increased.

At the heart of this argument is the belief that once a university has complied with prong two or three of the test, it should not have to make any additional changes in its athletic offerings to ensure that it stays in compliance. Such a result is neither possible nor desirable. A static test for compliance would fail to capture the core of Title IX—that men and women deserve equal athletic opportunity. The meaning of equal athletic opportunity for any given institution depends on the changing circumstances at that institution. It would hardly be equitable if a school were allowed to maintain compliance with Title IX simply because it had complied with prong two earlier by adding women's teams, but then subsequently halted expansion of women's opportunities despite growing interest among women to play sports. Indeed, the prong two standard, which permits an institution to come into compliance merely by making progress toward equalization of women's opportunities, is unusually lenient among civil rights laws. Similarly, if an institution fully accommodated women's athletic interest ten years ago under prong three, this fact alone should not render an institution in compliance if women currently have unmet athletic interests and receive disproportionately fewer athletic opportunities. Even compliance with prong one is not static, as enrollment may fluctuate or athletic offerings may change, requiring institutions who choose to comply under prong one to accommodate those changes in order to stay in compliance.

Rather than providing any valid reasons for altering the three-part test, the argument that prongs two and three ultimately will require proportionality is simply another effort to make proportionality, and by extension quotas, the focus of the debate.

b. *The Misuse of the "Quota" Label.* Even if substantially proportionate participation rates were the single or primary measure of compliance, the quota label would still be inappropriate. The argument that requiring substantially proportionate participation rates establishes a quota system which grants preferential treatment to women has been heavily relied upon by Title IX opponents without regard to its inapplicability to intercollegiate athletics. Advocates of this position have relied on analogies to other educational benefits to attack the use of proportionality in athletics. They argue that the use of proportionality as a measure of equity in intercollegiate athletics is tantamount to invoking quotas requiring a particular racial or gender balance in academic departments, band, or other academic or extracurricular activities. This argument obscures the fundamental reality that competitive athletics stands alone as virtually the only educational program or activity covered by Title IX which offers separate opportunities on the basis of sex.

Virtually all intercollegiate athletic programs sponsor sex-segregated teams. Unlike in employment, where men and women compete against one another for the same jobs, male and female college athletes compete separately for slots on male and female teams. While there are no inherent limits on the percentage of women or men who may fill the jobs available in a particular workplace, the nature of intercollegiate athletics itself sets gender-based limits on the percentage of men and the percentage of women who may participate in the program. Because intercollegiate athletic programs offer sex-separate teams, the selection of teams, hiring of coaches, budgeting, and recruiting together set a quota by determining the percentage of male and female athletes who will be allowed to participate in the program. Consequently, while the use of the word quota to describe the substantially proportionate participation rate measure in intercollegiate athletics makes for provocative rhetoric, it is not accurate because the university itself sets a quota for the percent-age of males and females who may participate in intercollegiate athletics. The rele-vant question is not whether there should be a gender-based quota in intercollegiate athletics, but whether universities should continue to reserve 67% of their varsity athletic slots for men and only 33% for women, or whether it should more closely parallel the percentages of men and women attending the university.

c. *The Relative Interest Argument.* The implicit assumption underlying the quota or reverse discrimination argument is that the three-part test is unfair to men because it assumes that men and women are equally interested in sports. If it can be shown that men are more interested in playing sports than women, the ar-gument continues, then the three-part test actually discriminates against men. This argument has repeatedly surfaced in the *Cohen* litigation, where Brown has attempted to use surveys to show that its provision of fewer athletic opportunities for women reflects women's lesser interest in sports, so that increasing women's share of opportunities would discriminate against men. In the argument advanced by Brown, if 500 men and 250 women are interested and able to play sports, the university should only have to accommodate both genders in proportion to their respective interest. Under this scenario, offering 100 slots for men to play sports and 50 to women would comply with Title IX.

The rejection of this argument by the courts in *Cohen*, both by the First Circuit during the preliminary injunction stage of the litigation and by the district court during the trial on the merits, demonstrates a number of its failings. First, and most significantly, there is no conceivable measure of interest that fully accounts for the fact that women have had, and continue to have, significantly fewer oppor-tunities to participate in interscholastic and intercollegiate sports in this country....

....

Any measure that purports to compare the interest of women and men in par-ticipating in sports will be affected by the present mix of opportunities for men and women. For example, the answers given by high school students to questions about what college sports they want to participate in will inevitably be affected by what sports they have had a chance to play in high school. These answers, in turn, will have been influenced by their opportunities for college athletic scholarships and the mix of sports offered at the college level.

No survey population avoids this problem. For example, as the district court rec-ognized in *Cohen*, any survey of the student body will be driven by the university's athletic offerings, recruiting practices, admissions preferences, and athletic scholar-ships, if available. Particularly at Division I schools that rely on recruiting to select their intercollegiate athletes, the results of a survey of athletic interest in the student body is predetermined by the university's selection of sports and recruiting prac-tices. For example, if a university recruits twice as many men as women for its in-tercollegiate athletic offerings, a survey which finds more men than women who claim to be interested in participating in intercollegiate athletes is not a true mea-sure of relative interest. Similarly, a survey of student applicants to a university will be skewed by that university's existing opportunities. Students who want to partici-pate in a sport not offered at a particular university may not apply there.

The largest potential survey pool, all high school graduates qualified for admis-sion to a university, is also inadequate as a survey population. In addition to the difficulties involved in identifying and surveying such a potentially large popula-tion, this grouping does not escape problems inherent in the use of such surveys as an objective measure of interest. Because opportunities for girls in interscholastic athletics continue to be limited at the high school level, a comparative survey of the relative athletic interest in this pool by gender will reflect the disparity in opportunities provided at both the high school and college level. In a world where men receive nearly twice as many college athletic scholarships as women, the incentive for sports participation at the high school and college levels cannot be considered equal. Adopting a relative interest standard, which cannot take into account the discriminatory differences in athletic opportunities provided to men and women, will only solidify existing inequities in opportunity.

In addition to the insurmountable problems of identifying an appropriate survey population, no objective and reliable measure of interest exists to quantify an individual's actual interest in participating in intercollegiate athletics. Survey questions cannot accurately determine whether a person who reports to have interest in a particular sport would actually participate in intercollegiate athletics if given the opportunity, nor can surveys differentiate between interest in participating in intramural, club, or intercollegiate athletic programs....

As a practical matter, requiring student-plaintiffs to first assess relative athletic interest among men and women in some survey population before bringing a Title IX claim would create an unworkable standard. Applying this requirement, student-plaintiffs would have to first assess the relative interest between men and women on their campus before filing a Title IX complaint. The existing three-part test, on the other hand, enables student-plaintiffs to rely on outwardly visible indicia of unmet interest, such as a successful women's club program, to demonstrate unmet interest under the third prong without conducting a campus-wide relative interest survey. Students will typically be unable to afford the cost of such surveys and analysis, and may have difficulty finding legal representation that will pay the costs of expert witnesses required to assess relative interest.

The argument that relative interests of men and women in sports can be accurately measured independent of disparities in existing opportunities is also contrary to the intent and purposes underlying Title IX, as well as past experience. Congress enacted Title IX against a backdrop of overwhelming evidence of sex discrimination in education. Shortly after Title IX was enacted, intercollegiate athletics became a focal point in congressional debates over Title IX. Congressional debates on the Title IX regulations in 1975 focused on the athletics regulations and recognized persistent and widespread discrimination against women in intercollegiate athletics. In documenting this discrimination, Congress recognized that women's athletic interest and ability had been, and was being, suppressed by their limited opportunities.

Similarly, the Policy Interpretation, which was the product of an extensive notice and comment period during which the agency received over 10,000 comments, also recognizes the link between interest and opportunity, stating that "(p)articipation in intercollegiate sports has historically been emphasized for men but not women. Partially as a consequence of this, participation rates of women are far below those of men."[175] Limiting women's athletic opportunities to their present levels based on some measure of the current relative interest between men and women, where women's interest continues to be suppressed by limited opportunities, would contravene this recognition.

---

175. 44 Fed. Reg. 71,413, 71,419 (1979).

Women have experienced and continue to experience discrimination in all of the elements of intercollegiate athletic programs that develop interest and ability — recruitment among high school athletes, scholarships, prestige, operational support, publicity, and the opportunity to participate in a competitive program. Consequently, without a level playing field, any measure purporting to compare men's and women's interest in intercollegiate athletics will simply reinforce the existing disparity in opportunities.

History has proven that athletic interest and ability expand as new opportunities are created. The refrain from the movie Field of Dreams could well describe the history of women's athletics in this country—if you build it, they will come. As schools began to create women's athletic programs in response to Title IX, participation by female students in organized sports soared, increasing by 600% at the high school level between 1971 and 1978. Women's athletic participation at the college level also sustained huge increases as Title IX created new athletic opportunities for women. In 1971, prior to the enactment of Title IX, less than 32,000 women played varsity sports at the college level. In 1993-94, over 105,000 college women competed in NCAA sports. Women's interest in participating in sports has always kept pace with expansions in women's athletic opportunities.

d. *Reverse Discrimination Claims in the Courts....*

i. *Reverse discrimination claims under Title IX.* Claims by male athletes challenging the elimination of a men's sport under Title IX are subject to the same three-part test that courts have applied to Title IX claims by female athletes. However, because the three-part test focuses on the opportunities provided to the underrepresented sex, at most institutions discrimination claims brought by male athletes will not succeed under Title IX. For example, male athletes who sue their university for dropping a men's sport will not be able to carry their burden of proof on the first prong if the athletic opportunities allocated to men overall are not substantially fewer than men's share of enrollment. Because a school need only comply with one of three parts of the test to comply with Title IX, reverse discrimination claims will fail under prong one of the test where men are not the underrepresented sex, without regard to prongs two or three.

Court decisions have applied this analysis in rejecting Title IX challenges brought by male athletes to university decisions eliminating men's teams. For example, in *Kelley v. University of Illinois*,[184] male swimmers challenged the University's decision to eliminate varsity men's swimming, while retaining the varsity women's swimming program, under both Title IX and the Equal Protection Clause of the Fourteenth Amendment....In applying the three-part test to the plaintiffs' Title IX claim, the Seventh Circuit ruled that the male swimmer's rights were not violated because men were not the underrepresented sex, and therefore could not succeed on prong one of the test.

Similar reasoning was applied to reject a Title IX claim by male athletes in *Gonyo v. Drake University*.[186] In *Gonyo*, male wrestlers challenged their University's decision to discontinue its men's varsity wrestling team on both Title IX and equal protection grounds....

184. 35 F.3d 265 (7th Cir. 1994).
186. 879 F. Supp. 1000 (S.D. Iowa 1995).

The courts' rejection of Title IX claims by male athletes challenging the elimination of a particular men's sport where men remain overrepresented in the overall athletics program properly reflects Title IX's focus on the rights of men and women as athletes, rather than as members of particular teams. This balance reflects the policy determination that an overall program comparison is a superior and more flexible test than requiring team-by-team equivalence — a standard which would require the men's and women's athletic programs to mirror one another. A team-by-team approach would frequently disadvantage women because the greater opportunities and benefits provided to men who play football would have no counterpart in the women's athletics. Moreover, men and women may have differing levels of interest in particular sports, and a team-by-team comparison may not properly reflect those different interests. For example, at a particular institution, women may have more interest in playing volleyball than soccer, while men may prefer soccer to volleyball. Rather than requiring that institution to offer the same sport to both groups, the current standard permits the school to offer volleyball to women and soccer to men, while treating both sets of athletes comparably. Consequently, male athletes challenging their university's decision to drop their sport under Title IX will not succeed where the opportunities provided to male athletes overall are underrepresentative.

Courts have also rejected reverse discrimination arguments by universities challenging the three-part test itself as a violation of Title IX in defending against Title IX suits by female athletes. In defending such cases, universities have argued that courts should reject the DOE's three-part test as a valid interpretation of Title IX because it violates § 1681(b) of the Act. Section 1681(b) provides that:

> Nothing contained in subsection (a) of this section shall be interpreted to require any education institution to grant preferential or disparate treatment to the members of one sex on account of an imbalance which may exist with respect to the total number or percentage of persons of that sex participating in or receiving the benefits of any federally supported program or activity, in comparison with the total number or percentage of persons of that sex in any community, State, section, or other area. Provided, that this subsection shall not be construed to prevent the consideration in any hearing or proceeding under this chapter of statistical evidence tending to show that such an imbalance exists with respect to the participation in, or receipt of the benefits of, any such program or activity by the members of one sex.[192]

Both Brown University and Colorado State University argued that the three-part test mandates statistical balancing in violation of this provision. But both the First and Tenth Circuits rejected this argument on the ground that the three-part test provides three independent avenues for Title IX compliance and does not mandate proportionality.

In addition to the reasoning of the First and Tenth Circuits, the argument that the three-part test constitutes preferential treatment in violation of § 1681(b) should be rejected for another reason. This section was designed to prohibit quotas in university admissions and hiring, and does not apply to the use of substantial proportionality as a measure of equity in the context of intercollegiate athletics, which by virtue of offering sex-separate teams itself requires a particular

---

192. 20 U.S.C. § 1681(b) (1994).

gender ratio of participants. An institution which provides intercollegiate athletic opportunities for each gender in numbers substantially proportionate to enrollment is not granting preferential or disparate treatment to the members of either sex, as prohibited under § 1681(b). Because intercollegiate athletics is a sex- segregated activity, gender is already a requirement for participation on an athletic team. Rather than requiring preferential or disparate treatment based on gender, requiring the offering of substantially proportionate opportunities in this context is a measure of equal treatment and nondiscrimination.

ii. *Reverse discrimination claims under the Equal Protection Clause....*

In equal protection challenges by male athletes whose teams have been eliminated, courts have ruled that the application of Title IX to a university program which results in the elimination of a men's team, with no corresponding elimination of a women's team, does not violate equal protection. For example, in *Kelley*, the Court of Appeals for the Seventh Circuit upheld the three-part test as applied to the University based on Congress' broad powers to remedy past discrimination. The court concluded that, to the extent that the three-part test requires a school to consider gender in reducing its athletic offerings, such consideration of gender is substantially related to the important government interest of remedying sex discrimination in intercollegiate athletics and therefore complies with equal protection. Similarly, the court in *Gonyo* rejected the equal protection claim of the male wrestlers, holding that the consideration of gender in decreasing athletic programs complies with equal protection because it properly assists members of the underrepresented sex, as is permissible under the Supreme Court's decision in Mississippi University for *Women v. Hogan.*[201]

Institutions defending Title IX claims have also failed to establish that the three-part test violates equal protection. In *Cohen*, Brown argued that by requiring the full and effective accommodation of the athletic interests of the underrepresented sex, without regard to whether the institution is fully accommodating the interests of overrepresented sex, the three-part test accords preferential treatment to women in violation of equal protection. The Court of Appeals for the First Circuit rejected this argument for two reasons. First, the court rejected Brown's view of the three- part test as conferring preferential treatment. The court observed that Brown's characterization of the test as preferential treatment assumes that, given equal opportunity, women are less interested in participating in varsity sports than men. The court explicitly rejected this assumption. Second, the court held that even if the test did constitute a gender preference, it would still pass constitutional muster because it fits within Congress' design to remedy extensive discrimination against women in intercollegiate sports. Like the courts in *Kelley* and *Gonyo*, the First Circuit relied on *Metro Broadcasting v. FCC*[206] in support of its deference to Congress' broad powers to remedy past discrimination.

Both rationales relied on by courts in rejecting reverse discrimination challenges to the propriety of the elimination of men's teams and to the three-part test are justified under equal protection principles. First, neither the three-part test nor its application to a university's decision to reduce its athletic offerings constitutes a gen-

---

201. 458 U.S. 718 91982); *see also Gonyo*, 879 F. Supp. at 1006.
206. 497 U.S. 547 (1990).

der-based classification which disadvantages men as a group under the Equal Protection Clause. In the world of intercollegiate athletics, a decision to drop a team will always have a gender-based component because of the existence of sex- separate teams. Because reverse discrimination claimants do not challenge the sex-based classification of separate men's and women's athletic teams, their challenge rests on the characterization of a decision to drop a men's team as a gender-based classification that disadvantages men. However, dropping a men's athletic team is not a gender-based classification that disadvantages men when men continue to retain the lion's share of athletic opportunities. Rather, such a decision is a gender-based classification that lessens the existing gender-based preference in favor of men, and therefore does not discriminate against men under the Equal Protection Clause.

Second, even if the three-part test or its application to athletic cutbacks was viewed as a gender-based classification that disadvantages men for equal protection purposes, it would still be constitutionally permissible because it is designed to remedy past discrimination against women in intercollegiate sports. Courts rejecting reverse discrimination claims on this ground have relied in part on Congress' broad powers to remedy discrimination upheld under *Metro Broadcasting*. This past term, in *Adarand Constructors, Inc. v. Pena*,[212] the Supreme Court overruled its holding in *Metro Broadcasting* that Congress is entitled to greater deference than state and local governments in enacting race-based affirmative remedial measures. However, the Court's recent decision in *Adarand* should not change the result in reverse discrimination challenges to the three-part test or its applications.

As an initial matter, *Adarand* should have no effect on the analysis of gender-based classifications designed to remedy discrimination against women. In *Adarand*, the Court applied strict scrutiny to race-based affirmative remedial measures enacted by Congress, which is the standard used by courts to evaluate racial discrimination. As long as gender-based classifications which discriminate against women are subjected to a lesser standard of intermediate scrutiny, it would defy common sense to apply strict scrutiny to gender-based classifications designed to remedy discrimination against women.

Moreover, even if strict scrutiny were extended to gender-based discrimination against women, the use of gender as a factor in determining how to decrease athletic offerings in an athletics program that provides more offerings to men should easily survive even strict scrutiny. Analyzed under strict scrutiny, a gender-based classification would be permissible if it was narrowly tailored to serve a compelling government interest. Remedying ongoing discrimination against women in an athletics program is undoubtedly a compelling state interest. Unlike the race-based affirmative action plan in *Croson*, which did not survive strict scrutiny because it was premised on correcting general societal discrimination rather than discrimination in the affected industry, the use of gender in this context directly addresses the discrimination by the affected institution itself.

The use of gender in cutting athletic offerings which are already slanted toward men is also narrowly tailored toward furthering the compelling state interest in remedying the school's discrimination against women athletes. Because intercollegiate athletics, unlike the construction industry involved in *Croson*, provide sex-segregated opportunities, gender is a necessary component of any plan to redress

---

212. 115 S. Ct. 2097 (1995).

discrimination in the allocation of athletic opportunities between men and women. Indeed, where an institution has decided to reduce athletic offerings in a program that provides more opportunities to men, the fit between the use of a gender-based classification to reduce men's rather than women's opportunities, and the goal of remedying ongoing institutional discrimination against women, could not be closer.

2. *Football is Unique: The Third Sex Rationale.* Another argument advanced by Title IX opponents to weaken the standards that have been applied by the DOE and the courts is that the three-part test does not take into account the unique particularities of the sport of football. Because the average football squad has between 85 and 100 players, football's large numbers are blamed for the failure of many schools to satisfy the substantial proportionality prong of Title IX compliance. In addition, football proponents claim that football's ability to generate revenue, coupled with the size of the squads and the fact that it is a sport played only by men, justifies taking football out of the mix in calculating whether substantially proportionate opportunities are available to women.

Neither the large size of football teams nor the fact that the sport is played primarily by men justifies treating it differently than any other sport. The large size of a football squad does not make football players a third sex. Institutions can offer an equivalent number of opportunities for women to participate in athletics by offering several women's teams. Precisely because football provides so many opportunities for men to play sports, many institutions will have to offer more sports for women than men to provide an equal opportunity for men and women to participate in athletics. Moreover, while football is played primarily by men, there are a number of sports now played primarily by women in this country, including volleyball, field hockey, and synchronized swimming with which to counter such imbalance. There is no shortage of sports for women to play to balance out the opportunities provided to male athletes by football. Indeed, the three-part test is sufficiently flexible to take into account the different sizes of sports and different sports interests of men and women by evaluating equal opportunity on a program-wide basis, rather than on the basis of a team-by-team comparison.

Finally, the argument that football's revenue-producing capabilities justify an exemption from Title IX is also unpersuasive. In fact, the vast majority of NCAA football programs lose more money than they bring in. Over 80% of football programs run a net deficit. Even in Division I-A and I-AA, the most competitive divisions which are beneficiaries of lucrative television contracts, 62% of football programs on average have annual deficits of $1 million in Division I-A and $664,000 in Division I-AA. Moreover, it is unclear why the capacity of an educational program to earn a profit should entitle it to special treatment under Title IX. Congress rejected precisely such a rationale in 1975 in defeating the Javits Amendment.

. . . .

III. CONCLUSION

In the past few years, women have made significant and long-awaited progress in achieving an equal opportunity to participate in intercollegiate athletics. Courts have unanimously adopted the DOE's three-part test for compliance with Title IX. As a result, women have succeeded in obtaining court orders requiring their schools to add additional women's teams and preventing their schools from cutting teams. But because of these successes, and a more conservative political environment in Congress, Title IX has come under attack by proponents of college football and other men's sports claiming that, as interpreted by the DOE and the courts, the law discriminates against men. Their argument is premised on the assertion that men are more interested in sports than women, and therefore deserve disproportionately more athletic opportunities. This assertion is unsupported by the evidence and has been soundly rejected in the courts.

---

3. Violence in Intercollegiate Athletics

Timothy Davis & Tonya Parker, Student-Athlete Sexual Violence Against Women: Defining the Limits of Institutional Responsibility
55 Washington & Lee Law Review 55 (1998)*

. . . .

II. A Propensity for Sexual Aggression?

A. *Empirical Research*

Prior to 1990, researchers devoted little attention to assessing whether there is a positive connection between participation in college athletics and sexual assault. The growing, yet still limited, body of research conducted since then has not reached incontrovertible conclusions regarding such an association. The recent undertakings, however, have contributed to the development of what appears to be two principal schools of thought. While deploring acts of sexual aggression, some authorities argue that college athletes are no more prone to commit violent acts against women than other males in American society. According to this view, the notoriety athletes receive in the popular press creates the misleading impression that athletes have a greater propensity to commit violent acts against women. Adherents to this view also argue that the empirical data has failed sufficiently to support assumptions that the violent overtones of football, hockey, and other sports are integral to the other parts of athletes' lives.

Other authorities adopt the contrary position that "athletes appear to be disproportionately involved in incidents of sexual assault on college campuses."[37] Two factors appear particularly important to the authorities holding this contrary position. First, although adherents to this view recognize that sexual violence is the product of multiple variables, they identify the subculture of which athletes are a part as a significant contributor to an athlete's slightly greater propensity to engage in sexual violence. "[A]ggression on the playing field, sexist language and attitudes in the locker room, and an inordinate need to prove one's maleness can

---

    37. Crossett et al., *supra* note 32, at 135.

combine in complex ways to predispose some male athletes towards off-the-field hostility."[39] Second, researchers argue that the existing research establishes that athletes may be slightly more prone to violence.

Even those who ascribe to the view that athletes are disproportionately involved in sexual assaults, however, warn against extracting concrete conclusions and overly broad generalizations from existing research. Both the limited body of research and the scientific methodology utilized therein underlies their call for caution. For instance, a 1995 study reported that "athletes appear to be disproportionately involved in incidents of sexual assault on college campuses."[42] In reaching this conclusion, however, the study's authors emphasized its limitations. Most notably, the finding was based on a limited survey, and the disproportionate number is not overwhelming. They also noted a desire to avoid overstating the problem as many commentators in the popular press have done. In this regard they dispelled the notion that the disproportion reaches the high levels (thirty-three percent) reported by many scholars and journalists.

In sum, the empirical research has failed to provide unchallenged evidence of an athlete's propensity for sexual aggression against women. The data has established the need for a comprehensive inquiry into the relationship between participation in athletics and sexual violence.

B. *Sport's Influence in Shaping Cultural Values*

The inconclusiveness of research attempting to establish a relationship between athletic participation and sexual violence underscores the need to exercise restraint to avoid unfairly labeling and stereotyping athletes. It is equally important, however, not to marginalize the problem of male athlete sexual violence against women. Indeed, overemphasis on the question of the propensity of athletes, in comparison to non-athletes, to engage in acts of sexual aggression risks obscuring an important reality: the impact of athlete violence against women may exceed its actual quantifiable prevalence. As the following discussion demonstrates, the potentially disproportionate influence of acts of sexual aggression by athletes against women is intimately tied to the role afforded sport and its participants in American society.

1. *Sport's Reinforcement of Cultural Themes*

Like other institutions, sport reflects and reinforces cultural themes, both empowering and harmful, that pervade our society. For instance, values generally considered positive and empowering, such as those associated with hard work and success, are disseminated through sport. Commenting on why sports-related opportunities must be expanded for women, Norma Cantu, Assistant Secretary for Civil Rights in the Justice Department, asserts that the "values we learn from participation in sports [include] teamwork, standards, leadership, discipline, work ethics, self- sacrifice, pride in accomplishment, [and] strength of character."[50]

On the other hand, sport as a microcosm of society also possesses and thereby reinforces the negative qualities of the society that it reflects. In this regard, participation in sport is one of multiple social mechanisms that introduces boys to con-

---

39. Melnick, *supra* note 35, at 33.

42. Crossett et al., *supra* note 32, at 135.

50. *See* Rodney K. Smith, *When Ignorance is Not Bliss: In Search of Racial and Gender Equity in Intercollegiate Athletics*, 61 Mo. L. Rev. 329, 340 (1996) (quoting Norma Cantu).

ceptualizations of maleness. In this sense, involvement in sport constitutes a "gendering process" inasmuch as the values and ideology that reside in sport are not gender neutral. "Through sports, boys are trained to be men, to reflect all the societal expectations and attitudes surrounding such a rigid role definition."[56] Thus, as a social institution, sport represents an external dynamic that socializes boys and helps to sculpt their developing gender identities.

Commenting on the influence of sport in shaping gender identity, some feminist scholars argue that the values residing within sport contribute to the construction of male identity in ways that are harmful to women. This perspective is captured in the following comment:

> [S]port is an institution that creates and reproduces male power and domination in this culture.... [S]port serves as a central site for the production of male supremacy and hypermasculinity, not only in sport, but in the larger social order. Perhaps most important is the direct connection between sport as a cult of masculinity and gender relationship built on power, domination, and control.... [A] central element of the sport experience for men is equating manhood and masculinity with attitudes and behaviors that demean and devalue women.[59]

....

Despite sport's significance, it is inappropriate to cast sport as the primary influence with respect to the production and reproduction of masculine identity. Indeed, sport is merely one of the features of the "wider social structure that affect the relative power chances of the sexes."[62] Yet, it is generally believed that "assaultive behavior is learned behavior[ ] and that abuse against women builds on traditional assumptions about gender roles."[63] Therefore, to the extent that sport perpetuates such patterns of behavior through the reinforcement of traditional gender roles, it represents one of the strands that nurture the attitudes and beliefs that produce sexual violence by athletes.

2. *The Impact of Athletes' Behavior—Real or Imagined*

The status afforded athletes in American society may exacerbate the potentially harmful influence of sport in shaping cultural attitudes that contribute to athlete violence against women. "Because star athletes are held in such high esteem, they frequently find themselves worshiped by their adoring publics."[64] A consequence of this adoration is that athletes are afforded a place in society which, at least historically, has given them and the public the perception that they are impervious to the standards that dictate the behavior of others. Privileged status, when combined with other factors, produces a distorted or unrealistic view of interpersonal relationships.

This privileged status may be more pernicious than merely contributing to shaping the multiple aspects, including social relationships, of the lives of individ-

---

56. *See id.* at 20 (footnote omitted) (quoting sociologists Donald Sabo and Ross Run-Fola).

59. Mary Jo Kane & Lisa J. Disch, *Sexual Violence and the Reproduction of Male Power in the Locker Room: The "Lisa Olson Incident,"* Soc. Sport J., Dec. 1993, at 331, 334 (citations omitted).

62. *Id.*

63. Rhode, *supra* note 22, at 244.

64. Melnick, *supra* note 35, at 33.

ual athletes. Sociologists argue that the conduct of athletes extends beyond their peers to influence the behavior and attitudes of men, particularly the young, in the general population. On one hand, this influence could be expected given the enormous efforts devoted to packaging, exposing, and promoting athletes for commercial purposes. Mass media produce images that heighten the visibility of athletes and increase the likelihood that their conduct will have a disproportionate impact on shaping cultural values.

On the other hand, undue emphasis on athletes as a primary source of demeaning sexual attitudes toward women can inappropriately shift focus from institutional and structural contributors to such attitudes. As explained below, using the label role model may inadequately describe the impact of athletes in shaping cultural attitudes because to do so may not only be theoretically unsound, but may risk diverting attention from addressing structural factors that result in athlete violence against women.

The role model concept has been invoked in discourse regarding the influence of athletes in matters ranging from drugs to violence against women. In the latter context, one commentator observed:

> [I]t doesn't really matter whether athletes commit violence against women at a rate greater than the general population.... What I am concerned about is the enormous effect athletes have as role models on some men. When we see stories on a consistent basis, as we have, that prominent athletes have done terrible things and sometimes it gets papered over, that sends a message to some men that maybe it's really kind of OK—and really it might be kind of cool. That's the message we have to turn around.[74]

Professor Adeno Addis explores the genealogy of the role model concept and the circumstances giving rise to its emergence as a term increasingly invoked in social and legal contexts. According to Addis, the term role model is invoked with increasing frequency without solid empirical footing. He argues the role model concept is inappropriately used — particularly in the case of athletes and entertainers — to describe individuals who fall outside of the legitimate conceptualizations of "role model."

Addis identifies two traditional circumstances — the "role imitation" view and "comprehensive" view — where invocation of the role model concept is "empirically informed, logically sound, or normatively defensible."[79] Under the role imitation conceptualization, a role model provides an example in a specific field, such as a lawyer serving as a role model for law students. In contrast, the comprehensive conceptualization refers to "an individual who provides a comprehensive example in relation to 'a wider array of behaviors and values.'"[81] Thus, a comprehensive role model includes individuals who may influence certain people through aspects of their lives that "transcend a particular (professional) role."[82] Addis adds that two limitations set the boundaries under which it is appropriate to invoke role model in the comprehensive context: the role model and follower must

---

74. Eric Brady, *Study Searches for Tie Between Sport, Violence*, USA TODAY, Oct. 4, 1995, at 1 (quoting then ABA President Roberta Cooper Ramo).
79. *Id.* at 1459.
81. *Id.* at 1393 (quoting MERTON, *supra* note 75, at 356-58).
82. Addis, *supra* note 72, at 1393.

be "tied by physical proximity and by an authority-vulnerability social nexus."[83] He adds that "[i]n the absence of physical presence and the authority-vulnerability nexus, the role model follower only emulates the role model in relation to the specific role for which he or she is known."[84]

....

Having defined the circumstances under which it is proper to invoke the role model concept, Addis explains the basis for his objection to the too frequent invocation of the comprehensiveness conceptualization of role model to describe the perceived influence of groups of persons including athletes. He observes that

> focusing on the behaviors and actions of certain individuals and groups to explain social decay may allow those in positions of power to avoid dealing with the institutional and structural conditions that led to social decline.... It is easier for those in power to blame black athletes or a televison program than to take responsibility for these structural and institutional problems which they have helped create or sustain.[87]

The modern world of mass media and mass merchandising causes one to question Addis's differentiation of role specific and comprehensive role models. For example, perhaps the images created by mass media exposure allow what would have traditionally been considered a specific role model to have a comprehensive influence despite the absence of interaction between the role model and follower. In this sense, Addis's conceptualizations may be too narrowly defined. What is significant for our purposes, however, is Addis's concern that undue focus on the influence of athletes in shaping cultural attitudes toward women risks "emphasiz[ing] individuals and individual acts to the exclusion of institutions and collective acts and constraints."[89]

Assuming that athletes are instrumental in shaping cultural attitudes that translate into violence against women, steps should be taken to counteract such influence. Not to hold athletes accountable—whether they are in the professional or college ranks—sends an unattended message, particularly to men, of the acceptability of sexual violence against women. Yet, undue emphasis on the conduct of athletes may unintentionally divert attention from the institutional and structural conditions that contribute to such attitudes.

3. *Summary*

The enormous popularity and accessibility of sports in America makes sport a key component of our current gender order. Consequently, events that transpire in sport, including athlete violence against women, contribute significantly to shaping our cultural attitudes concerning the degree to which such conduct is deemed socially reprehensible. Despite its significance, however, sport constitutes merely one of the social institutions that is constructed by and subsequently aids in establishing gender order in society. Similarly, athletes represent mere components of the social institution of sport. Therefore, while it is important that individual per-

---

83. *Id*. at 1411.

84. *Id*. at 1403 (quoting Axel Honneth, *Integrity and Disrespect: Principles of a Conception of Morality Based on the Theory of Recognition*, 20 POL. THEORY 187, 189 (1992).

87. *Id*.

89. Addis, *supra* note 72, at 1384.

petrators be held accountable for their conduct, accountability should extend to a broader institutional level.

In short, one should view challenging patterns in sport that contribute to violence against women as part of an overall effort to transform other social institutions, including our colleges and universities. One commentator adroitly stated: "As long as . . . both sexes are socialized to accept male aggression and female passivity, abuse will remain pervasive. Changing the conditions that foster violence requires changing cultural perspectives and priorities. It demands sustained challenges to media presentations, educational programs, and social services."[94]

III. Title IX as a Means of Recourse

. . . . [A detailed discussion of the availability of Title IX as a means of recourse in teacher-to-student and peer-to-peer sexual harassment claims is omitted. — ed.].

C. Institutional Liability for Peer Harassment: The Collegiate Level

. . . .

2. Brzonkala v. Virginia Polytechnic and State University

Brzonkala v. Virginia Polytechnic & State University[282] (*Brzonkala I*) is the other case in which a court has examined the applicability of Title IX in a case of peer harassment in the collegiate context. In addition, it is the only case that involves sexual harassment by student-athletes against a woman student. Ms. Brzonkala alleged that she was brutally raped by two members of the Virginia Polytechnic and State University (VPI) football team in a room located on the third floor of her dormitory. Subsequent to the incident, Ms. Brzonkala filed charges against both athletes under the school's sexual assault policy. VPI conducted a disciplinary hearing, and only one of the athletes, Antonio Morrison, was found guilty of abusive conduct and suspended for two semesters. Morrison appealed the decision. Without notifying Ms. Brzonkala, VPI set aside the suspension and allowed Morrison to return to school the following semester on a full athletic scholarship. Upon learning that VPI permitted Morrison to return, Ms. Brzonkala canceled plans to return to VPI to complete her education.

Based on these factual assertions, the United States District Court for the Western District of Virginia interpreted Brzonkala's Title IX complaint as alleging that VPI participated in creating a hostile educational environment by allowing the student-athlete to return to campus while the plaintiff was still a student. In response to Brzonkala's complaint, the court ruled that a Title IX claim based on student-to-student harassment brought against the university is actionable. Next, the court articulated a two prong test for determining what constitutes a hostile environment: (1) conduct that objectively creates a hostile or abusive environment, and (2) the victim's subjective perception that an environment is abusive. Applying this test, the *Brzonkala I* court held that the plaintiff's hostile environment claim was premature because it was based on her fear of future reprisal that had not actually materialized.

---

94. *Id.*
282. 935 F. Supp. (W.D. Va. 1996).

On appeal in *Brzonkala v. Virginia Polytechnic Institute and State University*[293] (*Brzonkala III*), the United States Court of Appeals for the Fourth Circuit considered whether Ms. Brzonkala stated a Title IX claim against VPI pursuant to hostile environment and disparate treatment theories. Relying on Title VII jurisprudence and cases which have adopted Title VII analysis in Title IX litigation, the court concluded that an "educational institution's handling of a known sexually hostile environment is actionable" under Title IX.[295] In so holding, the Fourth Circuit severely criticized the Fifth Circuit's "deeply flawed analysis" in *Rowinsky*. Arguing that *Rowinsky* incorrectly framed the issue in terms of liability for acts of third parties, the court stated:

> [I]n a Title IX hostile environment action a plaintiff is not seeking to hold the school responsible for the acts of third parties (in this case fellow students). Rather, the plaintiff is seeking to hold the school responsible for its own actions, i.e. that the school "knew or should have known of the illegal conduct and failed to take prompt and adequate remedial action." ... Therefore, the entire focus of Rowinsky's analysis as to whether a school may be held responsible for the acts of third parties under Title IX misses the point. Brzonkala does not seek to make [VPI] liable for the acts of third parties. She seeks only to hold the school liable for its own discriminatory actions in failing to remedy a known hostile environment.[297]

Having found that peer hostile environment claims are actionable under Title IX, the court turned to whether Ms. Brzonkala alleged facts were sufficient to establish VPI's liability for a hostile environment claim. The court adopted a Title VII standard of liability and articulated the test as "whether Brzonkala has alleged facts sufficient to support an inference that [VPI] 'knew or should have known of the illegal conduct and failed to take prompt and adequate remedial action.'"[298] Applying this test, the appellate court rejected the district court's finding that, because Ms. Brzonkala failed to return to campus, a hostile environment never occurred. The court reasoned that the district court failed to recognize that the rape of Ms. Brzonkala created a hostile environment and that VPI was aware of this environment and failed to properly remedy it. According to the court, "[g]iven the seriousness of the harassment acts, the total inadequacy of [VPI's] redress, and Brzonkala's reasonable fear of unchecked retaliation including possible violence, Brzonkala did not have to return to the campus the next year and personally experience a continued hostile environment."[300]

. . . .

---

293. Nos. 96-1814, 96-2316, 1997 WL 785529 (4th Cir. Dec. 23, 1997).

295. *Id.* at *5.

297. *Id.* at *7 (citations omitted).

298. *Id.* at *9.

300. *Id.* at *9.

Part IV

Tort Liability

Introduction

The application of tort law to sports epitomizes the broader question raised in Chapter 1, *supra*, as to whether there is a unique body of sports law or merely the application of tort principles to sports. Many torts law classes cover *Hackbart v. Cinncinatti Bengals*, Inc., 435 F. Supp. 352 (D. Colo. 1977), *rev'd* 601 F. 2d 516 (10th Cir. 1979). A professor may engage first-year law students in a Socratic dialogue about whether fundamental tort principles apply in the sports setting or whether sports has its own unique set of assumptions that require different rules, if not results. This chapter does not attempt directly to answer that question. Rather it presents some of the scholarship of legal scholars who have analyzed liability issues related to injuries suffered by athletes while participating in sports activity. Section (1) discusses general standards of liability. Section (2) covers the liability of colleges and universities, while Section (3) discusses the liability of medical professionals who treat athletes in connection with their participation in sports activity.

Section (1) contains an excerpt from an article by Professor Ray Yasser that delineates the standard causes of action brought by athletes injured in the playing arena. These causes of action apply whether the defendant is another athlete, a university or a professional team. Professor Yasser's article is followed by Professor Eugene Bjorklun's discussion of the defense of assumption of risk. Students may find that sports is one of those areas in which the principles underlying affirmative defenses set the standard of liability. Some students may ponder whether the tort policy of compensating victims tends to be more important than deterrence. That idea appears in Section (2) in Professor William Baker's discussion of the duties of colleges and universities to participants. The article by Professor Cathy Jones next explores the responsibility of the athlete in preventing or limiting injuries to self. She writes about medical treatment issues, particularly who among potential decision-makers is best suited to determine the appropriate treatment and whether the athlete should return to competition. Professor Matthew Mitten examines the other side of that coin in Section (3) where he analyzes the liability of physicians who treat injured athletes.

Chapter 13

Liability of Participants

1. Standard of Care

Ray Yasser, In the Heat of Competition: Tort Liability of One Participant to Another; Why Can't Participants Be Required to Be Reasonable?
5 Seton Hall Journal of Sport Law 253 (1995)[*]

....

Generally, an athlete so injured can base an action to recover on three theories: (1) an intentional tort such as battery or assault, (2) recklessness, and (3) negligence. Even though decisions that allow a simple negligence cause of action can be found in jurisdictions stretching from Washington state to Connecticut to Louisiana, the prevailing view appears to be that the participant to participant sports injury case requires at least recklessness.

II. INTENTIONAL TORTS

A simple definition of battery is the intentional, unprivileged, harmful or offensive contact by the defendant with the person of another. An assault is committed when the defendant, without privilege, intentionally places the plaintiff in apprehension of an immediate harmful or offensive touching. Sports activities are rife with what arguably can be termed assaults and batteries. A review of the cases indicates that a defense of privilege is often the key issue in such litigation. The *Restatement (Second) of Torts* categorizes privileges in terms of whether they are consensual or nonconsensual.[9] Commonly accepted nonconsensual privileges include self-defense, defense of others, and defense of property. In sports, the consent privilege weighs heavily.

As a starting point, in a series of cases beginning around the turn of the century the courts dealt with the issue of consent in the "mutual combat" context. The courts were repeatedly faced with the task of determining precisely to what risks a voluntary participant consents. The intentional tort theory is the clearest basis for an action, as the available defenses are well established and generally agreed on. The prevailing view is that although participation in an athletic contest involves manifestation of consent to those bodily contacts which are permitted by the rules of the game and foreseeable, an intentional act causing injury, which goes beyond

---

9. RESTATEMENT (SECOND) OF TORTS § 10 (1965).

what is ordinarily permissible in an unforeseeable way, is an assault and battery for which recovery may be had.

. . . .

Clearly no court disputes the view that an intentional tort theory is a viable cause of action in the sports participant to participant context, with the caveat that a defense of privilege may prevail.

III. RECKLESSNESS

Recklessness is conduct that creates a higher degree of risk than that created by simple negligence. The defense of assumption of risk may be a defense to the recklessness-based cause of action.

The decisions of the Illinois Appellate Court are illustrative of the handling of the recklessness cause of action in the sports context. A soccer match between two amateur high school teams was the setting for *Nabozny v. Barnhill*.[18] Barnhill, a forward, entered the opposing goalkeeper's penalty area and kicked the plaintiff, Nabozny, in the head as he was receiving a pass. The contact caused permanent skull and brain damage to Nabozny. Barnhill's action was a violation of the F.I.F.A. rules, which prohibited a player from making contact with a goalkeeper in possession of the ball in the penalty area. The defendant in this case was alleged to have been negligent; this was the first Illinois case involving organized athletic competition where one of the participants was so charged. The trial court's decision directing a verdict for defendant Barnhill was reversed, and a new trial was ordered. It is important to note, however, that the plaintiff did not recover on a negligence theory. The Illinois appellate court revisited this issue on five year intervals for the next ten years.

In 1980, the court again held that the plaintiff in a sports injury case must show something worse than ordinary negligence on the part of the defendant.[20] The plaintiff in the case, Oswald, was injured when he was kicked while playing basketball in a required high school gym class. The court went out of its way to distinguish the cause of action in this case from that in the non-contact sport context case by stating that "participants in bodily contact games such as basketball assume greater risks than do golfers and others involved in non-physical contact sports."[21]

In 1985, the Illinois appellate court again addressed liability in the participant to participant sports injury case.[22] Since the court based its ruling on a negligence analysis, however, a discussion of the rationale is reserved for the treatment of "negligence" cases to follow.

Finally, in 1994 an Illinois appellate court revisited the issue in *Lundrum v. Gonzalez*.[23] The plaintiff in *Lundrum* was playing first base in an informal softball game. The defendant ran into the plaintiff while running the bases, causing him to fall on his shoulder and sustain serious injury. Relying on *Nabozny*, the court concluded that the plaintiff could not recover, since he had not shown wilful or wanton conduct on the part of the defendant.

---

18. 334 N.E.2d 258 (Ill. App. Ct. 1975).
20. Oswald v. Township High School Distr. No. 214, 406 N.E.2d 157 (Ill. App. Ct. 1980).
21. *Id.* at 160.
22. Ramos by Ramos v. City of Countryside, 45 N.E.2d 418 (Ill. App. Ct. 1985).
23. 629 N.E.2d 710 (Ill. App. Ct. 1994).

In *Hackbart v. Cincinnati Bengals, Inc. (Hackbart I)*,[25] a Denver Bronco defensive player (Hackbart) was severely injured after a Cincinnati pass was intercepted near the goal line. Hackbart attempted to block a Bengal offensive player (Clark) and fell to the ground. Clark, "acting out of anger and frustration, but without specific intent to injure...stepped forward and struck a blow with his right forearm to the back of the kneeling plaintiff's head." Hackbart sustained a neck injury and sought recovery on the theories of reckless misconduct and failure of the Bengals to instruct and control Clark. The trial court held that the plaintiff could not recover because professional football is inherently violent and because adequate sanctions were available through the imposition of monetary penalties and expulsion from the game.

Hackbart II[27] reversed the trial court's findings and conclusions. The Tenth Circuit Court of Appeals found that "there are no principles of law which allow a court to rule out certain tortious conduct" simply because it occurs in a generally rough game. Additionally, the questioned conduct by Clark was explicitly prohibited by the rules of the game. The appellate court also ruled that the appropriate standard for liability was recklessness, where intent cannot be shown. The plaintiff Hackbart was entitled to have the case tried on the assessment of his rights and not on the trial court's determination that "as a matter of social policy the game was so violent and unlawful that value lines could not be drawn."[30]

In *Gauvin v. Clark*,[31] the standard of care that participants owe one another was again at issue, this time in the setting of a hockey game. Clark "butt-ended" Gauvin by taking the back end of his hockey stick and striking Gauvin in the abdomen, causing serious injuries. The court ruled that Clark was not liable because he had not acted recklessly, reasoning that preclusion of liability where there is only negligence furthers the policy that "vigorous and active participation in sporting events should not be chilled by the threat of litigation."

Bourque v. Duplechin[33] involved injuries suffered by a second baseman in a summer league softball game. Bourque, the second baseman, was standing five feet away from the base when he was hit under the chin and severely injured by the base runner, Duplechin. A double play throw had forced Duplechin out, but he continued to run toward Bourque at full speed. To make contact with the second baseman, Duplechin left the basepath. Although the defendant alleged that Bourque had assumed the risk of injury, the court concluded that the runner's "negligent" conduct was not a risk assumed by softball players. Duplechin was found liable and Bourque recovered for his injuries.

Bourque is really more accurately viewed as a case in which the defendant was liable because he was reckless and not because he was negligent. The court pointed out that the sports participant assumes "all risks incidental to that particular activity which are obvious and foreseeable" but does not assume "the risk of injury from fellow players acting in an unexpected or unsportsmanlike way with a reckless lack of concern for others participating."[34] The thrust of the *Bourque*

---

25. 435 F. Supp. 352 (D. Colo. 1977).

27. Hackbart v. Cincinnati Bengals, Inc. (Hackbart II), 601 F.2d 516 (10th Cir. 1979).

30. *Hackbart I*, 435 F. Supp. at 355.

31. 537 N.E.2d 94 (Mass. 1989).

33. 331 So.2d 40 (La. Ct. App. 1976).

34. *Id*. at 42.

opinion was that the sports participant invariably assumes the risks created by the co-participant's negligence but not necessarily by his recklessness.

The relevant case law now clearly supports the view that an injured sports participant can recover on a showing of recklessness or intention. The suggestion in *Hackbart I* that the sports participant is insulated from tort liability has been almost universally discredited. *Hackbart II* reflects the modern view that recklessness is an appropriate cause of action.

The outcome of the litigation will often depend on the availability of the defenses. In the recklessness context, the primary defense is akin to assumption of risk. It is interesting to note, however, that other defenses to a recklessness-based cause of action have not been clearly delineated. The practitioner would be well advised to plead the well established intentional tort defenses of consent, self-defense, defense of others, and defense of property, along with the well established negligence defenses of assumption of risk and contributory negligence, and let the court decide.

IV. NEGLIGENCE

No court in the land would hold that intentional conduct fails to state a cause of action; none have said that recklessness is not a basis for recovery; but many have stated that negligence is insufficient.

Nabozny, *Hackbart I*, *Hackbart II*, and *Gauvin* articulate the view that the simple negligence claim should fail. Although negligence was pleaded in *Nabozny*, the opinion stressed that "a player is liable if his conduct is such that it is either deliberate, wilful or with a reckless disregard for the safety of the other player."[37] The implication of *Nabozny* is that simple negligence will not suffice. The plaintiff in *Hackbart* did not rely on a negligence theory. As the *Hackbart II* court pointed out, "this [was] in recognition of the fact that subjecting another to unreasonable risk of harm, the essence of negligence, is inherent in the game of football."[38] *Gauvin* rejected the negligence cause of action in accepting recklessness as the appropriate minimum standard. Some courts have held that ordinary negligence will not support a cause of action in such contact sports as "pickup" basketball, an informal game of touch football, or even an unorganized neighborhood game. One court ruled that actions in a juvenile game of "bombardment" failed to support a negligence action.[42]

Yet a growing number of jurisdictions are rejecting this approach and allowing the negligence action. One reason for this may be that, as *Hackbart II* notes, the distinction between recklessness and negligence is not bright-line.

Generally the courts have taken one of two positions: 1) that more than negligence is required to state a cause of action or 2) that negligence is sufficient for recovery. As the discussion on recklessness has shown, the language used to differentiate negligence from "more" generally includes phrases such as "recklessness or wilful" or "recklessness or wanton."

What is really going on in these cases is that courts are struggling to figure out whether or not they will allow a simple negligence cause of action. By now it should be fairly obvious that this is one of the battle lines in the "torts in sports"

---

37. *Nabozny*, 334 N.E.2d at 261.
38. *Hackbart II*, 601 F.2d at 520.
42. Ramos by Ramos, 45 N.E.2d at 418.

debate. But the courts are also grappling with the more general problem of what makes the conduct reckless (or wanton or wilful) in the first place? If the conduct can be declared intentional or reckless, its a slam dunk. If it is negligence at most, the situation is more comparable to shooting at a moving basket—a tough shot to make.

The basis of negligence as a cause of action is conduct that results in an unreasonable risk of harm to another. Of course, almost all human activities involve some risk of harm. The gist of a negligence-based claim is that the conduct involves a risk of harm that is not outweighed by the benefits to be derived from engaging in the conduct. Increasingly, the courts have shown a willingness to allow the application of this principle in the participant to participant sports injury as they do in virtually any other area of our lives.

In a 1993 decision, the Wisconsin Supreme Court ruled that liability in the sports injury case may be based on negligence, depending on the specific circumstances.[47] Robert F. Lestina, the plaintiff, was injured in a collision with the defendant, Leopold Jerger. Lestina was playing an offensive position for his recreational soccer team and Jerger was the goal keeper for the opposing team. Jerger, the defendant, apparently ran out of the goal area and collided with the plaintiff. The plaintiff alleged that the defendant "slide tackled" him in order to prevent him from scoring. The plaintiff seriously injured his left knee and leg in the collision.

While the Wisconsin Supreme Court acknowledged that relatively few sports cases have held that a plaintiff may recover on proof of negligence, it ruled in this case that negligence is an appropriate standard to govern cases involving injuries during recreational team contact sports.

For a time, New Jersey also adopted the negligence standard for sports injury cases in *Crawn v. Campo*.[49] In *Crawn*, the appellate court held that ordinary negligence, rather than reckless conduct, was the appropriate standard to be applied in a participant to participant sports injury case.

Plaintiff Michael Crawn, playing catcher in a pick-up softball game, was injured in a collision at home plate with defendant John Campo, an opposing base runner. The lower court ruled, on the basis of *Gauvin* and *Marchetti*, that intentional conduct or reckless disregard of the safety of others was required to give rise to a cause of action in a participant to participant sports related injury. This of course had been the trend. But in overruling the trial court the appellate court lined itself up with *Lestina*. The court persuasively reasoned that the only two settings in which New Jersey courts have recognized a negligence immunity is in special situations that involve the exercise of parental authority or the "fireman's rule."[50]

New Jersey has however abandoned the simple negligence standard. Relying on *Nabozny*, the Supreme Court of New Jersey held that the duty of care required in establishing liability in recreational sports should be based on a standard of reckless or intentional conduct, rather than negligence.[51]

---

47. Lestina v. West Bend Mut. Ins. Co., 501 N.W.2d 28, 33 (Wis. 1993).

49. 630 A.2d 368 (N.J. Super. Ct. App. Div. 1993).

50. *Id.* at 375. The "fireman's rule" allows a fireman or policeman to recover for injuries that result from hazards that are inherent or incidental to the performance of their duties only if intentional or wilful misconduct can be shown.

51. Crawn v. Campo, 136 N.J. 494, 508 (1994).

Connecticut joined the ranks of those jurisdictions allowing a negligence cause of action in 1989. In *Babych v. McRae*,[52] the plaiintiff, Wayne Babych, alleged that the defendant, Ken McRae, a fellow professional hockey player, struck the plaintiff across his right knee with a hockey stick during a game, causing the plaintiff to suffer personal injuries and financial losses. In holding that negligence is a legally sufficient cause of action when one professional sports participant is injured by another, the court rejected the New York decision in *Turcotte v. Fell*,[53] which held that negligence is not actionable when one professional sports participant injures another. *Babych* ruled that there was no analogous Connecticut case law barring a negligence cause of action in sports participant to participant cases.

As early as 1976, the Missouri Court of Appeals accepted negligence as a viable cause of action in sports related injuries.[55] In *Niemczyk*, the plaintiff and the defendant were participating in a softball game in Bell City, Missouri. The plaintiff was a member of a team from Bell City, and the defendant was a member of a team from Fisk, Missouri. The plaintiff, a base runner, was running from first base to second when the defendant ran across the infield and collided with the plaintiff in the base path. The court accepted negligence as a cause of action in this instance. It held that "whether one player's conduct, causing injury to another, constitutes actual negligence hinges upon the facts of the individual case."[56]

In 1992, The Louisiana Court of Appeals also held that negligence was a viable cause of action in the sports injury case.[57] The plaintiff, Patrick Hendry, was engaged in a game of racquetball with Robert Panek and Stephen Schoelmann. Hendry was hit in the face with Panek's racket, when Panek swung the racket too wide after backhanding a ball. The court held that voluntary participants in sporting activities have a duty to play with sportsmanlike conduct, according to the rules of the game, and to refrain from acts which are unforeseeable and which evidence wanton or reckless disregard for the other participants. Thus, the court apparently accepted everything from a negligence standard to a recklessness standard in the sports context.

In *Ginsberg v. Hontas*,[59] the plaintiff was playing second base in a recreational softball game. Defendant was sliding into second base, and a collision occurred between the plaintiff and the defendant, fracturing the plaintiff's right leg. The court held that the plaintiff failed to prove by a preponderance of the evidence that the defendant was negligent in his play during the game. The appellate court affirmed the lower court's conclusion that the plaintiff failed to establish that defendant had acted negligently. The court went on to state however, that "[t]he duty owed by the defendant in instant matter is a common duty, the duty to act reasonably under the circumstances."[60] One may reasonably conclude that since the court based its decision on the plaintiff's failure to meet his burden of proof, and not on a finding that the plaintiff's theory was based on a non-viable cause of action, negligence is in fact a viable cause of action in Louisiana. Unfortunately,

---

52. 567 A.2d 1269 (Conn. Super. Ct. 1989).

53. 502 N.E.2d 964 (N.Y. 1986).

55. Niemczyk v. Burleson, 537 S.W.2d 737 (Mo. Ct. App. 1976).

56. *Id*. at 741.

57. Hendry v. U.S. Fidelity and Guar. Ins. Co., 594 So.2d 584 (La. Ct. App. 1992).

59. 545 So. 2d 1154 (La. App. 4th Cir. 1989).

60. *Id*. at 1155.

the court obfuscated a clear understanding of the matter by mixing negligence language with that of recklessness in stating that "[i]n this softball game defendant owed the plaintiff the duty to act reasonably, that is to play fairly according to the rules of the game and to refrain from any wanton, reckless conduct likely to result in harm or injury to another."[61]

In a 1986 decision, the Washington Court of Appeals allowed the negligence claim for sports injuries.[62] *Kladnick* involved an injury caused on a skating rink. While it was not a "heat of competition" case, the court expressed its ruling in terms that encompass sports cases as a whole, saying that those who participate in sports or amusements are taken to assume known risks of being hurt, although they are not deemed to have consented to unsportsmanlike rule violations which are not part of the game. Thus, the court here bases its ruling, not on the inappropriateness of a negligence cause of action, but rather on an assumption of risk defense.

There are in fact a number of older opinions from which it can be inferred that the court would allow a negligence cause of action. While these are not all "heat of competition" cases, they do involve the sports context and give some insight into the courts' reasoning on the application of negligence principles to the actions of sports participants. In these cases, the courts typically talk about the assumption of risk defense to the negligence cause of action rather than declaring that negligence fails to state a cause of action in the first place.

Florida so held in 1983, when it stated that express assumption of risk is a viable defense to a negligence action in the context of a contact sport.[64] The plaintiff, Kuehner, brought a negligence action against the defendant, Green. Kuehner had been injured as the result of a karate take-down maneuver executed by Green during a sparring exercise at Green's home. The court appears to adopt the view that negligence is a viable cause of action in a contact sport. The court found that the plaintiff had subjectively recognized the danger of the take-down maneuver called a "leg sweep."

Similarly, Minnesota, Michigan, Wisconsin, Louisiana and California have turned, in the sports injury case, to analysis of defenses to negligence, rather than of failure of negligence to state a cause of action in the first place. In *Lutterman v. Studer*,[66] the plaintiff tried out for the 7th grade baseball team. On the first day of practice, the students were moved indoors because of rain. During a simulated batting drill, the bat slipped out of the defendant's hand and struck the plaintiff on the left side of his head. The court held that in the sports context, as well as other contexts, even where there is a finding of negligence, proximate cause usually presents a jury issue. Thus, the court allowed a deliberation by the jury on the negligence cause of action.

In *Carey v. Toles*[68], the plaintiff, James Carey, age 15, and the defendant, Edward Toles, age 13, were engaged in an afternoon pick-up baseball game. Toles, a right handed batter, hit the ball into right field and started to run. He threw his bat which hit Carey, who was on the sidelines between home plate and first base. Carey's injuries required extensive surgery on his mouth and jawbone and the re-

---

61. *Id.*

62. Ridge v. Kladnick, 713 P.2d 1131 (Wash. Ct. App. 1986).

64. Kuehner v. Green, 436 So. 2d 78 (Fla. 1983).

66. 217 N.W.2d 756 (Minn. 1974).

68. 151 N.W.2d 396 (Mich. Ct. App. 1967).

placement of nine teeth. The court ruled that whether a minor baseball player was negligent in throwing a bat after hitting a ball and whether a minor plaintiff was contributorily negligent in standing on the sidelines are jury questions. The appellate court remanded for a new trial based on an improper jury instruction regarding the assumption of risk as it relates to negligence. Note that the court did not rule that negligence in the sports context fails to state a cause of action.

In *Ceplina v. South Milwaukee Sch. Bd.*,[70] a minor plaintiff, Rosemary Ceplina, was injured when she was struck in the face with a baseball bat swung by the minor defendant, James Pauwels. Both were 6th grade students. The court held that as a general rule, the existence of negligence is a question of fact which is to be decided by the jury. The court expressed the belief that the jury should decide what the defendant's duty was and whether or not it was breached, as opposed to the court deciding this issue as a matter of law.

In the two Louisiana cases,[72] the Louisiana Court of Appeals held that even if there was negligence on the part of the defendant, the plaintiff had assumed the risk of injury resulting from negligence. Once again, the logical inference is that, since defenses to the negligence action are analyzed by the court, negligence must be recognized as a viable cause of action.

In *Tavernier v. Maes*[73], the plaintiff and defendant were part of a family picnic at a public park. The plaintiff was playing second base and the defendant was running from first to second. The defendant slid into second base, colliding with the plaintiff, which resulted in the fracture of both the outer and inner bones of the plaintiff's left ankle. The court held that in the sports context, as well as others, one of the key issues in regard to the assumption of risk defense is "what did the plaintiff know and when did he know it." The court allowed a negligence cause of action but gave a jury instruction of assumption of risk as well. In *Hoyt v. Rosenberg*[75], the plaintiff, Marilyn Hoyt, 11 years old, and the defendant, Jack Rosenberg, 12 years old, were playing "kick the can," a form of the old game of hide and seek, with two other children. The rules are not crucial to understanding this game, but essentially one had to "kick the can" to be the winner. The defendant kicked the can with some force, striking the plaintiff in the face, and causing her to lose the use of one eye. The court held that in deciding whether there had been a failure of a minor to use ordinary care to avoid injury to other children, the test is not what an adult would have done or what the results indicate should have been done, but what an ordinary child in that situation would have done. By its holding the court indicates that it would allow a negligence cause of action in this informal youth "contest."

As pointed out in the material on "recklessness," courts have at times gone out of their way to distinguish the cause of action in the contact as opposed to the non-contact sports injury case, by stating that "participants in bodily contact games such as basketball assume greater risks than do golfers and others involved in non-physical contact sports."[77]

---

70. 243 N.W.2d 183 (Wis. 1976).

72. Benedetto v. Travelers Ins. Co., 172 So. 2d 354 (La. Ct. App. 1965); Gaspard v. Grain Dealers Mut. Ins. Co., 131 So. 2d 831 (La. Ct. App. 1961).

73. 51 Cal. Rptr. 575 (Ct. App. 1966).

75. 182 P.2d 234 (Cal. Ct. App. 1947).

77. Oswald, 406 N.E.2d at 160. [A substantial discussion and citation to golf cases is omitted. —ed.].

When negligent conduct proximately causes harm, a prima facie case is established. The main defenses to a negligence-based claim are contributory negligence and assumption of risk. Each of these defenses once operated as a complete bar to the negligence claim. Comparative negligence legislation now applicable in most states has changed this common law rule. Under comparative negligence statutes, a contributorily negligent plaintiff is not necessarily precluded from recovery. A negligence-based claim in sports may be won or lost over the availability of an assumption of risk defense. As with consent in the intentional tort action, the assumption of risk defense will require the court to determine the nature of the risks that the willing participant assumes.

The best advice to a practitioner representing an injured sports participant is to plead the three causes of action in the alternative. This would be done in the same manner as one would plead breach of warranty, negligence, and strict liability on behalf of a consumer injured by a defensive product.

V. CONCLUSION

A growing number of states appear to recognize negligence as a viable cause of action in the "heat of competition" context. In almost every area of our lives we are exposed to liability if we act in a negligent manner and cause harm to others. For the most part, our social compact says that unreasonable conduct which causes physical harm is actionable. This rule of liability is firmly grounded in social policy. The exposure to liability serves to deter unreasonably risky behavior and to compensate the injured.

. . . .

Does it make sense, then, to insulate a negligent sports participant from liability to a physically injured co-participant? Is sports deserving of such solicitude? Are there really convincing policy reasons to insulate a sports participant from liability for physical harm caused by negligence?

The courts that require an injured sports participant to prove recklessness (and thus protect the "merely" negligent actor) do so on the theory that sports, like speech, needs "breathing room." But the evidence is accumulating that, on every level of competition, participants need to be restrained and not emboldened. From kids' sports to professional sports, sportsmanship, fair play and reasonable restraint are lost values. Grotesque showmanship, unethical means to win, and reckless unconcern mar the landscape of sport. Sports participants don't need breathing room; they should rather have their feet held to the liability fire.

. . . .

Eugene C. Bjorklun, Assumption of Risk and Its Effect on School Liability for Athletic Injuries
55 Education Law Reporter 349 (1989)*

. . . .

ASSUMPTION OF RISK

In each of the preceding cases, defendants claimed or could have claimed that they should not be held liable for damages because the athletes assumed the risk of injury. This defense of assumption of risk holds that "a plaintiff who fully understands a risk of harm to himself...and who nevertheless voluntarily chooses...to accept it, is not entitled to recover for harm within that risk."

Assumption of risk does not have universal acceptance. In some states, it has been expressly abolished on the basis that "...reasonableness of conduct should be the basic consideration in all negligence cases." In other states, although courts have not expressly abolished it, judicial disapproval has been clearly stated on the grounds that "...it adds nothing to modern law except confusion...." Thus, assumption of risk as a defense against liability is not available in some states. In those states where it is available, it can be either implied or expressed.

Implied Assumption of Risk

In implied assumption of risk, three criteria must be met: (1) the injured party had some actual knowledge of the danger; (2) the injured party understood and appreciated the risk; and (3) the injured party voluntarily accepted the risk. The burden of proving that these conditions existed is on the defendant and is a matter for the injury to decide.

One difficulty for defendants in proving implied assumption of risk in athletic injuries at the secondary level relates to the age of the students. Frequently, they are minors, not held to the same standard of care for their own safety as that required of an adult. The standard of care of minors for their own safety also varies according to the minor's age and experience. As a general rule, age 14 is a dividing line. Crook states, "...at 14 years of age an infant is presumed to have sufficient capacity and understanding to be sensible of danger and have the power to avoid it."

Thus, students under 14 who participate in athletic activities may or may not have assumed the risks, depending on their mental maturity. It may be difficult to convince a jury that middle school or junior high school students are mature enough to meet the criteria of assumption of risk described previously. For high school students, the defendant's task may be less difficult. However, the standard of care for students 14 years and older is "...that of a child of his age and capacity and not the standard of care of an adult."

Proving to a jury's satisfaction that a student had assumed the risks in participating in an athletic activity still does not ensure freedom from liability for the student's injury. Students assume only the known risks inherent in the activity, not risks that are not ordinary and inherent parts of the activity. Thus, if the student's injury was caused by the negligence of the defendants, it did not occur as the result of an ordinary and inherent aspect of the activity. Students do not assume the risks of harm caused by the negligence of school personnel; school personnel may be held liable for damages for injuries caused by their breaches of owed duties of care.

Express Assumption of Risk

A second type of assumption of risk occurs when one expressly agrees to accept the risks. Express assumption of risk has been defined in this way: "A plaintiff who by contract or otherwise expressly agrees to accept a risk of harm arising from defendant's negligence or reckless conduct cannot recover for such harm, unless the agreement is invalid as contrary to public policy." Disclaimers, waivers, or liability releases are used by a variety of businesses and other enterprises, including public schools. Because of the possibility of catastrophic injury and large damage awards, some school districts have begun using statements of risk that students and their parents/guardians are required to sign as a condition of participation. A typical statement of risk that a student must sign is as follows:

> I am aware competing or practicing in any athletic activity can be a dangerous activity involving risk of injury. I understand that the dangers and risks of competing and practicing in the activity include, but are not limited to, death, neck and spinal injury which may result in complete or partial paralysis, brain damage, injury to virtually all bones, joints, ligaments, muscles, tendons, and other aspects of the muscular-skeletal system, and injury or impairment of future abilities to earn a living, to engage in other business, social, and recreational activities and generally to enjoy life.
>
> If I am a participant in baseball, hockey, softball, football, basketball, or wrestling, I specifically acknowledge that it is a contact sport involving even greater risk of injury than other sports.
>
> Because of the possible dangers of participating in the activities, I recognize the importance of following the coaches' instructions regarding playing techniques, training and other team rules, and agree to obey such instructions.
>
> In consideration of the School District's permitting me to try out for and to engage in all activities related to the team, including, but not limited to, trying out, practicing, or participating in that activity, I hereby assume all risks associated with participation.

A similar statement in which the parent or guardian agrees "to assume all risks associated" with the student's participation also must be signed before the student is allowed to participate.

Several questions in regard to the use of such statements of risk arise: (1) Are they valid waivers of liability for injuries caused by negligence? (2) Can school districts deny students the opportunity to participate in athletics if they or their parents/guardians refuse to sign them? (3) Are they of value in convincing a jury that a student assumed the risks inherent in an athletic activity?

In regard first to their validity as waivers of liability, the definition of an express assumption of risk given earlier suggests that it is indeed possible for one to enter into a contract that waives claims of liability for injuries caused by another's negligence. However, since most secondary school students are minors, such a waiver would be difficult to enforce. This is not because minors do not have the power to enter into contracts; they do. However, in most states, minors can disavow a contract at any time during their minority or within a reasonable time after reaching majority unless the contract is for "necessities." Since it is unlikely that participation in athletics would be viewed as a necessity (food, shelter, clothing, etc.), the minor could disavow the statement of risk as a contract pretty much at will. Neither would the parent or guardian's signature on the statement of risk constitute a waiver of liability for the student, because "a next friend or guardian may not ordinarily waive the rights of an infant...."[40]

Thus, risk statements signed by minor students would have little validity as liability waivers, but what about those signed by their parents or guardians and

---

40. Part 2 Waiver, 28 Am. Jur. 2d Escrow 836, 838.

those signed by students who have reached the age of majority? Under the definition of express assumption of risk, adults may waive liability claims against another for negligence. Thus, parents or guardians may waive their own claims for damages for an injury to the student arising from another's negligence, but may not waive the student's claim to damages. Similarly, students who are no longer minors could waive their claims to damages for injuries resulting from another's negligence. However, this action is possible only if the waiver is not contrary to public policy because "the public interest may not be waived." A consideration of whether or not such risk statements are contrary to public policy leads into the additional question of whether or not school districts can require them to be signed as a condition of participation. A recent decision by the Supreme Court of Washington in *Wagenblast v. Odessa School District* may provide the answers to both questions.[42]

In *Wagenblast,* two school districts, Odessa and Seattle, required students and their parents/guardians to sign standardized forms that released the school district and its employees from liability for any negligence arising out of the athletic program. The court held that requiring students and their parents/guardians to sign these forms as a condition to participation was not permissible, because the releases are "...invalid because they violate public policy."

In reaching this conclusion, the court used a test the California Supreme Court developed for determining whether or not such waivers violate public policy. The test consists of six criteria and an invalid waiver exhibits some or all of them: (1) a type of business generally thought suitable for public regulation; (2) the party seeking the waiver is engaged in performing a public service; (3) the party is willing to perform the service for any member of the public who wants it; (4) the party seeking the waiver has a decisive advantage in bargaining strength against the members of the public who want the service; (5) in using this superior bargaining power, the party uses a standardized contract and makes no provision whereby the public can obtain protection against negligence; and (6) as a result of the use of the waiver, the party seeking the service is placed under the control of the other party and subject to the carelessness of that party and its agents.

Applying these criteria to the use of the waivers by the Odessa and Seattle school districts, the court found all of them present as follows: (1) interscholastic sports are regulated and are a fit subject for public regulation; (2) interscholastic sports in public schools are a matter of public importance; (3) interscholastic sports programs are open to all students who meet skill and eligibility standards; (4) school districts have a clear and disparate bargaining strength, because no alternative program in interscholastic athletics exists that is free and available to students and their parents; (5) students and their parents have no choice but to sign the forms or be barred from participation; (6) the natural relationship of athlete and coach places the student under the coach's control and subjects her/him to the risk of injury due to the coach's carelessness. For these reasons, the court held that the waivers used by the school districts were invalid because they violated public policy.

Thus, school districts cannot use the statement of risk forms as a condition to participation if they purport to waive liability for injuries resulting from negli-

---

42. Wagenblast v. Odessa School Dist., 110 Wash.2d 845, 758 P.2d 968 [48th Ed. Law. Rep. 676] (1988).

gence. Likewise, because they are invalid as against public policy, a parent, guardian, or non-minor student whose signature has been obtained would not be precluded from using for damages for such injuries.

Since these risk statements are invalid as waivers of liability for injuries resulting from negligence, are they any value in avoiding awards of damages against school districts and school personnel? If is possible that a risk statement used to inform the participant of known risks in the activity may be useful in convincing a jury that the participant was informed of the inherent risks and assumed them. In other words, if the risk statement does not purport to be a waiver of liability for negligence, but is rather a vehicle for giving the participant full knowledge and appreciation of the risks inherent in the activity and the opportunity to voluntarily accept them, the statement may be helpful in using the defense of assumption of risk. However, it also should be noted that injuries that do not result from negligence are not actionable to begin with.

CONCLUSIONS AND IMPLICATIONS

....

Assumption of risk will not provide a way for school districts and school personnel to avoid liability for their negligence. Implied assumption of risk only applies to the ordinary risks inherent in the activity. A student who participates in athletics assumes only those risks and not the risks arising out of the negligence of the school district or the coaches. Since damages can be awarded only based on negligence, an injury inherent (or non-negligent) in the activity is unlikely to result in a damage award. Thus, implied assumption of risk is relatively meaningless.

In addition, express assumption of risk, whereby students and their parents sign waivers of liability for claims against school districts and school personnel for their negligence, are equally useless. These waiver forms are merely contracts, and a minor can disavow most contracts at will. Thus, the statement of risk signed by a minor student has no validity if the student decides to disavow it. Those waivers signed by adult parents, guardians, and students also are unenforceable because they are contrary to public policy. Having them signed by students and parents/guardians as an informational device may be permissible (though not very useful in avoiding liability), but requiring them to be signed as a condition of participation is not.

Therefore, school personnel should not place their faith in assumption of risk as a way to avoid or minimize their liability. Instead, they should focus their efforts on avoiding negligence by discharging their owed duties of care. Rather than insisting that students and parents sign statements of risk, school personnel should insist that their programs incorporate adequate instruction and supervision of the participants. They should ensure that the participants have been given adequate equipment and that proper medical attention will be given to those who are injured. In devoting attention to these matters, school districts are more likely to avoid liability for injury than by relying on assumption of risk. Such an effort will reduce the incidence and severity of sports injuries, which is indeed the primary objective.

2. Liability of Colleges and Universities

William H. Baker, Injuries to College Athletes: Rights and Responsibilities
97 Dickinson Law Review 655 (1993)*

....

II. Tort Liability of Colleges and Universities

A. *State Institutions*

....

Many states have followed the same approach as the federal government — unless they have consented to being sued, the doctrine of sovereign immunity applies. State laws vary insofar as they drift away from the doctrine of sovereign immunity. The vast majority of states permit suits in tort although they vary as to the circumstances under which suit may be brought and as to the amount which may be recovered.

....

If a state has retained an area of immunity, that immunity also will be available to agencies of the state, such as corporations, boards, and commissions, assuming that those bodies are performing functions of the state. This immunity for subsidiary agencies of a state applies to educational institutions as well as prisons, hospitals and other state activities. Accordingly, unless a particular state statute provides to the contrary, state colleges and universities, as state agencies, would come under the same state immunity provisions as the state itself.

Even though most of the states have abandoned the concept of strict sovereign immunity, some states distinguish between governmental and proprietary activities. In *Louitt v. Concord School District*,[31] separate actions were brought against the school district, the superintendent of schools, the principal of a high school, and teacher-coaches for the death of one student and permanent injuries resulting to another because of heat prostration suffered during football practice. The court held that the football program was a governmental rather than a proprietary function. The court pointed out that the athletic programs of the school district had operated at a loss for the preceding five years. The school district, the superintendent, and the principal, accordingly, were held to be immune from liability, but the court held that the teacher-coaches could be personally liable if the death and injury resulted from their negligence. They would be unable to stand behind the shield of sovereign immunity.

As illustrated in *Louitt*, governmental immunity can be interpreted in such a way that it covers a broad spectrum of activities. For example, in Michigan, if the function in question is "expressly or impliedly mandated or authorized by constitution, statute or other law", it is treated as a governmental function and state immunity applies. The distinction between governmental and proprietary activities

---

31. 228 N.W. 2d 479 (Mich. App. 1975).

is most significant, however, not at the state level, but at the municipal level. Municipal immunity often is applied to governmental actions, but not to proprietary activities.

State statutes might be worded in such a way that sovereign immunity is waived only in very narrow specific factual situations. In *Andy Lowe v. Texas Tech. University*,[34] the Texas Tort Claims Act provided for the waiver of governmental immunity in three areas: use of publicly owned automobiles, defect of premises, and injuries that arise out of conditions or use of property. The plaintiff, a college football player, alleged that he injured his knee because the coaching staff, managers, and trainers of Texas Tech failed to furnish him with proper equipment and braces. The Supreme Court of Texas held that the plaintiff's allegations stated a case within the waiver of statutory immunity arising from some condition or use of personal property, as required by the Texas statute.

B. Private Institutions

There is no general rule that will apply to all states with respect to the question of immunity of private institutions from tort liability. There are a few older cases which held that private schools are immune from tort liability. These cases often turned on the view that the funds of a charitable organization should not be used to satisfy tort claims because such funds were given to accomplish certain charitable goals for the public good....

Some states have departed from the view that charitable institutions are immune from tort liability, either by enacting statutes or through case law. In fact, many states have followed the view for some time that private institutions are not immune from tort liability. In Illinois, for example, *Parks v. Northwestern University*, no longer represents the law. In 1950, the case of *Moore v. Moyle et al. (Bradley Polytechnic Institute)*,[43] held that where trust funds or insurance was available to satisfy a tort claim, no immunity would be recognized. In 1959, the case of *Molitor v. Kaneland Community Unit District*,[45] ruled against allowing immunity and the trust fund theory. The court there noted that public education has become a big business and that one can no longer justify school immunity on a protection of public funds theory. The *Molitor* Court held that it does not make sense to determine whether or not educational funds are being put to a proper or improper use based on the availability of trust funds. The question of a proper school expenditure should be determined first, without regard to the funds that might be available to satisfy a tort judgment. The court noted that courts which have abandoned immunity have not had to shut down their schools because their funds have been depleted and indicated that if trust funds can be used to pay insurance premiums, they also should be available to pay the liability directly, if no insurance exists.

....

Some states take an intermediate position between immunity and full liability. For example, some state courts have held such institutions liable in tort but limited judgments to the value of non-trust assets. Other courts have distinguished between the charitable and non-charitable activities of an institution and have

---

34. 540 S.W.2d 297 (Tex. 1976).
43. 405 Ill. 555 (1950).
45. 18 Ill. 2d 11 (1959).

found immunity only when the activity in question is charitable in nature. But if the activity is of a commercial nature, these jurisdictions have found such institutions liable. Still other courts have distinguished between negligence attributable directly to the school itself and the negligence of employees of the institution. The negligence of an employee could be imputed under the doctrine of respondeat superior.

The court in *Morehead College v. Russell* distinguished between the types of trust funds held by an institution. Charitable trust funds could not be reached for the negligence of employees of the institution under the doctrine of respondeat superior, but funds which were not charitable in nature (tuition of students and insurance) could be reached. Furthermore, negligence of a corporate or administrative nature permits utilizing trust funds because the negligence was committed by the trustees who had the responsibility, under the charter, of managing the institution. A private institution could be liable, however, for the failure to use due care in hiring personnel. With respect to the question of whether employees of a charitable institution can be held liable for negligence even though the institution itself is immune, the general rule is that an agent is not entitled to the protection of his principal's immunity even if the agent is acting on behalf of his principal. Some cases have distinguished between tort actions brought by beneficiaries of the institution and actions brought by strangers. It has been held that immunity from tort liability does not extend to suits brought by strangers. On the other hand, immunity may be recognized even where tort actions are brought by strangers.

C. Insurance

Regardless of whether or not public or private universities are legally liable to compensate athletes for athletic injuries, adequate insurance coverage can be used to protect the interests of athletes. Insurance coverage varies, and in many instances, if the insurance carried by the school is not sufficiently comprehensive, the athlete or his parents may want to carry insurance to make certain that any injury will be compensated. Effective August 1, 1992, the National Collegiate Athletic Association (NCAA) announced that it would pay 100% of the premiums to cover athletes at member schools with catastrophic athletics injury insurance. The commitment by the NCAA was projected through August 1, 1995. The new program covers student-athletes, trainers, managers and cheerleaders for injuries suffered while participating in or traveling to and from scheduled games and practice sessions that are part of sanctioned intercollegiate athletics.

There are numerous benefits available under this insurance coverage. The plan provides lifetime rehabilitation, medical and dental expenses and also provides lifetime monthly loss of earnings benefits, up to $2,000 per month. Under the plan, payments would begin twelve months after the athlete has sustained the injury. This insurance coverage also includes a college education benefit which would pay the cost of the students' remaining college expenses incurred in acquiring a degree. However, the payments are conditioned upon commencing his education within fifteen years after the injury has taken place and completing the degree within fifteen years after returning to school. Other benefits provided by the plan include:

> 1. A maximum amount of $125,000 during the first decade for remodeling or adapting living quarters or vehicles and $50,000 during the second decade.

2. A provision for nursing benefits at the individual's home and other daily living expenses up to the maximum of $50,000 per year.

3. Expenses of up to $30,000 to compensate for family counseling, training and travel related to the injury. This benefit is also intended to assist the parents of the injured student-athlete by compensating them for wages which they might have lost during the period following the injury.

4. Benefits up to $100,000 to assist the injured athlete because of inability to purchase medical insurance.

5. A $10,000 accidental-death benefit.[59]

In addition, the NCAA has approved a program which will make it easier for exceptional student-athletes to receive disability insurance coverage. This program is designed to cover student athletes with professional potential who are engaged in intercollegiate football, basketball or baseball at NCAA institutions. For example, the program will cover a football player if he is projected to be selected in the first two rounds of the next National Football League Draft. In the case of basketball and baseball players, they are included in the program if they are projected for selection in the first round drafts of the National Basketball Association or one of the major league baseball drafts.

This insurance coverage is intended to protect the exceptional student-athlete with respect to both permanent total disability and temporary total disability. The maximum coverage provided under this insurance is $2,700,000 in the case of basketball, $1,800,000 in the case of football and $900,000 in the case of baseball. There is also a $10,000 accidental death and dismemberment benefit.

Under this program, student-athletes who qualify are automatically approved for a loan at a very competitive interest rate. Loans are to be repaid when the student-athlete signs a professional contract or, if injury occurs, when the benefits under the policy are paid. If a professional contract is not signed or if benefits under the disability policy are never paid, the loan would be repaid when the insurance coverage no longer exists. The primary purpose of this program is to protect talented student-athletes against future loss of earnings as a professional, because of disabling injuries or sickness which occur while the student is participating in college athletics.

With respect to injuries to students-athletes who are not covered by either of the above programs, universities vary as to the type of insurance coverage provided. The University of Wisconsin-Madison, for example, self-insures its students-athletes. The University of Kansas attempts to use the insurance policies of the student-athletes' families. One problem with this method is that families of many student athletes may not have insurance, and even if they do, their policies may not cover athletics injuries. This is a subject which student athletes and their parents will want to discuss with the particular universities.

.... [Discussions of waiver and denial of rights to participate and possible Rehabilitation Act and ADA claims are omitted. — ed.].

IV. Injuries During Athletic Competition

A. *Injuries Caused by Athletes*

....

---

59. NCAA News, June 24, 1992, Volume 29, No. 25.

2. *Liability of College or University*, — Even if a player willfully, wantonly or recklessly injures a player on an opposing team and thereby becomes liable to the injured player, the university for whom the tortfeasor is playing, would not ordinarily be liable in tort for the injury (assuming there is no immunity). The potential liability of the university would turn on the question of agency and whether or not the player causing the injury was acting as an agent of the university at the time of the injury. One of the few cases which involved this question is *Hanson v. Kynast*.[138] During a lacrosse game, an Ohio State player, Allen, scored a goal whereafter he was body-checked from behind by Kynast of the Ashland team. When Allen fell to the ground, Kynast allegedly taunted him. At that point, Hanson, of Ohio State, wanting to protect his teammate Allen, ran up behind Kynast and grabbed Kynast in a bear hug. Kynast then twisted his body and flipped Hanson off of his back. Hanson's head hit the ground and the incident resulted in Hanson becoming a quadriplegic. Kynast was not on an athletic scholarship at Ashland, and he used his own equipment when playing lacrosse. The university did not request or require him to play. He received no compensation of any kind for playing. In *Hanson*, the plaintiff argued that a principal-agent relationship existed between Kynast and Ashland University because of the control that the lacrosse coach had over Kynast and because beneficial publicity resulted to Ashland because of Kynast's participation on the lacrosse team.

The court in *Hanson* concluded that lacrosse was part of the total educational experience offered by Ashland University to its students and that when students decided to attend Ashland and accept the various activities offered by the university, a contractual arrangement between students and the university arose. The court noted that one of the key factors in finding an agency relationship is whether or not the services in question were performed in the course of the principal's business. In this case, said the court, the business of the university is educating students, and Kynast, by playing lacrosse, was not participating in that business. He was merely participating in an activity offered by the university. Other factors relied on by the court to show that no agency relationship existed were the fact that Kynast was not compensated by the university and that the university did not supply any equipment required for Kynast's performance. The control exercised by the lacrosse coach was held to be incidental to the educational experience of playing lacrosse which Kynast participated in on a voluntary basis. It was merely a form of guidance necessary to see that the students had a proper chance to benefit from the opportunity to play on the lacrosse team. The direction offered by the coach did not amount to the control required to establish an agency relationship. In addition, lacrosse was not an income producing sport and Kynast's participation in lacrosse was not for the purpose of accomplishing an objective for the university—it was simply part of the total educational experience of attending the university. There also was no evidence that Ashland got any benefit from the publicity associated with its lacrosse team. For these reasons, the court held that the doctrine of respondeat superior was not applicable.

. . . .

Charles Edwin Brown, Jr. v. Neil Day,[159] was a similar case. In *Charles Edwin Brown, Jr.*, Brown was a member of the Wilmington College soccer team, and was

---

138. 494 N.E.2d 1091 (Ohio 1986).
159. 588 N.E.2d 973 (Ohio 1990).

injured by Day who ran up behind him toward the end of the game and knocked him to the ground. Subsequently, Brown sued Tiffin University alleging that its coaches were negligent in their supervision of Day and that the university was negligent in its supervision of its sports program. The allegation pivoted on the fact that the university and its coach knew of Day's propensity for violence but, nevertheless, allowed him to play. In *Charles Edwin Brown, Jr.,* the court referred to the concurring opinion of Judge Holmes in *Hanson* which suggested that universities can be liable where they allow a student with a known propensity for violence to play. But in *Charles Edwin Brown, Jr.,* although the allegation was made of negligent supervision for letting Day play when it was known that he had a propensity for violence, there was no evidence presented that Day had ever committed similar violent acts in previous soccer games. Although there was evidence of prior unsportsmanlike conduct, that was held not to rise to the level of a propensity for violence.

It seems that the court in *Townsend v. State of California*[165] was not aware of the *Hanson* case when it reached its decision. Townsend was a case which involved a basketball game between San Jose State University and U.C.L.A. in which a San Jose player struck a U.C.L.A. player with his fists causing physical injury. An argument was made in that case that because intercollegiate athletics are "big business," the athletes should be considered as employees or agents of their universities under the doctrine of respondeat superior. The statutory law in California provided that a public entity is liable for injuries caused by an employee acting within the scope of employment. In *Townsend*, the court referred to *Van Horn v. Industrial Acc. Com.,*[169] which involved a college football player who was killed in a plane crash while traveling with the team. He had been receiving financial assistance from a fund created by a private booster club as well as from the university, and his widow was successful in getting workers' compensation benefits because there was a finding that the deceased had a contract of employment with the university. But in *Van Horn*, the court indicated that athletic scholarships alone do not make a student-athlete an employee. If that were the case, students who never agreed to be employees would be denied a right to sue for damages. After the *Van Horn* case, the California legislature amended the Labor Code to exclude from the definition of an employee any student participating in amateur athletics as part of a university program even though a recipient of a scholarship, travel expenses, meals, equipment, uniforms or other benefits customarily given to college athletes.

In *Townsend*, the court concluded that college athletic programs are not a "business" and that public policy prohibits exposing universities to suits arising out of athletic injuries because of the great financial burden such suits would place on the funds available in the state for educational purposes. *Townsend* is in line with the concurring opinion in *Hanson* in finding that college athletes are not ordinarily in an employment relationship. This seems to be a sound and realistic approach because universities are educational institutions, and their athletic programs are a part of the total educational experience in which students may participate. A university does not have the kind of control over athletes which an employer ordinarily has over employees. Furthermore, the athletes are not engaged in the pursuit of business activities for the university. Most of the teams at a uni-

---

165. 191 Cal. App.3d 1530 (1987).
169. 219 Cal. App.2d 457 (1963).

versity are a financial drain on the school and do not produce any revenue. In most cases, only the football and basketball teams produce revenue. At many schools, even those programs are not financially successful. Therefore, it seems clear that the primary purpose of the institution in running its intercollegiate athletic program is not to produce revenue but to enhance the school's overall educational activity.

. . . .

B. The Supervision of Athletes — Role of the University

1. Activities—. . . .

. . . .

Where there is negligent supervision by the employees of a university, or if the university is negligent in hiring or retaining incompetent employees to supervise athletic activities, the university can be held liable under the doctrine of respondeat superior. Schools are becoming more sensitive to the need to hire qualified athletic supervisors. Some high schools are hiring only college-educated trainers who are certified by the National Athletic Trainers Association, and players and coaches are being instructed on how to recognize injuries and what to do about them. Players are often carefully instructed with respect to the rules to be followed. Also, equipment is being carefully assigned and checked for fit and proper use. If an instructor requests that a student perform some particular physical or athletic activity with which the student is unfamiliar and which has a risk of injury, the school could be held liable for a failure of the instructor to properly instruct the student as to the correct procedure for safely performing the activity.

. . . .

2. Equipment.—Students participating in athletic activities sponsored by the university should be furnished with proper equipment for use in those activities. The equipment should be maintained properly and periodically checked to determine its condition. No one should be permitted to practice or play who does not have proper equipment. In *Lowe v. Texas Tech University*, 540 S.W.2d 297 (1976), [sic] a varsity football player alleged that he suffered a knee injury because he had been furnished equipment, uniforms and pads which were improper or otherwise defective. In Texas, immunity under the Texas Tort Claims Act was waived where the injury arose from some condition or some use of tangible property, and the court in *Lowe* held that the allegations stated a case within the statutory waiver of immunity under the statute.

Failure to periodically inspect athletic equipment can lead to injuries and possible liability. In *Tiemann v. Independent School District 6740*,[202] the plaintiff was injured when she vaulted over a vaulting horse in physical education class. The handles on the horse had been removed leaving two half-inch diameter holes on the surface of the horse. The plaintiff caught a finger in one of the holes as she vaulted over the horse and was injured when she fell on the wooden floor. The primary issue was whether the evidence was sufficient to permit the case to go to the jury without any expert testimony being offered. The court indicated that there is no question as to the standard of care owed. The court in *Tieman* stated that: "A school owes a duty to its students to use reasonable care to inspect and

---

202. 331 N.W.2d 250 (Sup. Ct. of Minn. 1983).

maintain its premises and equipment and to protect its students from an unreasonable risk of harm."[203] It held that expert testimony was not necessary, because a lay jury was capable of determining whether a teacher using ordinary care would permit students to use a horse having two holes on its surface.

Of course, there is no duty to provide equipment to protect an athlete from risks of which all athletes are aware and which commonly are part of the sport. There also are situations where equipment provides a certain amount of risk but also provides a certain amount of safety. In *Johnson v. Municipal University of Omaha*,[205] a wooden box was placed beneath pole vault standards for support, and the plaintiff was injured while pole vaulting when he fell on the box. There was substantial testimony that the wooden box served a useful purpose, and even though there was some risk involved in using the box, the risk did not outweigh the usefulness of the box, and the court held that the evidence did not present a question for the jury.

3. *Premises.*—If the facilities provided are such that an obstruction is present on the playing field which, although visible to the players, might not be noticed in the excitement of competition, the institution can be held liable. That was the result reached in a case where a student at State Teachers College was playing in a baseball game and ran into a metal flagpole while chasing a fly ball.[208] The same result was reached in a case where a game of frisbee was being played on a gymnasium court between two college teams. The game was not an official game of the two schools, and it seems that the janitor of the school in question admitted the students to the gym. One of the walls, which was five to eight feet from one of the goal lines, had glass doors in the center of it. One of the players ran into the glass doors and lacerated his arm. The court held that the jury could have concluded that the defendant should reasonably have foreseen the plaintiff's presence in the gym, and the jury could find that the defendant had a duty to protect users of the gym from the dangers of the glass doors. Furthermore, the jury could find that this breach of duty was the proximate cause of the accident.

. . . .

Cathy J. Jones, College Athletes: Illness or Injury and the Decision to Return to Play
40 Buffalo Law Review. 113 (1992)*

I. INTRODUCTION

On March 4, 1990, Hank Gathers, one of the nation's premier college basketball players, collapsed during an intercollegiate conference tournament game. He was pronounced dead two hours later. The cause of death was given as "cardiomyopathy, a heart muscle disorder of unknown cause that damaged both lower heart chambers, or ventricles."

---

203. Kingsley v. Independent School District No. 2, Hill City, 312 Minn. 572 (1977).
205. 187 Neb. 24 (1971).
208. Scott v. State of New York, 158 N.Y.S.2d 617 (Ct. Cl. 1956).

Gathers' fatal collapse was not the first indication of his heart disease. He had fainted during a game on December 9, 1989. Following the earlier collapse, Gathers was admitted to a hospital where he underwent diagnostic testing. He was diagnosed as having exercise-induced ventricular tachycardia. He was placed on 240 milligrams per day of propranolol (also known as inderal), a standard cardiac drug, and on December 21, 1989, was cleared to return to basketball by an internal medicine specialist at the hospital where his condition had been diagnosed.

What transpired after Gathers' December diagnosis and treatment is disputed. Following an autopsy which showed that at the time of his death Gathers had only 26 nanograms of propranolol per milliliter in his blood, the Medical Examiner concluded that the amount was less than a therapeutic dose. This conclusion gave rise to the speculation that Gathers had not been taking the medication, or at least had not been taking it in therapeutic amounts, near the time of his death. There is apparently no dispute that the amount of propranolol Gathers was taking had been reduced a number of times from the initial dosage of 240 milligrams per day to 120 milligrams per day and finally to 80 milligrams per day at the time of his death. There *is* dispute over whether Gathers, himself, or Paul Westhead, his coach at Loyola Marymount, requested the reduction.

On March 7, 1990, the *Los Angeles Times* reported that Gathers had failed to keep an appointment for a treadmill stress test the week before he died and that he was suspected of not taking his medication. An unidentified cardiologist quoted by the *Los Angeles Times* also reported that Gathers had been advised not to play basketball any longer.

A $32.5 million lawsuit filed by Gathers' family against Westhead and 12 other Loyola Marymount University officials and doctors, and a subsequent suit filed on behalf of Gathers' son, alleged, among other things, that Gathers was not told his heart condition was potentially fatal and that the propranolol was repeatedly decreased at the request of Westhead, who believed the medication was causing Gathers to perform below his potential. Furthermore, the Gathers' family attorney, Dr. Bruce G. Fagel, has asserted that Gathers did not miss a treadmill stress test and that family members had seen him taking his medication.

Hank Gathers represents only one of a number of college athletes who have been injured or have died while engaging in athletic contests while "knowing" of preexisting physical conditions which could lead to serious injury or death.

.... [Discussion of incidents involving athletes, Tony Penny, Marc Buoniconti, Mark Tingstad and Mark Seay is omitted. — ed.].

While the catastrophic results experienced or potentially experienced by these five athletes are fortunately not typical of the experiences of most college athletes, the examples share a common theme that is potentially relevant to every college athlete. All five had been diagnosed as having a preexisting medical condition that could subject them to serious injury or death if they continued to pursue their athletic careers, and all five wanted to continue their careers. All five were ultimately cleared, by physicians and by university officials, to return to play. Two of the five died while engaging in their chosen sports activities (albeit one, Penny, while he was no longer a student); two were paralyzed, one permanently. At least two, Gathers and Penny, had high hopes of lucrative professional careers following their college playing days. All, by standard legal definitions, were adults when they chose to continue playing their sports. Two, Penny and Seay, sued those whom they believed responsible *for trying to prevent them from returning* to athletics. Two, the representatives of Gathers' family and Buoniconti, sued the universities and team physicians following their catastrophes alleging, among other things, *that they should not have been cleared to play.*

Shortly before Hank Gathers died, I had completed work on an article in which I examined the doctrine of informed consent to medical treatment, both in its theory and its practice. In that article, I had concluded that even though the law claims to believe in patient autonomy and self-determination and purports to protect patients' decision-making powers in the context of medical care, neither law nor medicine does so. Rather, once mandating that physicians make certain disclosures to patients, the law then does little or nothing to require or even encourage health care providers to ensure that their patients understand the information disclosed; similarly, the law neither requires nor encourages patients to make decisions concerning their health care. I rejected the reasons given by health care providers in support of their beliefs that patients are unable or unwilling to make such decisions. I argued that the doctrine of informed consent in the context of medical treatment is a goal worth pursuing and I suggested a number of ways in which that goal might be furthered. Specifically, I proposed that health care providers take steps to ensure that their patients understand the information necessary to make decisions and also that patients be encouraged to make and be supported in making those decisions. In addition to suggesting that patients make those decisions, I also proposed that they be held responsible for those decisions, leaving patients the right to sue health care providers for medical malpractice only if the providers were actually negligent in making the required disclosures or in performing the agreed upon diagnostic or therapeutic procedures. I believed my ideas, although certainly subject to debate, were worth trying in the context of competent adult patients seeking medical treatment.

And then Hank Gathers died. I began to wonder if my ideas about the theory and practice of the doctrine of informed consent to medical treatment, which I previously thought applicable to all competent adults, would hold up in the context of college athletics. College athletes, while legally adults, are nevertheless quite young. That youth may contribute not only to an immature ability to make decisions, but also to feelings of immortality and invincibility—that is, even if the athletes' conditions could result in dire consequences to someone else, the athletes believe those consequences could not happen to them because they are young and strong. Furthermore, the reports of pressures imposed on college athletes—to perform and to win—by coaches, other students and teammates, alumni/ae, university officials, and themselves are legion.

I wondered, therefore, whether my theory now must be revised in the context of college athletes. Maybe athletes, because of their youth, their strength, their (in)ability to resist certain pressures, could not understand the information presented to them and/or could not voluntarily, as that word is to be understood in the informed consent context, make decisions concerning their own medical care and their athletic careers.

If college athletes cannot make such decisions, however, other questions arise. Who should be delegated the responsibility for making those decisions? And who should bear the responsibility if an athlete who is cleared to return to play is subsequently injured or dies for reasons attributed to the medical condition and the athletic activity? If athletes are not cleared to play, may they sue—the physician, the coach, the university—and if so, what relief would they request and on what theories would their requests be based?

.... [A general discussion of the law of informed consent is omitted. — ed.].

IV. COLLEGE ATHLETES AND DECISIONMAKING

A. *The Context of the Decision*

Decisions concerning the diagnosis and medical treatment of college athletes may arise in at least three specific contexts: preparticipation physical examinations (occurring either before play begins or before a previously injured or ill player is authorized to return to play), therapeutic treatment once a player has become ill or has been injured, and administration of drugs.

1. *Diagnosis and Treatment* The purpose of the physical examination administered to athletes prior to their initial participation in athletic activities is to determine whether they are fit to withstand the physical challenges of the sport. The NCAA's policy concerning such examinations states: "Before student-athletes accept the rigors of any organized sport, their health status should be evaluated. Such an examination should determine whether the student-athlete is prepared to engage in a particular sport."[118] The NCAA's *Sports Medicine Handbook* describes procedures relating to both medical evaluation of student athletes and maintenance of the athletes' medical records:

> 1. A preparticipation medical evaluation should be required upon a student-athlete's initial entrance into the institution's intercollegiate athletics program. This *initial evaluation* should include a review of the student-athlete's health history and a relevant physical exam.
>
> 2. Medical records should be maintained during the student-athlete's collegiate career and should include:
>
> a.   A record of injuries and illnesses, whether sustained during the competitive season or the off-season;
>
> b.   Referrals for consultation or treatment;
>
> c.   Subsequent care and clearances, and
>
> d.   A completed yearly health status questionnaire.
>
> 3. An exit examination or evaluation at the conclusion of the student-athlete's participation in a particular sport at that institution is also recommended. Providing there is a continuous awareness of the health status of the student-athlete, the traditional annual preparticipation physical examination of all student-athletes is not believed to be necessary.[119]

There is little uniformity in the performance of preparticipation or return to play physicals. While major universities may have full time "sports physicians" on their staffs, many colleges and universities rely on university physicians in general or physicians from the community in which the college is located. Few team physicians are truly "experts" in "sports medicine." Many are internists or family practitioners. The thoroughness of the physical examination, itself, also varies.

---

118. NCAA Sports Medicine Handbook, *supra* note 45, Policy No. 1, § 1.
119. *Id.*, Policy No. 2, § 3.

The American Medical Association recommends that preparticipation physicals include a urinalysis, hemoglobin test, tuberculin test, and chest x-ray, the latter to detect cardiac problems or pulmonary disease. While certainly an examining physician (or a physician's assistant) would check a student athlete's heart beat and blood pressure, and may generally screen the athlete's vision, hearing, and balance, time and expense make unlikely the performing of more complicated procedures. For the young, apparently healthy athlete who reports no prior health problems, preexisting medical conditions, or injuries, such a general preparticipation physical examination would probably be reasonable under the circumstances. If, of course, the athlete does report a preexisting condition or if the general physical uncovers a potential problem, for example, an irregular heartbeat, the physician would be under a duty to advise the athlete of the potential problem, to perform a more complete examination relative to the condition or refer the athlete to an appropriate specialist who could perform such an examination, and to refuse to clear the athlete for play until such an examination had been performed and the athlete informed of the results.

Examinations following illness or injury tend to raise more complex issues. Because the athlete has been ill or injured, the physician is on notice that a general examination may not be sufficient before clearing the athlete to return to play. If, for example, an athlete has suffered a cervical injury, examination and clearance by an orthopedist and/or a neurologist may be in order. Similarly, if an athlete has been diagnosed as having a cardiac related disorder, examination and clearance by a cardiologist should be required.

Whatever the stage at which the physical is performed, the guiding principle in determining a school's or a physician's liability should be whether the examination and subsequent disclosure of information was reasonable under the circumstances. Accidents will happen notwithstanding the degree of care used. But if an athlete shows signs of illness or injury, a different type of examination may be mandated than that required for an apparently healthy athlete with no prior history of illness or injury.

. . . .

2. *Decision to Play.* . . . [Discussion of assumption of the risk and waiver is omitted. — ed.]

. . . .

Issues relating to informing adequately a college athlete about medical care and a subsequent return to play following illness or injury should be no different from the informed consent issues relevant to any competent adult patient agreeing to undergo diagnosis and treatment and then returning to life's activities. That is not to say that there are no problems with transmission and comprehension of the necessary information. The information may be complex; athletes, just as patients, will be of varying degrees of intelligence and they may be overcome by anxiety or feelings of denial that prevent them from "hearing" or remembering the information conveyed.

Just as with medical patients, however, there are ways to improve the athlete's comprehension of information. For example, the team physician or athletic representative could provide information in writing as well as orally concerning medical conditions, treatments, risks, and alternatives, as well as information associated with return to play decisions. Conversations between physicians or school officials and athletes could be tape recorded so the athlete could hear as many

times as necessary the information and the warnings. Physicians or college officials could test an athlete's comprehension of the information provided by requiring the athletes to write in their own words what they understand the information
conveyed to mean. Athletes could be accompanied during such conferences with
physicians or school officials by another adult of their choice who may help them
frame questions or later help to refresh their recollections concerning the information provided. Just as with medical patients in general, none of these suggestions
is guaranteed to insure that the athlete knows and understands all the information
necessary for informed decisionmaking about medical treatment and return to
play. In all probability, however, a combination of these techniques will enable the
athlete to comprehend the information better than will a general conversation
with a physician or school official and an all-purpose, catch-all waiver form.

Equally problematic to the question of whether athletes know and appreciate
the information concerning medical treatment and return to play is whether, because of age and pressures from within and without, they can voluntarily choose
to accept the risks associated with treatment and play.

B. *The Decisionmaker: Athlete or Surrogate?*

1. *The Argument for the Athlete as Decisionmaker* Unlike prior times when the
doctrine of *in loco parentis* was one of the principles regulating the college/stu-
dent relationship, educational institutions and society in general, with the support
of the law, regard college-age students as adults with the same rights and responsibilities that attend all adults. College students or college-age students are entitled
to vote, marry, enlist in the military, and engage in many other "adult" activities
without the consent of a parent or guardian. Outside the context of college athletics, college-age students are certainly accorded the status of competent adults in
terms of making health care decisions. The treatment accorded college students,
including athletes, in these contexts supports the position that college athletes
should be treated as competent adults in terms of decisions relating to medical
treatment and return to play. That is not, however, the only reason for doing so.

One of the goals of the educational process is to help the student mature into a
responsible person who will make positive contributions to society. To authorize
someone other than the athlete to make decisions in the medical care and return
to play context would impact adversely on the student's autonomy. As the *Baldwin v. Zoradi* Court said, in the context of refusing to impose duties on educational institutions in relation to students and alcohol, infringing on the students'
autonomy would not be "in the best interests of society.... The transfer of prerogatives and rights from college administrators to the students is salubrious when
seen in the context of a proper goal of postsecondary education—the maturation
of the students. Only by giving them responsibilities can students grow into responsible adulthood."[171]

At least two courts have held in the context of students with physical disabilities that the students or the students and their parents are the appropriate decisionmakers when deciding whether the students should be permitted to engage in
contact sports.[172] In *Wright v. Columbia University*, the court entered a temporary

---

171. Baldwin v. Zoradi, 176 Cal. Rptr. at 818.
172. Wright v. Columbia Univ., 520 F. Supp. 789 (E.D. Pa. 1981); Poole v. South Plainfield Bd. of Educ., 490 F. Supp. 948 (D.N.J. 1980).

restraining order allowing a student with sight in only one eye to play college football. In doing so, the court stated that Wright not only had presented expert evidence that football did not pose a substantial risk of injury to his sight, but also he had testified that he seriously considered and appreciated the risks incident to playing football with impaired vision and he willingly accepted those risks. The court found Wright, who had been an outstanding high school athlete despite his impaired vision, to be mature and capable. The court also found that Wright and his parents were willing to release Columbia from any liability should he suffer injury to his sight while playing football and that the Columbia coaching staff supported his request to play. While calling Columbia's concern for the student's sight "laudable," the court nevertheless found that the results of such concern were inconsistent with the protection afforded Wright by Section 504 of the Rehabilitation Act.

Poole v. South Plainfield Board of Education involved a former high school student with only one kidney who sued for damages because he had been denied the opportunity to take part in the school's interscholastic wrestling program. At the time Poole wanted to wrestle, he clearly was a minor and his parents were the primary decisionmakers for such matters. The court found that Poole's decision to wrestle was protected by Section 504. Even though injury to the healthy kidney would have lead to "grave consequences," the court said, so might other injuries which could have affected Poole or any other member of the wrestling team. As did the student and his parents in *Wright*, Poole and his parents had consulted experts—their family doctor, a specialist in sports medicine, and the wrestling coach at Lehigh University, a traditional wrestling powerhouse—about the types and frequencies of injuries encountered by wrestlers. Poole's parents had also offered to waive any potential liability of the school district should their son be injured wrestling. In characterizing the rights and responsibilities of the parties in *Poole*, the court said:

> This is a young man who, with his parents' support and approval, wishes to live an active life despite a congenital defect. The Board's responsibility is to see that he does not pursue this course in a foolish manner. They therefore have a duty to alert Richard and his parents to the dangers involved and to require them to deal with the matter rationally.
>
> ....
>
> Whatever duty the Board may have had towards Richard was satisfied once it became clear that the Pooles knew of the danger involved and rationally reached a decision to encourage their son's participation in interscholastic wrestling.[183]

There are strong arguments, then, for allowing athletes to make their own decisions concerning medical treatment and return to play. In almost all other contexts they are treated as adults, with the right to make decisions about the most important issues affecting their lives. Furthermore, the exercising of such rights and responsibilities is something that society wants not only to protect but also to encourage. The question remains, however, whether the pressures upon college athletes are so great that the law should carve out an exception to their autonomy. That is, should the law say that within the narrow context of decisions relating to some or all illnesses or injuries and to decisions relating to return to play follow-

---

183. *Id.* at 954.

ing such illness or injury, the athlete should be declared incompetent to make such decisions and a surrogate named to make those decisions on the athlete's behalf?

2. *The Argument for a Surrogate Decisionmaker* One legitimate reason exists for appointing a surrogate to make decisions for college athletes concerning medical treatment and return to play. The pressures on college athletes, especially those in revenue producing sports at Division I universities, are so great that any decision the athlete makes must be suspect as not being truly voluntary. The pressures on the athlete come from within and from without.

It is not uncommon for athletes to "play hurt." Some do it for the love of the game. Others because "much of [the] athlete's life has been dedicated to fulfilling an athletic dream" or perhaps a more personal dream....

....

Athletes themselves admit, frequently after suffering injury, that they believed themselves to be invincible and that someone else should have protected them from their own decisions....

....

In addition to athletes' feelings of invincibility which may lead them to play hurt or to return to play following injury, media attention may encourage them to do so, as well....

....

If personal dreams, feelings of invincibility, and media attention are not enough to give highly rated college athletes incentive to return to play too soon or to return when they never should because of serious illness or injury, the lure of professional sports contracts is an incentive. Those college football and basketball players drafted by professional teams could secure contracts paying them millions of dollars over a several year period....

....

All of the internal pressures affecting athletes' desire — or need — to play while hurt can only be exacerbated by the pressures from outside sources. Successful revenue producing athletic programs are important to universities as a whole. Colleges and universities earn huge sums based upon post season tournament play. And, television coverage has become an increasingly important source of college sports revenue.... The more successful a school's football or basketball program, the more television exposure the team receives and, accordingly, the more money it makes. A recent report indicated that the nation's major college football conferences, inspired by contracts such as that between Notre Dame and NBC, are "raiding" other conferences and attempting to draw nonconference schools into "super-conferences," giving those conferences and those schools a larger network television audience and more television revenue. Widespread television coverage also enhances an institution's ability to recruit prized high school athletes.

Coaches, individually, may pressure their star athletes to "play hurt" or to return to play too soon following illness or injury. Coaches, too, feel pressure from their institutions to develop highly successful (in terms of won-loss record) revenue producing sports programs, and many reap great personal benefits from these programs.

Finally, college athletes — and their parents — may be subject to pressure from athletic "boosters...."

....

The "trickle down" effect as it affects college athletes is real: colleges pressure coaches to produce winning programs, athletes to perform, doctors to heal injuries quickly; coaches pressure athletes and doctors; other players, wanting their teams to be successful, pressure peers to "play hurt"; injured players, themselves, apprehensive that they will lose their spot in the starting lineup or their stage to perform for the professional scouts, play when hurt and urge physicians to do whatever is necessary to help them perform. "It is...debatable as to whether or not the usual disciplinary authority of the coach, the pressure of school spirit, the probable odium attached to a refusal to play, both by...fellow-players and... school mates, might not...rob" an athlete of volition in terms of decisions relating to return to play after illness or injury.

Perhaps a physician can disclose to an athlete relevant information about the athlete's medical condition, suggested treatment, and the benefits, risks, and alternatives, not only to the proposed treatment but also to a return to play. Perhaps, too, an athlete can comprehend that information and appreciate the risks involved in returning to play in a manner sufficient to make an informed decision. Still, the concern is legitimate that the pressures on the athlete are so great that the "voluntariness" of any decision to return to play is suspect. In resolving the question, however, of whether a surrogate would be a better decisionmaker than an athlete, even given the problems with the athlete as decisionmaker, it is important to consider the advantages and disadvantages attached to those who could serve as a surrogate and the standards by which a surrogate would decide whether the athlete could return to play.

C. The Surrogate as Decisionmaker

1. *Who Should Be the Surrogate?* The logical choices of a surrogate decisionmaker for a college athlete would be the athlete's parent(s), coach, physician, or a specially appointed "athlete advocate."

An athlete's parents or guardians would clearly be the most obvious choice to act as surrogate decisionmaker in terms of health care decisions and return to play. In most instances they know their children and have their children's best interests in mind more than any other person. Throughout the child's life, the parents have acted as surrogate decisionmakers so it is only natural that they continue to do so. The difficulty, of course, with allowing parents to act as surrogate decisionmakers is that they might vicariously be affected by some of the same pressures affecting the athlete — for example, the desire to see the child succeed or the lure of financial remuneration if the child is a professional prospect. Once again, then, the decision may not be entirely "voluntary," even if made by the athletes' parents.

Coaches are candidates to be substitute decisionmakers because they, too, usually know their athletes well and have the athletes' best interests at heart. Some coaches and athletes have almost a parent-child relationship. Coaches are inappropriate as substitute decisionmakers, however, because of the inherent conflict of interest present when they need their star athletes to play and play at peak performance in order to enhance the team's chances of winning and, accordingly, the coach's reputation and all that is associated with that reputation.

The third logical substitute decisionmaker would be the physician treating the athlete. Despite the physician's ethical obligations in treating athletes as patients, several problems are present when the physician is the surrogate decisionmaker. The first is the physician's status and his or her relationship with the athlete.

While in theory the physician has a physician-patient relationship with the athlete, as with any other patient, the realities of the physician's employment situation may indicate otherwise. Generally, the athlete has not chosen any particular physician. Either the physician is an employee of the college or university or more likely, especially for smaller institutions, the physician is an independent contractor hired for a limited time to perform preparticipation physicals, attend home games, and accept referrals. This type of "as needed" relationship may not in many instances provide physicians with the information — medical or otherwise — they may acquire and use in making recommendations for patients when they work with patients on a long term basis. And, since few team physicians are "sports medicine specialists," they may not understand the psychology of the athlete "determined to play at all costs."

A second problem which may arise were the physician to be the surrogate decisionmaker is the conflict of interest between the college or university which pays the physician's fee and the athlete receiving the care. College or university officials through, for example, coaches, athletic directors, or trainers, could pressure physicians to prescribe specific treatments or return athletes to play before they are ready because they want their star athletes in action in order to improve the team's performance and, accordingly, the school's reputation and revenue producing opportunities. Physicians are subject to pressures from others — families, boosters, and athletes, themselves, — to treat athletes quickly and return them to play. And, physicians, themselves, are often fans of the team and want the team to succeed.

Overall, then, despite their professional obligations to their patients, team physicians may not know the athletes well, may have at least the appearance of divided loyalties between those who pay their salaries and those whom they serve, and may be subject to pressures from a number of sources, including the patients, to treat athletes and return them to play expediently, rather than effectively.

One powerful incentive for the physician *not* to treat the athlete expediently rather than effectively would, of course, be the threat of a malpractice action against the physician if the athlete were to suffer subsequent injury or illness which could be connected to the physician's treatment of the athlete. That incentive could, however, cause the physician to treat the athlete too conservatively or to make decisions concerning return to play based on fear of liability rather than on the medical condition, capabilities, and best interests of the athlete. The team physician does not appear to be an appropriate substitute decisionmaker.

The final possible substitute decisionmaker would be an "athlete advocate" employed by the university to work with athletes and to help protect their interests. In theory, the concept of the advocate sounds good. In the health care and return to play context, the advocate could help athletes understand their conditions and the various risks, benefits, and alternatives associated with treatment and return to play. The advocate could gather all information relevant to the decisions being made — medical information concerning the athlete's condition and proposed treatment, the risks of a return to play, the athlete's wishes — and could make the decision which would best serve the athlete's interests.

In reality, however, the advocate is not necessarily any better equipped or any less pressured than the athletes themselves, or any of the other potential surrogates. No one knows the athlete as well as the athlete does. No one understands the medical information as well as the physician. Although the advocate, by definition, must work with athletes free from pressures imposed by the employer (the university) or by any of the university's employees (coaches, athletic directors or trainers), academic advisors or tutors in relatively the same position have been pressured or punished in the past for causing athletes to become ineligible for play.

Ideally, any of these persons chosen as a surrogate decisionmaker for ill or injured athletes would enter into a consultative process with the others. Parents, coaches, physicians, advocates, all with the same theoretical goal of serving the athlete's best interests, should share information and concerns in an attempt to reach the most appropriate result. They should also, of course, consult with the athlete.

Assuming that a surrogate is appointed to make decisions for the athlete concerning medical care and return to play, by what standard should the surrogate be guided?

2. *What Should Be the Standard?* Surrogate decisionmakers have traditionally been authorized to apply one of two standards, one subjective, the other objective, in making decisions for those unable to make decisions for themselves. Both standards are problematic when applied to the college athlete presumed competent for every decisionmaking scenario except that concerning medical treatment and return to play.

A subjective, substituted judgment standard is frequently applied in surrogate decisionmaking situations, particularly if there is evidence of the decision the incompetent would make if competent to decide. In fact, the purpose behind the substituted judgment standard is to effectuate the decision the incompetent would have made if competent. Factors to be considered by the substitute decisionmaker include the incompetent's preferences (expressed while competent) concerning the decision to be made; the incompetent's religious beliefs; the impact of any decision on the incompetent's family; the probability of adverse side effects of any treatment chosen; the consequences if a decision is made to decline treatment (or return to play); the prognosis with a particular treatment (or a decision to return to play).

These factors could certainly all be ascertained and weighed in the surrogate's attempt to decide what treatment and play decisions the athlete would make if competent to do so, but such a weighing process would be unnecessary. Most instances of incompetency in which the substituted judgment approach has been followed have involved cases in which incompetents were either physically or mentallyincapable of communicating their preferences to the surrogates. In the case of the college athlete that is clearly not true. The athletes are capable of expressing their precise wishes concerning return to play. It is rather because *we do not trust* the athlete's decisionmaking abilities that we have turned to a surrogate decisionmaker. In that case, perhaps an objective, reasonable person approach to substitute decisionmaking would be appropriate.

The purpose behind the objective substitute decisionmaking standard is to serve the best interests of the incompetent, based not on what the incompetent would have wanted, but rather on what the reasonable person acting under the same or similar circumstances would have chosen. The objective approach is basically a weighing of the benefits and burdens associated with the various alternatives available to the decisionmaker. Applying the best interests standard to the college athlete is problematic, however, because the objective standard is generally held to be appropriate where the surrogate is unable to determine what the incompetent's preferences would have been. That is clearly not the case with college athletes who can tell surrogates exactly what they want. The objective standard is further problematic in instances where the "incompetent's" wishes are known. The purpose behind substitute decisionmaking is, in part, to recognize that incompetents, like those who are competent, have rights of self-determination and autonomy that deserve to be exercised, by others, if not by the person himself or herself. There is something incongruous about saying we will allow a substitute decisionmaker to exercise a college athlete's right of self-determination and then ignoring the express wishes of the athlete.

The true difficulty with college athletes and decisionmaking is, of course, not that the athletes are incompetent, but that we do not trust the decision they might make. In the health care context, health care providers and institutions frequently have disagreed with decisions that competent adults have made. Traditionally, the law has recognized four "compelling state interests" that could be advanced against competent adults' decisions concerning their own medical care: preserving life, preventing suicide, protecting the interests of innocent third parties, and preserving the integrity of the medical profession. With the exception of protecting the interests of innocent third parties, generally minor children who will be left dependent if their parent or guardian should die, the courts have come to give precedence to the rights of competent adults to make decisions concerning their own bodies and their own health care, even if such decisions would result in death. Those decisions, however, might be distinguishable from the situation of the relatively healthy college athlete. In those cases where courts have found a competent adult's medical treatment decision sufficiently important to override the state's or the medical profession's interest in preserving life, the patients have generally been near death or suffering from terminal or intolerable physical conditions. The continued exceptions to these decisions, however, are the cases in which patients who are Jehovah's Witnesses refuse blood transfusions. There, even though the patients are often not suffering from terminal or intolerable conditions, the courts have supported the patients' wishes to decline treatment, even in the face of death.

One of the questions for the law, then, will be to determine whether the state's overriding interest in the preservation of life would prohibit a college athlete from effectuating a decision which could lead to permanent injury or death, or whether the athlete cases will be treated similarly to the Jehovah's Witnesses cases in which the competent adult's decision will be respected notwithstanding the possible outcome of the decision.

The final question in relation to the surrogate decisionmaker is whether the surrogate should be held responsible if the athlete is injured subsequent to the surrogate's decision to allow the athlete to return to play.

3. *Liability of the Surrogate* Three possibilities exist for imposing liability on the surrogate if a medical treatment or return to play decision results in subsequent injury to the athlete: the surrogate could be immune from liability for injuries resulting from any decision; the surrogate could be held strictly liable for any such injuries; or the surrogate could be judged by an objective standard and be held liable for subsequent injuries only if he or she failed to exercise reasonable care in making the decision.

While a decision to hold a surrogate immune from liability could induce more persons to be willing to be surrogates and could facilitate their decisionmaking, immunity may remove the incentive necessary to exercise great care in making the decision. While we would hope that the surrogate, regardless of the standard employed to make the decision, would act only in the best interests of the athlete, immunity from liability may make the outside pressures from the athlete, the athlete's family, the college or university and its employees and supporters, harder to resist.

Strict liability, of course, raises the opposite problem. If a surrogate were to be held liable for subsequent injury to an athlete even though the surrogate used all due care in making the decision, few persons would choose to be surrogates and those who did might be very reluctant ever to authorize an athlete to return to play. The logical solution to the question of surrogate liability, then, would be to hold the surrogate to a reasonable person standard. That standard would encourage a surrogate to use care in gathering information concerning the athlete's medical condition, athletic activities, and other matters relevant to the decision, in discussing that information in a thoughtful manner with others — parents, school officials, and the athlete — who could aid in the decisionmaking process, and in reaching a decision that would serve the athlete's health and athletic interest. The standard would not be so strict, however, that it would discourage the surrogate from ever authorizing the athlete to return to play.

Before offering a proposal to answer the questions of who should be the ultimate decisionmaker when an ill or injured athlete needs medical treatment and wants to return to play, and under what circumstances, if any, should an athlete be denied the opportunity to compete, I will address the issue of the athlete's recourse if he or she or the surrogate decides that a return to play is appropriate and the college or university says "No."

....[Discussion of the statutory right to participate via the Rehabilitation Act and the ADA is omitted. — ed.].

---

3. Liability of Medical Personnel

Matthew Mitten, Team Physicians and Competitive Athletes: Allocating Legal Responsibility for Athletic Injuries
55 University of Pittsburgh Law Review 129 (1993)*

I. INTRODUCTION

....[Discussion of the competitive athlete's desire and legal right to play is omitted. — ed.].

IV. TEAM PHYSICIAN'S CONFLICTING RESPONSIBILITIES

One commentator has defined a "team physician" as "a physician who undertakes to render professional medical services to athletic participants and whose services are either arranged for or paid for at least in part by an institution or entity other than the patient, the patient's family, or some surrogate." Under this de-

---

finition, a "team physician" includes one who volunteers gratuitously or is selected by a team to perform preparticipation physicals paid for by the player.

Team physicians are generally either family practitioners or orthopedic surgeons. Other specialists such as internists, cardiologists, pediatricians, dermatologists and gynecologists also practice sports medicine. Currently, the American Board of Medical Specialties does not recognize a specialized practice area for sports medicine. However, the American Osteopathic Association is considering a proposal to establish a certification board for sports medicine.

A physician certified by the American Board of Emergency Medicine, Internal Medicine, Family Practice or Pediatrics may earn a certificate of added qualification in sports medicine by passing a written examination. Physicians may also obtain training in sports medicine by serving a one-year fellowship offered by various clinics.

With the absence of a board-certified specialty in sports medicine, standardized education or training requirements, team physicians have diverse backgrounds and differing levels of experience in caring for athletes. Medical science lacks conclusive scientific and clinical data for certain medical conditions. Therefore, the team physician, perhaps with the assistance of consulting specialists, must make an individualized evaluation of the medical risks of participation for each competitive athlete. Sports medicine guidelines formulated by medical specialty groups and organizations provide recommendations regarding whether an athlete should play with a particular medical condition, but also recognize the importance of the examining physician's clinical judgment and the athlete's unique physiology in determining the appropriate course of action. Sports medicine physicians may disagree regarding the nature and magnitude of the risks of athletic participation with a particular medical condition. They may also disagree as to whether participation in a sport is medically reasonable.

. . . .

Although the team physician is selected and paid by an athletic team, he or she must provide medical treatment and advice consistent with an individual athlete's best health interests because there is a physician-patient relationship between them. The physician-patient relationship is consensual in nature and both the physician and athlete must demonstrate by agreement or conduct their willingness to enter into such a relationship. If the athlete seeks medical advice or treatment and the team physician undertakes to provide either, the physician owes the athlete a duty of care even though the team selects or pays the physician or benefits from the medical care rendered to the athlete.

. . . .

Athletic teams must use reasonable care in operating their programs and protecting the health and safety of their players. Professional and amateur team officials generally rely on the opinion of the team physician, and her chosen consulting specialists regarding the medical risks of participation and the athlete's physical ability to compete in a sport. Team officials generally grant the team physician the authority to medically disqualify a competitive athlete from a sport.

Recent litigation challenging medical clearance recommendations, diagnoses, and injury treatment procedures by sports medicine physicians has created uncertainty regarding the nature and scope of the team physician's legal obligations. Athletes have sued team physicians for refusing to medically clear them to play a sport. On the other hand, some team physicians have been sued for clearing athletes to play when participation results in the athlete's death or injury, providing inadequate medication or equipment, or failing to disclose the long-term effects of playing with a medical condition or injury to the athlete's health. The threat of lawsuits challenging sports medicine decisions and practices looms over team physicians, whether they deny or permit participation. Controlling legal principles need to be established.

V. TEAM PHYSICIAN'S LEGAL RESPONSIBILITY

This section first considers the team physician's duty to screen athletes for potentially harmful medical conditions, properly diagnose their condition, and provide appropriate medical treatment. A physician's responsibility to provide sound medical clearance recommendations and inform an athlete of the risks of athletic participation and medical treatment will then be discussed. Finally, the circumstances under which team physicians may be immune from malpractice claims will be discussed.

A. Screening, Diagnosis, and Treatment

This section discusses general medical malpractice principles and their application to sports medicine. The traditional legal standard of requiring a team physician to follow customary sports medicine practice is then examined. The adoption of "accepted sports medicine practice" as the controlling legal standard is proposed as a better alternative.

1. General Principles

During the care of a patient, a physician "must have and use the knowledge, skill and care ordinarily possessed and employed by members of the [medical] profession in good standing." Malpractice liability is based on harm caused by a physician's negligent conduct in light of the general knowledge and skill of the medical profession. The law generally permits the medical profession to establish the bounds of appropriate physician care and treatment under the circumstances.

Until the middle of this century, the standard of care was based on the medical practices in the defendant physician's local community. Physicians were required to exercise the level of care prevailing in the locality where they practiced. The rationale for this rule was to avoid treating rural physicians unfairly by holding them to the standard of doctors practicing in large cities, who generally had more modern treatment facilities and better access to knowledge of medical advances.

Most states have now modified this locality rule because of advances in communication and transportation as well as the wide availability of medical literature. These advances enable all physicians to keep abreast of medical developments. For general practitioners, states have either broadened the relevant geographical community to include localities of similar size or treated the defendant physician's local community as merely one factor to be considered in determining the standard of care. For specialists, the trend is to apply a national standard of care because national specialty certification boards, standardized training and certification procedures exist.

Courts have not recognized sports medicine as a separate medical specialty, presumably because there is no national medical specialty board certification or standardized training. Some commentators argue that the team physician should be held to the standard of a "reasonably competent general practitioner" unless he provides services performed exclusively by specialists or holds himself out as possessing special competence in sports medicine.[105] Others assert that the team physician should be treated as a specialist aware of "fundamentals which all practicing specialists in sports medicine should know, based on the types of athletes with whom the physician is involved."[106] A team physician implicitly holds herself out as having special competence in sports medicine and therefore should be held to this higher standard. Team physicians also should conform to the standard of care corresponding to their actual specialty training; for example, an orthopedic surgeon should be held to the standard of an orthopedist specializing in sports medicine.

A national standard of care for team physicians is preferable to a local community standard because appropriate care should not vary with the geographic location of sports medicine care and treatment. For example, proper treatment of a sprained ankle should be the same whether occurring during a home or away game.

2. Customary Sports Medicine Practice

The applicable legal standard of physician conduct is "good medical practice" within the physician's type of practice. In other words, what is commonly done by physicians in the same specialty generally serves as the standard by which a physician's conduct is measured. Courts traditionally have equated "good medical practice" with what is customarily and usually done by physicians under the circumstances. This rule has been adopted because medical decisions require professional judgment, and it has been considered infeasible to permit lay jurors "to evaluate the ethical quality of the trade-offs that a doctor must make in the diagnosis and treatment of patients."[111]

There are few reported cases discussing the appropriate standard of care for evaluating and diagnosing an athlete's physical condition and treating his injuries. There have been several allegations of physician negligence in providing medical care to athletes. Allegations include physician failure to discover latent injuries or physical defects, medically unjustified administration of drugs to enable athletic participation, and improper treatment of athletic injuries.

To avoid malpractice liability, courts traditionally have required a physician to follow customary sports medicine practice. In *Rosensweig v. State*,[115] a boxer died from a brain hemorrhage after being knocked unconscious during a boxing match. One of the allegations by the decedent's estate was that physicians negligently failed to discover a brain injury he suffered in a prior fight. The New York Court of Claims held the State of New York liable based on the examining physicians' negligence. The court found that merely giving the decedent an electroencephalogram and a standard pre-fight physical exam was negligent under the circumstances.

An intermediate appellate court reversed the finding of negligence liability because the examining physicians had provided the decedent with the customary pre-fight medical examination. This court refused to hold these physicians to

---

105. King, *supra* note 65, at 695.

106. Russell, *supra* note 68, at 306-07; *see also* Weistart & Lowell, *supra* note 86, § 8.08, at 986-87.

111. Keeton, *supra* note 97, at 359.

115. 146 N.Y.S.2d 589 (Ct. Cl. 1955), *rev'd*, 171 N.Y.S.2d 912 (N.Y. App. Div. 1958), *aff'd*, 158 N.E.2d 229 (N.Y. 1959).

some other standard of care. The New York Court of Appeals affirmed the appellate court's decision on other grounds.

3. Accepted Sports Medicine Practice

The use of custom as the legal standard in a medical malpractice case has been criticized as difficult to determine, unduly deferential to a mere professional habit, and uncertain to produce optimal health care. Some commentators have argued that a better approach would require conformity to an "accepted practice" professional standard of care, which has been adopted by some courts. Under this standard, acceptable practices constituting medical care consistent with physicians' collective reasonable expectations are controlling. In other words, what should have been done under the circumstances, not what is commonly done, controls.

The accepted practice standard would have several advantages in the sports medicine context. It focuses on the current state of the medical art, rather than the historical conduct of sports medicine physicians. It enables a physician to deviate from an undesirable custom inconsistent with his best judgment, thereby facilitating the development of sound sports medicine practices. It also alleviates the need to search for a discernible custom among a diverse group of sports medicine physicians, and provides a standard absent such a custom. Some recent sports medicine malpractice cases appear to adopt the "accepted practice" standard of care rather than the customary medical practice standard developed by the *Rosensweig* appellate court.

In providing medical care to a competitive athlete, the team physician should adhere to accepted sports medicine standards under the circumstances. The level of competition at which an athlete is playing appears to be a relevant factor in determining the accepted medical practice. Professional and college players receive more comprehensive medical examinations because of the extreme physical demands of these levels of play and the economic ability of teams to pay for extensive examinations. Players at these levels also may be able to recover from injuries more rapidly because of their superior conditioning, physical development and team-provided rehabilitation.

Conversely, youth and high school athletic activities generally are less physically demanding. It may not be economically feasible to provide extensive medical examinations to all participants, especially those who, based on a screening examination, do not appear to be medically at risk. Due to their still-developing bodies, different rehabilitation procedures and longer periods of inactivity may be appropriate for these athletes.

A physician generally does not warrant the correctness of a diagnosis or success of a treatment, and a doctor is not liable for honest mistakes of judgment if the appropriate diagnosis or treatment is in reasonable doubt. In some instances it may be necessary to consult with specialists, and the team physician may be negligent for failing to do so. If there are various recognized methods of treatment, a physician may select the one she deems best, and is not liable for malpractice because some physicians utilize other alternatives.

Under these principles a team physician would not necessarily be liable for negligence if he misdiagnosed an athlete's physical condition. For example, if a physician erroneously concluded that Reggie Lewis had "the normal heart of an athlete," he would not be liable for a negligent diagnosis if he performed appropriate tests and merely made an honest mistake interpreting the results. A physician would be liable only if the diagnosis were not based on accepted medical practice.

Team physicians should be particularly careful regarding the use of anesthetics and pain killers to facilitate athletic participation. Medication to relieve pain masks the seriousness of an injury, and may cause aggravation or reinjury of a preexisting condition. In prescribing drugs to athletes, team physicians should follow accepted medical practices regarding the appropriate type and dosage of pharmaceutical treatment. They should prescribe drugs to enable athletic participation only if doing so is consistent with an athlete's best health interests. If physicians prescribed a non-therapeutic dosage of heart medication for Hank Gathers to enable him to play college basketball games at a higher level, this should constitute actionable negligence.

B. Medical Clearance Recommendations

This section assumes that an athlete's medical condition has been properly diagnosed and addresses the circumstances under which the team physician should be held liable for providing medical clearance to play a sport.

Sports medicine physicians have primary responsibility for medically clearing athletes to participate in sports or return to play. By having responsibility for such an important medical decision, they also should assume legal responsibility for harm to an athlete resulting from failure to conform to accepted sports medicine practices. The legal standard of care should provide an incentive for physicians to provide a sound medical clearance recommendation to an athlete without unduly inhibiting or second guessing the exercise of their professional judgment in individual cases.

Athletes have sued team physicians and other sports medicine physicians for alleged negligent medical clearance recommendations. In *Rosensweig v. State*,[139] one of the allegations was that examining physicians improperly cleared a boxer to fight less than two weeks after he was knocked out in a prior fight. Relying on conclusive expert testimony that good medical practice requires a six-week to two-month suspension from fighting for boxers suffering a knockout or severe head beating in a prior fight, the New York Court of Claims found that these physicians were negligent.

The Court of Claims refused to recognize the physicians' claimed defense of adherence to the professional custom of not suspending a boxer if the attending physician at the boxer's prior fight medically cleared him to resume boxing. It observed that such an unsound custom

> calls for a doctor, who at the time is the sole master of the patient's fate, to discard his own medical knowledge and experience, to push aside his own observations and to submerge his own conscience, to defer to the judgment of someone else. This type of reasoning opens the door to such tragic and foreseeable consequences that we hold it to be negligence.[142]

On appeal, a New York intermediate appellate court reversed the lower court's finding of negligence. The appellate court held that medically clearing the boxer to fight was "an honest error of judgment" insufficient to impose medical malpractice liability.

---

139. 146 N.Y.S.2d 589 (Ct. Cl. 1955), *rev'd*, 171 N.Y.S.2d 912 (App. Div. 1958), *aff'd*, 158 N.E.2d 229 (N.Y. 1959).

142. *Id.*

In *Mikkelsen v. Haslam*,[144] the plaintiff alleged that a physician negligently provided her with medical clearance to snow ski after hip replacement surgery. The jury found the physician negligent based on undisputed testimony that advising a total hip replacement patient that skiing is permissible "is a departure from orthopedic medical profession standards."[145]

. . . .

To enhance the quality and consistency of sports medicine practice, medical societies and specialty boards have promulgated medical eligibility guidelines for use by physicians making athletic participation recommendations. Sports generally are characterized by the intensity and type of physical exertion required as well as the nature of contact or collision inherent in the sport. The law should encourage the development of sports medicine participation guidelines and physician adherence to them by giving such guidelines appropriate deference.

Guidelines should be developed that reflect the medical profession's consensus regarding the level of participation that may be permitted with a given medical condition. These guidelines should provide explicit guidance to physicians, facilitate the provision of quality health care, and improve self-regulation of the medical profession. Guidelines have the beneficial effect of pooling medical knowledge, distilling research and clinical experience, and enabling physicians to base participation recommendations on something other than their own background and experience.

Commentators have advocated that applicable guidelines or standards should constitute some evidence or conclusive evidence of the standard of care in malpractice cases. Furthermore, courts have admitted standards and guidelines established by national medical associations as evidence of good medical practice.

If a medical society's participation standard or guideline reflects accepted practice based on the medical state of the art at the time of clearance to play a sport, it should be judicially treated as conclusive evidence of proper care if followed by the team physician. Such guidelines are the product of a physician consensus regarding the medical risks of participation in a sport based on existing scientific data and clinical experience. They provide objective guidance to a team physician encountering psychological or economic pressure from a competitive athlete or third party to take action inconsistent with the athlete's physical well being.

Judicial recognition of medical standards and guidelines as the legal standard of care would inform physicians what the law expects of them and prevent retrospective second guessing of the team physician's conduct by lay jurors. This proposal would encourage sports medicine physicians to engage in self-regulation and formulate collectively determined principles to guide an eclectic group of team physicians.

Physician adherence to outdated sports medicine guidelines should not be a recognized defense. Standards should be updated and modified periodically as the practice of sports medicine evolves to promote the health and safety of athletes and prevent unnecessary exclusion from sports activities. Giving legal effect only to guidelines consistent with the medical state of the art provides an incentive to medical organizations to revise them consistent with advances in sports medicine.

To provide the flexibility necessary for individualized medical care of an athlete, guidelines could permit variations in individual circumstances consistent

---

144. 764 P.2d 1384 (Utah Ct. App. 1988).
145. *Id.* at 1386.

with acceptable medical practices. This will allow a team physician to exercise his or her own clinical judgment to protect the competitive athlete's health without unnecessarily restricting athletic participation. The jury may need to consider whether the team physician's participation recommendation is within the range of acceptable medical practices established by the guidelines. It is, however, important to consider the alleged negligence in light of existing circumstances at the time of medical clearance, not in light of an after-the-fact tragedy.

Non-compliance with an applicable sports medicine guideline should not necessarily be a breach of the team physician's duty of care. Even if there is a deviation, no physician negligence should be found if a considerable number of recognized and respected physicians disagree with the scientific basis of the standard, or a departure from the standard is justified based on the athlete's individual medical condition and physiology. This would permit a team physician to make a participation recommendation consistent with an athlete's physical health and safety.

If there is no applicable medical guideline, or if a team physician deviates from an applicable guideline, accepted sports medicine practice under the circumstances should be the legal standard of care. Professional custom should not be controlling because it may not exist in the diverse field of sports medicine and may reflect non-medical factors because of competing loyalties faced by the team physician. The bounds of acceptable sports medicine practice should be limited by the team physician's paramount obligation to protect the competitive athlete from medically unreasonable risks of harm.

In making a participation recommendation, the team physician should only consider the athlete's medical best interest. The physician may appropriately consider the following factors: the intensity and physical demands of a sport; the athlete's unique physiology; whether the athlete has previously participated in the sport with his physical condition; available clinical evidence; the probability and severity of harm from athletic participation with the subject condition; and whether medication or protective equipment will minimize the health risks of participation.

The team physician should not permit the athlete's strong desire to play or the coach's obsession with winning to override his professional judgment and ethical obligation to protect the competitive athlete's health. The team physician should refuse to clear an athlete to participate if she believes there is a significant medical risk of harm from participation, irrespective of the team's need for the player or the player's psychological or economic motivation to play.

In cases in which there is an uncertain potential for life-threatening or permanently disabling harm, it appears advisable to err on the side of caution and recommend against athletic participation. Even if the team physician approves athletic participation by a competitive athlete with a physical abnormality or injury because of his opinion that there is no medically unreasonable risk, he should fully explain all material risks of playing to the athlete.

A team physician should not be held negligent for refusing to medically clear an athlete to participate in sports with a properly diagnosed injury, physical disability or medical condition. In *Penny v. Sands*,[170] Anthony Penny alleged that a cardiologist was negligent for withholding medical clearance to play college bas-

---

170. Complaint (D. Conn. Filed May 3, 1989) (No. H89-280) (voluntarily dismissed by Penny before the court decided the merits of his claims).

ketball with a potentially life-threatening heart condition. Even if an applicable medical organization guideline generally allows participation, legal recognition of such claims would unduly impair the team physician's professional judgment and may cause her to place greater weight on legal rather than medical considerations. The athlete may seek a second medical opinion, as Anthony Penny did, if he disagrees with the team physician's participation recommendation. This second opinion may provide him with a legal right to play the desired sport.

. . . . [A discussion of informed consent to risks of athletic participation and medical treatment is omitted. — ed.].

D. Immunity Issues

In some instances, team physicians may be immune from legal liability for malpractice claims brought by athletes. Several states have enacted qualified immunity statutes protecting volunteer team physicians from negligence liability arising from the rendering of emergency care to athletes. Some states have expanded their Good Samaritan laws to include physicians rendering emergency care at athletic events. These statutes are designed to encourage physicians to volunteer their services to elementary and high school athletic programs. Statutory immunity generally covers only team physicians who provide emergency medical care in good faith and without compensation to an athlete with an apparent life-threatening condition or serious injury. Wilful or wanton emergency treatment or gross negligence by the physician is not immune from liability. Pre-participation physical exams, general non-emergency medical care rendered to athletes, and physician decisions regarding whether an athlete may return to a game are not normally subject to immunity.

Team physicians employed by public universities may be protected by state law qualified immunity covering discretionary acts of public officials. In *Sorey v. Kellett*,[208] the Fifth Circuit held that this doctrine barred suit against a team physician alleging negligent medical treatment of a college football player. The court relied upon Mississippi law providing immunity to state-employed physicians for discretionary aspects of administered medical care.

Professional athletes' claims against team physicians for negligent medical care may be barred by state workmen's compensation laws. In *Hendy v. Losse*,[210] a professional football player sued team physicians for negligently diagnosing and treating a knee injury suffered during a game and advising him to continue playing football. In dismissing these claims, the California Supreme Court held that California's workmen's compensation law bars tort suits between co-employees for injuries caused within the scope of employment. The court found that plaintiff and defendant were both employed by the San Diego Chargers and that the defendant acted within the scope of his employment in treating the plaintiff. Thus, the plaintiff's exclusive remedy for his harm was workmen's compensation.

Some workmen's compensation laws do not bar tort claims for work-related injuries aggravated by fraudulent concealment of the existence of the injury. Claims for fraudulent concealment of medical information against professional team physicians, similar to those raised in *Krueger v. San Francisco Forty Niners*, are actionable.[215]

---

208. 849 F.2d 960 (5th Cir. 1988).
210. 819 P.2d 1 (Cal. 1992).
215. *See supra* notes 196-98 and accompanying text.

A professional team physician may be subject to a tort suit if she is found to be an independent contractor rather than an employee of a professional sports team covered by the workmen's compensation laws. Team physicians who are employees of professional teams are subject to common law tort claims for medical services provided to athletes that are outside the scope of the physician's employment agreement.

VI. COMPETITIVE ATHLETE'S RESPONSIBILITY

....[A discussion of contributory negligence and assumption of the risk is omitted.—ed.].

C. Allocation of Legal Responsibility

In providing medical care to a competitive athlete, if the team physician conforms to standards or guidelines established by a recognized medical association or specialty board or accepted sports medicine practice, the athlete should bear the harm resulting from athletic participation with a medical condition or injury if he or she is fully informed of the material risks. A team physician should not be held liable merely because his medical judgment was wrong or the athlete suffers unfortunate harm on the playing field. The athlete assumes the risk of harm that occurs from playing a sport despite receiving proper sports medicine care.

The team physician should bear substantial responsibility for harm caused by permitting non-medical factors such as the team's needs, player's stature, or economic considerations to impair the exercise of his professional judgment. Succumbing to these factors breaches the physician's paramount responsibility to protect the athlete's health. Fraudulently concealing material information about an athlete's medical condition or grossly deviating from accepted sports medicine principles to induce or enable an athlete to play a sport are extreme situations that would fall within this category. An award of punitive damages would be appropriate to deter and punish this irresponsible breach of the trust that an athlete places in the team physician.

In many instances, the team physician and a competitive athlete should share responsibility for harm resulting from playing with a medical condition or injury. The comparative negligence systems adopted by most states would apportion legal responsibility for harm caused by a team physician's deviation from good sports medicine practice and an athlete's failure to use reasonable care to protect his health or voluntary assumption of the known risks of playing.

Marc Buoniconti's negligence lawsuit against Dr. E.K. Wallace, Jr., the Citadel's team physician, is a case in which the application of comparative negligence principles may have resulted in a fairer result than the jury's conclusion that Buoniconti was not entitled to any damages for permanent paralysis suffered while making a tackle during a football game. Buoniconti asserted that Dr. Wallace failed to inform him of his spinal abnormality and permitted him to play with a serious neck injury and to use equipment that placed his neck in a position making it vulnerable to being broken. Dr. Wallace contended that Buoniconti's dangerous and illegal tackling technique, not any improper medical clearance or treatment, caused his injury.

The jury found Dr. Wallace not liable for Buoniconti's injuries, but implicit in the jury's finding is that Buoniconti assumed the risk of his tragic injury by choosing to play football with a painful neck injury. South Carolina is one of the few states that has not adopted comparative negligence principles. As a result, a jury finding of *any* contributory negligence or assumption of risk on Buoniconti's part would have barred *any* recovery against Dr. Wallace even if he were negligent. It is difficult to determine whether the jury reached this conclusion or merely found that Dr. Wallace did not provide negligent medical care.

Assuming the conduct of both Buoniconti and Dr. Wallace exposed Buoniconti to an unreasonable risk of harm and their actions jointly caused his tragic injury, they should share legal responsibility for such harm. In this manner, individual responsibility and legal accountability are consistent.

The following hypothetical illustrates a proposed application of comparative responsibility principles to athletic injuries in the sports medicine context. Assume the team physician discovers that a college soccer player has a heart condition during a pre-season physical examination. After performing some tests, the physician, who is a cardiologist, tells the athlete he does not believe his condition is serious enough to justify excluding him from soccer for medical reasons. The team physician warns the athlete not to overexert himself and prescribes medication for the athlete's heart condition to alleviate any adverse effects from engaging in strenuous exercise. Before continuing to play soccer, the athlete is examined by another respected cardiologist who agrees with the team physician's diagnosis but believes that the medical risks of playing soccer with his heart condition are unreasonable. This cardiologist recommends against playing a strenuous competitive sport.

The university's athletic director requires medical clearance from the team physician before allowing the athlete to play on the school's soccer team. The team physician does so but requires the athlete to sign a waiver releasing him from any legal liability (including negligent medical care) for future harm including death or serious permanent injury arising out of the athlete's medical condition while playing soccer. One week later the athlete dies of cardiac arrest during soccer practice.

This article's proposed application of comparative responsibility principles would resolve a negligence suit against the team physician as follows. The waiver should be judicially declared invalid to the extent it purports to release the team physician from all liability for negligent medical care of the athlete. If expert medical testimony supports a jury finding that the team physician's participation recommendation fell outside of the bounds of good sports medicine practice by a competent cardiologist under the circumstances, he should be liable for some percentage of the harm caused by his negligence.

The athlete also should bear some legal responsibility for choosing to play soccer with a known heart condition. The athlete was warned not to play soccer by another cardiologist although the team physician medically cleared him to play. The law should require an athlete to incur some legal responsibility for voluntarily choosing to play with a known, potentially fatal condition. The athlete's age and maturity, level of competition, and degree of awareness of the material risks of playing based on information provided by the team physician and other consulting physicians should be considered by the jury in apportioning the athlete's percentage of responsibility.

VII. CONCLUSION

There currently are many sports medicine issues that are medically and legally unresolved. Because of the strong psychological and economic rewards of athletic participation, competitive athletes sometimes are willing to take serious health risks by playing a chosen sport with a physical abnormality or injury. Although often faced with conflicting loyalties to the team and athlete, a team physician must provide medical care consistent with the athlete's best health interests and not allow non-medical considerations to influence her judgment. A competitive athlete must use reasonable care to protect his own health and carefully consider the possibility of unfortunate consequences such as permanent injury or even death that may result from athletic participation with a known injury or medical condition.

The team physician and a competitive athlete should work together to develop a trusting relationship to safely promote the athlete's health and avoid unnecessary exclusion from athletic competition. An individualized, thoughtful and practical consideration of the demands of participation in a particular sport and potential harmful effects on an athlete's health is required. Hopefully the number of avoidable tragedies on the playing field will be reduced if competitive athletes and team physicians adhere to their individual moral and legal obligations.

....

Part V

Drug Testing

Introduction

Illegal drug use in American society represents a major public policy issue for Congress, state legislatures, and law enforcement officials. Efforts to crack-down on drug traffickers are understandable, but public policy over the past twenty years has sought to stem the tide by targeting users. A major approach to reducing drug abuse is drug testing in the workplace, and more recently in the schools. The lawfulness of drug testing has been challenged, generally unsuccessfully, in every arena in which it has been introduced. These challenges have targeted the infringement of personal privacy but have also been motivated by the risk of losing employment. In sports, athletes risk the permanent loss of eligibility for use of prohibited substances. No one disputes that athletes who use drugs may pose a threat to others and themselves and that such athletes should be subjected to some form of sanction. However, considerable controversy revolves around the extent to which governing associations, commissioners, owners and school officials may infringe on personal privacy to ascertain drug use. Relatedly, disagreement exists over the appropriate sanctions for athlete use of prohibited drugs.

The articles in this chapter address the legal issues raised in challenges in the sports arena. Steven Ludd opens the chapter with an overview of privacy issues and the concomitant legal issues in professional, collegiate and high school athletics. A student note analyzes the legality of drug testing programs in colleges and high schools after the Supreme Court's decision in *Vernonia School District 47J v. Acton* in 1995.

While constitutional issues are paramount in the collegiate and high school setting, collective bargaining issues rise to the forefront in professional athletics. The rights of professional athletes are determined by the collective bargaining agreement and applicable labor laws. Professor Ethan Lock examines the extent to which owners are required to resolve drug related matters through the collective bargaining process in the National Football League. Lock's analysis is applicable to all professional sports, a point demonstrated in a subsequent article by Professors Glenn Wong and Richard Ensor regarding the authority of the commissioner to impose mandatory drug testing or to discipline players for drug use under Major League Baseball's collective bargaining agreement. The section concludes with an article by Jennifer Johnson about the related issue of HIV testing. The legal issues in the HIV context are similar but the social policy issues vary because public health issues are added to the balancing equation.

This chapter does not cover drug testing in Olympic sports. The focus of articles on the subject tends to be directed at international law jurisdictional issues and the dispute resolution mechanisms of the complex Olympics governing structure. Accordingly, the issue of drug testing in Olympic sports is covered in Chapter 15.

Other noteworthy articles include: John J. Bursch, Note, *The 4 R's of Drug Testing in Public Schools: Random Is Reasonable and Rights Are Reduced*, 80 MINN. L. REV. 1221 (1996); Donald Crowley, *Student Athletes and Drug Testing*, 6 MARQ. SPORTS L. J. 95 (1995).

Chapter 14

Drug Testing

1. General Considerations

Steven O. Ludd, Athletics, Drug Testing and the Right to Privacy: A Question of Balance
34 Howard Law Journal 599 (1991)*

....

Over the last few years the very foundation of high school, collegiate and professional sports have been shaken by the invasion of drug use. In reaction to this malady, high schools, colleges and universities, and many professional sports associations have instituted various drug testing programs. While legal standards for these segments of American athletics differ, most of the drug testing programs rely upon some form of mandatory random testing. Whether the program is established by a local board of education, the National Collegiate Athletic Association (NCAA), or the National Basketball Association (NBA), each body has made participation in athletic competition contingent upon passing whatever drug test has been administered....

....

PROTECTION OF PERSONAL AUTONOMY AND AMERICAN SPORT:
THE CONSTITUTIONAL PARAMETERS

There can be little debate that the government has the constitutional power and responsibility to protect the health and welfare of its citizens. But, as this article has suggested, in fulfillment of this obligation government may not disregard other equally important constitutional mandates. Whether or not random mandatory drug testing of American athletes will withstand constitutional review is totally dependent upon the nature of the governmental entity requiring the drug testing program, the procedures instituted to test the athletes, the strength of the public policy arguments justifying such a program, and the type of athletic enterprise under review. Because American sport is often separated into three categories: professional; collegiate; and high school, we will examine the impact of the aforementioned considerations for constitutional review within the special context of each category of athletic enterprise in this country.

A. *Professional Sport*

As was mentioned earlier, the three most often articulated reasons offered to justify mandatory drug testing programs are: 1) the health and welfare of the athletes, 2) the need to maintain the integrity of the sport, and 3) the importance of protecting the public's financial interest in some forms of sporting activities. Yet, the importance of each of these considerations to the three levels of athletic competition in this country may be significantly different. Professional sport in America is unquestionably a business venture.

Literally millions of dollars provided by both the private and public sector support the functioning of professional football, baseball, basketball, hockey, and horse racing. Indeed, the economic health of some American cities rises or falls with the departure or arrival of professional sport teams. Professional sport is big business. The relationship between the athletes participating in professional sport and the owners, private or public or some combination thereof, is significantly distinct from the two other levels of athletic competition in this country.

Similar to many business enterprises, the legal relationship in professional sport is almost entirely governed by contractual principles. Therefore, while considerations of the health and safety and protection of the integrity of the particular sport are sometimes offered to justify one rule or another by owners associations, it is fair to suggest that the driving force behind rulemaking in professional sport is profit making. Thus, the creation of drug testing programs in professional athletics has often been the by-product of collective bargaining between owners and players associations. Consequently, very few cases challenging random mandatory drug testing in professional sport have been brought before the courts.

While one can only speculate as to future judicial determinations concerning the constitutionality of random mandatory drug testing in professional athletics, if the courts apply the same reasoning that has been applied to other private employment situations where such testing has been required by employers, the courts have generally searched the record to determine whether collective bargaining agreements had been entered into where employees agreed to such testing. In such cases the courts appear to be willing to accept the agreement as binding, thus, short circuiting full blown constitutional review of the drug testing programs.

It would appear then that because professional sport is for the most part perceived by the courts as a private business enterprise regulated by traditional contractual principles and bound by collective bargaining agreements, competing constitutional interests such as individual rights to privacy and protections against self-incrimination will not be considered as important as they might be in public governmental employment situations or in other cases concerning direct governmental involvement with athletic activities such as public university athletic programs or high school athletics.

B. *Collegiate Sport*

While many of the requirements for close judicial scrutiny of mandatory random drug testing may be absent in professional sport, there can be little question that public university athletic programs are forms of state action which activate the mandates of the Bill of Rights. Indeed, when the issue of random mandatory drug testing is taken out of the traditional employment situation and placed into a governmental/educational environment, the balancing of competing constitutional interests becomes much more complex. Public welfare arguments such as the health and welfare of the athletes, the integrity of the sport, and the protection of public financial contributions to the individual university must be now measured against the impact that such testing programs will have upon the educational process, the privacy rights of the student-athlete, and the selective application of the tests upon only one segment of the student population. Unfortunately, the courts have offered little guidance as to the comparative constitutional weight associated with these competing interests. Yet, if the few lower court decisions addressing random mandatory drug testing of athletes when coupled with accepted principles of constitutional law, an understanding of the major components of future judicial decision making can be constructed.

As was noted earlier, before an individual can call upon the protection of the Bill of Rights, he/she must demonstrate to the reviewing court that the case involves some form of state or governmental restriction of his/her liberty. In determining whether state action exists the court must ask the question: Is the challenged conduct fairly attributable to conduct which has been traditionally the prerogative of government? Because education falls well within the purview of state governmental action, any requirement upon students at a public university or college, including drug testing of athletes, should be construed as a form of state action which constitutionally activates the protections of the Bill of Rights. Presuming that the reviewing court finds random mandatory drug testing programs by state universities and colleges to be a form of state action justifying the application of the constitutional protections, what process will the court utilize in determining the weight of the student athlete's argument that his/her right to privacy has been violated by such state sanctioned programs?

In establishing the corresponding constitutional weights associated with such a claim by a student athlete a reviewing court will determine whether the testing program is reasonably related to a legitimate governmental interest. If so, it is likely that the court will place significant importance upon the public policy arguments mentioned above. However, if the reviewing court does not find that the drug testing program is within the delegated powers of the state university or college, it may require them to demonstrate that there exists some compelling state interest justifying such a program.

Because random mandatory drug testing directly confronts the constitutional protections against unreasonable searches and seizures found in the fourth amendment, it is likely that a reviewing court will examine why the traditional requirement of probable cause or reasonable suspicion should not be applied in the drug testing of collegiate athletes. Such a burden of proof may be extremely difficult for state universities and colleges to carry.

In the blood and urinalysis cases mentioned earlier in this article, the courts have been inconsistent in requiring probable cause, or now termed "individual suspicion." The determining factor appears to be the specific job responsibility of the public employee, or the workplace environment. In situations where the employee is performing duties which entail a high degree of care such as, bus or train operators, or fire fighters, the courts have generally concluded that individual suspicion is not required for random mandatory drug testing. But, these types of cases are easily distinguishable from intercollegiate athletics.

While the judicial process of balancing public safety with individual employee rights may, as in the cases cited above, require the courts to broadly apply the "reasonableness" standard of the fourth amendment, no valid comparison can be posited in relation with intercollegiate athletic competition. Public safety simply does not demand that college athletes line up at urinals. But, so the argument goes, there are other public welfare concerns that necessitate a judicial waiver of the "reasonableness" requirement such as the importance of protecting the health of the athletes, and the overall integrity of the sport. These arguments can only be evaluated in the context of the special governmental function that state universities and colleges perform. As was indicated above, a reviewing court may address these arguments by asking the question: Is the university's random mandatory drug testing program reasonably related to a legitimate governmental objective? Or, more precisely, does state sponsored higher education require such programs?

In response, it could be suggested that state universities are required to be paternalistic in many of its actions. Whether the issue involves standards of academic performance, student conduct in residential halls, or rules regulating the overall institutional environment, university officials must set standards to protect the health and safety of the student body. While anyone familiar with campus life cannot dispute the importance of establishing and fairly enforcing rules of conduct, the courts generally refuse to legitimize the actions of university officials which reach beyond accepted principles of higher education.

. . . .

HIGH SCHOOL ATHLETICS

If some protection of student athletes constitutional right to privacy has begun to emerge in young athletes, this trend is not occurring in cases of random mandatory drug testing of interscholastic athletics. In fact, in one of the most recent decisions from the federal judiciary, it appears that high school student athletes may be required to withstand even more intrusion into their personal autonomy than their counterparts in intercollegiate athletics.

In *Schaill v. Tippecanoe County School Corp,*[107] the United States Court of Appeals for the Seventh Circuit upheld a lower court determination that the school district could institute a random urinalysis testing program of its interscholastic athletes and cheerleaders. The testing program required all students desiring to participate in interscholastic competition and their parent or guardian to sign a consent form agreeing to submit to urinalysis if chosen on a random basis. If the student tested positive he/she could be suspended from some or all varsity competition, depending on the number of offenses. Two student athletes challenged the program contending that the program was an unconstitutional search and a violation of their right to privacy because the program did not require probable cause and a warrant.

What was not surprising, based upon the federal judiciary's recent decisions in employment drug testing, was that the Court of Appeals rejected the student athletes contention that probable cause and a warrant were required in cases involving non-criminal matters. What was surprising was the court's analysis and conclusion as to what constituted "reasonableness" under the fourth amendment absent even individual suspicion of drug use by the students to be tested.

. . . .

---

107. Schaill v. Tippecanoe County School Corp., 864 F.2d 1309 (7th Cir. 1988).

It appears that the court was satisfied that because the location for excretion was a toilet stall rather than an open urinal that privacy considerations were protected by this "less intrusive means." Additionally, the court reasoned that because participation in athletic programs almost always requires some form of "communal undress" that every student athlete understands that he/she cannot expect as much privacy as he/she might in other situations. Ultimately, the court concluded, that because interscholastic sport is dominated by numerous obligations of student athletes in regard to minimum grade point averages, residency and eligibility requirements, not to mention the high visibility of drug testing of collegiate and professional athletes, no student could reasonably have, "strong expectations of privacy with respect to urine tests."

....

The final rationale provided by the *Schaill* court for the warrantless search is that the school system's testing program is simply an administrative search which presumes a form of implied consent. Presumably, Judge Cudahy believed that the facts of this particular case were analogous to previous cases where warrantless administrative searches were held constitutional by the Supreme Court of the United States. Using the balancing test required in cases involving such searches, the court here believed that because a student athlete's refusal, "to submit to testing will not result in loss of employment, criminal penalties, or any academic penalty whatsoever...," that privacy expectations could be balanced away for the more important interest of the school authorities to prevent potential drug use.

....

Regardless of whether one supports or rejects the decision reached in *Schaill v. Tippecanoe County School Corp.*, there can be little doubt that interscholastic athletics will be vulnerable to mandatory drug testing programs and to subsequent challenges by student athletes until more balanced judicial approaches are provided.

....

---

2. Intercollegiate and High School Sports

Eric N. Miller, Comment, Suspicionless Drug Testing of High School and College Athletes After Acton: Similarities and Differences

45 University of Kansas Law Review 301 (1996)*

I. INTRODUCTION

In June of 1995, the United States Supreme Court held random, suspicionless drug testing of high school and elementary school athletes to be constitutional.[1] Although the Supreme Court had ruled on suspicionless drug testing in other set-

---

    1. Veronia Sch. Dist. 47J v. Acton, 115 S. Ct. 2386, 2396 (1995).

tings, this was the Court's first ruling on the constitutionality of random testing of athletes in either college, high school, or elementary school. Because the Court failed to note a difference in purpose between high school and collegiate testing policies, as it should have, it did not find random testing of high school athletes to be unconstitutional.

....

II. BACKGROUND

....

B. *Cases Preceding* Acton

In 1989, the United States Supreme Court first dealt with suspicionless drug testing in two landmark employment cases, *National Treasury Employees Union v. Von Raab*[38] and *Skinner v. Railway Labor Executives' Ass'n.*[39] In *Von Raab*, the United States Customs Service implemented a policy whereby employees seeking a transfer or a promotion to certain positions had to undergo urinalysis testing. This urinalysis testing was required for transfer or promotion into positions that met any one of three criteria.

The first criterion was met when the position included direct involvement in drug enforcement. Part of any drug agent's duties is not only to have direct contact with people who traffic drugs, but also to seize different types of contraband. The job of being a drug agent is thus fraught with temptation, and it is imperative that agents be drug free.

The second criterion was met when the position required the employee to carry a firearm. As the Commissioner of Customs pointed out, "public safety demands that employees who carry deadly arms and are prepared to make instant life or death decisions be drug free."

The final criterion was met when the position involved the handling of "classified" material. The Commissioner noted that this classified material might fall into the wrong hands if accessible to employees who were susceptible to blackmail because of their own drug abuse.

The petitioners in *Von Raab* challenged the drug testing program on the grounds that it violated their Fourth Amendment guarantee against unreasonable searches. The Court held that suspicionless testing of persons applying for positions or promotions to positions involving either drug enforcement or the carrying of a firearm is reasonable. The Court found that the Government had a compelling interest in preventing drug users from operating in such positions. The Court also found that this compelling interest outweighed the privacy expectations of individuals applying for such positions or promotions. Finally, the Court reasoned that the individuals had a diminished expectation of privacy because of the "special, and obvious, physical and ethical demands of those positions." The Court, however, refused to decide on whether suspicionless testing of employees who would be handling "classified" information was reasonable or not.

In *Skinner*, the Federal Railroad Administration, under the statutory authority of the Secretary of Transportation, promulgated regulations to deal with the

---

38. 489 U.S. 656 (1989).
39. 489 U.S. 602 (1989).

problem of alcohol and drug abuse on railroads. Among other provisions, the regulations called for suspicionless drug testing of any employees who were involved in a train accident involving the death of "any on-duty railroad employee." The Railway Labor Executives' Association challenged the regulations on constitutional grounds. The Supreme Court held that railroad employees involved in a train accident had a diminished expectation of privacy. The Court weighed this diminished expectation of privacy against the compelling Government safety interests served by the urinalysis testing and held that suspicionless testing in this situation was reasonable. Further, the Court also held that the compelling governmental interests would be "significantly hindered" if the railroad were required to base urinalysis testing on suspicion of drug use.

III. ANALYSIS

Drug testing of athletes became popular only as recently as the 1983 Pan American Games. Soon thereafter, the United States Olympic Committee adopted the idea of testing athletes for drugs. Today, with drug use considered one of society's worst evils, drug testing of athletes has become more popular than ever. According to one source, "The pill, capsule, vial and needle have become fixtures of the locker room as athletes increasingly turn to drugs in the hope of improving athletic performances."

There are three different situations in which student athletes may be subjected to random, suspicionless drug testing. First, a student may be tested by his or her high school, elementary school, or school district. Second, a college student may be tested by the NCAA. Finally, a college student may be tested by his or her own college or university.

With the decision in *Acton*, the Supreme Court indicated its belief that random, suspicionless drug testing of high school and elementary school athletes is basically the same as random, suspicionless drug testing of intercollegiate athletes. Current law holds suspicionless testing to be constitutional in both settings.

The implementation of a drug testing policy for high school and elementary school athletes, however, is much different from the implementation of a drug testing policy for intercollegiate athletes. In high school drug testing, as in *Acton*, the goals of a drug testing program are different than the goals of an intercollegiate drug testing program. While the goal of most intercollegiate drug testing programs is to ensure fair competition and eliminate drug use among intercollegiate athletes, the goal of most high school programs is not to ensure fair competition or eliminate drug use only among athletes, but to eliminate drug use among all students....

A. *Elementary and Secondary School Drug Testing Programs*

1. General Principles

As recently as 1990, drug testing of students at the high school and elementary school level was uncommon. In fact, until that time, the National Federation of State High School Associations had recommended against the drug testing of high school students. But due to the combination of steroid use and increased glorification of recreational drug use, schools all around the country have implemented drug testing programs over the past several years.

As noted above, those testing programs must pass Fourth Amendment scrutiny. The Court in *New Jersey v. T.L.O.*[70] held that public elementary and secondary school officials are "state officers" within the meaning of the Fourteenth Amendment. Thus, the Fourth Amendment requirement that a search be reasonable is applicable to drug testing programs implemented by high schools and elementary schools.

2. The *Acton* Decision

Vernonia School District 47 J v. Acton,[73] decided in June of 1995, is the leading case dealing with the constitutionality of random drug tests in public secondary schools. In the fall of 1989, the school district of Vernonia, Oregon, implemented a drug testing policy for students participating in athletics. The express purpose of the policy was to prevent student athletes from using drugs, to protect the student athlete's health and safety, and to provide those who use drugs with assistance programs.

In 1991, the respondent, James Acton, refused to sign the drug testing consent form required of all athletes. Because of this, he was denied the opportunity to play on his seventh grade football team. Acton and his parents subsequently filed suit against the school district, challenging the drug testing policy on Fourth and Fourteenth Amendment grounds.

The United States Supreme Court upheld the constitutionality of the school district's policy. In so doing, the Court effectively applied the same balancing factors that were used in *Delaware v. Prouse*[79] to determine whether the search was reasonable.

3. Nature of the Privacy Interest in *Acton*

The first factor that the Court looked at was the nature of the privacy interests upon which the search intrudes. For several reasons, the Court found that, analogous to the employment situations in *Von Raab* and *Skinner*, school children should have reason to expect intrusions into their privacy. Essential to this finding, in the Court's view, was the fact that the individuals subjected to the drug testing policy were "(1) children, who (2) have been committed to the temporary custody of the State." The Court noted that students are routinely subjected to medical examinations such as vision and hearing screening, dental checks, and scoliosis screening. As such, according to the Court, students in a school environment have a lesser expectation of privacy than do members of the general population with respect to medical examinations.

Further, the Court noted that students who are athletes have even a lesser privacy expectation than do students who choose not to participate in athletics. In support of this, the Court pointed to the fact that athletes are required to submit to a preseason physical exam and are also exposed to an element of "communal undress" to which students who do not participate in athletics are not subjected. Based on these considerations, the Court reasoned that elementary and high school student athletes have a diminished expectation of privacy.

The Court failed to recognize, however, that not just athletes, but practically all high school students are subjected to the elements of communal undress. Almost

---

70. 469 U.S. 325 (1985).
73. 115 S. Ct. 2386 (1995).
79. 440 U.S. 648 (1979).

all schools undoubtedly require physical education classes where the students are subjected to the elements of communal undress in their respective locker rooms. Thus, it is hard to imagine how athletes have a lesser expectation of privacy than students who do not participate in athletics when all students are subjected to the elements of communal undress. In addition, even if athletes do somehow have a lesser expectation of privacy because of the elements of communal undress, "it is unreasonable to assume that merely because athletes undress in the presence of one another, they somehow expect to be visually monitored by a stranger while they urinate."[90] It is also important to note that while "[u]ndressing in a communal locker room is permissive, . . . monitored urination is compulsory."[91] Further, the fact that students are children who have been committed to the temporary custody of the state may not be as important a consideration when, as James Acton's parents did, the parents of the athlete who does not consent to the testing also object to the random testing.

4. Character of the Intrusion in *Acton*

The Court next turned to the character of the intrusion that the respondents were challenging. The Court noted that urinalysis intrudes upon what has traditionally been a very private function. The degree of the intrusion, however, is at least partially determined by the manner in which the urine sample is taken. Under the school district's policy, male students remain fully clothed and, if they are visually observed, are only observed from behind. Female students are allowed to produce their urine samples in a closed stall with only aural monitoring. The Court noted that these conditions were practically the same as the conditions that students face in school restrooms everyday. The Court thus found that the intrusion in obtaining the urine sample was minimal.

It may be true that if the conditions of obtaining the sample were nearly identical to those encountered in public restrooms everyday, the effect on the privacy interests of student athletes would be negligible. The Court, however, refused to recognize that the conditions were not nearly identical. When a student uses the school restroom in everyday life there is no school official standing nearby making sure that the student urinates as there is when an athlete is being tested for drugs. Although the school official may not visually watch the tested athlete urinate, he or she does listen and make sure that the student does in fact urinate. This undoubtedly adds an uncomfortableness not normally found in everyday school restrooms. According to one source, "The process of monitoring urination invades deep-seated privacy expectations. Urination is one of the most private activities in our society." This suggests that the intrusion upon the athletes' privacy interests was not as minimal as the Court thought it to be.

The information disclosed by the urinalysis is another possible intrusion upon the privacy interests of student athletes. The Court found it significant that the testing policy set up by the Vernonia School District only disclosed whether a student was using drugs, and not whether the student had any other disease or med-

---

90. Karen E. Crummy, Note, *Urine or You're Out: Student-Athletes' Right of Privacy Stripped in* Hill v. NCAA, 29 U.S.F. L. REV. 197, 217 (1994) (citing Hill v. NCAA, 865 P.2d 633, 694 (Cal. 1994). (Mosk, J., dissenting)).

91. Stephen F. Brock et al., *Drug Testing College Athletes: NCAA Does Thy Cup Runneth Over?*, 97 W. VA. L. REV. 53, 105 (1994).

ical condition. The Court, however, did acknowledge some concern that the testing policy required students to reveal any medications they were taking in advance of the urinalysis.

Based on the Court's findings that the intrusion in obtaining the urinalysis sample was minimal and the urinalysis testing only revealed whether or not a student athlete was using drugs, the Court held that the governmental intrusion into the lives of the students was not significant.

5. Nature of Governmental Concern in *Acton*

The Court in *Acton* next examined the nature and immediacy of the governmental concern at issue to determine the reasonableness of the drug testing policy. As to the nature of the governmental concern at issue, the Court pointed out that although *Skinner* and *Von Raab* each held the governmental concern to be "compelling," that level of concern need not be present in order to uphold the constitutionality of a search. Rather, the Court stated that the governmental concern must be such as to justify the particular search at hand.

Next, the Court determined that the nature of the governmental concern at issue in *Acton* was important, and perhaps even compelling. "Deterring drug use by our Nation's schoolchildren is at least as important as enhancing efficient enforcement of the Nation's laws against the importation of drugs, which was the governmental concern in *Von Raab* ... or deterring drug use by engineers and trainmen, which was the governmental concern in *Skinner*."

As to the immediacy of the government concern, the Supreme Court did not question the district court's conclusion that the drug problem in the Vernonia School District had reached "epidemic proportions." Over a four and a half year period, however, the school district had tested five hundred students and had positive results in only twelve of those tests. Despite this fact, the Court found that the Vernonia School District had a very serious and immediate drug problem.

6. Effectiveness of the Program in *Acton*

The final factor that the *Acton* Court looked at in determining the reasonableness of the school district's drug testing program was the effectiveness of the program for addressing the governmental concern. This is where the biggest problem with the school district's drug testing policy occurs. The Court stated that "[i]t seems to us self-evident that a drug problem largely fueled by the 'role model' effect of athletes' drug use, and of particular danger to athletes, is effectively addressed by making sure that athletes do not use drugs." The Court thus found that the policy effectively addressed the governmental concern. There would be little doubt as to the Court's finding if the true goals of Vernonia School District's drug policy were its stated goals: to prevent student athletes from using drugs, to protect student athletes' health and safety, and to provide student athlete drug users with assistance programs.

There is some controversy, however, about whether the school district's stated goals were actually the true goals of the drug testing policy. Of particular importance is the fact that the Vernonia School District's policy didn't include testing the athletes for anabolic steroids. This fact suggests that protecting the health and safety of student athletes was not the school district's chief concern.

Steroids are dangerous, addictive, and deadly drugs. According to one source, anabolic steroids are, or at least should be, the drug of greatest concern in high school drug testing situations. There is evidence that anabolic steroids pose higher health risks than recreational drugs such as marijuana. Estimates show that as many as 500,000 high school males use steroids, and that forty percent of these users are so-called "hard-core" users. Another commentator indicated that approximately one-half of the estimated steroid users in America are adolescents. Further, "the detrimental effects of steroids on the liver, the cardiovascular system, the male and female reproductive systems and the psyche of the athlete have all been conclusively established." The most serious of these side effects is the damage to the liver. Other serious problems include the possibility of heart attacks, sexual changes, and mental disturbance. Recognizing all of these documented dangers, for the school district not to test for steroids and then say that protection of the district's student athletes and elimination of drug use among those athletes was the primary goal of the testing program defies logic.

In addition, although the policy only tested athletes and the stated goals of the policy were narrowly aimed at athletes, there was evidence suggesting that the school district was actually trying to get rid of drug use among the entire student body. On this point, several teachers in the Vernonia School District testified that the true goals of the policy were to limit disciplinary problems in the classroom and to limit the growth and glorification of drug use among the entire student body.

Also, it is important to note that the original version of the Vernonia School District's drug testing policy would have tested all students who were involved in extracurricular activities. This undoubtedly would have included more students in the testing pool and indicates that the district's concern was broader than eliminating the drug use among the athletes alone. In fact, there is evidence that the original version of Vernonia's drug testing program would have subjected nearly all of the district's students to the possibility of being tested, while the version actually implemented by the district affected only about half of the student body. The school district's reluctance to implement this original version of the testing program, however, probably stemmed from the decision in *Brooks v. East Chambers Consolidated Independent School District,*[132] where a federal district court held random testing of all students involved in extracurricular activities to be unconstitutional.

. . . .

It thus appears likely that the principal goal of the school district in implementing the drug testing policy was to eliminate drug use among the entire student body. As such, this casts serious doubt on the constitutionality of the school district's testing policy. If the school district's actual governmental concern was drug use among the entire student body, testing only the athletes did not effectively further its governmental concern.

. . . .

B. *The Drug Testing Program of The NCAA*

1. Specifics of the Program

. . . . Although the NCAA enacted a rule in 1973 prohibiting drug use by student athletes, a suspicionless drug testing program of student athletes was not en-

---

132. 730 F. Supp. 759 (S.D. Tex. 1989), *aff'd sub nom.* Brooks v. East Chambers County Sch., 930 F.2d 915 (5th Cir. 1991).

acted until 1986. In response to a nationwide survey of college athletes on drug use, the NCAA, at its 1986 national convention, adopted a drug testing policy. The policy prohibited drug use by college athletes "in several categories, including: (1) psychomotor and nervous system stimulants; (2) anabolic steroids; (3) alcohol and beta blockers (in rifle events only); (4) diuretics; and (5) street drugs." According to the NCAA, these banned substances are "generally purported to be performance-enhancing and/or potentially harmful to the health and safety of the student-athlete."[154]

Under the policy, any student athlete who sought to participate in any NCAA-sponsored competition had to sign a statement and consent form agreeing to be tested for drugs. The policy stated that all student athletes involved in any championship event or postseason bowl game could potentially be tested.

The policy had two stated goals. First, the NCAA wanted to safeguard the integrity of athletic competition.

Second, the NCAA wanted to protect the health and safety of its athletes.

2. Applicability of NCAA Drug Testing Decisions to Elementary and Secondary School Drug Testing Decisions

Drug testing conducted by the NCAA is not subject to Fourth Amendment scrutiny because the NCAA is not a state actor for the purposes of the Fourteenth Amendment.[159] At least one commentator believes that when conducting drug tests of student athletes, the NCAA is a government actor and subject to the Fourth Amendment. But following the Court's decision in *Tarkanian*, most student challenges to random, suspicionless drug testing by the NCAA have been brought on the basis that the testing violated state constitutions and state right to privacy laws. The test for reasonableness used by state courts, however, is closely related to the test used in *Acton*. It is thus useful to examine the NCAA's testing policy and to determine, based on *Acton*, how the Court would rule on such a policy if it were challenged.

The leading case on drug testing by the NCAA is *Hill v. NCAA*.[162] In *Hill*, several student athletes from Stanford University sued the NCAA on the grounds that the NCAA's drug testing policy violated their right to privacy under the California constitution. The university intervened and adopted the students' position. The court held that the NCAA's drug testing policy did not violate the students' state constitutional rights to privacy.

In reaching this result, the court analyzed three factors: first, the privacy expectations of the athletes, second, the seriousness of the invasion by the testing policy, and third, what the court termed the "competing interests." In this "competing interests" category, the court looked at the stated goals of the drug testing policy and compared those goals with the policy itself. These three factors are very closely related to the factors that the Supreme Court outlined in *Prouse* and used to decide *Acton*. Thus, the NCAA's drug testing policy was examined in *Hill*

---

154. Anthony Saler, *Nonconstitutional Privacy Based Challenges to NCAA Drug Testing*, 1 SPORTS L.J. 303, 305 (1994) (quoting NCAA DRUG-TESTING/EDUCATION PROGRAMS, at 7 (1993-94).

159. *See* NCAA v. Tarkanian, 488 U.S. 179, 193-99 (1988).

162. 865 P.2d 633 (Cal. 1994).

under the same factors as the Vernonia School District's drug testing was reviewed in *Acton*.

3. The Reasonableness Factors in *Hill v. NCAA*

In looking at the expectations of privacy of student athletes, the *Hill* court noted several things that gave the students a diminished expectation of privacy. First, the court noted that merely by participating in athletics, athletes have a diminished expectation of privacy in both their internal and external bodily condition. Further, the court noted that the advance notice and opportunity to consent to testing elements of the NCAA's testing policy further diminished the athletes' expectations of privacy. Thus, the court found that although random urinalysis implicates privacy interests, those privacy interests are seriously diminished in the student athlete context. The court, however, also noted that although the privacy interests of student athletes are diminished, those interests are not necessarily de minimis.

The second factor that the court considered was the seriousness of the intrusion in the privacy interests of the student athletes. NCAA policy requires direct observation of urination by a monitor. The court found this to be a serious intrusion of student athletes' privacy interests. Further, the court stated that the seriousness of this intrusion, despite the fact that student athletes have a decreased expectation of privacy, justified further inquiry into the "competing interests" of the NCAA policy.

In analyzing the competing interests, the court looked at the stated goals of the policy and compared those goals with the policy itself. The stated goals of the NCAA's testing policy were to safeguard the integrity of intercollegiate athletic competition and to protect the health and safety of student athletes. The court stated that the NCAA's drug testing policy was reasonably calculated to further its stated goals. First, the drug testing program was "reasonably calculated to further [the NCAA's] legitimate interest in maintaining the integrity of intercollegiate athletic competition." Second, the court stated that because the NCAA sponsors intercollegiate athletic events which involve risks of injury, the NCAA effectively created situations for injuries resulting from drug use. As such, the court stated that the NCAA may attempt to protect those athletes involved in intercollegiate athletics, and that this drug testing program does that. Given that the drug testing policy furthered the stated goals of the NCAA, the court held that the policy did not violate the Stanford student athletes' state constitutional rights to privacy despite the serious intrusion into their privacy interests that it represented.

4. Comparing *Acton* and *Hill*

There are several differences between the drug testing programs involved in *Acton* and *Hill*. First, the goals of the testing programs were different. The goals of the testing program in *Hill* were to ensure fair competition and to protect intercollegiate athletes. The evidence in *Acton* indicates that the true goal of the Vernonia School District's testing program was to eliminate drug use among its entire student body. By testing athletes, the drug testing program in *Hill* was narrowly tailored to achieve its goals. In contrast, the drug testing program in *Acton* was narrowly tailored toward athletes not to achieve the testing program's goals, but rather to pass constitutional scrutiny.

Second, the NCAA's drug testing program tested athletes for use of anabolic steroids. This supports the proposition that the testing program's actual goals included ensuring fair competition and the safety of student athletes. By comparison, the Vernonia School District did not test its athletes for the use of anabolic steroids, in spite of the fact that protecting student athletes was one of the stated goals of its testing program.

Hill was decided using essentially the same balancing factors as were used to decide *Prouse* and *Acton*. Unlike *Acton*, *Hill* demonstrates that random suspicionless drug testing of athletes can be effective and constitutional in some situations. The analysis, however, requires paying special attention to the specifics and goals of the test.

C. Drug Testing Programs By Colleges And Universities

A state college or university is a state actor within the meaning of the Fourteenth Amendment. Therefore, the Fourth Amendment's requirement that a search be reasonable applies to state colleges and universities. "When [a state university] decides to impose a serious disciplinary sanction...it must comply with the Due Process Clause of the Fourteenth Amendment to the Federal Constitution."[191] Therefore, a drug testing policy at a state college or university could be required to pass the *Acton* reasonableness test.

1. A State University Testing Program Examined: *University of Colorado v. Derdeyn.*

The leading case on college-or university-implemented drug testing programs is *University of Colorado v. Derdeyn.*[192] In 1984, the University of Colorado began a drug-testing program for its student athletes. The original testing program required a urine test for certain drugs at each annual physical and also randomly throughout the year. Over the next several years, the university amended and revised its program several times. The third amendment, in 1988, included several changes in the program. The major change was that random urinalysis was replaced with random "rapid eye examination" (REE) testing. Urinalysis was performed only after finding a reasonable suspicion that an athlete had used drugs. Under the new program, a failure to perform well on an REE provided the school with a reasonable suspicion of drug use. Thus, if a student athlete did not perform well on an REE, he or she was required to undergo a urinalysis.

Several athletes at the university filed a class action suit against the university challenging the constitutionality of the drug testing program. The court held that the testing program of the university was unconstitutional. In so doing, the court balanced the degree by which the university's drug testing program intruded on the reasonable expectations of privacy of student athletes against the magnitude of the governmental interests served by the program.

In determining the degree by which the university's drug testing program intrudes on the reasonable expectations of privacy of student athletes, the court acknowledged that nonvoluntary, random, suspicionless drug testing always intrudes on an individual's privacy interests. The court also noted, however, that the magnitude of the intrusion can vary in different situations. Factors that help courts determine the magnitude of the intrusion include the place and manner in

---

191. NCAA v. Tarkanian, 488 U.S. 179, 192 (1988).
192. 863 P.2d 929 (Colo. 1993).

which the urine sample is collected, whether the individual works in a closely regulated industry, and whether the individual is subject to frequent medical exams.

The university argued that the magnitude of the intrusion was minimal, and cited six reasons supporting this argument: (1) that collection of the urine sample was done in a closed stall with only aural monitoring, (2) that student athletes are normally subjected to urine tests in annual physicals, (3) that student athletes submit to extensive on-campus regulation of their behavior, (4) that they must already submit to the NCAA's drug testing program, (5) that the consequences of refusing to be tested are not severe, and (6) that positive test results are kept confidential. The court, after analyzing each one of these arguments, concluded that the university's random testing policy resulted in a clearly significant intrusion.

The university also asserted several governmental interests in continuing its drug testing program, including the following: (1) preparing its athletes for drug testing in NCAA championship events, (2) promoting the integrity of its athletic program, (3) preventing drug use by other students who look to athletes as role models, (4) ensuring fair competition, and (5) protecting the health and safety of intercollegiate athletes. The court concluded that, unlike the organizations in *Skinner* and *Von Raab*, the university asserted no significant governmental interest in public safety or national security. This, combined with the university's failure to prove that the student athletes had a diminished expectation of privacy, led the court to hold the university's drug testing program unconstitutional.

2. Subjecting *Derdeyn* to the *Acton* Analysis

. . . .

The first factor in the *Acton* balancing test is the nature of the privacy interest upon which the search intrudes. In this case, the intrusion was minimized by the fact that the student athletes being tested were subjected only to aural, not visible, monitoring. Further, student athletes have a diminished expectation of privacy because they must routinely have physical examinations and are subjected to the idea of "communal undress" in their respective locker rooms. On this point, it is important to note that the idea of "communal undress" in the intercollegiate athletic situation is different from the "communal undress" in high school athletics. In the high school situation, required physical education classes subject practically all students to the elements of communal undress. Thus, high school athletes do not have lesser expectations of privacy compared to other students who do not participate in athletics. In the collegiate situation, however, there are no required physical education classes at most colleges and universities. Because of this, college students who do not participate in athletics may never encounter the elements of communal undress. Thus, college athletes should have lesser expectations of privacy than their fellow college classmates who do not participate in athletics.

Further, with the heightened visibility and vast media attention given to intercollegiate athletics in today's society, college athletes' vital statistics and injuries are made much more public than are the statistics and injuries of high school and elementary school students. This gives the college athlete even lesser expectations of privacy.

The next factor the Supreme Court used in deciding *Acton* was the character of the intrusion. As noted in *Acton*, subjecting individuals to urinalysis testing intrudes on a very private excretory function. Important in the analysis of this intrusion, however, is the manner in which the urinalysis is taken. Under the university's testing program, athletes were allowed to provide urine specimens in "a private and enclosed area." A monitor remained outside and checked the specimen afterward for tampering. This method of obtaining the urine specimen—at least for male athletes—is more relaxed than the method used in *Acton*. Because the Supreme Court in *Acton* found the intrusion in obtaining the urine sample to be minimal, the university's policy in obtaining the urine specimen undoubtedly would also be considered a minimal intrusion.

In addition, under the university's policy, the test results were only given to a handful of school administrators. This minimizes the intrusion upon the student athlete's privacy interests even more. When this is combined with the university's relaxed methods of obtaining the urine specimens, the university's drug testing policy would almost assuredly pass the character of the intrusion test outlined in *Acton*.

The third factor used to decide *Acton* was the nature and the immediacy of the governmental concern at issue. Only three of the interests cited by the university are truly governmental concerns. Those three are ensuring fair competition, preventing drug use among other students who view athletes as role models, and protecting the health and safety of intercollegiate athletes. The other two interests cited by the university—preparing its athletes for drug testing in NCAA championship events and promoting the integrity of its athletic programs—are more in the nature of personal interests of the university's athletic programs.

. . . .

The last, and perhaps most important, factor used to decide *Acton* was the effectiveness of the means implemented in meeting the government's concerns. Once again, the governmental concerns of the university's drug testing policy were to prevent drug use by other students who look to athletes as role models, to ensure fair competition, and to protect the health and safety of intercollegiate athletes. Although at first blush these goals seem to be the exact same goals of the drug testing program enacted by the school district in *Acton*, there is an important distinction between the *Acton* and *Derdeyn* cases. That distinction is that the stated goals of the drug policy enacted by the university in *Derdeyn* really were the true goals of the testing policy, whereas in *Acton*, as stated above, the stated goals of the drug testing program enacted by the school district were not the true goals of the testing policy.

In addition, the implementation of the drug testing program by the university furthers every one of the goals, especially the goals of ensuring fair competition and protecting the health and safety of intercollegiate athletes. Of particular importance to these two goals is deterring the use of performance-enhancing drugs such as steroids. Steroids can not only give an athlete a distinct strength advantage over an opponent, but, as discussed above, can also be very dangerous to the health and safety of the athlete who uses them. Because the university's drug testing policy was set up to detect the use of anabolic steroids, it undoubtedly helps ensure fair competition while at the same time protecting the health and safety of student athletes.

Therefore, although the court in *Derdeyn* held the drug testing policy implemented by the University of Colorado to be unconstitutional, if tested by the standards used in *Acton*, the policy would most likely be found constitutional.

. . . .

IV. CONCLUSION

Because the true goal of the Vernonia School District in implementing its drug testing policy was to eliminate drug use among the district's entire student body and not just among the athletes of the school, the district's policy of testing only the athletes in the school district should have been held unconstitutional. The fact that high school and elementary school athletes do not have a lesser expectation of privacy than other high school and elementary school students suggests that a drug testing policy involving the whole student body might be constitutionally better than one involving only athletes.

. . . .

When analyzed under the balancing tests used to decide *Acton*, both the NCAA's drug testing policy and the individual drug testing policies of state colleges and universities are constitutional. The goals of these policies are to ensure fair competition in athletics and protect the safety of student athletes. The testing of athletes effectively furthers the attainment of those goals. Such programs are "legally defensible because [they are] intended to protect the health and welfare of the student-athlete and to assure equal competition in NCAA championships and NCAA-certified postseason games."[240] This is in contrast to high school and elementary school testing situations like *Acton*, where the goal is to eliminate drug use among an entire student body. In the high school and elementary school testing situation, because the testing of athletes does not effectively further elimination of drug use among the entire student body, suspicionless testing policies are unconstitutional.

. . . .

---

3. Professional Sports

Ethan Lock, The Legality Under the National Labor Relations Act of Attempts by National Football League Owners to Unilaterally Implement Drug Testing Programs
39 University of Florida Law Review 1 (1987)*

. . . .

III. TESTING AS MANDATORY VERSUS NON-MANDATORY SUBJECT OF COLLECTIVE BARGAINING

A. *Introduction*

One of the most controversial aspects of the drug testing programs proposed in professional sports involves management's right under the NLRA to unilaterally implement these programs. . . .

---

240. Teagarden, *supra* note 9, at 1008 (quoting *Strict Drug Testing Program Put in Place*, THE NCAA NEWS, Sept. 29, 1986, at 1).

.... Management's right to implement random drug testing without first bargaining with the union depends on the classification of drug programs as either a mandatory or a permissive subject of collective bargaining.

If drug programs fall within the scope of mandatory bargaining, management will violate the NLRA if it unilaterally adopts a drug program without first bargaining with the union. Both parties have an obligation to bargain over mandatory subjects, and a failure to do so constitutes a refusal to bargain under either subsection 8(a)(5) or 8(b)(3). Either party also has the right, with respect to mandatory subjects, to insist on its position to impasse and even back its position with a strike or lockout. Thus, both management and the union could, at the bargaining table, refuse a drug program proposed by its opponent and, at the same time, use economic weapons to pressure the other party to accept its own proposal.

Non-mandatory or permissive subjects may be proposed by either party. Yet, neither party is obligated to bargain over or discuss such subjects. The proponent of a non-mandatory subject can neither bargain to impasse nor resort to the use of economic weapons to obtain its demands. In effect, management can unilaterally implement decisions falling outside the scope of mandatory bargaining and the union is precluded from either demanding bargaining over the matter or striking to compel management to modify its decision.

An employer's willingness to discuss non-mandatory terms during collective bargaining does not change its statutory obligations. Thus, even if an employer bargains over and agrees to a permissive term, that term is unenforceable under the NLRA. In other words, the employer can breach the contract without violating the NLRA. Clearly, a determination that a subject is mandatory significantly impacts the bargaining relationship between the parties with respect to that particular subject.

B. *Scope of Mandatory Bargaining*

1. Statutory Language

The NLRA was designed to eliminate "obstructions to the free flow of commerce ... by encouraging the practice and procedure of collective bargaining."[108] This policy is theoretically enforced by the unfair labor practice provisions of the Act. Thus, an employer commits an unfair labor practice under section 8(a)(5) by refusing to bargain collectively, while a union's refusal to bargain violates section 8(b)(3).

The duty to bargain collectively is defined in section 8(d). Under this provision, both employers and unions are obligated to meet at reasonable times and confer in good faith with respect to wages, hours, and other terms and conditions of employment. Parties are free to bargain over any legal subject. Yet, Congress specifically limited the duty to bargain to those matters involving "wages, hours, and other terms and conditions of employment."

....

2. Supreme Court Precedents

....

---

108. 29 U.S.C. § 151 (1982).

In *Fibreboard Paper Products Corp. v. NLRB*,[123] the employer unilaterally decided to subcontract maintenance work performed by unit employees. At the expiration of the labor contract, the employer terminated the maintenance employees. The NLRB held that the employer was obligated to bargain over both the decision to subcontract and the effects of that decision. The Supreme Court, affirming the NLRB's decision, relied on several factors to find that the employer's decision to subcontract was a mandatory subject of bargaining.

The Court noted that employer decisions resulting in terminations fell within the broad meaning of "terms and conditions of employment." The Court stressed that the purposes of the NLRA were furthered by bringing matters "of vital concern to labor and management" within the bargaining framework established by Congress. Industrial practice indicated that subcontracting was a topic commonly contained in collective bargaining agreements, thus providing additional support for the decision. Significantly, the Court noted that the employer's decision to subcontract neither altered the company's basic operation nor required any capital investment. Thus, requiring an employer to bargain over this matter "would not significantly abridge his freedom to manage the business."

Justice Stewart, in his concurring opinion, interpreted conditions of employment less expansively than the majority....Stewart stated:

> Nothing the Court holds today should be understood as imposing a duty to bargain collectively regarding such managerial decisions, which lie at the core of entrepreneurial control. Decisions concerning the commitment of investment capital and the basic scope of the enterprise are not themselves primarily about conditions of employment, though the effect of the decision may be necessarily to terminate employment.[128]

The Supreme Court considered the scope of mandatory bargaining again in *First National Maintenance Corp. v. NLRB*.[129] The employer in that case supplied maintenance and cleaning services to commercial customers in the New York City area. A group of employees who serviced a particular nursing home voted in a Board-sanctioned election to be represented by a union. Without bargaining with the newly-elected union, the employer terminated its service to the nursing home and subsequently discharged all the employees.

Although it found no anti-union animus, the NLRB held that the employer's decision to terminate its service and the effects of that decision were mandatory subjects of bargaining. Thus, the employer violated section 8(a)(5) of the NLRA by failing to bargain in good faith over those decisions. The employer appealed the NLRB's finding that the decision to terminate service was a term or condition of employment. The Second Circuit upheld the NLRB's ruling. The Supreme Court held that an employer's decision to terminate part of its business for purely economic reasons was outside the scope of mandatory bargaining, and reversed the NLRB.

The Court, in its analysis of the scope of mandatory bargaining, identified three basic types of management decisions. Certain decisions, such as those in-

---

123. *Fibreboard*, 379 U.S. at 204-07.
128. *Id.*
129. 452 U.S. 666 (1981).

volving promotional expenditures, product design and financing arrangements, "have only an indirect and attenuated impact on the employment relationship" and thus fall outside the scope of mandatory bargaining. Other decisions, such as those pertaining to work rules and layoffs, have a direct and almost exclusive impact on the employer-employee relationship. These types of decisions are mandatory subjects. More troublesome for purposes of distinguishing mandatory from non-mandatory subjects are those decisions that directly impact on employment and are primarily economic decisions involving a change in the scope and direction of the enterprise. Decisions such as the one made by the employer in *First National Maintenance* to terminate part of a business fall into this category.

The Court acknowledged that decisions of this nature necessarily implicate significant employee and employer interests. Nonetheless, the Court avoided weighing these competing interests. Instead, it stated that an employer should be required to bargain over such decisions only if the benefit to labor-management relations and the collective bargaining process outweighs the burden placed on an employer's ability to conduct business.

The Court balanced the employer's "need for unencumbered decision making" with the benefit to labor-management relations. The Court recognized that a fundamental purpose of the Act was to promote industrial peace by bringing problems of vital concern to labor and management within the collective bargaining framework established by Congress. Yet, the Court stressed that management had to be free from the constraints of the bargaining process to the extent necessary to run a profitable business. The Court also noted that business exigencies frequently required employers to act with speed, flexibility, and secrecy. Noting that the employer's decision in *First National Maintenance* represented a significant change in operations, the Court concluded that the employer's need to operate freely regarding an economic decision to terminate part of its business outweighed the incremental benefit that might be gained through union participation in making such a decision.

C. *Analysis of Drug Programs in the Context of Professional Sports Under Existing Case Law*

1. Application of National Labor Relations Board and Lower Court Precedents

. . . .

The NLRB recently interpreted *First National Maintenance* in *Otis Elevator*.[146] In *Otis*, the employer decided to transfer some of its work to another of its plants. Although the employer disregarded the union while making this relocation decision, the NLRB upheld the employer's unilateral action. In an extremely broad reading of *First National Maintenance*, the NLRB held that all decisions affecting the scope and direction of an enterprise are exempted from bargaining and from the *First National Maintenance* Court's balancing test. In the NLRB's opinion, only those decisions in which labor costs are the determining factor would fall within the scope of mandatory bargaining.

Both the NLRB and the courts have interpreted "terms and conditions of employment" to include most provisions that deal with the employer-employee rela-

---

146. 269 N.L.R.B. 891 (1984).

tionship. Thus, most rules that regulate how employees perform their work are considered terms and conditions of employment. Included in this category are several bargaining subjects that bear some resemblance to the drug testing programs proposed in the professional sports industry.

For example, decisions involving employee health and safety protection on the job are clearly mandatory subjects of collective bargaining.... Safety considerations are such an important condition of employment that an employer may not modify safety rules without first bargaining with the union even when the employer is obligated by law to conform its conduct to specific minimum safety standards. Disciplinary rules are also generally mandatory subjects of bargaining. Thus, it is an unfair labor practice for an employer to unilaterally implement systems of discipline. Similarly, an employer must bargain over the criteria for demotion or a change in status of its employees.

The requirements of continued employment are perhaps the most literal of "terms and conditions of employment." Accordingly, employer decisions to terminate employees, like disciplinary rules, are mandatory subjects of bargaining. An employer may not unilaterally establish the allowable causes of discharge or the grievance procedures under which employer decisions involving discharges will be reviewed. In fact, the scope of "requirements of continued employment" is not limited to discharges for cause. An employer is generally obligated to bargain over other issues involving the tenure of its employees, including where and in what sequence layoffs occur and the age for forced retirement.

In connection with disciplinary rules and terminations, various testing programs constitute "terms or conditions of employment" and are thus mandatory bargaining topics. For example, the NLRB held that an employer may not unilaterally institute a polygraph test requirement for its employees, if results of the test could be the basis for disciplinary action or if refusal to submit to testing could result in automatic discharge. Likewise, an employer cannot unilaterally implement mandatory physical examinations for its employees as part of attendance control procedures either as a condition of continued employment or if the results of the examinations could be the basis for discharge.

The NLRB's treatment of each of these subjects suggests that drug testing programs proposed by professional sports leagues constitute mandatory subjects of bargaining. Drug abuse in professional sports clearly implicates valid employee safety concerns. The use of drugs during an athletic contest endangers the safety of all players. For example, amphetamines would tend to make players more intense and more aggressive and, thus, would be hazardous to users as well as nonusers. Former major league pitcher Doc Ellis, who under the influence of LSD pitched a no-hitter for the Pittsburgh Pirates, has publicly admitted that he became more aggressive and frequently threw at batters while on drugs. Cocaine, which also increases a person's heart rate, could presumably have a similar effect on players. Injuries might also result from marijuana or any other drug that might diminish a player's concentration during the contest.

The most controversial element of the proposed drug programs has been mandatory random testing. In addition, these programs have typically incorporated a system of progressive penalties for first, second, and third time offenders. The penalties include temporary suspension, suspension without pay, and permanent suspension.

The safety considerations associated with drug use, as well as the disciplinary and testing aspects of the drug programs in professional sports, suggest that these programs are mandatory bargaining topics. An alternative argument exists, however, to compel bargaining over drug programs. These programs appear to fall within the scope of mandatory bargaining under the Supreme Court's balancing test in *First National Maintenance*.

2. Application of Supreme Court Precedents

a. Categories of Management Decisions

Of the three categories of management decisions identified by the Court in *First National Maintenance*, the drug-testing programs proposed in professional sports more closely resemble that category of management decisions almost exclusively affecting the employer-employee relationship than the type of economic decision primarily affecting a change in the scope or direction of the enterprise. As noted above, the programs typically incorporate disciplinary measures affecting player job security and conditions of continued employment. In an effort to justify the implementation of random drug testing, management expressed a belief that drug use by players will ultimately undermine fan support and the financial survival of professional sports. Presumably, management would categorize a program designed to eliminate drug use as an economic decision primarily affecting the scope and direction of the enterprise.

This categorization is untenable for two reasons. First, an attempt to eliminate drug use in professional sports hardly constitutes a change in the scope or direction of business in the same manner as do terminations, partial closings, or decisions to invest in labor-saving machinery. The institution of a league-wide drug testing program would neither change the basic operation of a professional sports league nor require a significant capital investment. Thus, a drug program simply does not appear to be the type of management decision that lies at the "core of entrepreneurial control."

Second, and perhaps more important, a decision to implement a drug program does not appear to be the type of business exigency that must remain outside the bargaining process in order to enable management to run a profitable business. Despite management's concern that drugs are threatening the economic survival of professional sports, no evidence exists to support the theory that drug use by professional athletes will have any short run economic impact on professional sports leagues. To the contrary, industry revenues have increased during the past decade.

Amphetamines, pain killers, and steroids have been a part of professional sports for many years. More recently, street drugs have also become part of the industry. In 1985, a federal investigation revealed widespread cocaine use among major league baseball players. Rumors of cocaine use by NFL players also surfaced in 1985. Prior to the 1986 season, Cleveland Browns safety Don Rogers died of a cocaine overdose. Stories of cocaine use in the NBA have been well publicized for years. In 1985, several players were suspended from NBA play because of their involvement with cocaine. Nonetheless, professional sports franchises appear to be flourishing economically. Gate receipts and television ratings are strong and each of the three major professional sports leagues (NFL, MLB and NBA) has publicly discussed the possibility of expansion in the near future. The tremendous increase in gate receipts and network and non-network television revenues during the past decade suggests that fans have been indifferent to professional athletes' use of drugs. If eliminating drug use is actually fundamental to the survival or basic direction of professional sports leagues, these facts are difficult to explain.

b. Analysis Under First National Maintenance Balancing Test—Benefits to Labor-Management Relations and Collective Bargaining

Drug testing programs also appear to fall within the scope of mandatory bargaining under the Supreme Court's balancing test in *First National Maintenance*. The *First National Maintenance* test requires management to bargain if the benefits to labor-management relations and the collective bargaining process outweigh the burden placed on the employers' ability to conduct business. Admittedly, employers have a legitimate interest in controlling employees' drug use. Yet, the Court's language in *First National Maintenance* and the existence of other employer remedies to control the use of drugs suggest that the benefits derived from collective bargaining outweigh management's need to take unencumbered or unilateral actions.

The *First National Maintenance* court noted that the fundamental goal of the NLRA was to promote industrial peace. Designating certain matters as "mandatory subjects of bargaining" helps achieve industrial peace by bringing problems of vital concern to labor and management within the bargaining framework established by Congress. In the Court's opinion, collective bargaining results in better decisions for labor, management, and society as a whole. The Court's opinion presumes the subject proposed for discussion is amenable to resolution through the bargaining process.

The *First National Maintenance* Court concluded that decisions "essential for the running of a profitable business" are not amenable to collective bargaining. These types of decisions are excluded from collective bargaining to protect the employer's right to determine the scope and direction of its enterprise. Unlike decisions affecting the scope or direction of an enterprise, however, drug programs require neither swift nor unilateral action. As noted above, drug use by professional athletes appears to have had no immediate impact on industry revenues. In addition, the implementation of a drug program neither requires an investment of capital nor changes the basic direction of an enterprise.

At the same time, drug use is clearly a problem of vital concern to labor and management. Without minimizing management's interest in controlling drug use, it is inaccurate and patronizing to suggest that drug use by athletes is a "vital concern" only for management. Drug use by players clearly implicates legitimate health and safety concerns.

Drugs can also have a significant economic impact on players. Although average yearly salaries in professional sports exceed average salaries in most other industries, professional athletes have relatively short careers. The average career in the NFL, for example, is approximately four and one-half years. Drug use could conceivably shorten a player's career by contributing to injury, eroding the player's skills or subjecting the player to suspension or expulsion from the league. A one-year suspension or an injury that shortens a player's career by one year reduces an average career by almost twenty-five percent. Obviously, drug use can have a tremendous impact on a player's career earning potential. Thus, the subject of drugs is a "vital concern" for players.

In addition, current practice in the industry suggests that drug programs is a topic amenable to collective bargaining. In both *Fibreboard* and *First National Maintenance*, the Court acknowledged that current labor practice was not a "binding guide" for courts to determine the scope of mandatory bargaining. Nonetheless, the Courts cited industry practice as an indication of what was feasible through collective bargaining. The *Fibreboard* Court noted that employer decisions to subcontract had long been viewed as matters particularly well-suited for resolution within the structure of collective bargaining. Furthermore, the industrial practice of bargaining over this type of decision demonstrated the "amenability of such subjects to the collective bargaining process."

The Court in *First National Maintenance* also cited industry practice to support its finding that termination decisions fell outside the scope of mandatory bargaining. The Court noted that provisions giving unions the right to participate in the decisionmaking process concerning alteration of the scope of an enterprise were relatively rare. This evidence, in the Court's opinion, weighed against mandatory bargaining.

....

c. Analysis Under *First National Maintenance* Balancing Test—Management's Interest

Under the *First National Maintenance* balancing test, the benefits to the collective bargaining process must be weighed against management's right to protect its investment and unilaterally determine the scope or direction of its enterprise. Although drug use appears to have no short term impact on industry revenues, and drug programs do not affect the fundamental operation of an enterprise, employers have a legitimate interest in the quality of their employee's job performance. Whether that interest gives an employer the right to unilaterally adopt a drug testing program, however, is debatable.

The NLRA imposes a duty to bargain over many subjects about which employers have legitimate reasons for wanting to bargain. Thus, *Fibreboard* required the employer to bargain over a decision to "contract out" even though the employer had a legitimate economic interest in making its decision. In *Medicenter*, the NLRB ruled that polygraph testing was a mandatory subject of bargaining, even though the employer had legitimate concerns over vandalism. The employer's interest in detecting and preventing illegal activity did not justify its refusal to bargain.[189] Similarly, the Third Circuit in *CIBA-Geigy Pharmaceutical* found that physical examinations were a mandatory subject despite employer claims that testing was necessary to meet production schedules.[190]

Even assuming that an employer's interest in maximizing job performance permits the employer to unilaterally adopt a drug program, the unique nature of the professional sports industry distinguishes sports franchise owners from employers in other industries. Within the context of professional sports, an owner's need for unilateral action with regard to drug testing is diminished by the availability of other remedies. Because of the collective nature of athletic contests, unions and players recognize that a player's value to any particular team depends not only on the player's skill level, but also on the nature of the skills and the player's attitude, conduct, age, and relationship with teammates. Thus, the employment relationship in professional sports presumes that teams retain the discretion to make nec-

---

189. *Medicenter*, 331 N.L.R.B. at 676.
190. *CIBA-Geigy*, 114 L.R.R.M. at 3635.

essary personnel changes in search of the right combination of talent, attitude, and leadership to produce a winning team.

Teams typically retain broad powers to terminate a player's employment under the Standard Player Contract. Paragraph 11 of the NFL Player Contract, for example, allows the team to terminate a player's contract at any time if, in the sole judgment of the team, the player's skill is unsatisfactory as compared with other players or if the player has engaged in personal conduct reasonably judged by the club to adversely affect or reflect on the team....

In light of this wide range of discretion, a player will not be able to challenge a team's decision to terminate the player for failure to observe club rules or for lack of skill. Since a player's performance or conduct need only be unsatisfactory in the sole judgment of the club, the team is not obligated to support personnel decisions with objective proof. Each team may exercise unfettered discretion to terminate any players using or suspected of using drugs.

Admittedly, the use of drugs might be a league-wide problem that ultimately requires a league-wide solution. Nonetheless, since teams can unilaterally rid themselves of players with drug problems, owners need not take immediate, unilateral league-wide action. To the extent that owners perceive drug use as a public relations cancer likely to undermine fan support or destroy the league, each owner has a remedy with respect to individual drug users, pending negotiation with the union of a league-wide program.

An individual team owner will usually become aware of drug problems on the team before the fans or media do. Occasionally, however, a team owner might not learn of an individual player's problem until the public does. This undoubtedly has been true in the case of some player arrests. In either case, the owner can communicate the team's position on drug use by taking immediate action and terminating that player's contract. Thus, no business exigency exists to justify unilateral action by management.

Moreover, team owners historically delegate to the league commissioner significant authority over player discipline, disputes between players and teams, and inter-team controversies. Although players' associations have, through collective bargaining, successfully reduced the scope of the commissioners' role in player-team disputes, league commissioners have uniformly retained the right to fine or suspend players for conduct detrimental to the integrity of, or public confidence in, the sport.

Paragraph 15 of the NFL Player Contract, for example, permits the commissioner to fine or suspend the player or terminate his contract if the player

> [a]ccepts a bribe or agrees to throw or fix an NFL game; fails to promptly report a bribe offer or an attempt to throw or fix an NFL game; bets on an NFL game; knowingly associates with gamblers or gambling activity; uses or provides other players with stimulants or other drugs for the purpose of attempting to enhance on-field performance; or is guilty of any other form of conduct reasonably judged by the League Commissioner to be detrimental to the League or professional football.... [199]

The procedural requirements for commissioner action under paragraph 15 are outlined in article VIII of the 1982 collective bargaining agreement.

---

199. NFL PLAYER CONTRACT, ¶ 15.

The NFL Commissioner, through the power granted to him under the integrity-of-the-game clause contained in the NFL Player Contract, appears to be well-suited to deal with isolated instances of misconduct that threaten the integrity of the game. In 1983, NFL Commissioner Rozelle suspended Baltimore Colts quarterback Art Schlichter for two years for gambling. The same year, Rozelle suspended Ross Browner, Pete Johnson, E. J. Junior, and Greg Stemrick for four games because of their involvement with cocaine. None of these suspensions was challenged by the NFLPA and all seemed to be appropriate situations for Commissioner Rozelle to invoke his powers under paragraph 15 of the Player Contract and article VIII of the collective bargaining agreement. Yet the appropriateness of commissioner action in these instances hardly legitimizes league-wide action by the commissioner. In fact, the ability of the commissioner to discipline known drug users further reduces the need for unilateral adoption of a league-wide drug program.

D. *Analysis of Drug Programs in Context of Professional Sports Under Product Market Theory*

1. Application of Product Market Theory

One year after the *First National Maintenance* decision, Michael Harper published an article in the Virginia Law Review that attempted to clarify the scope of mandatory bargaining. The article reconciled the *First National Maintenance* decision with a clear but limited principle that could be predictably and uniformly applied to all bargaining cases. Harper proposed to exclude from compulsory bargaining all employer decisions that determine the nature, quantity, pricing, and marketing of products.

To support his product market theory, Harper argued that prohibiting employees from exerting any direct control over the product market was consistent with the NLRA. In addition, Harper cited a strong social policy, not subordinated by the NLRA, in favor of allowing consumers to decide which goods employers produce by expressing their preference in the marketplace. Consumers, not employees, should influence management's product market decisions. Unlike the *First National Maintenance* test, Harper's product market theory was based on the desirability of insulating product market decisions from the collective bargaining process rather than weighing employer and collective bargaining interests.

Whatever the merits of Harper's product market theory in the normal industrial setting, the theory conflicts with the purposes of the NLRA when applied to employees whose performance is the marketed product. For example, the NLRB and the courts have consistently held that safety concerns are conditions of employment within the meaning of the NLRA and, thus, are mandatory subjects of bargaining. The product market theory, however, excludes safety issues from mandatory bargaining in situations where employee risk formed part of the product. As a result, this theory would have a dramatic impact on the scope of collective bargaining in the professional sports industry.

    ....

3. Product Image

Despite the above cases, management's interest in controlling drug use can be distinguished from its interest in playing surfaces and the rules of the game. A drug program is not part of product design in the same manner that rules and playing surfaces represent aspects of product design. Drug use by players is arguably an aspect of product image rather than product design.

The exclusion from mandatory bargaining of those management decisions that affect the image of a product is perhaps the most appealing application of Harper's product market theory within the context of professional sports. Harper suggests that employer decisions concerning the identity and behavior of employees, like product design decisions, should remain outside the scope of mandatory bargaining when the identity and behavior of the employees define the marketed product. Employers should not have to bargain over product image or quality. Employers should, according to Harper, be able to unilaterally set personnel standards that define the product.

Authority exists to support the position that decisions that affect the image and quality of an employer's product should be excluded from the scope of mandatory bargaining. In *Newspaper Guild of Greater Philadelphia, Local 10, v. NLRB*,[265] a publisher attempted to unilaterally institute an ethics code that restricted its employees from participating in certain community or political activities and from receiving gifts from protected news sources. The stated purposes of the code were to maintain the paper's standards of integrity and objectivity and to protect its quality and credibility. The union claimed that the code was a condition of employment and filed an unfair labor practice charge after management refused to bargain over the matter.

The administrative law judge ruled that the code was a mandatory bargaining subject and ordered the employer to bargain. The NLRB agreed that the employer had a duty to bargain over the penalty provisions of the code but held that the employer had no duty to bargain over the code's substantive provisions. The penalty provisions affected employment security and fell within the scope of mandatory bargaining. In the NLRB's opinion, however, the code itself represented the newspaper's attempt to preserve the quality of its publication. It was, therefore, a management prerogative.

The D.C. Circuit Court of Appeals rejected the NLRB's distinction between a decision to institute a code and the penalties under the code. In its opinion, these matters were inseparable. Both were either mandatory or non-mandatory subjects of bargaining. At least with respect to news publications, however, the court recognized the non-mandatory nature of image and quality concerns. It found that credibility was a central element of the newspaper's ultimate product and, relying on Justice Stewart's concurring opinion in *Fibreboard*, concluded that the protection of a paper's editorial integrity lay "at the core of publishing control."

In a footnote to its decision, the *Newspaper Guild* court specifically declined to consider whether credibility and integrity were as fundamental to the scope of commercial enterprises not possessing the special characteristics of a news publication. Yet an argument of this nature is not untenable. Within the context of professional sports, professional athletes are clearly identified by the public with the product that is being marketed by professional sports leagues. Presumably, sports franchise owners would argue that drug use by professional athletes affects the quality and image of the product offered to the fans.

---

265. 636 F.2d 550 (D.C. Cir. 1980).

Ironically, management has contributed to the use of drugs in professional sports. Drugs and alcohol have for many years been associated with the industry. Breweries advertise heavily in professional sports. Beer is sold at most athletic stadiums and athletes frequently appear in beer commercials. More significantly, teams have historically used and abused amphetamines, painkillers, cortisone, and steroids. As recently as 1986, Commissioner Rozelle specifically stated that his proposed drug testing program would not include testing for steroids.

In addition, management's attempts to publicly pressure players to accept random drug testing fosters the image of professional athletes as drug users. There have, of course, been several instances of drug abuse by individual athletes. Nonetheless, many athletes do not use drugs, and resent both management's and the public's perception of athletes as drug abusers. Fans and the media interpret the players' refusal to accept testing as evidence that players either have something to hide or feel that drug abuse is not a serious problem.

Regardless of management's contribution to the presence of drugs in the industry and the public's perception of athletes as drug users, management clearly has a legitimate right to protect the image and quality of professional sports. Yet this right to protect its product does not necessarily give management the right to unilaterally implement a drug testing program. As noted above, management typically has the ability under the standard player contract to protect the image of the game by terminating drug users' contracts. Additionally, drug use involves significant employee interests as well as image concerns. Thus, unilateral action is justified only when management must act immediately in order to protect its product. Since drug use in professional sports has had no immediate impact on industry revenues, there appears to be no reason to relieve management of its obligation to bargain over this subject.

Finally, no evidence exists to suggest that drug testing will eliminate drug use in professional sports or change the image of professional athletes as drug users. The owners' argument that testing will deter drug use might have some validity. But cocaine leaves the body within a few days of use. Thus, unless tests are conducted every few days, players with drug problems will be inclined to use drugs immediately after being tested.

E. *Effects Bargaining*

Management's most persuasive argument to exclude drug programs from the scope of mandatory bargaining is that players' drug use affects the image and quality of the product offered to the market. Thus, drug testing is a matter that lies at the core of entrepreneurial control. As noted above, various factors, including the existence of other employee remedies, weaken the argument. Regardless of the validity of its argument, however, management may still have an obligation to bargain over the type of program currently proposed in professional sports. A determination that drug programs are not mandatory bargaining subjects will not necessarily relieve management of its obligation to bargain over the effects of those programs.

The Court and the NLRB have held that an employer's right to take unilateral action with respect to non-mandatory bargaining subjects does not permit the employer to unilaterally control the effects of that action. The NLRB's conclusion in *First National Maintenance* that the employer had an obligation to bargain over both its decision to terminate and the effects of that decision indicate that the NLRB recognized a distinction between these two types of employer decisions. On appeal, the Supreme Court also recognized this distinction. Although it held that the decision to close the plant was not a mandatory subject, the Court found that the employer did have an obligation to bargain over the effects of that decision.

The Court cited its own language in *Fibreboard* where it observed that section 8(d) covered terminations of employment that resulted from closing an operation. The Court also noted that the union must be given the opportunity to bargain over terminations resulting from closings as part of the effects bargaining mandated by section 8(a)(5). Because it had a legitimate interest in matters of job security, the union was entitled to offer concessions, information, or alternatives to management in an attempt to forestall or prevent the termination of jobs.

The NLRB reached a similar result in *Newspaper Guild*.[289] In that case, the NLRB found that the employer was obligated to bargain over the penalties imposed for violations of an ethics code even though the code itself was a nonmandatory bargaining subject. The D.C. Circuit's reversal of the NLRB's holding suggests that management's obligations with respect to effects bargaining are no more clearly defined than its obligations under the language of the NLRA.

The circuit court refused to distinguish for bargaining purposes the penalty provisions of the code from the code's substantive provisions. In its opinion, that distinction was "contrary to reason and at war with the practical considerations of collective bargaining." As a practical mater, the Court reasoned that penalties could not be separated under the NLRA from the substantive provisions they were designed to enforce.

Whether the *First National Maintenance* and *Newspaper Guild* decisions can be reconciled is unclear. Although a decision to terminate differs from product image or quality decisions, both cases involved employer decisions that fell outside the scope of mandatory bargaining. Similarly, significant employee interests were at stake in each case. On the other hand, for bargaining purposes, it could be far easier to separate the effects of a decision to terminate from the actual decision to terminate than to separate the penalties enforcing a set of rules from those rules.

A strong argument could be made that management should, at a minimum, have an obligation to bargain over the effects of a drug program. Determining the scope of "effects bargaining" presumably involves the same type of balancing test used by the Court in *First National Maintenance*. Once again, although the employer interests at stake may be significant, no evidence exists to suggest that management needs to take immediate, unilateral action to protect its product. At the same time, the penalties or "effects" under the proposed programs clearly implicate matters of "vital concern" to employees. Because professional athletes have such short careers, any type of suspension is an appropriate subject for collective bargaining. Thus, players should, at the very least, have the right to demand bargaining over the mechanics and penalties of a league-wide drug program.

.....

---

289. Newspaper Guild, Local 10 v. NLRB, 636 F.2d 550 (D.C. Cir. 1980).

Glenn M. Wong and Richard J. Ensor, Major League Baseball and Drugs: Fight the Problem or the Player?
11 Nova Law Review 779 (1987)*

. . . .

IV. The Ueberroth Era Begins

Whether because of public relations concerns, or a deepening problem, much time has initially been spent by the MLB's new Commissioner, Peter V. Ueberroth, on solving the league's drug-related issues. The new commissioner was appointed on March 3, 1984 and assumed office on October 1, 1984. Prior to the appointment, Ueberroth had been executive director of the Los Angeles Olympic Games, were he had run the highly successful, if very commercial, 1984 Olympic Games. The soon to be Commissioner noted during the press conference announcing his new position that in regards to drugs in MLB, "[b]aseball has a responsibility to fight drugs, not fight players."

However, Ueberroth would not be involved in the first decision concerning drug testing during his tenure. Former Commissioner Kuhn's efforts to initiate and develop the joint drug program between the MLB and the MLBPA were deemed insufficient in October, 1985 by the owners who dropped the program. Ueberroth did not directly participate in the owners' decision to drop Kuhn's drug program.

Reacting in part to a major federal drug probe in Pittsburgh, Ueberroth subsequently called for a comprehensive mandatory drug-testing program. The program mandated testing for those employed by the commissioner's office, the club's front office staffs and employees, and the umpires, as well as all minor league players.

On May 15, 1985, Commissioner Ueberroth announced his first set of drug testing guidelines. In a subsequent memo sent by Ueberroth on June 18, 1985, the commissioner outlined the policy as follows:

1. Preparations are complete for the implementation of the testing program.

2. Testing for Minor League players and umpires will commence during the month of July and continue through the end of each League season.

3. Testing for remaining Major and Minor League personnel will begin in August and continue through November 1985.

4. For 1986 and years thereafter, testing will commence in March and continue through October for all affected personnel.

The program will operate under the following guidelines:

a. Individuals subject to testing include all Minor League umpires and playing personnel; all full-time, year-round administrative and management personnel employed in Minor Leagues and by Major League Baseball; and all Major League managers, coaches, trainers and umpires;

. . . .

d. The cost for the administration of this program will be borne by the Major Leagues Central Fund;

---

e. Samples will be taken at Major and Minor League ballparks and at the administrative offices of Major and Minor League management personnel. Samples will be divided into two containers, one for analysis and the other stored for confirmatory tests, if required. Laboratory analysis will be conducted at a fully competent facility under the supervision of Dr. Daly and Dr. Jasper;

f. Samples will be tested for the following controlled substances: cocaine, amphetamines, marijuana, heroin and morphine. Amphetamines will not be considered an illegal drug if an individual has a legal prescription;

g. Positive test results will be provided to Dr. Daly. He will then authorize a confirmatory analysis. If positive, Dr. Daly (or an appropriate designee) will thereafter contact the individual involved to make arrangements for appropriate evaluation and treatment if necessary;

h. At the time of collection samples will be coded. The results of all tests will be kept confidential;

i. There will be no discipline or penalties for initial positive test results. Test results will not become a part of an employee's permanent employment record;

j. Positive test results will occasion evaluation and rehabilitative treatment if necessary. Wherever appropriate, this will be done in conjunction with our Employee Assistance Programs.

Ueberroth further advised that "Major League players are not covered by the program and will not be participating in it." In addition, the Commissioner stressed, "Reiterate to all affected personnel that the objectives of this program are not punitive.... Our objective is to deter drug use, not punish anyone who may be involved with it." In July, 1985 the first set of drug tests was administered to those MLB personnel who had agreed to the plan.

. . . .

Nothing dramatized the degree of drug involvement more than the Pittsburgh drug trials that were held in September just as the 1985 season entered into the American and National Leagues Championship Series and the World Series. The trial involved Curtis Strong, a Philadelphia resident accused of selling cocaine to MLB players. In the first week of Strong's trial, Lonnie Smith of the Kansas City Royals described under a grant of immunity his introduction to cocaine in the major leagues and how the drug was purchased and distributed in MLB. In a succession of days some of MLB's most well-known players including Keith Hernandez, Dale Berra, Enos Cabell, Dave Parker, and John Milner also testified under immunity about drug use in baseball.

While no MLB player was charged in the Pittsburgh case, by the time the trial ended in late September and Curtis Strong had been convicted and sentenced to 10 years imprisonment, it seemed to many fans that professional baseball had been judged guilty. Because of this perceived guilt by association, Commissioner Ueberroth decided to take further steps in his attack upon professional baseball's drug abuse problem.

While maintaining the same drug testing procedure that he had implemented in 1985 for all MLB personnel except the players, Commissioner Ueberroth decided to implement the following measures as well in the pre-1986 baseball season: conditional punishment for those players involved in the trial including mandatory testing for continued playing eligibility, and second, a renewed push for voluntary drug testing by all MLB players.

Initially, Commissioner Ueberroth had attempted to deal with the Pittsburgh situation in September 1985 by asking all MLB players directly whether they would submit to voluntary testing. This approach bypassed any involvement with the MLBPA. The MLBPA remained unconvinced of the Commissioner's intent. The MLBA was especially concerned about how Ueberroth's program would operate. While Commissioner Ueberroth quickly reconsidered his tactics and decided to seek MLBPA input for his plan, it soon became obvious that the plan was stalled. This stall was brought on in part because the MLBPA reasoned that drug testing by its very nature presumed guilt on the part of players. In late December 1985, the plan was rejected outright by the MLBPA.

Commissioner Ueberroth then instituted his penalties against the players who testified or were implicated at the Pittsburgh drug trials after first holding individual meetings with the players involved during January 1986. On February 28, 1986 the Commissioner announced his decision concerning these players:

> 1. Seven players were given the choice of either being suspended for one year, or instead donating ten percent of their salaries for one season to a drug prevention program(s) in their hometown, agree to random drug testing for the remainder of their careers, and contribute 100 hours of community service for each of the next two years.
> 2. Four players were given the option of a 60-day suspension at the start of the 1986 season, or instead donate five percent of their salary for one year, submit to random drug testing for the rest of their careers, and contribute 50 hours of community service for each of the next two years.
> 3. Ten other players were given the option of facing suspension or submitting to drug testing.

. . . .

While reaction to the decision was mixed, all 21 players did quickly agree to the penalties. . . .

. . . .

Despite the players decisions to go along with Ueberroth, the MLBPA decided to file a grievance on behalf of the association as a whole for arbitration of the Commissioner's decision concerning the players involved with the Pittsburgh trial. . . .

In April 1986, Ueberroth again attempted to institute a drug testing program for MLB players. The MLBPA again rejected the plan while awaiting the outcome of arbitration hearings over the issue of including random testing clauses in guaranteed and non-guaranteed contracts, as well as the Pittsburgh trial grievance.

V. The Robert's Drug Clause Arbitration Decision

The first major drug testing related issue to be decided utilizing arbitration under Commissioner Ueberroth involved mandatory drug testing clauses in guaranteed and non-guaranteed MLB player contracts. The controversy had begun in November 1985 when the owner's Player Relations Committee again suggested adding one of two clauses to individual player's contract which would have required mandatory random drug testing. The MLBPA filed their grievance on January 6, 1986 and it was heard the following April before baseball's new impartial arbitrator Thomas T. Roberts.

Initially, Roberts had to decide a grievance filed on behalf of Joel Youngblood of the San Francisco Giants. Youngblood had negotiated a guaranteed contract with the Giants and then refused to sign it when a mandatory drug testing clause was added. He subsequently reconsideredand agreed to sign. However, by that time the Giants claimed that they had withdrawn their offer. Youngblood sought to have the Giants honor the offer and filed a grievance.

In a March 1986 decision, Roberts ruled in favor of Youngblood....

It thus remained for Roberts to resolve the larger issue. In a much delayed July 1986 decision, Roberts ruled in favor of the MLBPA stating that, "The drug testing clauses... are in violation of Article II of the Basic Agreement." He stated further that, "Any such clauses must be negotiated with the Players Association." Soon after rendering his decision, Roberts was fired by the owners' Player Relations Committee as baseball's impartial arbitrator.

Roberts' decision focused on Article II of MLB's collective bargaining agreement. Article II states that the MLBPA is "the sole and exclusive collective bargaining agent for all Major League Players... with regard to all terms and conditions of employment." Exceptions to this general rule are allowed only for special covenants between the player and his club that "provide benefits beyond those found in the Uniform Player's Contract." The issue thus centered on whether drug testing was an additional benefit to the player....

The owners based their right to test players for drugs on Article XX of baseball's CBA that states, "Nothing in this agreement shall be construed to restrict the rights of the Clubs to manage and direct their operations... except as specifically limited by the terms of the Agreement." The owners reasoned that since drug testing was not discussed in baseball's CBA and since there was no prohibition concerning drug testing in the CBA that they should be allowed to utilize drug testing clauses as special covenants to the players contracts. This was especially valid because physicals were already required within the CBA.

In his decision, Roberts pointed out that past attempts to institute non-drug testing related special covenants in players contracts had been deemed violations of the CBA where the purpose was to bypass the MLBPA as the players' exclusive bargaining agent. Roberts noted that such actions would be inconsistent with the provisions of baseball's CBA, since:

> Article II on its face prohibits the individual negotiation of special covenants uniform in nature and applicable to substantially all players who desire to negotiate a new contract so long as those special covenants provide no actual or potential additional benefits to the player. A unilaterally imposed condition of employment may not be sanctioned if it is inconsistent with the provisions of the Basic Agreement or does not provide "additional benefits" to the player within the meaning of that phrase as it appears in Article II.

Roberts found that the clauses had been imposed unilaterally by the owners and were not voluntary....

Reviewing the nature of both the guaranteed and non-guarantted contracts, Roberts noted that in the case of the later, whether voluntary or not, the inclusion of the language in the contract created a previously non-existent affirmative duty to be tested until the "player repudiates his stated agreement to submit to testing...." A similar duty is created in guaranteed contracts, Roberts held, because even though such contracts traditionally prohibited certain conduct, never before had they sought to "create an affirmative duty such as that called for here, i.e., the production of urine samples for analysis in the absence of cause." As such,

Roberts held that non-guaranteed contracts drug testing clauses "are prohibited by Article II of the Basic Agreement unless first negotiated with the Players Association." In guaranteed contracts, Roberts held that the clauses are prohibited because "drug testing clauses may not be brought into compliance with Article II through the device of relating them to other clauses that do in fact afford a benefit."

Jennifer L. Johnston, Note, Is Mandatory HIV Testing of Professional Athletes Really the Solution?
4 Health Matrix 159 (1994)*

AS THE PATHS OF LAW AND MEDICINE so often intertwine, so too do the paths of sports and medicine. Since adeptness in sports requires "vigorous bodily exertion," an uncommonly high degree of physical fitness and an exposure to physical risks not incurred by most, routine medical practices become fundamental to sports. In fact, athletes grow accustomed to physical examinations and medical procedures as a necessary part of the sporting life. However, in the latter part of 1991, when the results of one such medical examination of a well-known professional athlete were announced, shockwaves were sent through the world of sports, causing such discourse and debate that the paths of sports and medicine came to intersect with a third path — that of the law.

The issue was the mandatory Human Immunodeficiency Virus ("HIV") testing of athletes by their teams and leagues. The announcement was that of the now-retired National Basketball Association ("NBA") superstar, Earvin "Magic" Johnson. For the first time, a professional athlete known and revered throughout the world had contracted the deadly HIV virus through unsafe heterosexual activity. The fears which were brought to the forefront of the minds of the members of the sports community with this single, yet devastating, announcement of HIV infection in their community were multiplied less than one month later. On December 3, 1991, two Canadian physicians in Montreal, Quebec, announced that a young woman who had died of AIDS two years prior, had disclosed to them that she had had sexual intercourse with between thirty and seventy different players of the National Hockey League ("NHL"). With the possibility that ten percent of all NHL players were exposed to the HIV virus by one woman, fears escalated. Concern grew that this deadly epidemic was reaching into the sports arena, so often considered a fantasy world.

The subject of mandatory HIV testing of athletes was not brought forth by the general public in an effort to protect the general populace from transmission from a specific "high risk" population. Nor was the proposal an effort to exclude HIV-positive athletes from the spotlight of celebrity. In fact, the general public has hardly been involved in the debate at all. Rather, it has been a debate largely internal to the sports industry itself. Not only the coaches and owners of certain professional sports teams, but also a number of well-respected professional athletes themselves, have called for the institution of mandatory testing policies for

---

all athletes within their respective leagues. The reason is fear — fear that players are at risk of contracting the virus every day at work, from blood-to-blood contact during the not uncommon injuries and fights on the playing field. This fear may or may not be legitimate, but so long as it exists there will be debate.

Although to date, none of North America's four major professional sports leagues has adopted a mandatory HIV testing policy, some leagues' players' associations have introduced the testing issue into collective bargaining discussions. Furthermore, a number of individual teams have initiated mandatory testing policies. Opponents of mandatory HIV testing in athletics have labelled such policies "a hysterical reaction," very "simplistic," and "a kneejerk response." Furthermore, they question the effectiveness and legality of such policies.

   ....

III. HIV ANTIBODY TESTING

   ....

B. Analysis to be Applied to the Professional Athlete Testing Proposal

In an effort to analyze the legalities and ethics of a proposed mandatory HIV testing policy of a professional sports club or league to be applied to its players, this note will use a variation of the analytical criteria provided by Harvard Law Professor Martha A. Field. As Lawrence O. Gostin suggested, "attempts to evaluate each proposal [for HIV screening of a particular population] without a systematic theory of analysis could reach inconsistent results."[100]

Field provides several general principles for guiding the analysis and evaluation of testing proposals:

> First, the purpose of testing must be ethically acceptable.... Second, the proposed use of test results must contribute to the program's goal.... Third, the test program must be the least restrictive or intrusive means for attaining the program's purpose.... Fourth, the benefit to public health must warrant the extent of intrusion into personal liberties.[101]

   ....

The first principle remains largely unchanged. Does the proposed testing policy serve an ethically acceptable purpose? The second question attempts to blend Field's second and third principles by asking if mandatory testing is necessary and effective for achieving that purpose. My third question for analysis differs greatly from Field's fourth. Field evaluated proposed screening policies proposed to be put into effect by government entities (generally). Such government actions require a constitutional analysis. Conversely, as the professional sports teams and leagues are both a part of the private business sector, the Constitution does not, generally speaking, provide the grounds for complaints of individuals who may feel oppressed by their employers. However, the individual rights of the professional athlete, as developed in state, federal and common law, deserve attention in the analysis of this issue. For this reason, the third question asks if a mandatory testing policy in professional sports violates the individual rights of the athlete?

---

100. Gostin, *supra* note 82, at 21.
101. Field, *supra* note 5, at 64-65.

Under this variation of the Field analysis, a conclusion that mandatory HIV testing of professional athletes would be both ethical and legal is warranted only if all three questions received a well-reasoned affirmative answer.

IV. AN ETHICALLY ACCEPTABLE PURPOSE?

Ethics is the first issue that must be addressed when evaluating a proposal for mandating HIV testing of all players on a particular team or in a particular league. What is the true purpose for the testing policy, and is it ethically acceptable? As ethics are merely a "system or code of morals," the question arises as to what should constitute "ethically acceptable?" For purposes of this analysis, this note will utilize the well-known system of ethics known as utilitarianism. In order to be considered "ethically acceptable" under this doctrine, a proposal for mandatory testing should be able "to bring about the greatest happiness of the greatest number." Therefore, the utility of mandatory testing must be determined as to the impact on the athlete himself, the teammates, the opponents, the coaches and other team management, the team trainers, the team physician(s), the owner(s) of the team, the player's family, the viewing audience and other fans and the general public.

Proponents of mandatory HIV testing in professional sports are likely to claim that their policy will prevent, or help to prevent, the transmission of the HIV virus, at least within the sports community itself. Most would agree with Field's statement that both "[p]rotecting public health and preventing transmission of HIV are acceptable purposes...."[104] Under the utilitarian approach, preventing HIV transmission, even if only within the sports community, would bring great benefit to an enormous number of persons; therefore, this general purpose easily could be argued to be ethically acceptable for purposes of this analysis.

Protection of the HIV-infected player is the second purpose which proponents would suggest is served by mandatory testing. This arguably could mean that the team which tests all players hopes to protect its investment in any player testing positive by providing the necessary medical treatment and drugs, such as AZT, to prolong the player's career. Although not necessarily a purely humanitarian gesture, the protection of a business investment or an "asset" clearly would be considered ethically acceptable under some systems of ethics, such as Materialism. From the utilitarian view, it may be argued that this purpose is ethically acceptable as it provides the greatest happiness to the greatest number. For example, the player who has worked for many years in an attempt to achieve his dream of being a professional athlete may continue to live this dream; team management and owner(s), teammates, the viewing audience and fans of the team may continue to receive the benefits inherent in this player's continued efforts as a part of a team; and the family of the player continues to receive the benefits inherent in the player's theoretically longer career and life. It should be noted that, although this purpose is on its face ethically acceptable, it may lead to discriminatory practices if the team's management takes an overly paternalistic approach to protecting players, such as limiting a player's actual involvement in the game "for his own good."

Another purpose which some proponents may argue that mandatory HIV testing achieves is the protection of other players, coaches and trainers when manage-

---

104. Field, *supra* note 5, at 64.

ment knows to use certain precautions when dealing with an HIV-positive player. Although this appears to be ethically acceptable, this purpose is somewhat suspect. In team sports, especially those with a level of contact which might make them "bloody" sports, universal precautions should be taken regardless of whether anyone is HIV-positive on the team. Safeguarding those who take care of a player, perhaps after an injury, raises issues similar to the HIV testing debate in the health care setting. The conclusion reached by Professor Gostin regarding screening health care patients and staff is equally pertinent to the sports setting. He states:

> The relatively low level of risk in the health care setting does not justify a wide scale screening program. Even if a screening program is implemented, its utility may be questionable. The health care worker should use the strictest precautions to avoid contracting HIV from the body fluids... [.] These precautions include using rubber gloves if the worker has a cut or open sore, and avoiding parenteral exposure. Health care workers should *always* be cautious in handling blood, body fluids, and items soiled with these substances.[110]

The final purpose to be discussed involves the determination of fitness for the sport. Contractually, the player has represented that his "general overall state of physical well-being is such that he can endure the rigors of professional sports training and competition," so monitoring all aspects of the player's health which may affect his ability to perform under the contract is clearly an ethically acceptable purpose on its face. Arguments supporting this conclusion under Utilitarianism would be quite similar to those discussed earlier supporting the acceptance of the purpose of protecting an HIV-infected athlete. Although this purpose may appear ethically acceptable, this fitness requirement in the standard player contract could easily be used as a front for discriminatory practices.

Although some of these purposes arguably may be a mere front for discrimination against HIV-positive athletes, which is clearly ethically unacceptable, proponents of mandatory testing in professional sports argue that these purposes are acceptable, even under utilitarian principles. Assuming that these individuals are correct and that an ethically acceptable purpose is served by mandatory HIV testing, one must next determine if mandatory testing is necessary and effective for achieving that purpose.

V. NECESSARY AND EFFECTIVE FOR ACHIEVING A PURPOSE?

The determination of whether mandatory HIV testing of all professional athletes, in a particular league or on a certain team, is necessary and effective for achieving a purpose depends upon the given purpose for the testing policy. For example, as has already been discussed, the safeguarding of players and staff by knowing to use certain precautions does not necessitate mandatory testing. In fact, mandatory testing would not be effective in safeguarding others, because HIV-infected players could test negative during the latency period and still be able to transmit the virus to others. Furthermore, as Field states, "the false sense of security and reduced precautions that testing can breed pose a serious difficulty with a testing program."[114]

---

110. Gostin, *supra* note 83, at 37-38 (emphasis added).
114. *Id.* at 60.

On the other hand, two other purposes are effectively achieved by mandatory testing. If a team wishes to determine the fitness of a player or desires to protect the team's investment in each athlete (by supplying the appropriate medical care and AZT to those testing positive), HIV testing of all athletes is necessary. In each case, the team's owners are, to some extent, protecting their investment. Therefore, anything less than mandatory testing would be ineffective for these purposes.

Although the broadly stated purpose of preventing transmission of the HIV virus is the most likely to go uncontested as ethically acceptable, its vagueness leaves much room for debate as to whether mandatory testing is necessary, or even effective, for preventing transmission. The first question that arises is whether the transmission sought to be prevented is potential transmission during the game. Or, is the purpose to also prevent transmission on or off the playing field, perhaps by encouraging behavior modification? If the goal is to answer the latter, it would be difficult to prove that mandatory testing is necessary, or even effective. Although mandatory testing arguably would allow a larger number (theoretically one-hundred percent) to know their HIV status than a voluntary testing proposal would, a number of variations for voluntary testing and education programs could be proposed which could be as effective, or more effective, in modifying behavior to prevent transmission. With such equally effective options available, mandatory testing would not seem to be necessary to achieve the purposes defined above.

Should one define the purpose of mandatory testing as the prevention of transmission only on the playing field, the analysis becomes a little more complex. First, the issue of the risk of transmission during play must be touched upon. Some argue that there is no true risk, and therefore no need for mandatory testing. Those in the sports community who advocate mandatory testing of professional athletes often base their fears of transmission on very small theoretical possibilities, coupled with generalizations of athletes' opportunities for unsafe promiscuous sexual behavior....

. . . .

Therefore, it could be argued that mandatory testing is ineffective for reducing the spread of the virus through transmission on the playing field, as experts currently think that that risk is "extremely unlikely." Mandating HIV testing for athletes is an extreme solution to what is currently considered by experts a practically nonexistent problem. Therefore, the necessity of a mandatory testing policy is called into question.

For the sake of the ensuing legal argument, this note will assume that a mandatory testing program whereby a team routinely tests each of its players pursuant to team rules (incorporated into the standard player contract) is both necessary and effective for preventing the transmission of the HIV virus on the playing field. The issue then becomes whether such a policy effectively could prevent the risk of transmission without violating the players' individual rights.

VI. NON-VIOLATIVE OF INDIVIDUAL RIGHTS?

Individual rights of the athletes which clearly must be protected are established by state statutes, federal legislation and the common law. The four legal issues which will be discussed in this section are: the common law right to privacy, the state statutory issues of consent and confidentiality and the freedom from employment discrimination, as illustrated by the federally-enacted Americans with Disabilities Act.

A. The Common Law Privacy Issue

The broadest of an individual athlete's individual rights likely to be affected by a mandatory HIV testing policy is his right of privacy. This right of privacy generally has been defined as:

> The right to be let alone; the right of a person to be free from unwarranted publicity.... The right of an individual... to withhold himself and his property from public scrutiny, if he so chooses.[121]

As Professor Gostin states, "[s]creening necessarily entails a restriction on individuals' rights to privacy; it involves blood sampling and the collection of sensitive information."[122] Proponents of mandatory testing of professional athletes may argue that an athlete's acceptance of the standard player contract and its corresponding rules negates any invasion of privacy. The physical nature of sport, as has been discussed earlier, requires certain medical examinations and blood tests to determine, for example, whether a player is physically fit to play as required by his contract and whether a player is abusing drugs as is prohibited by team and league rules. Therefore, it may be argued that a player's individual right to privacy is abandoned when he signs a contract, and thereby agrees to abide by team policies. Furthermore, the athlete's privacy interest is, arguably, no more violated by the HIV testing than by any other routine medical tests required by team and league policies. In fact, if the purpose of the testing policy is to determine a player's fitness to play, a player arguably has obligated himself to prove his fitness under the contract by subjecting himself to such testing, if necessary.

On the other hand, an HIV test is unlike any other blood test. In the modern world, persons who are HIV-positive are oftentimes discriminated against. "Fear, bigotry and lack of understanding are largely responsible for the consequences that can flow from a positive test result. The response is due in large part to other parties' fear that the infection will be transmitted."[124] Furthermore, the information collected should be considered more sensitive than that acquired through other medical and physical examinations, due to the fact that the virus is generally spread through some sort of "risky behavior" which oftentimes illustrates a person's most private lifestyle choices. Although it may be conceded that an athlete agreed to abide by the rules and policies of the team and league when he signed his lucrative contract, we, as a society, must begin to think about how far this should be allowed to go. To what extent may a professional athlete bargain away his individual rights?

In summary, it is clear that the individual athlete's right of privacy is intruded upon by a team or league which mandates HIV testing. But the issue remains whether or not that intrusion should be permitted, as it appears that such invasions of privacy are commonly (and often expressly) accepted by the athlete himself as part and parcel of the "big league" contract.

---

121. BLACK'S LAW DICTIONARY 1075 (6th ed. 1990).
122. Gostin, *supra* note 83, at 21.
124. Field, *supra* note 5, at 45.

B. The State Statutory Issue of Consent

.... [T]he majority of states have enacted legislation requiring some form of consent for an individual to be tested for HIV antibodies. These statutes require varying levels of consent, ranging from actual "consent" to "informed consent" to "written and informed consent." It appears that such statutes are meant to prevent the very type of policy at issue in this note — the mandatory HIV testing of a class of persons such as employees. It, therefore, appears that in some states the mandatory testing of professional athletes by their respective teams and/or leagues would constitute a prima facie violation of state law.

However, this is not necessarily true. When a professional athlete signs the standard player contract, he agrees to abide by the league and team rules and policies, which conceivably would include any mandatory HIV testing policy. Although the NLRA requires the employer team to bargain with players collectively about terms and conditions of employment, once a collective bargaining agreement is reached, it is binding on all players signing the standard player contract, whether or not they specifically agree with the bargain reached. Therefore, it is theoretically possible for an individual athlete to sign a standard player contract, which could be seen as providing consent for HIV testing, without individually agreeing with the issue of "mandatory" HIV testing.

This leads directly to the issue of whether or not such a testing policy is actually "mandatory." Proponents of such testing argue that it is not truly mandatory as consent is implied when the player accepts his contract. Arguably, the player may choose not to be tested as a condition of his employment by refusing to sign a contract with such a team or in such a league. On the other hand, one must remember the years of hard work leading to a professional sports contract, the handsome monetary rewards which often accompany such a contract and the not uncommon factors of youth, inexperience and lack of other realistic opportunities. Even when a young, inexperienced athlete is adequately represented by an agent, it appears to be fair to say that the athlete will choose to fulfill his dream and continue to play his sport. This may mean that he is required to consent to rules which are not generally applied to the general public, such as curfews, medical exams, routine drug testing and, arguably, routine HIV testing.

The idea that consent is provided upon acceptance of the standard player contract incorporating the rules of the team and league, might logically pass muster in a jurisdiction requiring simple "consent" to testing. This argument becomes more obtuse when dealing with those jurisdictions requiring "informed" or "written and informed" consent to testing. In such jurisdictions the team or league conceivably would need to require under its contract that the player sign a separate consent form after being informed of the testing procedures and potential impact of the results. Would this be sufficient to meet the requirements set forth by a state statute requiring written and informed consent, such as that of Pennsylvania? That statute states: "no HIV-related test shall be performed without first obtaining the informed written consent of the subject. Any consent shall be preceded by an explanation of the test, including its purpose, potential uses, limitations and the meaning of its results." This question will likely be left to the courts.

When answering the question whether teams or leagues can require a player to provide informed consent for testing, the purposes behind the legal doctrine of informed consent should serve as a guide....

. . . .

Although proponents of testing are likely to argue that a player gives up, to a certain extent, his right to individual autonomy when it comes to his health and fitness, when he signs the contract, arguably true informed consent may not be given under penalty of losing a "big league" contract.

In conclusion, it appears possible for a team or league to finesse a mandatory HIV testing policy so as not to violate state consent statutes. This is theoretically true even in those states requiring the strictest form of consent, which is both informed and written. Although such a testing policy appears to be a creative possibility for a sports team or league counsel, such a policy defeats the purposes of the legal doctrine of informed consent. Once again, to what extent may a professional athlete bargain away his individual rights to play his sport and to earn a living?

C. The State Statutory Issue of Confidentiality

When evaluating any HIV testing policy, it is essential to determine how the results of such tests will be used. Simply put, a mandatory HIV testing policy cannot be created in a vacuum, and "[t]he value of testing as a strategy to combat AIDS depends completely on how the information from tests will be used."[133] One key issue which many state legislatures have examined is that of the confidentiality of the test results.

A proposed mandatory testing policy affecting all professional athletes on a particular team or in a certain league must be artfully devised so as not to violate any state confidentiality statute. This appears to be very difficult in sports. In order to fulfill the theoretical purposes discussed in Part IV, a wide variety of individuals, such as coaches, trainers, team physicians and team owners, as well as possibly the teammates and opponents, are likely to have access to HIV results. This is analogous to the situation seen in the military, which has put into effect a mandatory testing policy:

> Even when a screening program purports to ensure it, confidentiality may be difficult to maintain. For example, in the military, the guarantee of confidentiality is ineffective in practice. "Confidential" test information can be released to the commander of the infected soldier, medical personnel, spouses, local authorities and others on a "need to know" basis. Moreover, the consequences typically associated with testing HIV-positive in the military, such as reassignment or restricted duties, can act as a signal to others of a soldier's infected status. *The military example illustrates that when rules designed to maintain confidentiality are not tightly drawn and narrowly tailored, they become meaningless.*

In order to evaluate effectively a mandatory testing proposal for professional sports, one must look beyond the face of the policy to determine if it will in practice preserve the confidentiality of the individual athletes tested. Clearly, in the sports business, there is much room for violation of particular state confidentiality statutes.

D. The Federal Freedom from Employment Discrimination Issue

Once again the proposal for mandatory testing of athletes must be examined in the context of the intended uses of the results. Clearly, positive HIV antibody test

---

133. Field, *supra* note 5, at 37.

results may be used in various ways. The only ethically acceptable uses are those which are in line with the ethically acceptable purposes for mandatory testing discussed in Part IV. The use of such results to discriminate against members of a team or league, or potential members (by terminating a player's contract solely on grounds of his HIV status, by failing to offer an HIV-positive player a new contract, or by reducing or eliminating an athlete's playing time) is not only unethical, but also illegal. Such discrimination against an HIV-infected athlete is illegal under the Americans with Disabilities Act ("ADA").

The ADA states that an employer shall not "discriminate against a qualified individual with a disability because of the disability of such individual in regard to job application procedures, the hiring, advancement, or discharge of employees, employee compensation, job training, and other terms, conditions, and privileges of employment." The legislative history of the ADA and its corresponding regulations explains that HIV infection and AIDS are to be considered "disabilities" under the Act.

In the realm of professional sports the issue of discrimination is especially noteworthy. As was stated previously, professional sports teams have very broad discretion to terminate or suspend a player. One acceptable cause for such termination is that the athlete is not physically fit for the rigors of the sport. Clearly, a team may finesse its way into terminating the contract of an HIV-positive player through this cause. However, if discriminatory practices ensue from a mandatory testing program, the ADA arguably would protect the individual athlete's right to be free from such discrimination in employment.

The problem, though, occurs in the fact that athletic employment is very different from other types of employment due to its physical nature. It can be argued that the mandatory testing of professional athletes may slip through a loophole in the ADA. One commentator has noted that:

> To be protected from discrimination, the person with disabilities must be able to perform essential job functions to a reasonable standard.... [E]mployers may not use pre-employment medical examinations except to determine whether an employee can 'perform job-related functions.' Similarly, current employees cannot be required to undergo medical examinations except for job-related reasons. One standard specifically included in the law in response to fears of contagion is that employers 'may include a requirement that an individual shall not pose a direct threat to the health or safety of other individuals in the workplace.'[140]

This brings the analysis back to the issue of whether there is truly a risk of transmission from blood-to-blood contact during contact on the playing field. Those who argue that there is, and who advocate mandatory testing, are likely to contend that there is a direct threat to the health and safety of other players and training staff. They may argue that a termination of such a player's contract or even a modification of his usual playing status is therefore allowable under the ADA. Furthermore, they may question whether an HIV-infected athlete is able to perform job-related functions, due to the effects of the virus on the player's immune system.

Although discrimination against employees with the virus is clearly prohibited, in general, by the ADA, a mandatory testing policy for professional athletes is not

---

140. CLOSEN ET AL., *supra* note 5, at 32.

necessarily violative of the ADA merely because of the potential for discriminatory practices resulting from the test results. The statute expressly gives employers the right to conduct pre-employment medical examinations to determine whether the employee can perform job-related duties. An employer also can require current employees to undergo medical exams for job-related reasons. Clearly, in the professional sports context, both of these types of medical examinations are completed to ensure the continued physical fitness of the players. The ADA seems to imply that such examinations may include HIV testing, so long as it is conducted for job-related reasons. Further, the ADA appears to imply that an employer may test for HIV antibodies so as not to allow an employee to pose a direct threat to the health or safety of others in the workplace.

Although mandatory testing of professional athletes for HIV antibodies appears to be legal under the ADA, if narrowly tailored to fit this loophole, the fact remains that such testing is likely to result in discriminatory practices due to the great discretion of team management to terminate employment. The existence of such a loophole in the ADA may allow a team to lawfully discriminate against HIV-positive athletes, but such discrimination arising out of mandatory testing may be considered in many ethical systems, including Utilitarianism, to be unethical.

. . . .

Part VI

Olympic Sports

Introduction

Legal scholarship in international sports law has increased over the last two decades. James Nafziger published his pioneering work "International Sports Law" in 1988. Aaron Wise and Bruce Meyer added "International Sports Law and Business" in 1997. This chapter is generally limited to articles that explore public international law issues related to the Olympics movement, but scholarship in private international law is increasing as well. Some of the most exciting scholarly contributions have been made by students, a fact that bodes well for the future of legal scholarship in this area. This chapter highlights those contributions with three student authored pieces.

The 1960s, '70s and '80s saw legal issues arise in the Olympic movement that were related to the impact of the foreign policy concerns of participating countries. These issues included the refusal by the Canadian government to admit Taiwanese athletes to participate in the 1976 Olympiad, the boycott of the 1980 Moscow Games by the United States, the Soviet boycott of the 1984 Los Angeles Games, and the worldwide boycott of South African athletes. During the 1990s, the focus shifted to issues relating to drug testing, athletic eligibility and dispute resolution. Professor Nafziger has described this transformation in *International Sports Law: A Replay of Characteristics and Trends*, 86 AM. J.INT'L L. 489 (1992).

The first excerpt in this chapter sets forth the international legal structure of the Olympic Movement and introduces the Amateur Sports Act of 1978. It touches briefly on the Butch Reynolds' dispute that is described more fully in the second excerpt, a student comment by Melissa R. Biting. She examines the arbitration mechanisms in place before and after the Butch Reynolds' dispute. Together the two articles present the legal regime that governs the eligibility of athletes from around the world who desire to participate in the Olympics. It remains unresolved whether the domestic law of an individual country can be used by an athlete to trump the Olympic regime.

The foregoing articles provide a flavor of international sports law issues, but they are not exhaustive. The Olympic Movement presents many questions relating to its governance and jurisdictional conflicts between its rules and the domestic law of participating countries. Some of these issues are covered in other recent articles including: Carter Anne McGowan, *Rough Around The Edges: Professionalism, Eligibility, And The Future Of Figure Skating*, 6 SETON HALL J. SPORT L. 501 (1996); Sara Lee Keller-Smith and Sherri A. Affrunti, *Going For The Gold: The Representation Of Olympic Athletes*, 3 VILL. SPORTS & ENT. L.J. 443 (1996); Edward E. Hollis, *The United States Olympic Committee And The Suspension Of Athletes: Reforming Grievance Procedures Under The Amateur Sports Act Of 1978*, 71 IND. L.J. 183 (1995); Comment, *The Growing Entertainment And Sports Industries Internationally: New Immigration Laws Provide For Foreign Athletes And Entertainers*, 12 MIAMI ENT. & SPORTS L. REV. 207 (1994/1995); Robert N. Davis, *Ambushing The Olympic Games*, 3 VILL. SPORTS & ENT. L.J. 423 (1996).

Chapter 15

Olympic Sports

1. Due Process

David B. Mack, Note, Reynolds v. International Amateur Athletic Federation: The Need for An Independent Tribunal in International Athletic Disputes
10 Connecticut Journal International Law 653 (1995)*

....

I. THE STRUCTURE OF INTERNATIONAL SPORTS LAW

A. *The Olympic Charter*

What is international sports law? Is there such a concept? At present international sports law is in large part a "patchwork of hard and soft law cultivated by the Olympic Movement," although a more structured pattern of international administration and dispute resolution is emerging. At the center of the Olympic Movement is the Olympic Charter, adopted in 1894, which "best evidence[s] international custom pertaining to sports competition."[3]

Although it may be the closest thing to a comprehensive international sports law statute, the Olympic Charter is on the whole vaguely and idealistically worded. One legal scholar has described it as "lack[ing] legal clarity and consistency,...[as] not even a coherent statute, but simply a collection of various texts."[6] Nevertheless, despite the ambiguity and the vagueness of the Charter,

> [i]t appears...that many states have deferred to the rules and general processes of the Olympic Movement to define a soft, but influential and growing body of international sports law. Although the acceptance of this body of law is not universal, and instances of disobedience all too common, the elements of international custom—repetition, duration and adherence under legal impulsion (*opinio juris*)—are present. Thus, the Olympic Charter, together with decisions and practices related to it, constitute the best evidence of a general practice of states and other international actors in and around the sports arena.[7]

---

3. James Nafziger, *International Sports Law: A Replay of Characteristics and Trends*, 86 Am. J. Int'l L. 489, 489 (1992).

6. Christoph Vedder, *The International Olympic Committee: An Advanced Non-Governmental Organization and the International Law*, 27 Ger. Y.B. Int'l L. 233, 240 (1984).

7. Nafziger, *supra* note 4, at 35.

B. *The International Olympic Committee (IOC)*

The IOC, created by the Congress of Paris of 23rd June 1894, is entrusted with the control and development of the modern Olympic games. The IOC governs the Olympic Movement and owns the rights over the Olympic Games. The Charter declares the IOC the "supreme authority" on all questions concerning the Olympic Games and the Olympic Movement, including matters of discipline.

Enhancing the IOC's power is the fact that any entity wishing to participate in the Olympic Movement must abide by the Rules of the Olympic Charter, as interpreted and enforced by the IOC. For example, Rule 1.2 states that "any person or organization belonging in any capacity whatsoever in the Olympic Movement is bound by the provisions of the Olympic Charter and shall abide by the decisions of the IOC. The breadth of the IOC's authority is further defined in Rule 25, which authorizes the IOC to impose sanctions on IFs, NOCs, and individual athletes and teams.

Thus, "by means of its authority under the Olympic Charter, the IOC has autonomously created a federative law for the entire Olympic Movement, binding not only the IOC itself, but all parts of the Olympic Movement, including individual participants."

C. *Legal Status of the IOC*

The IOC is incorporated under Swiss law as a nonprofit society with legal status. Rule 19 of the Charter establishes that the IOC is a body corporate under international law having juridical status and perpetual succession. Although the IOC purports to have legal personality under both national and public international law, it is debatable whether such declarations of international personality are accurate. It certainly is clear that the IOC, being nongovernmental, cannot in itself compel governmental obedience. "When the IOC is faced with non-participation of teams for political reasons or the [denial] of Olympic freedoms [to athletes], it is directly or indirectly subject to state powers."[17] For example, in the event of a boycott, the IOC suffers from its Charter's severe deficiency which, corresponding to the highly idealistic and unpolitical character of the Olympic Movement, neglects to take into consideration the significance of states in the modern Olympics. As a result, when push comes to shove, the IOC is powerless with regards to the states.

Unfortunately, it is well-recognized that governments use sports as an instrument in foreign policy. The most obvious and common example has been the boycott. Almost from its inception, the Olympic Games have been riddled with boycotts. The most memorable examples were the East-West boycotts of the 1980 Games in Moscow and the 1984 Games in Los Angeles. It would seem at first glance that boycotts are inconsistent with the Olympic Charter. Rule 3 of the Charter provides that "[a]ny form of discrimination with regard to a country or a person on grounds of race, religion, politics, sex, or otherwise is incompatible with belonging to the Olympic Movement." Also, Rule 9 declares the Games as competitions between athletes and teams, and not between countries. In addition, the National Olympic Committees are obliged under Rule 31.5 to remain "autonomous" and to "resist all pressures of any kind, including those of a political, religious or economic nature."

---

17. Vedder, *supra* note 6, at 248.

Despite these provisions, boycotts do not necessarily violate international law. "[B]oycotts may be acceptable, in some circumstances, as reprisal measures against illegal acts by another state."[23] For example, discrimination by states against South African athletes in the 1980s was a legitimate response to the racially discriminatory policies of the South African government.

Another example of a state's use of sports as a political weapon is the Canadian government's refusal to grant visas to Taiwanese athletes to participate in the 1976 Games in Montreal. The Canadian government rejected the designation of Taiwanese athletes as representatives of the People's Republic of China, a rejection which was motivated by Canada's anxiety over disturbing its relationship with China, its largest wheat importer. Professor James Nafziger criticized the Canadian government's decision as a "particularly flagrant violation of international custom." First, Canada violated its express commitment to the IOC "that all parties representing the National Olympic Committees recognized by the IOC will be free to enter Canada." Second, Canada's government violated the Olympic Charter's anti-discrimination provision. Finally, Canada violated the Olympic provision that "no legal condition or regulation may be valid in opposition to [IOC] Rules."

Fortunately, for the sake of the smooth operation of the Olympic Games, conflicts between an individual state's policies and the Charter primarily have been resolved in favor of the latter. States usually have given deference to the IOC as the enforcer of the Olympic Charter and have themselves been willing to subordinate their own law and policies to the Olympic Rules. For example, Australia admitted Soviet athletes to the 1956 Games in Melbourne despite the fact that it did not recognize the Soviet Union, and further objected to the latter's invasion of Hungary. Likewise, France permitted East Germans to participate in the 1968 Winter Olympics even though doing so directly violated NATO regulations. A final example is the United States' issuing visas to Cuban athletes to participate in the 1987 IOC-sponsored Pan-American Games in Indianapolis despite the fact that the United States and Cuba did not maintain diplomatic relations.

Thus, for the most part, countries have deferred to the general principles outlined in the Olympic Charter and have respected the autonomy of the IOC, thereby permitting sports competition to proceed smoothly in the international arena. The vagueness and ambiguity of the Charter, coupled with the IOC's lack of authority to compel governmental obedience, nevertheless leaves the framework and stability of international sports law vulnerable to the political whims of participating governments.

D. *Other Institutional Actors*

The preceding section concerned the general adherence of individual states to the Olympic Charter and the IOC. Where does the athlete fit into this larger framework? Lost in the discussion of the participating countries' use of sport as a political tool is the fact that the athletes are usually, if not always, the pawns in the chess match between the particular country and the IOC. Where is an athlete, such as Butch Reynolds, supposed to look for redress in the event of a dispute, for example over his or her eligibility? Unfortunately, the Olympic Charter, for all its

---

23. NAFZIGER, *supra* note 4, at 103.

flowery and lofty language, does not provide much hope. To answer this question, a discussion of the other institutional players in the Olympic Movement—the International Federations (IFs), the National Governing Bodies (NGBs), and the National Olympic Committees (NOCs)—is required.

1. International Federations (IFs)

International federations (IFs) are associations of national sports federations which control their respective sport worldwide. For example, the International Amateur Athletic Federation (IAAF) governs international track & field events, and its members are national federations that govern the sport on a national level.[37] The federation that governs track & field in the United States is U.S.A. Track & Field.

The ability of each IF to maintain control over the sport on an international level is critical to the success of the Olympic Movement and international sports competition on the whole. As such, IFs are granted extremely broad authority under the Olympic Charter to govern their respective sports:

> In order to promote the Olympic Movement, the IOC may recognize as IFs international non-governmental organizations administering one or several sports at the world level and encompassing organizations administering such sports at a national level. As far as the role of the IFs within the Olympic Movement is concerned, their statutes, practice and activities must be in conformity with the Olympic Charter. Subject to the foregoing, each IF maintains its independence and autonomy in the administration of its sport.[39]

The roles of the IFs are equally broadly defined, with the degree of specificity resembling the IOC's powers under the Charter.

The role of the IFs is to:

> establish and enforce the rules concerning the practice of their respective sports and to ensure their application; ensure the development of their sports throughout the world; contribute to the achievement of the goals set out in the Olympic Charter; establish their criteria of eligibility to enter the competitions of the Olympic Games in conformity with the Olympic Charter, and to submit these to the IOC for approval; assume the responsibility for the technical control and direction of their sports at the Olympic Games and at Games under the patronage of the IOC; provide technical assistance in the practical implementation of the Olympic Solidarity programme.[40]

Of vital importance to athletes is the role the IFs play in establishing eligibility criteria for individual athletes, in particular the criteria relating to drug abuse. Each IF is directed under the Charter to establish its own eligibility criteria, which must be in conformity with the Olympic Charter and approved by the IOC. More importantly, the application to the eligibility criteria lies with the IFs. The ability of each IF to establish its own eligibility criteria necessarily results in the lack of a uniform eligibility code and therefore unequal treatment of athletes. Although each IF's criteria require IOC approval, that does not prevent one IF's disciplinary rules from being stricter or more lenient than those of another IF. Nor does IOC approval preclude discrepancies in IFs' grievance procedures.

---

37. The IAAF was founded in 1914 and is the oldest of any IF.
39. OLYMPIC CHARTER, Rule 29.
40. *Id.* at Rule 30.

The Olympic Charter and its By-Laws establish a Medical Code which, among other things, "provide[s] for the prohibition of doping, establish[es] lists of the classes of prohibited medicaments and procedures, provide[s] for the obligation for competitors to submit themselves to medical controls and examinations and make[s] provision for sanctions to be applied in the event of a violation of such Medical Code." Unlike most other provisions of the Charter, the Medical Code and the rules regarding doping control are quite specific. In addition, the Charter establishes a Medical Commission, which is assigned to "elaborate the IOC Medical Code ... [and] to implement the IOC Medical Code in accordance with the instructions of the IOC Executive Board." The complexity and detail of the IOC Medical Code does not, however, necessarily result in uniformity, for under By-Law 2.2 to Rule 48, an athlete must "submit to medical controls and examinations carried out in conformity with the provisions of the IOC Medical Code *and with the relevant rules of the IFs concerned.*" Thus, the IFs' rules, especially their grievance procedure provisions, play a vital role and can lead to disparate treatment of athletes from sport to sport.

2. National Governing Bodies (NGBs)

A National Governing Body (NGB) is essentially the same type of institution as an international federation, except that the NGB governs the sport on a national rather than international basis. NGBs are members of the IFs, however, and therefore must comply with the IF's rules, which in turn must be approved by the IOC as being consistent with the Olympic Charter. In fact, NGBs are more than members, they are the agents of the IF in their respective countries. Thus, if the NGB acts in a way which an IF finds is inconsistent with its rules, the NGB endangers its membership with the IF, and moreover jeopardizes the eligibility of the athletes it represents.

3. National Olympic Committees (NOCs)

Under the Olympic Charter, the NOCs' mission is "to develop and protect the Olympic Movement in their respective countries, in accordance with the Olympic Charter." "The NOCs have the exclusive powers for the representation of their respective countries at the Olympic Games and at the regional, continental or world multi-sports competitions patronized by the IOC." In addition, to be eligible to compete, each athlete must be a member of his or her NOC, which in turn must be recognized by the IOC as the national representative body.

Thus, in order to participate in any international sporting event over which the IOC has authority, several conditions must be satisfied: (1) the athlete must be a member of his or her NGB; (2) the NGB must be a member of the governing IF; (3) the IF must be recognized by the IOC; (4) the athlete must be a member of his or her NOC; and (5) the NOC must be recognized by the IOC.

E. *The Amateur Sports Act of 1978: A Brief Summary*

1. Legislative History and Statutory Analysis

The Amateur Sports Act of 1978 (the "Act") represents the legislative foundation to an organized, modern, and competent Olympic program in the United States. The impetus to the Act's passage was a series of needless administrative mistakes surrounding the United States Olympic team in the 1972 Munich Games. The Act established the United States Olympic Committee (USOC) as a corporation and defined its purposes and powers in connection with amateur athletics on both the national and international level. It also created guidelines and requirements for the recognition of national governing bodies, and also provided a procedural mechanism for the disqualification of a NGB for failure to comply with the eligibility requirements.

Of significant importance with respect to the Butch Reynolds dispute are the Act's dispute resolution provisions, which manifest the intent of Congress to prevent judicial interference with the authority of the USOC to determine the eligibility of United States athletes in amateur athletic competition. For example, the Act declares that the object of the USOC shall be to "exercise exclusive jurisdiction, either directly or through its constituent members of committees, over all matters pertaining to the participation of the United States in the Olympic Games,"[55] and to "provide for the swift resolution of conflicts and disputes involving amateur athletes, [NGBs], and amateur sports organizations, and [to] protect the opportunity of any amateur athlete...to participate in amateur athletic competition." In addition, in order for a sports organization to be recognized as a NGB, it must agree to "submit...to binding arbitration in accordance with the commercial rules of the American Arbitration Association [AAA] in any controversy involving its recognition as a [NGB]...or involving the opportunity of any amateur athlete...to participate in amateur athletic competition."

The Act's legislative history also indicates an intent to keep United States courts out of disputes between an athlete, the NGB, and the USOC. Congress expressly rejected an amendment to the Act that would have provided special jurisdiction in United States district courts for certain injunction proceedings. In addition, Congress struck an amendment to the bill which would have authorized arbitrators to issue subpoenas and to petition district courts for enforcement of their awards.

2. Judicial Interpretation

For the most part, United States courts have followed the intent of Congress and have held that an athlete aggrieved by a decision of his or her NGB or of the USOC must contest these decisions according to the procedural guidelines of the USOC constitution, as dictated by the Act. In *Michels v. United States Olympic Committee*,[60] the court held that an athlete had no private cause of action under the Act to contest his suspension by his NGB, which had been upheld by the USOC. Michels, an American amateur weightlifter, competed in the Pan American Games, at which time he tested positive for drugs. The International Weightlifting Federation (IWF) immediately suspended Michels, which precluded him from competing for a position on the American weightlifting team scheduled to compete in the 1984 Olympics. Michels sued the USOC, the IWF, and the United States Weightlifting Federation (USWF), claiming that the test results were invalid and that the defendants were required to conduct a hearing regarding his claim. Specifically, Michels alleged that (1) the USOC violated the Amateur Sports Act, (2) the IWF violated its own constitution and by-laws, and (3) all three defendants had engaged in a group boycott in violation of the Sherman Act. The district court granted Michels' motion for a preliminary injunction, requiring the

---

55. 36 U.S.C. § 391-96.
60. 741 F.2d 155 (7th Cir. 1984).

USOC and the USWF to name Michels as an alternate to the team subject to the determination of Michels' rights by the IOC. The USOC and USWF appealed the injunction. The appellate court held that "the legislative history of the Act clearly reveals that Congress intended not to create a private cause of action under the Act," and therefore dissolved the district court's injunction. Thus, the only tribunal—outside either the USWF or USOC—authorized to hear Michels' dispute was the AAA.

Similarly, in *DeFrantz v. United States Olympic Committee*,[66] the court rejected a private cause of action under the Act. In *DeFrantz*, twenty-five athletes sought an injunction to prevent the USOC from carrying out a resolution not to send an American team to participate in the 1980 Summer Games in Moscow. The court concluded "that the USOC not only had the authority to decide not to send an American team to the Summer Olympics, but also that it could do so for reasons not directly related to sports considerations." Moreover, the court held that the Act does not guarantee an athlete the right to compete in the Olympics if the USOC decides not to send an American team, and therefore the plaintiffs had no "right" under the Act to bring an action in court.

Thus, *Michels* and *DeFrantz* support the proposition that the Amateur Sports Act of 1978 intended to keep the courts out of eligibility disputes between an athlete, his or her NGB, and the USOC.

Other courts (including the *Reynolds* court), however, have held that participation in USOC and/or NGB administrative procedures is merely a prerequisite to bringing a suit in court. Once an athlete exhausts these remedies, some courts have held, an athlete may proceed to the courts, notwithstanding the legislative history.

Thus, courts following *Michels* and *DeFrantz* have held that the Amateur Sports Act serves as an outright bar to a court hearing a dispute between an athlete and his or her NGB and/or the USOC. In contrast, a few courts more recently have held that exhaustion of administrative procedures is only a prerequisite to litigation in the courts.

3. Alternative Arguments

The fact that a majority of courts have held that the Act does not establish a private cause of action does not necessarily foreclose a court from hearing a dispute between an athlete and an NGB. One may attempt to circumvent the legislative history and judicial interpretation of the Act by asserting a state law contract claim rather than a violation of the Act. It is well established that the constitution, bylaws, rules and regulations of voluntary associations—such as an NGB—constitute a contract between an association's members. An athlete may allege that the NGB's rules and regulations—which incorporate the Amateur Sports Act—constitute a contract and that the suspension of an athlete's membership without a hearing is a breach of that contract. Thus, this argument perhaps would allow an athlete to bring before the court the Amateur Sports Act—and the issue of his or her eligibility—without asserting a private cause of action under the Act.

. . . .

---

66. 492 F. Supp. 1181 (D.D.C), *aff'd without opinion*, 701 F.2d 221 (D.C. Cir. 1980).

4. Application of the Act to International Federations

Regardless of one's interpretation of the Amateur Sports Act, however, it is important to keep in mind that the Act only governs disputes between an athlete, a NGB and the USOC. Although Congress intended to keep the courts out of disputes between parties governed by the Act, Congress also was cognizant of the fact that administrative procedures were not available to resolve disputes between an athlete and a party other than his or her NGB or the USOC, such as an international federation. Section 382b Resolution of Disputes "also makes it clear that only members of the USOC are subject to provisions in the USOC's constitution and by-laws which govern the disputes contemplated by this section. The USOC is not granted authority to subject non-members to arbitration or its internal procedures for resolving disputes."[81] Thus, there is no guarantee under the Act that a dispute between an athlete such as Butch Reynolds, and an IF, such as the IAAF, will proceed within an administrative framework consistent with the Constitution of the United States. While it may be reasonable and prudent for courts to refrain from intervening in disputes between an athlete and his or her NGB—disputes governed by the constitutionally sound administrative procedures outlined in the USOC constitution and by-laws—the courts should not behave so deferentially with respect to disputes between an athlete and his or her international federation. As long as it is constitutional for a court to exercise jurisdiction over the international federation, the courts should do so to ensure that the athlete has been treated fairly and equally.

. . . . [A substantial discussion of Butch Reynolds' dispute with the IAAF is omitted. — ed.].

III. THE SHORTCOMINGS OF INTERNATIONAL SPORTS LAW

Reynolds' dispute with the IAAF has raised several important issues and questions. First, should the courts of any country—let alone the United States—interfere in a dispute of this type? The answer to this question requires a balancing of two interests: the interests of the IFs in having complete autonomy over their respective sports versus an athlete's interest in receiving procedural due process. The second major question is whether there is a solution which requires neither granting autonomy to the IFs nor forcing IFs to defend themselves in courts around the world.

A. *Should Courts Intervene in International Sports Disputes?*

Courts of this country (and others) must intervene in a Reynolds-type dispute. Where the only law that governs these disputes is the internal rules of the federation itself, which in most cases fail to provide an athlete with adequate procedural safeguards, a court must step in to ensure the athlete an opportunity to present his or her case to an independent tribunal.

. . . .

B. *Treatment of Other Athletes*

The IAAF, in the midst of the Reynolds dispute, did overturn the suspensions of two other world-class athletes: Katrin Krabbe, a German sprinter, and James Do-

---

81. H.R. Rep. No. 1627, *supra* note 58, at 15.

erhing, a United States shotputter. The circumstances surrounding these athletes' suspensions reveal, however, that the stakes were not as high as they were with respect to Reynolds' ban.

Krabbe, the women's world champion in the 100 and 200 meters, along with fellow Germans Silke Moeller and Grit Breuer, were suspended by the German federation (DLV) on February 15, 1992, for allegedly manipulating their urine samples after being tested while training in South Africa. The DLV subsequently lifted the suspension because the federation's own rules failed to provide for random out-of-competition testing. The IAAF referred the case to its own Arbitration Panel, which upheld the decision to lift the ban, again citing the "technicality" of the absence in DLV's rules of a random drug testing provision. The Krabbe case is distinguishable from that of Reynolds because it did not call into question the testing procedures of the IAAF, but rather involved an oversight by a national federation. There is a difference between the IAAF admitting the failure of a member national federation to adopt consistent rules and admitting that its own testing procedures are substantially suspect.

Doehring was suspended in December 1990 for two years when a urine sample revealed testosterone excess. TAC initially rejected Doehring's appeal. A hearing before an AAA arbitrator, however, later revealed that the seal on one of Doehring's urine samples had been broken, although the arbitrator said it was highly likely Doehring used testosterone. TAC, fifteen months into a two-year ban, lifted the suspension. The IAAF accepted TAC's decision, citing a "technicality," i.e., the broken seal.

Although the Doehring case also involved the testing procedures of the IAAF, the lifting of the suspension was less damaging to the IAAF than it would have been in the Reynolds dispute. The IAAF was able to admit it was wrong without being accused of having labeled an innocent man a drug-user. Not only did the AAA arbitrator emphasize his decision was based on a technicality, but also Doehring, apart from his troubles with TAC and the IAAF, had been arrested, convicted, and sentenced to five years' probation in 1991 for amphetamine distribution. Thus, the IAAF, although certainly dismayed about having to overturn the suspension of a proven drug abuser, could take solace in the fact that its drug prevention system was sound—it had caught the right man—and that, but for a minor mistake, its offender would have served his entire suspension.

In contrast, absolving Reynolds of any wrongdoing would have required the IAAF to swallow the fact that its doping prevention system, in addition to the IOC's, was seriously flawed and could not distinguish between drug-free and drug-abusing athletes. It was not a simple mistake, such as a broken seal, that obscured the test results. As Reynolds' advocates established, the errors involved were more substantial and could not be characterized as "technical," as they were in the Doehring and Krabbe cases.

The Reynolds' case is more akin to that of Randy Barnes than it is to either Krabbe or Doehring. Barnes, a shotputter, was suspended following a meet in Sweden in 1990 after his urine sample tested positive for the steroid methyltestosterone. Both TAC and the IAAF upheld the suspension despite evidence of illegitimate drug-testing procedures in a report of a TAC official present when Barnes' "B" sample was tested. In addition, the 3-2 TAC opinion outwardly acknowledged the shortcomings of the IAAF's internal procedures vis-a-vis the United States judicial system. Similar to the Reynolds case, the IAAF could not back down with a simple explanation that its drug testing procedures were susceptible to the occasional minor error. Rather, the IAAF would have had to openly criticize the fundamental integrity of its program on the whole.

C. *Balancing of Interests*

One may argue that the Reynolds case is unique and would question the need to overhaul the system for the sake of a few athletes. The IAAF would argue that all that is needed is more stringent internal supervision of the drug laboratories. The problem, however, lies not in the ability of the IAAF or other IFs to carefully handle drug samples. Rather, the fundamental concern is that when an IF botches a drug test, the athlete's fate rests in the hands of the IF itself, which, depending on the circumstances, may or may not be willing to acknowledge its mistake.

The international federations undoubtedly have a strong interest in maintaining complete control over their respective sports. Vesting autonomy in the federation facilitates the swift and efficient resolution of disputes and provides for a uniform body of law within the sport. Such centrality of control is important to the fight against doping, especially "given the development of 'camouflage' chemicals that are absorbed to 'purify' the athlete of traces of performance-enhancing drugs in time for a given competition."

The federation's interests must, however, be weighed against the interest of the athlete to present his or her case to an independent tribunal. Most federations' procedural rules traditionally deem the federation itself to be the final authority. For example, IAAF Rule 20(4) provides: "The decision of the [IAAF] Arbitration Panel shall be final and binding on all parties, and on all members of the I.A.A.F., and no right of appeal will lie from the Arbitration Panel's decision."[157] While the IAAF's rules prohibit a member of the IAAF Council or of an IAAF Committee from being nominated to the arbitration panel, the members of the Panel are elected by the IAAF Congress itself, thereby permitting the IAAF to place on its panel arbitrators who are likely to be more sympathetic to the organization's concerns than to those of the athlete. Thus, any claim that the IAAF panel is independent is an illusion. An athlete in Reynolds' position is placed in a nearly impossible situation:

> The federation in question has generally existed for decades if not generations, and has, without any outside influence, developed a more or less complex and entirely inbred procedure for resolving disputes.... [T]he procedures devised by most sports federations seem to be so connected to the organization that no outsider has the remotest chance of standing on an equal footing with his adversary, which is of course the federation itself. To speak of a *consensual process* here seems an abuse of language.[160]

As the Reynolds case demonstrates, a positive test result for drugs can ruin an athlete's career, and in addition may irreparably damage his or her reputation and financial well-being. Because the stakes are so high, the monopolistic control of the federation must—at least until the fundamental procedural unfairness is alleviated—yield to the jurisdiction of the courts, notwithstanding the deficiencies of the judicial system.

---

157. IAAF Rule 20(4), *reprinted in* Addendum to Appellee's Brief, *supra* note 47.
160. Paulsson, *supra* note 155, at 13.

The courts also must intervene because there is no body of law other than the international federation's internal rules which govern a Reynolds-type dispute. Although the Olympic Charter arguably represents a comprehensive set of international sports standards, the ambiguous language of the Charter is an inappropriate guide to a technical dispute. Moreover, even if the lofty principles of the Charter could be a source of relief in a specific dispute, an athlete will find himself in a similar predicament if the IOC refuses to act on his behalf against the IF.

.... [A discussion of the Court of Arbitration for Sport is omitted. — ed.].

CONCLUSION

The district court and the Sixth Circuit should be commended for their intervention in the Reynolds dispute. The interests of the athlete in preserving his reputation and career, and moreover being afforded an opportunity to prove his case before an independent tribunal, far outweigh the interests of the international federation in maintaining complete control over its sport. While granting broad authority to the IFs is admittedly necessary, especially given the difficulty they face in preventing doping, providing an appeal to an independent body such as the CAS would do little to undermine the IFs' control over their sports, yet would go far toward instituting procedural safeguards for the athletes. The Olympic Charter should be amended to require IFs to include in their internal rules a provision granting the athlete the right to appeal a decision of the federation to the CAS.

---

2. Arbitration of Disputes

Melissa R. Bitting, Comment, Mandatory, Binding Arbitration for Olympic Athletes: Is the Process Better or Worse for "Job Security"?
25 Florida State University Law Review 655 (1998)*

....

II. HISTORY

....

C. Need for Resolution

With so many overlapping jurisdictions, resolution of eligibility disputes can prove to be complex, lengthy, and expensive. At the international level, differences in the selection process among NOCs, coupled with the difficulties facing a national court that is trying to obtain jurisdiction over an international body allegedly violating an athlete's national citizen rights, can quickly turn athletic eligibility into a confusing morass. The nature of athletic competition, however, requires quick decisions. If one athlete cannot compete, another is always ready to

---

fill the position. Once the race is run, the opportunity is gone. Especially when a spot on the Olympic team hangs in the balance or when the chance to win an Olympic gold medal may be denied, lengthy court battles are not a valid option. As discussed below, the Butch Reynolds court battle played out as a worst-case scenario that put the sports world on notice that it had to find a better solution.

1. The Controversy That Would Not Go Away: Butch Reynolds and the International Amateur Athletic Federation Square Off

After competing in a track and field event in Monte Carlo in August 1990, Butch Reynolds submitted to a random drug test. The individual world record holder in the 400 meters and gold and silver medalist in the 1988 Olympics tested positive for trace amounts of the steroid Nandrolone, a drug prohibited by the International Amateur Athletic Federation (IAAF). Banned by the IAAF from all international track competitions for two years, Reynolds was effectively shut out of any opportunity to compete in the 1992 Olympics. The United States NGB for track and field, then called The Athletics Congress (TAC), offered a hearing to Reynolds, but no date had been set when Reynolds filed suit in Ohio, alleging that the test was given negligently and provided incorrect results. Having failed to exhaust all administrative remedies, and finding no state action that would implicate due process rights under the Fifth Amendment, the district court dismissed the due process claim and stayed any further proceedings until the administrative remedies were exhausted. On appeal, the entire case was dismissed because Reynold's failure to exhaust administrative remedies prior to filing suit left the district court without subject matter jurisdiction.

In an effort to exhaust his administrative remedies, Reynolds, following the procedures outlined in the Amateur Sports Act and the USOC Constitution, submitted his dispute to an American Arbitration Association panel. The arbitrator's decision completely cleared Reynolds. The IAAF, however, did not honor the arbitrator's findings because the arbitration did not conform to IAAF rules; thus, the ban was not lifted. In compliance with IAAF procedure, Reynolds appealed to TAC, and that body also cleared Reynolds, finding that "substantial doubt" had been cast on the validity of the drug test.

Refusing to change its decision, the IAAF initiated another independent arbitration on the theory that TAC had "misdirected itself." Conducted in London, the home base of operations for the IAAF, this arbitration panel concluded that the tests were valid, and as there was "no doubt" about Reynolds' guilt, the two-year ban stayed in place.

Reynolds then filed another action in the Southern District of Ohio that claimed breach of contract, breach of contractual due process, defamation, and tortious interference with business relations. Reynolds wanted monetary damages and a temporary restraining order that would permit him to run races prior to the United States Olympic trials. The IAAF denied that the district court had jurisdiction and refused to appear. Reynolds qualified for the trials. Three days before the trials, the district court conducted a hearing on Reynolds' eligibility to compete, but the IAAF again refused to appear. Despite a favorable lower court ruling, Reynolds had to submit an emergency motion to Supreme Court Justice John Paul Stevens to preserve his opportunity to compete in the trials.

The IAAF threatened to bar from the Olympics every athlete who competed with Reynolds in the trials, but eventually the USOC and the IAAF reached an agreement that allowed Reynolds to compete and to qualify as a relay alternate. However, the IAAF would not allow Reynolds to actually compete in the Olympics and added four months to the two-year ban as a penalty for competing in the United States trials.

In the action for monetary damages, the IAAF again refused to appear, and Reynolds was awarded $27,356,008, with more than $20,000,000 of the award as punitive damages. When Reynolds began garnishment proceedings in 1993 against corporations with ties to the IAAF, the Association finally appeared before the district court to argue lack of jurisdiction. Four years after the original eligibility dispute arose, this final suit for damages was dismissed for lack of personal jurisdiction. The Olympics had come and gone. The endorsement opportunities had disappeared. Efforts to comply with conflicting regulations from an NGB and an IF proved fruitless for an athlete trying to compete.

2. Arbitration as a Possible Solution

The courts are not the ideal forum to settle athletic disputes. Speed is of the essence. As the long and tortuous history of the Butch Reynolds saga shows, international parties can throw a wrench into American judicial processes, and the lack of clear and definite procedures to handle disputes can confuse those who try to comply with the rules.

Mandatory arbitration may offer a partial solution. Within the United States, arbitration in sports has been a workable solution. The American Arbitration Association has provided several arbitrations within forty-eight hours of the complaint being filed. General Counsel and Director of Legal Affairs for the USOC, Ronald T. Rowan, reported that since 1983, 109 athletes have filed claims that they had been denied the chance to make the Olympic or Pan-American Team, and of those complaints that could not be resolved, forty-three have gone to arbitration.[50] Twenty-three of those forty-three arbitration cases have been decided in favor of the athlete. Athletes appear to have at least an opportunity to defend their rights to compete.

Realizing the need to inject consistency and fairness in the resolution of international sports disputes, the IOC created the International Council of Arbitration for Sport (ICAS) to "facilitate the settlement of sports-related disputes through arbitration and to ensure the protection of the rights of the parties in the context of the arbitration of disputes connected with sport." This newly formed group is based in Switzerland, and generally operates under Swiss law. The ICAS took center stage during the summer Olympic Games in Atlanta when, for the first time, all athletes, coaches, and officials had to agree to submit their disputes to ICAS procedures for mandatory and binding arbitration as a pre-condition to participation in the Olympics.

D. The Olympic Entry Clause

Particularly worried that athletes competing in the Atlanta Games would seek relief in the courts of the United States for their disputes, the IOC added a clause to the entry form that said that any dispute would go, in accordance with ICAS procedures, to the Court of Arbitration for Sport (CAS) for "final and binding ar-

---

50. *See id.* at 410.

bitration."[55] The form continued: "[T]he decisions of CAS shall be final, non-appealable and enforceable. I shall not institute any claim, arbitration or litigation, or seek any other form of relief in any other court or tribunal." Any athlete refusing to sign the entry form was denied the opportunity to compete.

When 11,000 athletes from 197 countries showed up to compete in Atlanta, the team of arbitrators sent by the ICAS were also in town, ready to "provide athletes with a fair, fast, independent and inexpensive way of resolving disputes." Typical controversies frequently involve drug testing or general eligibility requirements. Often, the mere threat of litigation by athletes had been enough to prevent governing organizations from trying to impose sanctions on an athlete. The system put into place in Atlanta was ostensibly designed to handle the concerns of both athletes and Olympic governing officials.

Although arbitration is gaining popularity as a quicker and less costly alternative to litigation of sports-oriented controversies, a mandatory waiver of rights to seek redress, particularly the clause included on the Olympic entry form discussed above, may be subject to attack. For many Olympic caliber athletes, training and competing in their chosen sport is their job-their means of supporting them-selves and their families. As a result, any contract agreement between the athlete/employee and governing officials/employer should be subject to standard contract analysis.

. . . . [Discussion of the financial aspects of athletic participation by Olympic athletes is omitted. — ed.].

IV. EVALUATING THE ENFORCEABILITY OF CONTRACTS REQUIRING MANDATORY ARBITRATION

A. *The United States Supreme Court*

The U.S. Supreme Court adheres to a "liberal federal policy favoring arbitration agreements."[89] The Court found that Congress explicitly created the Federal Arbitration Act (FAA) to "overcome an anachronistic judicial hostility to agreements to arbitrate."[91] The Court also espoused the view that the FAA mandates that "any doubts concerning the scope of arbitrable issues should be resolved in favor of arbitration." The pertinent language of the FAA reads:

> A written provision in . . . a contract evidencing a transaction involving commerce to settle by arbitration a controversy thereafter arising out of such contract . . . or an agreement in writing to submit to arbitration an existing controversy arising out of such a contract . . . shall be valid, irrevocable, and enforceable, save upon such grounds as exist at law or in equity for the revocation of any contract.[93]

Commerce, for purposes of the FAA, is defined to mean "commerce among the several States or with foreign nations . . . but nothing herein contained shall apply to contract of employment of . . . any other class of workers engaged in foreign or interstate commerce."[94]

---

55. ATLANTA COMM. FOR THE OLYMPIC GAMES, ENTRY BY NAME 1 (1996).

89. Mitsubishi Motor Corp. v. Soler Chrysler-Plymouth, Inc., 473 U.S. 614, 625 (1985) (quoting Moses H. Come Mem'l Hosp. v. Mercury Constr. Corp., 460 U.S. 1, 24 (1983)).

91. *Mitsubishi*, 473 U.S. at 625 n.14 (citations omitted).

93. 9 U.S.C. § 2 (1994).

94. *Id.* § 1.

Despite this announced preference for arbitration, the Court may scrutinize employment contracts that contain mandatory arbitration clauses. In *Gilmer v. Interstate/Johnson Lane Corp.*,[95] the Court explicitly refused to address whether the FAA excludes "all contracts of employment" from its coverage. The *Gilmer* Court did, however, touch on the issue of unequal bargaining power between employers and employees and stated that "[m]ere inequality in bargaining power" would not convince the Court that employment arbitration agreements should never be enforceable. Instead, the Court said that unequal bargaining power claims would have to be resolved on a case-by-case basis.

Gilmer was not a unanimous decision, and Justice Stevens argued, in a vigorous dissent, that "arbitration clauses contained in employment agreements are specifically exempt from coverage of the FAA...."

....

Furthermore, Justice Stevens stated that the Court too readily dismissed the problem of inequality of bargaining power. In an arbitration case decided seven years prior to *Gilmer*, the Court warned that "courts should remain attuned to well-supported claims that the agreement to arbitrate resulted from the sort of fraud or overwhelming economic power that would provide grounds "for the revocation of any contract."[103] However, when Gilmer, a sixty-two-year-old employee, tried to challenge an arbitration agreement that he had signed as a condition of employment, the Court found "no indication...that Gilmer...was coerced or defrauded into agreeing to the arbitration clause."[104]

....[Discussion of other mechanisms for revocation (e.g., fraud, duress, and unconscionability) that could impact the enforcement of contracts with mandatory arbitration provisions is omitted.—ed.].

C. Application in the Olympic Context

Olympic athletes do not have any meaningful choice in deciding whether to sign the entry form. If an athlete does not sign the form, the athlete does not compete. For whatever reason an athlete wants to appear in the Olympics—fulfillment of personal training or competition goals, completing requirements for monetary support, or simply accepting what may be a once-in-a-life-time chance to participate in a time-honored tradition of excellence—the only way to make that coveted appearance is to sign the form. The Olympic Charter mandates that every person involved with the Olympics accept the "supreme authority of the IOC" and agree to be bound by the IOC's rules. An individual athlete will not have the power to resist the demands of the IOC and still retain the right to compete.

The Olympic arbitration clause on the entry form is a take-it-or-leave-it proposition. However, the contract between the athlete and the IOC is not per se invalid. Other factors, such as the impartiality of arbitrators, may be considered in tandem with the adhesion to determine enforceability.

Arguably, Olympic athletes have no reasonable alternative to agreeing to mandatory and binding arbitration. As discussed earlier in this Comment, athletes depend on participation in the Olympics to support themselves or to fulfill terms

---

95. 500 U.S. 20 (1990).

103. Mitsubishi Motors Corp. v. Solar Chrysler Plymouth, 473 U.S. 614, 627 (1985) (quuoting 9 U.S.C. § 2 (1985).

104. *Gilmer*, 500 U.S. at 33.

of commercial endorsements. The opportunity to compete in the Olympics in any one given sport only occurs once every four years. Although there are exceptions, an athlete may have only one chance at the Olympic Games. That one shot is now tied to a waiver of the right to access the courts to settle disputes.

Finally, both the 1996 United States Olympic Team Code of Conduct and Grievance Procedures require the participant's signature; a parent or guardian must sign for participants of minority age. According to the General Counsel for the USOC, "there is no contractual obligation on the part of an athlete under 18 years of age." If it is true that an under age athlete has "no contractual obligation," then the child athlete could arguably initiate proceedings outside of the Olympic agreement regardless of any parental signature. If there was no contract created with the child, the parental validation argument would not apply.

. . . .

V. THE CURRENT OLYMPIC ARBITRATION SYSTEM

A. Developing the Process

Operating since 1983, the CAS was originally designed to accept only cases in which all parties involved in a dispute agreed to submit to its jurisdiction. Promoted as an independent organization made up of 150 arbitrators representing thirty-seven countries, the CAS is headquartered, along with the IOC, in Lausanne, Switzerland. All CAS arbitrators are "persons with legal training and recognized competence with regard to sport. Their experience enables the arbitrators to facilitate the settlement of disputes by offering a solution adapted to the sporting context." Because Swiss private international law governs CAS proceedings, the Swiss federal Supreme Court heard a 1993 challenge to a CAS award and affirmed the power of the CAS to validly bind parties to its decisions. However, the Swiss Supreme Court also recommended that the CAS reduce its level of dependency on the IOC. As a result, in 1994, the 102nd IOC session approved the creation of the ICAS to replace the IOC as the supervisor and financier of the CAS.

ICAS is composed of twenty members, consisting of a mixture of representatives of the IFs, ANOCs, and the IOC. The members must sign a declaration "undertaking to perform their functions in a personal capacity, with total objectivity and independence, and in conformity with the provisions of the Code of Sports-Related Arbitration." In an effort to further guarantee impartiality and independence of CAS arbitrators, the ICAS members are prohibited from serving as a CAS arbitrator or as counsel to any party appearing before the CAS.

Although the CAS is a permanent body, a short-term arbitration process was created to specifically address issues arising during the Atlanta Olympic Games, and as discussed, the IOC demanded that as a condition of competing, all disputes be resolved, through ICAS procedures, by the CAS. From its list of CAS arbitrators, ICAS created an Ad Hoc Division (AHD) of CAS and sent approximately twelve arbitrators to Atlanta to settle disputes on the spot. A panel of three arbitrators heard each case.

Filing a written application with the AHD office starts the arbitration process. Upon receipt of the paperwork, the President of the AHD chooses a panel of three arbitrators from the AHD. Subject to time constraints, the parties to the arbitration are allowed to have counsel. The AHD panel must reach a decision within twenty-four hours of filing, but in the case of extreme urgency, such as exclusion from impending competition, a stay may be immediately issued so that the competition can proceed as planned. If the determination is later made that an athlete should have been excluded, the athlete would be disqualified, and the results changed accordingly.

The AHD panels must review each case in light of the Olympic Charter, the applicable rules of each sport and the NOC, and "general principles of law," but the ICAS rules do not define "general principles of law." If any part of the dispute cannot be resolved, the unresolved issues proceed to a regular CAS process, but the same panel that heard the dispute at the Olympics remains assigned to the dispute. "A final award by the AHD is immediately enforceable because it is not subject to appeal."

B. Arbitration at the Atlanta Games

The AHD heard six disputes during the 1996 Atlanta Olympic Games, and no lawsuits were filed as a result of any AHD decisions. Four of the arbitrations required the AHD to determine whether an athlete would be excluded from competition or be allowed to continue. Two athletes whose eligibility was contested were allowed to compete, and two athletes accused of drug use were allowed to keep their medals. One athlete's disqualification, based on a referee's decision, was upheld.

One AHD decision resolved a dispute between the United States NGB for swimming and the Irish NOC. The United States wanted Irish swimmer Michelle Smith disqualified from the 400-meter free-style when the Irish NOC tried to substitute Smith into the 400-meter freestyle after the entry deadline. The IF for swimming, FINA, initially refused to allow the substitution, but when FINA was informed that the IOC was not strictly enforcing the entry deadline, FINA reversed its decision and allowed Smith to enter. The three-member AHD panel met for two hours and ruled in favor of the Irish swimmer.

In another decision, the CAS panel overruled an IOC decision to strip medals from two Russian athletes who tested positive for the drug bromantan. The IOC argued that bromantan was a performance-enhancing stimulant, but Russian Olympic officials countered that the drug was neither a stimulant nor officially on the banned list. The AHD panel discovered that athletes in the 1988 and 1992 Olympics had used bromantan, and it heard testimony from the AHD-appointed medical expert that lack of data made it impossible to predict the quantitative effect of bromantan. Acknowledging that bromantan was not specifically designated in the IOC Medical Code of prohibited substances, and dissatisfied with the medical evidence about the stimulant qualities of bromantan, the AHD panel decided to let the Russian athletes keep their medals.

A French boxer who was disqualified by a referee for allegedly punching an opponent below the belt also tried to initiate an AHD arbitration. The AHD panel refused to accept the application and noted "that the referee's decision was purely a technical one and as such was not the type of decision that the panel should review." Absent a showing of an error or an intentionally malicious act, the French boxer could not gain access to the arbitration process.

. . . .

VI. CONCLUSION

An athlete has much more to lose when her eligibility is at stake than does the IOC. The IOC will make sure that the Games go on with or without any one given athlete, but that one athlete has no-where else to go for Olympic competition. The IOC is in the difficult position of maintaining the highest overall standards for the Olympics, yet the IOC should also be aware of the fairness concerns of individual athletes.

The Olympic arbitration process has the potential to fairly address the overlapping jurisdictional disputes that often plague competition. However, requiring as a condition of eligibility that an athlete agree not to challenge a CAS award in court means that particular attention must be paid to the fairness of the process. The courts caution for vigilance against adhesion and duress. Neutral arbitrators are also essential. Mandatory, binding arbitration may not be a panacea for all the concerns of Olympic athletes, but given the unique circumstances of the fast-paced world of sports competition, it may offer the most viable option to quickly settle disputes.

———————

Index